ASPEN PUBLISHERS

Fundamentals of Securities Regulation, Fifth Edition

by Louis Loss, Joel Seligman and Troy Paredes

Fundamentals of Securities Regulation is a concise one-volume treatise that provides essential information covering a wide array of topics concerning securities law. This compendium reviews the most significant aspects of securities regulation.

The Fifth Edition of *Fundamentals of Securities Regulation* incorporates the statutory changes provided by the Sarbanes-Oxley Act, officially codified as The Public Company Accounting Reform and Corparate Responsibility, including the creation of the new Public Company Accounting Oversight Board and new Section 15D, which addresses Securities Analysts and Research Reports. The Sarbanes-Oxley Act also has led to substantial changes in the federal securities rules and regulations.

2010 Cumulative Supplement Highlights

New legislative, regulatory, and case law developments are analyzed in the 2010 Cumulative Supplement.

Highlights include:

- SEC's guidance as to how companies can use their websites to provide information to investors, particularly under the 1934 Act (Chapter 2, §B.6.h).

- SEC's adoption of rule amendments to permit risk/return summary information to be downloaded through XBRL directly into spreadsheets and analyzed in a variety of ways using commercial off-the-shelf software and adoption of rule and form amendments to allow applicants for EDGAR access codes using Form ID to submit authenticating documents in PDF rather than by fax (Chapter 2, §C.6).
- New section (Chapter 2, §D.2.h) discussing SEC policy on security ratings including:
  - SEC's proposal to amend Rule 17g-2(d) to require NRSROs to disclose ratings actions histories for all credit ratings issued on or after June 26, 2007 at the request of the obligor being rated or the issuer, underwriter, or sponsor of the security being rated and proposed a certification requirement under Rule 17g-5(e);
  - SEC's proposed rule amendments to impose additional requirements on NRSROs to address the integrity of their credit rating procedures and methodologies;
  - SEC's proposed amendments to Regulation FD to permit the disclosure of material nonpublic information to NRSROs regardless of whether they make their ratings publicly available.
- Discussion of the Final Report of the Advisory Committee on the Auditing Profession (Chapter 2, §D.3.d).
- SEC's adoption of rule amendments to the cross-border rules which are intended to facilitate more cross-border transactions by easing previous regulatory requirements (Chapter 2, §E.2.a).
- SEC's adoption of rule amendments to the Rule 12g3-2(b) exemption to exempt a foreign private issuer from having to register under §12(g) based on the submission to the SEC of specified information published by the issuer outside the United States (Chapter 2, §E.2.b).

- SEC's adoption of Rule 151A under the 1933 Act and Rule 12h-7 under the 1934 Act to define the terms *annuity contract* and *optional annuity contract* under the 1933 Act and to exempt insurance companies from filing reports under the 1934 Act with respect to indexed annuities and other securities registered under the 1933 Act provided that they are regulated by State insurance law and not publicly traded (Chapter 3, §A.1.f).

- Discussion of the Obama Administration's proposed outline of a comprehensive framework for OTC derivatives (Chapter 3, §A.1.l).

- SEC's proposal to modify Rule 14a-8 and permit shareholder proposals that relate to the procedures for director nominations and add new Rule 14a-11 to permit nomination of up to 25 percent of the board to a shareholder or group of shareholders that owns 1, 3, or 5 percent of a corporation's stock (Chapter 6, §C.4.c).

- Overview of the September 2008 Report from the SEC Office of Inspector General regarding the SEC's oversight of Bear Stearns and Related Entities and the simultaneous termination of The Consolidated Supervised Entity Program (Chapter 8, §A.1).

- SEC's adoption of amendments to Regulation SHO to eliminate the options market maker exception to the close-out requirement of Regulation SHO, adoption of new Rule 10b-21 substantially as proposed to address fails to deliver that had been associated with *naked* short selling, adoption of interim final Temporary Rule 204T of Regulation SHO to address abusive *naked* short selling in all equity securities, and proposed amendments to Regulation SHO with alternative short sale price tests and with alternative SEC circuit breakers that would apply to a particular security, rather than the entire market (Chapter 8, §B.3.b).

- Discussion of the latest Federal Circuit Court cases dealing with scienter (Chapter 9, §B.6).

- Discussion of the latest Federal Circuit Court cases addressing the Securities Litigation Uniform Standards Act's (SLUSA) pre-emption of state law (Chapter 11, §B).

- Discussion of the latest Federal Circuit Court cases addressing aiding and abetting a Rule 10b-5 violation (Chapter 11, §D.1.c).

- Discussion of the United States Supreme Court decision *Ashcroft v. Iqbal* (Chapter 11, § D.2.c).

- Overview of the Bernard Madoff cases and their implications (Chapter 13, §B.1).

This cumulative supplement contains an updated Table of Cases.

9/09

For questions concerning this shipment, billing, or other customer service matters, call our Customer Service department at 1-800-234-1660.

For toll-free ordering, please call 1-800-638-8437.

© 2009 Aspen Publishers. All Rights Reserved.

FUNDAMENTALS OF SECURITIES REGULATION

2010 Supplement

ASPEN PUBLISHERS

FUNDAMENTALS OF SECURITIES REGULATION
Fifth Edition

2010 Supplement

LOUIS LOSS
Late William Nelson Cromwell Professor of Law
Harvard University

JOEL SELIGMAN
President
University of Rochester

TROY PAREDES
Professor of Law
Washington University
School of Law

AUSTIN   BOSTON   CHICAGO   NEW YORK   THE NETHERLANDS

This publication is designed to provide accurate and authoritative information in regard to the subject matter covered. It is sold with the understanding that the publisher is not engaged in rendering legal, accounting, or other professional services. If legal advice or other professional assistance is required, the services of a competent professional person should be sought.

—From a *Declaration of Principles* jointly adopted by a Committee of the American Bar Association and a Committee of Publishers and Associations

© 2009 Estate of Louis Loss, Joel Seligman, and Troy Paredes
Published by Aspen Publishers. All Rights Reserved.

No part of this publication may be reproduced or transmitted in any form or by any means, eletronic or mechanical, including photocopy, recording, or any information storage or retrieval system, without permission in writing from the publisher. Requests for permission to reproduce content should be directed to the Aspen Publishers website at *www.aspenpublishers.com*, or fax a letter of intent to the permissions department at 212-771-0803.

ISBN 978-0-7355-8103-6

Printed in the United States of America

1 2 3 4 5 6 7 8 9 0

About Wolters Kluwer Law & Business

Wolters Kluwer Law & Business is a leading provider of research information and workflow solutions in key specialty areas. The strengths of the individual brands of Aspen Publishers, CCH, Kluwer Law International and Loislaw are aligned within Wolters Kluwer Law & Business to provide comprehensive, in-depth solutions and expert-authored content for the legal, professional and education markets.

CCH was founded in 1913 and has served more than four generations of business professionals and their clients. The CCH products in the Wolters Kluwer Law & Business group are highly regarded electronic and print resources for legal, securities, antitrust and trade regulation, government contracting, banking, pension, payroll, employment and labor, and healthcare reimbursement and compliance professionals.

Aspen Publishers is a leading information provider for attorneys, business professionals and law students. Written by preeminent authorities, Aspen products offer analytical and practical information in a range of specialty practice areas from securities law and intellectual property to mergers and acquisitions and pension/benefits. Aspen's trusted legal education resources provide professors and students with high-quality, up-to-date and effective resources for successful instruction and study in all areas of the law.

Kluwer Law International supplies the global business community with comprehensive English-language international legal information. Legal practitioners, corporate counsel and business executives around the world rely on the Kluwer Law International journals, looseleafs, books and electronic products for authoritative information in many areas of international legal practice.

Loislaw is a premier provider of digitized legal content to small law firm practitioners of various specializations. Loislaw provides attorneys with the ability to quickly and efficiently find the necessary legal information they need, when and where they need it, by facilitating access to primary law as well as state-specific law, records, forms and treatises.

Wolters Kluwer Law & Business, a unit of Wolters Kluwer, is headquartered in New York and Riverwoods, Illinois. Wolters Kluwer is a leading multinational publisher and information services company.

ASPEN PUBLISHERS SUBSCRIPTION NOTICE

This Aspen Publishers product is updated on a periodic basis with supplements to reflect important changes in the subject matter. If you purchased this product directly from Aspen Publishers, we have already recorded your subscription for the update service.

If, however, you purchased this product from a bookstore and wish to receive future updates and revised or related volumes billed separately with a 30-day examination review, please contact our Customer Service Department at 1-800-234-1660, or send your name, company name (if applicable), address, and the title of the product to:

**Aspen Publishers
7201 McKinney Circle
Frederick, MD 21704**

Important Aspen Publishers Contact Information

- To order any Aspen Publishers title, go to *www.aspenpublishers.com* or call 1-800-638-8437.
- To reinstate your manual update service, call 1-800-638-8437.
- To contact Customer Care, e-mail *customer.care@aspenpublishers.com*, call 1-800-234-1660, fax 1-800-901-9075, or mail correspondence to Order Department, Aspen Publishers, PO Box 990, Frederick, MD 21705.
- To review your account history or pay an invoice online, visit *www.aspenpublishers.com/payinvoices*.

CONTENTS

Preface   *xix*

CHAPTER 1

BACKGROUND OF THE SEC STATUTES

A.	Of Bubbles and Giants	1
B.	State Regulation of Securities	2
	1. The Uniform Securities Acts	2
	2. New York and California	9
	3. Selective Federal Preemption: The National Securities Markets Improvement Act of 1996	10
	a. Securities Offerings and Reporting	10
D.	A Telescopic Preview of the SEC Statutes	11
	4. Public Utility Holding Company Act of 1935	11
	6. Investment Company Act of 1940	11
	a. The *Investment Company* Concept	11
	(ii) Unit Investment Trusts	11
	c. Registration and Regulatory Provisions	12
	(v) Adequate and Feasible Capital Structures	12
	(vi) Financial Statements and Accounting	13
F.	The Securities and Exchange Commission	20
	2. The Commission's Staff	20

CONTENTS

CHAPTER 2

FEDERAL REGULATION OF THE
DISTRIBUTION OF SECURITIES

A.	Distribution Techniques	23
	2. Firm Commitment	23
	5. Shelf Registration	23
	6. Auctions	30
	7. Securities Underwriting in General	32
B.	The Basic Prohibitions of §5	33
	1. The Statutory Pattern	33
	3. The Jurisdictional Base of §5	41
	4. The Prefiling Period	42
	b. "Beating the Gun"	42
	5. The Waiting Period	55
	c. The *Tombstone Ad* [§2(a)(10)(b), Rule 134]	55
	d. The Preliminary Prospectus [§10(a), Rule 430]	57
	e. The Summary Prospectus [§10(b), Rule 431]	58
	(ii) Investment Companies	58
	f. Free Writing Prospectus and Electronic Road Shows [Rules 164 and 433]	58
	6. The Posteffective Period	66
	f. The Dealer's Exemption	66
	h. Electronic Delivery of Prospectus	67
	i. Registration of Underlying Securities in Asset Backed Securities Transactions	78
C.	The Registration Procedure: A Study in Administrative Technique	79
	1. The Statutory Pattern	79
	2. The Preeffective Period	80
	b. The Price Amendment or Rule 430A	80
	c. Acceleration	80
	d. The Base Prospectus and Rule 430B	81
	6. Electronic Filing	82

CONTENTS

- D. Contents of the Registration Statement and Prospectus (Herein of the SEC's Accounting Role) ... 84
  1. Integration of the Disclosure Provisions of the 1933 and 1934 Acts ... 84
  2. Regulation S-K (Nonfinancial Data) ... 85
     a. Commission Policy on Forward Looking Statements [Item 10(b); Sec. Act §27A; Sec. Ex. Act §21E] ... 85
     c. Item 103: Legal Proceedings ... 87
     d. Item 303: Management's Discussion and Analysis of Financial Condition and Results of Operations ... 88
     e. Item 304: Disagreements with Accountants on Accounting and Financial Disclosure ... 88
     f. Item 402: Executive Compensation ... 89
     g. Plain English and Differential Disclosure ... 112
     h. Item 10(h): Commission Policy on Security Ratings ... 113
  3. Financial Statements — The SEC and Accounting (Herein of Regulation S-X) ... 126
     b. The Commission and Accounting Standard Setting ... 126
     c. The Commission and Auditing ... 127
     d. The Sarbanes–Oxley Act ... 128
- E. International Offerings ... 140
  2. Offerings from a Foreign Country into the United States ... 140
     a. The Foreign Integrated Disclosure System ... 140
     b. Exchange Act Disclosure Provisions ... 153
  3. Offerings from the United States into a Foreign Country [Regulation S] ... 155

CONTENTS

CHAPTER 3

COVERAGE OF THE SECURITIES ACT OF 1933:
DEFINITIONS AND EXEMPTIONS

A. Definitions	157
1. *Security* [§2(a)(1)]	157
a. Introduction	157
b. Debt Instruments	157
(i) Notes	157
(iii) Bank Certificates of Deposit	158
c. Oil, Gas, or Other Mineral Rights	158
d. Investment Contracts	158
(i) Elements of the *Howey* Investment Contract Test	159
(iii) Partnerships	161
e. Stock	162
(i) Investment Contract Analysis	162
f. Insurance Products	163
j. Equipment Trust Certificates	164
k. Guarantees	165
l. Warrants, Options, and Futures	165
3. *Underwriter* [§2(a)(11)]	168
b. Purchasing from an Issuer	168
B. Exempted Securities	169
1. Exempted Securities versus Exempted Transactions	169
b. Fraud Provisions	169
c. Burden of Proof	169
2. Securities of Public Authorities and Banks [§3(a)(2)]	169
a. Federal Government	169
C. Exempted Transactions	170
1. Integration	170
5. *Small* Issues	172
a. Statutory Exemptions [§3(b), 3(c), 4(6)]	172
6. Limited Offerings	174
b. Regulation D	174

CONTENTS

		(i)	Rule 501(a) — Accredited Investor Definition	174
		(iii)	Rule 502(c) — Limitations on Manner of Offering	174
		(v)	Rules 503 and 507 and Form D — Notice of Sales	175
	7.	Trading Exemptions		175
		a.	Transactions by Persons Other Than Issuers, Underwriters, or Dealers [§4(1)]	175
D.	Resales of Control and Restricted Securities			176
	1.	Resales after Private Offerings		176
		b.	First Tier Buyer's Problems	176
	2.	Rule 144		176
	3.	Rule 144A		178
	4.	The Resale Problem in Other Contexts under the 1933 Act		180
		b.	Mergers and Similar Events [Rule 145]	180

CHAPTER 4

PROTECTIVE COMMITTEE REFORM: THE TRUST INDENTURE ACT OF 1939 AND SEC FUNCTIONS UNDER THE BANKRUPTCY CODE

B.	The SEC's Functions in Bankruptcy Proceedings		181
	2.	The Commission's Present Role under Chapter 11	181
		b. SEC Participation	181

CONTENTS

CHAPTER 6

REGISTRATION AND POSTREGISTRATION PROVISIONS OF THE 1934 ACT

A.	Registration	183
	4. Exemptions	183
	c. Section 12(h)	183
	5. Nonstatutory Requirements of the Exchanges and the NASD	184
	a. In General	184
	b. Voting Rights Standards	184
B.	Reporting Requirements	189
	1. In Connection with Exchange Act Registration	189
	a. Annual Reports	189
	b. Quarterly and Current Reports	190
	d. Management Report and Internal Controls	193
	3. Administrative Proceedings	245
	a. Voluntary Delisting	245
C.	Proxies	248
	1. The Problem (Herein of Costs of Solicitation)	248
	2. The Statutory Provisions and General Proxy Rules	249
	c. Coverage, Definitions, and Exemptions	249
	4. Contested Solicitations and Security Holder Proposals	270
	c. Security Holder Proposals [Rule 14a-8]	270
	5. False or Misleading Statements [Rule 14a-9]	282
	a. In General	282
	b. Materiality	283
	6. Securities Held in *Street Name* or *Nominee Name* [§14(b)]	286
D.	Tender Offers	287
	2. The Williams Act and Other Federal Securities Laws	287
	b. Beneficial Ownership Reports [§§13(d), 13(g)]	287
	(i) Group	287

CONTENTS

		c. Tender Offers [§14(d), Related Rules, and Schedules]		288
		(iv) Substantive Requirements		288
E.	Insider Trading			296
	3.	Section 16(b): From the *Objective* to the *Subjective*		296
		a. In General		296
		d. Derivative Securities		296
	7.	Definitions		297
		c. *Beneficial Owner*		297
	8.	Exemptions		297
		e. Section 16 Exemptive Rules		297
F.	Sarbanes–Oxley Act Amendments			298
	1.	Prohibitions on Loans		298
	4.	Forfeiture of Executive Bonuses Following Misconduct		298

CHAPTER 7

REGULATION OF THE SECURITIES MARKETS

A.	Structure of the Securities Markets			299
	1.	Introduction		299
	2.	The Stock Markets		325
		c. The Consolidated Reporting System		326
		(iii) Regulation NMS		326
	3.	The Over-the-Counter Market		352
		a. Nasdaq		352
		c. Order Execution		354
	4.	Options Markets		354
		a. Stock Options		354
C.	Securities Associations			354
	2.	The National Association of Securities Dealers		354

CONTENTS

D.	Brokerage Commission Rate Regulation	355
	1. Antitrust Generally	355
	2. Commission Rate Regulation	362
E.	Clearance and Settlement	364

CHAPTER 8

REGULATION OF BROKERS, DEALERS, AND INVESTMENT ADVISERS

A.	Broker-Dealer Registration	365
	1. The Changing Environment	365
	3. Definitions of *Broker* and *Dealer* [§§3(a)(4), 3(a)(5)]	396
	d. Banks and Other Depository Institutions	396
	5. Qualifications and Discipline	397
	a. Grounds for Proceeding	397
	(iv) Willful Violations	397
	8. Research Analysts	397
	a. The Global Settlement	397
	b. NASD and NYSE Rules	400
B.	Broker-Dealer Substantive Regulation	402
	2. Inspections	402
	3. Short Sales	402
	b. SEC Short Sale Rules	402
C.	Investment Advisers	405
	2. Definition of *Investment Adviser*	405
	b. Exclusions	405
	(iv) Brokers and Dealers	405

CHAPTER 9

FRAUD

A.	Common Law and SEC *Fraud*	415
	2. The Relation between SEC *Fraud* Concepts and Common Law Deceit	415

CONTENTS

B.	Issuers and *Insiders*	416
	4. The Fraud Element	416
	a. The *Disclose or Abstain* Rule	416
	b. Issuers' Activities	416
	(ii) Regulation FD	416
	(iii) The Duty to Update and the Duty to Correct	417
	5. The Duty Element	417
	c. Tippers and Tippees	417
	(i) The *Dirks* Standard	417
	6. Scienter	418
	7. Scope of Rule 10b-5	421
	b. In Connection with a Purchase or Sale	421
	8. Rule 14e-3	422
	9. Special *Insider Trading* Sanctions	422
	a. Disgorgement	422
C.	Brokers and Dealers	423
	1. Unreasonable Spreads	423
	a. The *Shingle* Theory and Markups	423
	2. Broker-Dealer Fiduciary Duties	423
	b. Determination of Fiduciary Status	423
	3. Duty to Investigate and the Suitability Doctrine	424
	a. Penny Stock Suitability Requirements [Rule 15g-9]	424
D.	Fraud by Investment Advisers	427

CHAPTER 10

MANIPULATION

D.	Manipulation of the Over-the-Counter Market under the SEC Statutes	433
E.	Stabilization	435

xv

CONTENTS

2.	Activities by Distribution Participants [Rule 101]	435
	a. Basic Prohibitions	435
6.	Short Sales in Connection with an Offering [Rule 105]	437

CHAPTER 11

CIVIL LIABILITY

B.	Blue Sky Laws and the Securities Litigation Uniform Standards Act of 1998	441
C.	SEC Statutes	448
	2. Securities Act of 1933	448
	b. Section 12(a)(2)	448
	(iv) Secondary Trading	448
	d. Section 11: Misstatements or Omissions in Registration Statement	449
	(i) Elements of the Action	449
	(iii) Comparison with Common Law Actions and §12(a)(2)	455
	3. Securities Exchange Act of 1934: Express Liabilities	455
	4. Securities Exchange Act of 1934: Implied Liabilities	456
	a. Theory and Scope	456
	c. Tender Offers	459
	(i) Standing	459
	d. Rule 10b-5	459
	(i) Reliance and Causation	459
	(ii) Damages and Rescission	471
	5. Investment Company Act of 1940	471
D.	General Provisions	473
	1. Secondary Liability	473
	a. Controlling Persons	473
	b. *Repondeat Superior*	475
	c. Aiding and Abetting	475

CONTENTS

2. Defenses		489
a. Statutes of Limitations		489
(i) Express Liabilities		489
(ii) Implied Liabilities		490
(iii) Sarbanes–Oxley Act Amendments		493
c. Failure to Plead Fraud with Particularity		495
d. *In Pari Delicto* and Unclean Hands		512
3. Arbitration and Nonwaiver Provisions		513
4. Class Actions		514
7. Indemnification, Contribution, and Insurance		515
8. Attorneys' Fees and Security for Costs		516

CHAPTER 12

GOVERNMENT LITIGATION

B. Criminal Prosecution		519
1. SEC Penal Provisions		519
2. *Willfully* and *Knowingly*		520
3. Relevant Provisions of the Criminal Code		520
C. Judicial Review of SEC Orders		520

CHAPTER 13

SEC ADMINISTRATIVE LAW

A. Securities Lawyers		527
1. Requirements for Practicing		527
2. The Securities Lawyer in General		527
B. Investigation		528
1. The Statutory Provisions and the Commission's Procedures		528
C. Quasijudicial Proceedings		539
D. Statutory Remedies		539

CONTENTS

    2. Cease and Desist Orders   539
    3. Corporate Bar Orders   540

CHAPTER 14

CONFLICT OF LAWS, PROCEDURAL ASPECTS, AND *GLOBALIZATION*

A. Jurisdiction and Venue   541
    1. Subject Matter Jurisdiction   541
    5. Criminal Actions   541
C. International Aspects   542
    1. Choice of Law   542

Table of Cases   *543*

PREFACE

Recent publication of a Fourth Edition of *Securities Regulation* began with a new coauthor, Troy Paredes. Troy also will be the coauthor of *Fundamentals of Securities Regulation*, beginning with the 2007 Annual Supplement. For me there is an extraordinary significance to this continuity. Louis Loss started Yale Law School in 1934, the year the Securities and Exchange Commission itself began. He started a 15 year career at the Commission in 1937. His career and scholarship stretch back to the very dawn of modern securities regulation. When I began work with Louis as coauthor in 1984, I was very much his junior and benefited immensely from the chance to learn from the master in the field. He remarked to me more than once that our interest in codification and in treatise scholarship had begun at roughly the same point in our lives. Now, decades later, I am the senior coauthor and joined by an extraordinary new scholar in securities regulation who also started at approximately the same age as I did. Troy Paredes, who graduated from the Yale Law School like Louis, has already begun to make his mark as a securities and corporate scholar with significant articles such as Blinded by the Light: Information Overload and Its Consequences for Securities Regulation, 81 Washington University Law Quarterly 417 (2003); A Systems Approach to Corporate Governance Reform: Why Importing U.S. Corporate Law Isn't the Answer, 45 William & Mary Law Review 1055 (2004); and On the Decision to Regulate Hedge Funds: The SEC's Regulatory Philosophy, Style, and Mission, 2006 University of Illinois Law Review.

In June 2008, Troy Paredes was confirmed as a Commissioner of the Securities and Exchange Commission. This is a richly deserved recognition of his outstanding scholarship. I look forward to working with him after he returns from his service at the

PREFACE

SEC. Until then, *Fundamentals* and its Annual Supplements will continue on schedule.

Troy Paredes worked on *Fundamentals* and its Annual Supplements while a Professor of Law at Washington University School of Law before being sworn in and taking office as a Commissioner of the SEC. The views expressed in *Fundamentals* and its Annual Supplements reflect the views of Troy Paredes, Joel Seligman, and the late Louis Loss and do not necessarily reflect those of the SEC or other Commissioners.

Let me acknowledge my gratitude to Lynne Hasman, who is responsible for the typing of this Annual Supplement, and to Beth Cross-Wilhelm for her cite checking.

This Annual Supplement speaks generally as of June 1, 2009, although there are occasional references to later materials.

JS

August 2009

CHAPTER 1

BACKGROUND OF THE SEC STATUTES

A. OF BUBBLES AND GIANTS

P. 3, new note 11.1, end 1st full par. In 2006 the Companies Act 2006 was adopted. The very lengthy Companies Act 2006, running approximately 700 pages, ushers in sweeping change across all aspects of corporate governance in the United Kingdom.

Part 28 of the Companies Act 2006 now governs takeovers and gives the Takeover Panel certain statutory authority and obligations. The City Code on Takeovers and Mergers was correspondingly revised.

P. 4, end 1st full par. The Investment Company Institute and Securities Industry and Financial Markets Association reported in *Equity and Bond Ownership in America, 2008* that during the first quarter of 2008 it was estimated that 47 percent of U.S. households (54.4 million) owned equities and/or bonds. Id. at 1. The fraction of households owning equities rose from 32 percent in 1989 to 53 percent in 2001 before retreating in 2008. Id. at 7. The increase in equity and bond ownership between 1989 and 2001 is "directly related to increasing [defined contribution] retirement plan coverage." Id. at 22.

1

B. STATE REGULATION OF SECURITIES

1. THE UNIFORM SECURITIES ACTS

P. 24, after 1st par. Where does the combination of NSMIA and the new Uniform Securities Act leave coordination of federal and state law today?

After NSMIA the federal securities laws employ three separate methods to coordinate federal-state securities laws:

(1) Specified aspects of the registration and periodic reporting of covered securities, broker-dealer regulation, and investment adviser registration and regulation are *preempted* in full or in part by NSMIA.

(2) Enforcement remains subject to *concurrent federal and state regulation* under express provisions preserving the jurisdiction of state securities commissions. The Securities and Securities Exchange acts, for example, specifically save "all other rights and remedies that may exist at [state] law or in equity." See Sec. Act §16(a); Sec. Ex. Act §28(a); *accord:* Sec. Act §18; Inv. Adv. Act §222; Inv. Co. Act §50.

(3) Section 19(d)(1) of the Securities Act of 1933 authorizes the SEC to cooperate, coordinate, and share information with "any association composed of duly constituted representatives of State governments whose primary assignment is the regulation of the securities business within those States," an elaborate way of referring to the North American Securities Administrators Association (NASAA) that operates in both Canada and the United States.

The harmonization of these different types of United States federal-state securities coordination methods functions differently with respect to policy development, enforcement, and regulatory flexibility.

Policy Development

Sections 19(d)(2) and (3) of the Securities Act stress a federal policy that emphasizes "maximum uniformity in Federal and

State regulatory standards." In particular cooperation is encouraged by §19(d)(3) between the SEC and NASAA in three specified areas:

(A) the sharing of information regarding the registration or exemption of securities issues applied for in the various States;

(B) the development and maintenance of uniform securities forms and procedures; and

(C) the development of a uniform exemption from registration for small issuers which can be agreed upon among several States or between the States and the Federal Government. The Commission shall have the authority to adopt such an exemption as agreed upon for Federal purposes. Nothing in this Act shall be construed as authorizing preemption of State law.

In recent years, cooperation has been a mantra of both United States federal–state securities policy development and efforts by the states to harmonize state policies.

The 2002 version of the Uniform Securities Act includes §608, a reciprocal provision to §19(d) of the Securities Act of 1933. Section 608(b)(2) of the 2002 Act provides that the securities administrators "shall, in its discretion, take into consideration in carrying out the public interest…maximizing uniformity in federal and state regulatory standards."

Consistent with the intent of such provisions as §19(d) of the Securities Act of 1933 and §608 of the 2002 Uniform Securities Act, the SEC and NASAA have adopted uniform forms (for example, Form BD for broker-dealer registration; Form ADV for investment adviser registration); cooperated with the NASD on one stop filing procedures for broker-dealers (the WebCRD or Central Registration Depository) and investment advisers (the IARD or Investment Advisers Registration Depository); and worked jointly to adopt the Uniform Limited Offering Exemption (by 2003 adopted in 50 of 53 U.S. state jurisdictions), which works in tandem with the SEC's Regulation D securities registration exemptions.

Critical aspects of joint policy development are less formal. Section 19(d)(4) further specifies that "in order to carry out these

P. 24

policies and purposes," the SEC "shall conduct an annual conference as well as other meetings to which, among others, NASAA representatives shall be invited to participate." Since 1984 these annual conferences on federal securities registration have addressed a wide array of mutual concerns.

The NASAA has been a particularly frequent and influential commenter on SEC rule and form proposals. NASAA is a membership organization of United States state and Canadian province securities regulators, with a centralized staff in Washington, D.C., that holds annual and other meetings and frequently adopts statements of policy and resolutions, as well as provides comment letters to the SEC and testimony to the United States Congress.

The degree of federal–state cooperation in securities regulation should not be overstated. There are important policy differences on occasion between the SEC and the NASAA or among the states themselves. As significant as policy differences has been the enthusiasm of the SEC Chairmen for working with the states. To cite a significant recent illustration of both points, in October 1995, SEC Chair Arthur Levitt announced his opposition to the initial version of what became the 1996 NSMIA Act in a speech to NASAA that urged cooperation in six areas: investment advisers, investment companies, registration of brokers, examination of brokers, registration of corporate securities, and enforcement authority. NASAA representatives were disappointed both by the substance of what Levitt urged and with the lack of prior consultation. From NASAA's point of view Levitt appeared to be compromising traditional areas of investor protection. Levitt viewed NSMIA itself as a compromise between the initial bill earlier introduced and the NASAA position. J. Seligman, The Transformation of Wall Street: A History of the Securities and Exchange Commission and Modern Corporate Finance, 674–681 (3d ed. 2003).

To put this in different terms, the SEC has not acted as if constrained by the statutory emphasis on cooperation when responding to emerging market needs when they are time sensitive. But as a general matter the Commission is required by the federal Administrative Procedure Act to employ notice and comment processes before adopting new rules. The statutory emphasis on federal-state cooperation has generally become part of this analysis. While states' comments are taken seriously, so are those of other federal agencies, industry, and investors.

For the most part the SEC has largely deferred to the states on intrastate and local policy issues. It was striking, for example, that the SEC did not participate in the 1978–1985 unsuccessful effort to rewrite the Uniform Securities Act and did not attempt to impose any policy position not required by federal statute in the 1998–2002 effort to do the same.

Enforcement

Enforcement remains the area of federal and state securities law that contains the most complete degree of concurrent regulation. While the United States Congress in the Private Securities Litigation Reform Act of 1995 and the Securities Litigation Uniform Standards Act of 1998 limited private securities class actions at both the federal and state level, NSMIA expressly preserved state securities commission authority "to investigate and bring enforcement actions with respect to fraud or deceit, or unlawful conduct ...in connection with...securities transactions." Sec. Act §18(c)(1). Indeed §102(a) of the Securities Litigation Uniform Standards Act of 1998 attempted to augment state enforcement power with a hortatory provision calling for reciprocal subpoena enforcement.

The major issues with respect to federal–state securities enforcement have been at the level of lore rather than law. There is an implicit nonstatutory assumption that the states will largely enforce intrastate and smaller claims and that the SEC will primarily enforce interstate and larger claims. States bring a larger volume of enforcement actions than does the SEC, but these actions tend to be smaller (in terms of the dollar amounts), involve individual defendants, and often relate to failures to register securities, individual broker-dealers, or individual investment advisers. SEC enforcement actions tend to be larger (in terms of dollar amounts), involve multiple defendants, and relate to a wider range of claims. Occasionally there has been frustration with this nonstatutory assumption either because particular states have been inadequately funded to perform a meaningful enforcement role, or when the SEC has expressed concerns about *interstate* claims such as the 2002 settlement that New York State Attorney General Eliot Spitzer negotiated with Merrill Lynch concerning its research analysts' misconduct. Merrill Lynch, Spitzer Reach Interim Deal; New Securities Research Disclosures Ordered, 34 Sec. Reg. & L. Rep. (BNA) 647 (2002). As a general matter the two most serious ongoing enforcement issues have been inadequate enforcement budgets in many states and periodically at the SEC. When there are significant increases in fraud, as there appeared to be in late 1990s, many states and the SEC can be overwhelmed. This can lead to inconsistent policy with respect to interstate cases.

At the same time, the New York State criminal case against research analysts is a useful illustration of a key virtue of concurrent enforcement. Precisely because the states also had investigatory and enforcement powers, one state was able to take up the slack and initiate what became a $1.4 billion settlement with ten leading broker-dealer firms. Wall St. Agrees to $1.4 Billion Payment, Broad Reforms, Resolving Conflict Charges, 34 Sec. Reg. & L. Rep. (BNA) 2037 (2002). Ultimately the SEC worked with the NASAA, NASD, and the State of New York on the Global Research Analyst Settlement. SEC Press Rel. 2003-54 (Apr. 28, 2003).

Regulatory Flexibility

At a statutory level there is a sharp distinction between topic areas where federal law preempts state law (such as merit regulation standards applied to covered securities) and concurrent regulation where state rulemaking authority is largely unfettered.

In practice the distinction is somewhat less sharp. Under §18(b)(3) of the Securities Act, for example, the SEC could significantly expand the categories of securities preempted from state merit standards by adopting a rule defining the term *qualified purchaser*. NASAA opposed an initial SEC proposal that would have reached natural persons with net worth of $1 million *or* income of $200,000 because NASAA believed this would increase the risk of defrauding natural persons. To date the SEC has desisted in either adopting the proposal or reproposing it.

On the other hand, when states are not subject to NSMIA's preemptive provisions, the states have often taken, as an SEC report explained, "significant actions to enhance uniformity in regulating offerings of securities that are both 'covered' and 'not covered.'" These included coordinated review of filings, a uniform registration statement for offerings that are exempt at the federal level, and statements of policy on a number of review issues that enhance uniformity of review in the states. SEC Rep., Uniformity of State Regulatory Requirements for Offerings of Securities that Are Not "Covered Securities" (1997).

The basis for this dulling of the state rulemaking authority distinction between preemptive and concurrent statutory provisions seems threefold.

First, implicitly both federal and state securities laws share common purposes to maximize investor protection while minimizing interference with capital formation. Cf. Sec. Act §19(c)(2)(B) & (C); Unif. Sec. Act (2002) §608(b)(1) & (3).

Second, at least since the 1956 Uniform Securities Act, most of the states have recognized that support for uniform state standards and coordination with federal law further reduces the likelihood of federal preemption. Cf. Unif. Sec. Act (1956) §415; Unif. Sec. Act (2002) §608(a). This point was powerfully illustrated when the failure of the states to agree with the securities industry on a common approach to merit review and securities registration exemptions prompted Congress in 1996 to enact NSMIA. Before NSMIA, but after the 1994 congressional elections, NASAA did create a Task Force on the Future of State and Federal Securities Regulation (including the author), whose primary implicit purpose was to find compromise positions acceptable to both NASAA and proponents of federal preemption and to discourage the United States Congress from acting. The political landscape was so significantly changed by the 1994 United States congressional elections that this effort at compromise failed.

Third, pivotal aspects of state securities law, particularly with respect to novel products or practices, repose in NASAA statements of policy, which can be adopted at the state law level as state rules or guidelines. See NASAA Rep. ¶¶351–3841. Currently there are over 60 such NASAA statements. The flexibility that these statements provide in the rapidly changing securities marketplace has been recognized as essential to securities regulation not only by NASAA, but also by such industry representatives as the Securities Industry Association (SIA) and the American Bar Association (ABA). Both the SIA and the ABA endorsed the new Uniform Securities Act (2002), including §203, which authorizes the securities administrator to grant additional exemptions and waivers and §204(a), which in specified instances, authorizes the administrator to deny, suspend, revoke, condition or limit existing exemptions.

While the United States federal–state system of securities regulation may appear reticulate, if not byzantine, a core reality is that it generally has worked well. Both the SEC and the states perceive advantages to having more, rather than fewer, regulators involved, particularly to review filings, conduct examinations, and bring enforcement actions. Both the SEC and the states have usually recognized that contradictory state policies or conflicts with the SEC may deter investment in the United States and strengthen the case for federal preemption. Both the SEC and the states take pride in the growth of the U.S. securities market and the number of direct and indirect investors under a regulated federal–state system.

Given these institutional realities, both the SEC and NASAA have emphasized consultation, whether formally through periodic conferences, or less informally through NASAA comments on SEC rule and form proposals, or meetings or telephone calls on specific topics such as enforcement cases. It is the informal shared values and coordination that is pivotal to making the U.S. system work as well as it does.

To be sure there are costs to the concurrent system of regulation. There can be redundant regulatory efforts including multiple fees for securities issuers and professionals. Federal and state policies can also be contradictory as they were with respect to state merit regulation of securities issues or the initial different enforcement strategies with respect to investment analysts. Both the federal government and the states can rationalize underfinancing securities regulation on the logic that it is addressed by a different layer of government. This has been a particularly challenging question with enforcement actions in states that have inadequate enforcement budgets. Coordination with 50 states can delay federal rule or form adoption and may be complex given different state policies. The significance of these types of costs varies over time. But, on balance, even with these costs, the United States federal–state model of securities regulation has generally been perceived to work well. See generally Donaldson Reinforces Message: State Enforcement Welcome, with Caveats, 35 Sec. Reg. & L. Rep. (BNA) 1559 (2003); Donaldson Reassures State Regulators that SEC Not Looking to Diminish Powers, 35 id. 1560.

By 2006, 12 states beginning with Missouri in 2003, as well as Hawaii, Idaho, Indiana, Iowa, Kansas, Maine, Minnesota, Oklahoma, South Carolina, South Dakota and Vermont, as well as the Virgin Islands had adopted the Uniform Securities Act (2002). To date the major debate over enactment concerns whether variable products should be excluded from the definition of security. Variable Annuity Industry under Scrutiny for Exchange Sales, Market Timing Abuses, 36 Sec. Reg. & L. Rep. (BNA) 425 (2004).

2. NEW YORK AND CALIFORNIA

P. 28 n.32, end note. After enactment of the Sarbanes-Oxley Act of 2002, California amended §1502 (subsequently amended further and adding §1502.1) and §2117 (subsequently amended further and adding §2117.1) of the California Corporations Code to require publicly traded corporations to file an annual statement disclosing, among other things, their independent auditor; any nonaudit services provided by the auditor during the two most recent fiscal years; the annual compensation paid to each director and to the five highest compensated officers who are not directors; and a description of any loans made to a director at a preferential rate during the two most recent fiscal years.

California also adopted §2207 of the California Corporations Code, requiring a corporation to notify in writing the state attorney general or the appropriate government agency, as well as the corporation's shareholders, if the corporation has knowledge of certain acts, including "actual knowledge that any officer, director, manager, or agent of the corporation" has made or issued in any report or prospectus any "material statement or omission that is false and intended to give the shares of stock in the corporation a materially greater or a materially less apparent market value than they really possess."

California further adopted new §25,404, making it "unlawful for any person to knowingly alter, destroy, mutilate, conceal, cover up, falsify, or make a false entry in any record, document, or tangible object with the intent to impede, obstruct, or influence the administration or enforcement of [the Corporate Securities Law of 1968]." California also stiffened the penalties under §25,540. Other states similarly adopted so-called "mini-Sarbanes-Oxley Acts." See generally French & Soderquist, State Responses to Corporate Corruption: Thirteen Mini Sarbanes-Oxley Acts, 32 Sec. Reg. L.J. 167 (2004).

3. Selective Federal Preemption: The National Securities Markets Improvement Act of 1996

a. Securities Offerings and Reporting

P. 29, after callout for note 37. In Brown v. Earthboard Sports USA, Inc., 481 F.3d 901 (6th Cir. 2007), the Sixth Circuit, reversing the district court, held that NSMIA only preempts state securities laws for those offerings that "actually qualify" as covered securities. It is not enough, according to the court, that the offering purported to be made pursuant to Rule 506 of Regulation D, a safe harbor under §4(2) of the 1933 Act. The offering would actually have to satisfy Rule 506's requirements for NSMIA to preempt the relevant state registration requirements. For the court to have held otherwise would have enabled issuers effectively to expand NSMIA's preemptive reach by simply claiming that an offering was pursuant to Rule 506 and making certain required filings with the SEC under Regulation D.

D. A TELESCOPIC PREVIEW OF THE SEC STATUTES

4. PUBLIC UTILITY HOLDING COMPANY ACT OF 1935

P. 47, end 1st par. The Energy Policy Act of 2005, 119 Stat. 594, repealed the Public Utility Holding Company Act of 1935. The Energy Policy Act replaced the 1935 Act with the Public Utility Holding Company Act of 2005. The 2005 Holding Company Act substantially overhauls the regulation of public utility holding companies, with the effect of easing the regulatory burden on the electric industry, and transfers authority from the SEC to the Federal Energy Regulatory Commission, which will administer the 2005 Act, and to relevant state commissions.

6. INVESTMENT COMPANY ACT OF 1940

a. The *Investment Company* Concept

(ii) *Unit Investment Trusts*

P. 48, new pars. after 3d full par. In March 2007 the SEC issued its Report on Refunds, Sales Practices and Revenues from Periodic Payment Plans, which was required by §4(c) of the Military Personnel Financial Services Protection Act, P.L. 109-290, 120 Stat. 1317 (2006). The Report summarized at 4–6:

> On September 29, 2006, Congress enacted the Military Personnel Financial Services Protection Act of 2006 (*Act*) to protect members of the Armed Forces from unscrupulous practices regarding sales of insurance, financial, and investment products. Among other things, the Act prohibited the issuance and sale of new periodic payment plan certificates after October 29, 2006, without invalidating any rights or obligations under a certificate sold

before that date. It also required the Securities and Exchange Commission (*Commission*) to prepare a report on various matters relating to broker-dealers and the sale of periodic payment plans over the five-year period preceding submission of the report, from 2002 to 2006 (the *report period*)....

Periodic payment plans are managed and sponsored by investment company complexes. The number of plan sponsors of periodic payment plans has also declined since 1970. In that year approximately 80 sponsors offered periodic payment plans. By 2002, the beginning of the report period, only nine sponsors were in operation, with two of them holding 75% of plan assets....

Any recommendations:...Congress directed the Commission, after such consultation with the Secretary of Defense as the Commission considers appropriate, to describe any legislative or regulatory recommendations to improve sales practices on military installations. Several legislative and regulatory initiatives have already been adopted, including the prohibition on sales of periodic payment plans; the on-going initiatives by the Department of Defense; the continuing oversight by the Commission and the NASD of broker-dealers that sell securities to military personnel; and the Commission and NASD's active program of investor education for uniformed military personnel. In light of these active initiatives, which have already achieved considerable success, the Commission has no further legislative or regulatory recommendations to make at this time.

c. Registration and Regulatory Provisions

(v) *Adequate and Feasible Capital Structures*

P. 57 n.42, end note. In 2006 the Commission adopted new rules concerning fund of funds investments. See Inv. Co. Act Rel. 27,399, 88 SEC Dock. 816 (2006) (adoption). The Commission adopted new Rules 12d1-1, 12d1-2, and 12d1-3 under the 1940 Investment Company Act. The Rules address the ability of a registered investment company to invest in shares of another investment company. The Commission also adopted amendments to Forms N-1A, N-2, N-3, N-4, and N-6 to require that prospectuses of funds of funds disclose the expenses investors in the acquiring fund will bear, including the expenses of any acquired funds.

(vi) *Financial Statements and Accounting*

P. 59, new par., after 2d full par. In 2003, Eliot Spitzer, the New York Attorney General, settled State of N.Y. v. Canary Capital Partners, LLC, in which a hedge fund agreed to pay $40 million after civil allegations were filed alleging an unlawful trading scheme involving several leading mutual funds. N.Y.A.G. Launches Probe of Fund Industry; Hedge Fund Pays $40M to Resolve Claims, 35 Sec. Reg. & L. Rep. (BNA) 1505 (2003).

Subsequently, several instances of improper trading by mutual fund executives or favored customers and failure to give customers appropriate discounts were widely reported. See, e.g., Labaton, SEC's Oversight of Mutual Funds Is Said to Be Lax, N.Y. Times, Nov. 16, 2003, at 1. The SEC was further criticized by Spitzer for a rushed settlement with Putnam Investments. Spitzer, Regulation Begins at Home, N.Y. Times, Nov. 17, 2003, at A23.

Chairman Donaldson testified to a House hearing in late October 2003 that market timing and late trading abuses by mutual funds were "quite widespread…more widespread than we originally anticipated." Donaldson Says Improper Trading in Mutual Funds "Quite Widespread," 35 Sec. Reg. & L. Rep. (BNA) 1806 (2003).

In December 2003 the Commission proposed amendments to Form N-1A to require open end management investment companies to provide enhanced disclosure regarding breakpoint discounts on front end sales loads. Inv. Co. Act Rel. 26,298, 81 SEC Dock. 2581 (2003) (proposal).

Separately the Commission circulated a concept Release requesting comments on several mutual fund transaction cost issues. Inv. Co. Act Rel. 26,313, 81 SEC Dock. 2600 (2003).

In 2004 the Commission adopted amendments to Forms N-1A, N-3, N-4, and N-6 to require mutual funds to disclose their policies with respect to frequent purchases and redemptions of fund shares. The Commission also adopted amendments to Forms

N-1A and N-3 to require specified variable annuities to explain the circumstances and effects of any use of fair value pricing. Inv. Co. Act Rels. 26,287, 81 SEC Dock. 2553 (2003) (proposal); 26,418, 82 SEC Dock. 2357 (2004) (adoption).

In Inv. Co. Act Rel. 26,288, 81 SEC Dock. 2553 (2003) (proposal to amend Rule 22c-1), the Commission proposed a time limit on the purchase of redeemable fund shares to prevent the receipt of an order after the time that the fund establishes for the calculation of its net asset value to prevent unlawful late trading in fund shares. Cf. Key Groups Oppose SEC Proposal on Providing Same-Day Price to Fund Shares, 36 Sec. Reg. & L. Rep. (BNA) 296 (2004).

In July 2004 the Commission adopted several new Investment Company Act governance rules. Inv. Co. Act Rels. 26,323, 81 SEC Dock. 3414 (2004) (proposal); 26,520, 83 SEC Dock. 1384 (2004) (adoption). Collectively the rule amendments would require that the covered funds usually have a board with at least 75 percent independent directors; that an independent director be chair of the fund board; that the board conduct an annual self-assessment; that the independent directors meet at least once each quarter without any interested persons present; that the independent directors be authorized to hire staff to help fulfill the board's fiduciary duties; and that the board retain copies of written materials that directors consider in approving advisory companies under §15 of the Investment Company Act. Commissioners Atkins and Glassman dissented from the requirements that 75 percent of the board be independent and that one independent director be chair.

The District of Columbia Court of Appeals later granted in part the Chamber of Commerce's petition for review. Chamber of Commerce of United States of Am. v. SEC, 412 F.3d 133 (D.C. Cir. 2005). The Court agreed with the SEC that it had authority to adopt the requirement of 75 percent independent directors and an independent Chair, but agreed with the Chamber that the SEC failed to adequately consider the costs that mutual funds would incur in complying with the new standards or alternatives to the independent Chair requirement. The Commission subsequently readopted the Rule on a 3-2 vote.

BACKGROUND OF THE SEC STATUTES   P. 59

In August 2005, the court stayed the 75 percent independent director and independent chair requirements pending court review. Chamber of Commerce of United States of Am. v. SEC, Order No. 05-1240 (D.C. Cir. 2005).

In early April 2006, the District of Columbia Circuit again ruled against the Commission. The federal appeals court found that the Commission did not follow proper procedures in readopting the mutual fund governance rules requiring more board independence. See Chamber of Commerce of United States of Am. v. SEC, Order No. 05-1240 (D.C. Cir. 2006). The court, though, allowed the Commission a limited opportunity to address the procedural shortcomings by reopening the record for comment on the cost of the 75 percent independent director and independent chair requirements.

In June 2006 the Commission did request additional comment. See Inv. Co. Act Rel. 27,395, 88 SEC Dock. 622 (2006). See also SEC Press Rel. 2006-95 (June 13, 2006) (announcing that the Commission had filed a status report with the D.C. Circuit concerning the Commission's mutual fund board independence rules). In response to two reports prepared by the SEC's Office of Economic Analysis that were made public, the Commission in December 2006 reopened the comment period, which had closed in August 2006 under the SEC's June 2006 request for comment. See Inv. Co. Act Rel. 27,600, 89 SEC Dock. 1894 (2006).

The Commission also adopted new rules and other rule amendments to require broker-dealers to provide their customers with point of sale information regarding the costs and conflicts of interests that arise from the distribution of mutual fund shares, unit investment trust interests, and municipal fund securities. Inv. Co. Act Rel. 26,464, 82 SEC Dock. 3441 (2004) (adoption).

In March 2004, the Commission settled the largest market timing and late trading case to date with Bank of America and two FleetBoston Financial Corporation subsidiaries. The settlement aggregated $675 million in a combination of disgorgement and civil penalties. BOA, FleetBoston Agree on $675 Million to Resolve SEC, N.Y. Charges over Abuses, 36 Sec. Reg. & L. Rep. (BNA) 513 (2004). See also Putnam to Pay $110M to Resolve Charges Its Employees Engaged in Marking Timing, 36 id. 663.

15

P. 59

In 2004, the Commission adopted amendments to Forms N-1A, N-2, N-3, and N-CSR to identify portfolio team managers, disclose potential conflicts of interest, and disclose the portfolio manager compensation structure and securities ownership. Inv. Co. Act Rels. 26,383, 82 SEC Dock. 1149 (2004) (proposal); 26,533, 83 SEC Dock. 1802 (2004) (adoption).

In 2005, the Commission further adopted Rule 22c-2 to permit mutual funds to impose a two percent fee on the redemption of shares purchased within the previous seven days. Inv. Co. Act Rels. 26,375A, 82 SEC Dock. 1419 (2004) (proposal); 26,782, 84 SEC Dock. 3664 (2005) (adoption).

In 2006 the Commission voted a different amendment of Rule 22c-2. See Inv. Co. Act Rels. 27,255, 87 SEC Dock. 1341 (2006) (proposal); 27,504, 88 SEC Dock. 3127 (2006) (adoption). These Rule 22c-2 amendments limit the types of intermediaries with which funds must enter into shareholder information agreements, address the application of Rule 22c-2 when there are *intermediary chains*, and clarify what impact the failure of a fund to obtain an agreement with any of its intermediaries has. The shareholder information agreements enable fund managers to determine which investors, if any, are trading in violation of the fund's limits on short-term trading. The amendments also extended certain compliance dates from 2006 to 2007.

In 2004, the Commission, on a three to two vote, adopted new rules requiring that hedge fund advisers register under the Investment Adviser Act. Inv. Adv. Act Rel. 2266, 83 SEC Dock. 1124 (2004) (proposal); 2333, 84 SEC Dock. 1032 (2004) (adoption).

As of 2004, there were approximately 8000 registered investment advisers who managed more than $23 trillion in client assets. Id. at 1125. While the diversity of investment advisers was strikingly broad, it did not include hedge funds.

Under the Investment Advisers Act §203(b)(3), *private* advisers (i) with fewer than 15 clients during the past 12 months, (ii) who do not hold themselves out generally to the public as an investment adviser, or (iii) who are not advisers to a registered investment company are exempt from registration under the Investment Advisers Act.

Hedge funds have often claimed exemption under §203(b)(3) by creating pooled investment vehicles, such as limited partnerships, business trusts or corporations (each of which the Commission counted as a single client), even when a substantial number of natural persons invested in the investment vehicle.

The Commission adopted Rule 203(b)(3)-2 to require investment advisers to count each shareholder, limited partner, member or beneficiary of a *private fund* to determine the availability of the §203(b)(3) exemption. *Private funds* are defined in Rules 203(b)(3)-1(d)(1)–(3) to mean a company:

> (i) That would be an investment company under section 3(a) of the Investment Company Act of 1940 but for the exception provided from that definition by either section 3(c)(1) or section 3(c)(7) of such Act;
>
> (ii) That permits its owners to redeem any portion of their ownership interests within two years of the purchase of such interests; and
>
> (iii) Interests in which are or have been offered based on the investment advisory skills, ability or expertise of the investment adviser.

(2) Notwithstanding paragraph (d)(1) of this section, a company is not a private fund if it permits its owners to redeem their ownership interests within two years of the purchase of such interests only in the case of:

> (i) Events you find after reasonable inquiry to be extraordinary; and
>
> (ii) Interests acquired through reinvestment of distributed capital gains or income.

(3) Notwithstanding paragraph (d)(1) of this section, a company is not a private fund if it has its principal office and place of business outside the United States, makes a public offering of its securities in a country other than the United States, and is regulated as a public investment company under the laws of the country other than the United States.

Rule 203(b)(3)-2 is, in effect, an exception to Rule 203(b)(3)-1, see infra at 334-335, which is a safe harbor that provides only a corporation, general partnership, limited liability company, trust or other legal entity will be counted as a client when the investment adviser provides advice based on the investment objective of the entity, rather than individual investment objectives of the beneficial owners.

The Rule 203(b)(3)-2 exception to Rule 203(b)(3)-1 is based on three characteristics shared by virtually all hedge funds. First, the private fund must be an investment company required to register under the Investment Company Act but for the specified §§3(c)(1) and (7) exceptions. This condition would exclude advisers to many business organizations such as insurance companies, broker-dealers, and publishers.

Second, a company would be a private fund only if it permitted redemption within two years of the purchase or an interest. The redeemability requirement would exclude investment advisers who advise private equity and venture capital funds, as well as other funds that require long term commitments of capital. Unlike hedge funds, funds with longer term temporal commitments have not been a major enforcement concern for the Commission.

Third, private fund interests are offered on the basis of the ongoing investment advisory skills, ability, or expertise of the investment adviser.

The Commission also adopted amendments to several other Investment Advisers Act rules, including relief from a recordkeeping requirement in Rule 204-2; application of the performance fee exemption in Rule 205-3 for earlier established hedge funds; Rule 206(4)-2, the adviser custody rule, and Form ADV.

Commissioners Atkins and Glassman dissented from the hedge fund registration requirement, writing in part:

> Our main concerns with this rulemaking can be broadly divided into the following categories:
>
> • There are many viable alternatives to this rulemaking that should have been considered....

- The pretext for the rule does not withstand scrutiny....
- The Commission's limited resources will be diverted.

Id. at 1087–1088.

In June 2006 the District of Columbia Court of Appeals in Goldstein v. SEC, 451 F.3d 873 (D.C. Cir. 2006), vacated the SEC Hedge Fund Rule as an arbitrary rule, criticizing among other things the Commission's failure to adequately justify departing from an earlier interpretation of §203(b)(3).

The Commission did not appeal *Goldstein*. See SEC Press Rel. 2006-135 (Aug. 7, 2006). Nor did the Commission attempt to fashion a revised rule that might pass muster requiring hedge fund managers to register under the Investment Advisers Act. Rather, in 2007 the SEC adopted a different set of rules impacting hedge funds. See Inv. Adv. Act Rels. 2576, 89 SEC Dock. 1938 (2006) (proposal); 2628, 90 SEC Dock. 938 (2007) (adoption); see infra ch. 9.D. The Commission summarized the rule amendments in the proposal Release as follows:

> First, we are proposing to adopt a new antifraud rule under the Advisers Act that would clarify, in light of a recent court decision [*Goldstein*], the Commission's ability to bring enforcement actions under the Advisers Act against investment advisers who defraud investors or prospective investors in a hedge fund or other pooled investment vehicle.
>
> Second, we are proposing a rule that would revise the requirements for determining whether an individual is eligible to invest in certain pooled investment vehicles. We are concerned that the definition of *accredited investor*, which certain privately offered investment pools (*private pools*) use in determining whether an individual is eligible to invest in the pool, may not provide sufficient protections for investors. We are therefore proposing to define a new category of accredited investor called *accredited natural person*, which is designed to help ensure that investors in these types of funds are capable of evaluating and bearing the risks of their investments.

89 SEC Dock. at 1940.

In February 2007 the President's Working Group on Financial Markets (*PWG*)—chaired by the Treasury Secretary and consisting of the chairmen of the Federal Reserve Board, the SEC, and the Commodity Futures Trading Commission—issued a set of principles and guidelines concerning private pools of capital, which include hedge funds. A copy of the Agreement Among PWG and U.S. Agency Principals on Principles and Guidelines Regarding Private Pools of Capital is available on the Treasury Department's Web site at http://www.treas.gov/press/releases/hp272.htm. The PWG advanced a market-oriented approach to hedge fund oversight that relies on market discipline both to protect hedge fund investors and to ensure that the pools of capital undertake effective investment and operational risk management. Cf. Paredes, On the Decision to Regulate Hedge Funds: The SEC's Regulatory Philosophy, Style, and Mission, 2006 U. Ill. L. Rev. 975 (urging market discipline over government regulation).

See generally GAO, Hedge Funds: Regulators and Market Participants Are Taking Steps to Strengthen Market Discipline, but Continued Attention Is Needed (GAO-08-200, Jan. 2008).

F. THE SECURITIES AND EXCHANGE COMMISSION

2. THE COMMISSION'S STAFF

P. 68 n.7, end note. In 2003, the Commission made fiscal year 2004 adjustments under §6(b) under the Securities Act of 1933, as well as §§13(e) and 14(a) under the 1934 Act, raising the rate to $126.70 per million and raising the rate to $39.00 per million under §§31(b) & (c) of the 1934 Act. Sec. Ex. Act Rel. 47,768, 80 SEC Dock. 147 (2003).

Early in 2004, the SEC sought a $913 million budget for FY 2005, as part of the President's budget, 12.5 percent above the SEC's recently enacted FY 2004 budget of $811.5 million. In FY 2004 the Commission anticipated adding 842 positions. The FY 2004 budget would add 106 additional staff. SEC Releases FY 2005 Budget Information, SEC Press Rel. 2004-2011; Bush Asks

12.5 Percent Increase for SEC in a Vote for Strong Wall Street Presence, 36 Sec Reg. & L. Rep. (BNA) 234 (2004).

The fiscal year 2005 adjustment to §§31(b) and (c) changed the fee rates to $32.90 per million. Sec. Ex. Act Rel. 49,634, 82 SEC Dock. 2613 (2004).

In the fiscal year 2005, the fee rates applicable under §6(b) of the 1933 Act and §§13(e) and 14(g) of the 1934 Act were changed to $117.70 per million.

Separately the Commission adopted Rule 31 and Form 31 to govern the calculation, payment, and collection of fees under §31. Sec. Ex. Act Rel. 49,928, 83 SEC Dock. 502 (2004) (adoption). Under the Accountability of Tax Dollars Act of 2002, P.L. 107-289, 31 U.S.C. §3515, beginning in the 2004 fiscal year, the SEC is required to prepare financial statements audited by an outside auditor. The new Rule and Form facilitate the ability of the SEC to calculate §31 fees and assessments consistent with the 2002 Act.

In February 2007 the Commission announced that the SEC would reduce the fees it charges. The fees to register securities were cut over 71 percent; the fees on securities transactions were cut over 50 percent. See SEC Press Rel. 2007-24 (Feb. 16, 2007); SEC Press Rel. 2006-64 (May 3, 2006) (announcing billion dollar fee cut for fiscal year 2007).

In 2004 the Commission published a 2004–2009 Strategic Plan. The Plan began by generalizing about Commission resources:

> The agency's staff of almost 4,100 monitor and regulate a securities industry that includes SROs (including 13 securities exchanges, 11 clearing agencies, NASD and the Municipal Securities Rulemaking Board), more than 7,000 broker-dealers, 900 transfer agents, and almost 500 municipal and government securities dealers. In 2003, the volume traded on U.S. exchanges and Nasdaq exceeded $22 trillion and 850 billion shares.
>
> The Commission also regulates more than 35,000 investment company portfolios (including mutual funds, closed-end funds, unit investment trusts, exchange-traded funds, and interval funds, and variable insurance products), more than 8,200 federally registered advisers, and 28 registered public utility holding companies.
>
> Each year, the Commission accepts, processes, and disseminates to the public more than 600,000 documents from companies and

individuals that are filed through the agency's Electronic Data Gathering, Analysis, and Retrieval (EDGAR) system. These filings include the annual reports of more than 12,000 reporting companies, which comprise up to eighteen million pages annually.

Id. at 9.

P. 69, end 1st par. In 2007 the SEC announced a new Office of Interactive Disclosure. That same year, the Division of Market Regulation was renamed the Division of Trading and Markets. In 2008 a new Office of Collections and Distributions was set up.

CHAPTER 2

FEDERAL REGULATION OF THE DISTRIBUTION OF SECURITIES

A. DISTRIBUTION TECHNIQUES

2. FIRM COMMITMENT

P. 85 n.10, end note. The SEC announced that, beginning in August 2004, it would publically release comment letters and filer responses to disclosure filings reviewed by the Divisions of Corporation Finance and Investment Management. SEC Press Rel. 2004–89 (June 24, 2004).

5. SHELF REGISTRATION

P. 89, end 3d par. In 2004, as part of its Regulation AB Release, Sec. Act Rel. 8518, 84 SEC Dock. 1624 (2004) (adoption), the Commission adopted Rule 15d-22 to require annual and other reports with respect to asset backed securities registered under Rule 415(a)(1)(x).

As part of the public offering reforms the Commission adopted in 2005, the Commission revised, and in many respects relaxed, the shelf offering process. The SEC, for example, relaxed the two year formula. In particular, for shelf offerings under Rule

415(a)(1)(x) and for continuous offerings under Rule 415(a)(1)(ix) that are registered on Form S-3 or F-3, the Commission eliminated the provision in Rule 415(a)(2) that limits the amount of securities registered to "an amount which, at the time the registration statement becomes effective, is reasonably expected to be offered and sold within two years from the initial effective date of the registration." This limit remains in place, though, for business combination offerings under Rule 415(a)(1)(viii) and for continuous offerings under Rule 415(a)(1)(ix) that are not registered on Form S-3 or F-3.

The SEC did adopt a new sort of three year formula, though. Under new Rule 415(a)(5), the shelf registration statement for offerings under Rule 415(a)(1)(ix) and (x), as well as the shelf registration statement for mortgage related securities offerings under Rule 415(a)(1)(vii), can only be used for three years after the initial effective date of the registration statement under which the securities are being offered and sold. In other words, a new registration statement must be filed every three years. The three year period is subject to a limited extension, however. Securities covered by the old registration statement may still be offered and sold until the earlier of the effective date of the issuer's new registration statement or 180 days after the third anniversary of the initial effective date of the old registration statement. Also, a continuous offering of securities covered by the old registration statement that started within three years of the initial effective date may continue until the effective date of the new registration statement, so long as such offering is permitted under the new registration statement. (Filings of a new registration statement with respect to automatic shelves, discussed below, are effective immediately under Rule 462(e), so the 180-day extension period does not apply.) Rule 415(a)(6) further provides that even though a new shelf registration statement must be filed for shelf offerings under Rules 415(a)(1)(vii), (ix), and (x) every three years, unsold securities under the prior registration statement and any fees already paid in connection with such unsold securities may be carried over and included as part of the new registration statement that is filed.

When originally adopted, Rule 415(a)(1)(x) covered securities registered on Form S-3 or F-3 "which are to be offered and sold on a continuous or delayed basis." The Commission's 2005 amendments to Rule 415 relaxed this provision to allow primary offerings on Form S-3 or F-3 also to occur "immediately" after effectiveness of a shelf registration statement. Rule 415(a)(1)(x), accordingly, now covers "[s]ecurities registered (or qualified to be registered) on Form S-3 or Form F-3...which are to be offered and sold on an immediate, continuous or delayed basis by or on behalf of the registrant, a majority-owned subsidiary of the registrant or a person of which the registrant is a majority-owned subsidiary." In practice, this change allows for immediate takedowns of securities off the shelf.

Another relaxation of the shelf offering process included in the Commission's 2005 public offering reforms concerns so-called *at the market offerings*, which Rule 415(a)(4), prior to the 2005 amendments, defined as "an offering of securities into an existing trading market for outstanding shares of the same class at other than a fixed price on or through the facilities of a national securities exchange or to or through a market maker otherwise than on an exchange." Under Rule 415(a)(4) as in effect prior to the 2005 amendments, an at the market offering had to satisfy a number of requirements, including (i) the offering must come within Rule 415(a)(1)(x), (ii) where voting stock is registered, the amount of securities registered must not exceed 10 percent of the aggregate market value of the registrant's outstanding voting stock held by non-affiliates, (iii) the securities must be sold through an underwriter or underwriters, and (iv) the underwriter or underwriters must be named in the prospectus included in the registration statement. Under the amended Rule, the restrictions on primary at the market offerings have been eliminated, except that the offering still must come within Rule 415(a)(1)(x). The amended Rule also revises the definition of *at the market offering* to mean "an offering of equity securities into an existing trading market for outstanding shares of the same class at other than a fixed price."

The most significant change to the shelf registration process concerns automatic shelf registration for well-known seasoned issuers, a new category of issuer included as part of the 2005 SEC public offering reforms. Rule 405 defines a *well-known seasoned issuer* (or *WKSI*) as follows:

[A]n issuer that, as of the most recent determination date determined pursuant to paragraph (2) of this definition:

(1)(i) Meets all the registrant requirements of General Instruction I.A. of Form S-3 or Form F-3 and either:

(A) As of a date within 60 days of the determination date, has a worldwide market value of its outstanding voting and non-voting common equity held by non-affiliates of $700 million or more; or

(B)(1) As of a date within 60 days of the determination date, has issued in the last three years at least $1 billion aggregate principal amount of non-convertible securities, other than common equity, in primary offerings for cash, not exchange, registered under the [Securities] Act; and

(2) Will register only non-convertible securities, other than common equity, and full and unconditional guarantees permitted pursuant to paragraph (1)(ii) of this definition unless, at the determination date, the issuer also is eligible to register a primary offering of its securities relying on General Instruction I.B.1 of Form S-3 or Form F-3; and

(3) Provided that as to a parent issuer only, for purposes of calculating the aggregate principal amount of outstanding non-convertible securities under paragraph (1)(i)(B)(1) of this definition, the parent issuer may include the aggregate principal amount of non-convertible securities, other than common equity, of its majority-owned subsidiaries issued in registered primary offerings for cash, not exchange, that it has fully and unconditionally guaranteed, within the meaning of Rule 3-10 of Regulation S-X in the last three years.

(ii) Is a majority-owned subsidiary of a parent that is a well-known seasoned issuer pursuant to paragraph (1)(i) of this definition and, as to the subsidiaries' securities that are being or may be offered on that parent's registration statement:

(A) The parent has provided a full and unconditional guarantee, as defined in Rule 3-10 of Regulation S-X, of the payment obligations on the subsidiary's securities and the securities are non-convertible securities, other than common equity;

(B) The securities are guarantees of:

(1) Non-convertible securities, other than common equity, of its parent being registered; or

(2) Non-convertible securities, other than common equity, of another majority-owned subsidiary being registered where there is a full and unconditional guarantee, as defined in Rule 3-10 of Regulation S-X, of such non-convertible securities by the parent; or

(C) The securities of the majority-owned subsidiary meet the conditions of General Instruction I.B.2 of Form S-3 or Form F-3.

(iii) Is not an ineligible issuer as defined in [Rule 405].

(iv) Is not an asset-backed issuer as defined in Item 1101 of Regulation AB.

(v) Is not an investment company registered under the Investment Company Act of 1940 or a business development company as defined in section 2(a)(48) of the Investment Company Act of 1940.

(2) For purposes of this definition, the determination date as to whether an issuer is a well-known seasoned issuer shall be the latest of:

(i) The time of filing of its most recent shelf registration statement; or

(ii) The time of its most recent amendment (by post-effective amendment, incorporated report filed pursuant to section 13 or 15(d) of the Securities Exchange Act of 1934, or form of prospectus) to a shelf registration statement for purposes of complying with section 10(a)(3) of the [Securities] Act (or if such amendment has not been made within the time period required by section 10(a)(3) of the [Securities] Act, the date on which such amendment is required); or

(iii) In the event that the issuer has not filed a shelf registration statement or amended a shelf registration statement for purposes of complying with section 10(a)(3) of the [Securities] Act for sixteen months, the time of filing of the issuer's most recent annual report on Form 10-K or Form 20-F (or if such report has not been filed by its due date, such due date).

Automatic shelf registration provides additional flexibility to WKSIs offering and selling securities and allows WKSIs to tap capital markets even more quickly. The principal features of an automatic shelf registration are as follows. Automatic shelf registration involves filings on Form S-3 or F-3 and is available at the option of eligible WKSIs; a WKSI is not obligated to use the automatic shelf registration process. The automatic shelf registration process permits WKSIs to register unspecified amounts of securities on Form S-3 or F-3 without indicating whether the offering is a primary offering or a secondary offering on behalf of selling security holders. As the SEC explained in the adoption Release, a WKSI that is such because it meets the $700 million public float threshold can use an automatic shelf for any registered offering, other than for business combination transactions. An issuer that is a WKSI because it meets the $1 billion nonconvertible securities issuance threshold can also register any such offering for cash using the automatic shelf process if such issuer is eligible to register a primary offering on Form S-3 or F-3 under General Instruction I.B.1 of such Form. However, a WKSI that only is a WKSI based on satisfying the $1 billion nonconvertible securities threshold but that is ineligible to register a primary offering on Form S-3 or Form F-3 under General Instruction I.B.1 of these Forms may use the automatic shelf procedure to register only securities offerings for cash of nonconvertible securities, other than common equity, whether or not the securities are investment grade. Forms S-3 and F-3 were amended such that automatic shelf issuers are now also allowed, through an expansion of the so-called unallocated shelf procedure, to register classes of securities without allocating the mix of securities registered between the issuer, its eligible subsidiaries, or selling security holders.

Under Rule 462, a registration statement is immediately effective upon filing under automatic shelf registration without any SEC review of the filing; an issuer may not defer effectiveness. Amended Rule 401(g) provides that an automatic shelf registration statement and any posteffective amendment thereto is deemed filed on the proper form unless and until the Commission notifies the issuer that the Commission objects to the issuer's use of such form. Accordingly, as the SEC highlighted in the adoption Release, unless notified by the Commission, an issuer can proceed with its offering with certainty that the issuer has used the proper form for registration. The SEC clarified in the adoption Release that if the SEC notifies an issuer that the issuer is not eligible to use the automatic shelf procedure, securities sold before the SEC notification will not have been sold in violation of §5 of the 1933 Act. Under Rule 413, a WKSI may add additional classes of securities and may add securities of eligible majority-owned subsidiaries to an automatic shelf registration statement already in effect by filing a posteffective amendment to the registration statement. The posteffective amendment will become immediately effective upon filing, as provided under Rule 462.

Along the lines described earlier with respect to certain other shelf registrations, Rule 415(a)(5) requires issuers to file a new automatic shelf registration statement every three years. The new registration statement will effectively restate the issuer's old registration statement and amend it as the issuer determines is needed. The new automatic shelf registration statement will be effective immediately, and any unused fees paid or unsold securities registered may be carried forward to the new registration statement under Rule 415(a)(6). Accordingly, a securities offering begun under the old automatic shelf registration statement can continue without interruption.

WKSIs may pay filing fees in connection with an automatic shelf registration statement at any time prior to a takedown or on a pay-as-you-go basis with filing fees due at the time each takedown off the shelf occurs. Fees paid on a pay-as-you-go basis are calculated in the appropriate amount given the date and the amount of the particular takedown with respect to which fees are being paid.

Although prospectuses are covered in more detail below, some important points should be noted here when it comes to what may be omitted from a prospectus that is part of an automatic shelf registration offering. Under current Rule 409 under the 1933 Act, a WKSI may omit from a base prospectus information that is unknown and not reasonably available. Under Rule 430B, a WKSI may also omit from an automatic shelf registration statement the following information: (i) whether the offering is a primary or secondary offering; (ii) the plan of distribution for the securities; (iii) a description of the securities registered other than an identification of the name or class of the securities (i.e., such identifications of the securities as *debt, common stock, preferred stock,* etc.); and (iv) the names of any selling security holders. This is not to say that investors are forever without this information. Issuers generally can add information to a prospectus under automatic shelf registration through any of the following means of disclosure: (a) a posteffective amendment to the registration statement; (b) a prospectus filed pursuant to Rule 424(b); or (c) incorporation by reference to 1934 Act reports of the issuer.

P. 90 n.26, end note. As part of the rulemaking resulting in the SEC's 2005 public offering reforms, the Commission requested comment in the proposal Release as to whether it should reevaluate the factors discussed in Rule 176, which would include Rule 176(g) for underwriters. For example, the introduction of the automatic shelf registration presents new concerns regarding the extent of underwriter due diligence requirements under §11. The SEC ultimately decided to make no changes to Rule 176 to address this or any other matter. See generally Coffee, A Section 11 Safe Harbor?, N.Y. L.J., Sept. 15, 2005, at 7.

In WorldCom, Inc. Sec. Litig., 346 F. Supp. 2d 628 (S.D.N.Y. 2004), a high profile case receiving a great deal of attention, Judge Cote addressed the underwriters' due diligence obligations with respect to the financial statements that were incorporated into two WorldCom bond offerings. Judge Cote's opinion included a thoroughgoing analysis of Rule 176 and underwriters' due diligence obligations in the context of shelf offerings.

6. AUCTIONS

P. 91, after 1st full par. The Dutch auction technique for distributing securities, discussed in the context of shelf offerings under Rule 415, began to develop in more recent years as an alternative to more traditional bookbuilding in nonshelf offerings, particularly in initial public offerings of equity securities.

To the extent that the auction method works as predicted in pricing an offering, there should not be a sizable price spike that follows once the security starts trading publicly in the aftermarket. Put differently, the Dutch auction model is said to remedy, or at least ameliorate, any underpricing of the offering that finds the issuer leaving money on the table, so to speak. Indeed, enormous price spikes were part and parcel of the abusive IPO practices that occurred during the technology stock bubble of the latter half of the 1990s. The expectation of a sizable *pop* in the company's stock price after its initial public offering animated favoritism in the allocation process, such as spinning. It should also be noted that underwriting fees tend to be considerably less in a Dutch auction offering than in a traditional underwriting.

In 2004, in the largest and highest-profile Dutch auction public offering to date, Google Inc. filed a particularly notable nonshelf IPO registration statement. A self-styled *Letter from the Founders* included in Google's registration statement explained:

> Informed investors willing to pay the IPO price should be able to buy as many shares as they want, within reason, in the IPO, as on the stock market.
>
> It is important to us to have a fair process for our IPO that is inclusive of both small and large investors. It is also crucial that we achieve a good outcome for Google and its current shareholders. This has led us to pursue an auction-based IPO for our entire offering. Our goal is to have a share price that reflects a fair market valuation of Google and that moves rationally based on changes in our business and the stock market....
>
> Many companies have suffered from unreasonable speculation, small initial share float, and boom-bust cycles that hurt them and their investors in the long run. We believe that an auction-based IPO will minimize these problems.
>
> An auction is an unusual process for an IPO in the United States. Our experience with auction-based advertising systems has been surprisingly helpful in the auction design process for the IPO. As in the stock market, if people try to buy more stock than is available, the price will go up. And of course, the price will go down if there aren't enough buyers. This is a simplification, but it captures the basic issues. Our goal is to have an efficient market price — a rational price set by informed buyers and sellers — for our shares at the IPO and afterward. Our goal is to achieve a relatively stable price in the days following the IPO and that buyers and sellers receive a fair price at the IPO.

Notably, after going public at a price of $85 per share, Google's stock closed the first day of trading at around $100. By early 2006,

Google's stock price had skyrocketed to over $450 per share, in large part on the strength of the company's stellar earnings. By the start of the second quarter of 2006, Google was trading at around $400 per share.

To date, Dutch auction offerings remain a rare event compared to more traditional underwritten offerings. It remains to be seen whether this will change and Dutch auction offers will become more common as the Internet continues to play an increasingly significant role in the public offering process and as securities markets become increasingly democratized with the growth of the so-called *investor class* in the United States.

P. 91, renumber subsection 6 as subsection 7.

7. SECURITIES UNDERWRITING IN GENERAL

P. 92 n.28, end note. The Securities Industry and Financial Markets Association (SIFMA) Fact Book at 4, 10-11 (2008) reported:

> The securities industry raised $3.6 trillion in capital for U.S. businesses in the United States in 2007, 7.5 percent below the record-setting 2006 level of more than $3.9 trillion in corporate underwriting, private placements and medium term notes. The growth of capital raised has been exceptional in recent years, with $16.3 trillion in capital raised in the past five years (2003-2007), exceeding that raised over the prior 15 years.
>
> Corporate debt market issuance, including straight corporate and convertible bonds, asset-backed and non-agency mortgage-backed securities, and private placements, totaled $3.0 trillion in 2007, 9.8 percent below the record set in 2006. . . .
>
> The primary equity markets raised a record of $247.5 billion, 29.9 percent above the 2006 total. Initial public offering (IPO) volume excluding closed-end funds rose to $50.7 billion in 2007, up nearly 10 percent from the prior year. Closed-end fund IPOs totaled $38.9 billion, up a staggering 23.1 percent from 2006. This is the greatest magnitude increase since closed-end IPO volume rose 222 percent in 2002 from the 2001 level. The combined value of closed-end fund IPOs issued during the past five years exceeds the combined amount raised in the previous

20 years. Follow-on issuance totaled $96.4 billion in 2007, the fourth consecutive $90 billion-plus issuance year recorded, although slightly below the 2006 level.

In the years before the 2008 stock market crash, there was a continuing high level of U.S. corporate underwritings:

Year	Number of Issues	Value ($ Billions)
2002	7524	1,900.5
2003	8843	2,469.9
2004	9367	2,891.2
2005	9738	3,401.5
2006	9927	3,935.8
2007	7631	3,639.2

B. THE BASIC PROHIBITIONS OF §5

1. THE STATUTORY PATTERN

P. 97, new pars., after 3d par. In 2005 the SEC adopted significant reforms that significantly revamped the process by which companies register securities and issue them to the public (referred to hereafter as the *2005 public offering reforms*). Sec. Act Rels. 8501, 83 SEC Dock. 4 (2004) (proposal); 8591, 85 SEC Dock. 2871 (2005) (adoption); 8591A (2006) (technical amendments). These reforms represent one of the most important reformations of the registration and offering process accomplished in one fell swoop in recent decades. The following also provides an overall summary of the reforms impacting the way in which issuers and other offering participants are allowed to communicate with the market during a public offering subject to §5 of the Securities Act.

The SEC's overall objective was to modernize the securities offering and communications processes. Two developments, in particular, argued in favor of updating the regulatory regime that

P. 97

governs how issuers offer their securities to the public. The first development centers on technological advances affecting securities markets. The SEC explained in the adoption Release:

> ...[S]ignificant technological advances over the last three decades have increased both the market's demand for more timely corporate disclosure and the ability of issuers to capture, process, and disseminate this information. Computers, sophisticated financial software, replaced, to a larger extent, paper, pencils, typewriters, adding machines, carbon paper, paper mail, travel, and face-to-face meetings relied on previously. The rules we are adopting today seek to recognize the integral role that technology plays in timely informing the markets and investors about important corporate information and developments.

85 SEC Dock. at 2880.

The second development motivating the adoption of the 2005 public offering reforms centers on the important role that a public company's 1934 Act filings play in keeping the market up-to-speed and informed about an issuer and its securities. The SEC again explained in the adoption Release:

> The role that a public issuer's Exchange Act reports play in investment decision making is a key component of the rules we are adopting today. Congress recognized that the ongoing dissemination of accurate information by issuers about themselves and their securities is essential to the effective operation of the trading markets. The Exchange Act and underlying rules have established a system of continuing disclosure about issuers that have offered securities to the public, or that have securities that are listed on a national securities exchange or are broadly held by the public. The Exchange Act rules require public issuers to make periodic disclosures at annual and quarterly intervals, with other important information reported on a more current basis. The Exchange Act specifically provides for current disclosure to maintain the timeliness and adequacy of information disclosed by issuers, and we have significantly expanded our current disclosure requirements consistent with the provision in the Sarbanes-Oxley Act of 2002 that "[e]ach issuer reporting under Section 13(a) or 15(d)...disclose to the public on a rapid and current basis such additional information

concerning material changes in the financial condition or operations of the issuer...as the Commission determines...is necessary or useful for the protection of investors and in the public interest."

A public issuer's Exchange Act record provides the basic source of information to the market and to potential purchasers regarding the issuer and its management, business, financial condition, and prospects. Because an issuer's Exchange Act reports and other publicly available information form the basis for the market's evaluation of the issuer and the pricing of its securities, investors in the secondary market use that information in making their investment decisions. Similarly, during a securities offering in which an issuer uses a short-form registration statement, an issuer's Exchange Act record is very often the most significant part of the information about the issuer in the registration statement.

With the enactment of the Sarbanes-Oxley Act and our recent rulemaking and interpretive actions, we have enhanced significantly the disclosure included in issuers' Exchange Act filings and accelerated the filing deadlines for many issuers. The following are examples of recent regulatory actions that have improved the delivery of timely, high-quality information to the securities markets by issuers under the Exchange Act:

- Requiring the establishment of disclosure controls and procedures;
- Requiring a public issuer's top management to certify the content of periodic reports and highlight their responsibilities for and evaluation of the issuer's disclosure controls and procedures and internal control over financial reporting;
- Modifying the approach to current disclosure by increasing significantly the types of events that must be reported on a current basis and shortening the time for filing current reports;
- Approving listing standard changes intended to improve corporate governance and enhance the role of the audit committee of the issuer's board of directors with regard to financial reporting and auditor independence; and
- Providing further interpretive guidance regarding the content and understandability of Management's Discussion and Analysis of Financial Condition and Results of Operation (MD&A) — a disclosure item we believe is at the core of a reporting issuer's periodic reports.

P. 97

Many of the recent changes to the Exchange Act reporting framework provide greater rigor to the process that issuers must follow in preparing their financial statements and Exchange Act reports. Senior management now must certify the material adequacy of the content of periodic Exchange Act reports. Moreover, issuers, with the involvement of senior management, now must implement and evaluate disclosure controls and procedures and internal controls over financial reporting. Further, we believe the heightened role of an issuer's board of directors and its audit committee provides a structure that can contribute to improved Exchange Act reports.

...We believe that the enhancements to Exchange Act reporting described above enable us to rely on these reports to a greater degree in adopting our rules to reform the securities offering process.

85 SEC Dock. at 2880–2881.

In short, securities markets are more informed at any given moment about an issuer and its securities as a result of technological advances and enhanced reporting under the Exchange Act, aside from the particular disclosures required by the federal securities laws in connection with a specific registered offering. Such developments, then, allow for the liberalization of the offering process and communications with investors and potential investors during a registered offering without compromising investor protection.

The SEC expressed its belief that the 2005 public offering reforms will:

- Facilitate greater availability of information to investors and the market with regard to all issuers;
- Eliminate barriers to open communications that have been made increasingly outmoded by technological advances;
- Reflect the increased importance of electronic dissemination of information, including the use of the Internet;
- Make the capital formation process more efficient; and
- Define more clearly both the information and the timeliness of the availability of information against which a seller's statements are evaluated for liability purposes.

85 SEC Dock. at 2880.

The SEC provided the following summary of the relaxed communication rules ushered in as part of the 2005 public offering reforms:

> Today, we are adopting rules that relate to the following:
>
> - Regularly released factual business information;
> - Regularly released forward-looking information;
> - Communications made more than 30 days before filing a registration statement;
> - Communications by well-known seasoned issuers during the 30 days before filing a registration statement;
> - Written communications made in accordance with the safe harbor in Securities Act Rule 134; and
> - Written communications (other than a statutory prospectus) by any eligible issuer after filing a registration statement.
>
> The following table provides a brief overview of the operation of the new and amended rules....

	Could it be an "offer" as defined in Section 2(a)(3)?	Is it a "prospectus" as defined in Section 2(a)(10)?	Is it a prohibited prefiling offer for purposes of Section 5(c)?	Is it a prohibited prospectus for purposes of Section 5(b)(1)?
Regularly Released Factual Business Information	Yes	No	Rule defines it as not an offer for Section 5(c) purposes	Section 5(b)(1) relates only to "prospectuses" — it is not applicable

continues

Regularly Released Forward-Looking Information	Yes	No	Rule defines it as not an offer for Section 5(c) purposes	Section 5(b)(1) relates only to "prospectuses" — it is not applicable
Communications Made More Than 30 Days Before Filing of Registration Statement	Yes	Possibly, based on facts and circumstances	Rule defines it as not an offer for Section 5(c) purposes	Section 5(b)(1) does not apply in the prefiling period — it is not applicable
Well-Known Seasoned Issuers — Oral Offers Made Within 30 Days of Filing of Registration Statement	Yes	No	Is exempted from prohibition of Section 5(c)	Section 5(b)(1) does not apply in the prefiling period — it is not applicable
Well-Known Seasoned Issuers — Written Offers Made Within 30 Days of Filing of Registration Statement	Yes	Yes. It also is a free-writing prospectus	Is exempted from prohibition of Section 5(c)	Section 5(b)(1) does not apply in the prefiling period — it is not applicable

Well-Known Seasoned Issuers — Free Writing Prospectuses Used Before Filing of Registration Statement	Yes	Yes	Is exempted from prohibition of Section 5(c)	Section 5(b)(1) does not apply in the prefiling period — it is not applicable
Identifying Statements in Accordance with Rule 134	Yes	No	Section 5(c) is not applicable, as Rule 134 relates only to the period after the filing of a registration statement	Section 5(b)(1) relates only to "prospectuses" — it is not applicable
All Eligible Issuers — Free Writing Prospectuses Used After Filing of Registration Statement	Yes	Yes	Section 5(c) is not applicable, as it does not apply in the post-filing period	Section 5(b)(1) will be satisfied, as the free writing prospectus will be a permitted Section 10(b) prospectus

....

The new and revised rules we are adopting establish a communications framework that, in some cases, will operate along a spectrum based on the type of issuer, its reporting history, and its equity market capitalization or recent issuances of fixed income securities.

Thus, under the rules we are adopting, eligible well-known seasoned issuers will have freedom generally from the gun-jumping provisions to communicate at any time, including by means of a written offer other than a statutory prospectus. Varying levels of restrictions will apply to other categories of issuers. We believe these distinctions are appropriate because the market has more familiarity with large, more seasoned issuers and, as a result of the ongoing market following of their activities, including the role of market participants and the media, these issuers' communications have less potential for conditioning the market for the issuer's securities to be sold in a registered offering. Disclosure obligations and practices outside the offering process, including under the Exchange Act, also determine the scope of communications flexibility the rules give to issuers and other offering participants. The cumulative effect of the rules under the gun-jumping provisions is the following:

- well-known seasoned issuers are permitted to engage at any time in oral and written communications, including use at any time of a free writing prospectus, subject to enumerated conditions (including, in specified cases, filing with us). [Rule 163]
- all reporting issuers are permitted, at any time, to continue to publish regularly released factual business information and forward-looking information. [Rule 168]
- non-reporting issuers are permitted, at any time, to continue to publish regularly released factual business information that is intended for use by persons other than in their capacity as investors or potential investors. [Rule 169]
- communications by issuers more than 30 days before filing a registration statement are not prohibited offers so long as they do not reference a securities offering that is or will be the subject of a registration statement. [Rule 163A]
- all issuers and offering participants are permitted to use free writing prospectuses after the filing of the registration statement, subject to enumerated conditions (including, in specified cases, filing with us). [Rules 164 and 433]
- a broader category of routine communications regarding issuers, offerings, and procedural matters, such as communications about the schedule for an offering or about

account-opening procedures, are excluded from the definition of "prospectus." [Rule 134]
- the exemptions for research reports are expanded. [Rules 137, 138, and 139]

...[A] number of these rules include conditions of eligibility. Most of the new and amended rules, for example, are not available to blank check companies, penny stock issuers, or shell companies.

The rules we are adopting today ensure that appropriate liability standards are maintained. For example, all free writing prospectuses have liability under the same provisions as apply today to oral offers and statutory prospectuses. Written communications not constituting prospectuses will not be subject to disclosure liability applicable to prospectuses under Securities Act Section 12(a)(2). This result will not affect their status for liability purposes under other provisions of the federal securities laws, including the anti-fraud provisions.

85 SEC Dock. at 2891–2893.

3. THE JURISDICTIONAL BASE OF §5

P. 101 n.9, end note. For other recent examples, see also Geiger v. SEC, 363 F.3d 481, 485 (D.C. Cir. 2004) (in finding a §5(c) violation, court rejected defendant's claim that he did not *offer* to sell securities during prefiling period but "merely accepted outstanding offers" from market makers to buy, and court cited authority to the effect that "price quotations" are commonly understood as inviting an offer); SEC v. Cavanagh, 155 F.3d 129, 134–136 (2d Cir. 1998) (negotiation of final terms for sale of securities previously issued to management was an offer in violation of §5(c)); Goldman, Sachs & Co., Sec. Act Rel. 8434, 83 SEC Dock. 442 (2004) (Goldman Sachs violated §5(c)'s prohibition against prefiling offers when a Goldman Sachs official spoke to the press on behalf of Goldman Sachs to correct a public perception regarding the use of the money to be raised in a yet-to-be-filed public offering).

For an additional case amplifying aspects of a §5 violation, see SEC v. Universal Express, Inc., 475 F. Supp. 2d 412, 422 (S.D.N.Y. 2007).

4. THE PREFILING PERIOD

b. "Beating the Gun"

P. 106, after 1st full par. After amendment in 2005, Rule 135 provides:

(a) *When notice is not an offer.* For purposes of section 5 of the [Securities] Act only, an issuer or a selling security holder (and any person acting on behalf of either of them) that publishes through any medium a notice of a proposed offering to be registered under the [Securities] Act will not be deemed to offer its securities for sale through that notice if:

(1) *Legend.* The notice includes a statement to the effect that it does not constitute an offer of any securities for sale; and

(2) *Limited notice content.* The notice otherwise includes no more than the following information:

(i) The name of the issuer;

(ii) The title, amount and basic terms of the securities offered;

(iii) The amount of the offering, if any, to be made by selling security holders;

(iv) The anticipated timing of the offering;

(v) A brief statement of the manner and the purpose of the offering, without naming the underwriters;

(vi) Whether the issuer is directing its offering to only a particular class of purchasers;

(vii) Any statements or legends required by the laws of any state or foreign country or administrative authority; and

(viii) In the following offerings, the notice may contain additional information, as follows:

(A) *Rights offering.* In a rights offering to existing security holders:

(1) The class of security holders eligible to subscribe;

(2) The subscription ratio and expected subscription price;

(3) The proposed record date;

(4) The anticipated issuance date of the rights; and

(5) The subscription period or expiration date of the rights offering.

(B) *Offering to employees.* In an offering to employees of the issuer or an affiliated company:

(1) The name of the employer;

(2) The class of employees being offered the securities;

(3) The offering price; and

(4) The duration of the offering period.

(C) *Exchange offer.* In an exchange offer:

(1) The basic terms of the exchange offer;

(2) The name of the subject company;

(3) The subject class of securities sought in the exchange offer.

(D) *Rule 145(a) offering.* In a [Rule] 145(a) offering:

(1) The name of the person whose assets are to be sold in exchange for the securities to be offered;

(2) The names of any other parties to the transaction;

(3) A brief description of the business of the parties to the transaction;

(4) The date, time and place of the meeting of security holders to vote on or consent to the transaction; and

(5) A brief description of the transaction and the basic terms of the transaction.

(b) *Correction of misstatements about the offering.* A person that publishes a notice in reliance on this [Rule] may issue a notice that contains no more information than is necessary to correct inaccuracies published about the proposed offering.

Put differently, a notice of proposed offering that contains disclosures in addition to those provided for in Rule 135 will not qualify for the Rule's safe harbor.

PP. 107–108   2010 SUPPLEMENT

PP. 107–108, 1st full par., substitute: 2005 Rules 137–139 were amended.

Each of these Rules refers to the publication or distribution of a *research report*, a term that needs to be unpacked before moving on to consider the Rules in chief. *Research report* is defined in each of the Rules as a "written communication...that includes information, opinions, or recommendations with respect to securities of an issuer or an analysis of a security of an issuer, whether or not it provides information reasonably sufficient upon which to base an investment decision." Rule 405, in turn, defines *written communication* as "any communication that is written, printed, a radio or television broadcast, or a graphic communication." It is worth stressing that, given the definition of *research report*, the research safe harbors under Rules 137–139 do not apply to oral communications. Unpacking the definition of *research report* still further, the term *graphic communication* is defined in Rule 405 to include "all forms of electronic media, including, but not limited to, audiotapes, videotapes, facsimiles, CD-ROM, electronic mail, Internet Web sites, substantially similar messages widely distributed (rather than individually distributed) on telephone answering or voice mail systems, computers, computer networks and other forms of computer data compilation. Graphic communication shall not include a communication that, at the time of the communication, originates live, in real-time to a live audience and does not originate in recorded form or otherwise as a graphic communication, although it is transmitted through graphic means."

Rule 137 presently permits a broker or dealer to publish or distribute "in the regular course of its business" research reports regarding the securities of an issuer which is the subject of an offering pursuant to a registration statement that the issuer proposes to file, has filed, or that is effective. In particular, so long as the Rule's conditions are satisfied, the terms *offers, participates,* or *participation* in the definition of *underwriter* in §2(a)(11) of the Securities Act will not apply to the publication or distribution of the broker-dealer research report. Prior to the 2005 amendments to Rule 137, the Rule only applied to the publication or distribution by brokers or dealers of "information, opinions or recommendations" related to the securities of a registrant required to file reports pursuant to §13 or

§15(d) of the 1934 Act which also proposed to file, had filed, or had an effective registration statement under the 1933 Act. In other words, Rule 137 has been expanded to apply to the securities of both reporting and nonreporting issuers, subject to certain specified exceptions. That is, neither the issuer nor any of its predecessors may be or have been during the past three years a blank check company, a shell company (other than a business combination shell company), or a penny stock issuer.

Consistent with the prior version of the Rule, in order to fall within Rule 137, the broker or dealer (and any affiliate) distributing the research report, as well as the person (and any affiliate) that has published the report, (a) must not participate or propose to participate in the distribution of the securities that are or will be the subject of the registered offering, and (b) in connection with the publication or distribution of the research report, must not receive, directly or indirectly, any consideration from, or act under any direct or indirect arrangement or understanding with, (i) the issuer, (ii) a selling security holder, (iii) any participant in the distribution of the securities that are or will be covered by the registration statement, or (iv) any other person interested in such securities. Rule 137 does provide an exception, though, when it comes to certain payments. In particular, Rule 137 generally allows payment of the regular price being paid by the broker or dealer for independent research or the regular subscription or purchase price for the research report.

Rule 138 was substantially amended in 2005. Rule 138 presently provides that, for purposes of §§2(a)(10) and 5(c) of the 1933 Act and so long as certain conditions are met, a broker's or dealer's publication or distribution of research reports about an issuer's securities will not constitute an offer for sale or offer to sell a security which is the subject of an offering pursuant to a registration statement that the issuer proposes to file, has filed, or that is effective, even if the broker or dealer is or will be participating in the registered offering. One notable condition is that (i) the research report relates solely to the issuer's common stock, or debt securities, or preferred stock convertible into its common stock, while the offering involves solely the issuer's nonconvertible debt securities or nonconvertible, nonparticipating preferred stock; or

(ii) the research report relates solely to the issuer's nonconvertible debt securities or nonconvertible, nonparticipating preferred stock, while the offering involves solely the issuer's common stock, or debt securities, or preferred stock convertible into its common stock. Another notable condition of Rule 138 is the requirement that the broker or dealer have previously published or distributed research reports on the types of securities in question in the regular course of its business. The requirement that the broker or dealer have published or distributed research on the same types of securities as those securities that are the subject of the research reports is new to the 2005 amendments.

The Rule generally covers research reports on all reporting issuers that are current in filing their periodic reports under the 1934 Act. Before amendment, Rule 138 provided a foreign private issuer must meet the registrant requirements of Form F-3 (other than the reporting history provisions of the Form), meet certain minimum float requirements or investment grade securities provisions of Form F-3, and have had its securities traded for at least 12 months on a designated offshore securities market. The Rule now applies to a foreign private issuer if such issuer has had its equity securities trading on a designated offshore securities market for at least 12 months or has a worldwide market value of outstanding common equity held by nonaffiliates of $700 million or more; meets the requirements of Form F-3 (other than the reporting history provisions of the Form); and either satisfies the public float threshold of Form F-3 or is issuing nonconvertible investment grade securities meeting the applicable provisions of such Form.

Rule 139 is the most significant of this series of rules. So long as certain specified conditions are satisfied, Rule 139 permits a broker or dealer to publish or distribute a research report about an issuer or any of its securities without such report, for purposes of §§2(a)(10) and 5(c) of the 1933 Act, constituting an offer for sale or an offer to sell a security of the issuer that is the subject of an offering pursuant to a registration statement that the issuer proposes to file or has filed, or that is effective, even if the broker or dealer is participating or will participate in the registered offering of such securities.

For issuer-specific research reports to fall within Rule 139, the issuer (i) must be current in filing its required periodic reports under the 1934 Act and (ii) at the later of the time of filing its most recent Form S-3 or Form F-3 or the time of its most recent amendment to such registration statement for purposes of complying with §10(a)(3) of the 1933 Act or, if no Form S-3 or Form F-3 has been filed, at the date of reliance on Rule 139, must meet the requirements of Form S-3 or Form F-3 and either at such date meet the minimum float provisions of such Forms or, at the date of reliance on Rule 139, be, or if a registration statement has not been filed, later be, offering securities meeting the requirements for the offering of investment grade securities pursuant to General Instruction I.B.2. of Form S-3 or Form F-3, or at the date of reliance on Rule 139, must be a well-known seasoned issuer, other than a majority-owned subsidiary that is a well-known seasoned issuer by virtue of paragraph (1)(ii) of the definition of well-known seasoned issuer under Rule 405. The Rule also applies to a foreign private issuer if such issuer (a) meets the requirements of Form F-3 (other than the reporting history provisions), (b) satisfies the public float threshold of Form F-3 or is issuing nonconvertible investment grade securities meeting the provisions of General Instruction I.B.2. of Form F-3, and (c) has had its equity securities trading on a designated offshore securities market for at least 12 months or has a worldwide market value of outstanding common equity held by nonaffiliates of $700 million or more.

Furthermore, in order to fall within Rule 139, the broker or dealer must publish or distribute the research report in the regular course of its business. Additionally, the subject research report must not represent the initiation of publication of research about the issuer or its securities or the reinitiation of coverage by the broker or dealer of such issuer or its securities. The 2005 amendments did away with the earlier requirement that the research also be contained in a publication distributed with *reasonable regularity*. In other words, Rule 139 no longer includes a *reasonable regularity* requirement.

Rule 139 also addresses more general industry reports (i.e., research reports that are not limited to a particular issuer or its securities but that cover an entire industry and mention the issuer). Such industry reports fall within Rule 139 and thus do not constitute an offer of a particular issuer's securities for purposes of §§2(a)(10) and 5(c) of the 1933 Act if, in addition to the issuer satisfying various eligibility requirements, (i) the research report includes similar information for a substantial number of issuers in the issuer's industry or subindustry or contains a comprehensive list of securities currently recommended by the broker or dealer, (ii) the analysis regarding the issuer or its securities is given no materially greater space or prominence in the publication than what is given to other issuers or securities, and (iii) the broker or dealer publishes or distributes research reports in the regular course of its business and, at the time of the publication or distribution of the research report, is including similar information about the issuer or its securities in similar reports. Amended Rule 139 deletes the prior requirement that the broker-dealer research report be no more favorable to the issuer or its securities than the broker-dealer's last report.

The SEC's 2005 public offering reforms ushered in a number of additional regulatory changes that further relaxed communications leading up to and during a securities offering. Many of these developments also helped clarify the types of communications that are permissible without running afoul of §5 of the 1933 Act.

First, Rule 168 creates a nonexclusive safe harbor that permits a reporting issuer, as well as asset backed issuers and certain nonreporting foreign private issuers, to continue to publish or disseminate regularly released factual business and forward-looking information at any time, including leading up to and during a registered offering, without running afoul of the prohibition against gunjumping. Rule 168 provides that, for purposes of §§2(a)(10) and 5(c) of the 1933 Act, the regular release or dissemination by or on behalf of an issuer of communications containing factual business or forward-looking information will not constitute an offer to sell or an offer for sale of a security which is being offered under a registration statement that the issuer proposes to file or has filed, or that is effective if: (i) the issuer is required to file reports under §13 or §15(d) of the 1934 Act; (ii) the issuer is a foreign private issuer that meets the requirements of Form F-3 (other than the reporting history provisions of the Form), either satisfies the public float threshold of Form F-3 or is issuing nonconvertible investment grade securities meeting the applicable provisions of such Form, and either has had its equity securities trading on a designated offshore securities market for at least 12 months or has a worldwide market value of outstanding common equity held by nonaffiliates of $700 million or more; or (iii) the issuer is an asset backed issuer or a depositor, sponsor, or servicer (as Item 1101 of Regulation AB defines such terms) or an affiliated depositor, even if such person is not the issuer. The issuer, however, must not be a registered investment company or a business development company.

Further, in order for the disclosure to be regularly released or disseminated within the meaning of Rule 168, the issuer (or other eligible persons if the issuer is an asset backed issuer) must have previously released or disseminated the same type of information in the ordinary course of its business; and the timing, manner, and form in which the information is released or disseminated must be consistent in material respects with similar past releases or disseminations. These conditions help ensure that the information is not being disclosed to condition the market for the issuer's registered offering.

Rule 168 defines *factual business information* as factual information about the issuer, its business or financial developments, or other aspects of its business; advertisements of, or other information about, the issuer's products or services; and dividend notices.

The Rule defines *forward-looking information* as:

- projections of the issuer's revenues, income (loss), earnings (loss) per share, capital expenditures, dividends, capital structure, or other financial items;
- statements about the issuer management's plans and objectives for future operations, including plans or objectives relating to the products or services of the issuer;
- statements about the issuer's future economic performance, including statements of the type contemplated by the management's discussion and analysis of financial condition and results of operation described in Item 303 of Regulations S-B and S-K or the operating and financial review and prospects described in Item 5 of Form 20-F; and

- assumptions underlying or relating to any of the above information.

There is, however, an important exclusion. That is, the Rule 168 safe harbor does not cover communications containing information about the registered offering or that are disclosed as part of the offering activities in the registered offering.

For purposes of Rule 168, a communication is made *by or on behalf of the issuer* if the issuer or its agent or representative, other than an offering participant who is an underwriter or dealer, authorizes or approves the release or dissemination before it is made.

Second, Rule 169 creates a nonexclusive safe harbor from §2(a)(10)'s definition of *prospectus* and §5(c)'s prohibition on pre-filing offers for certain communications of regularly released factual business information by reporting and nonreporting issuers, other than registered investment companies and business development companies. In particular, Rule 169 provides that, for purposes of §§2(a)(10) and 5(c) of the 1933 Act, the regular release or dissemination by or on behalf of an issuer of communications containing factual business information will not constitute an offer to sell or an offer for sale of a security by the issuer that is the subject of an offering under a registration statement that the issuer proposes to file or has filed, or that is effective if: (i) the issuer has previously released or disseminated the same type of information in the ordinary course of its business; (ii) the timing, manner, and form in which the information is released or disseminated is consistent in material respects with similar past disclosures; and (iii) the information is disclosed for intended use by persons, such as customers and suppliers (other than in their capacities as investors or potential investors in the issuer's securities), by the issuer's employees or agents who historically have provided such information.

Rule 169 defines *factual business information* falling within its safe harbor as (a) factual information about the issuer, its business or financial developments, or other aspects of its business, and (b) advertisements of, or other information about, the issuers' products or services. Rule 169's safe harbor, however, does not apply to communications containing information about the issuer's registered offering or to communications disclosed as part of the offering activities in the registered offering. It is also worth highlighting that, unlike Rule 168, Rule 169 does not apply to forward-looking information. As with Rule 168, a communication under Rule 169 is *by or on behalf of the issuer* if the issuer or its agent or representative, other than an offering participant who is an underwriter or dealer, authorizes or approves the disclosure before it is made.

Third, Rule 163A creates a nonexclusive bright-line safe harbor for certain communications that are made more than 30 days before an issuer files a registration statement. In particular, except for certain specified communications, in all registered offerings by an issuer, any communication made by or on behalf of an issuer more than 30 days before the registration statement is filed will not constitute an offer to sell, offer for sale, or offer to buy the securities under the registration statement for purposes of §5(c) if (i) the communication does not reference a securities offering that is or will be the subject of a registration statement (other than this restriction, Rule 163A does not regulate the content of communications covered by the Rule) and (ii) the issuer takes reasonable steps within its control to prevent further distribution or publication of such communication during the 30 days immediately before the registration statement is filed. Consistent with Rules 168 and 169, a communication is made "by or on behalf of" an issuer under Rule 163A if the issuer or an agent or representative of the issuer, other than an offering participant who is an underwriter or a dealer, authorizes or approves the communication before it is made. In other words, Rule 163A does not cover communications by offering participants other than the issuer, such as underwriters or dealers. The logic of the Rule is that the 30-day time period allows for a sufficient *cooling off* period if the communication does in fact stimulate the market's interest in the offering. Further, as the SEC explained in the adoption Release, "Because the Rule does not permit information about a securities offering that is or will be the subject of a registration statement, the communications made in reliance on the Rule are less likely to be used to condition the market for the issuer's securities. In addition, the communications are still subject to...the anti-fraud provisions [of the federal securities laws]."

Fourth, as part of the 2005 public offering reforms, the SEC fashioned the new *free writing prospectus*, a concept that has relevance throughout the offering process, including during the prefiling period, the focus here. Except as otherwise specifically provided or the context otherwise requires, a *free writing prospectus* is defined under Rule 405 as any written communication that constitutes an offer to sell or a solicitation of an offer to buy the securities relating to a registered offering that is used after the registration statement in respect of the offering is filed (or, in the case of a well-known seasoned issuer, whether or not the registration statement is filed) and is made by means other than: (i) a prospectus satisfying the requirements of §10(a) of the 1933 Act, Rule 430, Rule 430A, Rule 430B, Rule 430C, or Rule 431; (ii) a written communication used in reliance on Rule 167 and Rule 426; or (iii) a written communication that constitutes an offer to sell or solicitation of an offer to buy such securities that falls within the exception from the definition of prospectus in clause (a) of §2(a)(10) of the 1933 Act.

Rule 163 establishes a nonexclusive safe harbor that in effect permits offers to be made by or on behalf of a WKSI (but not other issuers) during the prefiling period without violating §5(c). In particular, Rule 163 provides that in a securities offering by or on behalf of a WKSI that will be or is at the time intended to be registered, an offer by or on behalf of such WKSI is exempt from §5(c)'s prohibition against offers to sell, offers for sale, or offers to buy its securities before a registration statement has been filed so long as certain conditions are satisfied as summarized below. A communication is made *by or on behalf of an issuer* if the issuer or its agent or representative, other than an offering participant who is an underwriter or dealer, authorizes or approves the communication before it is made. In other words, underwriters and dealers cannot avail themselves of Rule 163. Rule 163(a)(1) provides that any written communication that is an offer made in reliance on

Rule 163's exemption will be a free writing prospectus and a prospectus under §2(a)(10) relating to a public offering of the securities to be covered by the registration statement.

Under Rule 163(b), any such free writing prospectus that is an offer made in reliance on the Rule must contain a specified legend that notifies potential investors that the issuer may file a registration statement (including a prospectus) with the Commission for the offering to which the communication relates and that instructs potential investors to read the relevant prospectus before investing, as well as any other SEC filings the issuer has made. The legend must also indicate how potential investors can obtain a prospectus. Notably, the Rule provides a limited opportunity to cure a failure to meet the legend requirement. An immaterial or unintentional failure to include the required legend in a free writing prospectus will not result in a §5(c) violation or the inability to rely on Rule 163's exemption if: (i) a good faith and reasonable effort was made to comply with the legend requirement; (ii) the free writing prospectus is amended to include the required legend as soon as practicable after the omitted or incorrect legend is discovered; and (iii) if the free writing prospectus has been transmitted without the required legend, the free writing prospectus is subsequently retransmitted with the legend by substantially the same means as, and directed to substantially the same potential investors to whom, the free writing prospectus was originally transmitted.

In addition, for Rule 163 to apply, the issuer generally must file the free writing prospectus with the SEC promptly upon filing the registration statement or an amendment thereto covering the securities that have been offered in reliance on the Rule's exemption. If no such registration statement or amendment is filed, then the free writing prospectus does not have to be filed with the Commission. There is limited opportunity to cure any failure to satisfy this filing condition. An immaterial or unintentional failure to file or delay in filing the free writing prospectus will not result in a §5(c) violation or the inability to rely on Rule 163's exemption if a good faith and reasonable effort was made to comply with the filing requirement and the free writing prospectus is filed as soon as practicable after the failure to file is discovered.

P. 108

Rule 163's exemption from §5(c) does not apply to communications relating to business combination transactions subject to Rule 165 or 166, communications by a registered investment company, or communications by a business development company.

P. 108, new par, after 2d par. In 2004, as part of the Commission's Regulation AB adopted Release, Sec. Act Rel. 8518, 84 SEC Dock. 1624, 1698-1700 (2004) (adoption), the Commission also adopted a new Rule 139a safe harbor provision which provides in part:

> The publication or distribution by a broker or dealer of information, an opinion or a recommendation with respect to asset-backed securities meeting the criteria of General Instruction I.B.5 of Form S-3 shall not be deemed to constitute an offer for sale or offer to sell S-3 ABS registered or proposed to be registered for purposes of sections 2(a)(10) and 5(c) of the Act, even if such broker or dealer is or will be a participant in the distribution of the registered securities [if specified conditions are met similar to those required under Rule 139 and if registered securities are proposed to be offered, offered, or part of an unsold allotment or subscription, the information, opinion or recommendation, does not contain any *ABS informational or computation material* as defined in Reg. S-K Item 1101].

A new Rule 167 lists securities conditions under which ABS informational and computation material may be used after the effective date of an ABS security registration statement and before sending a §10(a) final prospectus without violating §5(b)(1). New Rule 426 requires filings of Rule 167 prospectuses on Form 8-K.

Rule 139a was amended in 2005 in light of the SEC's changes to Rule 139 deleting the prior Rule 139 requirement that a research report regarding an issuer or its securities can only be included in an industry report if the broker-dealer's last publication contained a recommendation as or more favorable to the issuer or any class of its securities. The comparable requirement included in Rule 139a(c) for asset backed securities was deleted, and paragraphs (d) and (e) of Rule 139a were redesignated as paragraphs (c) and (d). However, although the *reasonable regularity* requirement was also deleted from Rule 139, a comparable requirement in paragraph (a) of Rule 139a was not deleted as part of the 2005 public offering reforms.

5. THE WAITING PERIOD

c. The *Tombstone Ad* [§2(a)(10)(b), Rule 134]

P. 112, 1st full par., substitute: After a registration statement has been filed with the Commission, Rule 134 permits a communication limited to some or all of the following categories of information without such communication constituting a *prospectus* or *free writing prospectus*:

- The names of selling security holders, if then disclosed in the prospectus that is part of the filed registration statement;
- The names of securities exchanges or other securities markets where any class of the issuer's securities are, or will be, listed;
- The ticker symbols, or proposed ticker symbols, of the issuer's securities;
- The CUSIP number as defined in Rule 17Ad-19(a)(5) of the Securities Exchange Act of 1934 assigned to the securities being offered; and
- Information disclosed in order to correct inaccuracies previously contained in a communication permissibly made pursuant to Rule 134.

Rule 134 was amended in 2005 as part of the SEC's public offering reforms to expand the amount of information that Rule 134 allows to be communicated during the waiting period.

A communication used pursuant to Rule 134 must contain the following: (a) if the registration statement has not yet become effective, a specified statement to the effect that a registration

P. 112

statement has been filed with the SEC but has not yet become effective and that the securities covered by the registration statement may not be sold nor may offers to buy be accepted before the registration statement becomes effective; and (b) the name and address of one or more persons from whom a written §10 prospectus (other than a free writing prospectus), including, when required, a price range, may be obtained. There is a limited exception to this requirement, however. That is, it is not necessary to include the information described in the immediately preceding (a) and (b) if the communication that contains the information permitted by Rule 134(x) does no more than state from whom and include the uniform resource locator (URL) where a written prospectus that meets the requirements of §10 of the 1933 Act (other than a free writing prospectus) may be obtained, identify the security, state its price, and state by whom orders will be executed, or (y) is accompanied or preceded by a prospectus or a summary prospectus (other than a free writing prospectus) which satisfies §10's requirements, including a price range where required, at the date of such communication. In other words, the one item of information that must be included in every tombstone ad, whether the old fashioned or the expanded variety, is the identity of at least one person from whom a §10 prospectus may be obtained—the one exception being the case where the prospectus actually accompanies or precedes the ad.

Rule 134(d) allows a communication sent or delivered to any person in reliance on the Rule if such communication is accompanied or preceded by a prospectus that satisfies §10's requirements (other than a free writing prospectus), including a price range where required, to solicit from the recipient of the communication an offer to buy or an indication of interest if the communication contains a statement to the effect that no offer to buy can be accepted and no part of the purchase price can be received until the effective date and any such offer can be withdrawn or revoked, without any obligation or commitment of any kind, at any time prior to notice of its acceptance after the effective date. Otherwise, Rule 134 does not permit a sender of the communication to solicit an offer to buy or an indication of interest.

Under Rule 134(f), for purposes of Rule 134, an active hyperlink to a §10 prospectus in an electronic Rule 134 notice satisfies the requirement that the prospectus accompany or precede that notice in cases when such requirement must be met. It should be noted, though, that a hyperlink or URL may not be to an address with information other than the types of information that Rule 134 allows. Rule 134(e) also provides that a §10 prospectus that is included in any Rule 134 communication remains a prospectus for all purposes of the 1933 Act.

Rule 134(g) provides that the Rule does not apply to a registered investment company or a business development company.

In 2007 the Commission replaced Rule 498 with a new version of Rule 498 that permits mutual funds to satisfy the statutory prospectus delivery obligation under the 1933 Act by distributing a summary prospectus and providing the statutory prospectus online. The new Rule 498 requires a fund to send the statutory prospectus in paper or by e-mail on request. Sec. Act Rel. 8998,__ SEC Dock.__ (2009) (adoption).

d. The Preliminary Prospectus [§10(a), Rule 430]

P. 113, text after 1st full par., substitute:

> The information in this prospectus is not complete and may be changed. We may not sell these securities until the registration statement filed with the Securities and Exchange Commission is effective. This prospectus is not an offer to sell these securities and it is not soliciting an offer to buy these securities in any state where the offer or sale is not permitted.

The legend must be prominent and in a print type that is easy to read.

P. 115 2010 SUPPLEMENT

e. The Summary Prospectus [§10(b), Rule 431]

(ii) *Investment Companies*

P. 115, add at end of par. In 2003 the Commission eliminated the Rule 134 provisions that applied specifically to investment companies and enhanced investment company disclosure under Rule 482 and amended several Investment Company Act forms. The SEC emphasized in the adoption Release that with the elimination of the *substance of which* requirement from Rule 482, mutual funds would no longer need to rely on Rule 134. Indeed, presently Rule 134(e) expressly states that the Rule does not apply to registered investment companies.

f. Free Writing Prospectus and Electronic Road Shows [Rules 164 and 433]

P. 115, add new pars. after 3d full par. Before addressing the substantive rules that govern the use of free writing prospectuses and electronic road shows, it is worth first explaining two important definitions, adopted by the SEC in 2005 as part of the Commission's public offering reforms. The definitions of *written communication* and *graphic communication* more precisely distinguish between written and oral communications. These definitions provide some needed clarity and certainty in light of recent technological developments that often make it difficult to distinguish between written and oral communications. The ability to so distinguish has important implications for gunjumping under §5 of the 1933 Act.

Rule 405 defines *written communication* as "any communication that is written, printed, a radio or television broadcast, or a graphic communication as defined in [Rule 405.]" The term *graphic communication*, in turn, is defined in Rule 405 to include "all forms of electronic media, including, but not limited to, audiotapes, videotapes, facsimiles, CD-ROM, electronic mail, Internet Web sites, substantially similar messages widely distributed (rather than individually distributed) on telephone answering or voice mail systems, computers, computer networks and other forms of computer data compilation. Graphic communication shall not include a communication that, at the time of the communication, originates live, in real-time to a live audience and does not originate in recorded form or otherwise as a graphic communication, although it is transmitted through graphic means."

It should be made clear that any communication that is not a *written communication* is an oral communication.

Regarding voicemails, the SEC added that an individual voicemail from a live telephone call will not constitute a written communication, but that broadly disseminated or blast voicemail messages will constitute a written communication.

The concept of a free writing prospectus, which originated as part of the SEC's public offering reforms adopted in 2005, was introduced earlier insofar as a free writing prospectus can be used by a WKSI under certain circumstances during the prefiling period. A free writing prospectus can also be used after the registration statement has been filed as provided under Rules 164 and 433, the focus here. The free writing prospectus allows greater flexibility when it comes to making written offers.

Rule 164 provides that so long as certain conditions set forth in Rule 433 are satisfied, after the filing of the registration statement, a free writing prospectus of an eligible issuer or any underwriter, dealer, or other offering participant will constitute a §10(b) prospectus for purposes of §5(b)(1) of the 1933 Act. Put differently, a free writing prospectus may be used during the waiting period without violating §5(b)(1)'s prohibition on the use of a prospectus that is not a statutory prospectus once the registration statement has been filed.

Rule 433(a) provides that a free writing prospectus, which can contain information the substance of which is not included in the registration statement, that satisfies the conditions of Rule 433 is a prospectus permitted under §10(b) of the 1933 Act for purposes of §§2(a)(10), 5(b)(1), and 5(b)(2) of the 1933 Act. The rest of Rule 433 sets forth the key conditions that must be satisfied for a free writing prospectus to be used after the filing of the registration statement. These conditions relate to the delivery or availability of the statutory prospectus when the free writing prospectus is used; the information that the free writing prospectus contains; legend requirements; filing requirements; and record retention requirements.

First, in terms of prospectus delivery and availability requirements, in offerings of securities of a seasoned issuer or a well-known seasoned issuer (WKSI), the issuer or other offering participant in the offering may use a free writing prospectus in registered securities offerings once a registration statement regarding the offering has been filed containing a §10 statutory prospectus, other than a prospectus that satisfies §10 as a summary prospectus permitted under Rule 431 or as a permitted free writing prospectus. There is no requirement that the statutory prospectus actually be delivered in order to use the free writing prospectus. However, as described further below, there is a legend requirement designed to notify recipients of a free writing prospectus that a registration statement has been filed and how the statutory prospectus can be obtained.

The prospectus delivery and availability requirements are more demanding for nonreporting issuers and unseasoned issuers. In short, the statutory prospectus must actually be delivered prior to or with the free writing prospectus. For nonreporting issuers and unseasoned issuers, if (a) the free writing prospectus is or was prepared by or on behalf of or used or referred to by an issuer or other offering participant, (b) the issuer or other offering participant has or will give consideration for the dissemination (in any format) of the free writing prospectus, including any published article, publication, or advertisement, or (c) §17(b) of the 1933 Act requires disclosure that consideration has been or will be given by the issuer or other offering participant for any activity described in §17(b) in connection with the free writing prospectus, then a free writing prospectus may be used in an offering if (x) the registration statement has been filed for the offering and it includes a §10 statutory prospectus, including a price range where required by rule, other than a prospectus that satisfies §10 as a summary prospectus permitted under Rule 431 or as a permitted free writing prospectus, and (y) the free writing prospectus is preceded or accompanied by the most recent such statutory prospectus. Put simply, in these cases, anyone receiving a free writing prospectus must actually be provided the most recent statutory prospectus; simply indicating the availability of the statutory prospectus is not enough. Consequently, it might be infeasible to disseminate the free writing prospectus broadly other than in an electronic form. The prospectus delivery requirement will be satisfied if an electronic free writing prospectus includes an active hyperlink to the §10 prospectus. There is no need to get any advance consent of recipients for such electronic delivery.

The second set of conditions on the use of a free writing prospectus after the filing of the registration statement relates to the information contained in a free writing prospectus. Other than as provided below, there are no content conditions under Rules 164 and 433 for a free writing prospectus used after the filing of a registration statement. Under Rule 433(c), a free writing prospectus can contain information the substance of which is not contained in the registration statement if the information does not conflict with information contained in the registration statement, including any prospectus or prospectus supplement that is part of the registration statement and not superseded or modified, or any of the issuer's reports filed with or furnished to the SEC under §13 or §15(d) of the 1934 Act that the registration statement incorporates by reference and that are not superseded or modified.

Further, the free writing prospectus must contain substantially the following legend:

> The issuer has filed a registration statement (including a prospectus) with the SEC for the offering to which this communication relates. Before you invest, you should read the prospectus in that registration statement and other documents the issuer has filed with the SEC for more complete information about the issuer and this offering. You may get these documents for free by visiting EDGAR on the SEC Web site at www.sec.gov. Alternatively, the issuer, any underwriter or any dealer participating in the offering will arrange to send you the prospectus if you request it by calling toll-free 1-8-[xx-xxx-xxxx].

P. 115

The legend may also provide an e-mail address to request the documents and may indicate that the documents also are available on the issuer's Web site and include the Internet address and the particular location of the documents on the Web site.

Under Rule 164(c), an immaterial or unintentional failure to include the specified legend in a free writing prospectus as required under Rule 433 will not result in a violation of §5(b)(1) of the 1933 Act or the inability to rely on Rule 164(i) if a good faith and reasonable effort was made to comply with the legend condition; (ii) if the free writing prospectus is amended to include the specified legend as soon as practicable after discovery of the omitted or incorrect legend; and (iii) if transmitted without the legend, if the free writing prospectus is retransmitted with the legend by substantially the same means as, and directed to substantially the same prospective purchasers to whom, the free writing prospectus was originally transmitted.

Third, Rule 433(d) sets forth certain filing conditions for use of a free writing prospectus. In order to use a free writing prospectus, except in certain cases, such prospectus or the information contained in it must be filed with the SEC no later than the date the free writing prospectus is first used. More particularly, subject to certain specified exceptions, the issuer must file with the SEC any *issuer free writing prospectus*; any *issuer information* contained in a free writing prospectus prepared by or on behalf of or used by any other offering participant (but not information prepared by or on behalf of a person other than the issuer on the basis of or derived from such issuer information); and a description of the final terms of the issuer's securities in the offering or of the offering contained in a free writing prospectus or portion thereof prepared by or on behalf of the issuer or any offering participant, after such terms have been established for all classes in the offering. Also subject to certain specified exceptions, any offering participant other than the issuer must file with the SEC any free writing prospectus that is used or referred to by such offering participant and distributed by or on behalf of such participant in a manner reasonably designed to lead to its broad unrestricted dissemination.

DISTRIBUTION OF SECURITIES　　　　　P. 115

Any filing with the Commission that Rule 433 requires generally must be made no later than the date the free writing prospectus is first used. However, under Rule 433(d)(5)(ii), a free writing prospectus or portion thereof that contains only a description of the final terms of the issuer's securities in the offering or of the offerings must be filed by the issuer within two days of the later of the date the final terms have been established for all classes of the offering and the date first used.

Rule 433(d)(1) makes clear that the free writing prospectus that is filed under the Rule will not be filed as part of the registration statement subject to §11 liability, although the free writing prospectus might still be a basis of liability under §12(a)(2) of the 1933 Act and the antifraud provisions of the federal securities laws.

Under Rule 164(b), any immaterial or unintentional failure to file or delay in filing a free writing prospectus as required under Rule 433 will not result in a violation of §5(b)(1) of the 1933 Act or the inability to rely on Rule 164 if a good faith and reasonable effort was made to comply with the filing requirement and the free writing prospectus is filed as soon as practicable after discovery of the failure to file.

Rule 433 also addresses road shows specifically, including electronic road shows. Rule 433(d)(8) concerns filing conditions as they apply to *road shows* conducted by issuers and underwriters to market securities offerings. First, two terms need to be defined. Rule 433(h) defines a *road show* as:

> [A]n offer (other than a statutory prospectus or a portion of a statutory prospectus filed as part of a registration statement) that contains a presentation regarding an offering by one or more members of the issuer's management (and in the case of an offering of asset-backed securities, management involved in the securitization or servicing function of one or more of the depositors, sponsors, or servicers (as such terms are defined in Item 1101 of Regulation AB) or an affiliated depositor) and includes discussion of one or more of the issuer, such management, and the securities being offered.

In turn, a *bona fide electronic road show,* such as might be conducted or Web cast over the Internet to investors, is defined as:

P. 115

[A] road show that is a written communication transmitted by graphic means that contains a presentation by one or more officers of an issuer or other persons in an issuer's management (and in the case of an offering of asset-backed securities, management involved in the securitization or servicing function of one or more of the depositors, sponsors, or servicers (as such terms are defined in Item 1101 of Regulation AB) or an affiliated depositor) and, if more than one road show that is a written communication is being used, includes discussion of the same general areas of information regarding the issuer, such management, and the securities being offered as such other road show or shows for the same offering that are written communications.

Under Rule 433(d)(8), a road show that is a written communication is a free writing prospectus, except that a written communication that is a road show generally does not have to be filed. In the case of a road show that is a written communication for an offering of common equity or convertible equity securities by a nonreporting issuer that is not required to file reports under §13 or §15(d) of the 1934 Act when the registration statement for the offering is filed, such a road show must be filed unless the issuer makes at least one version of a *bona fide electronic road show* available without restriction by means of graphic communication to any person, including any potential investor in the securities (and if there is more than one version of a road show for the offering that is a written communication, the version available without restriction is made available no later than the other versions).

Technology impacts the offering process through more ways than just electronic road shows. Issuers can post information on their Web sites or can link to others' Web sites that post information about the issuer or the issuer's offering. Rule 433(e) addresses these possibilities. Under Rule 433(e), an offer of an issuer's securities that is contained on the issuer's Web site or that is hyperlinked by the issuer to a third party's Web site is a written offer by the issuer. Accordingly, the filing conditions of Rule 433 generally apply to such an offer. That having been said, under Rule 433(e)(2), historical issuer information will not be considered a current offer of the issuer's securities and thus will not be a free writing prospectus, meaning that, among other things, the information will not have to be filed with the SEC, if the historical information is identified as such, is located in a separate section of the issuer's Web site containing historical information, has not been incorporated by reference into or otherwise included in a prospectus for the offering, and has not otherwise been used or referred to in connection with the offering.

The final condition for the use of a free writing prospectus after filing the registration statement concerns record retention. Rule 433(g) requires that issuers and other offering participants retain all free writing prospectuses they have used and that have not been filed with the SEC for three years after the initial bona fide offering of the securities in question. Under Rule 164(d), an immaterial or unintentional failure to retain a free writing prospectus will not result in a violation of §5(b)(1) of the 1933 Act or the inability to rely on Rule 164 if a good faith and reasonable effort was made to comply with the record retention condition.

Rule 433(f) separately addresses free writing prospectuses that are published or distributed by the media, which in recent years have played an increasingly important role in disseminating information about issuers and their offerings.

Under Rule 433(f), any written offer that includes information provided, authorized, or approved by or on behalf of the issuer or another offering participant and that is prepared and published or disseminated by a person unaffiliated with the issuer or other offering participant that is in the business of publishing, radio or television broadcasting, or otherwise disseminating written communications would be a free writing prospectus prepared by or on behalf of the issuer or such other offering participant. However, the Rule 433 conditions are modified for any such free writing prospectus. Namely, the prospectus delivery requirements for nonreporting and unseasoned issuers under Rule 433(b)(2)(i) will not apply and the legend and filing conditions under Rules 433(c)(2) and 433(d), respectively, will be deemed satisfied if (i) no payment is made and no consideration is given by or on behalf of the issuer or any other offering participant for the written communication or its dissemination, and (ii) the issuer or other offering participant in question files the written communication with the SEC, and includes in the filing the legend required by Rule

P. 115

433(c)(2), within four business days after the issuer or other offering participant becomes aware of the publication, radio or television broadcast, or other dissemination of the written communication. The free writing prospectus, however, does not have to be filed if its substance has previously been filed with the SEC. Additionally, any filing that is made may include information that the issuer or other offering participant reasonably believes is necessary or appropriate to correct information included in the written communication; and in lieu of filing the actual written communication as published or disseminated, the issuer or other offering participant may file a copy of the materials provided to the media, including transcripts of interviews or similar materials, so long as the copy or transcripts contain all the information given to the media.

P. 115, re-letter subsection f, State Blue Sky Laws, as subsection g.

6. THE POSTEFFECTIVE PERIOD

f. The Dealer's Exemption

P. 120 n.38, end note. As part of the 2005 public offering reforms, the SEC amended Rule 153 to account for the reality that many transactions occur other than on a stock exchange and for the fact that electronic filings of final prospectuses on EDGAR and other technological developments had, as the SEC put it, largely rendered the paper-based system upon which Rule 153 has been based "outmoded and unnecessary." As amended in 2005, Rule 153 provides that brokers or dealers who are effecting transactions on or through a registered national securities exchange or facility thereof, trading facility of a national securities association, or an alternative trading system will satisfy §5(b)(2)'s requirement to deliver a prospectus to the broker or dealer on the other side of the transaction if: (1) securities of the same class as the securities that are the subject of the transaction are trading on such exchange or facility thereof, trading facility of a national securities association, or alternative trading system; (2) the registration statement for the offering is effective and is not the subject of any pending proceeding or examination under §8(d) or §8(e) of the 1933 Act; (3) neither the issuer nor any underwriter or participating dealer is the subject of a pending proceeding under §8A of the 1933 Act in connection with the offering; and (4) the issuer has filed or will file with the SEC a final §10(a) prospectus.

P. 121, after 1st full par. Rule 174 was amended in 2005 as part of the SEC's 2005 public offering reforms to add new Rule 174(h) to the effect that, except for filings with regard to offerings by blank check companies under Rule 174(g), any obligation of a dealer under §4(3) and Rule 174 to deliver a prospectus may be satisfied by compliance with Rule 172, which implements the *access equals delivery* model adopted as part of the 2005 public offering reforms.

h. Electronic Delivery of Prospectus

P. 124, after 1st full par. In April 2000 the Securities and Exchange Commission published another Interpretive Release on Use of Electronic Media. Sec. Act Rel. 7856, 72 SEC Dock. 753 (2000). This Release stated in part:

I. Introduction

By facilitating rapid and widespread information dissemination, the Internet has had a significant impact on capital-raising techniques and, more broadly, on the structure of the securities industry....[M]any publicly traded companies are incorporating Internet-based technology into their routine business operations, including setting up their own web sites to furnish company and industry information. Some provide information about their securities and the markets in which their securities trade. Investment companies use the Internet to provide investors with fund-related information, as well as shareholder services and educational materials. Issuers of municipal securities also are beginning to use the

Internet to provide information about themselves and their outstanding bonds, as well as new offerings of their securities. The increased availability of information through the Internet has helped to promote transparency, liquidity, and efficiency in our capital markets....

II. Interpretive Guidance

A. Electronic Delivery

We first published our views on the use of electronic media to deliver information to investors in 1995. [Sec. Act Rel. 7233, 60 SEC Dock. 1091 (1995).] The 1995 Release focused on electronic delivery of prospectuses, annual reports to security holders and proxy solicitation materials under the Securities Act of 1933, the Securities Exchange Act of 1934 and the Investment Company Act of 1940. Our 1996 electronic media release [Sec. Act Rel. 7288, 61 SEC Dock. 2167 (1996)] focused on electronic delivery of required information by broker-dealers (including municipal securities dealers) and transfer agents under the Exchange Act and investment advisers under the Investment Advisers Act of 1940.

We believe that the framework for electronic delivery established in these releases continues to work well in today's technological environment. Issuers and market intermediaries therefore must continue to assess their compliance with legal requirements in terms of the three areas identified in the releases — notice, access and evidence of delivery. Although we believe that this framework continues to be appropriate, we provide below guidance that will clarify some regulatory issues relating to electronic delivery.

1. Telephone Consent

...[O]ne of the three elements of satisfactory electronic delivery is obtaining evidence of delivery. The 1995 Release provided that one method for satisfying the evidence-of-delivery element is to obtain an informed consent from an investor to receive information through a particular electronic medium. The 1996 Release stated that informed consent should be made by written or electronic means. Some securities lawyers have concluded that, based on the 1996 Release, telephonic consent generally is not permitted. Others have opined that telephonic consent may be permissible if an issuer or intermediary retains a record of consent.

...We are of the view...that an issuer or market intermediary may obtain an informed consent telephonically, as long as a record of that consent is retained. As with written or electronic consent, telephonic consent must be obtained in a manner that assures its authenticity.

2. Global Consent

The 1995 Release stated that consent to electronic delivery could relate to *all* documents to be delivered by or on behalf of a single issuer....

We believe that an investor may give a global consent to electronic delivery — relating to all documents of any issuer — so long as the consent is informed. Given the broad scope of a global consent and its effect on an investor's ability to receive important documents, we believe intermediaries should take particular care to ensure that the investor understands that he or she is providing a global consent to electronic delivery. For example, a global consent that is merely a provision of an agreement that an investor is required to execute to receive other services may not fully inform the investor. To best inform investors, broker-dealers could obtain consent from a new customer through an account-opening agreement that contains a separate section with a separate electronic delivery authorization, or through a separate document altogether. We believe that a global consent to electronic delivery would not be an informed consent if the opening of a brokerage account were conditioned upon providing the consent. Therefore, absent other evidence of delivery, we believe that if the opening of an account were conditioned upon providing a global consent, evidence of delivery would not be established.

Similarly, because of the broad scope of a global consent, an investor should be advised of his or her right to revoke the consent at any time and receive all covered documents in paper format....

Although a global consent must identify the various types of electronic media that may be used to constitute an informed consent, it need not specify the medium to be used by any particular issuer. Additionally, the consent need not identify the issuers covered by the consent. If the consent does identify the covered issuers, it also

P. 124

may provide that additional issuers can be added at a later time without further consent. Investors cannot be required to accept delivery via additional media at a later time without further informed consent.

3. Use of Portable Document Format

The 1995 Release stated that "the use of a particular medium should not be so burdensome that intended recipients cannot effectively access the information provided."...We believe that issuers and market intermediaries delivering documents electronically may use PDF if it is not so burdensome as effectively to prevent access. For example, PDF could be used if issuers and intermediaries:

- inform investors of the requirements necessary to download PDF when obtaining consent to electronic delivery; and
- provide investors with any necessary software and technical assistance at no cost.

4. Clarification of the "Envelope Theory"

The 1995 Release provided a number of examples designed to assist issuers and market intermediaries in meeting their delivery obligations through electronic media. One example provided that documents in close proximity on the same web site menu are considered delivered together. Other examples confirmed the proposition that documents hyperlinked to each other are considered delivered together as if they were in the same paper envelope. The premise underlying these examples has come to be called the "envelope theory."...

Nevertheless, some issuers and intermediaries believe that the envelope theory has created ambiguities as to appropriate web site content when an issuer is in registration. Some securities lawyers have expressed concern that if a Section 10 prospectus is posted on a web site, the operation of the envelope theory causes everything on the web site to become part of that prospectus. They also have raised concerns that information on a web site that is outside of the four corners of the Section 10 prospectus, but in close proximity to it, would be considered free writing.

Information on a web site would be part of a Section 10 prospectus only if an issuer (or person acting on behalf of the issuer, including an intermediary with delivery obligations) acts to make it part of the prospectus. For example, if an issuer includes a hyperlink within a Section 10 prospectus, the hyperlinked information would become a part of that prospectus. When embedded hyperlinks are used, the hyperlinked information must be filed as part of the prospectus in the effective registration statement and will be subject to liability under Section 11 of the Securities Act. In contrast, a hyperlink from an external document to a Section 10 prospectus would result in both documents being delivered together, but would not result in the non-prospectus document being deemed part of the prospectus. Issuers nevertheless may be subject to liability under Section 12 of the Securities Act for the external document depending on whether the external document is itself a prospectus or part of one.

With respect to the free writing concern, the focus on the location of the posted prospectus is misplaced. Regardless of whether or where the Section 10 prospectus is posted, the web site content must be reviewed in its entirety to determine whether it contains impermissible free writing....

B. Web Site Content

...

1. *Issuer Responsibility for Hyperlinked Information*

...Whether third-party information is attributable to an issuer depends upon whether the issuer has involved itself in the preparation of the information or explicitly or implicitly endorsed or approved of the information. In the case of issuer liability for statements by third parties such as analysts, the courts and we have referred to the first line of inquiry as the "entanglement" theory and the second as the "adoption" theory.

In the case of hyperlinked information, liability under the "entanglement" theory would depend upon an issuer's level of prepublication involvement in the preparation of the information. In contrast, liability under the "adoption" theory would depend upon whether, after its publication, an issuer, explicitly or implicitly, endorses or approves the hyperlinked information....

P. 124　　　　　　2010 SUPPLEMENT

a. Context of the Hyperlink

Whether third-party information to which an issuer has established a hyperlink is attributable to the issuer is likely to be influenced by what the issuer says about the hyperlink or what is implied by the context in which the issuer places the hyperlink. An issuer might explicitly endorse the hyperlinked information. For example, a hyperlink might be incorporated in or accompany a statement such as "XYZ's web site contains the best description of our business that is currently available"....

In the context of a document required to be filed or delivered under the federal securities laws, we believe that when an issuer embeds a hyperlink to a web site within the document, the issuer should always be deemed to be adopting the hyperlinked information. In addition, when an issuer is in registration, if the issuer establishes a hyperlink (that is not embedded within a disclosure document) from its web site to information that meets the definition of an "offer to sell," "offer for sale," or "offer" under Section 2(a)(3) of the Securities Act, a strong inference arises that the issuer has adopted that information for purposes of Section 10(b) of the Exchange Act and Rule 10b-5....

2. Issuer Communications During a Registered Offering

...

An issuer that is in registration should maintain communications with the public as long as the subject matter of the communications is limited to ordinary course business and financial information, which may include the following:

- Advertisements concerning the issuer's products and services;
- Exchange Act reports required to be filed with the Commission;
- Proxy statements, annual reports to security holders and dividend notices;
- Press announcements concerning business and financial developments;
- Answers to unsolicited telephone inquiries concerning business matters from securities analysts, financial analysts, security holders and participants in the communications field who have a legitimate interest in the issuer's affairs; and

- Security holders' meetings and responses to security holder inquiries relating to these matters.

Statements containing information falling within any of the foregoing categories, or an available Securities Act safe harbor, may be posted on an issuer's web site when in registration, either directly or indirectly through a hyperlink to a third-party web site, including the web site of a broker-dealer that is participating in the registered offering.

Although our original guidance was directed at communications by reporting issuers when in registration, it also should be observed by non-reporting issuers preparing to offer securities to the public for the first time. A non-reporting issuer that has established a history of ordinary course business communications through its web site should be able to continue to provide business and financial information on its site consistent with our original guidance. A non-reporting issuer preparing for its first registered public offering that contemporaneously establishes a web site, however, may need to apply this guidance more strictly when evaluating its web site content because it may not have established a history of ordinary-course business communications with the marketplace. Thus, its web site content may condition the market for the offering and, due to the unfamiliarity of the marketplace with the issuer or its business, investors may be unable to view the issuer's communications in an appropriate context while the issuer is in registration. In other words, investors may be less able to distinguish offers to sell an issuer's securities in a registered offering from product or service promotional activities or other business or financial information.

C. Online Offerings

1. Online Public Offerings

Increasingly, issuers and broker-dealers are conducting public securities offerings online, using the Internet, electronic mail and other electronic media to solicit prospective investors. Examples of these electronic communications include investor questionnaires on investment qualifications, broker-dealer account-opening procedures and directives on how to submit indications of interest or offers to buy in the context of a specific public offering. These developments present both potential benefits and dangers to investors. On the positive side, numerous "online brokers" appear to have begun to give individual investors more access to public offerings, including initial public offerings, or IPO's. Still, dangers accompany these expanded online investment opportunities. Retail investors often are unfamiliar with the public offering process generally, and, in particular, with new marketing practices that have evolved in connection with online public offerings. We are concerned that there may be insufficient information available to investors to enable them to understand fully the online public offering process. We also are concerned that investors are being solicited to make hasty, and perhaps uninformed investment decisions.

Two fundamental legal principles should guide issuers, underwriters, and other offering participants in online public offerings. First, offering participants can neither sell, nor make contracts to sell, a security before effectiveness of the related Securities Act registration statement. A corollary to this principle dictates that "[n]o offer to buy...can be accepted and no part of the purchase price can be received until the registration statement has become effective."

Second, until delivery of the final prospectus has been completed, written offers and offers transmitted by radio and television cannot be made outside of a Section 10 prospectus except in connection with business combinations. After filing the registration statement, two limited exceptions provide some flexibility to offering participants to publish notices of the offering. Following effectiveness, offering participants may disseminate sales literature and other writings so long as these materials are accompanied or preceded by a final prospectus. Oral offers, in contrast, are permissible as soon as the registration statement has been filed. Offering participants may use any combination of electronic and more traditional media, such as paper or the telephone, to communicate with prospective investors, provided that use of these media is in compliance with the Securities Act....

The SEC's 2005 public offering reforms also addressed the growing use of technology in securities offerings. Most notably for present purposes, the SEC adopted the *access equals delivery* model of delivering a final prospectus. Sec. Act Rels. 8501, 83 SEC Dock.

4 (2004) (proposal); 8591, 85 SEC Dock. 2871 (2005) (adoption). Rule 172(b), adopted in 2005 as part of the SEC's public offering reforms, provides that any obligation under §5(b)(2) of the 1933 Act for a final §10(a) prospectus to precede or accompany the carrying or delivery of a security is treated as satisfied if the issuer has filed with the SEC a prospectus for the offering that satisfies §10(a) of the 1933 Act or the issuer will make a good faith and reasonable effort to file such a final prospectus within the time required by Rule 424. If the issuer fails to file timely such a prospectus, the issuer must file the prospectus as soon as practicable.

The Commission, particularly under the leadership of Chairman Cox, has continued to move forward with its interactive data and XBRL initiative. See, e.g., SEC Press Rel. 2006-7 (Jan. 11, 2006) (announcing SEC incentives for companies to file financial reports using interactive data); SEC Press Rel. 2006-79 (May 23, 2006) (announcing more companies deciding to furnish SEC reports using interactive data); SEC Press Rel. 2006-99 (June 20, 2006) (announcing more companies using interactive data for financial statements); SEC Press Rel. 2006-139 (Aug. 14, 2006) (announcing SEC initiative to design enhanced Web-based research tools for investors); SEC Press Rel. 2006-158 (Sept. 25, 2006) (announcing the Commission had invested substantially in an initiative to "transform the agency's 1980s-vintage public company disclosure system from a form-based electronic filing cabinet to a dynamic real-time search tool with interactive capabilities"); SEC Press Rel. 2007-12 (Jan. 31, 2007) (announcing that the SEC voted to propose rule amendments to expand the interactive data voluntary program to include mutual funds); Sec. Act Rel. 8781, 89 SEC Dock. 2855 (2007) (proposal to extend the interactive data voluntary reporting program on EDGAR to include mutual fund risk/return summary information).

See also SEC Press Rel. 2006-61 (Apr. 25, 2006) (announcing replacement by SEC of many paper effectiveness orders with electronic notices); SEC Press Rel. 2006-93 (June 12, 2006) (announcement that over one million corporate and mutual fund reports are fully searchable online); SEC Press Rel. 2006-190 (Nov. 14, 2006) (SEC announces enhancement of online search capabilities on EDGAR).

P. 124

Undoubtedly, the regulation of securities markets will continue to evolve in response to technological developments. There is every reason to be confident that the offering and periodic disclosure processes will become increasingly efficient, promoting the goal of capital formation, as the SEC continues to account for the pervasiveness of the Internet and other technological advances.

In 2008, in response to the Federal Advisory Committee on Improvements to Financial Reporting, the Commission provided further guidance as to how companies can use their Web sites to provide information to investors, particularly under the 1934 Act. Sec. Ex. Act Rel. 58,288, 93 SEC Dock. 2623 (2008) (interpretive guidance). The Commission Release stated in part:

> Ongoing technological advances in electronic communications have increased both the markets' and investors' demand for more timely company disclosure and the ability of companies to capture, process and disseminate this information to market participants. Indeed, one of the key benefits of the Internet is that companies can make information available to investors quickly and in a cost-effective manner. Recently, we noted that approximately 80% of investors in mutual funds in the United States have access to the Internet in their homes. Investors are turning increasingly to electronic media and to company and third-party web sites as sources of information to aid in their investment decisions, particularly since many types of investment-related company information are available only in electronic form. We believe that the Internet has helped to transform the trading markets by enabling many retail investors to have ready access to company information....
>
> Our rules and interpretations that promote the use of web sites generally work in two different respects. First, when delivery of documents is required under the federal securities laws, we have encouraged the delivery in electronic format or recognized that electronic access can satisfy delivery — hence, prospectuses and proxy materials can be delivered or otherwise made available using electronic communications and the Internet in certain circumstances. Indeed with respect to proxy materials, certain companies are required to post their proxy materials on a specified, publicly accessible Internet web site (other than EDGAR) and provide record holders with a notice informing them that the materials are available and explaining how to access those materials. Second,

where disclosure of information is required under the Exchange Act, we have allowed companies to make such information available to investors on their web sites with their web sites serving, depending on the circumstance, as a supplement to EDGAR, as an alternative to EDGAR, or as a stand-alone method of providing information to investors independent of EDGAR.

When a company web site serves as a supplement to EDGAR, company information is available both on EDGAR and on the company's web site. We have promoted this supplemental use of web sites by requiring, for example, that:

- Companies disclose their web site addresses in annual reports on Form 10-K and state whether their Exchange Act reports are available on their web sites;
- Mutual funds disclose in their prospectuses whether shareholder reports are available on their web sites, and if not, why not;
- Companies make their Exchange Act reports available on their web sites as a condition to incorporating by reference previously filed reports into prospectuses filed as part of registration statements on Form S-1 or Form S-11;
- Companies post on their web sites, if they have one, all beneficial ownership reports filed by officers, directors and principal security holders under Section 16(a) of the Exchange Act; and
- Companies post on their web sites, if they have one, notice of their intent to delist or deregister their securities.

In addition, we have proposed in the Interactive Data Proposing Releases that companies that maintain web sites be required to post their interactive data files on their web sites.

In some situations, we have given companies the choice and flexibility of satisfying an Exchange Act disclosure requirement either by filing the disclosure on EDGAR or by making it available on the company's web site, thereby using company web sites as an alternative to EDGAR. For example:

- A company may disclose non-GAAP financial measures and Regulation G required information on its web site;
- An asset-backed issuer may post disclosure of static pool data on its web site rather than filing it on EDGAR;

77

P. 124   2010 SUPPLEMENT

- A company may provide its audit, nominating or compensation committee charters on its web site as an alternative to providing them in its proxy or information statement;
- A company may disclose a material amendment to its code of ethics, or a material waiver of a provision of its code of ethics, by posting the information on its web site rather than filing a Form 8-K; and
- A company may provide information regarding board member attendance at the annual shareholder meeting on its web site rather than in its proxy statement.

Finally, we have recently recognized that, in very limited circumstances, a company's web site can even serve as a stand-alone method of providing information to investors wholly independent of EDGAR. We have permitted certain foreign private issuers to use their web sites as the primary or stand-alone source of information about the company as a basis for maintaining an exemption from Exchange Act registration and reporting requirements, under certain circumstances.

i. Registration of Underlying Securities in Asset Backed Securities Transactions

P. 124 new par. after 1st full par. In 2004, the Commission adopted Rule 190 as part of (1) Regulation AB Release. Sec. Act Rel. 8518, 84 SEC Dock. 1624 (2004) (adoption). Rule 190(a) requires registration of the relevant underlying securities in an offering of asset backed securities where the asset pool includes securities of another issuer, unless the underlying securities are exempt under §3 or all of the following conditions are established:

(1) Neither the issuer of the underlying securities nor any of its affiliates has a direct or indirect agreement, arrangement, relationship or understanding, written or otherwise, relating to the underlying securities and asset-backed securities transaction;

(2) Neither the issuer of the underlying securities nor any of its affiliates is an affiliate of the sponsor, depositor, issuing entity or underwriter of the asset-backed securities transaction; and

DISTRIBUTION OF SECURITIES P. 125

(3) The depositor would be free to publicly resell the underlying securities without registration under the Act. For example:

(i) If the underlying securities are restricted securities, as defined in [Rule]144(a)(3), the underlying securities must meet the conditions set forth in [Rule]144(k) for the sale of restricted securities; and

(ii) The offering of the asset-backed security does not constitute part of a distribution of the underlying securities. An offering of asset-backed securities with an asset pool containing underlying securities that at the time of the purchase for the asset pool are part of a subscription or unsold allotment would be a distribution of the underlying securities. For purposes of this section, in an offering of asset-backed securities involving a sponsor, depositor or underwriter that was an underwriter or an affiliate of an underwriter in a registered offering of the underlying securities, the distribution of the asset-backed securities will not constitute part of a distribution of the underlying securities if the underlying securities were purchased at arm's length in the secondary market at least three months after the last sale of any unsold allotment or subscription by the affiliated underwriter that participated in the registered offering of the underlying securities.

C. THE REGISTRATION PROCEDURE: A STUDY IN ADMINISTRATIVE TECHNIQUE

1. THE STATUTORY PATTERN

P. 125, last par., substitute: In the Investor and Capital Markets Fee Relief Act of 2002, fees under §6(b) of the Securities Act were reduced to $92 per $1 million of the maximum aggregate price at which securities are proposed to be offered, with annual adjustments scheduled for 2003 to 2011 so that the rate required "is reasonably likely to produce aggregate fee collections...equal to the target offsetting collection amount for such fiscal year." P.L. 107-123, 115 Stat. 2390 (2002).

P. 131 — 2010 SUPPLEMENT

In 2008 the Commission also made largely technical amendments to its procedures for payments of fees under 1933 Act Rule 111, 1934 Act Rule 0-9, Trust Indenture Act Rule 7a-10, and Investment Company Act Rule 0-8. Sec. Act Rel. 8885, 92 SEC Dock. 1311 (2008). Mellon was replaced as designated lockbox depository by U.S. Bank.

2. THE PREEFFECTIVE PERIOD

b. The Price Amendment or Rule 430A

P. 131, after 1st full par. The 2005 public offering reforms amended Rule 424(b)(2), which now currently provides that a "prospectus that is used in connection with a primary offering of securities pursuant to Rule 415(a)(1)(x) or a primary offering of securities registered for issuance on a delayed basis pursuant to Rule 415(a)(1)(vii) or (viii) and that, in the case of Rule 415(a)(1)(viii) discloses the public offering price, description of securities or similar matters, and in the case of Rule 415(a)(1)(vii) and (x) discloses information previously omitted from the prospectus filed as part of an effective registration statement in reliance on Rule 430B, shall be filed with the Commission no later than the second business day following the earlier of the date of the determination of the offering price or the date it is first used after effectiveness in connection with a public offering or sales, or transmitted by a means reasonably calculated to result in filing with the Commission by that date."

As part of the 2005 public offering reforms, the SEC eliminated Rule 434 and made corresponding amendments to other rules, such as Rule 497, that referred to Rule 434.

c. Acceleration

P. 134, 1st full par., before last sentence. ; or (5) in the case of a significant secondary offering at the market, the registrant, selling security holders and underwriters have not taken sufficient measures to assure compliance with Regulation M.

P. 135, *new text after carryover par.*

d. The Base Prospectus and Rule 430B

Rule 430B was adopted as part of the 2005 public offering reforms. Rule 430B is the corollary to Rule 430A for shelf offerings insofar as Rule 430B allows certain information to be excluded from the base prospectus in certain Rule 415 shelf offerings. Rule 430B is understood largely to codify existing practice.

Rule 430B(a) provides that a prospectus filed as part of a registration statement for a shelf offering under Rule 415(a)(1)(vii) or (a)(1)(x) may omit information that is "unknown or not reasonably available" to the issuer pursuant to Rule 409. Rule 430B(a) further provides that a prospectus filed as part of an automatic shelf registration statement for offerings under Rule 415(a) (other than Rule 415(a)(1)(vii) or (viii)) also may omit information as to whether the offering is a primary offering or an offering on behalf of persons other than the issuer (or a combination thereof), the plan of distribution for the securities, a description of the securities registered other than an identification of the name or class of securities, and the identification of other issuers. Each such prospectus will be deemed to have been filed as part of the registration statement for purposes of §7 of the 1933 Act.

Under Rule 430B(b), a prospectus filed as part of a registration statement for shelf offerings under Rule 415(a)(1)(i) by an issuer that is eligible to use Form S-3 or F-3 for primary offerings pursuant to General Instruction I.B.1 (a) may omit the information described in Rule 430B(a) and (b) may also omit the identities of selling security holders and amounts of securities to be registered on their behalf if: (1) the registration statement is an automatic shelf registration statement; or (2) numerous conditions specified in Rule 430B(b)(2) are all satisfied.

Rule 430B(c) provides that a prospectus that omits information in reliance on Rule 430B meets the requirements of §10 of the 1933 Act for purposes of §5(b)(1), but such a prospectus that omits information does not meet the requirements of §10(a) of the 1933 Act for purposes of §5(b)(2), or §2(a)(10)(a) (i.e., the traditional free writing prospectus after the effective date).

Rule 430B(d) allows flexibility in how information omitted from a prospectus that is part of an effective registration statement may be included later in the prospectus. In particular, such omitted information may be included subsequently in the prospectus that is part of the registration statement by: (1) a posteffective amendment to the registration statement; (2) a prospectus supplement filed under Rule 424(b); or (3) subject to Rule 430B(h), if the applicable form permits, including the information in the issuer's reports filed under §13 or §15(d) of the 1934 Act that are incorporated or deemed incorporated by reference into the prospectus.

Rule 430B(e)–(g) concerns liability under §11 of the Securities Act. Most notably, these provisions, included below, provide that a prospectus supplement filed under Rule 424 will be deemed part of and included in the registration statement containing the base prospectus that the supplement relates to and reset the effective date of registration statements for purposes of §11 liability in certain instances.

6. Electronic Filing

P. 148, after 2d full par. On October 25, 2001, the SEC approved the first completely paperless securities offering for a variable annuity with the offering to be conducted solely through the issuer's Web site. Am. Separate Account 5 of Am. Life Ins. Co. of N.Y., Sec. Act Rel. 8027, 76 SEC Dock. 181 (2001). The Commission order was limited to the facts and circumstances of this offering but marked the first tentative step toward a paperless offering process. See Berenson & Menconi, To Boldly Go Where No Security Offering Has Gone Before: Paperless, 35 Rev. Sec. & Commodities Reg. 137 (2002).

In 2005 the Commission also adopted new Rule 313 under Regulation S-T and amended various other rules, the effect of which was to expand the information that the SEC requires certain investment companies to submit to the Commission electronically through the EDGAR system and to make it easier for investors to search open-end management company and insurance company separate account filings on EDGAR by requiring that certain open-end management investment companies and insurance company separate accounts identify in their EDGAR filings information regarding their series and classes (or contracts, in the case of separate accounts). The rule changes also made certain technical changes to the EDGAR system. See Sec. Act Rels. 8401, 82 SEC Dock. 1532 (2004) (proposal); 8590, 85 SEC Dock. 2849 (2005) (adoption).

In Sec. Act Rel. 8529, 84 SEC Dock. 2615 (2005) (adoption), the Commission adopted rule and form amendments to permit registrants to submit voluntarily supplemental "tagged" financial information using the eXtensible Business Reporting Language (XBRL). See also SEC Press Rel. 2005-64 (Apr. 26, 2005). This voluntary program would enable the Commission to evaluate the usefulness of data tagging to registrants, investors, the SEC, and the marketplace.

In 2009 the Commission adopted rule amendments to permit risk/return summary information to be downloaded through XBRL directly into spreadsheets and analyzed in a variety of ways using commercial off-the-shelf software. The interactive data would be required to be provided as exhibits to registration statements. The rule amendments also would permit investment companies to submit portfolio holdings information in the interactive data voluntary program without being required to submit other financial information. Sec. Act Rel. 9006, __ SEC Dock. __ (2009) (adoption).

In 2008 the Commission announced it would move to replace EDGAR over a three year period beginning in 2009 with a new Interactive Data Electronic Application (IDEA) system. SEC Plans Gradually to Replace EDGAR with New, Interactive, XBRL-Based IDEA, 40 Sec. Reg. & L. Rep. (BNA) 1330 (2008).

In 2009 the Commission adopted rule and form amendments to allow applicants for EDGAR access codes using Form ID to submit authenticating documents in PDF (Portable Document

Format) rather than by fax. Sec. Act Rel. 9013, ___ SEC Dock. ___ (2009) (adoption).

D. CONTENTS OF THE REGISTRATION STATEMENT AND PROSPECTUS (HEREIN OF THE SEC'S ACCOUNTING ROLE)

1. INTEGRATION OF THE DISCLOSURE PROVISIONS OF THE 1933 AND 1934 ACTS

P. 150, end 1st par. In 2007 the Commission adopted amendments to the eligibility requirements for the primary offering of securities using Forms S-3 and F-3. See Sec. Act Rels. 8812, 90 SEC Dock. 2333 (2007) (proposal); 8878, 92 SEC Dock. 513 (2007) (adoption).

In 2008 the Commission adopted Form S-11 amendments to permit historical incorporation by reference. Sec. Act Rels. 8871, 92 SEC Dock. 421 (2007) (proposal); 8909, 92 SEC Dock. 2997 (2008) (adoption).

In 2007 the Commission adopted a number of regulatory changes intended to relieve the regulatory burden on smaller companies and to afford smaller companies regulatory simplification. See Sec. Act Rels. 8819, 90 SEC Dock. 2732 (2007) (proposal); 8876, 92 SEC Dock. 436 (2007) (adoption). The SEC amended Regulation S-K, as well as both rules and forms under the Securities Act, Securities Exchange Act, and Trust Indenture Act. The SEC amended Regulation S-K Items 10, 101, 102, 201, 301, 302, 303, 305, 401, 402, 404, 407, 503, 504, 512, 601, 701, and 1118; Securities Act Rules 110, 138, 139, 158, 175, 405, 415, 428, 430B, 430C, 455, and 502; Exchange Act Rules 0-2, 0-12, 3b-6, 10A-1, 10A-3, 12b-2, 12b-23, 12b-25, 12h-3, 13a-10, 13a-13, 13a-14, 13a-16, 13a-20, 14a-3, 14a-5, 14a-8, 14c-3, 14d-3, 15d-10, 15d-13, 15d-14, 15d-20, and 15d-21; Securities Act Forms 0-1, S-1, S-3, S-4, S-8, S-11, 1-A, and F-X; Exchange Act Forms 0-1, 8-A, 8-K, 10, 10-Q, 10-K, 11-K, 20-F, and SE; Schedules 14A and 14C; and Regulation S-X Rules 210.3-01, 210.3-05, 210.3-10,

210.3-12, 210.3-14, 210.4-01, and 210.10-01. The SEC also added a new Regulation S-X Article 8 with the financial statement requirements for smaller reporting companies. Further, the Commission amended Trust Indenture Act Rules 0-11, 4d-9, and 10a-5 and Trust Indenture Forms Section 269.0-1. Finally, the SEC removed Regulation S-B and the forms associated with it, Forms SB-1, SB-2, 10-SB, 10-QSB, and 10-KSB. The Commission adopted the amendments substantially as proposed.

P. 153, end of 1st full par. In 2005, as part of the Commission's public offering reforms, the Commission eliminated Form S-2. Sec. Act Rels. 8591, 85 SEC Dock. 2871 (2005) (adoption); 8591A (2006) (technical amendments). The Commission simultaneously eliminated Form F-2. Because of the Form's historical place in the Commission's integrated disclosure framework, it is still important to outline Form S-2 as in effect prior to being rescinded.

In 2007 the Commission adopted amendments to the eligibility requirements for Forms S-3 and F-3 for primary offerings. See Sec. Act Rels. 8812, 90 SEC Dock. 2333 (2007) (proposal); 8878, 92 SEC Dock. 513 (2007) (adoption).

2. REGULATION S-K (NONFINANCIAL DATA)

a. Commission Policy on Forward Looking Statements [Item 10(b); Sec. Act §27A; Sec. Ex. Act §21E]

P. 165, new text end of page. In Asher v. Baxter Int'l, Inc., 377 F.3d 727 (7th Cir. 2004), the court declined to dismiss a complaint whose projections the defendant urged were shielded from liability by the PSLRA safe harbors. Judge Easterbrook wrote in part:

> Whether or not Baxter could have made the cautions more helpful by disclosing assumptions, methods, or confidence intervals, none of these is required. The PSLRA does not require the *most* helpful caution; it is enough to "identify[ ]important factors that could cause actual results to differ materially from those in the

forward-looking statement." This means that it is enough to point to the principal contingencies that could cause actual results to depart from the projection. The statute calls for issuers to reveal the "important factors" but not to attach probabilities to each potential bad outcome, or to reveal in detail what could go wrong; as we have said, that level of detail might hurt investors (by helping rivals) even as it improved the accuracy of stock prices.... Moreover, "if enterprises cannot make predictions about themselves, then securities analysts, newspaper columnists, and charlatans have protected turf. There will be predictions by persons whose access to information is not as good as the issuer's. When the issuer adds its information and analysis to that assembled by outsiders, the *collective* assessment will be more accurate even though a given projection will be off the mark." *Wielgos*, 892 F.2d at 514 (emphasis in original).

Yet Baxter's chosen language may fall short. There is no reason to think — at least, no reason that a court can accept at the pleading stage, before plaintiffs have access to discovery — that the items mentioned in Baxter's cautionary language were those thought at the time to be the (or any of the) "important" sources of variance. The problem is not that what actually happened went unmentioned; issuers need not anticipate all sources of deviations from expectations. Rather, the problem is that there is no reason (on this record) to conclude that Baxter mentioned those sources of variance that (at the time of the projection) were the principal or important risks. For all we can tell, the major risks Baxter knew that it faced when it made its forecasts were exactly those that, according to the complaint, came to pass, yet the cautionary statement mentioned none of them.

Moreover, the cautionary language remained fixed even as the risks changed. When the sterility failure occurred in spring 2002, Baxter left both its forecasts and cautions as is. When Baxter closed the plants that (according to the complaint) were its least-cost sources of production, the forecasts and cautions continued without amendment. This raises the possibility — no greater confidence is possible before discovery — that Baxter knew of important variables that would affect its forecasts, but omitted them from the cautionary language in order to depict the projections as more certain than internal estimates at the time made them. Thus this complaint could not be dismissed under the safe harbor, though we cannot exclude the possibility that if after discovery Baxter establishes that the cautions did reveal what were, *ex ante*, the major risks, the safe harbor may yet carry the day.

In Baron v. Smith, 380 F.3d 49, 53–54 (1st Cir. 2004), the court concluded that a press release announcing the filing of a voluntary reorganization was protected by the statutory safe harbor to the extent it contained forward-looking statements. See also Helwig v. Vencor, Inc., 251 F.3d 540, 558–562 (6th Cir. 2001).

It is conceivable that cautionary language could be so involved and lengthy as to lose some of its practical value to investors. In Stone & Webster, Inc. Sec. Litig., 414 F.3d 187, 211–213 (1st Cir. 2005), the court addressed mixed factual and forward-looking statements and also suggested that the cautionary language safe harbor gives a "license to defraud."

In SEC v. Merchant Capital, LLC, 483 F.3d 747, 767–769 (11th Cir. 2007), the court held that general cautionary language accompanying rosy projections was materially misleading when the performance history of the relevant partnerships was omitted.

c. Item 103: Legal Proceedings

P. 174 n.60, end note. For more recent illustrative cases concerning disclosures related to management integrity, as well as management competency, see, e.g., Suez Equity Investors, L.P. v. Toronto-Dominion Bank, 250 F.3d 87, 96–99 (2d Cir. 2001) (misstatements concerning managerial competency sufficient to establish loss causation; distinguishing Santa Fe Indus., Inc. v. Green, 430 U.S. 462 (1977)); Gebhardt v. ConAgra Foods, Inc., 335 F.3d 824, 829–830 (8th Cir. 2003) (GAAP violations impugning management's integrity); Greenhouse v. MCG Capital Corp., 392 F.3d 650, 657–660 (4th Cir. 2004) (finding that misstatements regarding a key manager's educational background were not material, although educational background may be material in some instances, and suggesting that the mere fact that educational background was misstated does not itself call into question

P. 179   2010 SUPPLEMENT

management's integrity so as to give rise to a material misstatement; distinguishing *Gebhardt*).

Item 406 of Regulation S-K now requires disclosures concerning a company's code of ethics.

d. Item 303: Management's Discussion and Analysis of Financial Condition and Result of Operations

P. 179, end indented text. In 2005 the Commission staff submitted to the President and to Congress the Report and Recommendations Pursuant to Section 401(c) of the Sarbanes-Oxley Act of 2002 On Arrangements with Off-Balance Sheet Implications, Special Purpose Entities, and Transparency of Filings by Issuers. A copy of the Report is available on the Commission Web site at http://sec.gov/news/studies/soxoffbalancerpt.pdf. The extensive staff report addresses two principal inquiries: (1) the extent of off-balance sheet arrangements; and (2) whether current financial statement disclosures adequately disclose such arrangements.

In December 2007 the staff of the Division of Corporation Finance sent a letter to certain public companies highlighting potential MD&A disclosures they may wish to make relating to certain off balance sheet arrangements. A copy of a form of the letter is available on the Commission's Web site at http://sec.gov/divisions/corpfin/guidance/cfoffbalanceltr1207.htm.

e. Item 304: Disagreements with Accountants on Accounting and Financial Disclosure

P. 180 n. 71, end note. Item 307, adopted in 2002 and as subsequently amended, provides for the disclosure of the "conclusions of the registrant's principal executive and principal financial officers, or persons performing similar functions, regarding the effectiveness of the registrant's disclosure controls and procedures (as defined in [Rule 13a-15(e) or Rule 15d-15(e) under the 1934 Act]) as of the end of the period covered by the report, based on the evaluation of these controls and procedures required by paragraph (b) of [Rule 15d-15 under the 1934 Act]."

Item 308, initially adopted in 2003, presently provides for disclosures regarding a report by management concerning the registrant's internal control over financial reporting; an attestation report of the registrant's registered public accounting firm regarding management's assessment of the registrant's internal control over financial reporting; and disclosures regarding certain changes in the registrant's internal control over financial reporting that have materially affected or that are reasonably likely to materially affect the registrant's internal control over financial reporting.

f. Item 402: Executive Compensation

P. 182 n.73 end note. In July 2003, Microsoft announced that it would stop issuing options and instead begin giving its 50,000 employees restricted stock. Guth & Lublin, Tarnished Gold: Microsoft Ushers Out Era of Options, Wall St. J., July 9, 2003, at A1.

New questions regarding executive compensation arose in the wake of NYSE Chairman Richard Grasso's resignation in September 2003 after revelations that he had received a retirement and deferred pay compensation package of at least $139.5 million and annual compensation as high as $30.6 million in 2001, sharply higher than the $2.2 million he received in 1995, his first year as Chairman. Morgenson & Thomas, Chairman Quits Stock Exchange in Furor over Pay, N.Y. Times, Sept. 18, 2003, at A1; Craig & Kelly, Weakened NYSE Must Face Challenges, Wall St. J., Sept. 18, 2003, at C1; Grasso Declines Additional $48 M; Details of Compensation Package Provided, 35 Sec. Reg. & L. Rep. (BNA) 1480 (2003).

In 2004, New York State Attorney General Eliot Spitzer filed a complaint under the New York Not-for-Profit Corporation Law challenging compensations and benefits paid to Richard Grasso on grounds that the amounts were not "reasonable" and "commensurate with the services rendered," that the compensation provider was beset with conflicts of interest and dominated by Grasso, and that there had been a lack of full disclosure. See New York AG Spitzer Sues Ex-NYSE Chairman Grasso Over Pay, 36 Sec. Reg. & L. Rep. (BNA) 997 (2004). A federal district court subsequently declined to remove the action from the New York courts. New York v. Grasso, 350 F. Supp. 2d 498 (S.D.N.Y. 2004); In Setback for Grasso, NYSE Suit Over Pay Package Returned to N.Y. Court, 36 Sec. Reg. & L. Rep. (BNA) at 2237.

In 2004, the IASB adopted a standard that requires covered companies to expense stock options. IASB Issues Standard Requiring Expensing of Stock Options; U.K. Board to Follow Suit, 36 Sec. Reg. & L. Rep. (BNA) 365 (2004).

Shortly later the FASB also proposed that companies be required to report stock options as an expense. Norris, Accounting Board Wants Options to be Reported as an Expense, N.Y. Times, Apr. 1, 2004, at C1; FASB Formally Proposes Requirement to Expense Employee Stock Compensation, 36 Sec. Reg. & L. Rep. (BNA) 642 (2004).

In December 2004, the FASB adopted revisions to Statement of FAS Standard No. 123 and required public entities to expense stock options at specified dates in 2005. See also FASB, Statement of Financial Accounting Standards No. 123 (revised 2004), Share-Based Payment: Frequently Asked Questions (Dec. 16, 2004).

Appendix B, Basis for Conclusions, explained why the FASB reconsidered FAS Statement No. 123, in ¶¶83, 84–85:

> B2. Statement 123 was issued in 1995. Its requirements for share-based employee compensation transactions were effective for financial statements for fiscal years beginning after December 15, 1995. As originally issued, Statement 123 established the fair-value-based method of accounting as preferable for share-based compensation awarded to employees and encouraged, but did not require, entities to adopt it. The Board's decision at that time was based on practical rather than conceptual considerations. Paragraphs 60 and 61 of Statement 123 stated:
>
> The debate on accounting for stock-based compensation unfortunately became so divisive that it threatened the Board's future working relationship with some of its constituents. Eventually, the

nature of the debate threatened the future of accounting standards setting in the private sector.

The Board continues to believe that financial statements would be more relevant and representationally faithful if the estimated fair value of employee stock options was included in determining an entity's net income, just as all other forms of compensation are included....

B4. Before 2002, virtually all entities chose to continue to apply the provisions of Opinion 25 rather than to adopt the fair-value-based method to account for share-based compensation arrangements with employees. The serious financial reporting failures that came to light beginning in 2001 led to a keen interest in accounting and financial reporting issues on the part of investors, regulators, members of the U.S. Congress, and the media. Many of the Board's constituents who use financial information said that the failure to recognize compensation cost for most employee share options had obscured important aspects of reported performance and impaired the transparency of financial statements.

B5. The increased focus on high-quality, transparent financial reporting stemming from the financial reporting failures in the early years of the 21st century created a growing demand for entities to recognize compensation cost for employee share options and similar instruments — a demand to which entities began to respond. As of March 2003, when the Board added this project to its agenda, 179 public companies had adopted or announced their intention to adopt the fair-value-based accounting method in Statement 123. By May 2003, that number had grown to 276 public companies, of which 93 were companies included in the Standard & Poor's (S&P) 500 Index; those companies represented 36 percent of the index based on market capitalization. By February 2004, the number had increased to 483 public companies, 113 of which represented 41 percent of the S&P 500 Index based on market capitalization, and by July 2004, the number had increased to 753 public companies.

Revised FAS Statement No. 123 requires in ¶¶1 and 16:

that the cost resulting from all share-based payment transactions be recognized in the financial statements. This Statement establishes fair value as the measurement objective in accounting for share-based payment arrangements and requires all entities to apply a fair-value-based measurement method in accounting for share-based payment transactions with employees except for equity instruments held by employee share ownership plans....

The measurement objective for equity instruments awarded to employees is to estimate the fair value at the grant date of the equity instruments that the entity is obligated to issue when employees have rendered the requisite service and satisfied any other conditions necessary to earn the right to benefit from the instruments (for example, to exercise share options). That estimate is based on the share price and other pertinent factors, such as expected volatility, at the grant date.

A variety of valuation techniques satisfy the criteria of Revised Statement No. 123 including the Black-Scholes-Merton formula, a lattice model, or a Monte Carlo simulation technique. Id. at ¶A13 n.48.

Paragraph 4 defined the scope of Revised Statement No. 123:

This Statement applies to all share-based payment transactions in which an entity acquires goods or services by issuing (or offering to issue) its shares, share options, or other equity instruments (except for equity instruments held by an employee share ownership plan) or by incurring liabilities to an employee or other supplier (a) in amounts based, at least in part, on the price of the entity's shares or other equity instruments or (b) that require or may require settlement by issuing the entity's equity shares or other equity instruments.

Revised Statement No. 123 includes specified disclosure requirements in ¶64:

An entity with one or more share-based payment arrangements shall disclose information that enables users of the financial statements to understand:

    a. The nature and terms of such arrangements that existed during the period and the potential effects of those arrangements on shareholders
    b. The effect of compensation cost arising from share-based payment arrangements on the income statement

c. The method of estimating the fair value of the goods or services received, or the fair value of the equity instruments granted (or offered to grant), during the period
   d. The cash flow effects resulting from share-based payment arrangements.

In 2003, the Commission approved the NYSE and NASD equity compensation plan amendments. Sec. Ex. Act Rel. 48,108, 80 SEC Dock. 1596 (2003) (adoption). The NYSE proposal adopts §303A(8) of the NYSE's Listed Company Manual to require shareholder approval of all equity compensation plans and material revisions to the plans with limited exemptions. The new Rule replaces a NYSE pilot program relating to broadly based stock options, found in §§312.01, 312.03, and 312.04 of the NYSE Listed Company Manual.

In Walt Disney Co. Deriv. Litig., 907 A.2d 693 (Del. Ch. 2005), after a 37 day trial Chancellor Chandler concluded that the Walt Disney directors did not breach their fiduciary duties or commit waste with respect to Michael Ovitz's compensation. The court was critical of CEO Michael Eisner but did not conclude that Eisner's actions should lead to liability for a violation of the duty of care by either Eisner or the board.

In 2006, in the first major Rule initiated by the Cox Chairmanship, the Commission proposed and then adopted amendments to the disclosure requirements for executive and director compensation, related party transactions, director independence, and securing ownership of officers and directors. Sec. Act Rels. 8655, 87 SEC Dock. 529 (2006) (proposal); 8732A, 88 SEC Dock. 2353 (2006) (adoption).

The rulemaking's centerpiece is the revamped executive compensation disclosure requirements under Item 402 of Regulation S-K. Item 402(a) delineates Item 402's scope. Item 402(a) generally "requires clear, concise and understandable disclosure of all plan and non-plan compensation" for *named executive officers* and directors. Item 402(a)(3) defines *named executive officers* as:

> (i) All individuals serving as the registrant's principal executive officer or acting in a similar capacity during the last completed fiscal year (*PEO*), regardless of compensation level;

P. 182   2010 SUPPLEMENT

(ii) All individuals serving as the registrant's principal financial officer or acting in a similar capacity during the last completed fiscal year (*PFO*), regardless of compensation level;
(iii) The registrant's three most highly compensated executive officers other than the PEO and PFO who were serving as executive officers at the end of the last completed fiscal year; and
(iv) Up to two additional individuals for whom disclosure would have been provided pursuant to paragraph (a)(3)(iii) of this Item but for the fact that the individual was not serving as an executive officer of the registrant at the end of the last completed fiscal year.

Item 402(a)(6) further defines the reach of Item 402 by defining a number of key terms, including *stock, option, stock appreciation rights (SARs), equity, plan, incentive plan, equity incentive plan, non-equity incentive plan, incentive plan award, date of grant, grant date,* and *closing market price*.

Item 402(b) provides for the new Compensation Discussion and Analysis (or *CD&A*). The CD&A recalls the MD&A required under Item 303 of Regulation S-K. "The purpose of the [CD&A] is to provide to investors material information that is necessary to an understanding of the registrant's compensation policies and decisions regarding the named executive officers." Instr. 1 to Item 402(b). In other words, the CD&A puts a registrant's executive compensation disclosures in context and provides investors with insight into the board's thinking when setting executive pay. For the context to be meaningful, the registrant must avoid resorting to boilerplate in the CD&A.

Item 402(b)(1) provides that the CD&A must "explain all material elements of the registrant's compensation of the named executive officers," including describing:

(i) The objectives of the registrant's compensation programs;
(ii) What the compensation program is designed to reward;
(iii) Each element of compensation;
(iv) Why the registrant chooses to pay each element;
(v) How the registrant determines the amount (and, where applicable, the formula) for each element to pay; and

(vi) How each compensation element and the registrant's decisions regarding that element fit into the registrant's overall compensation objectives and affect decisions regarding other elements.

Item 402(b) expressly acknowledges that the information disclosed in the CD&A will depend upon the particular facts and circumstances facing a registrant. That said, Item 402(b)(2) provides the following nonexclusive list of examples of material information that may be disclosed:

(i) The policies for allocating between long-term and currently paid out compensation;
(ii) The policies for allocating between cash and non-cash compensation, and among different forms of non-cash compensation;
(iii) For long-term compensation, the basis for allocating compensation to each different form of award (such as relationship of the award to the achievement of the registrant's long-term goals, management's exposure to downside equity performance risk, correlation between cost to registrant and expected benefits to the registrant);
(iv) How the determination is made as to when awards are granted, including awards of equity-based compensation such as options;
(v) What specific items of corporate performance are taken into account in setting compensation policies and making compensation decisions;
(vi) How specific forms of compensation are structured and implemented to reflect these items of the registrant's performance, including whether discretion can be or has been exercised (either to award compensation absent attainment of the relevant performance goal(s) or to reduce or increase the size of any award or payout), identifying any particular exercise of discretion, and stating whether it applied to one or more specified named executive officers or to all compensation subject to the relevant performance goal(s);
(vii) How specific forms of compensation are structured and implemented to reflect the named executive officer's individual performance and/or individual contribution to these items of the registrant's performance, describing the elements of individual performance and/or contribution that are taken into account;

P. 182

(viii) Registrant policies and decisions regarding the adjustment or recovery of awards or payments if the relevant registrant performance measures upon which they are based are restated or otherwise adjusted in a manner that would reduce the size of an award or payment;

(ix) The factors considered in decisions to increase or decrease compensation materially;

(x) How compensation or amounts realizable from prior compensation are considered in setting other elements of compensation (e.g., how gains from prior option or stock awards are considered in setting retirement benefits);

(xi) With respect to any contract, agreement, plan or arrangement, whether written or unwritten, that provides for payment(s) at, following, or in connection with any termination or change-in-control, the basis for selecting particular events as triggering payment (e.g., the rationale for providing a single trigger for payment in the event of a change-in-control);

(xii) The impact of the accounting and tax treatments of the particular form of compensation;

(xiii) The registrant's equity or other security ownership requirements or guidelines (specifying applicable amounts and forms of ownership), and any registrant policies regarding hedging the economic risk of such ownership;

(xiv) Whether the registrant engaged in any benchmarking of total compensation, or any material element of compensation, identifying the benchmark and, if applicable, its components (including component companies); and

(xv) The role of executive officers in determining executive compensation.

In the adoption Release, the Commission described the CD&A as "principles-based, in that it identifies the disclosure concept and provides several illustrative examples." The principles-based nature of the CD&A suggests that registrants should avoid a check-the-box approach to disclosure that narrowly focuses on the foregoing examples in deciding what to disclose. The above list is a starting point, not an end point, in considering what should be disclosed and analyzed.

The 2006 amendments to Item 402 build on prior Item 402's tabular disclosures. In particular, revised Item 402's tables cover three general categories of compensation, described in the adoption Release as:

> 1. compensation with respect to the last fiscal year (and the two preceding fiscal years), as reflected in a revised Summary Compensation Table that presents compensation paid currently or deferred (including options, restricted stock and similar grants) and compensation consisting of current earnings or awards that are part of a plan, and as supplemented by one table [Grants of Plan-Based Awards Table] providing back-up information for certain data in the Summary Compensation Table;
> 2. holdings of equity-based interests that relate to compensation or are potential sources of future compensation, focusing on compensation-related equity-based interests that were awarded in prior years and are *at risk*, as well as recent realization on these interests, such as through vesting of restricted stock or the exercise of options and similar instruments [Outstanding Equity Awards at Fiscal Year-End Table and Option Exercises and Stock Vested Table]; and
> 3. retirement and other post-employment compensation, including retirement and deferred compensation plans, other retirement benefits and other post-employment benefits, such as those payable in the event of a change in control [Pension Benefits Table and Nonqualified Deferred Compensation Table].

Item 402(c) provides for the Summary Compensation Table, which, according to the Commission, "continues to serve as the principal disclosure vehicle regarding executive compensation." A registrant must disclose for the registrant's named executive officers for each of the last three completed fiscal years the information required by Item 402(c)(2), which includes:

- the dollar value of the base salary (cash and noncash) that the named executive officer earned during the fiscal year covered (column c)).
- the dollar value of the bonus (cash and noncash) that the named executive officer earned during the fiscal year covered (column (d));

P. 182

- for stock awards, the dollar amount recognized for purposes of financial statements for the fiscal year in accordance with Statement 123R (column (e));
- for option awards, with or without tandem stock appreciation rights, the dollar amount recognized for purposes of financial statements for the fiscal year in accordance with Statement 123R (column (f));
- the dollar value of all earnings for services performed during the last fiscal year pursuant to awards under nonequity incentive plans and all earnings on any outstanding awards (column (g));
- the sum of the changes in the value of accumulated benefits under defined benefit and actuarial pension plans and above-market or preferential earnings on compensation deferred on a non-tax-qualified basis (column (h));
- all other compensation that the registrant could not properly report in any other column of the Summary Compensation Table (column (i)); and
- the dollar value of total compensation—that is, the sum of all amounts reported in columns (c) through (i) for a named executive officer (column).

The tabular presentation of the information is to take the following form:

Summary Compensation Table

Name and Principal Position	Year	Salary ($)	Bonus ($)	Stock Awards ($)	Option Awards ($)	Non-Equity Incentive Plan Compensation ($)	Change in Pension Value and Nonqualified Deferred Compensation Earnings ($)	All Other Compensation ($)	Total ($)
(a)	(b)	(c)	(d)	(e)	(f)	(g)	(h)	(i)	(j)
PEO									
PFO									
A									
B									
C									

DISTRIBUTION OF SECURITIES　　　　P. 182

Perks are one of the more controversial aspects of executive compensation. Perks and other personal benefits must be disclosed in column (i) as part of All Other Compensation unless the "aggregate amount of such compensation is less than $10,000." The Item adds:

> Perquisites and personal benefits may be excluded as long as the total value of all perquisites and personal benefits for a named executive officer is less than $10,000. If the total value of all perquisites and personal benefits is $10,000 or more for any named executive officer, then each perquisite or personal benefit, regardless of its amount, must be identified by type. If perquisites and personal benefits are required to be reported for a named executive officer pursuant to this rule, then each perquisite or personal benefit that exceeds the greater of $25,000 or 10% of the total amount of perquisites and personal benefits for that officer must be quantified and disclosed in a footnote. The requirements for identification and quantification apply only to compensation for the last fiscal year. Perquisites and other personal benefits shall be valued on the basis of the aggregate incremental cost to the registrant. With respect to the perquisite or other personal benefit for which footnote quantification is required, the registrant shall describe in the footnote its methodology for computing the aggregate incremental cost. Reimbursements of taxes owed with respect to perquisites or other personal benefits must be included in column (i) and are subject to separate quantification and identification as tax reimbursements (paragraph (c)(2)(ix)(B) of this Item) even if the associated perquisites or other personal benefits are not required to be included because the total amount of all perquisites or personal benefits for an individual named executive officer is less than $10,000 or are required to be identified but are not required to be separately quantified.

The dividing line between when something is a perk for the executive's benefit as compared to conferred on the executive for the benefit of the business is often blurry. The Commission updated earlier interpretive guidance with the following in the adoption Release:

In the Proposing Release, we provided interpretive guidance about factors to be considered in determining whether an item is a perquisite or other personal benefit.

...[F]or decades questions have arisen as to what is a perquisite or other personal benefit required to be disclosed. We continue to believe that it is not appropriate for Item 402 to define perquisites or personal benefits, given that different forms of these items continue to develop, and thus a definition would become outdated. As stated in the Proposing Release, we are concerned that sole reliance on a bright line definition in our rules might provide an incentive to characterize perquisites or personal benefits in ways that would attempt to circumvent the bright lines. Many commenters sought additional or modified interpretive guidance, including guidance with respect to an item that is integrally and directly related to the performance of the executive's duties but has a personal benefit aspect as well. Accordingly, we are providing additional explanation regarding how to apply this guidance. The amendments we adopt today require perquisites and personal benefits to be disclosed for both named executive officers and directors. Further, the disclosure requirements we adopt regarding potential payments upon termination or change-in-control include disclosure of perquisites. Accordingly, this discussion also applies in the context of each of these disclosure requirements.

Among the factors to be considered in determining whether an item is a perquisite or other personal benefit are the following:

- An item is not a perquisite or personal benefit if it is integrally and directly related to the performance of the executive's duties.
- Otherwise, an item is a perquisite or personal benefit if it confers a direct or indirect benefit that has a personal aspect, without regard to whether it may be provided for some business reason or for the convenience of the company, unless it is generally available on a non-discriminatory basis to all employees.

We believe the way to approach this is by initially evaluating the first prong of the analysis. If an item is integrally and directly related to the performance of the executive's duties, that is the end of the analysis—the item is not a perquisite or personal benefit and no compensation disclosure is required. Moreover, if an item is integrally and directly related to the performance of an executive's duties under this analysis, there is no requirement to disclose any incremental cost over a less expensive alternative. For example, with respect to business travel, it is not necessary to disclose the cost differential between renting a mid-sized car over a compact car....

The concept of a benefit that is *integrally and directly related* to job performance is a narrow one. The analysis draws a critical distinction between an item that a company provides because the executive needs it to do the job, making it integrally and directly related to the performance of duties, and an item provided for some other reason, even where that other reason can involve both company benefit and personal benefit. Some commenters objected that *integrally and directly related* is too narrow a standard, suggesting that other business reasons for providing an item should not be disregarded in determining whether an item is a perquisite. We do not adopt this suggested approach. As we stated in the Proposing Release, the fact that the company has determined that an expense is an *ordinary* or *necessary* business expense for tax or other purposes or that an expense is for the benefit or convenience of the company is not responsive to the inquiry as to whether the expense provides a perquisite or other personal benefit for disclosure purposes. Whether the company should pay for an expense or it is deductible for tax purposes relates principally to questions of state law regarding use of corporate assets and of tax law; our disclosure requirements are triggered by different and broader concepts.

As we noted in the Proposing Release, business purpose or convenience does not affect the characterization of an item as a perquisite or personal benefit where it is not integrally and directly related to the performance by the executive of his or her job. Therefore, for example, a company's decision to provide an item of personal benefit for security purposes does not affect its characterization as a perquisite or personal benefit. A company policy that for security purposes an executive (or an executive and his or her family) must use company aircraft or other company means of travel for personal travel, or must use company or company-provided property for vacations, does not affect the conclusion that the item provided is a perquisite or personal benefit.

If an item is not integrally and directly related to the performance of the executive's duties, the second step of the analysis comes into play. Does the item confer a direct or indirect benefit that has a personal aspect (without regard to whether it may be provided for some business reason or for the convenience of the company)? If so, is it generally available on a non-discriminatory basis to all employees? For example, a company's provision of helicopter service for an executive to commute to work from home is not integrally and directly related to job performance (although it would benefit the company by getting the executive to work faster), clearly bestows a benefit that has a personal aspect, and is not generally available to all employees on a non-discriminatory basis. As we have noted, business purpose or convenience does not affect the characterization of an item as a perquisite or personal benefit where it is not integrally and directly related to the performance by the executive of his or her job.

A company may reasonably conclude that an item is generally available to all employees on a non-discriminatory basis if it is available to those employees to whom it lawfully may be provided. For this purpose, a company may recognize jurisdictionally based legal restrictions (such as for foreign employees) or the employees' *accredited investor* status. In contrast, merely providing a benefit consistent with its availability to employees in the same job category or at the same pay scale does not establish that it is generally available on a non-discriminatory basis to all employees.

Applying the concepts that we outline above, examples of items requiring disclosure as perquisites or personal benefits under Item 402 include, but are not limited to: club memberships not used exclusively for business entertainment purposes, personal financial or tax advice, personal travel using vehicles owned or leased by the company, personal travel otherwise financed by the company, personal use of other property owned or leased by the company, housing and other living expenses (including but not limited to relocation assistance and payments for the executive or director to stay at his or her personal residence), security provided at a personal residence or during personal travel, commuting expenses (whether or not for the company's convenience or benefit), and discounts on the company's products or services not generally available to employees on a non-discriminatory basis.

Beyond the examples provided, we assume that companies and their advisors, who are more familiar with the detailed facts of a particular situation and who are responsible for providing materially accurate and complete disclosure satisfying our requirements, can apply the two-step analysis to assess whether particular arrangements require disclosure as perquisites or personal benefits. In light of the importance of the subject to many investors, all participants should approach the subject of perquisites and personal benefits thoughtfully.

Item 402(d) requires the Grants of Plan-Based Awards Table. The tabular disclosures must include the following concerning each grant of an award to a named executive officer during the last completed fiscal year under any plan:

- the grant date for equity-based awards (column (b)); provided, that if the grant date is different than the date on which the board compensation committee (or other committee of the board of directors performing a similar function or the entire board) acts or is deemed to take action in making such grant, a separate column must be included between columns (b) and (c) showing such date of board action;
- the dollar value of the estimated future payout or the applicable range of estimated payouts (threshold, target, and maximum amount) on the satisfaction of the conditions under nonequity incentive plan awards granted in the fiscal year (columns (c) through (e));
- the number of shares of stock, or the number of shares of stock underlying options to be paid out or vested on the satisfaction of the conditions under equity incentive plan awards granted in the fiscal year, or the range of estimated shares of stock to be paid out, or the number of shares underlying options under the award (threshold, target, and maximum amount) (columns (f) through (h));
- the number of shares of stock granted in the fiscal year that do not have to be disclosed in columns (f) through (h) (column (i));
- the number of securities underlying options granted in the fiscal year that do not have to be disclosed in columns (f) through (h) (column (j));
- the per-share exercise price or base price of the options granted in the fiscal year (column (k)); provided, that if such price is less than the closing market price of the underlying

P. 182   2010 SUPPLEMENT

security on the grant date (i.e., the options are *in the money* when granted), an additional column showing the closing market price on the grant date must be added after column (k); and

- the grant date fair value of each equity award calculated according to Statement 123R (column (l)); provided, that if at any time during the last completed fiscal year, the registrant has repriced the options, stock appreciation rights, or similar option-like instruments awarded to a named executive officer, or has otherwise materially modified such awards, the incremental fair value, calculated as of the repricing or modification date in accordance with Statement 123R, with respect to that repriced of modified award shall be reported.

Registrants are to provide certain narrative disclosures that put into context the quantitative disclosures in the Summary Compensation Table and the Grants of Plan-Based Awards Table. Specifically Item 402(e) mandates a "narrative description of any material factors necessary to an understanding of the information disclosed" in such Tables. As with the CD&A, the narrative disclosures required here will depend upon the particular facts and circumstances a registrant faces. That said, Item 402(e)(1) provides the following list of illustrative examples of the kinds of information that may be disclosed:

(i) The material terms of each named executive officer's employment agreement or arrangement, whether written or unwritten;
(ii) If at any time during the last fiscal year, any outstanding option or other equity-based award was repriced or otherwise materially modified (such as by extension of exercise periods, the change of vesting or forfeiture conditions, the change or elimination of applicable performance criteria, or the change of the bases upon which returns are determined), a description of each such repricing or other material modification;
(iii) The material terms of any award reported in response to paragraph (d) of this Item, including a general description of the formula or criteria to be applied in determining the amounts payable, and the vesting schedule. For example, state where applicable that dividends will be paid on stock, and if so, the applicable dividend

rate and whether that rate is preferential. Describe any performance-based conditions, and any other material conditions, that are applicable to the award. For purposes of the [Grants of Plan-Based Awards Table] and the narrative disclosure required by paragraph (e) of this Item, performance-based conditions include both performance conditions and market conditions, as those terms are defined in [Statement 123R]; and
(iv) An explanation of the amount of salary and bonus in proportion to total compensation.

Other tables are also required. Item 402(f) requires the Outstanding Equity Awards at Fiscal Year-End Table. This Table generally requires disclosures regarding unexercised options, stock that is unvested, and equity incentive plan awards for named executive officers outstanding at the end of the last completed fiscal year for the registrant. In short, the Table reports information that allows investors to understand better a named executive officer's potential earnings. Item 402(f)(2) specifies that the registrant must report the following:

- award-by-award, the number of securities underlying unexercised options that are exercisable and that are not reported in column (d) (column (b));
- award-by-award, the number of securities underlying unexercised options that are not exercisable and that are not reported in column (d) (column (c));
- award-by-award, the total number of shares underlying unexercised options awarded under an equity incentive plan that have not been earned (column (d));
- the exercise or base price for the options reported in columns (b) through (d) (column (e));
- the expiration date for the options reported in columns (b) through (d) (column (f));
- the total number of shares that are unvested and that are not reported in column (i) (column (g));
- the aggregate market value of shares that are unvested and that are not reported in column (j) (column (h));

P. 182   2010 SUPPLEMENT

- the total number of shares, units, or other rights awarded under an equity incentive plan that are unvested and unearned, and the number of shares underlying such unit or right (column (i)); and
- the aggregate market or payout value of shares, units, or other rights awarded under an equity incentive plan that are unvested and unearned (column (j)).

The Option Exercises and Stock Vested Table under Item 402(g) provides information regarding amounts realized by named executive officers. Item 402(g)(2) requires disclosure of the following during the registrant's last completed fiscal year for each named executive officer:

- the number of securities received upon exercise (column (b));
- the aggregate dollar value realized upon the exercise of options or the transfer of an award for value (column c));
- the number of shares that have vested (column (d)); and
- the aggregate dollar value realized upon the vesting of stock or the transfer of an award for value (column (e)).

Item 402(h) also requires certain narrative disclosure to accompany the Pension Benefits Table. Item 402(h)(3) requires registrants to:

> Provide a succinct narrative description of any material factors necessary to an understanding of each plan covered by the tabular disclosure required by this paragraph. While material factors will vary depending upon the facts, examples of such factors may include, in given cases, among other things:
> (i) The material terms and conditions of payments and benefits available under the plan, including the plan's normal retirement payment and benefit formula and eligibility standards, and the effect of the form of benefit elected on the amount of annual benefits. For this purpose, normal retirement means retirement at the normal retirement age as defined in the plan, or if not so defined, the earliest time at which a participant may retire under the plan without any benefit reduction due to age;

(ii) If any named executive officer is currently eligible for early retirement under any plan, identify that named executive officer and the plan, and describe the plan's early retirement payment and benefit formula and eligibility standards. For this purpose, early retirement means retirement at the early retirement age as defined in the plan, or otherwise available to the executive under the plan;
(iii) The specific elements of compensation (e.g., salary, bonus, etc.) included in applying the payment and benefit formula, identifying each such element;
(iv) With respect to named executive officers' participation in multiple plans, the different purposes for each plan; and
(v) Registrant policies with regard to such matters as granting extra years of credited service.

Under Item 402(i)(2), the Nonqualified Deferred Compensation Table must report the following for each defined contribution or other plan that provides for deferring compensation on a non-tax-qualified basis:

- the dollar amount of aggregate named executive officer contributions during the last fiscal year (column (b));
- the dollar amount of aggregate contributions by the registrant during the last fiscal year (column (c));
- the dollar amount of aggregate earnings, including interest, accrued during the last fiscal year (column (d));
- the aggregate dollar amount of all withdrawals by and distributions to the named executive officer during the last fiscal year (column (e)); and
- the dollar amount of the total balance of the named executive officer's account at the end of the last fiscal year (column (f)).

Item 402(i)(3) requires certain narrative disclosures. Namely, registrants must:

Provide a succinct narrative description of any material factors necessary to an understanding of each plan covered by tabular disclosure required by this paragraph. While material factors will vary depending upon the facts, examples of such factors may include, in given cases, among other things:

(i) The type(s) of compensation permitted to be deferred, and any limitations (by percentage of compensation or otherwise) on the extent to which deferral is permitted;

(ii) The measures for calculating interest or other plan earnings (including whether such measure(s) are selected by the executive or the registrant and the frequency and manner in which selections may be changed), quantifying interest rates and other earnings measures applicable during the registrant's last fiscal year; and

(iii) Material terms with respect to payouts, withdrawals and other distributions.

Item 402(j) mandates enhanced disclosures regarding potential payouts to a named executive officer at, following, or in connection with the named executive officer's termination (including resignation, severance, retirement, or constructive termination), a change in control of the registrant, or a change in the named executive officer's responsibilities for the registrant. The disclosures do not need to be in a tabular format, although the registrant must provide quantitative disclosures.

Item 402(k) turns from named executive officer compensation to director compensation. For each registrant director, Item 402(k)(2) requires tabular disclosures of the following regarding director compensation for the registrant's last completed fiscal year:

- the amount of all director fees earned or paid in cash (column (b));
- for stock awards, the dollar amount recognized for financial statement purposes for the fiscal year in accordance with Statement 123R (column (c));
- for option awards, with or without tandem stock appreciation rights, the dollar amount recognized for financial statement purposes for the fiscal year in accordance with Statement 123R (column (d));
- the dollar value of all earnings for services performed during the registrant's fiscal year under nonequity incentive plans and all earnings on any outstanding awards (column (e));

- the sum of the changes in the value of the director's accumulated benefit under defined benefit and actuarial pension plans and above-market or preferential earnings on compensation deferred on a non-tax-qualified basis (column (f));
- all other director compensation for the fiscal year that the registrant could not properly report in any other Director Compensation Table column (column (g)); and
- the dollar value of total compensation — that is, the sum of all amounts reported in columns (b) through (g) with respect to each director (column (h)).

The Director Compensation Table takes the following form:

Director Compensation

Name	Fees Earned or Paid in Cash ($)	Stock Awards ($)	Option Awards ($)	Non-Equity Inventive Plan Compensation ($)	Change in Pension Value and Nonqualified Deferred Compensation Earnings	All Other Compensation ($)	Total ($)
(a)	(b)	(c)	(d)	(e)	(f)	(g)	(h)
A							
B							
C							
D							
E							

Item 402(k)(3) requires certain narrative disclosures that supplement the Director Compensation Table.

Item 403 supplements Item 402. Items 403(a)-(b) continue to require disclosures regarding the security ownership of any beneficial owner (including any *group* as defined under 1934 Act §13(d)(3)) who the registrant knows is the beneficial owner of more than 5 percent of any class of the registrant's voting securities and the security ownership of management, directors, and director nominees. These disclosures "provide investors with information regarding concentrated holdings of voting securities and management's equity stake in the company." Also Item 403(c)

P. 182   2010 SUPPLEMENT

continues to require certain disclosures regarding "arrangements, known to the registrant, including any pledge by any person of securities of the registrant or any of its parents, the operation of which may at a subsequent date result in a change in control of the registrant." The 2006 SEC rulemaking amended Item 403(b) by requiring a footnote or other disclosure reporting the number of shares pledged by management, directors, and director nominees.

In conjunction with amending its executive (and director) compensation disclosure requirements, the Commission also revised its related transaction disclosures. The SEC explained:

> [I]n addition to disclosure regarding executive compensation, a materially complete picture of financial relationships with a company involves disclosure regarding related party transactions. …Today we are amending Item 404…to streamline and modernize this disclosure requirement, while making it more principles-based. Although the amendments significantly modify this disclosure requirement, its purpose — to elicit disclosure regarding transactions and relationships, including indebtedness, involving the company and related persons and the independence of directors and nominees for director and the interests of management — remains unchanged.

Item 404(a) provides the general disclosure requirement for related person transactions. Item 404(a) directs registrants to:

> Describe any transaction, since the beginning of the registrant's last fiscal year, or any currently proposed transaction, in which the registrant was or is to be a participant and the amount involved exceeds $120,000, and in which any related person had or will have a direct or indirect material interest. Disclose the following information regarding the transaction:
> (1) The name of the related person and the basis on which the person is a related person.
> (2) The related person's interest in the transaction with the registrant, including the related person's position(s) or relationship(s) with, or ownership in, a firm, corporation, or other entity that is a party to, or has an interest in, the transaction.

(3) The approximate dollar value of the amount involved in the transaction.

(4) The approximate dollar value of the amount of the related person's interest in the transaction, which shall be computed without regard to the amount of profit or loss.

(5) In the case of indebtedness, disclosure of the amount involved in the transaction shall include the largest aggregate amount of principal outstanding during the period for which disclosure is provided, the amount thereof outstanding as of the latest practicable date, the amount of principal paid during the periods for which disclosure is provided, the amount of interest paid during the period for which disclosure is provided, and the rate or amount of interest payable on the indebtedness.

(6) Any other information regarding the transaction or the related person in the context of the transaction that is material to investors in light of the circumstances of the particular transaction.

The Instructions to Item 404(a) define the key terms of *related person*, *transaction*, and *amount involved*.

Two limitations on whether a related person transaction must be disclosed should be underscored. First, the amount involved must exceed $120,000. Before the 2006 amendments to Item 404, the financial threshold was $60,000. Second, the transaction must be *material* to the related person.

Item 404(b) mandates certain disclosures regarding the review, approval, or ratification of transactions with related persons. Among other things, such disclosures shine light on important corporate governance matters at companies. A registrant must describe its policies and procedures for reviewing, approving, or ratifying any related person transaction that must be disclosed under Item 404(a). Item 404(b)(1) expressly acknowledges that the disclosures a registrant must make depends on the circumstances, but goes on to offer the following nonexclusive list of examples of the types of material information about a registrant's policies and procedures that may be reported:

(i) The types of transactions that are covered by such policies and procedures;
(ii) The standards to be applied pursuant to such policies and procedures;

P. 186

(iii) The persons or groups of persons on the board of directors or otherwise who are responsible for applying such policies and procedures; and

(iv) A statement of whether such policies and procedures are in writing and, if not, how such policies and procedures are evidenced.

Additionally, the Commission adopted a new Item 407 requiring certain corporate governance-related disclosures, particularly disclosures concerning the composition and structure of boards of directors and the activities of key board committees. Item 407 consolidates prior SEC disclosure requirements and updates reporting obligations concerning director independence.

In short, Item 407 requires a number of disclosures that can be grouped into the following general categories:

- Item 407(a) requires disclosures regarding director independence;
- Item 407(b) requires disclosures regarding board meetings and committees, including board member attendance at meetings;
- Item 407(c) requires disclosures regarding the board nominating committee;
- Item 407(d) requires disclosures regarding the board audit committee, including disclosures concerning the audit committee financial expert;
- Item 407(e) requires disclosures regarding the board compensation committee, including disclosures concerning the so-called Compensation Committee Report; and
- Item 407(f) requires disclosures regarding the process, if any, that has been established for the registrant's security holders to communicate with the board.

g. Plain English and Differential Disclosure

P. 186, end text. As part of its 2005 public offering reforms, the Commission extended risk factor disclosures to certain Exchange Act reports. The Commission explained in the adoption Release:

We are adopting the proposed requirements for updated risk factor disclosure in quarterly reports because we believe that issuers who are required to file quarterly reports already need to undertake a review of changes in their operations, financial results, financial condition, and other circumstances in order to prepare the other portions of the quarterly report, including the financial statements and MD&A. Therefore, we believe that issuers should be able, on a quarterly basis, to update risk factors to reflect material changes from previously disclosed risk factors.

Sec. Act Rel. 8591, 85 SEC Dock. 2871, 2964-2965 (2005).

The size and complexity of SEC filings remains a concern, including for sophisticated investors, who may also struggle comprehending long, complex disclosure documents. See generally Paredes, Blinded by the Light: Information Overload and Its Consequences for Securities Regulation, 81 Wash. U. L.Q. 417 (2003) (analyzing the volume of information disclosure); Schwarcz, Rethinking the Disclosure Paradigm in a World of Complexity, 2004 U. Ill. Rev. 1 (analyzing the complexity of information disclosure).

As part of the Commission's 2006 amendments to its executive compensation, related person transaction, and other corporate governance disclosure obligations, the Commission adopted Rules 13a-20 and 15d-20 under the Securities Exchange Act providing for disclosures under Items 402, 403, 404, and 407 of Regulation S-K in Exchange Act reports to be made in plain English.

A copy of the Plain English Handbook is available on the Commission Web site at http://sec.gov/pdf/plaine.pdf.

h. Item 10(h): Commission Policy on Security Ratings

P. 187, after 2d par. In Sec. Ex. Act Rel. 59,343, __ SEC Dock. __ (2009) (proposal), the Commission proposed to amend Rule 17g-2(d) to require NRSROs to disclose ratings actions histories for all credit ratings issued on or after June 26, 2007, at the request of the obligor being rated or the issuer, underwriter, or sponsor of the security being rated. Under the proposed amendment, an NRSRO could delay for up to 12 months disclosing a rating action.

The Commission also reproposed amendments to Rules 17g-5(a) and (b):

(1) NRSROs that are hired by arrangers to perform credit ratings for structured finance products would need to disclose to other NRSROs (and only other NRSROs) the deals for which they were in the process of determining such credit ratings; (2) the arrangers would need to provide the NRSROs they hire to rate structured finance products with a representation that they will provide information given to the hired NRSRO to other NRSROs (and only other NRSROs); and (3) NRSROs seeking to access information maintained by the NRSROs and the arrangers would need to furnish the Commission an annual certification that they are accessing the information solely to determine credit ratings and will determine a minimum number of credit ratings using the information.

More specifically, under the re-proposed amendments, NRSROs that are paid by arrangers to determine credit ratings for structured finance products would be required to maintain a password protected Internet Web site that lists each deal they have been hired to rate. They also would be required to obtain representations from the arranger hiring the NRSRO to determine the rating that the arranger will post all information provided to the NRSRO to determine the rating and, thereafter, to monitor the rating on a password protected Internet Web site. NRSROs not hired to determine and monitor the ratings would be able to access the NRSRO Internet Web sites to learn of new deals being rated and then access the arranger Internet Web sites to obtain the information being provided by the arranger to the hired NRSRO during the entire initial rating process and, thereafter, for the purpose of surveillance. However, the ability of NRSROs to access these NRSRO and arranger Internet Web sites would be limited to NRSROs that certify to the Commission on an annual basis, among other things, that they are accessing the information solely for the purpose of determining or monitoring credit ratings, that they will keep the information confidential and treat it as material non-public information, and that they will determine credit ratings for at least 10% of the deals for which they obtain information. They also would be

DISTRIBUTION OF SECURITIES   P. 187

required to disclose in the certification the number of deals for which they obtained information through accessing the Internet Web sites and the number of ratings they issued that information during the year covered by their most recent certification.

Id. at __ [n.74].

The Commission in addition proposed a certification requirement under Rule 17g-5(e):

> An NRSRO, in order to access the Internet Web sites maintained by other NRSROs and the arrangers, would need to annually execute and furnish to the Commission the following certification:
> The undersigned hereby certifies that it will access the Internet Web sites described in §240.17g-5(a)(3) solely for the purpose of determining or monitoring credit ratings. Further, the undersigned certifies that it will keep the information it accesses pursuant to §240.17g-5(a)(3) confidential and treat it as material nonpublic information subject to its written policies and procedures established, maintained, and enforced pursuant to section 15E(g)(1) of the Act (15 U.S.C. 78o-7(g)(1)) and §240.17g-4. Further, the undersigned certifies that it will determine and maintain credit ratings for at least 10% of the issued securities and money market instruments for which it accesses information pursuant to §240.17g-5(a)(3)(iii), if it accesses such information for 10 or more issued securities or money market instruments in the calendar year covered by the certification. Further, the undersigned certifies one of the following as applicable: (1) In the most recent calendar year during which it accessed information pursuant to §240.17g-5(a)(3), the undersigned accessed information for [Insert Number] issued securities and money market instruments through Internet Web sites described in §240.17g-5(a)(3) and determined and maintained credit ratings for [Insert Number] of the such securities and money market instruments; or (2) The undersigned previously has not accessed information pursuant to §240.17g-5(a)(3) 10 or more times in a calendar year.
> The NRSRO would need to furnish this certification to the Commission each calendar year that the NRSRO seeks access to the NRSRO and arranger Internet Web sites. In addition, the NRSRO would be required to certify that it will determine and maintain credit ratings for at least 10% of the issued securities and money

115

P. 187

market instruments if it accesses information pursuant to the proposed rule 10 or more times in a calendar year. The use of the term *issued securities and money market instruments* is intended to address potential deals that are posted on the Internet Web sites but that ultimately do not result in final ratings because the arranger decides not to issue the securities or money market instruments. An NRSRO that accessed such information would not need to count it among the final deals that would be used to determine whether it met the 10% threshold.

Id. at __ [n.86].

The Commission proposed amending Regulation FD Rule 100(b)(2)(iii) to permit the disclosure of material nonpublic information to NRSROs regardless of whether they make their ratings publicly available.

After the Bear Stearns crisis, New York State Attorney General Andrew Cuomo reached agreement with Standard & Poor's, Moody's Investors Service and Fitch, Inc. on measures to *dramatically* boost independence from issuer. NY AG, Major CRAs Agree on Reforms to Boost Independence, 40 Sec. Reg. & L. Rep. (BNA) 901 (2008). Cf. Commission Staff's Examination of Select Credit Agencies, 2008 Fed. Sec. L. Rep. (CCH) ¶88,244 (2008).

In the wake of the 2007-2008 credit crisis, the Commission proposed rule amendments to impose additional requirements on NRSROs to address the integrity of their credit rating procedures and methodologies "in light of the role they played in determining credit ratings for securities collateralized by or linked to subprime residential mortgages." Sec. Ex. Act Rel. 57,967, 93 SEC Dock. 1266 (2008) (proposal). The proposal Release stated in part:

> Beginning in the early 2000s, originators started to increasingly make residential mortgage loans based on lower underwriting standards *(subprime loans)*. For the first few years there did not appear to be any negative repercussions from this lending practice. However, beginning in mid-2006, home values leveled off and soon began to decline, which, in turn, led to a corresponding increase in delinquencies and, ultimately, defaults in subprime loans. This marked increase in subprime loan delinquencies and,

ultimately, in defaults has had substantial adverse effects on the markets for, and market values and liquidity of, residential mortgage-backed securities (*RMBS*) backed by subprime loans and on collateralized debt obligations (*CDOs*) linked to such loans (collectively *subprime RMBS and CDOs*).

Moreover, the impacts from the troubles experienced by subprime loans extended beyond subprime RMBS and CDOs to the broader credit markets and the economy as a whole. As a result, the parties that participated in various parts of the process of making subprime loans, packaging them into subprime RMBS and CDOs, and selling these debt instruments, including mortgage brokers, loan originators, securities sponsors and underwriters, and NRSROs have come under intense scrutiny....

The purpose of the Credit Rating Agency Reform Act of 2006 (the *Rating Agency Act*), enacted on September 29, 2006, is to "improve ratings quality for the protection of investors and in the public interest by fostering accountability, transparency, and competition in the credit rating industry." The operative provisions of the Rating Agency Act became applicable upon the Commission's adoption in June 2007 of a series of rules implementing a registration and oversight program for credit rating agencies that register as NRSROs....

The growth in the origination of subprime loans began in the early 2000s. For example, Moody's reports that subprime loans amounted to $421 billion of the $3.038 trillion in mortgages originated in 2002 (14%) and $640 billion of the $2.886 trillion in mortgages originated in 2006 (22%). This growth was facilitated by steadily rising home values and a low interest rate environment. In addition, increases in the breadth of the credit risk transfer markets as a result of new investors willing to purchase credit based structured finance products provided an opportunity for lenders to originate subprime loans and then move them off their balance sheets by packaging and selling them through the securitization process to investors as subprime RMBS and CDOs. The investors in subprime RMBS and CDOs included domestic and foreign mutual funds, pension funds, hedge funds, banks, insurance companies, special investment vehicles, and state government operated funds.

This *originate to distribute* business model created demand for residential mortgage loans, including subprime loans. For example, according to Moody's, of the approximately $2.5 trillion worth of mortgage loans originated in 2006, $1.9 trillion were securitized in RMBS and approximately 25%, or $520 billion worth, of these loans were categorized as subprime. The demands of the loan securitization markets encouraged lenders to lower underwriting standards to maintain a steady volume of loans and to use less traditional products such as adjustable rate, negative amortization, and closed-end second lien mortgages....

The creation of an RMBS begins by packaging a pool of mortgage loans, usually numbering in the thousands, and transferring them to a bankruptcy remote trust. The trust purchases the loan pool and becomes entitled to the interest and principal payments made by the borrowers. The trust finances the purchase of the loan pool through the issuance of RMBS. The monthly interest and principal payments from the loan pool are used to make monthly interest and principal payments to the investors in the RMBS.

The trust typically issues different classes of RMBS (known as *tranches*) offering a sliding scale of coupon rates based on the level of credit protection afforded to the security. Credit protection is designed to shield the tranche securities from loss of interest and principal arising from defaults of the loans backing the RMBS. The degree of credit protection afforded a tranche security is known as its *credit enhancement* and is provided through several means. The primary source of credit enhancement is subordination, which creates a hierarchy of loss absorption among the tranche securities. For example, if a trust issued securities in 10 different tranches of securities, the first (or senior) tranche would have nine subordinate tranches, the next highest tranche would have eight subordinate tranches and so on down the capital structure. Losses of interest and principal experienced by the trust from delinquencies and defaults among loans in the pool are allocated first to the lowest tranche until its principal amount is exhausted and then to the next lowest tranche and so on up the capital structure. Consequently, the senior tranche would not incur any loss until the principal amounts from all the lower tranches have been exhausted through the absorption of losses from the underlying loans.

A second form of credit enhancement is over-collateralization, which is the amount that the principal balance of the mortgage pool underlying the trust exceeds the principal balance of the tranche securities issued by the trust. This excess principal creates an additional *equity* tranche below the lowest tranche security to absorb losses. In the example above, the equity tranche would sit

DISTRIBUTION OF SECURITIES　　　　　P. 187

below the 10th tranche security and protect it from the first losses experienced as a result of defaulting loans.

A third form of credit enhancement is excess spread, which consists of the amount by which the interest derived from the underlying loans in the aggregate exceeds interest payments due to investors in the tranche securities in the aggregate plus the administrative expenses of the trust such as fees due the loan servicer as well as premiums due on derivatives contracts and bond insurance. In other words, the excess spread is the amount that the monthly interest income from the pool of loans exceeds the weighted average interest due to the RMBS bondholders. This excess spread can be used to build up loss reserves or pay off delinquent interest payments due to a tranche security.

A fourth form of credit enhancement sometimes employed is bond insurance. When used, bond insurance is typically purchased only for the senior RMBS tranche.

The creation of a typical CDO is similar to that of an RMBS. A bankruptcy remote trust is created to hold the CDO's assets and issue its securities. The underlying assets, however, are generally debt securities rather than mortgage loans....

In recent years, CDOs have been some of the largest purchasers of subprime RMBS and the drivers of demand for those securities. For example, according to Fitch, the average percentage of subprime RMBS in the collateral pools of CDOs it rated grew from 43.3% in 2003 to 71.3% in 2006. Generally, the CDOs holding subprime RMBS issued fell into one of two categories: high grade and mezzanine. High grade CDOs are generally defined as those that hold RMBS tranches with AAA, AA, or A credit ratings, whereas mezzanine CDOs are those that hold RMBS tranches rated predominantly BBB. Securities issued by mezzanine CDOs pay higher yields than those issued by high grade CDOs since the BBB-rated RMBS underlying the mezzanine CDOs pay higher yields than the AAA to A rated RMBS underlying high grade CDOs. In addition to CDOs holding subprime RMBS, a market for CDOs holding other CDOs that held subprime RMBS developed in recent years. These debt instruments are known as *CDOs-squared*.

As the market for mortgage related CDOs grew, CDO issuers began to use credit default swaps to replicate the performance of subprime RMSBs and CDOs. In this case, rather than purchasing subprime RMBS or CDOs, the CDO entered into credit default swaps referencing subprime RMBS or CDOs, or indexes on RMBS. These CDOs, in some cases, are composed entirely of credit default swaps (*synthetic CDOs*) or a combination of credit default swaps and cash RMBS (*hybrid CDOs*). The use of credit default swaps allowed the CDO securities to be issued more quickly, since the issuer did not have to wait to accumulate actual RMBS for the underlying collateral pool....

A key step in the process of creating and ultimately selling a subprime RMBS and CDO is the issuance of a credit rating for each of the tranches issued by the trust (with the exception of the most junior *equity* tranche). The credit rating for each rated tranche indicated the credit rating agency's view as to the creditworthiness of the debt instrument in terms of the likelihood that the issuer would default on its obligations to make interest and principal payments on the debt instrument. To varying degrees, many investors rely on credit ratings in making the decision to purchase subprime RMBS or CDOs, particularly with respect to the senior AAA rated tranches. Some investors use the credit ratings to assess the risk of the debt instruments. In part, this may be due to the large number of debt instruments in the market and their complexity. Other investors use credit ratings to satisfy client investment mandates regarding the types of securities they can invest in or to satisfy regulatory requirements based on certain levels of credit ratings, or a combination of these conditions. Moreover, investors typically only have looked to ratings issued by Fitch, Moody's, and S&P, which causes the arrangers of the subprime RMBS and CDOs to use these three NRSROs to obtain credit ratings for the tranche securities they brought to market....

By mid-2006, however, the steady rise in home prices that had fueled this growth in subprime lending came to an end as prices began to decline. Moreover, widespread areas of the country began to experience declines whereas, in the past, poor housing markets generally had been confined to distinct geographic areas. The downturn in the housing market has been accompanied by a marked increase in delinquencies and defaults of subprime loans.

The increases in delinquency and default rates have been concentrated in loans made in 2006 and 2007, which indicates that borrowers have been falling behind within months of the loans being made. For example, by the fourth quarter of 2006, the percentage of subprime loans underlying RMBS rated by Moody's that were in default within six months of the loans being made stood at 3.54 percent, nearly four times the average six month default rate of 0.90 percent between the first quarter of 2002 and the second quarter of 2005. Similarly, default rates for subprime loans within 12 months of the loans being made rose to 7.39 percent as compared to 2.00 percent for the period from the first quarter of 2002 through the second quarter of 2005. Figures released by S&P show similar deterioration in the performance of recent subprime loans. According to S&P, the serious delinquency rate for subprime loans underlying RMBS rated by S&P within twelve months of the initial rating was 4.97 percent of the current aggregate pool balance for subprime RMBS issued in 2005, 10.55 percent for subprime RMBS issued in 2006, and 15.19 percent for subprime RMBS issued in 2007.

Along with the deterioration in the performance of subprime loans, there has been an increase in the losses incurred after the loans are foreclosed. According to S&P, the actual realized losses on loans underlying 2007 subprime RMBS after 12 months of seasoning were 65 percent higher than the losses recorded for RMBS issued in 2006 at the same level of seasoning.

The rising delinquencies and defaults in subprime loans backing the RMBS rated by the NRSROs has exceeded the projections on which they based their initial ratings. Furthermore, the defaults and foreclosures on subprime loans have resulted in realizable losses to the lower RMBS tranches backed by the loans and, correspondingly, to the lower CDO tranches backed by those RMBS. As discussed above, the reduction in the amount of monthly principal and interest payments coming from the underlying pool of subprime loans or, in the case of a CDO, RMBS tranches or other CDO tranches is allocated to the tranches in ascending order. In addition to directly impairing the affected tranche, the losses — by reducing the principal amount of these tranches — decreased the level of subordination protecting the more senior tranches. In other words, losses suffered by the junior tranches of an RMBS or CDO directly reduced the level of credit enhancement — the primary factor considered by NRSROs in rating tranched securities — protecting the senior tranches of the instrument. These factors have caused the NRSROs to reevaluate, and in many cases downgrade, their ratings for these instruments.

- As of February 2008, Moody's had downgraded at least one tranche of 94.2 percent of the subprime RMBS deals it rated

P. 187

in 2006 (including 100 percent of 2006 RMBS deals backed by subprime second-lien mortgage loans) and 76.9 percent of all subprime RMBS deals it rated in 2007. Overall, 53.7 percent and 39.2 percent of 2006 and 2007 tranches, respectively, had been downgraded by that time. RMBS tranches backed by first lien loans issued in 2006 were downgraded an average of 6.0 notches from their original ratings, while RMBS tranches backed by second-lien loans issued that year were downgraded 9.7 notches on average. The respective figures for 2007 first- and second-lien backed tranches were 5.6 and 7.8 notches.

- As of March 2008, S&P had downgraded 44.3 percent of the subprime RMBS tranches it had rated between the first quarter of 2005 and the third quarter of 2007, including 87.2 percent of second-lien backed securities. Downgrades to subprime RMBS issued in 2005 averaged four to six notches, while the average for those issued in 2006 and 2007 was 6.0 to 11 notches.

- As of December 7, 2007, Fitch had issued downgrades to 1,229 of the 3,666 tranches of subprime RMBS issued in 2006 and the first quarter of 2007, representing a par value of $23.8 billion out of a total of $193 billion. Subsequently, on February 1, 2008, Fitch placed all subprime first-lien RMBS issued in 2006 and the first half of 2007, representing a total outstanding balance of approximately $139 billion, on Rating Watch Negative.

The extensive use of subprime RMBS in the collateral pools of CDOs has led to similar levels of downgrade rates for those securities as well. Moreover, the use of subprime RMBS as reference securities for synthetic CDOs magnified the effect of RMBS downgrades on CDO ratings. Surveillance of CDO credit ratings has been complicated by the fact that the methodologies used by the NRSROs to rate them relied heavily on the credit rating of the underlying RMBS or CDOs. Consequently, to adjust the CDO rating, the NRSROs first have needed to complete their reviews of the ratings for the underlying RMBS or adjust their methodologies to sufficiently account for the anticipated poor performance of the RMBS. Ultimately, the NRSROs have downgraded a substantial number of CDO ratings.

DISTRIBUTION OF SECURITIES   P. 187

- Over the course of 2007, Moody's issued 1,655 discrete downgrade actions (including multiple rating actions on the same tranche), which constituted roughly ten times the number of downgrade actions in 2006 and twice as many as in 2002, previously the most volatile year for CDOs. Further, the magnitude of the downgrades (number of notches) was striking. The average downgrade was roughly seven notches as compared to a previous average of three to four notches prior to 2007. In the words of a March 2008 report by Moody's, "[T]he scope and degree of CDO downgrades in 2007 was unprecedented."
- As of April 1, 2008, S&P had downgraded 3,068 tranches from 705 CDO transactions, totaling $321.9 billion in issuance, and placed 443 ratings from 119 transactions, with a value of $33.8 billion, on CreditWatch negative, "as a result of stress in the U.S. residential mortgage market and credit deterioration of U.S. RMBS."
- By mid-December, 2007, Fitch had issued downgrades to 158 of the 431 CDOs it had rated with exposure to RMBS. Among the 30 CDOs with exposure to the subprime RMBS which "suffered the greatest extent and magnitude of negative rating migration," all but $82.7 million of the $20.7 billion in balance was downgraded.

The scope and magnitude of these downgrades has caused a loss of confidence among investors in the reliability of RMBS and CDO credit ratings issued by the NRSROs. This lack of confidence in the accuracy of NRSRO ratings has been a factor in the broader dislocation in the credit markets. For example, the complexity of assessing the risk of structured finance products and the lack of commonly accepted methods for measuring the risk has caused investors to leave the market, including the market for AAA instruments, particularly investors that had relied primarily on NRSRO credit ratings in assessing whether to purchase these instruments. This has had a significant impact on the liquidity of the market for these instruments.

In the wake of these events, the NRSROs that rated subprime RMBS and CDOs have come under intense criticism and scrutiny. It has been suggested that changes may be needed to address the conflicts of interest inherent in the process of rating RMBS and CDOs. The NRSROs that have been the primary ratings providers for subprime RMBS and related CDOs each operate under an *issuer-pays* model in which they are paid by the arranger to rate a proposed RMBS or CDO. The arranger has an economic interest in obtaining the highest credit rating possible for each security issued by the trust and the NRSRO has an economic interest in having the arranger select it to rate the next RMBS or CDO brought by the arranger to market. Observers have questioned whether, given the incentives created by this arrangement, the NRSROs are able to issue unbiased ratings, particularly as the volume of deals brought by certain arrangers increased in the mid-2000s. The above concerns are compounded by the arrangers' ability to *ratings shop*. Ratings shopping is the process by which an arranger will bring its proposed RMBS and CDO transaction to multiple NRSROs and choose, on a deal-wide or tranche-by-tranche basis, which two (or in some cases one) to use based on the preliminary ratings of the NRSROs.

In addition, the interaction between the NRSRO and the arranger during the RMBS and CDO rating process has raised concerns that the NRSROs are rating products they designed (i.e., evaluating their own work). A corporate issuer is more constrained in how it can adjust in response to an NRSRO to improve its creditworthiness in order to obtain a higher rating. In the context of structured finance products, the arranger has much more flexibility to make adjustments to obtain a desired credit rating by, for example, changing the composition of the assets in the pool held by the trust or the subordination levels of the tranche securities issued by the trust. In fact, an arranger frequently will inform the NRSRO of the rating it wishes to obtain for each tranche and will choose an asset pool, trust structure, and credit enhancement levels based on its understanding of the NRSROs' quantitative and qualitative models. The credit analyst will use the expected loss and cash flow models to, in effect, check whether the proposed assets, trust structure and credit enhancement levels are sufficient to support the credit ratings desired by the arranger.

Id. at 1267-1275.

Subsequently the Commission issued three related Releases.

First, in Inv. Co. Act Rel. 28,327, 93 SEC Dock. 1903 (2008) (proposal), the Commission proposed amendments to Rules 2a-7, 3a-7, 5b-3, and 10f-3 under the Investment Company Act and

Rule 206(3)-3T under the Investment Adviser Act to omit references to NRSRO ratings and, in all but one of these Rules, substitute alternative provisions to achieve the same purpose as the ratings.

The second Commission Release would replace 1933 and 1934 Act rule and form requirements that rely on security ratings with alternative requirements. Sec. Act Rel. 8940, 93 SEC Dock. 163-7 (2008) (proposal). Specifically the Commission proposed to amend Regulation S-K Items 10, 1100, 1112, and 1114, 1933 Act Rules 134, 138, 139, 168, 415, 436, Forms S-3, S-4, F-1, F-3, F-4, and F-9, and Schedule 14A under the 1934 Act.

The third Commission Release, Sec. Ex. Act Rel. 58,070, 93 SEC Dock. 1766 (2008) (proposal), amended other 1934 Act Rules and Forms, specifically Rules 3a1-1, 10b-10, 15c3-1, 15c3-3, Rules 101 and 102 of Regulation M, Regulation ATS, Form ATS-R, Form PILOT, and Form X-17A-5 Part IIB.

In the aftermath of the stock market crash that began in September 2008, criticism of rating agencies intensified. See Ratings Firms Testify on Revenue Sources as Lawmakers Note SEC's Oversight Failure, 40 id. 1731; U.S. Chamber Calls for Regulation of Credit Rating Agencies, Other Areas, 40 Sec. Reg. & L. Rep. (BNA) 1872 (2008); SEC Proposes Tough New Regime to Regulate Credit Rating Agencies, 40 id. 1883; Morgensen, Debt Watchdogs, Caught Napping, N.Y. Times, Dec. 7, 2008; Lawmaker [Sen. Jack Reed] Introduces Bill to Give SEC Greater Authority to Oversee Rating Firms, 41 Sec. Reg. & L. Rep. (BNA) 961 (2009); Kanjorski Calls for More Regulation, SEC Office Devoted to Rating Agencies, 41 id. 961; At Most U.S. Needs Three Regulators for Financial Industry, Reform Report Says, 41 id. 1008 (Comm. on Capital Mkt Rep., The Global Financial Crisis: A Plan for Regulatory Reform).

In National Century Fin. Enter., Inc., Inv., 580 F. Supp. 2d 630 (S.D. Ohio 2008), the court denied a motion to dismiss a claim against a credit rating agency whose assignment of a rating was communicated to investors in a private placement memorandum. Id. at 637-639. The court declined to estop liability on First

Amendment grounds, id. at 639-640, but did dismiss the claim for failure to plead scienter consistent with the *Tellabs* standard. Id. at 640-644.

The court further held that Moody's could be sued under Ohio law for negligent misrepresentation. Id. at 646-649, 652-656.

In Moody's Corp. Sec. Litig., 599 F. Supp. 2d 493, 508 (S.D.N.Y. 2008), the court declined to grant Moody's summary dismissal when a plaintiff called into question Moody's claim that it "maintains independence in its relationships with Issuers and other interested entities." The court also denied Moody's contentions that plaintiffs' allegations were inactionable puffery and held that statements made about Moody's methodologies were actionable. Id. at 508-510.

3. Financial Statements — The SEC and Accounting (Herein of Regulation S-X)

b. The Commission and Accounting Standard Setting

P. 191, end 3d full par. In 2007 the SEC appointed the Advisory Committee on Improvements to Financial Reporting to study financial reporting in the United States in an effort to identify opportunities to simplify financial reporting and make disclosures more understandable. See, e.g., SEC Press Rel. 2007-123 (June 27, 2007) (announcing the creation of the Committee).

The FASB's membership was cut from seven to five in 2008, along with other changes. See Leone, FASB Parent: Five Is More than Seven, CFO.com, Feb. 26, 2008, available at http://cfo.com/article.cfm/10756502?f=search.

In the aftermath of the stock market crash of 2008, mark-to-market accounting became controversial with more than 60 lawmakers asking that the SEC immediately suspend mark-to-market rules. Lawmakers Urge SEC to Suspend *Mark to Market* Rules Immediately (Press Rel. Sept. 30, 2008); but see Joint Statement of the Center for Audit Quality, the Council of Institutional

Investors and the CFA Institute Opposing Suspension of Mark-to-Market Accounting (Press Rel. Oct. 1, 2008); Wutkowski, Bernanke: Abandoning Fair Value Would Harm Markets (Sept. 23, 2008); FASB Agrees to Issue Quick Guidance on Fair Valuing Assets in Inactive Markets, 40 Sec. Reg. & L. Rep. (BNA) 1584 (2008); SEC, FASB Issue Fair Value Clarifications, 40 id. 1585; FASB Issues Guidance on Fair Value of Financial Assets in Inactive Markets, 40 id. 1713; SEC Announces 10/29 Roundtable to Discuss Mark-to-Market Accounting, 40 id. 1719; SEC Takes Steps to Launch Study of Fair Value's Impact on Credit Crisis, 40 id. 1667.

In April 2009 the FASB approved two staff interpretations on fair value and impairment of debt securities that were likely to ease accounting of troubled assets held by financial institutions. FASB Clears Guidance on Fair Value, Securities Impairments; Effective 2nd Quarter, 41 Sec. Reg. & L. Rep. (BNA) 631 (2009). See 157-4 Determining Fair Value when the Volume and Level of Activity for the Asset or Liability Have Significantly Decreased and Identifying Transactions Are Not Orderly; FAS 107-1 and APB 28-1, Interim Disclosures about Fair Value of Financial Instruments; FAS 115-2 and FAS 124-2, Recognition and Presentation of Other-than-Temporary Impairments. See also Mainly Praise for FASB Fair Value Guidance; Continual Doubts, Criticism of 0711 Changes, 41 Sec. Reg. & L. Rep. (BNA) 679 (2009).

c. The Commission and Auditing

P. 194 n.109, end note. In Ernst & Young, Init. Dec. Rel. 249, 82 SEC Dock. 2472 (2004), quoting the text, Chief Administrative Law Judge Murray found serious violations of independence Rule 2-01(b); see also Codification of Financial Reporting Policies §602.02.g, and Rule of Practice 102(e)(1)(iv)(B)(2). Judge Murray wrote in part:

> The overwhelming evidence is that during the relevant period, EY's day-to-day operations were profit-driven and ignored considerations of auditor independence in business relationships with PeopleSoft. EY's partners shared in the pooled revenues of the

firm's three practice areas, and each EY partner was evaluated annually on his or her achievement toward five preset goals, one of which was sales....

EY had no procedures in place that could reasonably be expected to deter violations and assure compliance with the rules on auditor independence with respect to business dealings with audit clients. As an expert in audits, EY knew or should have known that a worldwide firm with thousands of employees could not rely on voluntary compliance. The fact that EY relied on self-interested people to voluntarily raise independence issues and to file forms where positive responses would cause a loss of income are strong indications that EY was negligent.

Id. at 2477–2508.

Four sanctions were entered: (1) A cease and desist order; (2) disgorgement of $1,686,500 received by Ernst & Young for auditing between 1994 and 1999 and prejudgment interest of $729,302; (3) a requirement that an independent consultant be hired by Ernst & Young acceptable to the Division of Enforcement; and (4) a six month suspension of Ernst & Young from accepting new audit clients. Ernst & Young chose not to appeal this decision.

See also Royal Dutch Petroleum and the "Shell" Transport & Trading Co., p.l.c., Sec. Ex. Act Rel. 50,233, 83 SEC Dock. 1881 (2004) (related consent settlement).

d. The Sarbanes–Oxley Act

P. 200 n.127, end note. In 2003 a court appointed examiner in the Enron bankruptcy proceeding amplified the Powers Report's conclusions with respect to Arthur Andersen. Appendix B (Role of Andersen), Final Report of Neal Batson, Court-Appointed examiner, Enron Corp., Ch. 11, Case No. 01-16034 (AJG) (Bankr. S.D.N.Y. 2003). The Report concluded in part:

> [T]he evidence reviewed by the Examiner is sufficient for a factfinder to conclude that Andersen breached its duty of care and was negligent as to certain portions of work it performed for Enron. In

public statements and testimony, Andersen has acknowledged that it made material errors. The Examiner has reviewed evidence that suggests additional acts of negligence beyond those previously acknowledged. This includes evidence indicating Andersen's failure to discharge its duties in communicating with Enron's Audit Committee, as well as evidence indicating a failure to perform appropriate audit procedures to learn of facts that were critical to Andersen's understanding of the SPE transactions.

Beyond instances of negligence, the Examiner has also determined that a factfinder could conclude that, in connection with certain transactions, Andersen aided and abetted Enron officers in breaches of fiduciary duty. The evidence suggests that, on multiple occasions, Andersen accountants had actual knowledge of the wrongful conduct giving rise to breaches of fiduciary duty by Enron officers with respect to those transactions, and gave substantial assistance to those officers by: (i) approving accounting that made Enron's financial statements materially misleading; and (ii) not communicating to the Audit Committee in accordance with applicable standards.

In July 2004, the Justice Department filed a criminal complaint against Kenneth L. Lay and the SEC filed a separate civil complaint against him. United States v. Caviey et al., Cr. No. H-04-25 (S-2) (superseding indictment) (S.D. Tex. 2004); SEC v. Lay, Civil Action No. H-04-0284 (Harmon)(Second Amended Complaint) (S.D. Tex. 2004).

The criminal complaint alleged a conspiracy involving Lay, Jeffrey K. Skilling, Richard Causey and others. The complaint alleged that Lay, Skilling and Causey spearheaded an effort to conceal the true state of Enron. With respect to Lay, the complaint largely, but not exclusively, focused on the August to November 2001 time period. Counts 38 to 41 of the complaint also alleged that Lay had engaged in bank fraud over a period from 1999 to 2001.

The SEC Complaint emphasized false and misleading forms 10-K (FY 1999, 2000), 10-Q (3d Quarter 1999, 1st-3rd Quarters 2000, 1st-3rd Quarters 2001), registration statements (2000–2001) and Form 8-K (Nov. 9, 2001) and $90 million of stock sales by Lay in 2001. Lay and Skilling were convicted of most

P. 200

counts in 2006. Jury Finds Lay, Skilling Guilty of Fraud, Conspiracy in Enron Collapse, 38 Sec. Reg. & L. Rep. (BNA) 935 (2006).

See also with $2B J.P. Morgan Settlement, Recovery in WorldCom Suit Could Top $6B, 37 id. 507 (2005).

After filing two interim reports (dated November 4, 2002 and June 9, 2003), the Bankruptcy Court Examiner Dick Thornburgh published a 450 page Third and Final Report in WorldCom, Inc., Case No. 02-13533 (AJG) (Jan. 26, 2004). The Report explained in part:

> The Examiner believes that WorldCom has causes of action against a number of persons and entities that bear responsibility for WorldCom's injuries. The potential claims identified by the Examiner are briefly summarized as follows:
>
> - Claims for malpractice and negligence against KPMG to recover any interest and/or penalties paid by the Company to any state taxing authorities based upon the flawed advice KPMG provided to WorldCom in connection with the state tax minimization program. The Company may also have claims to require KPMG to return the millions of dollars in fees paid to KPMG for its flawed advice.
> - Claims for breaches of the fiduciary duties of loyalty and good faith against Mr. Ebbers for awarding investment banking business to Salomon and SSB in return for lucrative financial favors, including extraordinary allocations of shares in initial public offerings ("IPO's") from 1996 until August 2000 and extraordinary loan assistance in 2000–2002. The Examiner also believes that the Company has claims against Salomon and SSB for aiding and abetting Mr. Ebbers' breaches of his fiduciary duties.
> - Claims for breaches of the fiduciary duties of loyalty and good faith against Mr. Ebbers for accepting more than $400 million in loans from WorldCom at non-commercial interest rates and for accepting loans without disclosing his inability to repay them. The Examiner also believes that WorldCom has claims against the remaining former Directors for their breaches of their duties of care and loyalty in connection with such loans. WorldCom also has a claim

against Mr. Ebbers for breach of his April 30, 2002 Severance Agreement.
- Claims for fraud and breaches of fiduciary duties of loyalty and good faith against former Chief Financial Officer ("CFO") Scott Sullivan and those other former WorldCom employees who have pled guilty to crimes related to the Company's accounting irregularities. In addition, claims related to the accounting irregularities may exist against other former WorldCom personnel, including Mr. Ebbers.
- Claims for accounting malpractice or negligence and breach of contract against Arthur Andersen and certain of its former personnel based upon their failure to satisfy professional standards in their audits of WorldCom's financial statements for audit years 1999 through 2001.
- Claims for breaches of the fiduciary duties of loyalty and good faith against Messrs. Ebbers and Sullivan for causing WorldCom to proceed with the Intermedia merger amendment in February 2001 without proper authorization by the Company's Board of Directors. The Examiner also believes that WorldCom has claims against all other former Directors who later voted in favor of the Intermedia transaction for breaches of their fiduciary duty of care, based upon their failure to investigate whether to proceed with the Intermedia merger amendment and their failure to confront Messrs. Ebbers and Sullivan for authorizing the Intermedia merger amendment without Board approval.

Id. at 4–5.

In March 2005, a jury convicted Bernard Ebbers of nine counts of criminal culpability for WorldCom's $11 billion accounting fraud. Jury Convicts WorldCom's Ebbers of Directing $11 Billion Fraud Scheme, 37 id. 534.

In August 2004, a Special Committee of the Board of Directors of Hollinger Int'l, Inc. filed a 521 page report detailing allegations that Hollinger's former CEO Conrad M. Black and its former COO F. David Radler took more than $400 million in cash over a seven year period or 95.2 percent of Hollinger's adjusted net income during 1997 to 2003. Id. at 1. The Committee at the time of the report had already commenced a civil action in Illinois against Black, Radler and others seeking $1.25 billion in damages, see id. at 3. Separately the Delaware Chancery Court ruled that Conrad Black repeatedly breached the duty of loyalty he owed to Hollinger. Hollinger Int'l, Inc. v. Black, 844 A.2d 1022, 1028–1029 (Del. Ch. 2004).

P. 208 n.141, end note. Five years after the enactment of the Sarbanes-Oxley Act, Treasury Secretary Henry Paulson appointed the Advisory Committee on the Auditing Profession, co-chaired by former SEC Chair Arthur Levitt and Donald Nicolaisen. In October 2008 the Committee published its Final Report, which explained in part:

> Now in its sixth year of operations, with a budget of $145 million, mostly derived from fees charged to public companies, and nearly 500 employees, as of May 2008 the PCAOB has registered over 1,853 auditing firms, 863 of which are domiciled outside the United States in eighty-five countries, not all of which issue public company audit reports....
>
> In 2007, the PCAOB inspected 236 registered auditing firms and issued 170 reports on inspections conducted from 2004 through 2007. Ten U.S. firms and one Canadian firm are subject to annual inspections as they have over 100 public company audit clients. Currently, approximately 875 registered firms are subject to triennial PCAOB inspection; 230 of these firms are firms based in foreign jurisdictions....

National Auditing Firms by Number of SEC Audit Clients

Firms	SEC Audit Clients
Ernst & Young LLP	1,652
Deloitte & Touche LLP	1,304
PricewaterhouseCoopers LLP	1,222
KPMG LLP	1,044
Grant Thornton LLP	362
BDO Seidman LLP	342
McGladrey & Pullen LLP	160
Crowe, Chizek and Company LLP	108

The four largest firms each generated U.S. revenues in 2007 of over $5.4 billion, with the largest firm generating $9.8 billion. The four largest firms each have over 1,715 partners, 15,200 nonprofessional staff, and 22,000 total staff, with the largest firm having 2,760 partners, 29,700 professional staff, and 41,000 total staff. The next four largest firms each generated U.S. revenues in 2007 of over $480 million, with the largest of the midsize firms generating $1.389 billion. These midsize firms each have over 200 partners, 1,500 nonprofessional staff, and 2,300 total staff, with the largest of the midsize firms having 700 partners, 5,900 nonprofessional staff, and 8,200 total staff....

The larger auditing firms are all members of global networks of affiliates. The creation of these networks, dating to the early twentieth century and increasing and growing into this century, was a response to a number of factors: the emergence of multi-national companies, and differing legal regulations, accounting and auditing standards, and cultural environment.

...According to the *International Accounting Bulletin*, in 2006, the top fifteen auditing networks by revenue generated over a total of $100.4 billion in revenue. Each of the largest four networks, whose member firms include one of the four largest U.S. auditing firms by revenue, took in global revenues in 2007 in excess of $19.8 billion, with the largest network taking in $25.2 billion. These four networks each have over 7,200 partners, 92,000 non-partner professionals, and 123,000 total staff, with the largest network having 8,600 partners, 108,900 non-partner professionals, and 147,000 total staff....

Global revenue has doubled or nearly doubled at the largest four networks over the past five years. Note that the definition of the services provided, particularly *advisory services*, differs from network to network and may change from year to year in a single network. In fiscal year 2007, PricewaterhouseCoopers International Limited reported global revenues of $25.1 billion, divided among assurance ($13.1 billion or 52%), advisory ($5.7 billion or 23%), and tax ($6.3 billion or 25%)....

Network governance also tends towards an integrated, *single-visioned* global network rather than a mere grouping of autonomous firms, although much of the specific governance and operating decisions of the member firms remain local. For example, a board, comprised of thirty-five members appointed by

P. 208

member firms and regions, governs and an Executive team, comprised of nineteen senior members, manages Deloitte Touche Tohmatsu, a Swiss verein. The Executive team establishes the vision and strategy of the Deloitte network. The board approves the network's strategy, major transactions, and other significant initiatives and monitors ethical conduct. The board has a number of supporting committees: Governance; Risk Management: Audit and Finance; Membership Affairs; and CEO Evaluation and Compensation....

Most auditing firms offer a range of services beyond auditing work, including tax and consulting and advisory services. Consulting services both to audit and non-audit clients became a greater and greater source of the largest U.S. firms' revenue from 1975 through the late 1990s. In 1975 at the largest eight auditing firms, consulting services revenues ranged from 5% to 16% of total revenues or 11% on average. In 1998, these services made up from 34% to 70% or an average of 45% of the largest five firms' revenues....

Since Sarbanes-Oxley, the amount of non-audit fees paid by the largest public companies to their auditors has continued to drop. In 2002, non-audit fees comprised 50% of total fees paid by the largest public companies to their independent auditor. This figure fell to 27% in 2004 and further to under 20% in 2006....

The Committee recommends that regulators, the auditing profession, and others, as applicable, effectuate the following:

Recommendation 1. Urge the Securities and Exchange Commission (*SEC*), and Congress as appropriate, to provide for the creation by the Public Company Accounting Oversight Board (*PCAOB*) of a national center to facilitate auditing firms' and other market participants' sharing of fraud prevention and detection experiences, practices, and data and innovation in fraud prevention and detection methodologies and technologies, and commission research and other fact-finding regarding fraud prevention and detection, and further, the development of best practices regarding fraud prevention and detection....

Recommendation 2. Encourage greater regulatory cooperation and oversight of the public company auditing profession to improve the quality of the audit process and enhance confidence in the auditing profession and financial reporting.

The SEC, the PCAOB, and individual state boards of accountancy regulate the auditing profession. The SEC and the PCAOB enforce the securities laws and regulations addressing public company audits. Individual state accountancy laws in fifty-five jurisdictions in the United States govern the licensing and regulation of both individuals and firms who practice as certified public accountants. State boards of accountancy enforce these laws and also administer the Uniform CPA Examination. NASBA serves as a forum for these boards to enhance their regulatory effectiveness and communication.

The Committee believes that enhancing regulatory cooperation and reducing duplicative oversight of the auditing profession by federal and state authorities and enhancing licensee practice mobility among the states are in the best interest of the public and the effective operation of the capital markets. In this regard, the Committee recommends the following:

(a) Institute the following mechanism to encourage the states to substantially adopt the mobility provisions of the Uniform Accountancy Act, Fifth Edition (*UAA*): If states have failed to adopt the mobility provisions of the UAA by December 31, 2010, Congress should pass a federal provision requiring those states to adopt these provisions....

(b) Require regular and formal roundtable meetings of regulators and other governmental enforcement bodies in a cooperative effort to improve regulatory effectiveness and reduce the incidence of duplicative and potentially inconsistent enforcement regimes....

(c) Urge the states to create greater financial and operational independence of their state boards of accountancy....

Recommendation 3. Urge the PCAOB and the SEC, in consultation with other federal and state regulators, auditing firms, investors, other financial statement users, and public companies, to analyze, explore, and enable, as appropriate, the possibility and feasibility of firms appointing independent members with full voting power to firm boards and/or advisory boards with meaningful governance responsibilities to improve governance and transparency of auditing firms....

Recommendation 4. Urge the SEC to amend Form 8-K disclosure requirements to characterize appropriately and report every public company auditor change and to require auditing firms to notify the PCAOB of any premature engagement partner changes on public company audit clients....

P. 208   2010 SUPPLEMENT

Recommendation 5: Urge the PCAOB to undertake a standard-setting initiative to consider improvements to the auditor's standard reporting model. Further, urge that the PCAOB and the SEC clarify in the auditor's report the auditor's role in detecting fraud under current auditing standards and further that the PCAOB periodically review and update these standards....

Recommendation 6. Urge the PCAOB to undertake a standard-setting initiative to consider mandating the engagement partner's signature on the auditor's report....

Recommendation 7. Urge the PCAOB to require that, beginning in 2010, larger auditing firms produce a public annual report incorporating (a) information required by the EU's Eighth Directive, Article 40 Transparency Report deemed appropriate by the PCAOB, and (b) such key indicators of audit quality and effectiveness as determined by the PCAOB in accordance with Recommendation 3 in Chapter VIII of this Report. Further, urge the PCAOB to require that, beginning in 2011, the larger auditing firms file with the PCAOB on a confidential basis audited financial statements....

The Committee has also considered the EU's Eighth Directive, Article 40 Transparency Report, which requires that public company auditors post on their websites annual reports including the following information: legal and network structure and ownership description; governance description; most recent quality assurance review; public company audit client list; independence practices and confirmation of independence compliance review; continuing education policy; financial information, including audit fees, tax advisory fees, consulting fees; and partner remuneration policies. The Article 40 Transparency Report also requires a description of the auditing firm's quality control system and a statement by firm management on its effectiveness. Auditing firms and investors have expressed support for requiring U.S. auditing firms to publish reports similar to the Article 40 Transparency Report....

Members of the Committee engaged in extensive discussion regarding the possible impact of the current U.S. liability system on audit effectiveness and the continued sustainability of the public company auditing profession....

Over a twelve-year period, since the enactment of the Private Securities Litigation Reform Act of 1995, the six largest auditing firms have paid out $5.66 billion to resolve 362 cases related to public company audits, private company audits, and all other non-audit services, with 65% of the total ($3.68 billion) related to public company audits. Information provided by the six largest auditing firms indicates that the weighted average of "litigation and practice-protection costs" was 6.6 percent of these firms' revenues and 15.1% of these firms' audit-related revenues for the most recent fiscal year.

While claims can be large, some Committee members noted that the payments made by auditing firms upon settlement or final judgment are on average only a small percentage of the alleged claims. For example, over the 1996-2007 time period median settlements in shareholder class actions (a subset of litigation against auditing firms) in which an auditing firm was named as a defendant were 4.8% of the total estimate damages. Other Committee members noted that average settlement figures are less relevant to considering the sustainability of the major auditing firms than the possibility of a large litigation loss in the context of a very large claim....

Members of the Committee who believe that the catastrophic litigation risk faced by the auditors of public companies is an unacceptably severe hazard to auditing firms, to investors, and to the stability of the U.S. capital markets, requiring actions to reduce the hazard, expressed one or more of the following views:

- The information presented to the Committee amply demonstrates that the litigation environment, in which auditing firms operate, poses a significant threat to firms' sustainability. Data provided by the accounting profession and testimony from academics, legal, and insurance experts make clear that the threat of the loss of a major auditing firm due to litigation is real. Such a loss would threaten the sustainability of the public company auditing profession as a whole, with serious adverse consequences to the stability of our capital markets and the confidence and protection of investors.
- The profession faces catastrophic litigation risk different from that of other businesses. Under the U.S. litigation system, auditors are potentially liable for the entire drop in market capitalization of their public company audit clients. The average public company common stock capitalization has increased from approximately $1.375 billion in 1997 to

P. 208

$3.842 billion in 2007. This exposure is unrelated to the scope of any audit error or misconduct, and dramatically dwarfs audit fees.
- Claims today in securities class actions can be significant multiples of the capital of even the largest auditing firms.
- The private litigation system makes it very difficult for auditing firms to bring large cases to trial. Firms are forced to settle cases even where they believe the claims lack merit and they have strong defenses, because the size of the claims means that if the firm does not prevail at trial, the resulting award could destroy the firm. Firm management cannot prudently risk the fate of a firm on the outcome of a trial.
- Auditing firms have thus far been able to settle large claims for affordable amounts. However, there is no assurance or control system that assures the ability to do so in the future. That will depend on the voluntary willingness of claimants to negotiate reasonable settlements. Any single claimant seeking $500 million or more has the capacity to make unreasonable demands or to force trial. The uncertainty of litigation means that either could prove fatal to the firm. Settlement with an immediate payout of any of the claims at a level in excess of $500 million could result in the demise of any of the largest firms. It is not acceptable public policy to leave the health of our economy or the competitiveness of our capital markets to the unfettered discretion of any of dozens of claimants and their counsel.
- The threat of disproportionate, catastrophic liability is not necessary to preserve or enhance audit quality. Auditors have many incentives to perform audits to the best of their ability, without the added threat of catastrophic liability. Professional standards, PCAOB inspections and SEC enforcement activities, internal firm evaluations, ordinary civil liability based on actual misconduct, and reputational concerns, are all more than sufficient to ensure professional behavior.
- The threat of disproportionate liability can harm audit quality by discouraging the best and brightest from entering and remaining in public company auditing, inhibiting the use of professional judgment, impeding the evolution of more useful audit reports, and causing overly cautious audits or *defensive* auditing.

- The combination of catastrophic litigation risk and difficulty obtaining insurance exacerbates concentration in the profession. Smaller firms are reluctant to pursue public company clients to increase their market share given the disproportionate threat of liability.
- The U.S. capital markets are increasingly a part of a global capital market system and therefore any deliberations regarding litigation reform require forward-looking consideration of the impact of global factors. Concerns with regard to liability reform are not unique to the United States, as is evidenced by recent consideration of liability within the EU. Because the larger auditing firms operate through global networks that include U.S. firms, it is important that the U.S. system not remain stagnant and put U.S. firms, and markets, at a disadvantage.

Id. at V:2 to VIII:12.

The Report was endorsed by all but one of its 20 members. Former SEC Chief Accountant Lynn Turner dissented, stating in part:

> The Committee members were given the choice of either voting for the Report in its entirely and all recommendations therein, or dissenting. They were not given the opportunity to vote for or against individual recommendations. As a result, I dissent to the issuance of the Report as the Committee has voted to recommend that beginning in 2011, audited financial statements of the larger auditing firms will be provided to the Public Company Accounting Oversight Board solely on a confidential basis. At a time when the U.S. capital markets are reeling from a lack of transparency, trust and confidence, such a recommendation will not build trust in the auditing profession, but rather raise further doubts.

Id. at IX.1.

In Free Enter. Fund v. PCAOB, Case No. 1:06CV00217 (D.D.C. 2006), a conservative public interest organization and a small public accounting firm challenged the constitutionality of the creation of the PCAOB by the Sarbanes–Oxley Act of 2002.

The District Court subsequently rejected these claims. Free Enter. Fund v. PCAOB, 2007 WL 891,675 (D.D.C. 2007), *aff'd*, 537 F.3d 667 (D.C. Cir. 2008), *cert. granted*, 129 S. Ct. 2378 (2009).

P. 211

Constitutional challenges to the PCAOB were ultimately rejected by the District Court, see Free Enter. Fund v. Pub. Co. Accounting Oversight Bd., Civil Action No. 06-0217 (JR), 2007 WL 891675 (D.D.C. Mar. 21, 2007), a two-to-one majority of the District of Columbia Court of Appeals agreed, Free Enter. Fund v. Pub. Co. Accounting Oversight Bd., 537 F.3d 667, 669 (D.C. Cir. 2008).

The majority of the Court of Appeals concluded:

> We hold, first, that the Act does not encroach upon the Appointment power because, in view of the Commission's comprehensive control of the Board, Board members are subject to direction and supervision of the Commission and thus are inferior officers not required to be appointed by the President. Second, we hold that the for-cause limitations on the Commission's power to remove Board members and the President's power to remove Commissioners do not strip the President of sufficient power to influence the Board and thus do not contravene separation of powers, as that principle embraces independent agencies like the Commission and their exercise of broad authority over their subordinates.

Judge Kavanaugh dissented, characterizing this case as "the most important separation-of-powers case regarding the President's appointment and removal powers to reach the courts in the last 20 years." Id. at 685.

The Supreme Court subsequently granted certiorari.

E. INTERNATIONAL OFFERINGS

2. OFFERINGS FROM A FOREIGN COUNTRY INTO THE UNITED STATES

a. The Foreign Integrated Disclosure System

P. 211 n.4, end note. In 2005, the Commission adopted amendments to Form 20-F by adding a new Instruction G to allow an eligible foreign private issuer to omit from SEC filings for its first year of reporting under the International Financial Reporting Standards the earliest of three years of financial statements. Sec. Act Rel. 8567, SEC Dock. 406 (2005) (adoption).

In July 2007 the Commission proposed terminating the requirement that foreign private issuers preparing their financial statements in accordance with International Financial Reporting Standards (*IFRS*) as issued by the International Accounting Standards Board (*IASB*) reconcile such financial statements with U.S. GAAP. See Sec. Act Rel. 8818, 90 SEC Dock. 2694 (2007) (proposal); see also SEC Publishes Proposal to End IFRS Reconciliation with U.S. GAAP, 39 Sec. Reg. & L. Rep. (BNA) 1086 (2007).

Later in 2007 the SEC adopted rule amendments terminating the requirement that foreign private issuers using IFRS as issued by the IASB reconcile their financial statements to U.S. GAAP. Sec. Act Rel. 8879, 92 SEC Dock. 717 (2007) (adoption).

The SEC continues to focus on *mutual recognition*. In short, mutual recognition generally refers to the concept whereby foreign financial intermediaries, such as foreign broker-dealers and exchanges, could provide services and otherwise gain greater access to U.S. investors without having to comply with the full panoply of U.S. regulatory requirements. In effect, mutual recognition contemplates that the SEC would *recognize*, to one degree or another, the regulatory regime of a foreign country as a substitute for the United States federal securities laws. Mutual recognition, if put into practice, would likely require some sort of comparability analysis whereby the SEC would assess a foreign country's regulatory regime to validate that it is sufficiently comparable to that of the United States. A key goal of such a comparability assessment is to ensure that investor protection and market integrity are not compromised through mutual recognition. The SEC also likely would require reciprocal recognition by the foreign country.

In 2008 the SEC also proposed certain amendments designed to improve the reporting of foreign issuers, styled as *foreign issuer reporting enhancements*. Sec. Act Rel. 8900, 92 SEC Dock. 2107 (2008) (proposal).

In 2008 the Commission adopted amendments to the cross-border rules, specifically amending Rules 162, 800, and 802

P. 211   2010 SUPPLEMENT

under the Securities Act of 1933, and Rule 101 of Regulation S-T, and Rules 13d-1, 13e-3, 13e-4, 14d-1, 14d-11, 14e-5, and 16a-1 under the Securities Exchange Act of 1934, as well as Forms S-4, F-4, F-X, CB, and Schedule 13G and TO. Sec. Act Rels 8917, 93 SEC Dock. 466 (2008) (proposal); 8957, 94 SEC Dock. 339 (2008) (adoption). The amendments in general were intended to facilitate more cross-border transactions by easing previous regulatory requirements.

First, the Rule amendments revised the eligibility test for cross-border exemptions. Without changing the threshold percentages of United States ownership for reliance on the cross-border exemptions, the Commission changed the manner in which these percentages were calculated:

> No aspect of the Proposing Release generated more commentary, and more criticism, than this focus on beneficial ownership and the manner in which it must be calculated under our rules....[W]e are adopting an alternate test for such circumstances based, in part, on a comparison of the average daily trading volume [*ADTV*] of the subject securities in the United States as compared to worldwide trading over a twelve-month period. The trading volume percentages we established for the ADTV element of the alternate test are the same as those for existing hostile presumption. The ADTV element of the alternative test is supplemented by other factors, such as the acquiror's actual knowledge of the U.S. ownership percentage of the subject securities, based on reports filed by the target company and others, as well as information from third parties known to the acquiror....
>
> ...Under existing rules, acquirors are required to calculate U.S. ownership as of a set date — the 30th day before the commencement of a tender offer or before the solicitation for a business combination other than a tender offer. The revisions adopted change the reference date to the public announcement of the business combination transaction. For these purposes, we consider *public announcement* to be any oral or written communication by the acquiror or any party acting on its behalf, which is reasonably designed to inform or has the effect of informing the public or security holders in general about the transaction. Under our revised rules, an acquiror seeking to rely on the cross-border exemptions may calculate U.S. ownership as of any date no more

than 60 days before and no more than 30 days after the public announcement of the cross-border transaction.

The revised rules will allow the calculation to be accomplished based on a range of dates before public announcement of a business combination transaction because we believe that this will allow the parties to a business combination to determine and inform the markets of the treatment of U.S. target security holders at an earlier stage in the planning process. In addition, this change allows the calculation of U.S. ownership to be made before the target security holder base is affected by the public announcement....

We expanded the rule to permit the calculation as of a date no more than 30 days after announcement to address commenters' concerns about the confidentiality of the look-through analysis....

This 90-day range should be used in most cases. We recognize, however, that the 90-day range may not be enough time in some foreign jurisdictions, depending on the procedures available for obtaining beneficial ownership information. Therefore, our revised rules specify that where the issuer or acquiror is unable to complete the look-through analysis as of this 90-day period, it may use a date within 120 days before public announcement....

Our revised rules do not affect the percentages of target securities that may be beneficially owned by U.S. holders in order for a transaction to qualify for the exemption. The maximum U.S. ownership percentages remain at no more than 10 percent for reliance on Tier I and Rules 801 and 802 and no more than 40 percent for Tier II. The look-through analysis by which these percentages are calculated has changed, however. Our revised rules will no longer require that individual holders of more than 10 percent of the subject securities be excluded from the calculation of U.S. ownership. We believe this change will significantly expand the number of cross-border business combinations eligible for the exemptions, while still providing appropriate investor protections....

Although we are not providing an exhaustive list of the situations that would justify the use of the alternate test, we do recognize specific factual scenarios when the alternate test could be used. For example, in some foreign jurisdictions, security holder lists are generated only at fixed intervals during the year and are not otherwise available. In those circumstances, where the published information is as of a date outside the range specified in our revised rules, the alternate test may be used unless the acquiror or issuer otherwise has access to more current information....

P. 211

We also believe that an acquiror generally will be unable to conduct the required look-through analysis in the manner prescribed by our revised rules when the subject securities are in bearer form. In addition, in certain foreign jurisdictions, nominees may be prohibited by law from disclosing information about the beneficial owners on whose behalf they hold. Where this prohibition extends to the country of residence of the beneficial owners of the subject securities, we believe the alternate test for determining eligibility should be available. Even the issuer itself may be unable to conduct the required look-through analysis and thus may turn to the alternate test under our revised rules. In addition, where a business combination transaction is non-negotiated (not conducted pursuant to an agreement between the target and the acquiror), the acquiror need not conduct the look-through analysis under our revised rules. This is consistent with the existing rules, premised on the concept that a third party will generally have decreased access to ownership information without the cooperation of the target....

Under the revised eligibility test, most acquirors will be required to conduct the look-through analysis, as modified by the rule changes we adopt today and discussed above. Only where an acquiror is unable to conduct the required analysis because of specific circumstances may it turn to the other means of determining eligibility specified in the alternate test....

The first prong of our alternate test is based on a comparison of ADTV of the subject securities in the United States, as compared to worldwide ADTV. As revised, this element of the alternate test is satisfied where ADTV for the subject securities in the United States over a twelve-month period ending no more than 60 days before the announcement of the transaction is not more than 10 percent (40 percent for Tier II) of ADTV on a worldwide basis....

The revised rules provide acquirors with a range of dates by which they may do the comparison of U.S. and worldwide average daily trading volume. The comparison must be made over a twelve-month period ending no more than 60 days before the public announcement of the transaction....

The revised rules also require that there be a *primary trading market* for the subject securities, as that term is defined in our rules, in order for the acquiror in a negotiated transaction to rely on the alternate test as a result of being unable to conduct the look-through analysis. *Primary trading market* means that at least 55 percent of the trading volume in the subject securities takes place in a single, or no more than two, foreign jurisdictions during a recent twelve-month period. In addition, if the trading of the subject securities occurs in two foreign markets, the trading in at least one of the two must be larger than the trading in the United States for that class....

The second prong of the alternate test is that the acquiror must consider information about U.S. ownership levels that appear in annual reports or other annual information filed by the issuer with the Commission or with the regulator in its home jurisdiction. It may be disqualified from relying on the cross-border exemption sought if those reports or other filings indicate levels of U.S. ownership that exceed applicable limits for that exemption....

The annual report filed with the Commission by foreign private issuers subject to Exchange Act reporting requires disclosure of the percentage of the class held by U.S. persons. Not all foreign private issuers file annual reports with the Commission, however. For those who do not file with the Commission, reports filed in the home jurisdiction may or may not require disclosure of comparable information about U.S. ownership. However, the acquiror may have reason to know U.S. beneficial ownership figures for non-reporting issuers, which also must be taken into account pursuant to the final element of the eligibility test....

We refer to the final element in the new alternate test as the *reason to know* element. The existing hostile presumption test for non-negotiated transactions contains a similar element. This prong of the alternate test provides that an applicable cross-border exemption is not available, even where all other elements of the alternate test are met, if the acquiror *knows or has reason to know* that U.S. beneficial ownership levels exceed the limits for the applicable exemption....

We are adopting as proposed the limiting language in this revised instruction that makes it clear that knowledge or reason to know acquired after public announcement will not disqualify the acquiror from relying on the cross-border exemptions....

The changes to the eligibility test we adopt today also will apply to the calculation of U.S. ownership for rights offerings. Issuers may now calculate U.S. ownership as of a date no more than 60 days before and 30 days after the record date for the rights offering. Thus, issuers will have greater flexibility on the timing of the calculation of U.S. ownership within a range of dates; however, the reference point for the calculation will continue to be the record

P. 211

date for rights offerings, rather than the date of public announcement for business combinations. This is appropriate because the record date for a rights offering is more closely tied to the specific security holder base that may participate in the transaction.

... It is our understanding that many foreign private issuers continue to exclude U.S. holders from rights offerings available to all other security holders. To the extent that the revisions we adopt today make the exemption for rights offerings more readily available and facilitate the inclusion of U.S. holders, these changes may be useful in promoting our investor protection goals.

Therefore, we are adopting similar changes to the method of calculating U.S. ownership for purposes of the exemption for rights offerings as we adopt today for business combination transactions. This will allow issuers more time to conduct the U.S. ownership calculation at an earlier stage in the transaction planning process. In addition to the changes to the look-through analysis mandated under our revised rules, the alternate test for calculating U.S. ownership also will be available for issuers unable to conduct the look-through analysis.

Id. at 346-354.

Second, the Commission revised Rule 13e-3(g)(6) to expand the scope of the Rule 13e-3 exemption to cover a broader range of cross-border transactions. The adoption Release explained:

Existing Rule 13e-3(g)(6) exempts the parties engaged in an affiliated cross-border business combination transaction from the application of Rule 13e-3 where that transaction is structured as an issuer or third-party tender offer under the Tier I cross-border exemptions, or as a securities offering made pursuant to Securities Act Rule 802. Transactions such as cash mergers, compulsory acquisitions for cash, and schemes of arrangement not consummated under these rules could be subject to Rule 13e-3 even where they otherwise would have been eligible for the cross-border exemption from that rule, if structured under Tier I or Securities Act Rule 802.

We believe that the form of the transaction should not govern whether Rule 13e-3 applies to a cross-border transaction which otherwise would be eligible for the Tier I exemption from that rule; therefore, we proposed eliminating the limits on the kinds of cross-border transactions that could be covered under the exemption in

DISTRIBUTION OF SECURITIES P. 211

Rule 13e-3(g)(6). We are adopting this change as proposed. In order to qualify for the expanded exemption from Rule 13e-3, a party must meet all of the conditions for reliance on Rule 802 or Tier I. These conditions such as the requirement that U.S. security holders be treated at least as favorably as foreign security holders, will continue to safeguard the interests of U.S. holders. In addition, a party relying on revised Rule 13-3(g)(6) for affiliated transactions not conducted pursuant to Securities Act Rule 802 or Tier I must submit a Form CB to the same extent as would be required in a transaction conducted pursuant to those provisions. Because the party relying on the expanded cross-border exemption from Rule 13e-3 would have had an obligation to file a Schedule 13E-3, absent the expanded exemption, a Form CB (and Form F-X where the filer is foreign) will be required....

Id. at 354.

Third, Tier II exemptions were extended to Regulation 14E only offers where the exemptions would have been available if those offers were subject to Rule 13e-4 or Regulation D. Id. at 355.

Fourth, the Commission clarified the application of Tier II relief for multiple concurrent foreign offers consistent with a United States offer:

Because we believe the use of a multiple offer structure may be helpful in addressing procedural and technical conflicts between tender offer rules and practice, as well as procedural requirements between different jurisdictions, we see no reason to prohibit the use of more than one offer outside the United States in connection with the Tier II exemptions....We believe the resulting increased flexibility to resolve regulatory conflicts will promote our goal of facilitating the inclusion of U.S. investors in cross-border tender offers subject to multiple regulatory regimes outside of the United States.

...[T]he amendments we adopt today with respect to the use of a multiple offer structure under Tier II are not intended to permit the use of separate proration pools where such a structure is used in the context of a partial cross-border tender offer. Under the current as well as the revised rules, bidders who conduct separate foreign and U.S. offers to minimize the difficulties of complying with two different regulatory regimes applicable to the offer must pro

P. 211   2010 SUPPLEMENT

rate tendered securities on an aggregate basis, where required under U.S. rules.

Id. at 356.

Fifth, the Commission adopted amendments to allow a bidder in a Tier II cross-border tender offer to make the United States offer available to all ADR holders, including non-United States holders. Ibid.

Sixth, the Commission also adopted amendments allowing a bidder to include United States security holders in a foreign offer conducted under Tier II, when "(i) the laws of the foreign target company's home jurisdiction expressly prohibit the exclusion of any target security holders, including U.S. persons; and (ii) the offer materials distributed to U.S. persons fully and completely describe the risks to U.S. holders of participating in the non-U.S. offer." Id. at 357.

Seventh, the Commission adopted as proposed rule amendments permitting a bidder in a Tier II cross-border tender offer to suspend withdrawal rights during the counting of tendered securities and until the securities are accepted for payment.

Eighth, to address a source of conflict with foreign regulators, the Commission eliminated the time limits on the length of a subsequent offering period in the tender offer rules generally. See esp. Rule 14a-11. Id. at 358-359.

The Commission adopted a related rule change to allow a bidder in a Tier II cross-border tender offer to *bundle* and pay for securities within 20 days of the date of tender, rather than on a *rolling* basis as soon as they are tendered. Id. at 360.

The Commission also adopted a rule amendment to permit bidders in Tier II cross-border tender offers to pay interest on securities tendered during a subsequent offering period when required under foreign law. Id. at 361.

Ninth, the Commission also adopted rule amendments to facilitate *mix and match* cross-border tender offers under which bidders offer a mix of cash and securities in exchange for each target security, while permitting tendering holders to request a different proportion of cash or securities. The adoption Release underlined: "These elections by tendering holders are satisfied to the extent that other tendering security holders make offsetting elections for the opposite proportion of cash and securities, subject to a maximum amount of cash or securities that the bidder is willing to issue." Id. at 362.

Tenth, the Commission reaffirmed an earlier interpretive position and recognized a bidder's ability in a Tier II cross-border tender offer to waive or reduce a minimum acceptance condition without providing withdrawal rights.

Eleventh, again because of conflicts with foreign jurisdiction, the Commission amended Rules 13e-4 and 14d-1(d) to permit early termination of an initial offering period before its scheduled expiration, which also will terminate withdrawal rights.

Twelfth, the Commission codified three class exemptive letters in new Rules 14e-5(b)(11) and (b)(12): "purchases and arrangements to purchase securities of a foreign private issuer (1) pursuant to the non-U.S. tender offer for a cross-border tender offer where there are separate U.S. and non-U.S. offers; (2) by offerors and their affiliates outside of a tender offer; and (3) by financial advisor's affiliates outside of a tender offer." Id. at 366.

Thirteenth, the Commission expanded the ability to *early commence* an exchange offer by allowing all exchange offers including those for domestic target companies not subject to Rule 13e-4 or Regulation 14D to commence upon the filing of a registration statement registering the offer under specified conditions. Id. at 368.

Fourteenth, the Commission required that all Form CBs be submitted electronically. Id. at 370.

Fifteenth, the Commission extended the list of institutional investors in Rule 13d-1(b)(1)(ii) to include nondomestic institutions.

The adoption Release concluded with interpretive guidance on (1) the ability of bidders in tender offer for United States target companies to exclude foreign target holders in tender offer subject to the all-holders rules in Rules13e-4(f) and 14d-10, id. at 374-375. The guidance here was a reiteration of positions the Commission had taken since 1986.

Subsequently the Commission published a proposed rule to establish a Roadmap for the potential use of financial statements

149

P. 211

prepared in accordance with International Financial Reporting Standards (*IFRS*) by United States issuers. Sec. Act Rel. 8982, 94 SEC Dock. 1703 (2008) (proposal). "This Roadmap sets forth several milestones that, if achieved, could lead to the required use of IFRS by U.S. issuers in 2014 if the Commission believes it to be in the public interest and for the protection of investors." Ibid.

The proposal Release emphasized:

> The increasing acceptance and use of IFRS in major capital markets throughout the world over the past several years, and its anticipated use in other countries in the near future, indicate that IFRS has the potential to become the set of accounting standards that best provide a common platform on which companies can report and investors can compare financial information. Approximately 113 countries around the world currently require or permit IFRS reporting for domestic, listed companies.
>
> Foreign jurisdictions have chosen to require or allow IFRS for many different reasons. For example, in the European Union (the *E.U.*), prior to its requirement relating to IFRS applicable to companies incorporated and publicly traded in its Member States, accounting standards in each of the E.U. Member States generally were established individually in each jurisdiction. Further, each Member State would typically permit the use in its capital markets of accounting standards set in other jurisdictions, in addition to its own domestic accounting standards. IFRS provided a comment set of accounting principles under which all domestic listings in the E.U. could report. In Canada, accounting standard setters concluded that, given the increasing globalization of capital markets and other recent developments, that it was timely for public Canadian companies to adopt globally accepted, high-quality accounting standards by converging Canadian GAAP with IFRS over a transitional period, after which a separate and distinct Canadian GAAP would cease to exist as a basis of financial reporting for public companies. In Australia, the decision to adopt IFRS was part of a strategy to ensure consistency and comparability of Australian financial reporting with financial reporting across global financial markets. More countries have adopted IFRS, including Israel, and others have plans to allow it, including Brazil. The market capitalization of exchange listed companies in the E.U., Australia and Israel totals $11 trillion (or approximately 26% of global market

capitalization), and the market capitalization from those countries plus Brazil and Canada totals $13.4 trillion (or approximately 31% of global market capitalization).

Id. at 1707-1708.

Notably, the Commission proposed amendments to its rule that would allow certain United States issuers that meet specified criteria to file annual statements in accordance with IFRS, rather than U.S. GAAP, for use in their annual and other reports, including those made under §13(a) or 15(d). See generally id. at 1720-1722.

In 2008, the Commission adopted amendments to Rule 405 of Regulation C, Form F-1, Form F-3, and Form F-4 under the Securities Act of 1933, Form 20-F under the Securities Exchange Act of 1934, and Exchange Act Rules 3b-4, 13a-10, 13e-3, 15d-2, and 15d-10. Sec. Act Rels. 8900, 92 SEC Dock. 2107 (2008) (proposal); 8959, 94 SEC Dock. 403 (2008) (adoption). The adoption Release explained:

> The amendments will: (1) Permit foreign issuers to test their qualification to use the forms and rules available to foreign private issuers on an annual basis, rather than on the continuous basis that is currently required; (2) Accelerate the filing deadline for annual reports filed on Form 20-F by foreign private issuers under the Exchange Act by shortening the filing deadline from six months to four months after the foreign private issuer's fiscal year-end, after a three-year transition period; (3) Eliminate an instruction to Item 17 of Form 20-F that permits certain foreign private issuers to omit segment data from their U.S. GAAP financial statements; (4) Amend Rule 13e-3 under the Exchange Act by reflecting the new termination of reporting and deregistration rules for foreign private issuers; (5) Require foreign private issuers that are required to provide a U.S. GAAP reconciliation to do so pursuant to Item 18 of Form 20-F; and (6) Amend Form 20-F to require foreign private issuers to disclose information about changes in the issuer's certifying accountant, the fees and charges paid by holders of American Depositary Receipts (*ADRs*), the payments made by the depositary to the foreign issuer whose securities underlie the ADRs, and, for

P. 211   2010 SUPPLEMENT

listed issuers, the differences in the foreign private issuer's corporate governance practices and those applicable to domestic companies under the relevant exchange's listing rules.

Id. at 404.

With respect to the fifth of these amendments, the adoption Release stated:

> We are adopting amendments to eliminate the option to provide financial statements according to Item 17 of Form 20-F in annual reports and registration statements filed on that form. Currently, a foreign private issuer that is only listing a class of securities on a national securities exchange, or only registering a class of securities under Exchange Act Section 12(g), without conducting a public offering of those securities may provide financial statements according to Item 17 of Form 20-F....Under Item 17, a foreign private issuer must prepare its financial statements and schedules in accordance with U.S. GAAP, or IFRS as issued by the IASB. If its financial statements and schedules are prepared in accordance with another basis of accounting, the issuer must include a reconciliation to U.S. GAAP. This reconciliation must include a narrative discussion of reconciling differences, a reconciliation of net income for each year and any interim periods presented, a reconciliation of major balance sheet captions for each year and any interim periods, and a reconciliation of cash flows for each year and any interim periods. In contrast, if a foreign private issuer that presents its financial statements on a basis other than U.S. GAAP, or IFRS as issued by the IASB, provides financial statements under Item 18 of Form 20-F, it must provide all the information required by U.S. GAAP and Regulation S-X, in addition to the reconciling information for the line items specified in Item 17.
>
> To eliminate this distinction between the disclosure provided to the primary and secondary markets, we proposed amendments to require Item 18 information for foreign private issuers that are only listing a class of securities on an exchange, or only registering a class of securities under Exchange Act Section 12(g), without conducting a public offering.

Id. at 415.

P. 213, end 2d full par. Form F-2 was eliminated in 2005 as part of the SEC's public offering reforms.

b. Exchange Act Disclosure Provisions

P. 215, new text after 2d full par. In 2007 the Commission adopted new rules permitting termination of a foreign private issuer's registration of a class of securities under §12(g) of the Exchange Act and the duty to file reports under the Exchange Act. See Sec. Ex. Act Rels. 53,020, 87 SEC Dock. 13 (2005) (proposal); 55,540, 90 SEC Dock. 860 (2007) (adoption); 55,005, 89 SEC Dock. 1968 (2006) (reproposal). The operative rule is Rule 12h-6.

In 2008 the Commission proposed additional amendments to Rule 12g3-2. See Sec. Ex. Act Rel. 57,350, 92 SEC Dock. 1906 (2008) (proposal). In short, the proposal would permit a foreign private issuer to take advantage of the exemption under Rule 12g3-2(b) without having to submit certain information to the SEC in paper format, although the issuer would have to satisfy certain electronic publication obligations and meet other requirements. In particular, the proposal would amend not only Rule 12g3-2 but also Rule 15c2-11 and Forms 15, 15F, 40-F, and 6-K under the Exchange Act, along with Form F-6 under the 1933 Act.

In 2008 the Commission adopted the amendments to the Rule 12g3-2(b) exemption, Sec. Ex. Act Rel. 58,465, 94 SEC Dock. 68 (2008) (adoption), to exempt a foreign private issuer from having to register under §12(g) based on the submission to the SEC of specified information published by the issuer outside the United States. The exemption would allow the issuer to have its equity securities traded in the United States over-the-counter market, but will require the issuer to maintain a listing of its equity securities in a primary trading market outside the United States and to publish electronically in English specified non-United States disclosure documents.

Specifically, the rule amendments will enable a foreign private issuer to satisfy amended Rule 12g3-2(b) without having to submit a written application to the Commission so long as the issuer:

P. 215　　　　　　　　　　2010 SUPPLEMENT

- currently maintains a listing of the subject class of securities on one or more exchanges in its primary trading market, which is defined to mean, as proposed, that:
  - at least 55 percent of the trading in the subject class of securities on a worldwide basis took place in, on or through the facilities of a securities market or markets in a single foreign jurisdiction or in no more than two foreign jurisdictions during the issuer's most recently completed fiscal year; and
  - if a foreign private issuer aggregates the trading of its subject class of securities in two foreign jurisdictions, the trading for the issuer's securities in at least one of the two foreign jurisdictions is greater than the trading in the United States for the same class of the issuer's securities;
- the issuer is not required to file or furnish reports under Exchange Act Section 13(a) or 15(d), as proposed; and
- unless claiming the exemption upon or following its recent Exchange Act deregistration, the issuer has published in English specified non-U.S. disclosure documents, from the first day of its most recently completed fiscal year, on its Internet Web site or through an electronic information delivery system generally available to the public in its primary trading market.

The adopted rule amendments will require an issuer to maintain the Rule 12g3-2(b) exemption by electronically publishing the specified non-U.S. disclosure documents for subsequent years. An issuer will lose the exemption if it:

- fails to publish electronically the required non-U.S. disclosure documents;
- no longer meets the foreign listing/primary trading market condition; or
- incurs Exchange Act reporting obligations.

Id. at 72-73.

Conforming amendments were made to Form F-6 and Rule 15c2-11.

3. OFFERINGS FROM THE UNITED STATES INTO A FOREIGN COUNTRY [REGULATION S]

P. 227 n.30, end note. In SEC v. Autocorp Equities, Inc., 292 F. Supp. 2d 1310, 1327–1328 (D. Utah 2003), the court concluded:

> Although securities issued under Regulation S are exempt from the registration requirement, once the SEC has established a prima facie case for a Section 5 violation, the burden of proof shifts back to the defendant to establish that he has satisfied the requirements of the exemption. Furthermore, Regulation S does not exempt securities that are issued as "part of a plan to evade the registration provisions of the Securities Act."

In recent years, the SEC has frequently successfully litigated fraud cases against defendants who inappropriately relied on Regulation S when there has been a prima facie violation of the Securities Acts and the securities involved are "part of a plan to evade the registration provisions of the Securities Act." See, e.g., Geiger v. SEC, 363 F.3d 481, 488 (D.C. Cir. 2004) (transaction amounted to a design to evade registration when there was "[resort] to fraud"); SEC v. Autocorp Equities, Inc., 292 F. Supp. 2d 1310, 1327–1328 (D. Utah 2003); Charles F. Kirby, Init. Dec. No. 177, 2000 SEC LEXIS 2681 ("Regulation S is not available with respect to any transaction or series of transactions that, although in technical compliance with these rules, is part of a plan or scheme to evade the registration provisions of the [Securities Act]"); SEC v. Corporation Relations Group, Inc., Case No. 6:99-cv-1222-Orl.-28KRS (M.D. Fla. 2003) ("The evidence shows no confusion or misapprehension on the part of the defendants, but rather a calculated albeit failed attempt to evade a regulation that they well understood"). "Regulation S shelters only bona fide overseas transactions." SEC v. Softpoint, 958 F. Supp. 846, 860 (S.D.N.Y. 1997), *aff'd*, 159 F.3d 1348 (2d Cir. 1998). Regulation S is not available for "bogus" transactions. SEC v. Schiffer, 1998 Fed. Sec. L. Rep. (CCH) ¶90,247 (S.D.N.Y. 1998).

CHAPTER 3

COVERAGE OF THE SECURITIES ACT OF 1933: DEFINITIONS AND EXEMPTIONS

A. DEFINITIONS

1. SECURITY [§2(a)(1)]

a. Introduction

P. 231 n.1, end note. In states where the definition of the term *security* has been taken from the federal securities laws, state courts have looked to federal law to define it. See, e.g., Poyser v. Flora, 780 N.E.2d 1191 (Ind. 2003); Caldwell v. Texas, 95 S.W.3d 563 (Tex. Ct. App. 2003); but see King v. Pope, 91 S.W.3d 314 (Tenn. 2003) (following risk capital rather than *Howey* test).

b. Debt Instruments

(i) *Notes*

P. 239 n.20, end note. See also Fin. Sec. Assurance, Inc. v. Stephens, Inc., 500 F.3d 1276 (11th Cir. 2007), in which the court explained:

P. 241

We do not disagree that FSA acquired the bonds through operation of the insurance policy. However, although FSA became the *owner* of the bonds, it did not acquire a *security* because, by the [Official Statement's] own terms, FSA acquired no right to receive interest or principal in the bonds after disbursement. Under the [Official Statement], once the bonds or a portion of the bonds were redeemed, the owners of such bonds or portions thereof ceased to be entitled to any benefit or security under the Bond Resolution.

Id. at 1286 (citation omitted).

(iii) *Bank Certificates of Deposit*

P. 241 n.27, end note. In SEC v. U.S. Reservation Bank & Trust, 2008 Fed. Sec. L. Rep. (CCH) ¶94,804 (9th Cir. 2008), *cert. denied*, 547 U.S. 1193, the court held that an investment that consisted of a certificate of deposit and a profit sharing plan was a security.

c. Oil, Gas, or Other Mineral Rights

P. 243 n.35, end note. In SEC v. Shoreline Dev. Co., 2005 Fed. Sec. L. Rep. (CCH) ¶93,356 (9th Cir. 2005), *cert. denied*, 547 U.S. 1193, the court found that the defendants created fractional interests when they sold fractions of their interests in wells to the public.

d. Investment Contracts

P. 248 new n.38.1, 1st full par., end 1st sentence. In SEC v. Edwards, 540 U.S. 389, 394–395 (2004), the U.S. Supreme Court quoted this language from *Howey*, then added, quoting the text:

> Those laws were the precursors to federal securities regulation and were so named, it seems, because they were "aimed at promoters who 'would sell building lots in the blue sky in fee simple.'" 1 L. Loss & J. Seligman, Securities Regulation 36, 31–43 (3d ed. 1998)

(quoting Mulvey, Blue Sky Law, 36 Can. L. Times 37 (1916)). The state courts had defined an investment contract as "a contract or scheme for 'the placing of capital or laying out of money in a way intended to secure income or profit from its employment,'" and had "uniformly applied" that definition to "a variety of situations where individuals were led to invest money in a common enterprise with the expectation that they would earn a profit solely through the efforts of the promoter or [a third party]."

(i)   *Elements of the* Howey *Investment Contract Test*

P. 251 n.47, end note.   In SEC v. Edwards, 540 U.S. 389 (2004), the United States Supreme Court reversed a lower court holding that return on investment was not "derived solely from the efforts of others" when the purchaser had a contractual entitlement to the return. The Court's analysis of this issue described vertical relationships where the investing public was "attracted by representations of investment income" and the defendants were "unscrupulous marketers," id. at 394, and where the "investors have bargained for a return on their investment." Id. at 397.

In United States v. Leonard, 529 F.3d 83, 88-91 (2d Cir. 2008), the court cited the treatise and concluded that an interest in the LLC in the case was a security because of the expectation that the investors would perform a passive role "notwithstanding the organizational documents drafted to suggest active participation by members." Id. at 91.

P. 256, new text after carryover par.   In SEC v. Edwards, 540 U.S. 389 (2004), quoting the text, the Supreme Court held that the term *profits* would include a scheme that offered a contractual entitlement to a fixed, rather than a variable, return, writing in part:

> Thus, when we held that "profits" must "come solely from the efforts of others," we were speaking of the profits that investors seek on their investment, not the profits of the scheme in which they invest. We used "profits" in the sense of income or return, to

include, for example, dividends, other periodic payments, or the increased value of the investment.

There is no reason to distinguish between promises of fixed returns and promises of variable returns for purposes of the test, so understood. In both cases, the investing public is attracted by representations of investment income, as purchasers were in this case by ETS' invitation to "'watch the profits add up.'" [Citation deleted.] Moreover, investments pitched as low-risk (such as those offering a "guaranteed" fixed return) are particularly attractive to individuals more vulnerable to investment fraud, including older and less sophisticated investors. See S. Rep. No. 102–261, Vol. 2, App., p. 326 (1992) (Staff Summary of Federal Trade Commission Activities Affecting Older Consumers). Under the reading respondent advances, unscrupulous marketers of investments could evade the securities laws by picking a rate of return to promise. We will not read into the securities laws a limitation not compelled by the language that would so undermine the laws' purposes.

Respondent protests that including investment schemes promising a fixed return among investment contracts conflicts with our precedent. We disagree. No distinction between fixed and variable returns was drawn in the blue sky law cases that the *Howey* Court used, in formulating the test, as its evidence of Congress' understanding of the term. *Howey*, [328 U.S. 293 (1946), at 298, and n.4]. Indeed, two of those cases involved an investment contract in which a fixed return was promised. [Citing cases.]

None of our post-*Howey* decisions is to the contrary. In *United Housing Foundation, Inc. v. Forman*, 421 U.S. 837 (1975), we considered whether "shares" in a nonprofit housing cooperative were investment contracts under the securities laws. We identified the "touchstone" of an investment contract as "the presence of an investment in a common venture premised on a reasonable expectation of profits to be derived from the entrepreneurial or managerial efforts of others," and then laid out two examples of investor interests that we had previously found to be "profits." *Id.* at 852. Those were "capital appreciation resulting from the development of the initial investment" and "participation in earnings resulting from the use of investors' funds." *Ibid.* We contrasted those examples, in which "the investor is 'attracted solely by the prospects of a return'" on the investment, with housing cooperative shares, regarding which the purchaser "is motivated by a desire to use or consume the item purchased." *Id.*, at 852–853 (quoting

Howey, supra, at 300). Thus, *Forman* supports the commonsense understanding of "profits" in the *Howey* test as simply "financial returns on...investments." 421 U.S., at 853.

Concededly, *Forman*'s illustrative description of prior decisions on "profits" appears to have been mistaken for an exclusive list in a case considering the scope of a different term in the definition of a security, "note." See *Reves*, 494 U.S., at 68, n.4. But that was a misreading of *Forman*, and we will not bind ourselves unnecessarily to passing dictum that would frustrate Congress' intent to regulate all of the "countless and variable schemes devised by those who seek the use of the money of others on the promise of profits." *Howey*, 328 U.S., at 299....

The Eleventh Circuit's perfunctory alternative holding, that respondent's scheme falls outside the definition because purchasers had a contractual entitlement to a return, is incorrect and inconsistent with our precedent. We are considering investment *contracts.* The fact that investors have bargained for a return on their investment does not mean that the return is not also expected to come solely from the efforts of others. Any other conclusion would conflict with our holding that an investment contract was offered in *Howey* itself. 328 U.S., at 295–296 (service contract entitled investors to allocation of net profits).

We hold that an investment scheme promising a fixed rate of return can be an "investment contract" and thus a "security" subject to the federal securities laws.

Id. at 394–397.

(iii) *Partnerships*

P. 259 n. 73, end note. In Robinson v. Glynn, 349 F.3d 166 (4th Cir. 2003) an interest in a two person limited liability company was held not to be an investment contract when the plaintiff "was not a passive investor relying on the efforts of others, but a knowledgeable executive actively protecting his interest and position in the company." Id. at 172. The court also rejected the notion that the LLC membership interest was *stock* under Landreth Timber Co. v. Landreth, 471 U.S. 681 (1985), because: (1) the LLC membership interests did not share in profits in proportion to their interests; (2) the interests were not freely negotiable; (3) the interest could be pledged, but the pledgee would not acquire control rights; and (4) the interests were not called stock. Id. at 172–174.

e. Stock

(i) *Investment Contract Analysis*

P. 267 n.100, end note. In applying *Landreth* in a related context concerning commodities, one court, CFTC v. Zelener, 373 F.3d 861 (7th Cir. 2004), described the *Landreth* decision as follows:

> A business can be transferred two ways: the corporation may sell all of its assets, then liquidate and distribute to investors the cash received from the buyer; or the investors may sell their securities directly to the buyers. With sufficient care in drafting, these two forms may be made economically equivalent. This equivalence led to arguments that the sale of stock to transfer a whole business should not be regulated by the federal securities laws. Because the sale of assets would be governed by state contract law, it would upset expectations to handle the functionally equivalent transaction under federal law just because stock played a role. Many courts adopted this sale-of-business doctrine, but the Supreme Court rejected it, ruling that form must be respected....One reason is that the securities laws are *about* form....Another powerful reason was the need for certainty. The sale-of-business doctrine led to all sorts of questions. What if there were a significant minority shareholder? What if the new buyer did not plan to run the business as an entrepreneur? The list of questions turned out to be long and the uncertainty considerable....By taking form seriously the Supreme Court was able to curtail, if not eliminate, that uncertainty and promote sensible business planning.

Id. at 866.

Cf. SEC v. Merchant Capital, LLC, 483 F.3d 747, 754–766 (11th Cir. 2007) (registered limited liability partnership interests were investment contracts, applying Williamson v. Tucker, 645 F.2d 404 (5th Cir. 1981)).

f. Insurance Products

P. 272 n.110, end 2d par.   See also SEC v. Mutual Benefits Corp., 323 F. Supp. 2d 1337 (S.D. Fla. 2004), *aff'd*, 408 F.3d 737 (11th Cir. 2005) (viatical settlements were securities).

Cf. Ring v. AXA Fin., Inc., 483 F.3d 95 (2d Cir. 2007) (*children's term rider* that is "attached to a variable life insurance policy falling within the definition of a *covered security*" is not a *covered security* under SLUSA; explaining that "in determining whether a particular product is a security requiring registration as well as in determining whether a plaintiff may maintain a Rule 10(b) suit, we must disaggregate separate promises of a product or transaction").

P. 284, end 1st par.   In 2009 the Commission adopted Rule 151A under the 1933 Act and Rule 12h-7 under the 1934 Act to define the terms *annuity contract* and *optional annuity contract* under the 1933 Act and to exempt insurance companies from filing reports under the 1934 Act with respect to indexed annuities and other securities registered under the 1933 Act provided that they are regulated by State insurance law and not publicly traded. Sec. Act Rels. 8933, 93 SEC Dock. 1405 (2008) (proposal); 8996, ___ SEC Dock. ___ (2009) (adoption).

Under Rule 151A(a), the Commission will exclude from the §3(a)(8) exemption a contract subject to state insurance regulation if:

(1) The contract specifies that amounts payable by the issuer under the contract are calculated at or after the end of one or more specified crediting periods, in whole or in part, by reference to the performance during the crediting period or periods of a security, including a group or index of securities; and

(2) Amounts payable by the issuer under the contract are more likely than not to exceed the amounts guaranteed under the contract.

Rule 151A(b) then specifies to make the determination under Rule 151A(a)(2):

(1) Amounts payable by the issuer under the contract and amounts guaranteed under the contract shall be determined by taking into account all charges under the contract, including, without limitation, charges that are imposed at the time that payments are made by the issuer; and

(2) A determination by the issuer at or prior to issuance of the contract shall be conclusive, provided that:

(i) Both the methodology and the economic, actuarial, and other assumptions used in the determination are reasonable;

(ii) The computations made by the issuer in support of the determination are materially accurate; and

(iii) The determination is made not more than six months prior to the date on which the form of contract is first offered.

Rule 151A does not apply to any contract whose value varies according to the investment experience of a separate account. Rule 151A(c).

Rule 151A(a)(2) was aptly characterized by the Commission as a "principles-based approach." The Commission recognized "that a number of commenters expressed concern that the principles-based approach provides insufficient guidance regarding implementation and the methodologies and assumptions that are appropriate and could result in inconsistent determination by different insurance companies and present enforcement and litigation risk." Id. at __ [nn.108].

Subsequently SEC Chair Schapiro informed Congress that the Commission was reviewing the viatical market, now valued at $12 billion, to determine whether there is a need for additional regulation. Schapiro: SEC Will Review Viaticals Market to Determine if Closer Regulation Required, 41 Sec. Reg. & L. Rep. (BNA) 803 (2009).

j. Equipment Trust Certificates

P. 297, end carryover par. In 2004, the Commission defined *issuer* in §2(a)(4), in relation to asset backed securities in its Regulation AB Release. See Sec. Act Rel. 8518, 84 SEC Dock. 1624, 1654 (2004) (adoption). Rule 191(a)–(b) provide in relevant part:

(a) The depositor for the asset-backed securities acting solely in its capacity as depositor to the issuing entity is the *issuer* for purposes of the asset-backed securities of that issuing entity.

(b) The person acting in the capacity as the depositor specified in paragraph (a) of this section is a different issuer from that same person acting as a depositor for another issuing entity or for purposes of that person's own securities.

An identical definition was also adopted in Rule 3b-19 of the 1934 Act.

k. Guarantees

P. 297 n.182, end note. In Financial Security Assurance, Inc. v. Stephens, Inc., 450 F.3d 1257, 1263 (11th Cir. 2006), the court refused to grant a guarantor of bonds standing under Rule 10b-5 because §3(a)(10) of the 1934 Act does not include a guarantee in the definition of *security*. The guarantor had claimed that by guaranteeing bonds it had sold a security.

l. Warrants, Options, and Futures

P. 314, after 4th par. In November 2008 the President's Working Group announced a new policy to create central counterparties for OTC derivatives by year end. The same day the SEC, CFTC, and Federal Reserve System released a MOU intended to enhance cooperation and information sharing associated with this central counterparty. PWG, Regulators Work to Encourage Launch of CDS Clearinghouse by End of December, 40 Sec. Reg. & L. Rep. (BNA) 1869 (2008). See also Sec. Act Rel. 8999, __ SEC Dock. __ (2009) (temporary exemption for eligible credit default swaps to facilitate operation of central counterparties to clear and settle credit default swaps).

In the aftermath of the failure of Bear Stearns, Lehman Brothers, Fannie Mae, and Freddie Mac, SEC Chair Christopher Cox proposed regulating the $58 trillion market for credit default

P. 314   2010 SUPPLEMENT

swaps to address a "regulatory hole" "completely lacking in transparency" that "is ripe for fraud and manipulation." SEC Chairman Urges Lawmakers to Confer Authority to Regulate Credit Default Swaps, 40 Sec. Reg. & L. Rep. (BNA) 1531 (2008). See also Porteous & Martignon, Credit Default Swaps: Regulatory Storm Clouds Brewing, 40 id. 2070.

Subsequently the New York State Insurance Department on September 22, 2008 issued guidance that the structuring of credit default swaps may constitute "the doing of an insurance business" and issued best practices it expected to be implemented. N.Y. Announces New Monoline Standards Aimed at Improving Soundness of Insurer, 40 id. 1541. See also Cox Notes SEC Action in Swap Market, But Repeats Call for Congressional Action [on Credit Default Swaps], 40 id. 1633; Lawmakers Told Credit Default Swaps' Lack of Transparency Led to AIG's Fall, 40 id. 1640; Market Reintroduces Fourth Version of Bill to Improve Derivatives Regulation, 40 id. 1651.

On May 13, 2009, the Obama Administration proposed an outline of a comprehensive regulatory framework for OTC derivatives. U.S. Dep't of Treasury Press Rel. tg-129 (May 13, 2009). The Approach, in bullet point fashion, stated:

Objectives of Regulatory Reform of OTC Derivatives Markets

- Preventing Activities Within the OTC Markets From Posing Risk to the Financial System — Regulators must have the following authority to ensure that participants do not engage in practices that put the financial system at risk:
- The Commodity Exchange Act (*CEA*) and the securities laws should be amended to require clearing of all standardized OTC derivatives through regulated central counterparties (*CCP*):
    - CCPs must impose robust margin requirements and other necessary risk controls and ensure that customized OTC derivatives are not used solely as a means to avoid using a CCP.
    - For example, if an OTC derivative is accepted for clearing by one or more fully regulated CCPs, it should

create a presumption that it is a standardized contract and thus required to be cleared.

- All OTC derivatives dealers and all other firms who create large exposures to counterparties should be subject to a robust regime of prudential supervision and regulation, which will include:
  - Conservative capital requirements
  - Business conduct standards
  - Reporting requirements
  - Initial margin requirements with respect to bilateral credit exposures on both standardized and customized contracts

- Promoting Efficiency and Transparency Within the OTC Markets — To ensure regulators would have comprehensive and timely information about the positions of each and every participant in all OTC derivatives markets, this new framework includes:

- Amending the CEA and securities laws to authorize the CFTC and the SEC to impose:
  - Recordkeeping and reporting requirements (including audit trails).
  - Requirements for all trades not cleared by CCPs to be reported to a regulated trade repository.
  - CCPs and trade repositories must make aggregate data on open positions and trading volumes available to the public.
  - CCPs and trade repositories must make data on individual counterparty's trades and positions available to federal regulators.
  - The movement of standardized trades onto regulated exchanges and regulated transparent electronic trade execution systems.
  - The development of a system for the timely reporting of trades and prompt dissemination of prices and other trade information.
  - The encouragement of regulated institutions to make greater use of regulated exchange-traded derivatives.

- Preventing Market Manipulation, Fraud, and Other Market Abuses — The Commodity Exchange Act (*CEA*) and securities laws should be amended to ensure that the CFTC and the SEC have:
    - Clear and unimpeded authority for market regulators to police fraud, market manipulation, and other market abuses.
    - Authority to set position limits on OTC derivatives that perform or affect a significant price discovery function with respect to futures markets.
    - A complete picture of market information from CCPs, trade repositories, and market participants to provide to market regulators.
- Ensuring That OTC Derivatives Are Not Marketed Inappropriately To Unsophisticated Parties — Current law seeks to protect unsophisticated parties from entering into inappropriate derivatives transactions by limiting the types of counterparties that could participate in those markets. But the limits are not sufficiently stringent.
- The CFTC and SEC are reviewing the participation limits in current law to recommend how the CEA and the securities laws should be amended to tighten the limits or to impose additional disclosure requirements or standards of care with respect to the marketing of derivatives to less sophisticated counterparties such as small municipalities.

3. UNDERWRITER [§2(a)(11)]

b. Purchasing from an Issuer

P. 327 n.248, end note. See Berckeley Inv. Group, Ltd. v. Colkitt, 455 F.3d 195, 216 (3d Cir. 2006), quoting the text, that "a sell order given to a stock exchange broker results in an offer to the highest bidder in the world, which is certainly a 'public offering.'"

B. EXEMPTED SECURITIES

1. EXEMPTED SECURITIES VERSUS EXEMPTED TRANSACTIONS

b. Fraud Provisions

P. 343, new n.4.1, 1st full par. at 6th line. As later amended, exemption extends to §3(a)(14) as well as to §3(a)(2). Securities within §§3(a)(2) or (14) are exempt from §12(a)(2) liability. Lieberman v. Cambridge Partners, LLC, 2003–2004 Fed. Sec. L. Rep. (CCH) ¶92,650 (C.D. Pa. 2003).

c. Burden of Proof

P. 344 n.10, end note. See also State v. Andresen, 773 A.2d 328 (2001) (an exemption from registration is an affirmative defense to the charge of selling unregistered securities). For the comparable provision under the 2002 Uniform Securities Act, see §503(a) of the 2002 Act.

2. SECURITIES OF PUBLIC AUTHORITIES AND BANKS [§3(a)(2)]

a. Federal Government

P. 347, end page. A new era in the federal government's approach to government sponsored enterprises (GSEs) began in September 2008 when the federal government seized control of Fannie Mae and Freddie Mac, which then had $5.4 trillion of guaranteed mortgage backed securities and debt outstanding, more than 40 percent of the United States housing market. Federal Gov't Seizes Control of Fannie, Freddie Mac; GSEs Put in Conservatorship, 40 Sec. Reg. & L. Rep. (BNA) 1410 (2008).

C. EXEMPTED TRANSACTIONS

1. INTEGRATION

P. 363, end carryover par. In 2007 the Commission proposed amending the Regulation D safe harbor. Sec. Act Rel. 8828, 91 SEC Dock. 685, 704–705 (2007) (proposal). The Commission explained:

> The integration doctrine seeks to prevent an issuer from improperly avoiding registration by artificially dividing a single offering into multiple offerings such that Securities Act exemptions would apply to the multiple offerings that would not be available for the combined offering. The integration concept was first articulated in 1933 and was further developed in two interpretive releases issued in the 1960s. The interpretive releases clarified that determining whether a particular securities offering should be integrated with another offering requires an analysis of the specific facts and circumstances of the offerings. In our guidance, we identified five factors to consider in making the determination of whether the offerings should be integrated. In 1982, we included the five factors and established an integration safe harbor in Rule 502(a). We stated that the five factors relevant to the question of integration are:
>
>> Whether (1) the different offerings are part of a single plan of financing, (2) the offerings involve issuance of the same class of security, (3) the offerings are made at or about the same time, (4) the same type of consideration is to be received, and (5) the offerings are made for the same general purpose.
>>
>> Under the safe harbor, offers and sales more than six months before a Regulation D offering or more than six months after the completion of a Regulation D offering will not be considered part of the same offering. This provides issuers with a bright-line test upon which they can rely to avoid integration of multiple offerings....
>
> The current six-month time frame of the safe harbor in Rule 502(a) provides a substantial time period that has worked well to clearly differentiate two similar offerings and

provide time for the market to assimilate the effects of the prior offerings.... We recognize that increased volatility in the capital markets and advances in information technology have changed the landscape of private offerings. We remain concerned, however, that an inappropriately short time frame could allow issuers to undertake serial Rule 506-exempt offerings each month to up to 35 non-accredited investors in reliance on the safe harbor, resulting in unregistered sales to hundreds of non-accredited investors in a year. Such sales could result in large numbers of non-accredited investors failing to receive the protections of Securities Act registration. Our proposal seeks to strike an appropriate balance between the number of non-accredited investors allowed in an offering relying on the integration safe harbor and the non-public nature of that offering. It would be an anomalous result that an issuer could make an offering to hundreds of non-accredited investors in reliance on the integration safe harbor, triggering reporting requirements under the Exchange Act, without a public offering. We propose, therefore, to lower the safe harbor time frame to 90 days.... We believe 90 days is appropriate, as it would permit an issuer to rely on the safe harbor once every fiscal quarter.

The Commission provided the following interpretive guidance concerning Rule 152:

Consistent with Securities Act Rule 152, the staff of the Division of Corporation Finance, in its review of Securities Act registration statements, will not take the view that a completed private placement that was exempt from registration under Securities Act Section 4(2) should be integrated with a public offering of securities that is registered on a subsequently filed registration statement. Consistent with the staff's approach to this issue, we are of the view that, pursuant to Securities Act Rule 152, a company's contemplation of filing a Securities Act registration statement for a public offering at the same time that it is conducting a Section 4(a)-exempt private placement would not cause the Section 4(a) exemption to be unavailable for that private placement.

Id. at 703.

P. 391

2010 SUPPLEMENT

5. SMALL ISSUES

a. Statutory Exemptions [§§3(b), 3(c), 4(6)]

P. 391, new text after 1st full par. In 2007 the Commission adopted a number of regulatory changes intended to relieve the regulatory burden on smaller companies and to afford smaller companies regulatory simplification. Sec. Act Rels. 8819, 91 SEC Dock. 2732 (2007) (proposal); 8876, 92 SEC Dock. 436 (adoption). The Commission provided the following background and elaborated on the rulemaking in part in the Adoption Release:

...The new provisions:

- Establish a category of *smaller reporting companies* eligible to use our scaled disclosure requirements. The primary determinant for eligibility will be that the company have less than $75 million in public float. When a company is unable to calculate public float, however, such as if it has no common equity outstanding or no market price for its outstanding common equity exists at the time of the determination, the standard will be less than $50 million in revenue in the last fiscal year;
- Move 12 non-financial scaled disclosure item requirements [(1) Description of Business (Item 101); (2) Market Price of and Dividends on Registrant's Common Equity and Related Stockholder Matters (Item 201); (3) Selected Financial Data (Item 301); (4) Supplementary Financial Information (Item 302); (5) Management's Discussion and Analysis of Financial Condition and Results of Operations (Item 303); (6) Quantitative and Qualitative Disclosures about Market Risk (Item 305); (7) Executive Compensation (Item 402); (8) Transactions with Related Persons, Promoters and Certain Control Persons (Item 404); (9) Corporate Governance (Item 407); (10) Prospectus Summary, Risk Factors, and Ratio of Earnings to Fixed Charges (Item 503); (11) Use of Proceeds (Item 504); and (12) Exhibits (Item 601)] from

Regulation S-B into Regulation S-K. These scaled requirements will be available only for smaller reporting companies. The remaining 24 item requirements of Regulation S-B...are substantially the same as their corresponding Regulation S-K item requirements. We therefore are not amending them except in one minor instance...;
- Move the scaled financial statement requirements in Item 310 of Regulation S-B into new Article 8 of Regulation S-X, and amend these requirements to provide a scaled disclosure option for smaller reporting companies, requiring two years of balance sheet data instead of one year, and make other minor adjustments...;
- Permit smaller reporting companies to elect to comply with scaled financial and non-financial disclosure on an item-by-item or *a la carte* basis. As adopted, eligible companies may elect to follow scaled financial statement requirements or to provide the larger company financial statement presentation on a quarterly basis, rather than require companies to elect the full fiscal year's financial presentation in the first quarterly report of the fiscal year, as was proposed;
- Eliminate our current *SB* forms but allow a phase-out period for small business issuers transitioning to smaller reporting company status;
- Combine elements relating to the accelerated filer definition with qualifying standards for the smaller reporting company determination and transition provisions to promote uniformity and consistency with current regulations and, therefore, simplify regulation;
- Permit all foreign companies to qualify as *smaller reporting companies* if they otherwise qualify and choose to file on domestic company forms and provide financial statements prepared in accordance with U.S. Generally Accepted Accounting Principles (*US GAAP*); and
- Eliminate the transitional small business issuer format.

Id. at 439–440.

Other recent regulatory developments affect small business, although the impact of such developments is not limited to small business. For example, in 2007 the Commission liberalized the Rule 144 safe harbor for resales of restricted securities. Sec. Act

Rels. 8813, 91 SEC Dock. 2499 (2007) (proposal); 8869, 92 SEC Dock. 110 (2007) (adoption). The Commission also amended Rule 12h-1 under the Securities Exchange Act to, among other things, provide an exemption for issuers who do not file reports under the Exchange Act. Sec. Ex. Act Rel. 56,887, 92 SEC Dock. 190 (2007) (adoption). In addition, the Commission proposed certain amendments that would facilitate offerings under Regulation D, Sec. Act Rel. 8828, 91 SEC Dock. 685 (2007) (proposal), and also adopted amendments to Regulation D providing for the electronic filing of Form D. Sec. Act Rels. 8814, 91 SEC Dock. 2657 (2007) (proposal); 8891, 92 SEC Dock. 1498 (2008) (adoption).

6. LIMITED OFFERINGS

b. Regulation D

(i) *Rule 501(a) — Accredited Investor Definition*

P. 408 n.144, end note. For recent SEC proposals to amend the definition of *accredited investor* and add two new related categories of investor — *large accredited investor* and *accredited natural person* — see Sec. Act Rels. 8766, 89 SEC Dock. 1938 (2006); 8828, 91 SEC Dock. 685 (2007).

See also Sec. Act Rel. 8891, 92 SEC Dock. 1498 (2008) (adoption) (amending Rule 502(c) to address a matter concerning the ban on general solicitation and advertising presented by the SEC's rule adoption mandating the electronic filing of Form D).

(iii) *Rule 502(c) — Limitations on Manner of Offering*

P. 409, new n.146.1, end 1st par. In 2007 the Commission proposed a new Rule 507 under Regulation D to provide so-called *large accredited investors* greater latitude to advertise Regulation D offerings. Sec. Act Rel. 8828, 91 SEC Dock. 685 (2007) (proposal).

COVERAGE OF THE 1933 ACT   P. 413

See also Sec. Act Rel. 8891, 92 SEC Dock. 1498 (2008) (adoption) (amending Rule 502(c) to address a matter concerning the ban on general solicitation and advertising presented by the SEC's rule adoption mandating the electronic filing of Form D).

(v) *Rules 503 and 507 and Form D — Notice of Sales*

P. 410, 1st par., 4th line. The Commission adopted amendments in 2008 to require, among other things, the electronic filing of Form D and to amend Form D itself in various respects. Sec. Act Rel. 8891, 92 SEC Dock. 1498 (2008) (adoption). Before the rule change, five copies of the Form D had to be filed with the SEC.

P. 410 1st par., 2d sentence & n.148. *Delete.*

7. Trading Exemptions

a. Transactions by Persons Other Than Issuers, Underwriters, or Dealers [§4(1)]

P. 413, new n.155.1, end 2d full par. For ongoing developments concerning §4(1), see, for example, Geiger v. SEC, 363 F.3d 481 (D.C. Cir. 2004); SEC v. Kern, 425 F.3d 143 (2d Cir. 2005) (person who does not qualify for the Rule 144 safe harbor may still qualify for §4(1) exemption, although §4(1) exemption was unavailable in this case); SEC v. Cavanagh, 445 F.3d 105 (2d Cir. 2006) (stating that "sellers seeking a Section 4(1) exemption outside Rule 144 face a difficult standard" and finding that §4(1) exemption does not reach affiliates, including affiliates who "terminat[e] their affiliate status immediately prior to consummating the [unregistered] transaction," given the definition of *issuer* for purposes of §4(1)); Berckeley Inv. Group, Ltd. v. Colkitt, 455 F.3d 195 (3d Cir. 2006); SEC v. Phan, 500 F.3d 895 (9th Cir. 2007), citing the text.

175

D. RESALES OF CONTROL AND RESTRICTED SECURITIES

1. Resales after Private Offerings

b. First Tier Buyer's Problems

P. 429, new n.18.1, end text. Cf. Berckeley Inv. Group, Ltd. v. Colkitt, 455 F.3d 195, 214 (3d Cir. 2006) (discussing change-in-circumstances exception, citing the text).

2. Rule 144

P. 430, end 1st par., new text and n.18.2. In December 2007, the Commission adopted amendments to Rule 144. The Rule 144 changes shortened the holding period for restricted securities of issuers subject to 1934 Act reporting requirements to six months while maintaining the one-year holding period for restricted securities of nonreporting issuers; considerably eased the restrictions on resales by nonaffiliates; revised the Preliminary Note, although without intending any substantive impact; amended the manner of sale provisions and eliminated such restrictions for debt securities; amended the volume limitations for debt securities; raised the Form 144 filing triggers; and codified various staff interpretive positions.[18.2]

[18.2] Sec. Act Rels. 8813, 90 SEC Dock. 2499 (2007) (proposal); 8869, 92 SEC Dock. 110 (2007) (adoption).

With adoption of the 2007 Rule 144 amendments, nonaffiliates (or, more specifically, "any person who is not an affiliate of the issuer at the time of the sale, and has not been an affiliate during the preceding three months") may freely resell restricted securities after complying with the requisite holding period with one exception. That is, when selling restricted securities of reporting issuers, nonaffiliates are subject to the current public information requirements of Rule144(c) for an additional six months after the six-month holding period. The other non-holding period Rule 144 conditions no longer apply to the resale of restricted securities of reporting or nonreporting issuers by nonaffiliates. See Rule 144(b)(1).

COVERAGE OF THE 1933 ACT   P. 430

P. 430 2d par., next-to-last line before indented summary, substitute for "if six conditions are met:[22]":
…if specified conditions are met:[22]

Then substitute for indented material and accompanying footnotes:

(1) Current public information must be available about the issuer unless sales are limited to those made by nonaffiliates after one year.[23]

(2) When restricted securities of reporting issuers are sold, generally there must be a six month holding period.[24] When restricted securities of nonreporting issuers are sold, there is a one year holding period.

(3) When restricted securities of either a reporting or nonreporting issuer are resold by an affiliate after the six month or one year holding period, the affiliate may resell under Rule 144 in accordance with volume limitations on the amount of securities that may be sold,[25] manner of sale and Form 144 filing requirements.

(4) The rules for resales by nonaffiliates are similar. For restricted securities of reporting issuers, after six months, but before one year, there may be unlimited public resales under Rule 144 except that the current public information requirement applies. After one year, a nonaffiliate may make unlimited public results and need not comply with any provision of Rule 144. For restricted securities of nonreporting issuers, no resales are permitted by nonaffiliates for one year. After one year, there may be unlimited public resales by nonaffiliates of restricted securities of nonreporting issuers without compliance with any Rule 144 condition.[26]

(5) When the manner of sale requirement applies to a resale by an affiliate, sales must be made in a brokers' transaction as defined by §4(4) of the 1933 Act.[27]

(6) The Form 144 filing requirement is applicable to resales by an affiliate of 5,000 or more shares or units or with an aggregate value of $50,000 or more.[28]

P. 438

Rule 144 is not available for securities with no or minimal operations and no or minimal noncash assets.[29]

[22] Rule 144(b).
[23] Rule 144(c).
[24] Rule 144(d).
[25] Rule 144(e). Rule 144(e) aggregates restricted and nonrestricted securities sales for the purposes of calculating volume limitations.
[26] Rule 144(b).
[27] Rules 144(f)-(g). After the 2007 amendments, the manner of sale requirements no longer apply to resales by nonaffiliates.
[28] Rule 144(h).
[29] Rule 144(i).
[30] [Reserved.]

3. RULE 144A

P. 438 n.52, end note. Several authorities support the proposition that a §11 case cannot be brought against those who participate in a legitimate Rule 144A transaction. See also Safety-Kleen Bondholders Litig., 2002 U.S. Dist. LEXIS 26,735 (D.S.C. 2002); Hayes Lemmerz Int'l Inc. Equity Sec. Litig. v. Cucuz, 271 F. Supp. 2d 1007 (E.D. Mich. 2003); American High-Income Trust v. AlliedSignal, 329 F. Supp. 2d 534, 540–542 (S.D.N.Y. 2004). *Safety-Kleen*, in turn, relied on an amicus curiae letter from SEC General Counsel David M. Becker (Aug. 9, 2001).

Presumably these authorities do not address §11 or §12 liability when the Rule 144A transaction was not valid. *Livent*, see 151 F. Supp. 2d at 430–432, *Safety-Kleen Corp., supra* at * 3-4, and *Hayes Lemmerz*, 271 F. Supp. 2d at 1026–1029, did not question the propriety of the initial Rule 144A offerings. Similarly SEC General Counsel Becker's conclusion in his amicus curiae letter in *Safety-Kleen* is that "the concept of integration for Section 5 purposes is not relevant in this case" was expressly contingent upon the premise that: "plaintiffs, however, explicitly disclaim any assertion that the Rule 144A offering should have been registered."

COVERAGE OF THE 1933 ACT P. 438

Whether a Rule 144A transaction is valid itself may present a fact question for the trier of fact. Cf. *SEC v. Parnes*, 2001-2002 Fed. Sec. L. Rep. (CCH) ¶91,678 (S.D.N.Y. 2001) ("whether the proof is sufficient to establish a scheme to evade registration requirements and preclude application of the exemption is a question for trial"); Enron Corp. Sec., Deriv. & ERISA Litig., 310 F. Supp. 2d 819, 859-866 (S.D. Tex. 2004).

In Levi Strauss & Co. Sec. Litig., 527 F. Supp. 2d 965 (N.D. Cal. 2007), the court explained that an *Exxon Capital* exchange transaction did not give rise to §11 liability or §12(a)(2) liability, relying on Refco, Inc. Sec. Litig., 503 F. Supp. 2d 611 (S.D.N.Y. 2007).

The Interim Report of the Committee on Capital Markets Regulation (Nov. 30, 2006) described the growing significant of Rule 144A:

> The number of exchange-listed U.S. public offerings of international equity securities since the late 1990s has declined markedly, as the Rule 144A market has become foreign issuers' market of choice for U.S. equity issues. In 2005, foreign companies raised $83 billion in 186 equity issues in the Rule 144A market compared to $5.3 billion in 34 public offerings — that is, 90 percent of the volume of international equity issues in the United States were done in the private market. This compares with about a 50-50 split between these two markets in 1995.

Id. at 46.

In 2007 the Commission approved rule changes to reestablish PORTAL and allow participants to trade with one another in a closed system. Sec. Ex. Act Rel. 56,172, 91 SEC Dock. 606 (2007) (approval Release). The Commission approval Release explained in part:

> The PORTAL Market did not develop as anticipated. The Exchange believes this is, in part, because PORTAL securities could only be traded in the PORTAL Market and the original POR-TAL rules imposed trade reporting for all transactions in PORTAL securities at a time when there were no trade reporting requirements for privately-placed securities. In addition, Nasdaq believes PORTAL did not develop because it required use of cumbersome

P. 440   2010 SUPPLEMENT

technology for access to the PORTAL Market computer system for reporting purposes, which was a stand-alone computer system.

After nearly a decade, NASD filed a proposed rule change to delete many features of the PORTAL Market that had become obsolete including rules governing the registration of PORTAL Dealers, PORTAL Brokers, and PORTAL Qualified Investors and rules that were intended to regulate the quotation and trade reporting of PORTAL securities between PORTAL participants using the PORTAL system. Following approval of this proposed rule change, NASDAQ's primary role in the PORTAL Market became designating securities as PORTAL eligible which made those securities eligible for book entry services at The Depository Trust Company (*DTC*).

Nasdaq's PORTAL Proposal

Nasdaq has proposed an updated version of the PORTAL Market, which would operate as a facility of the Exchange. The proposed amendments to the PORTAL rules would: (i) establish qualification requirements for brokers and dealers that are Nasdaq members, and QIBs that wish to have access to PORTAL; and (ii) implement quotation, trade negotiation, and trade reporting functions in the PORTAL Market for PORTAL-designated securities. Many of the rules proposed by Nasdaq are substantially the same as those approved by the Commission when the PORTAL Market was first implemented by NASD in 1990.

4. The Resale Problem in Other Contexts under the 1933 Act

b. Mergers and Similar Events [Rule 145]

P. 440, new n.55.1, end page. In 2007 the Commission amended Rule 145 to jettison the presumptive underwriter concept except for Rule 145(a) transactions that involve shell companies, and conformed Rule 145(d) to Rule 144, which was amended at the same time as Rule 145. Sec. Act Rel. 8869, 92 SEC Dock. 110 (2007) (adoption).

CHAPTER 4

PROTECTIVE COMMITTEE REFORM: THE TRUST INDENTURE ACT OF 1939 AND SEC FUNCTIONS UNDER THE BANKRUPTCY CODE

B. THE SEC'S FUNCTIONS IN BANKRUPTCY PROCEEDINGS

2. THE COMMISSION'S PRESENT ROLE UNDER CHAPTER 11

b. SEC Participation

P. 449 n.4, end note. In Sherman v. SEC, 491 F.3d 948 (9th Cir. 2007), the SEC was held to have standing under Chapter 7 when the Commission was a creditor with respect to a disgorgement judgment. The court did not reach the question whether the Commission would also be a creditor with respect to a contempt judgment.

CHAPTER 6

REGISTRATION AND POSTREGISTRATION PROVISIONS OF THE 1934 ACT

A. REGISTRATION

4. EXEMPTIONS

c. Section 12(h)

P. 498, end page. In 2007 the Commission added Rules 12h-1(f) and (g) to exempt (1) stock options under written compensation stock option plans that are not required to file periodic reports under the 1934 Act and (2) stock options that are issued under written compensation plans when the issuer has an equity security underlying the stock options that is registered under §15(d). Sec. Ex. Act Rels. 56,010, 90 SEC Dock. 2881 (2007) (proposal); 56,887, 92 SEC Dock. 190 (2007) (adoption).

P. 502 2010 SUPPLEMENT

5. NONSTATUTORY REQUIREMENTS OF THE EXCHANGES AND THE NASD

a. In General

P. 502, new text, after 3d full par. In 2006 the SEC approved NYSE amendments eliminating the NYSE Listed Company Manual requirements that listed companies distribute an annual report to shareholders since Rule 14a-3 had made this requirement redundant for most NYSE listed United States companies subject to the proxy rules. Sec. Ex. Act Rels. 54,029, 88 SEC Dock. 769 (2006) (proposal); 54,344, 88 SEC Dock. 2240 (2006) (adoption).

b. Voting Rights Standards

P. 508, end text. In 2003, after amendments, the Commission approved new NYSE and NASD corporate governance standards. Sec. Ex. Act Rels. 47,672, 79 SEC Dock. 3074 (2003) (NYSE proposal); 47,516, 79 SEC Dock. 2407 (2003) (NASD proposal); 48,745, 81 SEC Dock. 1586 (2003) (adoption of both NYSE and NASD proposals). See also NYSE Listed Company Manual §303A Corporate Governance Listing Standards Frequently Asked Questions (Jan. 19, 2004), www.nyse.com.

As approved, after three amendments, the revised NYSE Manual of Listing Standards §303A(1) requires the board of each listed company to consist of a majority of independent directors.

Under §303A(2) no director would qualify as independent unless the board of directors determines that the director has no material relationship with the company. Specifically the NYSE tightened its definition of *independent director* in §303A(2)(b), as the adoption Release explained:

> First, a director who is an employee, or whose immediate family member is an executive officer, of the company would not be independent until three years after the end of such employment

relationship ("NYSE Employee Provision"). Employment as an interim Chairman or CEO would not disqualify a director from being considered independent following that employment.

Second, a director who receives, or whose immediate family member receives, more than $100,000 per year in direct compensation from the listed company, except for certain permitted payments, would not be independent until three years after he or she ceases to receive more than $100,000 per year in such compensation ("NYSE Direct Compensation Provision").

Third, a director who is affiliated with or employed by, or whose immediate family member is affiliated with or employed in a professional capacity by a present or former internal or external auditor of the company would not be independent until three years after the end of the affiliation or the employment or auditing relationship.

Fourth, a director who is employed, or whose immediate family member is employed, as an executive officer of another company where any of the listed company's present executives serve on that company's compensation committee would not be independent until three years after the end of such service or the employment relationship ("NYSE Interlocking Directorate Provision").

Fifth, a director who is an executive officer or an employee, or whose immediate family member is an executive officer, of a company that makes payments to, or receives payments from, the listed company for property or services in an amount which, in any single fiscal year, exceed the greater of $1 million, or 2% of such other company's consolidated gross revenues, would not be independent until three years after falling below such threshold....

The NYSE [defines] "immediate family member" to include a person's spouse, parents, children, siblings, mothers- and fathers-in-law, sons- and daughters-in-law, brothers- and sisters-in-law, and anyone (other than domestic employees) who shares such person's home. The NYSE [intended] references to "company" include any parent or subsidiary in a consolidated group with the company.

Sec. Ex. Act Rel. 48,745, 81 SEC Dock. at 1590–1591.

Nonmanagement directors, under §303A(3), would be required to meet at regular intervals without management.

Each listed company, under §303A(4)(a), would be required to have a nomination/corporate governance committee composed entirely of independent directors. The nominating/corporate governance committee, under §303A(4)(b), would be required to have a written charter that addresses the committee's purpose and responsibilities, and an annual performance evaluation of the nominating/corporate governance committee.

Each listed company would be required under §303A(5) further to have a compensation committee composed entirely of independent directors. The compensation committee similarly would be required to have a written charter that addressed the committee's purpose and responsibilities and to prepare an annual performance evaluation of the compensation committee. "The Compensation Committee also would be required to produce a compensation committee report on executive compensation, as required by Commission rules to be included in the company's annual proxy statement or annual report on Form 10-K filed with the Commission." Id. at 1591.

Revised §§303A(6) and (7) requires each NYSE-listed company to have a minimum three person audit committee that meets the independence standards of *both* §303A(2) and SEC Rule 10A-3. NYSE §303A(7) also requires each member of the audit committee to be *financially literate* as that term is interpreted by the full board or to become financially literate within a reasonable period of time after being appointed to the audit committee. In addition at least one member of the audit committee would be required to have accounting or related financial marketing expertise. Any person who satisfies the definition of *audit committee financial expert* in Item 401(e) of Regulation S-K is presumed to satisfy §303A(7)(a).

If a person serves on the audit committee of more than three public companies, each public company board would be required under §303A(7)(a) to determine that such simultaneous service would not impair the ability of the person to effectively serve on that company's audit committee. This determination must be disclosed.

Each audit committee, under §303A(7)(c), is required to have a written charter that addresses "(i) the committee's purpose; (ii) an annual performance evaluation of the audit committee; and (iii) the duties and responsibilities of the audit committee." Id. at 1592. The NYSE version of the charter at a minimum must include the substance of Rule 10A-3(b)(2)–(5):

> as well as the responsibility to annually obtain and review a report by the independent auditor; discuss the company's annual audited financial statement and quarterly financial statements with management and the independent auditor; discuss the company's earnings press releases, as well as financial information and earnings guidance provided to analysts and rating agencies; discuss policies with respect to risk assessment and risk management; meet separately, periodically, with management, with internal auditors (or other personnel responsible for the internal audit function), and with independent auditors; review with the independent auditors any audit problems or difficulties and management's response; set clear hiring policies for employees or former employees of the independent auditors; and report regularly to the board.

Ibid.

Section 303A(9) requires each listed company to adopt and disclose corporate governance guidelines that must include "director qualification standards; director responsibilities, director access to management and, as necessary and appropriate, independent advisors; director compensation; director orientation and continuing education; management succession; and annual performance evaluation of the board." Ibid.

In addition, §303A(10) requires each listed company to adopt and disclose a Code of Business Conduct and Ethics for directors, officers, and employees. Any waiver of this Code must be promptly disclosed. Commentary to §303A(10) discusses the most important topics to be addressed in the Code, which include "conflicts of interest; corporate opportunities; confidentiality of information; fair dealing; protection and proper use of company assets; compliance with laws, rules and regulations (including insider trading laws); and encouraging the reporting of any illegal or unethical behavior." Id. at 1593.

Under §303A(12)(a), the CEO of each listed company must certify that he or she is not aware of any violation of the NYSE's corporate governance listing standards. Under §303A(12)(b) the CEO must promptly notify the NYSE when any executive officer of the listed company becomes aware of *any* material noncompliance with any applicable provision of the new standards.

Section 303A(13) permits the NYSE to issue a public reprimand to any listed company that violates an NYSE listing standard.

There are exceptions to the requirement that a company have a majority of independent directors and nominating/corporate governance and compensation committee comprised entirely of independent directors for (1) any listed company of which more than 50 percent of its voting stock is held by an individual, group, or another company; (2) limited partnerships; and (3) companies in bankruptcy proceedings. Id. at 1593. The NYSE generally excepts from §303A management investment companies registered under the Investment Company Act. Ibid. A more limited series of exceptions is available for business development companies that are *not* registered under the Investment Company Act. Id. at 1594.

Except as otherwise required by Rule 10A-3, the new requirements would not apply to trusts, derivatives, special purpose securities, or listed companies listing only preferred or debt securities on the NYSE. Ibid.

Foreign private issuers would be permitted to follow home country practice except that these companies would be required to "(1) have an audit committee that satisfies the requirements of Rule 10A-3; (2) notify the NYSE in writing after any executive officer becomes aware of any non-compliance with any applicable provision; and (3) provide a brief, general summary of the significant ways in which its governance differs from those followed by domestic companies under NYSE listing standards." Ibid.

Nasdaq adopted somewhat similar, but less demanding, standards.

In 2004, the Commission approved rule changes to §303A of the NYSE Listed Company Manual. Sec. Ex. Act Rel. 50,625, 84 SEC Dock. 179 (2004) (adoption). The amendments, among other matters, addressed the definition of independent directors in §303A.02(b), added a new definition of executive officer in §303A-02(b)(i), and added a requirement that a nonmanaging director preside over each executive session.

In 2006 the SEC approved Nasdaq amendments to its definition of independent director in its Corporate Governance Standards. Sec. Ex. Act Rels. 54,333, 88 SEC Dock. 2217 (2006) (proposal); 54,583, 89 SEC Dock. 190 (2006) (adoption). The proposal would change the $60,000 threshold for independence to be based on *compensation* (which would include interest on a director savings account or contributions made to the political campaign of a director or family member).

B. REPORTING REQUIREMENTS

1. IN CONNECTION WITH EXCHANGE ACT REGISTRATION

a. Annual Reports

P. 509 n.2, end note. In 2007 the Commission proposed elimination of Forms 10-SB, 10-QSB, and 10-KSB to simplify reporting by smaller reporting companies. Sec. Act Rel. 8819, 90 SEC Dock. 2732 (2007) (proposal).

P. 511, end page. In 2005 the Commission adopted amendments to its accelerated filer deadlines for large accelerated filers. Sec. Act Rels. 8617, 86 SEC Dock. 660 (2005) (proposal); 8644, 86 SEC Dock. 2355 (2005) (adoption). The new Commission standard provides that large accelerated filers (those with a market value of outstanding voting and nonvoting common equity held by nonaffiliates of $700 million or more) will become subject to the accelerated filing transition schedule that will require Form 10-K annual reports to be filed within 60 days after the end of a fiscal year on or after October 15, 2006. Large accelerated filers would also remain subject to the current 40 day deadline for Form 10-Q reports rather than the further adopted 35 day deadline, and other accelerated filers would similarly continue under current deadlines (75 days after fiscal year end for Form 10-K annual reports and 40 days for Form 10-Q quarterly reports).

The proposal also would revise the definition of *accelerated filer* to permit an accelerated filer with less than a $50 million float to exit accelerated filer status and begin filing its annual and quarterly reports on a nonaccelerated filer basis. The proposals similarly would permit a *large accelerated filer* that has less than a $500 million float to promptly exit large accelerated filer status.

The adoption Release included the following chart depicting three tiers of filing deadlines that will take effect for fiscal years ending after December 15, 2005, as a result of the amendment:

Category of Filer	Revised Deadlines for Filing Periodic Reports	
	Form 10-K Deadline	**Form 10-Q Deadline**
Large Accelerated Filer ($700MM or more)	75 days for fiscal years ending before December 15, 2006 and 60 days for fiscal years ending on or after December 15, 2006	40 days
Accelerated Filer ($75MM or more and less than $700MM)	75 days	40 days
Non-accelerated Filer (less than $75MM)	90 days	45 days

Sec. Ex. Act Rel. 8644, 86 SEC Dock. at 2363–2364.

Conforming amendments were made to Regulation S-X Rules 3-01, 3-09, and 3-12 and the 1994 Act Rule 12b-2 definitions of *accelerated filer* and *large accelerated filer*.

b. Quarterly and Current Reports

P. 512 n.14, end note. Early in 2004 the Commission added eight new items to Form 8-K, expanded specified existing disclosures under that Form, and reorganized the required Form 8-K disclosure items into topical categories. Simultaneously the Commission shortened the Form 8-K filing deadline to two business days after the occurrence of a triggering event to better provide the "real time issuer disclosure" required by §409 of the Sarbanes-Oxley Act. Under Rule 12b-25 there is provision for an automatic two day business extension.

In the new topical reorganization, there are eight operative Form 8-K sections of disclosure items:

Section 1 — Registrant's Business and Operations

Item 1.01 Entry into a Material Definitive Agreement
Item 1.02 Termination of a Material Definitive Agreement
Item 1.03 Bankruptcy or Receivership

Section 2 — Financial Information

Item 2.01 Completion of Acquisition or Disposition of Assets
Item 2.02 Results of Operations and Financial Condition
Item 2.03 Creation of a Direct Financial Obligation or an Obligation under an Off-Balance Sheet Arrangement of a Registrant
Item 2.04 Triggering Events That Accelerate or Increase a Direct Financial Obligation or an Obligation under an Off-Balance Sheet Arrangement
Item 2.05 Costs Associated with Exit of Disposal Activities
Item 2.06 Material Impairments

Section 3 — Securities and Trading Markets

Item 3.01 Notice of Delisting or Failure to Satisfy a Continued Listing Rule or Standard; Transfer of Listing
Item 3.02 Unregistered Sales of Equity Securities
Item 3.03 Material Modifications to Rights of Security Holders

Section 4 — Matters Related to Accountants and Financial Statements

Item 4.01 Changes in Registrant's Certifying Accountant

P. 512   2010 SUPPLEMENT

Item 4.02 Non-Reliance on Previously Issued Financial Statements or a Related Audit Report or Completed Interim Review

Section 5 — Corporate Governance and Management

Item 5.01 Changes in Control of Registrant

Item 5.02 Departure of Directors or Principal Officers; Election of Directors; Appointment of Principal Officers

Item 5.03 Amendments to Articles of Incorporation or By-laws; Change in Fiscal Year

Item 5.04 Temporary Suspension of Trading under Registrant's Employee Benefit Plans

Item 5.05 Amendments to the Registrant's Code of Ethics, or Waiver of a Provision of the Code of Ethics

Section 6 — [Reserved]

Section 7 — Regulation FD

Item 7.01 Regulation FD Disclosure

Section 8 — Other Events

Item 8.01 Other Events

Section 9 — Financial Statements and Exhibits

Item 9.01 Financial Statements and Exhibits

The eight new Form 8-K disclosure Items are: Item 1.01, Entry into a Material Definitive Agreement; Item 1.02, Termination of a Material Definitive Agreement; Item 2.03, Creation of a Direct Financial Obligation or an Obligation under an Off-Balance Sheet Arrangement of a Registrant; Item 2.04, Triggering Events that Accelerate or Increase a Direct Financial Obligation or an Obligation under an Off-Balance Sheet Arrangement; Item 2.05, Costs Associated with Exit or Disposal Activities; Item 2.06, Material Impairments; Item 3.01, Notice of Delivery or Failure to Satisfy a Continued Listing Rule or Standard; Transfer of Listing; Item 4.02, Non-Reliance on Previously Issued Financial Statements or a Related Audit Report or Completed Interim Review.

The two items that were modified from existing disclosure requirements in periodic reports are Item 3.02, Unregistered Sales of Equity Securities, and Item 3.03, Material Modifications to Rights of Security Holders.

Many of the Form 8-K Items retain the substance of former Form 8-K Items: Item 1.03 retains the substance of former Item 3; Item 2.01 (former Item 2); Item 2.02 (former Item 12); Item 4.01 (former Item 4); Item 5.01 (former Item 1); Item 5.02 (former Item 6); Item 5.03 (former Item 5); Item 5.04 (former Item 11); Item 5.05 (former Item 10); Item 7.01 (former Item 9); Item 8.01 (former Item 5); and Item 9.01 (former Item 7).

The Commission also adopted a new limited safe harbor from public and private claims under §10(b) and Rule 10b-5 for a failure to file a Form 8-K regarding Items 1.01, 1.02, 2.03, 2.04, 2.05, 2.06, and 402(a). See also Sec. Ex. Act Rel. 49,424A, 83 SEC Dock. 1427 (2004) (technical amendments); Sec. Act Rel. 8518, 84 SEC Dock. 1624, 1723 (2004) (amendments for use of Form 8-K by asset backed issuers). See also Horwich, New Form 8-K and Real-Time Disclosure, 37 Rev. Sec. & Commodities Reg. 109 (2004).

P. 517, new text after 2d full par.

d. Management Report and Internal Controls

In June 2003 the Commission adopted new or amended provisions to Regulations S-B, S-K, and S-X; 1934 Act Rules 12b-15, 13a-14, 13a-15, 15d-14, and 15d-15; Forms 10-Q, 10-QSB, 10-K, 10-KSB, 20-F, 40-F; Investment Company Act Rules 8b-15, 30a-2, and 30a-3; and Forms N-CSR and N-SAR to implement the Sarbanes-Oxley Act §404 requirement that companies reporting under the 1934 Act include in their annual report a management report on the company's internal control over financial reporting. Sec. Ex. Act Rels. 46,701, 78 SEC Dock. 1907 (2002) (proposal); 47,986, 80 SEC Dock. 1014 (2003) (adoption). The Commission also amended 1934 Act Rules 13a-14 and 15d-14 and Investment Company Act Rule 30a-2 to require companies to file certifications mandated by §§302 and 906 of the Sarbanes-Oxley Act as

P. 517

exhibits to annual, semiannual, and quarterly reports. Id. at 1017. See also Sec. Ex. Act Rel. 47,551, 79 SEC Dock. 2558 (2003) (proposal).

To address confusion over the exact meaning of the phrase *internal control over financial reporting*, it was defined in 1934 Act Rules 13a-15(f), 15d-15(f), and similarly in Investment Company Act Rule 30a-2(d) to mean

> a process designed by, or under the supervision of, the issuer's principal executive and principal financial officers, or persons performing similar functions, and effected by the issuer's board of directors, management and other personnel, to provide reasonable assurance regarding the reliability of financial reporting and the preparation of financial statements for external purposes in accordance with generally accepted accounting principles and includes those policies and procedures that:
>
> (1) Pertain to the maintenance of records that in reasonable detail accurately and fairly reflect the transactions and dispositions of the assets of the issuer;
>
> (2) Provide reasonable assurance that transactions are recorded as necessary to permit preparation of financial statements in accordance with generally accepted accounting principles, and that receipts and expenditures of the issuer are being made only in accordance with authorizations of management and directors of the issuer; and
>
> (3) Provide reasonable assurance regarding prevention or timely detection of unauthorized acquisition, use or disposition of the issuer's assets that could have a material effect on the financial statements.

The adoption Release emphasized: "From the outset, it was recognized that internal control is a broad concept that extends beyond the accounting functions of a company." Sec. Ex. Act Rel. 47,986, 80 SEC Dock. at 1018. The new term was intended to be distinguishable from other uses of the term *internal* control. Id. at 1017–1019.

As amended, Regulations S-B and S-K Item 308 and Forms 20-F and 40-F require the company's annual report to include management's *"internal control over financial reporting"* report, specifically including:

(1) A statement of management's responsibility for establishing and maintaining adequate internal control over financial reporting for the registrant;

(2) A statement identifying the framework used by management to evaluate the effectiveness of the registrant's internal control over financial reporting as required by paragraph (c) of §240.13a-15 or 240.15d-15 of this chapter;

(3) Management's assessment of the effectiveness of the registrant's internal control over financial reporting as of the end of the registrant's most recent fiscal year, including a statement as to whether or not internal control over financial reporting is effective. This discussion must include disclosure of any material weakness in the registrant's internal control over financial reporting identified by management. Management is not permitted to conclude that the registrant's internal control over financial reporting is effective if there are one or more material weaknesses in the registrant's internal control over financial reporting; and

(4) A statement that the registered public accounting firm that audited the financial statements included in the annual report containing the disclosure required by this Item has issued an attestation report on management's assessment of the registrant's internal control over financial reporting.

As adopted, the Commission modified the final requirements to specify that management must base its evaluation of the effectiveness of the company's internal control over financial reporting on a suitable, recognized control framework that is established by a body or group that has followed due-process procedures, including the broad distribution of the framework for public comment.

The COSO Framework satisifies our criteria and may be used as an evaluation framework for purposes of management's annual internal control evaluation and disclosure requirements....The final rules require management's report to identify the evaluation framework used by management to assess the effectiveness of the company's internal control over financial reporting.

Sec. Ex. Act Rel. 47,986, 80 SEC Dock. at 1024.

P. 517   2010 SUPPLEMENT

The term *material weakness* has the same meaning in the adopted rules as in the definition under GAAS and attestation standards. Id. at 1025 and n.73.

Quarterly evaluations of internal controls over financial reporting can be less extensive than annual evaluations. Id. at 1026–1027. See also id. at 1028–1030. See Regulations S-B and S-K Item 308(c).

The Commission separately defined *disclosure controls and procedures* in 1934 Act Rules 13a-15(e) and 15d-15(e) and similarly in Investment Company Act Rule 30a-2(c), to mean

> controls and other procedures of an issuer that are designed to ensure that information required to be disclosed by the issuer in the reports that it files or submits under the Act is recorded, processed, summarized and reported, within the time periods specified in the Commission's rules and forms. Disclosure controls and procedures include, without limitation, controls and procedures designed to ensure that information required to be disclosed by an issuer in the reports that it files or submits under the Act is accumulated and communicated to the issuer's management, including its principal executive and principal financial officers, or persons performing similar decisions regarding required disclosure.

With respect to potential confusion between *internal control over financial reporting* and *disclosure controls and procedure*, the Commission explained:

> While there is substantial overlap between a company's disclosure controls and procedures and its internal control over financial reporting, there are both some elements of disclosure controls and procedures that are not subsumed by internal control over financial reporting and some elements of internal control that are not subsumed by the definition of disclosure controls and procedures.
>
> With respect to the latter point, clearly, the broad COSO description of internal control, which includes the efficiency and effectiveness of a company's operations and the company's compliance with laws and regulations (not restricted to the federal securities laws), would not be wholly subsumed within the definition of disclosure controls and procedures....

We agree that some components of internal control over financial reporting will be included in disclosure controls and procedures for all companies. In particular, disclosure controls and procedures will include those components of internal control over financial reporting that provide reasonable assurances that transactions are recorded as necessary to permit preparation of financial statements in accordance with generally accepted accounting principles.

Id. at 1027–1028.

Section 404 of the Sarbanes–Oxley Act exempts registered investment companies. See id. at 1034–1036. In its adoption Release, the SEC delayed the compliance date for foreign private issuers, id. at 1031; excluded asset backed issuers from its new requirements, id. at 1031–1032; provided extended compliance periods for small business issuers, id. at 1032; and afforded bank and thrift holding companies the option either to comply with the Commission's new rules implementing §404 or provisions in 12 C.F.R. part 363 [the FDIC Regulations], id. at 1032–1034.

For many boards of directors and outside auditors §404 has emerged as one of the key new responsibilities of the board. Under most state corporate law statutes, the board is "fully protected" when it relies on the report of an outside accountant or management. See Del. Gen. Corp. L. §141(e). Section 404 and the new SEC rules, in contrast, place responsibility on the management "to [establish] and [maintain] an adequate internal control structure and procedures for financial reporting" and to annually assess its effectiveness. The registered public accounting firm is required to attest to this assessment. §404(b).

To better harmonize §§302 and 906 of the Sarbanes–Oxley Act, the Commission also amended

> the exhibit requirements of Forms 20-F and 40-F and Item 601 of Regulations S-B and S-K to add the Section 302 certifications to the list of required exhibits. In the final rules, the specific form and content of the required certifications is set forth in the applicable exhibit filing requirement. To coordinate the rules requiring an evaluation of *disclosure controls and procedures and internal control over*

P. 517 2010 SUPPLEMENT

financial reporting, we are moving the definition of the term *disclosure controls and procedures* from Exchange Act Rules 13a-14(c) and 15d-14(c) and Investment Company Act Rule 30a-2(c) to new Exchange Act Rules 13a-15(c) and 15d-15(c) and Investment Company Act Rule 30a-3(c), respectively.

[Amended] Exchange Act Rules 13a-14 and 15d-14 and Investment Company Act Rule 30a-2... require the Section 906 certifications to accompany periodic reports containing financial statements as exhibits. We also are amending the exhibit requirements in Forms 20-F, 40-F and Item 601 of Regulations S-B and S-K to add the Section 906 certifications to the list of required exhibits to be included in reports filed with the Commission. In addition, we are amending Item 10 of Form N-CSR to add the Section 906 certifications as a required exhibit. Because the Section 906 certification requirement applies to periodic reports containing financial statements that are filed by an issuer pursuant to Section 13(a) or 15(d) of the Exchange Act, the exhibit requirement will only apply to reports on Form N-CSR filed under these sections and not to reports on Form N-CSR that are filed under the Investment Company Act only. A failure to furnish the Section 906 certifications would cause the periodic report to which they relate to be incomplete, thereby violating Section 13(a) of the Exchange Act. In addition, referencing the Section 906 certifications in Exchange Act Rules 13a-14 and 15d-14 and Investment Company Act Rule 30a-2 subjects these certifications to the signature requirements of Rule 302 of Regulation S-T.

Id. at 1038.

Subsequently the PCAOB adopted Audit Standard No. 2, An Audit of Internal Controls over Financial Reporting Performed in Conjunction with an Audit of Financial Statements. PCAOB Rel. No. 2004-001, 2003–2004 Fed. Sec. L. Rep. (CCH) ¶87,151 (Mar. 9, 2004). If approved by the SEC the new standard was estimated to increase audit costs by as much as 30-100 percent. Experts Split on Costs and Benefits of PCAOB's Proposed Audit Standard, 36 Sec. Reg. & L. Rep. (BNA) 163 (2004); Ernst & Young, Emerging Trends in Internal Controls: Initial Survey (Jan. 2004) (survey of 100 major companies found initial budgets of 10,000 to 200,000 new hours for §404 compliance).

Within weeks of the SEC approval of PCAOB Audit Standard No. 2, the PCAOB Staff published Staff Questions and Answers: Audit Internal Control over Financial Reporting (June 23, 2004). The SEC Office of the Chief Accountant & Division of Corporate Finance published a briefer Management Report on Internal Control over Financial Reporting and Disclosure in Exchange Act Periodic Reports: Frequently Asked Questions, 2004–2005 Fed. Sec. L. Rep. (CCH) ¶87,262 (Oct. 6, 2004), which focused on the impact of §404 on material acquisitions expected to close near the end of a fiscal year.

Subsequently, the Commission issued a Statement on Implementation of Internal Control Reporting Requirements (Press Rel. 2005-74 May 16, 2005).

The SEC Advisory Committee on Smaller Public Companies proposed in February 2006 to fully exempt from §404 (1) micro-cap companies (with equity capital below approximately $128 million and annual revenue less than $125 million) as well as (2) small cap companies (with equity capital between approximately $128 million and $787 million and less than $10 million in annual revenue). Former SEC Chair Arthur Levitt and former Federal Reserve Chair Paul Volcker sharply criticized this proposal for potentially removing an estimated 80 percent of all public companies subject to §404 38 Sec. Reg. & L. Rep. (BNA) 341 (2006). In April 2006 the Advisory Committee published its Final Report, with 33 recommendations.

In May 2006 the Commission announced several steps it intended to take to improve §404 implementation. Press Rel. 2006-75 (May 17, 2006). These steps include:

- **Guidance for Companies.** The Commission has received many requests for additional guidance for management on how to complete its assessment of internal control over financial reporting, as required by Section 404(a) of the Sarbanes-Oxley Act. To prepare for the issuance of management guidance, the Commission intends to take the following steps:
  - **Concept Release and Opportunity for Public Comment.** The Commission expects to issue a Concept

Release covering a variety of issues that might be the subject of Commission guidance for management. With the Concept Release, the Commission will solicit views on the management assessment process to ensure that the guidance the Commission ultimately proposes addresses the needs and concerns of all public companies. We will also seek input on the appropriate role of outside auditors in connection with the management assessment required by Section 404(a) of Sarbanes-Oxley, and on the manner in which outside auditors provide the attestation required by Section 404(b), to assist in our consideration of possible alternatives to the current approach.

- **Consideration of Additional Guidance from COSO.** The Commission has long been supportive of the Committee of Sponsoring Organizations of the Treadway Commission (COSO) as it works to provide guidance on COSO's 1992 Internal Control — Integrated Framework to address the needs of smaller companies. The Commission anticipates that this forthcoming guidance will help organizations of all sizes to better understand and apply the control framework as it relates to internal control over financial reporting. As the SEC develops guidance for management on how to assess its internal control over financial reporing, we will consider the extent to which the additional guidance that COSO provides is useful to smaller public companies in completing their Section 404(a) assessments.

- **Issuance of Guidance.** Commentary submitted to the Commission has suggested that management assessments under Section 404 have not fully reflected the top-down, risk-based approach the Commission intended. Building from the information gathered in response to the Concept Release, and from the anticipated COSO guidance, the Commission currently anticipates that it will issue guidance to management to assist in its performance of a top-down, risk-based assessment of internal control over financial reporting. To ensure that this guidance is of help to non-accelerated filers and smaller public companies, the Commission intends that this future guidance will be scalable and responsive to their individual circumstances. The guidance will also be sensitive to the fact that many companies have already invested substantial resources to establish and document programs and procedures to perform their assessments over the last few years. The form of the guidance has yet to be determined.

- **Revisions to Auditing Standard No. 2.** The PCAOB announced today that it intends to propose revisions to its Auditing Standard No. 2, An Audit of Internal Control over Financial Reporting Performed in Conjunction with an Audit of Financial Statements. Any final revision of AS No. 2 would be subject to SEC approval. The proposed revisions would:

    - Seek to ensure that auditors focus during integrated audits on areas that pose higher risk of fraud or material error;
    - Incorporate key concepts contained in the guidance issued by the PCAOB on May 16, 2005; and
    - Revisit and clarify what, if any, role the auditor should play in evaluating the company's process of assessing internal control effectiveness.

    The Commission will work closely with the PCAOB to ensure that the proposed revisions to AS No. 2 are in the public interest and consistent with the protection of investors.

- **SEC Oversight of PCAOB Inspection Program.** The PCAOB announced on May 1, 2006 that it would focus its 2006 inspections on whether auditors have achieved cost-saving efficiencies in the audits they have performed under AS No. 2, and on whether auditors have followed the guidance that the PCAOB issued in May and November 2005 urging them to do so. As part of the Commission's oversight of the PCAOB, the Commission staff inspects aspects of the PCAOB's operations, including its inspection program. Among other things, upon completion of the PCAOB's 2006 inspections, the staff will examine whether the PCAOB inspections of audit firms have been effective in encouraging implementation of the principles outlined in the PCAOB's May 1, 2006 statement.

P. 517

- **Extension of Compliance for Non-Accelerated Filers.** In order to permit non-accelerated filers and their auditors to have the benefit of the management guidance that the SEC intends to issue, and to have the opportunity to evaluate and implement the revisions that the PCAOB plans to make to AS No. 2, the Commission expects to issue a short postponement of the effective date of the Commission's rules implementing Section 404 for non-accelerated filers. It is anticipated that any such postponement would nonetheless require all filers to comply with the management assessment required by Section 404(a) of Sarbanes-Oxley for fiscal years beginning on or after Dec. 16, 2006.

In 2006 the Commission published a Concept Release to address §404. Sec. Ex. Act Rel. 54,122, 88 SEC Dock. 1173 (2006).

See also GAO: SOX Section 404 Beneficial, But Costs High for Small Companies, 38 Sec. Reg. & L. Rep. (BNA) 902 (2006); Concept Release on Internal Control "Prelude" to Management Guidance, SEC Says, 38 id. 1246 (2006); COSO Section 404 Guidance Aligns Companies, Auditors on Internal Controls, 38 id. 1247.

The Commission adopted a change in compliance date to December 31, 2007 for foreign private issuers that are accelerated filers, but not large accelerated filers, for amendments to Forms 20-F and 40-F that require such issuers to include in their annual reports an attestation report by the issuer's accounting firm or management's assessment on internal control over financial reporting. Sec. Act Rel. 8730A, 88 SEC Dock. 2005 (2006) (adoption).

In September 2006 testimony, SEC Chair Christopher Cox stated that he was "convinced that there are no irreparable problems with Section 404 implementation." Cox Says SOX §404 Problems Can Be Fixed; Discusses Exempting Community Banks' HCs, 38 Sec. Reg. & L. Rep. (BNA) 1611 (2006).

In November 2006 Treasury Secretary Henry Paulson offered his view in Remarks on the Competitiveness of U.S. Capital Markets at the Economic Club of New York, N.Y. (Nov. 20, 2006):

We responded to the corporate scandals with the Sarbanes-Oxley Act of 2002, new listing rules for public companies, and regulatory and legal enforcement actions to alter certain business practices. These changes have been extensive and significant, so it is quite naturally taking time for companies to understand, process, and implement the new rules and requirements. Many of the results have been positive. At the same time, as corporations, financial institutions, and regulators continue to adapt, questions are being raised about the long-term impact of these changes. Our goal is to preserve the integrity of our markets while maintaining their competitiveness....

Yet recently, in the wake of new, heightened regulatory and listing requirements for all public companies in the U.S., we have witnessed changes in IPO activity. Despite our strong economy and stock market, IPO dollar volume in the U.S. is well below the historical trend and below the trend and activity level in a number of foreign markets.

Moreover, existing public companies in the U.S. are deciding to forego their public status — with its attendant regulatory requirements — and go private. This is occurring in record numbers, at record volumes, and, as a percentage of overall public company M&A activity, is approaching levels we have not seen in almost 20 years. This development is being facilitated by ever-growing private pools of capital....

Some observers cite the decline of foreign IPOs in the U.S. market as an indicator of the competitiveness of our capital markets. We should go beyond the numbers and examine some of the possible reasons for this decline. Several factors contribute to the recent trends, including public policies in other countries. But several other contributing factors offer a framework to assess our own capital markets. These include:

- The development of markets outside the U.S., particularly in London and Hong Kong — and the ability of U.S. investors to participate in these offerings;
- A legal system in the U.S. that exposes market participants to significant litigation risk;
- A complex and confusing regulatory structure and enforcement environment;

P. 517

- And new accounting and governance rules which, while necessary, are being implemented in a way that may be creating unnecessary costs and introducing new risks to our economy....

A sophisticated legal structure — with property rights, contract law, mechanisms to resolve disputes, and a system for compensating injured parties — is necessary to protect investors, businesses and consumers. But our legal system has gone beyond protection. In 2004, U.S. tort costs reached a record quarter-trillion dollars, which is approximately 2.2 percent of our GDP. This is twice the relative cost in Germany and Japan, and three times the level in the UK. The consulting firm Towers-Perrin found that the tort system is highly inefficient, with only 42 cents of every tort dollar going to compensate injured plaintiffs. The balance goes to administration, attorney's fees, and defense costs. Inefficient tort costs are effectively a tax paid by shareholders, employees, and consumers. Simply put, the broken tort system is an Achilles heel for our economy. This is not a political issue, it is a competitiveness issue and it must be addressed in a bipartisan fashion....

Sarbanes-Oxley and Governance

When discussing the competitiveness of our markets, we should acknowledge that Sarbanes-Oxley and the related public company listing rules brought necessary reforms to our corporate governance and capital markets. These reforms are rooted in the basic principles that underpin a robust corporate governance system — accountability, transparency, and the need to identify and manage conflicts of interest.

These changes were necessary to rein in abuses. But significant changes always cause stress, and early implementation of new rules may produce uneven results. We must recognize the benefits of the new rules, and remain open-minded about how they affect the system, both positively and negatively. At this time, I do not believe we need new legislation to amend Sarbanes-Oxley. Instead, we need to implement the law in ways that better balance the benefits of the legislation with the very significant costs that it imposes, especially on small businesses.

By far the single biggest challenge with Sarbanes-Oxley is section 404, which requires management to assess the effectiveness of a company's internal controls and requires an auditor's attestation of that assessment. Companies should invest in strong internal controls and shareholders welcome this development because it is in their best interest. However, section 404 should be implemented in a more efficient and cost effective manner. It seems clear that a significant portion of the time, energy, and expense associated with implementing section 404 might have been better focused on direct business matters that create jobs and reward shareholders.

In the Interim Report of the Committee on Capital Market Regulation (Nov. 30, 2006), 22 corporate and financial leaders, including former NASD CEO Robert Glauber and NYSE President and Co-COO Catherine Kinney similarly provided an analysis of how to maintain and improve the competitiveness of United States Capital Markets.

The Report made several specific recommendations, including:

Section III: The Public and Private Enforcement System

...

14. Resolve Existing Uncertainties in Rule 10b-5 Liability. Although claims under Rule 10b-5 account for the vast majority of securities litigation, considerable uncertainty exists about many of the elements of Rule 10b-5 liability as a result of conflicting interpretations by courts. Recognizing that Rule 10b-5 cases are factually complicated, the SEC should attempt to provide more guidance, using a risk-based approach, where it is able to do so. This review should include materiality, *scienter* — the requisite knowledge the wrongdoer needs to have about his/her wrongdoing — and reliance....

17. Indict Entire Firms Only in Exceptional Circumstances. Extant guidelines of the U.S. Department of Justice (the *Thompson Memorandum*) on whether to prosecute a firm fail to take into account the damage to innocent employees and shareholders and, in some cases, to the entire economy. The Committee recommends that the Justice Department revise its prosecutorial guidelines so that firms are only prosecuted in exceptional circumstances of pervasive culpability throughout all offices and ranks....

19. Congress Should Explore Protecting Auditing Firms from Catastrophic Loss. The United States and the rest of the world are highly dependent on audit firms. Audit firms play a key role in ensuring the integrity of financial statements and the effectiveness of internal controls of public companies. The demise of another

U.S. audit firm would impose huge costs on U.S. shareholders. Also, the prospect of catastrophic liability can have a significant impact on auditing costs through the adoption of overly conservative practices. Taken to an extreme, these practices will continue to impact the competitiveness of the U.S. markets versus the European Union, even when worldwide accounting principles converge.

There are various approaches Congress could take in addressing this problem. One would be to create a safe harbor for certain defined auditing practices. Another approach would involve setting a cap on auditor liability in specified circumstances, an approach that some European countries already take and that the EU Commissioner for Internal Markets Charlie McGreevy has recommended the EU pursue. Any protection from catastrophic loss should be premised on a firm's satisfying minimum capital levels as a condition for receiving protection. After all, such protection is intended to remove the risk of catastrophic loss — not all liability.

Preventing damage awards against audit firms and their employees at a level that could destroy a firm would allow insurers to reenter this market. Insurance would be in the interest of both audit firms and shareholders. It would allow audit firms to price risk and create a source of recovery for shareholders....

20. Clarify Section 10A Liability. Section 10A of the Securities Exchange Act of 1934 (the *1934 Act*) requires auditors to undertake certain measures when they become "aware of information indicating that an illegal act...has or may have occurred." This provision has not to date resulted in auditor liability but has led auditors to require their issuer clients to conduct expensive and time-consuming investigations.

The language in Section 10A arguably is too broad and should be narrowed by Congress to focus on activities that pose a serious risk of harm to investors. In particular, the section could be amended as follows: (i) to apply only to *material* misstatements or omissions, which by definition are only those that affect investors' decisions; (ii) to limit liability only to situations where the misstatement implicates management's integrity; and (iii) to require auditors to investigate potential illegalities only when they uncover information indicating a *substantial likelihood* that an illegal act has been committed (currently the SEC's regulations under Section 10A do not distinguish information by level of probability that an illegal act has occurred). Such limited amendments would focus auditor responsibility under Section 10A on matters of true importance to investors....

21. Modify SEC Rule 176. The SEC should modify Rule 176, issued pursuant to Section 11 of the Securities Act, to make an outside director's good-faith reliance on an audited financial statement or an auditor's SAS 100 review report conclusive evidence of due diligence. Further, the modification could make good faith reliance by outside directors on representation of senior officers — after boardroom discussion — conclusive evidence of good faith as to other parts of the prospectus.

22. Modify SEC Indemnification Policy. Outside directors who have acted in good faith should also be insulated against out-of-pocket damages through changes in indemnification policy. The SEC could accomplish this by reversing its longstanding position that indemnification of directors for damages awarded in Section 11 actions is against public policy, at least insofar as the outside directors have acted in good faith. This change would help ensure the continued recruitment of high quality independent directors who play such a crucial role in corporate governance. This recommendation would not have the effect, however, of barring shareholder derivative suits against directors....

28. Develop Enhanced PCAOB and SEC Guidance.

The Committee recommends that the SEC and PCAOB further enhance guidance by:

- clarifying and permitting greater judgment as to the auditor's role in understanding and evaluating management's assessment process;
- confirming that auditors, in attesting to management's assessment, are not required to perform similar assessments to those needed in issuing their own opinions;
- reinforcing the appropriateness of the auditor's use of judgment throughout the audit of internal controls over financial reporting, including in the evaluation of strong indicators of material weakness;
- clarifying that the auditor attestation does not require the auditor to report separately on management's own internal control assessment process; and
- incorporating the frequently-asked questions guidance into the text of AS2.

In addition, the PCAOB should pursue its announced change in focus in its inspection process to consider auditor efficiency in its evaluations and should continue to take steps to provide timely, targeted feedback regarding the application of AS2. The PCAOB should accelerate the development of an Audit Guide for smaller issuers and could consider other measures — particularly in instances where an auditor is required to issue an adverse report due to a material weakness in internal control — that could help improve efficiencies.

29. Permit Multi-Year Rotational Testing and Increased Reliance on Work of Others. Consistent with the objective of focusing control reviews primarily on higher risk components of financial processes, the SEC and the PCAOB should give guidance to management and auditors to allow multi-year rotational testing, as part of an annual attestation. Critical components of financial processes and higher risk areas such as procedures for preparing the annual financial statements and related disclosures should be tested each year. For lower risk components of financial processes and other areas, such as certain elements of the information technology environment, management and the auditor should be allowed to use a multi-year rotational testing approach within an annual attestation....

30. Small Companies Should Either Be Subject to the Same (Revised) Section 404 Requirements as Large Companies or Congress Should Reshape 404 for Small Companies. In the near-term, application of Section 404 to non-accelerated files (companies with less than $75 million of market capitalization) should continue to be deferred until the changes in materiality, enhanced guidance, and multi-year rotational testing take effect. At such time, the SEC should reassess the costs and benefits of extending Section 404 to small companies. To the extent that the SEC finds that, even with the proposed reforms, the costs are still too high relative to the benefits, it should ask Congress to consider exempting small companies from the auditor attestation requirement of Section 404 while at the same changing the management certification requirement to one requiring reasonable belief in the adequacy of internal controls. Without the comfort of auditor attestation, management would not be able to make a stronger certification....

31. Do Not Apply Section 404 to Foreign Companies Subject to Equivalent Home Country Requirements. The Committee recommends that the SEC not apply Section 404 to foreign firms that

could demonstrate that they were subject to equivalent home country internal control regulation. The Committee also recommends that, in any event, the SEC should not apply the Section 404 review to the U.S. GAAP reconciliation. The Committee applauds the fact that the SEC has publicly reassured all concerned that Section 404 would not apply to a company listed only on an overseas exchange simply because that exchange is owned by a company incorporated in the United States.

Id. at 1-21.

Early in 2007, New York Senator Charles Schumer and New York City Mayor Michael Bloomberg published *Sustaining New York's and the US' Global Financial Services Leadership*, a study prepared by McKinsey & Company, in part based on interviews of more than 50 financial services industry CEOs and business leaders. The recommendations of this Report were similar to those in the Paulsen Report, and included:

> Recommendation 1 — Provide clearer guidance for implementing the Sarbanes-Oxley Act. The Securities and Exchange Commission (SEC) and the Public Companies Accounting Oversight Board (PCAOB), in consultation with business and public accounting firms, should follow through on their recently proposed revisions to the guidelines controlling the implementation of Section 404 of the Sarbanes-Oxley Act. Provided that, upon their adoption, they afford guidance beyond what is currently proposed with regard to the notion of *material weakness*, these proposals should ensure that the audit of internal controls takes a top-down perspective, is risk-based, and is focused on the most critical issues. The guidance should also enable auditors and management to exercise more judgment and emphasize materiality. Taking full account of the constructive observations that will result from the notice and comment periods to which both proposals are currently subject, the SEC and PCAOB should seek to implement the proposed revisions quickly and effectively, resisting pressure to dilute the recommendations, as doing so would severely undermine the proposals' important signaling benefits.
>
> Depending on the extent to which the revised guidelines empirically reduce the particularly significant compliance burden that Sarbanes-Oxley imposes on smaller companies, as explained in

more detail in Recommendation 2, the SEC may want to consider giving such companies the opportunity to *opt out* of the more onerous requirements of Sarbanes-Oxley, provided that this choice is conspicuously disclosed to investors. The SEC should also consider exempting foreign companies from certain parts of Sarbanes-Oxley, provided they already comply with sophisticated, SEC-approved foreign regulators. This would make US capital markets more attractive to smaller companies and foreign corporations without unduly jeopardizing investor protection and the quality of corporate governance. It would also address international concerns about the extraterritorial application of US regulations by showing appropriate deference to foreign regulators....

Recommendation 2 — Implement securities litigation reform. The SEC should make use of its broad rulemaking and exemptive powers to deter the most problematic securities-related suits. For example, the SEC could invoke Section 36 of the Securities Exchange Act of 1934, which effectively allows it to exempt companies from certain onerous regulations where it deems such exemptions to be in the public interest. Within the confines of the SEC's authority under the 1934 Act, the Commission therefore could, pursuant to a thorough cost/benefit analysis, choose to: limit the liability of foreign companies with US listings to securities-related damages proportional to their degree of exposure to the US markets; impose a cap on auditors' damages that would maintain the deterrent effect of large financial penalties while also reducing the likelihood of the highly concentrated US auditing industry losing another major player; and give smaller public companies the ability to *opt out* of some portions of Sarbanes-Oxley....

Recommendation 5 — Recognize IFRS without reconciliation and promote the convergence of accounting and auditing standards. The SEC should consider recognizing International Financial Reporting Standards (IFRS) without requiring foreign companies listing in the US to reconcile to US Generally Accepted Accounting Principles (GAAP). Similarly, the PCAOB should work with other national and international bodies towards a single set of global audit standards....

In December 2006 the Commission extended the compliance date until December 15, 2007 for smaller public companies to provide management reports on internal control over financial reporting as required by §404. Sec. Act Rel. 8760, 89 SEC Dock. 1611 (2006).

In 2007 the PCAOB adopted Audit Standard No. 5, *An Audit of Internal Control over Financial Reporting that Is Integrated with an Audit of Financial Statements,* to Supersede Audit Standard No. 2. Sec. Ex. Act Rel. 55,876, 90 Dock. 2161 (2007). The SEC subsequently approved Standard No. 5. SEC Unanimously OKs PCAOB AS5 for Use in Auditing Internal Controls, 39 Sec. Reg. & L. Rep. (BNA) 1190 (2007).

Audit Standard No. 5 provided in relevant part:

> 1. This standard establishes requirements and provides direction that applies when an auditor is engaged to perform an audit of management's assessment of the effectiveness of internal control over financial reporting (*the audit of internal control over financial reporting*) that is integrated with an audit of the financial statements.
> 2. Effective internal control over financial reporting provides reasonable assurance regarding the reliability of financial reporting and the preparation of financial statements for external purposes. If one or more material weaknesses exist, the company's internal control over financial reporting cannot be considered effective....
> 5. The auditor should use the same suitable, recognized control framework to perform his or her audit of internal control over financial reporting as management uses for its annual evaluation of the effectiveness of the company's internal control over financial reporting.
> 6. The audit of internal control over financial reporting should be integrated with the audit of the financial statements....
> 7. In an integrated audit of internal control over financial reporting and the financial statements, the auditor should design his or her testing of controls to accomplish the objectives of both audits simultaneously —
>
> > • To obtain sufficient evidence to support the auditor's opinion on internal control over financial reporting as of year-end, and

- To obtain sufficient evidence to support the auditor's control risk assessments for purposes of the audit of financial statements....

9. The auditor should properly plan the audit of internal control over financial reporting and properly supervise any assistants. When planning an integrated audit, the auditor should evaluate whether the following matters are important to the company's financial statements and internal control over financial reporting and, if so, how they will affect the auditor's procedures —

- Knowledge of the company's internal control over financial reporting obtained during other engagements performed by the auditor;
- Matters affecting the industry in which the company operates, such as financial reporting practices, economic conditions, laws and regulations, and technological changes;
- Matters relating to the company's business, including its organization, operating characteristics, and capital structure;
- The extent of recent changes, if any, in the company, its operations, or its internal control over financial reporting;
- The auditor's preliminary judgments about materiality, risk, and other factors relating to the determination of material weaknesses;
- Control deficiencies previously communicated to the audit committee or management;
- Legal or regulatory matters of which the company is aware;
- The type and extent of available evidence related to the effectiveness of the company's internal control over financial reporting;
- Preliminary judgments about the effectiveness of internal control over financial reporting;
- Public information about the company relevant to the evaluation of the likelihood of material financial statement misstatements and the effectiveness of the company's internal control over financial reporting;
- Knowledge about risks related to the company evaluated as part of the auditor's client acceptance and retention evaluation; and
- The relative complexity of the company's operations....

10. Risk assessment underlies the entire audit process described by this standard, including the determination of *significant accounts and disclosures* and *relevant assertions*, the selection of controls to test, and the determination of the evidence necessary for a given control.

11. A direct relationship exists between the degree of risk that a material weakness could exist in a particular area of the company's internal control over financial reporting and the amount of audit attention that should be devoted to that area. In addition, the risk that a company's internal control over financial reporting will fail to prevent or detect misstatement caused by fraud usually is higher than the risk of failure to prevent or detect error. The auditor should focus more of his or her attention on the areas of highest risk. On the other hand, it is not necessary to test controls that, even if deficient, would not present a reasonable possibility of material misstatement to the financial statements.

12. The complexity of the organization, business unit, or process, will play an important role in the auditor's risk assessment and the determination of the necessary procedures....

13. The size and complexity of the company, its business processes, and business units, may affect the way in which the company achieves many of its *control objectives*. The size and complexity of the company also might affect the risks of misstatement and the controls necessary to address those risks. Scaling is most effective as a natural extension of the risk-based approach and applicable to the audits of all companies. Accordingly, a smaller, less complex company, or even a larger, less complex company might achieve its control objectives differently than a more complex company.

14. When planning and performing the audit of internal control over financial reporting, the auditor should take into account the results of his or her fraud risk assessment. As part of identifying and testing entity-level controls,... the auditor should evaluate whether the company's controls sufficiently address identified risks of material misstatement due to fraud and controls intended to address the risk of management override of other controls. Controls that might address these risks include —

- Controls over significant, unusual transactions, particularly those that result in late or unusual journal entries;
- Controls over journal entries and adjustments made in the period-end financial reporting process;

P. 517 — 2010 SUPPLEMENT

- Controls over related party transactions;
- Controls related to significant management estimates; and
- Controls that mitigate incentives for, and pressures on, management to falsify or inappropriately manage financial results.

15. If the auditor identifies deficiencies in controls designed to prevent or detect fraud during the audit of internal control over financial reporting, the auditor should take into account those deficiencies when developing his or her response to risks of material misstatement during the financial statement audit, as provided in AU sec. 316.44 and .45....

17. For purposes of the audit of internal control, however, the auditor may use the work performed by, or receive direct assistance from, internal auditors, company personnel (in addition to internal auditors), and third parties working under the direction of management or the audit committee that provides evidence about the effectiveness of internal control over financial reporting. In an integrated audit of internal control over financial reporting and the financial statements, the auditor also may use this work to obtain evidence supporting the auditor's assessment of control risk for purposes of the audit of the financial statements....

19. The extent to which the auditor may use the work of others in an audit of internal control also depends on the risk associated with the control being tested. As the risk associated with a control increases, the need for the auditor to perform his or her own work on the control increases....

21. The auditor should use a top-down approach to the audit of internal control over financial reporting to select the controls to test. A top-down approach begins at the financial statement level and with the auditor's understanding of the overall risks to internal control over financial reporting. The auditor then focuses on entity-level controls and works down to significant accounts and disclosures and their relevant assertions. This approach directs the auditor's attention to accounts, disclosures, and assertions that present a reasonable possibility of material misstatement to the financial statements and related disclosures. The auditor then verifies his or her understanding of the risks in the company's processes and selects for testing those controls that sufficiently address the assessed risk of misstatement to each relevant assertion....

22. The auditor must test those entity-level controls that are important to the auditor's conclusion about whether the company has effective internal control over financial reporting. The auditor's evaluation of entity-level controls can result in increasing or decreasing the testing that the auditor otherwise would have performed on other controls.

23. Entity-level controls vary in nature and precision —

- Some entity-level controls, such as certain control environment controls, have an important, but indirect, effect on the likelihood that a misstatement will be detected or prevented on a timely basis. These controls might affect the other controls the auditor selects for testing and the nature, timing, and extent of procedures the auditor performs on other controls.
- Some entity-level controls monitor the effectiveness of other controls. Such controls might be designed to identify possible breakdowns in lower-level controls, but not at a level of precision that would, by themselves, sufficiently address the assessed risk that misstatements to a relevant assertion will be prevented or detected on a timely basis. These controls, when operating effectively, might allow the auditor to reduce the testing of other controls.
- Some entity-level controls might be designed to operate at a level of precision that would adequately prevent or detect on a timely basis misstatements to one or more relevant assertions. If an entity-level control sufficiently addresses the assessed risk of misstatement, the auditor need not test additional controls relating to that risk.

24. Entity-level controls include —

- Controls related to the control environment;
- Controls over management override;...
- The company's risk assessment process;
- Centralized processing and controls, including shared service environments;
- Controls to monitor results of operations;
- Controls to monitor other controls, including activities of the internal audit function, the audit committee, and self-assessment programs;

- Controls over the period-end financial reporting process; and
- Policies that address significant business control and risk management practices.

25. Control Environment. Because of its importance to effective internal control over financial reporting, the auditor must evaluate the control environment at the company. As part of evaluating the control environment, the auditor should assess —

- Whether management's philosophy and operating style promote effective internal control over financial reporting;
- Whether sound integrity and ethical values, particularly of top management, are developed and understood; and
- Whether the Board or audit committee understands and exercises oversight responsibility over financial reporting and internal control.

26. Period-end Financial Reporting Process. Because of its importance to financial reporting and to the auditor's opinions on internal control over financial reporting and the financial statements, the auditor must evaluate the period-end financial reporting process. The period-end financial reporting process includes the following —

- Procedures used to enter transaction totals into the general ledger;
- Procedures related to the selection and application of accounting policies;
- Procedures used to initiate, authorize, record, and process journal entries in the general ledger;
- Procedures used to record recurring and nonrecurring adjustments to the annual and quarterly financial statements; and
- Procedures for preparing annual and quarterly financial statements and related disclosures....

28. The auditor should identify significant accounts and disclosures and their relevant assertions. Relevant assertions are those financial statement assertions that have a reasonable possibility of

containing a misstatement that would cause the financial statements to be materially misstated. The financial statement assertions include —

- Existence or occurrence
- Completeness
- Valuation or allocation
- Rights and obligations
- Presentation and disclosure...

29. To identify significant accounts and disclosures and their relevant assertions, the auditor should evaluate the qualitative and quantitative risk factors related to the financial statement line items and disclosures. Risk factors relevant to the identification of significant accounts and disclosures and their relevant assertions include —

- Size and composition of the account;
- Susceptibility to misstatement due to errors or fraud;
- Volume of activity, complexity, and homogeneity of the individual transactions processed through the account or reflected in the disclosure;
- Nature of the account or disclosure;
- Accounting and reporting complexities associated with the account or disclosure;
- Exposure to losses in the account;
- Possibility of significant contingent liabilities arising from the activities reflected in the account or disclosure;
- Existence of related party transactions in the account; and
- Changes from the prior period in account or disclosure characteristics.

30. As part of identifying significant accounts and disclosures and their relevant assertions, the auditor also should determine the likely sources of potential misstatements that would cause the financial statements to be materially misstated. The auditor might determine the likely sources of potential misstatements by asking himself or herself "what could go wrong?" within a given significant account or disclosure.
31. The risk factors that the auditor should evaluate in the identification of significant accounts and disclosures and their relevant

P. 517   2010 SUPPLEMENT

assertions are the same in the audit of internal control over financial reporting as in the audit of the financial statements; accordingly, significant accounts and disclosures and their relevant assertions are the same for both audits....

33. When a company has multiple locations or business units, the auditor should identify significant accounts and disclosures and their relevant assertions based on the consolidated financial statements. Having made those determinations, the auditor should then apply the direction in Appendix B for multiple locations scoping decisions....

34. To further understand the likely sources of potential misstatements, and as a part of selecting the controls to test, the auditor should achieve the following objectives —

- Understand the flow of transactions related to the relevant assertions, including how these transactions are initiated, authorized, processed, and recorded;
- Verify that the auditor has identified the points within the company's processes at which a misstatement — including a misstatement due to fraud — could arise that, individually or in combination with other misstatements, would be material;
- Identify the controls that management has implemented to address these potential misstatements; and
- Identify the controls that management has implemented over the prevention or timely detection of unauthorized acquisition, use, or disposition of the company's assets that could result in a material misstatement of the financial statements....

36. The auditor also should understand how IT affects the company's flow of transactions. The auditor should apply paragraphs .16 through .20, .30 through .32, and .77 through .79, of AU sec. 319, *Consideration of Internal Control in a Financial Statement Audit*, which discuss the effect of information technology on internal control over financial reporting and the risks to assess....

37. Performing Walkthroughs. Performing walkthroughs will frequently be the most effective way of achieving the objectives in paragraph 34. In performing a walkthrough, the auditor follows a transaction from origination through the company's processes,

including information systems, until it is reflected in the company's financial records, using the same documents and information technology that company personnel use. Walkthrough procedures usually include a combination of inquiry, observation, inspection of relevant documentation, and re-performance of controls.

38. In performing a walkthrough, at the points at which important processing procedures occur, the auditor questions the company's personnel about their understanding of what is required by the company's prescribed procedures and controls. These probing questions, combined with the other walkthrough procedures, allow the auditor to gain a sufficient understanding of the process and to be able to identify important points at which a necessary control is missing or not designed effectively....

46. For each control selected for testing, the evidence necessary to persuade the auditor that the control is effective depends upon the risk associated with the control. The risk associated with a control consists of the risk that the control might not be effective and, if not effective, the risk that a material weakness would result. As the risk associated with the control being tested increases, the evidence that the auditor should obtain also increases....

47. Factors that affect the risk associated with a control include —

- The nature and materiality of misstatements that the control is intended to prevent or detect;
- The inherent risk associated with the related account(s) and assertion(s);
- Whether there have been changes in the volume or nature of transactions that might adversely affect control design or operating effectiveness;
- Whether the account has a history of errors;
- The effectiveness of entity-level controls, especially controls that monitor other controls;
- The nature of the control and the frequency with which it operates;
- The degree to which the control relies on the effectiveness of other controls (e.g., the control environment or information technology general controls);
- The competence of the personnel who perform the control or monitor its performance and whether there have been any changes in key personnel who perform the control or monitor its performance;

P. 517

- Whether the control relies on performance by an individual or is automated (i.e., an automated control would generally be expected to be lower risk if relevant information technology general controls are effective); and...
- The complexity of the control and the significance of the judgments that must be made in connection with its operation....

52. Timing of Tests of Controls. Testing controls over a greater period of timing provides more evidence of the effectiveness of controls than testing over a shorter period of time....

54. Extent of Tests of Controls. The more extensively a control is tested, the greater the evidence obtained from that test....

57. In subsequent years' audits, the auditor should incorporate knowledge obtained during past audits he or she performed of the company's internal control over financial reporting into the decision-making process for determining the nature, timing, and extent of testing necessary....

60. The auditor may also use a benchmarking strategy for automated application controls in subsequent years' audits....

61. In addition, the auditor should vary the nature, timing, and extent of testing controls from year to year to introduce unpredictability into the testing and respond to changes in circumstances....

63. The severity of a deficiency depends on —

- Whether there is a reasonable possibility that the company's controls will fail to prevent or detect a misstatement of an account balance or disclosure; and
- The magnitude of the potential misstatement resulting from the deficiency or deficiencies.

64. The severity of a deficiency does not depend on whether a misstatement actually has occurred but rather on whether there is a reasonable possibility that the company's controls will fail to prevent or detect a misstatement.

65. Risk factors affect whether there is a reasonable possibility that a deficiency, or a combination of deficiencies, will result in a misstatement of an account balance or disclosure. The factors include, but are not limited to, the following —

- The nature of the financial statement accounts, disclosures, and assertions involved;
- The susceptibility of the related asset or liability to loss or fraud;
- The subjectivity, complexity, or extent of judgment required to determine the amount involved;
- The interaction or relationship of the control with other controls, including whether they are interdependent or redundant;
- The interaction of the deficiencies; and
- The possible future consequences of the deficiency....

66. Factors that affect the magnitude of the misstatement that might result from a deficiency or deficiencies in controls include, but are not limited to, the following —

- The financial statement amounts or total of transactions exposed to the deficiency; and
- The volume of activity in the account balance or class of transactions exposed to the deficiency that has occurred in the current period or that is expected in future periods.

67. In evaluating the magnitude of the potential misstatement, the maximum amount that an account balance or total of transactions can be overstated is generally the recorded amount, while understatements could be larger. Also, in many cases, the probability of a small misstatement will be greater than the probability of a large misstatement.

68. The auditor should evaluate the effect of compensating controls when determining whether a control deficiency or combination of deficiencies is a material weakness. To have a mitigating effect, the compensating control should operate at a level of precision that would prevent or detect a misstatement that could be material....

69. Indicators of material weaknesses in internal control over financial reporting include —

- Identification of fraud, whether or not material, on the part of senior management;
- Restatement of previously issued financial statements to reflect the correction of a material misstatement;

P. 517　　2010 SUPPLEMENT

- Identification by the auditor of a material misstatement of financial statements in the current period in circumstances that indicate that the misstatement would not have been detected by the company's internal control over financial reporting; and
- Ineffective oversight of the company's external financial reporting and internal control over financial reporting by the company's audit committee.

70. When evaluating the severity of a deficiency, or combination of deficiencies, the auditor should also determine the level of detail and degree of assurance that would satisfy prudent officials in the conduct of their own affairs that they have reasonable assurance that transactions are recorded as necessary to permit the preparation of financial statements in conformity with generally accepted accounting principles. If the auditor determines that a deficiency, or combination of deficiencies, might prevent prudent officials in the conduct of their own affairs from concluding that they have a reasonable assurance that transactions are recorded as necessary to permit the preparation of financial statements in conformity with generally accepted accounting principles, then the auditor should treat the deficiency, or combination of deficiencies, as an indicator of a material weakness....

71. The auditor should form an opinion on the effectiveness of internal control over financial reporting by evaluating evidence obtained from all sources, including the auditor's testing of controls, misstatements detected during the financial statement audit, and any identified control deficiencies....

72. After forming an opinion on the effectiveness of the company's internal control over financial reporting, the auditor should evaluate the presentation of the elements that management is required, under the SEC's rules, to present in its annual report on internal control over financial reporting....

75. In an audit of internal control over financial reporting, the auditor should obtain written representations from management —

　　a. Acknowledging management's responsibility for establishing and maintaining effective internal control over financial reporting;

b. Stating that management has performed an evaluation and made an assessment of the effectiveness of the company's internal control over financial reporting and specifying the control criteria;
c. Stating that management did not use the auditor's procedures performed during the audits of internal control over financial reporting or the financial statements as part of the basis for management's assessment of the effectiveness of internal control over financial reporting;
d. Stating management's conclusion, as set forth in its assessment, about the effectiveness of the company's internal control over financial reporting based on the control criteria as of a specified date;
e. Stating that management has disclosed to the auditor all deficiencies in the design or operation of internal control over financial reporting identified as part of management's evaluation, including separately disclosing to the auditor all such deficiencies that it believes to be significant deficiencies or material weaknesses in internal control over financial reporting;
f. Describing any fraud resulting in a material misstatement to the company's financial statements and any other fraud that does not result in a material misstatement to the company's financial statements but involves senior management or management or other employees who have a significant role in the company's internal control over financial reporting;
g. Stating whether control deficiencies identified and communicated to the audit committee during previous engagements pursuant to paragraphs 77 and 79 have been resolved and specifically identifying any that have not; and
h. Stating whether there were, subsequent to the date being reporting on, any changes in internal control over financial reporting or other factors that might significantly affect internal control over financial reporting, including any corrective actions taken by management with regard to significant deficiencies and material weaknesses.

76. The failure to obtain written representations from management, including management's refusal to furnish them, constitutes a limitation on the scope of the audit....

P. 517

77. AU sec. 333, Management Representations, explains matters such as who should sign the letter, the period to be covered by the letter, and when to obtain an updated letter....

78. The auditor must communicate, in writing, to management and the audit committee all material weaknesses identified during the audit. The written communication should be made prior to the issuance of the auditor's report on internal control over financial reporting.

79. If the auditor concludes that the oversight of the company's external financial reporting and internal control over financial reporting by the company's audit committee is ineffective, the auditor must communicate that conclusion in writing to the board of directors.

80. The auditor also should consider whether there are any deficiencies, or combinations of deficiencies, that have been identified during the audit that are significant deficiencies and must communicate such deficiencies, in writing, to the audit committee.

81. The auditor also should communicate to management, in writing, all deficiencies in internal control over financial reporting (i.e., those deficiencies in internal control over financial reporting that are of a lesser magnitude than material weaknesses) identified during the audit and inform the audit committee when such a communication has been made....

82. The auditor is not required to perform procedures that are sufficient to identify all control deficiencies; rather, the auditor communicates deficiencies in internal control over financial reporting of which he or she is aware.

83. Because the audit of internal control over financial reporting does not provide the auditor with assurance that he or she has identified all deficiencies less severe than a material weakness, the auditor should not issue a report stating that no such deficiencies were noted during the audit.

84. When auditing internal control over financial reporting, the auditor may become aware of fraud or possible illegal acts. In such circumstances, the auditor must determine his or her responsibilities under AU sec. 316, Consideration of Fraud in a Financial Statement Audit, AU sec. 317, Illegal Acts by Clients, and Section 10A of the Securities Exchange Act of 1934....

85. The auditor's report on the audit of internal control over financial reporting must include the following elements —

a. A title that includes the word *independent*;
b. A statement that management is responsible for maintaining effective internal control over financial reporting and for assessing the effectiveness of internal control over financial reporting;
c. An identification of management's report on internal control;
d. A statement that the auditor's responsibility is to express an opinion on the company's internal control over financial reporting based on his or her audit;
e. A definition of internal control over financial reporting as stated in paragraph A5;
f. A statement that the audit was conducted in accordance with the standards of the Public Company Accounting Oversight Board (United States);
g. A statement that the standards of the Public Company Accounting Oversight Board require that the auditor plan and perform the audit to obtain reasonable assurance about whether effective internal control over financial reporting was maintained in all material respects;
h. A statement that an audit includes obtaining an understanding of internal control over financial reporting, assessing the risk that a material weakness exists, testing and evaluating the design and operating effectiveness of internal control based on the assessed risk, and performing such other procedures as the auditor considered necessary in the circumstances;
i. A statement that the auditor believes the audit provides a reasonable basis for his or her opinion;
j. A paragraph stating that, because of inherent limitations, internal control over financial reporting may not prevent or detect misstatements and that projections of any evaluation of effectiveness to future periods are subject to the risk that controls may become inadequate because of changes in conditions or that the degree of compliance with the policies or procedures may deteriorate;
k. The auditor's opinion on whether the company maintained, in all material respects, effective internal control over financial reporting as of the specified date, based on the control criteria;
l. The manual or printed signature of the auditor's firm;

P. 517

   m. The city and state (or city and country, in the case of non-U.S. auditors) from which the auditor's report has been issued; and
   n. The date of the audit report....

86. The auditor may choose to issue a combined report (i.e., one report containing both an opinion on the financial statements and an opinion on internal control over financial reporting) or separate reports on the company's financial statements and on internal control over financial reporting....

90. Paragraphs 62 through 70 describe the evaluation of deficiencies. If there are deficiencies that, individually or in combination, result in one or more material weaknesses, the auditor must express an adverse opinion on the company's internal control over financial reporting, unless there is a restriction on the scope of the engagement.

91. When expressing an adverse opinion on internal control over financial reporting because of a material weakness, the auditor's report must include —

- The definition of a material weakness, as provided in paragraph A7.
- A statement that a material weakness has been identified and an identification of the material weakness described in management's assessment....

92. The auditor should determine the effect his or her adverse opinion on internal control has on his or her opinion on the financial statements. Additionally, the auditor should disclose whether his or her opinion on the financial statements was affected by the adverse opinion on internal control over financial reporting....

93. Change in internal control over financial reporting or other factors that might significantly affect internal control over financial reporting might occur subsequent to the date as of which internal control over financial reporting is being audited but before the date of the auditor's report. The auditor should inquire of management whether there were any such changes or factors and obtain written representations from management relating to such matters, as described in paragraph 75h....

96. If the auditor obtains knowledge about subsequent events that materially and adversely affect the effectiveness of the company's

internal control over financial reporting as of the date specified in the assessment, the auditor should issue an adverse opinion on internal control over financial reporting (and follow the direction in paragraph C2 if management's assessment states that internal control over financial reporting is effective). If the auditor is unable to determine the effect of the subsequent event on the effectiveness of the company's internal control over financial reporting, the auditor should disclaim an opinion. As described in paragraph C13, the auditor should disclaim an opinion on management's disclosures about corrective actions taken by the company after the date of management's assessment, if any.

97. The auditor may obtain knowledge about subsequent events with respect to conditions that did not exist at the date specified in the assessment but arose subsequent to that date and before issuance of the auditor's report. If a subsequent event of this type has a material effect on the company's internal control over financial reporting, the auditor should include in his or her report an explanatory paragraph describing the event and its effects or directing the reader's attention to the event and its effects as disclosed in management's report.

98. After the issuance of the report on internal control over financial reporting, the auditor may become aware of conditions that existed at the report date that might have affected the auditor's opinion had he or she been aware of them. The auditor's evaluation of such subsequent information is similar to the auditor's evaluation of information discovered subsequent to the date of the report on an audit of financial statements, as described in AU sec. 561, *Subsequent Discovery of Facts Existing at the Date of the Auditor's Report*.

Appendix A included several definitions, including:

A7. A *material weakness* is a deficiency, or a combination of deficiencies, in internal control over financial reporting, such that there is a *reasonable possibility* that a material misstatement of the company's annual or interim financial statements will not be prevented or detected on a timely basis....

A11. A *significant deficiency* is a deficiency, or a combination of deficiencies, in internal control over financial reporting that is less severe than a material weakness, yet important enough to merit attention by those responsible for oversight of the company's financial reporting.

The Commission's adoption Release of its Interpretive Guidance, Sec. Act Rel. 8810, 90 SEC Dock. 2305 (2007), stated in part:

> The Interpretive Guidance is organized around two broad principles. The first principle is that management should evaluate whether it has implemented controls that adequately address the risk that a material misstatement of the financial statements would not be prevented or detected in a timely manner. The guidance describes a top-down, risk-based approach to this principle, including the role of entity-level controls in assessing financial reporting risks and the adequacy of controls. The guidance promotes efficiency by allowing management to focus on those controls that are needed to adequately address the risk of a material misstatement of its financial statements. The guidance does not require management to identify every control in a process or document the business processes impacting [Internal Control over Financial Reporting] ICFR. Rather, management can focus its evaluation process and the documentation supporting the assessment on those controls that it determines adequately address the risk of a material misstatement of the financial statements. For example, if management determines that a risk of a material misstatement is adequately addressed by an entity-level control, no further evaluation of other controls is required.
>
> The second principle is that management's evaluation of evidence about the operation of its controls should be based on its assessment of risk. The guidance provides an approach for making risk-based judgments about the evidence needed for the evaluation. This allows management to align the nature and extent of its evaluation procedures with those areas of financial reporting that pose the highest risks to reliable financial reporting (that is, whether the financial statements are materially accurate). As a result, management may be able to use more efficient approaches to gathering evidence, such as self-assessments, in low-risk areas and perform more extensive testing in high-risk areas. By following these two principles, we believe companies of all sizes and complexities will be able to implement our rules effectively and efficiently.

REGISTRATION UNDER THE 1934 ACT   P. 517

The Interpretive Guidance reiterates the Commission's position that management should bring its own experience and informed judgment to bear in order to design an evaluation process that meets the needs of its company and that provides a reasonable basis for its annual assessment of whether ICFR is effective. This allows management sufficient and appropriate flexibility to design such an evaluation process. Smaller public companies, which generally have less complex internal control systems than larger public companies, can use this guidance to scale and tailor their evaluation methods and procedures to fit their own facts and circumstances. We encourage smaller public companies to take advantage of the flexibility and scalability to conduct an evaluation of ICFR that is both efficient and effective at identifying material weaknesses....

The guidance in this release shall be effective immediately upon its publication in the Federal Register.

As a companion to this interpretive release, we are adopting amendments to Exchange Act Rules 13a-15(c) and 15d-15(c) and revisions to Regulation S-X. The amendments to Rules 13a-15(c) and 15d-15(c) will make it clear that an evaluation that is conducted in accordance with this interpretive guidance is one way to satisfy the annual management evaluation requirement in those rules. We are also amending our rules to define the term *material weakness* and to revise the requirements regarding the auditor's attestation report on ICFR. Additionally, we are seeking additional comment on the definition of the term *significant deficiency*....

A. The Evaluation Process

The objective of internal control over financial reporting (*ICFR*) is to provide reasonable assurance regarding the reliability of financial reporting and the preparation of financial statements for external purposes in accordance with generally accepted accounting principles (*GAAP*). The purpose of the evaluation of ICFR is to provide management with a reasonable basis for its annual assessment as to whether any material weaknesses in ICFR exist as of the end of the fiscal year. To accomplish this, management identifies the risks to reliable financial reporting, evaluates whether controls exist to address those risks, and evaluates evidence about the operation of the controls included in the evaluation based on its assessment of risk. The evaluation process will vary from company to company; however, the top-down, risk-based approach which is described in this guidance will typically be the most efficient and effective way to conduct the evaluation....

Under the Commission's rules, management's annual assessment of the effectiveness of ICFR must be made in accordance with a suitable control framework's definition of effective internal control. These control frameworks define elements of internal control that are expected to be present and functioning in an effective internal control system. In assessing effectiveness, management evaluates whether its ICFR includes policies, procedures and activities that address the elements of internal control that the applicable control framework describes as necessary for an internal control system to be effective. The framework elements describe the characteristics of an internal control system that may be relevant to individual areas of the company's ICFR, pervasive to many areas, or entity-wide....

1. Identifying Financial Reporting Risks and Controls

Management should evaluate whether it has implemented controls that will achieve the objective of ICFR (that is, to provide reasonable assurance regarding the reliability of financial reporting). The evaluation begins with the identification and assessment of the risks to reliable financial reporting (that is, materially accurate financial statements), including changes in those risks. Management then evaluates whether it has controls placed in operation (that is, in use) that are designed to adequately address those risks. Management ordinarily would consider the company's entity-level controls in both its assessment of risks and in identifying which controls adequately address the risks.

The evaluation approach described herein allows management to identify controls and maintain supporting evidential matter for its controls in a manner that is tailored to the company's financial reporting risks (as defined below). Thus, the controls that management identifies and documents are those that are important to achieving the objective of ICFR....

a. Identifying Financial Reporting Risks

Management should identify those risks of misstatement that could, individually or in combination with others, result in a material misstatement of the financial statements (*financial reporting risks*). Ordinarily, the identification of financial reporting risks begins with evaluating how the requirements of GAAP apply to the company's business, operations and transactions. Management must provide investors with financial statements that fairly present the company's financial position, results of operations and cash flows in accordance with GAAP. A lack of fair presentation arises when one or more financial statement amounts of disclosures (*financial reporting elements*) contain misstatements (including omissions) that are material.

Management uses its knowledge and understanding of the business, and its organization, operations, and processes, to consider the sources and potential likelihood of misstatements in financial reporting elements. Internal and external risk factors that impact the business, including the nature and extent of any changes in those risks, may give rise to a risk of misstatement. Risks of misstatement may also arise from sources such as the initiation, authorization, processing and recording of transactions and other adjustments that are reflected in financial reporting elements. Management may find it useful to consider *what could go wrong* with a financial reporting element in order to identify the sources and the potential likelihood of misstatements and identify those that could result in a material misstatement of the financial statements.

The methods and procedures for identifying financial reporting risks will vary based on the characteristics of the company. These characteristics include, among others, the size, complexity, and organizational structure of the company and its processes and financial reporting environment, as well as the control framework used by management. For example, to identify financial reporting risks in a larger business or a complex business process, management's methods and procedures may involve a variety of company personnel, including those with specialized knowledge. These individuals, collectively, may be necessary to have a sufficient understanding of GAAP, the underlying business transactions and the process activities, including the role of computer technology, that are required to initiate, authorize, record and process transactions. In contrast, in a small company that operates on a centralized basis with less complex business processes and with little change in the risks or processes, management's daily involvement with the business may provide it with adequate knowledge to appropriately identify financial reporting risks.

Management's evaluation of the risk of misstatement should include consideration of the vulnerability of the entity to fraudulent activity (for example, fraudulent financial reporting,

P. 517

misappropriation of assets and corruption), and whether any such exposure could result in a material misstatement of the financial statements. The extent of activities required for the evaluation of fraud risks is commensurate with the size and complexity of the company's operations and financial reporting environment....

b. Identifying Controls that Adequately Address Financial Reporting Risks

Management should evaluate whether it has controls placed in operation (that is, in use) that adequately address the company's financial reporting risks. The determination of whether an individual control, or a combination of controls, adequately addresses a financial reporting risk involves judgments about whether the controls, if operating properly, can effectively prevent or detect misstatements that could result in material misstatements in the financial statements. If management determines that a deficiency in ICFR exists, it must be evaluated to determine whether a material weakness exists....

Management may identify preventive controls, detective controls, or a combination of both, as adequately addressing financial reporting risks. There might be more than one control that addresses the financial reporting risks for a financial reporting element; conversely, one control might address the risks of more than one financial reporting element. It is not necessary to identify all controls that may exist or identify redundant controls, unless redundancy itself is required to address the financial reporting risks....

In addition to identifying controls that address the financial reporting risks of individual financial reporting elements, management also evaluates whether it has controls in place to address the entity-level and other pervasive elements of ICFR that its chosen control framework prescribes as necessary for an effective system of internal control. This would ordinarily include, for example, considering how and whether controls related to the control environment, controls over management override, the entity-level risk assessment process and monitoring activities, controls over the period-end financial reporting process, and the policies that address significant business control and risk management practices are adequate for purposes of an effective system of internal control. The control frameworks and related guidance may be useful tools for evaluating the adequacy of these elements of ICFR....

c. Consideration of Entity-Level Controls

Management considers entity-level controls when identifying financial reporting risks and related controls for a financial reporting element. In doing so, it is important for management to consider the nature of the entity-level controls and how those controls relate to the financial reporting element. The more indirect the relationship to a financial reporting element, the less effective a control may be in preventing or detecting a misstatement.

Some entity-level controls, such as certain control environment controls, have an important, but indirect, effect on the likelihood that a misstatement will be prevented or dated on a timely basis. These controls might affect the other controls management determines are necessary to adequately address financial reporting risks for a financial reporting element. However, it is unlikely that management will identify only this type of entity-level control as adequately addressing a financial reporting risk identified for a financial reporting element.

Other entity-level controls may be designed to identify possible breakdowns in lower-level controls, but not in a manner that would, by themselves, adequately address financial reporting risks. For example, an entity-level control that monitors the results of operations may be designed to detect potential misstatements and investigate whether a breakdown in lower-level controls occurred. However, if the amount of potential misstatement that could exist before being detected by the monitoring control is too high, the control may not adequately address the financial reporting risks of a financial reporting element.

Entity-level controls may be designed to operate at the process, application, transaction or account-level and at a level of precision that would adequately prevent or detect on a timely basis misstatements in one or more financial reporting elements that could result in a material misstatement of the financial statements. In these cases, management may not need to identify or evaluate additional controls relating to that financial reporting risk.

d. Role of Information Technology General Controls

Controls that management identifies as addressing financial reporting risks may be automated, depending upon IT functionality, or a combination of both manual and automated procedures. In these situations, management's evaluation process generally considers the design and operation of the automated or IT dependent application controls and the relevant IT controls over the applications providing the IT functionality. While IT general controls alone ordinarily do not adequately address financial reporting risks, the proper and consistent operation of automated controls or IT functionality often depends upon effective IT general controls. The identification of risks and controls within IT should not be a separate evaluation. Instead, it should be an integral part of management's top-down-risk-based approach to identifying risks and controls and in determining evidential matter necessary to support the assessment....

e. Evidential Matter to Support the Assessment

As part of its evaluation of ICFR, management must maintain reasonable support for its assessment. Documentation of the design of the controls management has placed in operation to adequately address the financial reporting risks, including the entity-level and other pervasive elements necessary for effective ICFR, is an integral part of the reasonable support. The form and extent of the documentation will vary depending on the size, nature, and complexity of the company. It can take many forms (for example, paper documents, electronic, or other media). Also, the documentation can be presented in a number of ways (for example, policy manuals, process models, flowcharts, job descriptions, documents, internal memorandums, forms, etc.)....

2. Evaluating Evidence of the Operating Effectiveness of ICFR

Management should evaluate evidence of the operating effectiveness of a control considers whether the control is operating as designed and whether the person performing the control possesses the necessary authority and competence to perform the control effectively. The evaluation procedures that management uses to gather evidence about the operation of the controls it identifies as adequately addressing the financial reporting risks for financial reporting elements...should be tailored to management's assessment of the risk characteristics of both the individual financial reporting elements and the related controls (collectively, ICFR risk). Management should ordinarily focus its evaluation of the operation of controls on areas positing the highest ICFR risk. Management's assessment of ICFR risk also considers the impact of entity-level controls, such as the relative strengths and weaknesses of the control environment, which may influence management's judgments about the risks of failure for particular controls.

Evidence about the effective operation of controls may be obtained from direct testing of controls and on-going monitoring activities. The nature, timing and extent of evaluation procedures necessary for management to obtain sufficient evidence of the effective operation of a control depend on the assessed ICFR risk. In determining whether the evidence obtained is sufficient to provide a reasonable basis for its evaluation of the operation of ICFR, management should consider not only the quantity of evidence (for example, sample size), but also the qualitative characteristics of the evidence. The qualitative characteristics of the evidence include the nature of the evaluation procedures performed, the period of time to which the evidence relates, the objectivity of those evaluating the controls, and, in the case of on-going monitoring activities, the extent of validation through direct testing of underlying controls. For any individual control, different combinations of the nature, timing, and extent of evaluation procedures may provide sufficient evidence. The sufficiency of evidence is not necessarily determined by any of these attributes individually.

a. Determining the Evidence Needed to Support the Assessment

Management should evaluate the ICFR risk of the controls...as adequately addressing the financial reporting risks for financial reporting elements to determine the evidence needed to support the assessment. This evaluation should consider the characteristics of the financial reporting elements to which the controls relate and the characteristics of the controls themselves....

Management's consideration of the misstatement risk of a financial reporting element includes both the materiality of the financial reporting element and the susceptibility of the underlying account balances, transactions or other supporting information to a misstatement that could be material to the financial statements. As the materiality of a financial reporting element increases in relation to the amount of misstatement that would be considered material to the financial statements, management's assessment of misstatement risk for the financial reporting element generally would correspondingly increase. In addition, management considers the extent to which the financial reporting elements include transactions, account balances or other supporting information that are prone to material misstatement. For example, the extent to which a financial reporting element: (1) involves judgment in determining the recorded amounts; (2) is susceptible to fraud; (3) has complex accounting requirements; (4) experiences change in the nature or volume of the underlying transactions; or (5) is sensitive to changes in environmental factors, such as technological and/or economic developments, would generally affect management's judgment of whether a misstatement risk is higher or lower.

Management's consideration of the likelihood that a control might fail to operate effectively includes, among other things:

- The type of control (that is, manual or automated) and the frequency with which it operates;
- The complexity of the control;
- The risk of management override;
- The judgment required to operate the control;
- The competence of the personnel who perform the control or monitor its performance;
- Whether there have been changes in key personnel who either perform the control or monitor its performance;
- The nature and materiality of misstatements that the control is intended to prevent or detect;
- The degree to which the control relies on the effectiveness of other controls (for example, IT general controls); and
- The evidence of the operation of the control from prior year(s).

For example, management's judgment of the risk of control failure would be higher for controls whose operation requires significant judgment than for non-complex controls requiring less judgment.

Financial reporting elements that involve related party transactions, critical accounting policies, and related critical accounting estimates generally would be assessed as having a higher misstatement risk. Further, when the controls related to these financial reporting elements are subject to the risk of management override, involve significant judgment, or are complex, they should generally be assessed as having higher ICFR risk.

When a combination of controls is required to adequate address the risks related to a financial reporting element, management should analyze the risk characteristics of the controls. This is because the controls associated with a given financial reporting element may not necessarily share the same risk characteristics....

b. Implementing Procedures to Evaluate Evidence of the Operation of ICFR

Management should evaluate evidence that provides a reasonable basis for its assessment of the operating effectiveness of the controls identified in Section II.A.1. Management uses its assessment of ICFR risk, as determined in Section II.A.2. to determine the evaluation methods and procedures necessary to obtain sufficient evidence. The evaluation methods and procedures may be integrated with the daily responsibilities of its employees or implemented specifically for purposes of the ICFR evaluation....

As the ICFR risk increases, management will ordinarily adjust the nature of the evidence that is obtained. For example, management can increase the evidence from on-going monitoring activities by utilizing personnel who are more objective and/or increasing the extent of validation through periodic direct testing of the underlying controls. Management can also vary the evidence obtained by adjusting the period of time covered by direct testing. When ICFR risk is assessed as high, the evidence management obtains would ordinarily consist of direct testing or on-going monitoring activities performed by individuals who have a higher degree of objectivity. In situations where a company's on-going monitoring activities utilize personnel who are not adequately objective, the evidence obtained would normally be supplemented with direct testing by those who are independent from the operation of the control. In these situations, direct testing of controls corroborates evidence from on-going monitoring activities as well as evaluates the operation of the underlying controls and whether they continue to adequately address financial reporting risks. When ICFR risk is assessed as low, management may conclude that evidence from on-going monitoring is sufficient and that no direct testing is required. Further, management's evaluation would ordinarily consider evidence from a reasonable period of time during the year, including the fiscal year-end.

In smaller companies, management's daily interaction with its controls may provide it with sufficient knowledge about their operation to evaluate the operation of ICFR. Knowledge from daily interaction includes information obtained by on-going direct involvement with and direct supervision of the execution of the control by those responsible for the assessment of the effectiveness of ICFR. Management should consider its particular facts and circumstances when determining whether its daily interaction with controls provides sufficient evidence to evaluate the operating effectiveness of ICFR. For example, daily interaction may be sufficient when the operation of controls is centralized and the number of personnel involved is limited. Conversely, daily interaction in companies with multiple management reporting layers or operating segments would generally not provide sufficient evidence because those responsible for assessing the effectiveness of ICFR would not ordinarily be sufficiently knowledgeable about the operation of the controls. In these situations, management would ordinarily utilize direct testing or on-going monitoring-type evaluation procedures to obtain reasonable support for the assessment.

Management evaluates the evidence it gathers to determine whether the operation of a control is effective. This evaluation considers whether the control operated as designed. It also considers matters such as how the control was applied, the consistency with which it was applied, and whether the person performing the control possesses the necessary authority and competence to perform the control effectively. If management determines that the operation of the control is not effective, a deficiency exists that must be evaluated to determine whether it is a material weakness.

c. Evidential Matter to Support the Assessment

Management's assessment must be supported by evidential matter that provides reasonable support for its assessment. The nature of the evidential matter may vary based on the assessed level of ICFR risk of the underlying controls and other circumstances. Reasonable support for an assessment would include the basis for management's assessment, including documentation of the methods and procedures it utilizes to gather and evaluate evidence.

The evidential matter may take many forms and will vary depending on the assessed level of ICFR risk for controls over each of its financial reporting elements. For example, management may document its overall strategy in a comprehensive memorandum that establishes the evaluation approach, the evaluation procedures, the basis for management's conclusion about the effectiveness of controls related to the financial reporting elements and the entity-level and other pervasive elements that are important to management's assessment of ICFR.

If management determines that the evidential matter within the company's books and records is sufficient to provide reasonable support for its assessment, it may determine that it is not necessary to separately maintain copies of the evidence it evaluates. For example, in smaller companies, where management's daily interaction with its controls provides the basis for its assessment, management may have limited documentation created specifically for the evaluation of ICFR. However, in these instances, management should consider whether reasonable support for its assessment would include documentation of how its interaction provided it with sufficient evidence. This documentation might include memoranda, e-mails, and instructions or directions to and from management to company employees....

The evidential matter constituting reasonable support for management's assessment would ordinarily include documentation of how management formed its conclusion about the effectiveness of the company's entity-level and other pervasive elements of ICFR that its applicable framework describes as necessary for an effective system of internal control.

3. Multiple Location Considerations

Management's consideration of financial reporting risks generally includes all of its locations or business units. Management may determine that financial reporting risks are adequately addressed by controls which operate centrally, in which case the evaluation approach is similar to that of a business with a single location or business unit. When the controls necessary to address financial reporting risks operate at more than one location or business unit, management would generally evaluate evidence of the operation of the controls at the individual locations or business units.

Management may determine that the ICFR risk of the controls ...that operate at individual locations or business units is low. In such situations, management may determine that evidence gathered through self-assessment routines or other on-going monitoring activities, when combined with the evidence derived from a centralized control that monitors the results of operations at individual locations, constitutes sufficient evidence for the evaluation. In other situations, management may determine that, because of the complexity or judgment in the operation of the controls at the individual location, the risk that controls will fail to operate is high, and therefore more evidence is needed about the effective operation of the controls at the location....

P. 517

B. Reporting Considerations

1. Evaluation of Control Deficiencies

In order to determine whether a control deficiency, or combination of control deficiencies, is a material weakness, management evaluates the severity of each control deficiency that comes to its attention. Control deficiencies that are determined to be a material weakness must be disclosed in management's annual report on its assessment of the effectiveness of ICFR. Control deficiencies that are considered to be significant deficiencies are reported to the company's audit committee and the external auditor pursuant to management's compliance with the certification requirements in Exchange Act Rule 13a-14.

Management may not disclose that it has assessed ICFR as effective if one or more deficiencies in ICFR are determined to be a material weakness. As part of the evaluation of ICFR, management considers whether each deficiency, individually or in combination, is a material weakness as of the end of the fiscal year....

The evaluation of the severity of a control deficiency should include both quantitative and qualitative factors....

Risk factors affect whether there is a reasonable possibility that a deficiency, or a combination of deficiencies, will result in a misstatement of a financial statement amount or disclosure. These factors include, but are not limited to, the following:

- The nature of the financial reporting elements involved (for example, suspense accounts and related party transactions involve greater risk);
- The susceptibility of the related asset or liability to loss or fraud (that is, greater susceptibility increases risk);
- The subjectivity, complexity, or extent of judgment required to determine that amount involved (that is, greater subjectivity, complexity, or judgment, like that related to an accounting estimate, increases risk);
- The interaction or relationship of the control with other controls, including whether they are interdependent or redundant;
- The interaction of the deficiencies (that is, when evaluating a combination of two or more deficiencies, whether the deficiencies could affect the same financial statement amounts or disclosures); and

- The possible future consequences of the deficiency.

Factors that affect the magnitude of the misstatement that might result from a deficiency or deficiencies in ICFR include, but are not limited to, the following:

- The financial statement amounts or total of transactions exposed to the deficiency; and
- The volume of activity in the account balance or class of transactions exposed to the deficiency that has occurred in the current period or that is expected in future periods.

In evaluating the magnitude of the potential misstatement, the maximum amount that an account balance or total of transactions can be overstated is generally the recorded amount, while understatements could be larger. Also, in many cases, the probability of a small misstatement will be greater than the probability of a large misstatement.

Management should evaluate the effect of compensating controls when determining whether a control deficiency or combination of deficiencies is a material weakness. To have a mitigating effect, the compensating control should operate at a level of precision that would prevent or detect a misstatement that could be material.

In determining whether a deficiency or a combination of deficiencies represents a material weakness, management considers all relevant information. Management should evaluate whether the following situations indicate a deficiency in ICFR exists and, if so, whether it represents a material weakness:

- Identification of fraud, whether or not material, on the part of senior management;
- Restatement of previously issued financial statements to reflect the correction of a material misstatement;
- Identification of a material misstatement of the financial statements in the current period in circumstances that indicate the misstatement would not have been detected by the company's ICFR; and
- Ineffective oversight of the company's external financial reporting and internal control over financial reporting by the company's audit committee.

P. 517

When evaluating the severity of a deficiency, or a combination of deficiencies, in ICFR, management also should determine the level of detail and degree of assurance that would satisfy prudent officials in the conduct of their own affairs that they have reasonable assurance that transactions are recorded as necessary to permit the preparation of financial statements in conformity with GAAP. If management determines that the deficiency, or combination of deficiencies, might prevent prudent officials in the conduct of their own affairs from concluding that they have reasonable assurance that transactions are recorded as necessary to permit the preparation of financial statements in conformity with GAAP, then management should treat the deficiency, or combination of deficiencies, as an indicator of a material weakness.

2. Expression of Assessment of Effectiveness of ICFR by Management

Management should clearly disclose its assessment of the effectiveness of ICFR and, therefore, should not qualify its assessment by stating that the company's ICFR is effective subject to certain qualifications or exceptions. For example, management should not state that the company's controls and procedures are effective except to the extent that certain material weakness(es) have been identified. In addition, if a material weakness exists, management may not state that the company's ICFR is effective. However, management may state that controls are ineffective for specific reasons.

3. Disclosures about Material Weaknesses

The Commission's rule implementing Section 404 was intended to bring information about material weaknesses in ICFR into public view. Because of the significance of the disclosure requirements surrounding material weaknesses beyond specifically stating that the material weaknesses exist, companies should also consider including the following in their disclosures:

- The nature of any material weakness,
- Its impact on the company's financial reporting and its ICFR, and
- Management's current plans, if any, or actions already undertaken, for remediating the material weakness.

Disclosure of the existence of a material weakness is important, but there is other information that also may be material and necessary to form an overall picture that is not misleading. The goal underlying all disclosure in this area is to provide an investor with disclosure and analysis that goes beyond describing the mere existing of a material weakness. There are many different types of material weaknesses and many different factors that may be important to the assessment of the potential effect of any particular material weakness. While management is required to conclude and state in its report that ICFR is ineffective when there are one or more material weaknesses, companies should also consider providing disclosure that allows investors to understand the cause of the control deficiency and to assess the potential impact of each particular material weakness. This disclosure will be more useful to investors if management differentiates the potential impact and importance to the financial statements of the identified material weaknesses, including distinguishing those material weaknesses that may have a pervasive impact on ICFR from those material weaknesses that do not.

4. Impact of a Restatement of Previously Issued Financial Statements on Management's Report on ICFR

Item 308 of Regulation S-K requires disclosure of management's assessment of the effectiveness of the company's ICFR as of the end of the company's most recent fiscal year. When a material misstatement of previously issued financial statements is discovered, a company is required to restate those financial statements. However, the restatement of financial statements does not, by itself, necessitate that management consider the effect of the restatement on the company's prior conclusion related to the effectiveness of ICFR.

While there is no requirement for management to reassess or revise its conclusion related to the effectiveness of ICFR, management should consider whether its original disclosures are still appropriate and should modify or supplement its original disclosure to include any other material information that is necessary for such disclosures not to be misleading in light of the restatement. The company should also disclose any material changes to ICFR, as required by Item 308(c) of Regulation S-K.

Similarly, while there is no requirement that management reassess or revise its conclusion related to the effectiveness of its disclosure controls and procedures, management should consider

P. 517

whether its original disclosures regarding effectiveness of disclosure controls and procedures need to be modified or supplemented to include any other material information that is necessary for such disclosures not to be misleading. With respect to the disclosures concerning ICFR and disclosure controls and procedures, the company may need to disclose in this context what impact, if any, the restatement has on its original conclusions regarding effectiveness of ICFR and disclosure controls and procedures.

5. Inability to Assess Certain Aspects of ICFR

In certain circumstances, management may encounter difficulty in assessing certain aspects of its ICFR. For example, management may outsource a significant process to a service organization and determine that evidence of the operating effectiveness of the controls over that process is necessary....

Id. at 2307–2319.

The Commission's adoption of confirming amendments in Rules 13a-15(c) and 15d-15(d) and Item 308 of Regulations S-B and S-K was in Sec. Act Rel. 8809, 90 SEC Dock. 2289 (2007) (adoption). This Release also adopted amendments to Regulation S-X, most significantly 1-02(p), a new definition of *material weakness* that provides:

The term *material weakness* is a deficiency, or a combination of deficiencies, in internal control over financial reporting...such that there is a reasonable possibility that a material misstatement of the registrant's annual or interim financial statements will not be prevented or detected on a timely basis.

An identical definition of *material weakness* was also made to Rule 12b-2.

In Sec. Act Rel. 8811, 90 SEC Dock. 2331 (2007), the Commission requested additional comments on the term *significant deficiency*, which is likely to be the basis of a future definition in the SEC rules.

In January 2007 the GAO published Securities and Exchange Commission: Internal Control over Financial Reporting in

Exchange Act Periodic Reports of Non-Accelerated Filers and Newly Public Companies (GAO-07-305R).

In April 2007 the Commissioners endorsed recommendations offered by the staff for §404 and recommended that the SEC staff work with the PCAOB in this regard.

Subsequently in 2007 the SEC approved the PCAOB's Auditing Standard No. 5, An Audit of Internal Control over Financial Reporting That Is Integrated with an Audit of Financial Statements, replacing Auditing Standard No. 2, see Sec. Ex. Act Rel. 56,152, 91 SEC Dock. 522 (2007) (adoption); and adopted a definition of *significant deficiency*. See Sec. Act Rel. 8829, 91 SEC Dock. 726 (2007) (adoption). The PCAOB had earlier adopted Auditing Standard No. 5. See PCAOB Rel. 2007-005 (May 24, 2007).

In 2007 the Commission staff's Frequently Asked Questions, Management's Report on Internal Control over Financial Reporting and Certification of Disclosure in Exchange Act Periodic Reports was updated. A copy of the FAQs is available on the SEC's Web site at http://sec.gov/info/accountants/controlfaq.htm.

In October 2007 the PCAOB issued Preliminary Staff Views — An Audit of Internal Control That Is Integrated with an Audit of Financial Statements: Guidance for Auditors of Smaller Public Companies, a copy of which is available on the PCAOB's Web site at http://pcaob.org/standards/standards_and_related_rules/as5/guidance.pdf.

In early 2008 the SEC proposed delaying for an additional year smaller public company compliance with §404(b) and indicated that the staff had undertaken a cost-benefit analysis of §404(b) compliance. See Sec. Act Rel. 8889, 92 SEC Dock. 1485 (2008) (proposal); SEC Press Rel. 2008-8 (Feb. 1, 2008).

3. ADMINISTRATIVE PROCEEDINGS

a. Voluntary Delisting

P. 521, after 1st full par. In 2007 the Commission adopted new rules permitting termination of a foreign private issuer's registration of a class of securities under §12(g) and the duty to file reports under §13(a) or 15(d) of the 1934 Act. Sec. Ex. Act Rel. 55,540, 90 SEC Dock. 860 (2007) (adoption). As adopted Rule 12h-6 and the accompanying rule amendments:

- permit a foreign private issuer, regardless of size, to terminate its Exchange Act registration and reporting obligations regarding a class of equity securities, assuming it meets all the other conditions of Rule 12h-6, if, for a recent 12-month period, the U.S. ADTV of the subject class of securities has been no greater than 5 percent of its worldwide ADTV—rather than 5 percent of the ADTV in its primary trading market, as reproposed;
- permit an issuer to include off-market transactions, including transactions through alternative trading systems, when calculating its worldwide ADTV for a class of equity securities...as long as the trading volume information regarding the off-market transactions is reasonably reliable and does not duplicate other trading volume information regarding the subject class of securities;
- require an issuer to wait 12 months before filing its Form 15F in reliance on the trading volume standard if the issuer has delisted its class of equity securities from a national securities exchange or automated inter-dealer quotation system in the United States, or terminated a sponsored ADR facility and, at the time of delisting or termination, the U.S. ADTV of the subject class of securities exceeded 5 percent of its worldwide ADTV for the preceding 12 months;
- retain the 300-holder standard as an alternative to the trading volume standard for an equity securities issuer and as the quantitative standard for a debt securities issuer...
- exclude convertible debt and other equity-linked securities from the definition of equity security for the purpose of new Rule 12h-6's trading volume provision;
- require an equity securities registrant to have at least one year of Exchange Act reporting, be current in reporting obligations for that period, and have filed at least one Exchange Act annual report...;
- permit an issuer to count a special financial report filed pursuant to Exchange Act Rule 15d-2 as an Exchange Act

annual report for the purpose of the new rule's prior reporting condition;
- prohibit an issuer of equity securities from selling securities in the United States in a registered offering under the Securities Act, except as specified, during the 12 months preceding the filing of its Form 15F (the *dormancy condition*)...;
- require an issuer of equity securities to have maintained a listing of the subject class of securities for at least the 12 months preceding the filing of its Form 15F on one or more exchanges in a foreign jurisdiction that, either singly or together with the trading of the same class of the issuer's securities in another foreign jurisdiction, constitutes the primary trading market for those securities...;
- define primary trading market to mean that at least 55 percent of the trading in a foreign private issuer's class of securities that is the subject of Form 15F took place in, on or through the facilities of a securities market or markets in a single foreign jurisdiction or in no more than two foreign jurisdictions during a recent 12-month period, as long as the trading in at least one of the two foreign jurisdictions is larger than the trading in the United States for the same class of the issuer's securities;
- permit an equity securities issuer relying on the alternative 300-holder standard, or a debt securities issuer, to use a revised counting method that limits the inquiry regarding the amount of securities represented by accounts of customers resident in the United States to brokers, dealers, banks and other nominees located in the United States, the foreign private issuer's jurisdiction of incorporation, legal organization of establishment, and the one or two jurisdictions comprising the issuer's primary trading market if different from the issuer's jurisdiction of incorporation, legal organization or establishment...;
- permit an issuer of equity or debt securities to rely on the assistance of an independent information services provider when determining whether the issuer falls below the 300-holder standard...;
- permit a successor issuer meeting specified conditions to terminate its Exchange Act reporting obligations under new Rule 12h-6...;

- permit a foreign private issuer that filed a Form 15 and suspended or terminated its Exchange Act reporting obligations under the current exit rules before the effective date of Rule 12h-6 to terminate its Exchange Act reporting obligations under new Exchange Act Rule 12h-6, as long as, if regarding a class of equity securities, the issuer meets Rule 12h-6's listing condition and either the trading volume or alternative-300 holder condition or, if regarding a class of debt securities, the issuer meets the rule's 300-holder condition for debt issuers;
- extend the Rule 12g3-2(b) exemption to a foreign private issuer of equity securities, including a successor issuer and prior Form 15 filer, immediately upon its termination of reporting under Rule 12h-6, and require the issuer to maintain that exemption by publishing in English specified material home country documents required by Rule 12g3-2(b) on its Internet Web site or through an electronic information delivery system generally available to the public in its primary trading market...;
- permit a non-reporting company that has received or will receive the Rule 12g3-2(b) exemption, upon application to the Commission and not pursuant to Rule 12h-6, to publish its *ongoing* home country documents required under Rule 12g3-2(b) on its Internet Web site or through an electronic information delivery system rather than submit them in paper to the Commission; and
- permit an issuer that has filed a Form 15F to terminate its Exchange Act reporting obligations regarding a class of debt securities to establish the Rule 12g3-2(b) exemption for a class of equity securities upon the effectiveness of its termination of reporting under Rule 12h-6, by submitting an application for the Rule 12g3-2(b) exemption after filing its Form 15F.

C. PROXIES

1. THE PROBLEM (HEREIN OF COSTS OF SOLICITATION)

P. 534 n.17, end note. In The Case for Shareholder Access to the Ballot, 59 Bus. Law. 43, 46 (2003), Professor Bebchuk summarized the incidence of contested proxy solicitations between 1996 and 2002:

Year	Contested Solicitations	Contests Not over Election of Directors	Directors Contests over Sale, Acquisition, or Closed-End Fund Restructuring	Director Contests over Alternative Management Team
2002	38	5	19	14
2001	40	8	16	16
2000	30	6	17	7
1999	30	10	7	13
1998	20	1	6	13
1997	29	12	12	5
1996	28	11	8	9
TOTAL	215	53	85	77

2. THE STATUTORY PROVISIONS AND GENERAL PROXY RULES

c. Coverage, Definitions, and Exemptions

P. 539, new text, end page. In 2005 the Commission proposed amendments to Rules 14a-2, 14a-3, 14a-4, 14a-7, 14a-8, 14a-12, 14a-13, 14b-1, 14b-2, 14c-2, 14c-3, 14c-5, 14c-7, Schedule A, Schedule C, Form 10-K, Form 10-KSB, Form 10-Q, Form 10-QSB, and Form N-SAR to provide an alternative method for issuers and third persons to furnish proxy materials by posting them on the Internet. Shareholders would be given notice of the availability of the proxy materials and could obtain copies at no cost. These proposals would not apply to business combination transactions. All existing methods of furnishing proxy materials would continue to be available. Sec. Ex. Act Rel. 52,926, 86 SEC Dock. 2145 (2005) (proposal).

The proposal Release crisply summarized the immediate background of these proposals:

> In 2000, we discussed an "access equals delivery" model and an implied consent model as possible alternatives to the existing electronic delivery conditions. In our 2000 Interpretive Release, we described the "access equals delivery" model as one under which "investors would be assumed to have access to the Internet, thereby allowing delivery to be accomplished *solely* by an issuer posting a document on the issuer's or a third party's Web site." In that release, we also described the "implied consent" model as one that would allow an issuer to rely on electronic delivery if intended recipients did not affirmatively object when notified of the issuer's or intermediary's intention to deliver documents in an electronic format.
>
> We did not take action regarding either of those models in 2000. With the passage of five years and the increased use of the Internet as a means to quickly, reliably, and inexpensively disseminate information, we think it is again appropriate to consider the effect that technological developments have had on making information available and propose an alternative model for furnishing proxy materials.
>
> More than 10.7 million beneficial shareholders already have given their consent to electronic delivery of proxy materials and approximately 85% of their shares were voted electronically or telephonically during the 2005 proxy season. Moreover, recent data indicates that up to 75% of Americans have access to the Internet in their homes, and that this percentage is increasing steadily among all age groups.
>
> In connection with our recent Securities Offering Reform effort, we adopted new Securities Act Rule 172, which implements an "access equals delivery" model in the context of final prospectus delivery. Under Rule 172, a final prospectus is deemed to precede or accompany a security for sale for purposes of Securities Act Section 5(b)(2) so long as the company offering the security files with the Commission a final prospectus meeting the requirements of Securities Act Section 10(a) as part of the registration statement pursuant to Securities Act Rule 424.

> Investors will be able to access the electronically filed final prospectus on EDGAR, but no longer will receive a copy unless they request one.

Id. at 2148–2149.

The proposed rule changes were intended to similarly update the proxy system:

> We are proposing amendments to the proxy rules to update our regulatory framework to take advantage of communications technology and provide an alternative proxy model that could reduce the printing and mailing costs associated with furnishing proxy materials to shareholders. The proposed amendments would provide an alternative method for furnishing proxy materials to shareholders based on a "notice and access" model. Under the proposals, an issuer would be able to satisfy its obligations under the Commission's proxy rules by posting its proxy materials on a specified, publicly-accessible Internet Web site (other than the Commission's EDGAR Web site) and providing shareholders with a notice informing them that the materials are available and explaining how to access those materials. These proposals are intended to establish procedures that would promote use of the Internet as a reliable and cost-efficient means of making proxy materials available to shareholders. The proposed amendments would provide a new alternative to existing methods of furnishing proxy materials, which would not be affected by the proposal....
>
> The proposed amendments would require an issuer that is relying on the proposed "notice and access" model to provide a shareholder with a copy of the materials upon request (in papers or by e-mail, as requested). A soliciting person other than the issuer may choose not to provide a copy of its proxy materials to a requesting shareholder if the person is conducting a conditional "electronic only" proxy solicitation and soliciting proxy authority only from shareholders willing to electronically access the soliciting person's proxy materials.
>
> Under the proposed "notice and access" model, the issuer would be able to send a notice to shareholders (the "Notice of Internet Availability of Proxy Materials" or "Notice") at least 30 days before the meeting, or if no meeting is to be held, at least 30 days before the date the votes, consents, or authorizations may be used to effect a corporate action, indicating that the issuer's proxy materials are

available on a specified Internet Web site and explaining how to access those proxy materials. The Notice also would explain the procedure for requesting a copy of the materials, if a shareholder desires such a copy.

...The amendments would permit a soliciting person to choose to rely on the proposed model as a means of furnishing some proxy-related documents to shareholders and use other means, such as paper documents, with regard to other proxy-related materials. For example, an issuer could choose to use the "notice and access" model for its proxy statement and to furnish its annual report to security holders (commonly referred to as the "glossy annual report") in paper through the U.S. mail.

Id. at 2147.

Specifically the proposed alternative means would apply to:

- Notices of shareholder meetings;
- Schedule 14A proxy statements and consent solicitation statements;
- Proxy cards;
- Schedule 14C information statements;
- Annual reports to security holders;
- Additional soliciting materials; and
- Any amendments to such materials that are required to be furnished to shareholders.

Id. at 2149.

The proposal Release specifically stated with respect to the notice and access procedure:

To notify shareholders of the availability of the proxy materials on the specified Internet Web site, an issuer relying on the proposed "notice and access" model would have to send a Notice of Internet Availability of Proxy Materials to shareholders 30 days or more in advance of the shareholder meeting date or, if no meeting is to be held, 30 days or more in advance of the date that votes, consents, or authorizations may be used to effect the corporate actions to be voted on. The 30-day period is to provide shareholders with sufficient time to receive the Notice, request copies of the materials, if desired, and review the proxy materials prior to voting. We would view the Notice as additional soliciting material that would have to be filed with the Commission pursuant to Rule 14a-6(b) no later than the date it is first sent or given to shareholders.

The proposed Notice of Internet Availability of Proxy Materials and the notice of a shareholder meeting required under state corporation law could be combined together into a single document, unless prohibited by state law. The Notice could not be combined with any document other than the state law meeting notice. We believe that it is important for the Notice to be furnished in a way that brings it to each shareholder's attention. Therefore, whether or not combined with the state law meeting notice, the Notice of Internet Availability of Proxy Materials must be sent separately from other types of shareholder communications and may not accompany any materials other than the proxy card and return envelope.

The Notice of Internet Availability of Proxy Materials would have to include the following information in clear and understandable terms:

- A prominent legend in bold-face type that states:

   "**Important Notice Regarding the Availability of Proxy Materials for the Shareholder Meeting to Be Held on [insert meeting date].**
    - **This communication presents only an overview of the more complete proxy materials that are available to you on the Internet. We encourage you to access and review all of the important information contained in the proxy materials before voting.**
    - **The [proxy statement] [information statement] [annual report to shareholders] [proxy card] are available at [insert Web site address].**
    - **If you want to receive a paper or e-mail copy of these documents, you must request one. There is no charge to you for requesting a copy. Please make your request for a copy as instructed below on or before [insert a date that is two weeks or more before the meeting date] to facilitate timely delivery. If you hold your shares through a broker, bank, or other intermediary, you must request delivery of a copy of the proxy materials through that intermediary, but it likely will take longer

P. 539 2010 SUPPLEMENT

to receive your materials through an intermediary than directly from the company."
- The date, time and location of the meeting or, if corporate action is to be taken by written consent, the earliest date on which the corporation action may be effected;
- A clear and impartial identification of each separate matter intended to be acted upon and the issuer's recommendations regarding those matters, but no supporting statements;
- A list of the materials being made available at the specified Web site; and
- (1) a toll-free telephone number, and (2) an e-mail address where the shareholder can request a copy of the proxy materials.

Only the information specified above and, if it is being combined with the state law meeting notice, any information required by state law, could be included in the Notice. To ensure that the Notice is clear and understandable, it would have to meet substantially the same plain English principles as apply to key sections of Securities Act prospectuses pursuant to Securities Act Rule 421(d).

Id. at 2150.

The proposal Release also elaborated on the Internet Web site:

All proxy materials to be furnished through the "notice and access" model, other than additional soliciting materials, would have to be posted on a specified Internet Web site by the time the issuer sends the Notice of Internet Availability of Proxy Materials to shareholders. These materials would have to remain on that Web site and be accessible to shareholders through the time of the related shareholder meeting, at no charge to the shareholder. ...[T]he Notice must clearly identify the Internet Web site address at which the materials are available. The Internet Web site address must be specific enough to lead shareholders directly to the proxy materials, rather than to the home page or other section of the Web site on which the proxy materials are posted, so that shareholders do not have to browse the Web site to find the materials. The Internet Web site that an issuer uses to electronically furnish its proxy materials to shareholders must be a publicly accessible Internet Web site other than the Commission's EDGAR Web site.

There are two primary reasons why we propose not to allow use of the EDGAR Web site for this purpose. First, issuers are not required to furnish their glossy annual reports to the Commission using the EDGAR system. Most issuers, therefore, furnish paper copies of these annual reports to the Commission. Even with respect to the issuers that choose to furnish the annual report to the Commission via EDGAR, they generally omit graphics included in the paper version, such as charts and tables, from their EDGAR submissions. Second, it is our view that electronically posted proxy materials should be presented on the Internet Web site in a format that provides a substantially identical version of those materials, including all charts, tables, graphics, and similarly formatted information, as otherwise furnished to shareholders in a different medium such as paper. Currently, the EDGAR system accepts documents only in ASCII or HTML format. Further, documents filed on EDGAR may omit or describe, but generally do not replicate, some disclosures, including charts and graphs. As a result, merely hyperlinking from the specified publicly accessible Internet Web site to the filing on the Commission's EDGAR system would not satisfy the requirement.

Id. at 2154.

Notably the proposed proxy revisions also apply to intermediaries such as banks circulating materials to beneficial owners under Rules 14a-13, 14b-1, and 14b-2, id. at 2156–2159, and to soliciting persons other than issuers who proceed under Rules 14a-7 and 14a-12, id. at 2159–2162.

In 2007 the Commission adopted amendments to the proxy rules substantially as proposed that permit issuers and other persons to furnish proxy materials to shareholders by posting them on an Internet Web site *and* notifying shareholders of the availability of the proxy materials. Sec. Ex. Act Rel. 55,146, 89 SEC Dock. 2489 (2007) (adoption).

This is a voluntary system. Issuers and shareholders and other persons conducting their own proxy solicitations are not required to participate. The Commission later adopted amendments to Rules 14a-7, 14a-16, 14b-1, 14b-2, 14c-2, and 14c-3 to *require* that issuers and other soliciting persons furnish proxy materials on an Internet Web site and provide shareholders with notice of the

P. 539 2010 SUPPLEMENT

availability of the proxy materials. Sec. Ex. Act Rels. 55,147, 89 SEC Dock. 2525 (2007) (proposal) 56,135, 91 SEC Dock. 345 (2007) (adoption).

The initial adoption Release explained:

> Under the final rules...an issuer may satisfy its obligations under the Commission's proxy rules to furnish proxy materials to shareholders in connection with a proxy solicitation by posting its proxy materials on a publicly-accessible Internet Web site (other than the Commission's EDGAR Web site) and sending a Notice of Internet Availability of Proxy Materials (*Notice*) to shareholders at least 40 calendar days before the shareholder meeting date indicating that the proxy materials are available and explaining how to access those materials. Shareholders must have a means to execute a proxy as of the time on which the Notice is sent. The Notice also must explain how a shareholder can request a copy of the proxy materials and how a shareholder can indicate a preference to receive a paper or e-mail copy of any proxy materials distributed under the notice and access model in the future. An issuer may not send a proxy card along with the Notice; however, 10 calendar days or more after sending the Notice, the issuer may send a proxy card to shareholders. If an issuer chooses to send a proxy card without a copy of the proxy statement under this provision, a copy of the Notice must accompany the proxy card so that recipients will be notified again about the Web site on which the proxy statement is accessible. Finally, the notice and access model may not be used in conjunction with a proxy solicitation related to a business combination transaction.
>
> Shareholders and other persons conducting their own proxy solicitations may rely on the notice and access model under requirements substantially similar to the requirements that would apply to issuers. As a result, these rules may have the effect of reducing the cost of engaging in a proxy contest. However, unlike the requirements for an issuer, a soliciting person other than the issuer may selectively choose the shareholders from whom it desires to solicit proxies without the need to send an information statement to all other shareholders.
>
> The new rules do not affect the availability of other means of providing proxy materials to shareholders, such as obtaining affirmative consents for electronic delivery pursuant to existing

Commission guidance. Thus, an issuer may rely on affirmative consents to furnish proxy materials to some shareholders, and rely on the notice and access model to furnish the materials to others....

Under Rule 14a-16(a), an issuer may furnish a proxy statement under Rule 14a-3(a), or an annual report under Rule 14a-3(b) by sending a Notice of Internet Availability of Proxy Materials 40 calendar days or more before the date of relevant votes, consents, or authorizations. All materials identified in the Notice must be publicly accessible, and free of charge at the Web site address specified in the Notice on or before the time the Notice is sent and continue to be available on the Web through the conclusion of the meeting of shareholders. Rule 14a-16(b)(1). Materials on the Web site must be presented in a format that is convenient either for reading online or printing on paper. Rule 14a-16(c)(1).

The Notice of Internet Availability is required by Rule 14a-16(d) to contain:

(1) A prominent legend in bold-face type that states:

Important Notice Regarding the Availability of Proxy materials for the Shareholder Meeting to Be Held on [insert meeting date].

1. This communication presents only an overview of the more complete proxy materials that are available to you on the Internet. We encourage you to access and review all of the important information contained in the proxy materials before voting.

2. The [proxy statement] [information statement] [annual report to security holders] [[is/are] available at [insert Web site address].

3. If you want to receive a paper or e-mail copy of these documents, you must request one. There is no charge to you for requesting a copy. Please make your request for a copy as instructed on or before [insert a date] to facilitate timely delivery.;

(2) The date, time, and location of the meeting or, if corporate action is to be taken by written consent, the earliest date on which the corporate action may be effected;

(3) A clear and impartial identification of each separate matter intended to be acted on and the soliciting person's recommendations regarding those matters, but no supporting statements;

(4) A list of the materials being made available at the specified Web site;

(5) A toll-free telephone number, an e-mail address, and an Internet Web site where the security holder can request a copy of the proxy statement, annual report to security holders, and form of proxy, relating to all of the registrant's future security holder meetings and for the particular meeting to which the proxy materials being furnished relate;

(6) Any control/identification numbers that the security holder needs to access his or her form of proxy;

(7) Instructions on how to access the form of proxy, provided that such instructions do not enable a security holder to execute a proxy without having access to the proxy statement and, if required by [Rule]14a-3(b), the annual report to security holders; and

(8) Information on how to obtain directions to be able to attend the meeting and vote in person.

The Notice of Internet Availability may not be combined with another document unless the other document is required by state law. Rule 14a-16(e)(1).

Similarly, Rule 14a-16(f)(1) specifies that the Notice of Internet Availability must be sent separately from most other types of security holder communications including the form of proxy. The form of proxy only may be sent ten or more calendar days after the Notice of Internet Availability. Rule 14a-16(h). If the form of proxy is not accompanied or preceded by a copy of the proxy statement and annual report that is required by Rule 14a-3(b), then the registrant must accompany the form of proxy with a Notice of Internet Availability. Ibid.

Plain English is required by Rule 14a-16(g).

At no cost, the registrant is required by Rule 14a-16(j)(1) to send by first class mail or other reasonably prompt means a paper copy of the proxy statement, information statement, annual report to shareholders, and form of proxy, to the extent any of these documents is required, to any record holder or responder bank requesting such a copy within three business days after receiving the request. Under Rule 14a-16(j)(2) there is a similar obligation to provide electronic copies.

The intermediary is required to provide specified information in its Notice that is applicable only to beneficial owners:

- (1) A toll-free telephone number of the intermediary or its agent, (2) an e-mail address of the intermediary or its agent, and (3) an Internet Web site of the intermediary or its agent where the shareholder can request a copy of the proxy materials, for all meetings and for the particular meeting to which the Notice relates;
- Any control/identification numbers that the beneficial owner needs to access his or her request for voting instructions;
- Instructions on how to access the request for voting instructions on the Web site of the intermediary or its agent, provided that such instructions do not enable a beneficial owner to provide voting instructions without having access to the proxy statement and annual report;
- Information on how to obtain directions to be able to attend the meeting and vote in person; and
- A brief description, if applicable, of the rules that permit the intermediary to vote the securities if the beneficial owner does not return his or her voting instructions.

The intermediary's Notice must contain instructions on how to access the request for voting instructions on the Web site of the intermediary or its agent. Such information should include any control or identification numbers necessary for the beneficial owner to provide voting instructions. However, the intermediary's Notice cannot include a means, such as a telephone number, which would enable the beneficial owner to provide voting instructions without having access to the proxy statement and annual report. A telephone number that a beneficial owner can use to provide voting instructions may be provided on the Internet Web site on which the request for voting instructions is posted (as well as on a paper request for voting instructions sent to shareholders 10 days or more after the intermediary's Notice was sent). Like an issuer, the intermediary cannot include a request for voting instructions with its Notice....

A solicitation in opposition to the issuer's proposals to be voted on at a shareholder meeting often is not initiated until after the issuer has filed its proxy statement....Therefore, the amendments require a soliciting person other than the issuer that is following the Notice and Access Model to send out its Notice by the later of: (1) 40 calendar days prior to the meeting; or (2) 10 calendar days after the issuer first sends out its proxy statement or Notice to shareholders....

The content of the Notice sent by a soliciting person other than the issuer could be different from the content of the issuer's Notice. For example, if a solicitation in opposition is launched before the issuer has sent its own proxy statement or Notice, the full shareholder meeting agenda may not be known to the soliciting person at the time it sends its Notice to shareholders. In such a case, the soliciting person must include the agenda items in its Notice only to the extent known.

Also, there may be circumstances in which a person soliciting proxies in opposition to the issuer may provide a partial proxy card, that is, a proxy card soliciting proxy authority only for the agenda items in which the soliciting person is interested rather than for all of the items, or presenting only a partial slate of directors. Typically, such a proxy would revoke any previously-executed proxy and the shareholder may lose his or her ability to vote on matters or directors other than those presented on the soliciting person's card. To prevent a shareholder from unknowingly invalidating his or her vote on those other matters, a person soliciting in opposition that is presenting such a card to shareholders must indicate clearly on its Notice whether execution of that card will invalidate the shareholder's earlier vote on the other matters or directors reflected on the issuer's proxy card....

In 2008 the Commission adopted amendments to Rules 14a-2, 14a-6, and 14a-8, new Rules 14a-17 and 14a-18, and amendments to Schedules 13G and 14A to include in proxy materials proposals for bylaw amendments regarding processes for nominating board candidates and to provide shareholders with additional information about proposal proponents and shareholders who nominate a candidate under the new procedures. Sec. Ex. Act Rels. 56,160, 91 SEC Dock. 544 (2007) (proposal); 57,172, 92 SEC Dock. 1202 (2008) (adoption).

Separately the Commission published a new interpretation to clarify the meaning of the Rule 14a-8(i)(8) exclusion of shareholder proposals related to the board. Sec. Ex. Act Rel. 56,161, 91 SEC Dock. 575 (2007) (proposal).

Both the rule proposals and the interpretation were a response to American Fed. of State, County & Mun. Employees v. American Int'l Group, Inc., 462 F.3d 121 (2d Cir. 2006).

The paired proposals were noteworthy for taking diametrically opposed views of shareholder access, with Chairman Cox siding both with Democrats Campos and Nazareth and separately with Republicans Atkins and Casey to precipitate a novel debate that subsequently took a quite unexpected turn when Campos resigned and Nazareth chose not to seek renomination. See SEC Votes to Issue Diametrically Opposed Proposals, 39 Sec. Reg. & L. Rep. (BNA) 1169 (2007).

The rule proposal Release stated in part:

> Rule 14a-8(i)(8) sets forth one of several substantive bases upon which a company may exclude a shareholder proposal from its proxy materials. Specifically, it provides that a company need not include a proposal that "relates to an election for membership on the company's board of directors or analogous governing body." The purpose of this provision is to prevent the circumvention of other proxy rules that are carefully crafted to ensure that investors receive adequate disclosure and an opportunity to make informed voting decisions in election contests. Last year, the U.S. Court of Appeals for the Second Circuit, in *American Federation of State, County and Municipal Employees, Employees Pension Plan v. American International Group, Inc.* [*AFSCME*] held that AIG could not rely on Rule 14a-8(i)(8) to exclude a shareholder bylaw proposal under which the company would be required, under specified circumstances, to include shareholder nominees for director in the company's proxy materials at subsequent meetings.
>
> The effect of the *AFSCME* decision was to permit both the bylaw proposal and, had the bylaw been adopted, subsequent election contests conducted under it, to *be* included in the company's proxy materials, but without compliance with the disclosure requirements of Rule 14a-12 solicitations. Because of the importance that we attach to the provision of meaningful disclosure to investors in election contests, we are revisiting the provisions of Rule 14a-8 in

P. 539

light of the *AFSCME* decision with a proposal that is designed to ensure that this objective is consistently achieved....

To achieve the mutually reinforcing objectives of vindicating shareholders' state law rights to nominate directors, on the one hand, and ensuring full disclosure in election contests, on the other hand, we are proposing revisions to Rule 14a-8(i)(8) that would permit a shareholder who makes full disclosure in connection with a bylaw proposal for director nomination procedures, including a proposal such as that in the *AFSCME* case, to have that proposal included in the company's proxy materials. The basis for the disclosure that we are proposing is the familiar Schedule 13G regime, under which certain passive investors that beneficially own more than 5% of a company's securities, report their ownership of a company's securities. We believe that using this well-understood system of disclosure should reduce compliance costs for companies and shareholders. In addition, because shareholders eligible to file under Schedule 13G must not have acquired or held their securities for the purpose of or with the effect of changing or influencing the control of the company, the opportunity to use Rule 14a-8 to inappropriately circumvent the disclosure and procedural regulations that are intended to apply in contested elections should be minimized.

Under the proposed amendments, if the proponents of a bylaw to establish a procedure for shareholder nominations of directors do not meet both the threshold for required filing on Schedule 13G, and the eligibility requirements to file on Schedule 13G, the proposal could then be excluded from the company's proxy materials under Rule 14a-8(i)(8). In this way, shareholders will be guaranteed the disclosure necessary to evaluate such proposals.

In light of the need for full disclosure where the possibility of control over a company is present, we believe that our decision to link the ability to include a bylaw proposal for director nominations in a company's proxy materials to the 5% threshold set by Section 13(d) of the Exchange Act addresses the basic policy concerns previously articulated by both Congress and the Commission. Moreover, because the proposed expansion of shareholders' ability to submit proposals under Rule 14a-8 would be limited to specific situations in which shareholders would be assured of appropriate disclosure and procedural protections, if the proposal did not meet the eligibility requirements of the amended rule, the

Commission's staff would continue to interpret the rule to permit companies to exclude the proposal.

Id. at 549.

Specifically, the Commission proposed an amendment to Rule 14a-8(i)(8) to enable shareholders to have their proposals for bylaw amendments regarding the procedures for nominating directors included in the company's proxy materials. The bylaw proposal would be required to be included in the proxy material if:

- The shareholder (or group of shareholders) that submits the proposal is eligible to file a Schedule 13G and files a Schedule 13G that includes specified public disclosures regarding its background and its interactions with the company;
- The proposal is submitted by a shareholder (or group of shareholders) that has continuously beneficially owned more than 5% of the company's securities entitled to be voted on the proposal at the meeting for at least one year by the date the shareholder submits the proposal; and
- The proposal otherwise satisfies the requirements of Rule 14a-8.

As amended, Rule 14a-8 would allow proponents of bylaw proposals to offer shareholder nomination procedures as they see fit. The only substantive limitations on such procedures would be those imposed by state law or the company's charter and bylaws. For example, the procedure could specify a minimum level of share ownership for those making director nominations that would be included in the company's proxy materials, specify the number of director slots subject to the procedure, or prescribe a method for the allocation of any costs — so long as both the form and substance of any such requirements were consistent with applicable state law and the company's charter and existing bylaw provisions. Likewise, the voting threshold required in order to adopt the bylaw would be determined by the thresholds set forth by state law or in the company's charter and bylaws with respect to the adoption of bylaws or bylaw amendments.

Id. at 550.

P. 539

To trigger these requirements, the Commission characterized as "an essential element...that the shareholder (or group of shareholders) proposing the bylaw provide disclosure about its own background, intent and course of dealings with the company to enable other shareholders to vote intelligently on the proposal." Id. at 550–551.

The Commission also proposed new Rule 14a-17 to require that the existing disclosure requirements for solicitations in opposition would apply to nominating shareholders and their nominees under *any* shareholder nomination procedure. "These disclosure requirements are found in Item 4(b), Item 5(b), Item 7, and Item 22(b) of Schedule 14A, and provide basic information regarding the nominating shareholder (or shareholder group) and nominee or nominees, including biography and shareholdings, other interests of the individuals (or group), methods and costs of the solicitation, and other information to enable voting shareholders to make an informed decision." Id. at 556.

Proposed Rule 14a-17(e), modeled on Rule 14a-8(l)(2), would provide that a shareholder who nominates a director under the proposed bylaw provision concerning the nomination of directors would be liable for any materially false statements in the disclosures included by the company in its proxy materials. The company itself would not be responsible for the shareholder's disclosures. Id. at 556.

Proposed Rule 14a-17(b) would require any nominating shareholder to provide to the company the disclosures required by Item 8A, 8B and 8C of Schedule 13G.

The Commission further proposed Rule 14a-18 to facilitate the use of electronic shareholder forums:

> We propose to facilitate greater online interaction among shareholders by removing obstacles in the current rules to the use of an electronic shareholder forum. To facilitate the establishment of such forums, which can be conducted and maintained in any number of ways, we propose to clarify that a company is not liable for independent statements by shareholders on a company's electronic shareholder forum. In addition, in order to enhance the efficacy of the forum, we propose to address any ambiguity concerning

whether use of an electronic shareholder forum could constitute a proxy solicitation.

Id. at 558–559.

The SEC also sought comment on requiring the inclusion of bylaw amendments concerning nonbinding shareholder proposals. Id. at 560.

In a separate proposal Release, Sec. Ex. Act Rel. 56,161, 91 SEC Dock. 575 (2007) (proposal), the Commission published an interpretation of the meaning of exclusion under Rule 14a-8(i)(8), as well as proposed amendments to Rule 14a-8(i)(8). This Release explained:

> In administering Rule 14a-8(i)(8), the staff has applied the following explanation of the election exclusion that the Commission gave in 1976 when it proposed the exclusion:
>
> > [T]he principal purpose of [Rule 14a-8(i)(8)] is to make clear, with respect to corporate elections, that Rule 14a-8 is not the proper means for conducting campaigns or effecting reforms in elections of that nature, since other proxy rules, including Rule 14a-11, are applicable thereto.
>
> In its application of the Commission's explanation, the staff has permitted companies to exclude any shareholder proposal that may result in a contested election. For purposes of Rule 14a-8, the staff has expressed the position that a proposal may result in a contested election if it is a means either to campaign for or against a director nominee or to require a company to include shareholder-nominated candidates in the company's proxy materials. The staff's position is consistent with the explanation that the Commission gave in 1976, and with the Commission's interpretation of the election exclusion.
>
> A recent decision by the U.S. Court of Appeals for the Second Circuit in *American Federation of State, County & Municipal Employees, Employees Pension Plan v. American International Group, Inc.*, addressed the application of the election exclusion. In that decision, the Second Circuit held that AIG could not rely on Rule 14a-8(i)(8) to exclude a shareholder proposal seeking to amend a company's bylaws to establish a procedure under which a company

would be required, in specified circumstances, to include shareholder nominees for director in the company's proxy materials. The Second Circuit interpreted the Commission's statement in 1976 as limiting the election exclusion "to shareholder proposals used to oppose solicitations dealing with an identified board seat in an upcoming election and reject[ing] the somewhat broader interpretation that the election exclusion applied to shareholder proposals that would institute procedures making such election contests more likely." It is the Commission's position that the election exclusion should not be limited in this way.

We are concerned that the Second Circuit's decision has resulted in uncertainty and confusion with respect to the appropriate application of Rule 14a-8(i)(8) and may lead to contested elections for directors without adequate disclosure. In this regard, not only are shareholders and companies unable to know with certainty whether a proposal that could result in an election contest may be excluded under Rule 14a-8(i)(8), but the staff also is severely limited in their ability to interpret Rule 14a-8 in responding to companies' notices of intent to exclude shareholder proposals. Therefore, to eliminate any uncertainty and confusion arising from the Second Circuit's decision, we are issuing this release to confirm the Commission's position that shareholder proposals that could result in an election contest may be excluded under Rule 14a-8(i)(8). We also are soliciting comment as to whether we should adopt proposed changes to Rule 14a-8(i)(8) to further clarify the rule's application. If clarification of the text of Rule14a-8(i)(8) would be helpful, we are seeking input as to whether the text of the proposed amendment provides adequate clarity.

Id. at 578.

Specifically, the new Commission interpretation of Rule 14a-8(i)(8) states:

...[T]he Commission stated clearly when it proposed amendments to Rule 14a-8 in 1976 that "Rule 14a-8 is not the proper means for conducting campaigns or effecting reforms in elections of that nature, since other proxy rules, including Rule 14a-11, are applicable thereto." Thus, Rule 14a-8 expressly was *not* intended to be a substitute, or additional, mechanism for conducting contested elections (the type of elections that would involve the *conducting [of] campaigns*), or for effecting reforms in contested elections (elections whose *nature* involves campaigns). Based on the foregoing, it is the Commission's view that a proposal may be excluded under Rule 14a-8(i)(8) if it would result in an immediate election contest (*e.g.*, by making or opposing a director nomination for a particular meeting) *or* would set up a process for shareholders to conduct an election contest in the future by requiring the company to include shareholders' director nominees in the company's proxy materials for subsequent meetings.

In the *AFSCME* opinion, the Second Circuit agreed with the Commission's view that shareholder proposals can be excluded under Rule 14a-8(i)(8) if they would result in an immediate election contest. The court, however, disagreed with the view that a proposal can be excluded under Rule 14a-8(i)(8) if it "establish[es] a process for shareholders to wage a future election contest."

We believe that the fact a proposal relates to the process for future elections rather than an immediate election is not dispositive in determining whether the election exclusion applies to the proposal. As the Commission stated in 1976, the express purpose of the election exclusion is to make clear that Rule 14a-8 is not a proper *means* to achieve election contests because *other proxy rules* are applicable to such contests. The use of Rule 14a-8 to require companies to include proposals that would require election contests to be conducted without compliance with the specific rules governing such contests would be contrary to the intent of the Commission's 1976 statement.

For these reasons, and to avoid such circumvention, the phrase *relates to an election* in the election exclusion cannot be read so narrowly as to refer only to a proposal that *relates to the current election*, or a particular election, but rather must be read to refer to a proposal that *relates to an election* in subsequent years as well. In this regard, if one looked only to what a proposal accomplished in the current year, and not to its effect in subsequent years, the purpose of the exclusion could be evaded easily. For example, such a reading might permit a company to exclude a shareholder proposal that nominated a candidate for election as director for the upcoming meeting of shareholders but not exclude a proposal that required the company to include the same shareholder-nominated candidate in the company's proxy materials for the following year's meeting.

P. 539

In implementing the Commission's intended meaning, the staff has taken care not to adopt an inappropriately broad reading of whether a proposal *relates to an election*, as such a reading would permit the exclusion of all proposals regarding the qualifications of directors, the composition of the board, shareholder voting procedures, and board nomination procedures. We agree with the staff's application of the exclusion in this regard, as an inappropriately broad reading of the exclusion would deny shareholder access to the company proxy materials under Rule 14a-8 with respect to a vast category of election matters of importance to shareholders that would not result in an election contest between management and shareholder nominees, and that do not present significant conflicts with the Commission's other proxy rules.

Our interpretation of the election exclusion is fully consistent with the Commission's statement in 1976, that the rule was not intended "to cover proposals dealing with matters previously not held not excludable by the Commission, such as cumulative voting rights, general qualifications for directors...". In the *AFSCME v. AIG* opinion, the Second Circuit inferred from this Commission statement that the Commission "reject[ed] the somewhat broader interpretation that the election exclusion applies to shareholder proposals that would institute procedures for making election contests more likely." Our view that Rule 14a-8(i)(8) allows companies to exclude shareholder proposals that could result in election contests without compliance with the contested election proxy rules is consistent with the Commission's statement in 1976. As explained above, the analysis under Rule 14a-8(i)(8) does not focus on whether the proposal would make election contests more likely, but whether the resulting contests would be governed by the Commission's proxy rules for contested elections. The Commission's references in 1976 to proposals relating to *cumulative voting rights* and *general qualifications for directors* simply reflect the long-held belief that these proposals generally do not trigger the contested elections proxy rules and therefore are not excludable under Rule 14a-8(i)(8). Accordingly, the Commission's 1976 statement should not be interpreted to mean that Rule 14a-8(i)(8) is inapplicable to proposals establishing procedures for elections generally.

Id. at 580–581.

The Commission also sought comment on whether it should amend Rule 14a-8(i)(8) to further clarify the meaning of the exclusion, by proposing to revise the language to read:

> If the proposal relates to a nomination or an election for membership on the company's board of directors or analogous governing body or a procedure for such nomination or election.
>
> We believe that the added references to *nomination* and *procedure* in the rule text will reflect more appropriate the purpose of the election exclusion. Further, if adopted, we would indicate clearly that the term *procedures* referenced in the election exclusion relates to procedures that would result in a contested election, either in the year in which the proposal is submitted or in subsequent years, consistent with the Commission's interpretation of the exclusion.

Id. at 582.

In late November 2007 a 3-to-1 majority of the Commission voted to adopt amendments to Rule 14a-8(i)(8) to permit exclusion of shareholder proposals to establish proxy access. Divided SEC Acts to Allow Exclusion by Firms of Shareholder Access Proposals, 39 Sec. Reg. & L. Rep. (BNA) 1818 (2007). See also Shareholders Would Reserve Proxy Access as Negotiation Tool, TIAA-CREF Official Says, 39 id. 1844.

In Sec. Ex. Act Rel. 56,914, 92 SEC Dock. 256 (2007) (adoption), a majority of the Commission voted to add the words *or a procedure for such nomination or election* to the end of Rule 14a-8(i)(8). In the adoption Release, the Commission specifically explained: "The term *procedures* in the election exclusion relates to procedures that would result in a contested election either in the year in which the proposal is submitted or in any subsequent year." Id. at 261. A Commission interpretation of Rule 14a-8(i)(8) amplified:

> Rule 14a-8(i)(8) permits exclusion of a proposal that would result in an immediate election contest (e.g., by making or opposing a director nomination for a particular meeting) or would set up a process for shareholders to conduct an election contest in the

future by requiring the company to include shareholders' director nominees in the company's proxy materials for subsequent meetings.

In the *AFSCME v. AIG* opinion, the Second Circuit took the view that a shareholder proposal may be excluded under Rule 14a-8(i)(8) if it would result in an immediate election contest, but that a proposal may not be excluded under Rule 14a-8(i)(8) if it "establish[es] a process for shareholders to wage a future election contest." As the Commission stated in 1976, however, the express purpose of the election exclusion is to make clear that Rule 14a-8 is not a proper *means* to achieve election contests because *other proxy rules* are applicable to such contests. We are acting today to state clearly that the phrase *relates to an election* in the election exclusion cannot be read so narrowly as to refer only to a proposal that relates to the current election, or a particular election, but rather must be read to refer to a proposal that *relates to an election* in subsequent years as well. In this regard, if one looked only to what a proposal accomplished in the current year, and not to its effect in subsequent years, the purpose of the exclusion could be evaded easily. For example, such a reading might permit a company to exclude a shareholder proposal that nominated a candidate for election as director for the upcoming meeting of shareholders, but not exclude a proposal that resulted in the company being required to include the same shareholder-nominated candidate in the company's proxy materials for the following year's meeting.

Id. at 260.

4. CONTESTED SOLICITATIONS AND SECURITY HOLDER PROPOSALS

c. Security Holder Proposals [Rule 14a-8]

P. 570, new text after 1st full par. In May 2009 the Commission proposed to modify Rule 14a-8 and permit shareholder proposals that relate to the procedures for director nominations.

On a 3-2 vote, the Schapiro Commission also proposed new Rule 14a-11 to permit nomination of up to 25 percent of the board to a shareholder or group of shareholders that owns 1, 3, or 5 percent of a corporation's stock (depending on the net assets of the firm). The minority shareholder's gross would do so without bearing the expense of the proxy solicitation.

In Sec. Ex. Act Rel. 60,089, __ SEC Dock. __ (2009), the Commission proposed new Rule 82a of Part 200 Subpart D — Information and Requests, and new Rules 14a-11, 14a-18, and 14a-19, new Regulation 14N and Schedule 14N, and amendments to Rule 13 of Regulation S-T, Rules 13a-11, 13d-1, 14a-2, 14a-4, 14a-6, 14a-8, 14a-9, 14a-12, and 15d-11, Schedule 14A, and Form 8K, under the Securities Exchange Act of 1934.

The key proposals were in new proxy Rule 14a-11 and in amendments to Rule 14a-8(i)(8). The proposal Release explained in part:

> Proposed Rule 14a-11 would apply to all companies subject to the Exchange Act proxy rules (including investment companies registered under Section 8 of the Investment Company Act of 1940), other than companies that are subject to the proxy rules solely because they have a class of debt registered under Section 12 of the Exchange Act. As proposed, a company would be subject to Rule 14a-11 unless applicable state law or a company's governing documents prohibits shareholders from nominating candidates for the board of directors. When a company's governing documents do prohibit nomination rights, shareholders who want to amend the provision may seek to do so by submitting a shareholder proposal....
>
> Today's proposal does not require a triggering event. Instead, Rule 14a-11 would apply to all companies subject to Exchange Act Section 14(a), other than companies that are subject to the proxy rules solely because they have a class of debt registered under Exchange Act Section 12....
>
> In seeking to balance shareholders' ability to participate more fully in the nomination and election process against the potential cost and disruption to companies subject to the proposed new rule, we are proposing that only holders of a significant, long-term interest in a company be able to rely on Rule 14a-11 to have disclosure about their nominees for director included in company proxy materials. We are proposing that the requirement for a company to include a shareholder's nominee or nominees for director in the

P. 570

company's proxy materials and on its form of proxy be based on a minimum ownership threshold, which would be tiered according to company size. Assuming the other conditions of proposed Rule 14a-11 are met, companies would not be able to exclude a shareholder nominee or nominees if the nominating shareholder or group:

- Beneficially owns, as of the date of the shareholder notice on Schedule 14N, either individually or in the aggregate:
    - For large accelerated filers as defined in Exchange Act Rule 12b-2, and registered investment companies with net assets of $700 million or more, at least 1% of the company's securities that are entitled to be voted on the election of directors at the annual meeting of shareholders (or, in lieu of such an annual meeting, a special meeting of shareholders);
    - For accelerated filers as defined in Rule 12b-2, and registered investment companies with net assets of $75 million or more but less than $700 million, at least 3% of the company's securities that are entitled to be voted on the election of directors at the annual meeting of shareholders (or, in lieu of such an annual meeting, a special meeting of shareholders); and
    - For non-accelerated filers as defined in Rule 12b-2, and registered investment companies with net assets of less than $75 million, at least 5% of the company's securities that are entitled to be voted on the election of directors at the annual meeting of shareholders (or, in lieu of such an annual meeting, a special meeting of shareholders);

- Has beneficially owned the securities that are used for purposes of determining the ownership threshold continuously for at least one year as of the date of the shareholder notice on Schedule 14N (in the case of a shareholder group, each member of the group must have held the securities that are used for purposes of determining the ownership threshold for at least one year as of the date of the shareholder notice on Schedule 14N); and
- Represents that it intends to continue to own those securities through the date of the annual or special meeting....

The tiered beneficial ownership thresholds that we are proposing represent an effort to balance the varying considerations and address the possibility that certain companies could be impacted disproportionately based on their size. In determining the proposed ownership thresholds, we considered two different samples of data on security ownership as an indicator of the ownership of securities that are entitled to be voted on the election of directors. First, we considered the current ownership make-up of a sample by an outside source of 5,327 companies that have held meetings between January 1, 2008 and April 15, 2009. In this sample, roughly 26% of the firms are classified as large accelerated filers, 35% are classified as accelerated filers, and 38% are classified as non-accelerated filers. The second sample is derived from CDA Spectrum and is based on filings of Forms 13F in third quarter of 2008. In this sample, roughly 26% of the firms are classified as large accelerated filers, 33% are classified as accelerated filers, and 40% are classified as non-accelerated filers.....

In addition, to rely on proposed Rule 14a-11 to have disclosure about their nominee or nominees included in the company proxy materials, a nominating shareholder or group must:

- Not acquire or hold the securities for the purpose of or with the effect of changing control of the company or to gain more than a limited number of seats on the board;
- Provide and file with the Commission a notice to the company on proposed new Schedule 14N of the nominating shareholder's or group's intent to require that the company include that nominating shareholder's or group's nominee in the company's proxy materials by the date specified by the company's advance notice provision or, where no such provision is in place, no later than 120 calendar days before the date that the company mailed its proxy materials for the prior year's annual meeting, except that if the company did not hold an annual meeting during the prior year, or if the date of the meeting has changed by more than 30 days from the prior year, then the nominating shareholder or group must provide notice a reasonable time before the company mails its proxy materials, as specified by the company in a Form 8-K filed within four business days after the company determines the anticipated meeting date pursuant to proposed Item 5.07; and

P. 570   2010 SUPPLEMENT

- Include in the shareholder notice on Schedule 14N disclosure about the amount and percentage of securities owned by the nominating shareholder or group, length of ownership of such securities, and the nominating shareholder's or group's intent to continue to hold the securities through the date of the meeting as well as intent with respect to continued ownership after the election, a certification that the nominating shareholder or group is not seeking to change the control of the company or to gain more than a limited number of seats on the board of directors, and disclosure meeting the requirements of Rule 14a-18.

...

We do not intend for proposed Rule 14a-11 to be available for any shareholder or group that is seeking to change the control of the issuer or to gain more than a limited number of seats on the board....

As proposed, a company would be required to include no more than one shareholder nominee or the number of nominees that represents 25 percent of the company's board of directors, whichever is greater. Where a company has a director (or directors) currently serving on its board of directors who was elected as a shareholder nominee pursuant to Rule 14a-11, and the term of that director extends past the date of the meeting of shareholders for which the company is soliciting proxies for the election of directors, the company would not be required to include in its proxy materials more shareholder nominees than could result in the total number of directors serving on the board that were elected as shareholder nominees being greater than one shareholder nominee or 25 percent of the company's board of directors, whichever is greater. We believe this limitation is appropriate to reduce the possibility of a nominating shareholder or group using the proposed new rule as a means to effect a change in control of a company or to gain more than a limited number of seats on the board by repeatedly nominating additional candidates for director....

Proposed Rule 14a-11(d)(3) would address situations where more than one shareholder or group would be eligible to have its nominees included in the company's form of proxy and disclosed in its proxy statement pursuant to the proposed rule. In those situations, the company would be required to include in its proxy statement and form of proxy the nominee or nominees of the first nominating shareholder or group from which it receives timely notice of intent to nominate a director pursuant to the rule, up to and including the total number of shareholder nominees required to be included by the company. Where the first nominating shareholder or group from which the company receives timely notice does not nominate the maximum number of directors allowed under the rule, the nominee or nominees of the next nominating shareholder or group from which the company receives timely notice of intent to nominate a director pursuant to the rule would be included in the company's proxy materials, up to and including the total number of shareholder nominees required to be included by the company....

Upon receipt of a shareholder's or group's notice of its intent to require the company to include in its proxy materials a shareholder nominee or nominees pursuant to Rule 14a-11, the company would determine whether any of the events permitting exclusion of the shareholder nominee or nominees has occurred. If not, the company would notify in writing the nominating shareholder or group no later than 30 calendar days before the company files its definitive proxy statement and form of proxy with the Commission that it will include the nominee or nominees. The company would be required to provide this notice in a manner that provides evidence of timely receipt by the nominating shareholder or group.

The company would then include disclosure regarding the shareholder nominee or nominees and the nominating shareholder or group in the company's proxy statement and include the name of the nominee on the company's form of proxy that is included with the proxy statement. With regard to the company's form of proxy, the company could identify any shareholder nominees as such and recommend how shareholders should vote for, against, or withhold votes on those nominees and management nominees on the form of proxy. The company would otherwise be required to present the nominees in an impartial manner in accordance with Rule 14a-4. Under the current rules, a company may provide shareholders with the option to vote for or withhold authority to vote for the company's nominees as a group, provided that shareholders also are given a means to withhold authority for specific nominees in the group. In our view, this option would not be appropriate where the company's form of proxy includes shareholder nominees, as grouping the company's nominees may make it easier to vote for all of the company's nominees than to vote for the shareholder nominees in addition to some of the company nominees. Accordingly, when a shareholder nominee is included, the proposed rules would not permit a company to provide shareholders the option of voting for or withholding authority to vote for the company nominees as a group, but would instead require that each nominee be voted on separately.

A company also would be required to include in its proxy statement, if desired by the nominating shareholder or group, a statement by the nominating shareholder or group in support of the shareholder nominee or nominees. In this regard, we believe that not only should a company be able to include a statement in support of the company nominees in its proxy statement, provided that it complies with Rule 14a-9, we also are of the view that a nominating shareholder or group should be afforded a similar opportunity. Accordingly, we are proposing to require a company to include a nominating shareholder's or group's statement of support for the shareholder nominee or nominees, so long as the statement of support does not exceed 500 words. This statement must be provided to the company in the shareholder notice on Schedule 14N....

A company may determine that it is not required under proposed Rule 14a-11 to include a nominee from a nominating shareholder or group in its proxy materials if it determines any of the following:

- Proposed Rule 14a-11 is not applicable to the company;
- The nominating shareholder or group has not complied with the requirements of Rule 14a-11;
- The nominee does not meet the requirements of Rule 14a-11;
- Any representation required to be included in the notice to the company is false or misleading in any material respect; or
- The company has received more nominees than it is required to include by proposed Rule 14a-11 and the nominating shareholder or group is not entitled to have its nominee included under the criteria proposed in Rule 14a-11(d)(3)....

As proposed, Rule 14a-11 would permit shareholders to aggregate their securities with other shareholders in order to meet the applicable minimum ownership threshold to nominate a director....

We are proposing an amendment to Rule 14a-8(i)(8), the election exclusion, to enable shareholders, under certain circumstances, to require companies to include in company proxy materials proposals that would amend, or that request an amendment to, a company's governing documents regarding nomination procedures or disclosures related to shareholder nominations, provided the proposal does not conflict with proposed Rule 14a-11. The proposal would have to meet the procedural requirements of Rule 14a-8 and not be subject to one of the substantive exclusions other than the election exclusion (e.g., the proposal could be excluded if the shareholder proponent did not meet the ownership threshold under Rule 14a-8).

As proposed, except as provided below in the codification of staff positions, revised Rule 14a-8(i)(8) would not restrict the types of amendments that a shareholder could propose to a company's governing documents to address the company's provisions regarding nomination procedures or disclosures related to shareholder nominations, although any such proposals that conflict with proposed Rule 14a-11 or state law could be excluded. We recognize that the proposed amendments to Rule 14a-8(i)(8) could result in shareholders proposing amendments that would establish procedures for nominating directors and disclosures related to such nominations that require a different ownership threshold, holding period, or other qualifications or representations than those proposed in Rule 14a-11.....

Proposed Rule 14a-19 would apply to a shareholder nomination for director for inclusion in the company's proxy materials made pursuant to procedures established pursuant to state law or by a company's governing documents. The proposed rule would require a nominating shareholder or group to include in its shareholder notice on Schedule 14N (which also would be filed with the Commission on the date provided to the company) disclosures about the nominating shareholder or group and their nominee that are similar to what would be required in an election contest....

Although we are proposing to amend Rule 14a-8(i)(8), we continue to believe that under certain circumstances companies should have the right to exclude proposals, related to particular elections and nominations for director from company proxy

277

P. 570

materials where those proposals could result in an election contest between company and shareholder nominees without the important protections provided by the disclosure and liability provisions otherwise provided for in the proxy rules. Rule 14a-8(i)(8) should not, however, be read so broadly such that the provision could be used to permit the exclusion of proposals regarding the qualifications of directors, shareholder voting procedures, board nomination procedures and other election matters of importance to shareholders that would not directly result in an election contest between management and shareholder nominees, and that do not present significant conflicts with the Commission's other proxy rules. Therefore, we propose to amend Rule 14a-8(i)(8) to codify certain prior staff interpretations with respect to the type of proposals that would continue to be excludable.

A company would be permitted to exclude a proposal under Rule 14a-8(i)(8) if it:

- Would disqualify a nominee who is standing for election;
- Would remove a director from office before his or her term expired;
- Questions the competence, business judgment, or character of one or more nominees or directors;
- Nominates a specific individual for election to the board of directors, other than pursuant to Rule 14a-11, an applicable state law provision, or a company's governing documents; or
- Otherwise could affect the outcome of the upcoming election of directors.

With regard to the language "otherwise could affect the outcome of the upcoming election of directors," we are seeking to address the fact that the proposed new language of the exclusion specifically addresses the particular types of proposals that we have traditionally seen in this area and that we believe are clearly excludable under the policy underlying the rule. With the broader proposed language, we are seeking to address new proposals that may be developed over time that are comparable to the four specified categories and would undermine the purpose of the exclusion. This broader language is generally consistent with the language of the other bases for exclusion in Rule 14a-8.

Id. at __ -__ [nn.104-277].

P. 573, new text, end page. In July 2003 the SEC Division of Corporation Finance published Staff Report: Review of the Proxy Process Regarding the Nomination and Election of Directors, 2003 Fed. Sec. L. Rep. (CCH) ¶86,938 (July 15, 2003), in response to a proposal of the American Federation of State, County, and Municipal Employees Pension Plan to require companies to include in their proxy materials the nominee of any shareholder or group of shareholders beneficially owning 3 percent or more of a company's outstanding common stock.

The Division recommended that the SEC seek public comment with respect to improved disclosure and conditional shareholder access to the nomination process. Id. at 87,886. With respect to conditional access, the Report specifically stated:

> The Division recommends that the Commission propose and solicit public comment on new proxy rules that would allow a shareholder or a group of shareholders to place their nominees in a company's proxy materials within the following parameters:
>
> - applicable state corporate law must provide the company's shareholders with the right to nominate a candidate for election as a director;
> - neither the candidacy nor the election of a shareholder nominee may otherwise violate, or cause the company to violate, controlling state law, federal law or listing standards;
> - the availability of a shareholder nomination process should be premised upon the occurrence of one or more triggering events that are objective criteria evidencing potential deficiencies in the proxy process such that shareholder views — especially those of a majority — may not otherwise be adequately taken into account;
> - there should be appropriate standards for independence of shareholder nominees;
> - there should be minimum standards with regard to shareholdings and the length of time those shares have been held by a nominating shareholder or shareholder group; and
> - there should be limitations on the total number or percentage of permitted shareholder nominees.

Id. at 32–33.

P. 573

In Sec. Ex. Act Rel. 48,626, 81 SEC Dock. 770 (2003) (proposal), the Commission proposed rules based on the Staff Report. The Commission proposed a new Rule 14a-11 that would permit a security holder holding individually or in a group that beneficially owns more than 5 percent of the registration securities to nominate one or more persons for the board, subject to a 500 word limit or the statement of support, provided that:

(1) Applicable state law does not prohibit the registrant's security holders from nominating a candidate or candidates for election as a director;

(2) One or more of the following events has occurred during the calendar year in which the meeting that is the subject of the proxy statement is being held or during either of the preceding two calendar years:

(i) At least one of the registrant's nominees for the board of directors for whom the registrant solicited proxies received "withhold" votes from more than 35% of the votes cast at an annual meeting of security holders (or, in lieu of an annual meeting, a special meeting) held after January 1, 2004, at which directors were elected (provided, that this event will be deemed not to occur with regard to any contested election to which [Rule] 14a-12(c) applies or an election to which this section applies); or

(ii) A security holder proposal providing that the registrant become subject to [Rule] 14a-11 that was submitted pursuant to [Rule] 14a-8 by a security holder or group of security holders that held more than 1% of the securities entitled to vote on that proposal for at least one year as of the date the proposal was submitted and provided evidence of such holding to the registrant, received more than 50% of the votes cast on that proposal at an annual meeting of security holders (or, in lieu of an annual meeting, a special meeting) held after January 1, 2004.

Under proposed Rule 14a-11(d)(l) a registrant is not required to include more than one nominee if there are fewer than eight directors; two if there are more than eight but fewer than 20; and three, if there are more than 20 directors.

Proposed Rule 14a-11 represented the first SEC rule that would have permitted direct shareholder nomination of directors. As such it was a significant proposal. The proposal was susceptible to criticism for the temporal delays that the triggering events would portend. The proposal Release was notable for not addressing SEC authority to adopt a director nomination rule, an issue that wisely might have been raised given Business Roundtable v. SEC, 905 F.2d 406 (D.C. Cir. 1990). See generally ABA Task Force Report on Proposed Changes in Proxy Rules and Regulations Regarding Procedures for the Election of Corporate Directors, 59 Bus. Law. 109, 130–136 (2003).

On December 22, 2003 the Business Roundtable filed a 76 page Comment on the SEC's proposed election contest rules stressing its belief "that the Commission lacks the statutory authority to adopt the Proposed Election Contest Rules." Detailed Comments Accompanying Letter to Jonathan G. Katz from Business Round Table Dec. 22, 2003, re: File No. S7-19-03, at 1.

In Qwest Communications Int'l Inc., 2004–2005 Fed. Sec. L. Rep. (CCH) ¶78,922 (avail. Feb. 7, 2005), Alan Beller, Director, Division of Corporation Finance, signed a no action letter response signaling that the Commission would not adopt proposed Rule 14a-11. Earlier, in Sec. Ex. Act Rel. 48,626, 81 SEC Dock. 770 (2003) (proposal), the staff was reported to have informed the Commission of its intention to take the position that a proposal under Rule 14a-8(i)(8) to adopt the procedures in the proposed Rule 14a-11 could not be excluded. In the 2005 letter, "given the passage of time," the staff now concluded that a proposal that a corporation comply with Proposed Rule 14a-11 could be excluded under Rule 14a-8(i)(8).

In American Fed. of State, County & Mun. Employees v. American Int'l Group, Inc., 462 F.3d 121 (2d Cir. 2006), the court held "that a shareholder proposal that seeks to amend the corporate bylaws to establish a procedure by which shareholder-nominated candidates may be included on the corporate ballot does not relate to an election within the meaning of the Rule and therefore cannot be excluded from corporate proxy materials under that regulation." Id. at 123.

The court rejected the position of the SEC articulated in an amicus brief that the plaintiff's proposal "related to an election" and could be excluded under Rule 14a-8(i)(8).

P. 576

The court agreed with the Commission that a shareholder proposal seeking to contest management nominees would be excludable under Rule 14a-8(i)(8). In contrast, the court declined to permit Rule 14a-8(i)(8) to exclude a proposal to establish a process for shareholders to wage a future election contest.

The court based the opinion, in part, on what it viewed as a change in the Commission's interpretation of Rule 14a-8(i)(8) in 1976 and 1990. The court stated in part:

> The 1976 Statement clearly reflects the view that the election exclusion is limited to shareholder proposals used to oppose solicitations dealing with an identified board seat in an upcoming election and rejects the somewhat broader interpretation that the election exclusion applies to shareholder proposals that would institute procedures making such election contests more likely....
>
> ... It was not until 1990 that the Division first signaled a change of course by deeming excludable proposals that *might* result in contested elections, even if the proposal only purports to alter general procedures for nominating and electing directors....
>
> Because the interpretation of Rule 14a-8(i)(8) that the SEC advances in its amicus brief — that the election exclusion applies to proxy access bylaws proposals — conflicts with the 1976 Statement, it does not merit the usual deference we would reserve for an agency's interpretation of its own regulations.

Id. at 128-129.

5. FALSE OR MISLEADING STATEMENTS [RULE 14a-9]

a. In General

P. 576, new text, end 1st sentence. See Makor Issues & Rights Ltd. v. Tellabs, Inc., 437 F.3d 588 (7th Cir. 2006), *rev'd on other grounds*, 551 U.S. 308 (2007) ("Mere sales puffery is not actionable under Rule 10b-5").

P. 576 n.139, end note. A determination of *buried facts* is fact specific. Cf. Benzon v. Morgan Stanley Distrib., Inc., 420 F.3d 598, 608 (6th Cir. 2005) ("All of the information from which Plaintiffs' claims regarding Defendants' failure to make statements regarding the relative merits of different class shares are drawn is available in Defendants' prospectuses").

Cf. Syncor Int'l, 2007 Fed. Sec. L. Rep. (CCH) ¶94,354 at 92,505 (9th Cir. 2007):

> Incomplete statements are misleading if they "affirmatively create an impression of a state of affairs which differs in a material way from the one that actually exists." [Citation omitted.] Defendants' statements meet this standard. By attributing Syncor's success solely to legitimate practices, defendants implicitly (and falsely) warranted that there were no illegal practices contributing to that success. [Citations omitted.]

In J&R Marketing, SEP v. General Motors Corp., 549 F.3d 384, 394 (6th Cir. 2008), the court added: "A company has to disclose additional information only when what it has disclosed would be rendered misleading without that additional information."

P. 577 n.145, end note. In Nolte v. Capital One Fin. Corp., 390 F.3d 311, 315 (4th Cir. 2004), the Fourth Circuit interpreted *Virginia Bankshares* to require a pleading "that the opinion expressed was different from the opinion actually held by the speaker." Here an allegation that a bank executive feared a bank would be deemed undercapitalized was insufficient to plead that he believed the company was undercapitalized. Id. at 316.

b. Materiality

P. 582 n.155, end note. In Vernazza v. SEC, 327 F.3d 851, 860 (9th Cir. 2003), the court concluded that "[t]he Commission correctly determined that the petitioners had a duty to disclose any potential conflicts of interest accurately and completely" and to recognize that an investment adviser's Shareholder Servicing Agreement created such a potential conflict.

See also SEC v. Merchant Capital, LLC, 483 F.3d 747, 770–772 (11th Cir. 2007) (it is materially misleading to omit disclosure of the personal bankruptcy of the 75 percent controlling investor and also materially misleading to omit disclosing a contemporaneous cease and desist order that prohibited sale of identical securities in California).

Cf. Derek L. DuBois, Sec. Ex. Act Rel. 48,332, 80 SEC Dock. 2403, 2405 (2003), a Commission opinion, in which it was held: "A prospective investor would consider it material that a salesperson who was recommending a particular investment was being compensated by a third party for doing so; as a result, the salesperson's recommendation might not be disinterested."

P. 588 n.186, end note. In Kapps v. Torch Offshore, Inc., 379 F.3d 207, 213 (5th Cir. 2004), the court elaborated:

> Specifically, we hold that the definition of *material* under Section 11 is not strictly limited to information that is firm-specific and non-public. While all material information need not be included in the registration statement, an issuer is not free to make material misrepresentations, or to omit material information that is either required to be disclosed by law or that is necessary to disclose in order to prevent statements made in the registration statement from being misleading.

P. 588 n.187, end note. In Gebhardt v. ConAgra Foods, Inc., 335 F.3d 824 (8th Cir. 2003), the court declined to dismiss a complaint on materiality grounds, stating in part:

> In addressing the circumstances of this case, the District Court held that "[i]n the total mix of information available to investors, the mere fact that ConAgra's revenues were overstated by 0.4 percent, during fiscal 1998–2000 was immaterial as a matter of law," and determined that the question of materiality could be decided against the plaintiffs as a matter of law....In our view, the quantity of a revenue overstatement, in and of itself, is not sufficient to be dispositive of this issue. Instead, we look at the total mix of data

available to investors, and place the misrepresented data in context. More than a revenue loss was involved here. There was also a loss in net income, a figure that may be of more significance to investors. Here, the complaint alleges that ConAgra overstated its net income for 1999 and 2000 by 8 percent. It is hard to say that a discrepancy of this magnitude is immaterial as a matter of law. In order to take this decision away from the jury, the circumstances must make it obvious why a reasonable investor would not be concerned about the facts misrepresented. In *Parnes*, we found it rational to conclude that investors attracted to an investment with high risk and the potential of high return are not going to be fazed by a small increase in risk. 122 F.3d at 547. No such circumstances are obvious in this case, and they rarely will be at the pleadings stage.

Id. at 830. In United States v. Nacchio, 519 F.3d 1140, 1164 (10th Cir. 2008), the court held:

> ...[W]e are asked to decide whether a risk that a company's revenue will fall $900 million short of its public guidance — a 4.2% shortfall — is necessarily immaterial to investors. Although it is a close question, we conclude that the answer is *no*. The 4.2% shortfall is close to the 5% rule of thumb embraced by the SEC, and there was enough evidence of additional factors that we cannot reject the possibility of materiality as a matter of law. See *Ganino*, 228 F.3d at 162-64; Staff Accounting Bulletin No. 99, 64 Fed. Reg. 45,150 (1999). The government argued that the shortfall had particular salience given the state of the economy and the industry. Mr. Nacchio himself had said in January that the *skittish market* was so *mercurial* that even a $50 million shortfall could create a 15-20% drop in stock price. Apple.'s Supp. App. exh. 559A. We think that if the evidence is viewed in the light most favorable to the government, a reasonable and properly-instructed jury could have concluded that information about a 4.2% shortfall, in the special circumstances of this case, was material.

See also Stavros v. Exelon Corp., 266 F. Supp. 2d 833, 841–842 (N.D. Ill. 2003) (declining to hold that 1.5 percent earnings per share error was immaterial on a pretrial motion).

P. 590 n.190, end 1st par. A court of appeals held that a reasonable jury could find a defendant criminally liable for insider trading when he exercised employee stock options after merger negotiations had begun. United States v. Mooney, 401 F.3d 940 (8th Cir. 2005).

In United States v. Mooney, 2004 Fed. Sec. L. Rep. (CCH) ¶92,874 at 94,154 (8th Cir. 2004), the court relied in part on call option purchases to conclude that a reasonable jury could find materiality. See also Media Gen., Inc. v. Tomlin, 387 F.3d 865, 870 (D.C. Cir. 2004) (testimony by counsel to a merger target that he would have wanted to know about expanded litigation claim was sufficient to defeat defendant motion to dismiss since "[a] major factor in determining whether information was material is the importance attached to it by those who know about it").

In contrast to SEC v. Sargent, 229 F.3d 68 (1st Cir. 2000), in SEC v. Happ, 392 F.3d 12 (1st Cir. 2004), sufficient circumstantial evidence was presented that defendant possessed and used material nonpublic information in deciding to sell stock when he did.

Whether omitted information is material may also involve the efficient market hypothesis. In Merck & Co. Sec. Litig., 432 F.3d 261, 268–271 (3d Cir. 2005), the court focused on the speed at which information was reflected in a stock price to analyze whether an omission was material. Citing Basic v. Levinson, 485 U.S. 224, 228 n.28 (1988), Burlington Coat Factory Sec. Litig., 114 F.3d 1410, 1425 (3d Cir. 1997), and Oran v. Stafford, 226 F.3d 275, 282 (3d Cir. 2000), the court concluded that new publicly available information should be absorbed "immediately following disclosure," although not necessary instantaneously. 432 F.3d at 269.

6. Securities Held in *Street Name* or *Nominee Name* [§14(b)]

P. 593, end page, new text. In 2006 the Commission approved NYSE rule changes to permit the elimination of the requirement that listed companies physically deliver annual reports to shareholders. Sec. Ex. Act Rel. 54,344, 88 SEC Dock. 2240 (2006) (adoption).

D. TENDER OFFERS

2. THE WILLIAMS ACT AND OTHER FEDERAL SECURITIES LAWS

b. Beneficial Ownership Reports [§§13(d), 13(g)]

(i) *Group*

P. 622 n.32, end note. For purposes of §13(d)(3) and Rule 13d-5(b)(1), actors need not have combined to form a group for all of the listed purposes. "Acquiring, holding, and disposing of are listed in the disjunctive." Roth v. Jennings, 489 F.3d 499, 508 (2d Cir. 2007). "The questions of (a) whether two or more persons act[ed] as a group or agreed to act together, and (b) whether their purpose was the acquisition, holding, or disposition of an issuer's equity securities are questions of fact." Ibid.

Nor need an agreement to act together be unconditional in order to support a finding that the actors constituted a group. Ibid. A group does not have to commit to any specific set of terms, and their agreement need not be expressly memorialized in writing. Ibid.

See generally CSX Corp. v. Children's Inv. Fund Management (UK), 562 F. Supp. 2d 511, 539 (S.D.N.Y. 2008), *aff'd*, 2008 U.S. App. LEXIS 19,788 (2d Cir. 2008): "Although Congress did not define the term, its intention manifestly was that the phrase [*beneficial ownership*] be construed broadly. The SEC did so in Rule 13d-3...." See generally id. at 539-552. Judge Kaplan concluded: "[T]here are substantial reasons for concluding that TCI is the beneficial owner of the CSX shares held as hedges by its short counterparties." Id. at 545.

P. 643   2010 SUPPLEMENT

In Hemispherx Biopharma, Inc. v. Johannesburg Consol. Inv., 553 F.3d 1351 (11th Cir. 2008), the court held that beneficial ownership is necessary to become a member of a group within the meaning of §13(d)(3).

c. Tender Offers [§14(d), Related Rules, and Schedules]

(iv) *Substantive Requirements*

P. 643 n.107, end note. In WHX Corp., Sec. Ex. Act Rel. 47,980, 80 SEC Dock. 1153 (2003), the Commission found a violation of Rule 14d-10(a)(1) when shareholders, unable to provide a proxy vote at a shareholder meeting, could not participate in a tender offer.

On appeal the District of Columbia Court of Appeals, reversed. WHX Corp. v. SEC, 362 F.3d 854 (D.C. Cir. 2004). The court gave "great deference" to the SEC standard for issuing a cease and desist order, citing KMPG Peat Marwick LLP, 289 F.3d 109 (D.C. Cir. 2002), but found that application of that standard here was arbitrary and capricious in the court's view:

> WHX committed (at most) a single, isolated violation of the rule, it immediately withdrew the offending condition once the Commission had made its official position clear, and the Commission has offered no reason to doubt WHX's assurances that it will not violate the rule in the future. In light of these factors, none of which the Commission seems to have considered seriously, the imposition of the cease-and-desist order seems all the more gratuitous.

WHX Corp. at 861.

Rule 14d-10 has occasioned two major interpretative challenges in the courts.

First, *when* does a tender offer occur under the Rule? The courts are divided between those that favor a flexible or functional approach such as Epstein v. MCA, Inc., 50 F.3d 644 (9th Cir. 1995), *rev'd on other grounds sub nom.* Matsushita Elec. Indus. Corp. v. Epstein, 516 U.S. 367; Gerber v. Computer Assoc. Int'l, Inc.,

303 F.3d 126 (2d Cir. 2002) and those that favor a more literal or bright line approach. See Lerro v. Quaker Oats Co., 84 F.3d 239 (7th Cir. 1996). Cf. Digital Island Sec. Litig., 357 F.3d 322 (3d Cir. 2004) (recognizing under *Lerro* that some payments made outside of the tender offer period may be so transparently fraudulent as to require them to be treated as made "during the tender offer"). The *Digital Island* case correctly recognizes that too rigid a rule can invite schemes to circumvent or "game" the rule. This does not appear to be consistent with the intent of the SEC in adopting Rule 14d-10, which appeared to cast a very wide net:

> Similarly, Section 14(d)(7) assures equality of treatment among all security holders who tender their shares by requiring that any increase in consideration offered to security holders be paid to all security holders whose shares are taken up during the offer. One of Congress' purposes in promulgating the provision was "to assure equality of treatment among all shareholders who tender their shares." These substantive provisions assume that offers will be made to all security holders and not just to a select few, and that offers will not be made to security holders at varying prices. Without the all-holders requirement and best-price provision, the specific protections provided by Sections 14(d)(6) and (d)(7) would be vitiated because an offeror could simply address its offer either to a privileged group of security holders who hold the desired number of shares or to all security holders but for different considerations. The all-holders requirement and best-price provision both are consistent with Congressional intent and complement the pro rata and equal price protections of the Williams Act.

Sec. Ex. Act Rel. 23,421, 36 SEC Dock. 96, 99–100 (1986).

Second, does Rule 14d-10 also apply to employment contracts between bidders and target company executives or solely to share purchases? Cf. Walther, Employment Agreements and Tender Offers: Reforming the Problem Treatment of Severance Plans Under Rule 14d-10, 102 Colum. L. Rev. 774 (2002).

In 2005 the Commission proposed amendments to the tender offer best-price Rules 13e-4 and 14d-10. Sec. Ex. Act Rel. 52,968, 86 SEC Dock. 2394 (2005) (proposal).

P. 643

Both Rules 13e-4(f)(8)(ii) and 14d-10(a)(2) were proposed to be amended to clarify that the best-price rules apply only to consideration offered and paid for securities tendered in a tender offer. This proposal was made in response to a conflict between courts that held that the best-price rule applies to all integral elements of a tender offer, including employment compensation, severance, and other employee benefits, see, e.g., Epstein v. MCA Inc., 50 F.3d 644 (9th Cir. 1995), *rev'd on other grounds sub nom.* Matsushita Elec. Indus. Co. v. Epstein, 516 U.S. 367 (1996), and courts that held that the best-price rule only applies to agreements between the time a tender offer formally commences and expires, see, e.g., Kramer v. Time Warner Inc., 937 F.2d 767 (2d Cir. 1991); Lerro v. Quaker Oats, 84 F.3d 239 (7th Cir. 1996); Digital Island Sec. Litig., 357 F.3d 322 (3d Cir. 2004).

The Commission neither subscribed to the integral-part nor to the bright-line test:

> We do not believe that the best-price rule should be subject to a strict temporal test. We also do not believe that all payments that are conditioned on or otherwise somehow related to a tender offer, including payments under compensatory or commercial arrangements that are made to persons who happen to be security holders, whether made before, during or after the tender offer period, should be subject to the best-price rule. Accordingly, we are proposing amendments to the best-price rule that do not follow the approach of either the integral-part or the bright-line test. Instead, the proposed amendments would refocus the determination as to potential violations of the best-price rule on whether any consideration paid to security holders for securities tendered into an offer is the highest consideration paid to any other security holder for securities tendered into the tender offer.
>
> The premise of the best-price rule is that bidders must pay consideration of equal value to all security holders for the securities that they tender in a tender offer. Accordingly, an analysis of the best-price rule must include a consideration of whether any security holders have been paid additional or different consideration for the securities they tendered in the offer.
>
> Our proposed amendments recognize that if purchases of securities are deemed to be made as part of a tender offer, then the consideration paid for all securities tendered in the offer must satisfy

the best-price rule. We propose to amend the best-price rule to establish clearly that it applies with respect to the consideration offered and paid for securities tendered in the tender offer. Specifically, we propose to revise the best-price rule to state that a bidder shall not make a tender offer unless "[t]he consideration paid to any security holder for securities tendered in the tender offer is the highest consideration paid to any other security holder for securities tendered in the tender offer." In doing so, the clause "for securities tendered in the tender offer" would replace the current clauses "pursuant to the tender offer" and "during such tender offer" to clarify the intent of the best-price rule.

Id. at 2398–2399.

The proposal is more precise in its use of the phrase "for securities tendered" rather than "pursuant to" a tender offer. Consideration paid for other arrangements, including compensation and commercial arrangements, accordingly would not be within the scope of the best-price rules.

Augmenting this proposed amendment was a proposed specific exemption to Rule 14d-10(c) for:

> The negotiation, execution or amendment of an employment compensation, severance or other employee benefit arrangement, or payments made or to be made or benefits granted or to be granted according to such arrangements, with respect to employees and directors of the subject company, where the amount payable under the arrangement: (i) relates solely to past services performed or future services to be performed or refrained from performing, by the employee or director (and matters incidental thereto), and (ii) is not based on the number of securities the employee or director owns or tenders.
>
> We believe that amounts paid pursuant to employment compensation, severance or other employee benefit arrangements should not be considered when calculating the price paid for tendered securities. These payments are made for a different purpose.

Id. at 2400.

The Commission also proposed a compensation committee safe harbor in Rule 14d-10(c) for bidders and subject companies

P. 643   2010 SUPPLEMENT

who enter employment compensation, severance, and employee benefits arrangements during a third-party tender offer subject to Rule 14d-10:

> The safe harbor provision would allow the compensation committee or a committee performing similar functions of the subject company's or bidder's board of directors, depending on whether the subject company or the bidder is the party to the arrangement, to approve an employment compensation, severance or other employee benefit arrangement and thus have it deemed to be an arrangement within the exemption of the proposed rule. The proposed safe harbor would require that the compensation committee or the committee performing similar functions be comprised solely of independent directors. Specifically, the proposals would add the following sentence to new proposed Rule 14d-10(c)(3):
>
> > For purposes of paragraph (c)(2) of this section, pursuant to this non-exclusive safe harbor, an arrangement shall be deemed an employment compensation, severance or other employee benefit arrangement if it is approved as meeting the requirements of paragraphs (c)(2)(i) and (ii) of this section by the compensation committee of the subject company's or bidder's (depending on whether the subject company or bidder is a party to the arrangement) board of directors. If that company's board of directors does not have a compensation committee, the arrangement shall be deemed an employment compensation, severance or other employee benefit arrangement if it is so approved by the committee of that board of directors that performs functions similar to a compensation committee. In each circumstance, the arrangement shall be deemed an employment compensation, severance or other employee benefit arrangement only if the approving compensation committee or the committee performing similar functions is comprised solely of independent directors.

Id. at 2402.

With respect to determining independence, the proposed revision would:

Include an instruction to Rule 14d-10(c)(3) providing that if the bidder or the subject company, as the case may be, is a listed issuer whose securities are listed on a registered national securities exchange or in an automated inter-dealer quotation system of a national securities association that has independence requirements for compensation committee members, the independence standards for compensation committee members as defined in the listing standards applicable to listed issuers should be used. Alternatively, if the bidder or the subject company is not a listed issuer, in determining whether a member of the compensation committee is independent, the bidder or subject company would use a definition of independence of a national securities exchange or a national securities association, so long as whatever definition is chosen is used consistently for all members of the compensation committee.

Id. at 2403.

In 2006 the amendments to Rules 13e-4 and 14d-10 were adopted generally as proposed. Sec. Ex. Act Rel. 54,684, 89 SEC Dock. 576 (2006) (adoption).

Rules 13e-4(f)(8)(ii) and 14d-10(a)(2) identically provided: "The consideration paid to any security holder for securities tendered in the tender offer is the highest consideration paid to any other security holder for securities tendered in the tender offer." The adoption Release underlined with respect to this basic best price standard: "The clause 'for securities tendered in the tender offer' would replace the clauses 'pursuant to the tender offer' and 'during such tender offer,' as the rule previously read, to clarify the intent of the best-price rule." Id. at 579-580. Specifically, the revised Rules neither were intended to follow the judicial integral-part or bright-line tests. "Instead," the adoption Release explained: "we proposed to change the language of the best-price rule so that only consideration paid to security holders for securities tendered into a tender offer will be evaluated when determining the highest consideration paid to any other security holder for securities tendered into the tender offer." Id. at 579.

P. 643

Identical language was also adopted in Rules 13e-4(f)(12) and 14d-10(d) to create an exemption from the basic best price standards for specified compensation arrangements and to create a safe harbor procedure to qualify for the exemption. Rule 13e-4(f)(12) provides:

(12)(i) Paragraph (f)(8)(ii) of this section shall not prohibit the negotiation, execution or amendment of an employment compensation, severance or other employee benefit arrangement, or payments made or to be made or benefits granted or to be granted according to such an arrangement, with respect to any security holder of the issuer, where the amount payable under the arrangement:

(A) is being paid or granted as compensation for past services performed, future services to be performed, or future services to be refrained from performing, by the security holder (and matters incidental thereto); and

(B) Is not calculated based on the number of securities tendered or to be tendered in the tender offer by the security holder.

(ii) The provisions of paragraph (f)(12)(i) of this section shall be satisfied and, therefore, pursuant to this non-exclusive safe harbor, the negotiation, execution or amendment of an arrangement and any payments made or to be made or benefits granted or to be granted according to that arrangement shall not be prohibited by paragraph (f)(8)(ii) of this section, if the arrangement is approved as an employment compensation, severance or other employee benefit arrangement solely by independent directors as follows:

(A) The compensation committee or a committee of the board of directors that performs functions similar to a compensation committee of the issuer approves the arrangement, regardless of whether the issuer is a party to the arrangement, or, if an affiliate is a party to the arrangement, the compensation committee or a committee of the board of directors that performs functions similar to a compensation committee of the affiliate approves the arrangement; or

(B) If the issuer's or affiliate's board of directors, as applicable, does not have a compensation committee or a committee of the board of directors that performs functions similar to a compensation committee or if none of the members of the issuer's or affiliate's compensation committee or committee that performs functions similar to a compensation committee is independent, a special committee of the board of directors formed to consider and approve the arrangement approves the arrangement; or

(C) If the issuer or affiliate, as applicable, is a foreign private issuer, any or all members of the board of directors or any committee of the board of directors authorized to approve employment compensation, severance or other employee benefit arrangements under the laws or regulations of the home country approves the arrangement.

Instruction 1 to this paragraph provides that for listed securities independence will be determined in compliance with the listing standards applicable to compensation committee members of the listed issuer.

This exception was premised on the Commission belief that the consideration paid for employment compensation, severance or other benefit arrangements should not be considered when calculating the price paid for securities under the base price Rules. Id. at 580.

In adopting the final Rule, the adoption Release noted:

> We have revised the proposed exemption for compensatory arrangements that meet specified substantive requirements to address a number of the comments received. We have expanded the persons who may enter into an employment compensation, severance or other employee benefit arrangement to include all security holders of the subject company, as opposed to only employees and directors of the subject company. We are also extending this exemption to issuer tender offers. Finally, we have modified the requirements of the exemption so that the amounts to be paid pursuant to an arrangement will have to be "paid or granted as compensation for past services performed, future services to be performed, or future services to be refrained from performing, by the security holder (and matters incidental thereto)" and may "not [be] calculated based on the number of securities tendered or to be tendered in the tender offer by the security holder."

Id. at 580.

E. INSIDER TRADING

3. SECTION 16(b): FROM THE *OBJECTIVE* TO THE *SUBJECTIVE*

a. In General

P. 687 n.30, end note. Similarly in At Home Corp. v. Cox Communications, Inc., 446 F.3d 403, 408 (2d Cir. 2006), *cert. denied*, 549 U.S. 953, the court declined to apply *Kern* to a garden variety insider allegedly engaged in a novel form of insider trading. "*Kern County* controls when the insider is atypical as well as the transaction."

d. Derivative Securities

P. 692 n.54, end note. In At Home Corp. v. Cox Communications, Inc., 446 F.3d 403 (2d Cir. 2006), *cert. denied*, 549 U.S. 953, the court concluded that the acquisition date of a put option is the only sale date if the option is ultimately exercised under a fixed price mechanism.

In Morrison v. Madison Dearborn Capital Partners III, L.P., 463 F.3d 312 (3d Cir. 2006), *cert. denied*, 549 U.S. 1246, the parties agreed that preferred stock convertible into common stock was a *call equivalent position* under Rule 16a-1(b), but held that an automatic adjustment to the conversion price of a derivative security is not a *purchase* for the purposes of §16(b).

Cf. Donoghue v. Centillium Communications, Inc., 2006 Fed. Sec. L. Rep. (CCH) ¶93,824 (S.D.N.Y. 2006), the court held that a defendant's failure to exercise an option cannot be characterized as a *sale*. The analysis followed Rule 16b-6 and Magma Power Co. v. Dow Chem. Co., 136 F.3d 316 (2d Cir. 1998). "[T]he acquisition of a fixed-price option — rather than its exercise — constitutes a *sale* or *purchase* for purposes of Section 16(b)." Id. at 90,120.

7. Definitions

c. *Beneficial Owner*

P. 704 n.86, end note. Under §16(b), a beneficial owner must hold a security both at the time of the purchase and sale or sale and purchase of the security. In Roth v. Jennings, 489 F.3d 499, 514 (2d Cir. 2007), however, the court held that not every member of a group must satisfy the purchase and sale requirement. It is sufficient if collectively these persons own more than 10 percent of the stock before any transaction leading to a short swing profit and at the time of the matching transaction. Ibid.

8. Exemptions

e. Section 16 Exemptive Rules

P. 719 n.126, end 1st par. In Dreiling v. American Express Co., 458 F.3d 942 (9th Cir. 2006), the court held that the 1996 amendment of Rule 16b-3(d) was validly adopted by the SEC. The court rejected the argument that the SEC could only adopt an exemption from Rule 16b-3 when "there is the mere possibility of abuse" and instead relied on "the SEC's 60-year experience with rules interpreting §16(b)." Id. at 951.

The court affirmed also the SEC interpretation of Rule 16b-3(d) as including "directions by deputization," specifically citing Blau v. Lehman and Feder v. Martin Marietta Corp. Id. at 952-953.

F. SARBANES–OXLEY ACT AMENDMENTS

1. Prohibitions on Loans

P. 726, new note 0, end 1st sentence. In 2004 the Commission adopted Rule 13k-1 to exempt an issuer that is a foreign bank or its parent from the §13(k) prohibition on insider lending. Sec. Ex. Act Rel. 48,481, 81 SEC Dock. 107 (2003) (proposal); 49,616, 82 SEC Dock. 2538 (2004) (adoption).

4. Forfeiture of Executive Bonuses Following Issuer Misconduct

P. 727, end page. In Digimarc Corp. Deriv. Litig., 549 F.3d 1223 (9th Cir. 2008), the court held that §304 does not imply a private cause of action.

CHAPTER 7

REGULATION OF THE SECURITIES MARKETS

A. STRUCTURE OF THE SECURITIES MARKETS

1. INTRODUCTION

P. 739, new text after 2d par.   In the aftermath of Richard Grasso's resignation as NYSE Chair, and a major enforcement action against NYSE specialists, questions concerning the NYSE system of governance received renewed attention. See, e.g., Cohen, Craig & Dugan, NYSE Trading Probe Took Late, Sharp Turn, Wall St. J., Oct. 17, 2003, at C1; see also Craig, Kelly & Dugan, NYSE Traders Are Subject of Investigation, Wall St. J., Mar. 4, 2004, at C1.

John Reed, former co-chair of Citigroup, was named interim chair of the NYSE in September 2003. Thomas & Labaton, New Roles and New Faces at the New York Stock Exchange, N.Y. Times, Oct. 17, 2003 at C1; Reed Defends Self-Regulation for NYSE, Outlines Plans for Election of New Board, 35 Sec. Reg. & L. Rep. (BNA) 1732 (2003).

In November Reed proposed and the NYSE membership approved several proposals to change NYSE governance. These proposals were subject to SEC review and approval. Reed proposed eight candidates for election to the reconstituted board: Madeleine K. Albright, Herbert M. Allison, Jr., Euan D. Baird, Marshall N. Carter, Shirley Ann Jackson, James S. McDonald, Robert B. Shapiro, and Sir Dennis Weatherstone. These new members were intended to serve until June 2004 after which the entire board would stand for election each June.

The Reed proposals to amend the NYSE Constitution envisioned both a streamlined board of directors with 6 to 12 directors and a board of executives, appointed by the board of directors, comprised of approximately 20 constituent representatives, balanced among the major broker-dealer firms, the floor community, lessor members, institutional investors, large public funds, and listed companies. The board of directors would select the Chairman and the CEO each June, although the Reed proposal did not resolve whether this would be one or two persons. The board of directors would meet no less than four times a year, Art. IV §6 of Proposed NYSE Constitution, and was empowered to delegate specified powers to committees or the board of executives. Art. IV §14. The board of directors would have authority for rulemaking, supervision, and listing of securities. Art. VIII. It would also be responsible for disciplinary proceedings, Art. IX, membership fees, Art. X, and arbitration, Art. XI.

Under the proposed Constitution, the Nominating and Governance, Human Resources and Compensation, Audit, and Regulatory Oversight and Regulatory Budget committees were required to consist solely of members of the board of directors. Art. IV §12(a).

There are also new proposed joint committees comprising both members of the board of directors and board of executives to address regulation and enforcement and listing standards. Art. IV §12(b).

The board of directors and board of executives were authorized further to meet in joint sessions several times a year.

The board of executives was intended to provide "reasonably balanced representation of the many communities that come together in the Exchange." Art. V §2(a). Cf. §6(b)(3) of Securities Exchange Act. The Chairman of the board of directors would also be Chairman of the board of executives. If there is a separate CEO he or she would also be a member of the board of executives.

> The Board of Executives members (other than the Chairman and Chief Executive Officer) shall be appointed by the Board at its

annual organizational meeting and shall consist of (i) at least six individuals who are either the chief executive or a principal executive officer of a member organization that engages in a business involving substantial direct contact with securities customers, (ii) at least two individuals who are either the chief executive or a principal executive officer of a specialist member organization, (iii) at least two individuals, each of whom spends a majority of his or her time on the Floor of the Exchange, and has as a substantial part of his or her business the execution of transactions on the Floor of the Exchange for other than his or her own account or the account of his or her member organization, but who shall not be registered as a specialist, (iv) at least two individuals who are lessor members who are not affiliated with a broker or dealer in securities, (v) at least four individuals who are either the chief executive or a principal executive officer of an institution that is a significant investor in equity securities, at least one of whom shall be a fiduciary of a public pension fund, and (vi) at least four individuals who are either the chief executive or a principal executive officer of a listed company....If the Board increases the size of the Board of Executives it shall strive to maintain approximately the same balance between Industry Members of the Board of Executives and other members of the Board of Executives as is represented above.

Art. V §2(b).

The board of executives shall meet at least six times each year.
Art. V §6(a).

The Reed proposal envisioned permitting the board of directions to fashion the role of the Chair. However, in Art. VI §2, the Restated Constitution does provide:

> The Chairman shall preside at all meetings of the Board and of the Board of Executives and shall decide all questions of order, subject, however, to an appeal to the Board; provided, however, that if the Chairman is also the Chief Executive Officer, he or she shall not participate in executive sessions of the Board. If the Chairman is not the Chief Executive Officer, he or she shall act as liaison officer between the Board and the Chief Executive Officer. In addition to his or her usual duties, the Chairman shall make an Annual Report on the Exchange's activities to a Plenary Session.

Art. VI §1 specifies additional officers, including the Chief Regulatory Officer, one or more Vice Presidents (one or more of whom may be designated as Executive Vice Presidents or as Senior Vice Presidents or by other designations), a Secretary, a Treasurer, a Controller, and such other officers as the CEO may propose, subject to the approval of the board. Any office may be occupied by more than one individual.

The board of directors was also intended to maintain other advisory committees. NYSE Proxy Notice of Special Meeting at 8 (Nov. 4, 2003).

Reed emphasized the transparency of the revised board of directors:

> (1) Prior to the Annual Meeting, we will publish a proxy statement disclosing the Board Committee charters and the Committee reports on their activities for the year; membership on the Board, on the Board of Executives, and on the various standing and advisory Committees; the facts establishing each Board member's independence, including any non-director relationship between Board members and the NYSE itself and any material relationships among Board members; and Board compensation.
>
> (2) We will publicly disclose information regarding the means by which members and investors may communicate with the NYSE's non-management directors.
>
> (3) The annual report of the Human Resources & Compensation Committee will detail compensation decisions for the top five officers, the existence of any contracts for these individuals and the compensation for the top management team as a whole. The Committee will detail the competitive comparisons and performance judgments that guided their recommendations.
>
> (4) The Nominating & Governance Committee will explain its nominations and make public the procedures that are in place to ensure that appropriate potential nominees are found and considered.
>
> (5) The Board of Directors will detail the considerations that lead to membership on the Board of Executives, and the current membership. A report of the activities of the Board of Executives will be included in the proxy statement.

(6) The various advisory committees of the NYSE will be identified and described, and their members listed in the proxy statement.

(7) An annual report detailing the charitable activities of or on behalf of the Exchange, including the activities of the NYSE Foundation, will be included with the proxy statement.

(8) A report disclosing NYSE political activities, including a list of political contributions made by any NYSE PAC, will be made available prior to the annual meeting.

John Reed Letter to NYSE Members, Nov. 4, 2003, at 3–4.

Two days earlier the *Wall Street Journal* published a front page article describing a 40 page SEC staff report that sharply criticizes the NYSE for laxity in the investigation and discipline of specialists. The Staff Report allegedly concluded that over 22 billion shares were improperly traded over three years, costing investors $155 million. Solomon & Craig, SEC Blasts Big Board Oversight of "Specialist" Trading Firms, Wall St. J., Nov. 3, 2003, at A1. Subsequently the California Public Employees Retirement System (CalPERS) sued the NYSE and seven specialist firms over these practices. CalPERS Sues NYSE, Specialist Firms, Claiming Trading Practices Hurt Investors, 35 Sec. Reg. & L. Rep. (BNA) 2128 (2003); Two NYSE Specialist Firms Settle SEC, Exchange Allegations, 36 Sec. Reg. & L. Rep. (BNA) 331 (2004).

In December 2003 the SEC approved the NYSE reorganization as proposed. Sec. Ex. Act Rel. 48,946, 81 SEC Dock. 2676, 2685 (2003). The Commission concluded its approval of the NYSE reorganization somewhat tentatively:

> The Commission believes that the revised NYSE governance structure is one, but not the only, model for SRO governance consistent with the Act that would provide independence between the business side of the Exchange and its regulatory operations. Other self-regulatory structures or allocations of regulatory duties among SROs may offer advantages and disadvantages in terms of expertise, effectiveness, responsiveness, costs and, ultimately, investor protection. In considering the NYSE proposal, some commenters

have advocated the complete separation of market and SRO functions. In the Commission's view, the complete structural separation of the NYSE's — or any other SRO's — regulatory function cannot be accomplished by an individual SRO, but would require Commission or Congressional action on a market-wide basis.

The Commission is considering a regulatory initiative to assess possible steps to strengthen the framework for the governance of SROs. In addition, the Commission will continue to consider ways to improve the transparency of the governance procedures of all SROs. In this context, some of the transparency topics the Commission may examine include increasing the disclosure of information relating to compensation of SRO directors, officers and employees; regulatory performance (*e.g.*, number of enforcement actions); types and amounts of fines levied; financial information and financial results; and the operation of key committees.

Id. at 2690.

In 2004, the Commission published a detailed rule proposal with respect to stock market governance, Sec. Ex. Act Rel. 50,699, 84 SEC Dock. 444 (2004) (proposal), as well as a related Concept Release. Cf. Seligman, Cautious Evolution or Perennial Irresolution: Stock Market Self-Regulation during the First Seventy Years of the Securities and Exchange Commission, 59 Bus. Law. 1347 (2004).

The Concept Release emphasized the inherent conflicts between SRO functions and SRO members, market operations, listed issuers, and shareholders:

1. INHERENT CONFLICTS WITH MEMBERS

The SROs are responsible for promulgating and enforcing rules that govern all aspects of their members' securities business, including their financial condition, operational capabilities, sales practices, and the qualifications of their personnel. In fulfilling these functions, the SROs conduct examinations on the premises of their members, monitor financial and other operational reports, investigate potential violations of rules, and bring disciplinary proceedings when appropriate. In addition, SROs must surveil trading on any markets they operate to detect rule violations and other improper practices, such as insider trading and market manipulation. Unchecked conflicts in the dual role of regulating and serving can result in poorly targeted SRO rulemaking, less extensive SRO rulemaking, and under zealous enforcement of SRO rules against members....If [the SRO] regulatory staff is disinclined to regulate members, self-regulation will fail. Thus, to be effective, an SRO must be structured in such a way that regulatory staff is unencumbered by inappropriate business pressure.

Pressures that inhibit effective regulation and discourage vigorous enforcement against members can arise for a variety of reasons, including member domination of SRO funding, member control of SRO governance, and member influence over regulatory and enforcement staff. In addition, the economic importance of certain SRO members may create particularly acute conflicts, especially in light of the consolidation of some of the largest securities firms. For example, the number of NYSE specialist firms, which are control to the NYSE's auction trading model, has dropped from 27 in 1999 to 7 in 2002. One NYSE specialist firm in 2003 accounted for over 28% of total NYSE trading volume....

Thus, the current situation appears to be one in which a declining number of member firms are increasingly important to the business interests of their regulator SROs. The anecdotal evidence cited above could indicate that SROs have become more dependent on large members for their funding, potentially enabling those members to wield significant influence with respect to their regulator SROs. This creates the potential for failures by SROs to enforce rules against these members, especially when compared to enforcement against other smaller or less economically influential members, and SRO failures to develop rules that would disrupt the business practices of important members.

The PCX's proposal in 2001 to enter into an arrangement in which ArcaEx would become the PCX's equity trading facility presented a particularly complicated situation in which an SRO would be affiliated with a member. In the ArcaEx Approval Order, the Commission examined a variety of issues related to self-regulation, including the regulatory responsibilities of the PCX under the new structure and the potential for inherent conflicts to be exacerbated when an SRO is affiliated with a member. In addition, the Commission imposed certain requirements with respect to PCX and ArcaEx that were designed to ensure that the various functions of the affiliated broker-dealer were properly regulated.

P. 739

In an ArcaEx Approval Order, the Commission discussed the PCX's proposal that Wave Securities LLC ("Wave"), a wholly owned subsidiary of ArcaEx, would be a registered broker-dealer and a member of both the PCX and the NASD. Wave would have two primary functions with respect to ArcaEx. Specifically, Wave would act as an introducing broker for customers that were not PCX members and would provide sponsored access to ArcaEx. Wave would also provide an optional routing service for ArcaEx, and, as necessary, would route orders to other market centers from ArcaEx.

Under Section 6(b)(5) of the Exchange Act, the rules of a national securities exchange must not be designed to permit unfair discrimination between customers, issuers, brokers, or dealers. The Commission noted in the ArcaEx Approval Order that the potential for unfair discrimination may be heightened if a national securities exchange or its affiliate owns or operates a broker-dealer. This is because, the Commission stated, the financial interests of the exchange may conflict with its responsibilities as an SRO regarding the affiliated broker-dealer. Moreover, the Commission described the conflict of interest that may arise if a national securities exchange (or an affiliate) provides advantages to its broker-dealer that are not available to other members, or provides a feature to all members that was designed to give its broker-dealer a special advantage. These advantages, such as greater access to information, improved speed of execution, or enhanced operational capabilities in dealing with the exchange, might constitute unfair discrimination under the Exchange Act, the Commission concluded. Thus, the Commission required that the PCX not serve as the self-regulatory organization primarily responsible for examining the Wave broker-dealer....

2. Inherent Conflicts with Market Operations

In addition to conflicts with members, an SRO's regulatory obligations may conflict with the interests of its own or its affiliate's market operations. The SROs that operate markets...are responsible for promulgating rules that govern trading in their markets; establishing the necessary systems and procedures to monitor such trading; identifying instances of suspicious trading, such as potential insider trading and market manipulation; and enforcing the Exchange Act, the rules thereunder, and their own rules. If an SRO identifies potential misconduct involving persons or entities within its jurisdiction, the SRO is responsible for conducting a further investigation and bringing a disciplinary action when appropriate....

As competition among markets grows, the markets that SROs operate will continue to come under increased pressure to attract order flow. This business pressure can create a strong conflict between the SRO regulatory and market operations functions. Because increasing inter-market competition has provided members...with increasing flexibility as to where to direct order flow, SRO staff may be less inclined to enforce vigorously SRO rules that would cause large liquidity providers to redirect order flow....

While regulatory staff is responsible for carrying out self-regulatory obligations, they are also a component of a competitive business organization. As inter-market competition increases, regulatory staff may come under pressure to permit market activity that attracts order flow to their market. Market operations staff may also be less likely to cooperate and communicate with regulatory staff if they think such cooperation or communication will hinder their effort to attract order flow....

Another concern is the potential for SRO regulatory staff, in the course of developing rules and examining members, to become overly dependent on members for their understanding of market practices and to lose their independent perspective concerning these practices. A potential loss of objectivity could accompany the greater knowledge and expertise that result from having SRO regulatory staff interwoven with SRO market operations.

Also, SROs may have a tendency to abuse their SRO status by over-regulating members that operate markets that compete with the SRO's own market for order flow. Indeed, among other reasons, these concerns led the Commission to require the NASD to establish the Alternative Display Facility ("ADF"). Exchange Act rule 11Ac1-1 requires that SRO members communicate their best bids and offers to an SRO and in the late 1990s broker-dealer choice as to where to post quotes in Nasdaq securities was effectively limited to Nasdaq. Thus, certain users of Nasdaq were concerned that they would be put at a distinct competitive disadvantage if they were compelled to provide their best bids and offers to the exclusive Securities Information Processor ("SIP") for Nasdaq securities through the new SuperMontage system. These users argued that, not only would their quotes be subject to a competing market's trading rules, but that the situation would be rife for abuse because of Nasdaq functioning both as a regulator and competitor of the ECNs. Thus, before permitting the launch of Nasdaq's SuperMontage, the Commission required that the NASD provide an alternative, the ADF, to Nasdaq's SuperMontage on which to quote Nasdaq securities....

3. Inherent Conflicts with Issuers

Another potential SRO conflict is with listed issuers. The SROs promulgate and administer listing standards that govern the securities that may be traded in their markets. For corporate securities, these rules include minimum financial qualifications and reporting requirements for their issuers. Obtaining a listing on a prominent SRO market provides corporate issuers with enhanced visibility and prestige in the eyes of investors, as well as the appearance of a well-operated and well-regulated trading market for their securities. An active market for secondary trading serves not only its shareholders, but also the corporation itself through enhanced capital-raising capacities.

SRO listing standards also have a major role in corporate governance, particularly since the passage of the Sarbanes-Oxley Act....

As issuers are offered new alternatives as to markets on which to list their securities, SROs face increasing competitive pressure to gain and retain listings. As with SRO competition for members and order flow, competition for issuers may cause an SRO to fail to discharge its self-regulatory responsibilities properly. This can take the form of admitting to trading issuers that fail to satisfy initial listing standards; delaying the delisting of issuers that no longer satisfy maintenance standards; failing to enforce listing standards (including the new issuer corporate governance standards); and reducing (or even eliminating) listing fees. This competition also can reveal itself in an unwillingness to restrict issuer activities or impose requirements that may be more stringent than similar rules of competitor SROs....

4. INHERENT CONFLICTS WITH SHAREHOLDERS

Another significant conflict of interest for SRO responsibilities is with SRO shareholders. SRO demutualization raises the concern that the profit motive of a shareholder-owned SRO could detract from proper self-regulation. For instance, shareholder-owned SROs may commit insufficient funds to regulatory operations or use their disciplinary function as a revenue generator with respect to member firms that operate competing trading systems or whose trading activity is otherwise perceived as undesirable. Moreover, as with the inherent conflicts discussed above, this conflict can be exacerbated by increased intermarket competition.

A variety of ownership controls for demutualized SROs can potentially prevent some of these conflicts. Indeed, as previously noted, this concept release is being published in conjunction with the SRO Governance and Transparency Proposal, which would, if adopted, impose a variety of restrictions, including an effective restriction on revenue from regulatory operations being used to pay dividends to shareholders.

Id. at 624–631. See also id. at 633–646 (recent intermarket surveillance and funding stresses on SRO regulation).

To ensure fair administration of SRO governance, the Commission proposed identical new Rule 6a-5 applicable to national securities exchanges and new Rule 15Aa-3 applicable to registered securities associations:

> The proposals would apply to exchanges and associations minimum governance standards that are commensurate with standards required of listed issuers. Among other provisions, the proposed rules would require an exchange's or association's governing board to be composed of a majority of independent directors, with key board committees to be composed solely of independent directors....
>
> The proposed governance rules also would require each exchange and association to separate its regulatory function from its market operations and other commercial interests, whether through functional or organizational separation. Although a premise underlying self-regulation is that regulation works best when it is carried out in proximity to the regulated activity, it is

equally important that there be sufficient independence within the self-regulatory process to adequately check undue interference or influence from the persons or entities being regulated. In the Commission's view, the proposed rules would help insulate the regulatory activities of an exchange or association from the conflicts of interest that otherwise may arise by virtue of its market operations.

In addition, the proposed rules would require an exchange or association to establish ownership and voting limitations on the interest of its members that are brokers or dealers in the exchange, association, or a facility of the exchange or association through which the member is permitted to effect transactions. Members who trade on an exchange or through a facility of an exchange or association have traditionally had ownership interests in such exchange or facility. Recent developments, including the trend towards demutualization, have raised the concern that a member's interest could become so large as to cast doubt on whether the exchange or association could fairly and objectively exercise its self-regulatory responsibilities with respect to that member....The Commission believes that the proposed rules would help mitigate the conflicts of interest that could occur if a member were to control a significant stake in its regulator, and are necessary and appropriate to help ensure that an exchange or association can effectively carry out its statutory obligations under Section 6(b) or 15A(b) of the Exchange Act, respectively.

Id. at 455–456.

Proposed Rules 6a-5 and 15Aa-3 apply respectively to each national securities exchange and generally to each of its regulatory subsidiaries. Proposed Rule 6a-5(a); Proposed Rule 15Aa-3(a). There are exceptions for a national securities exchange registered under §6(g)(1) and a limited purpose national securities association under §15A(k)(1).

Proposed Rules 6a-5 and 15Aa-3 would impose identical substantive requirements with respect to each covered exchange and covered securities association.

Proposed Rules 6a-5(c)(1) and 15Aa-3(c)(1) would expressly require that the board of each national securities exchange and registered securities association be composed of a majority of independent directors. The proposal Release further notes: "SROs, of course, can elect to implement a greater proportion of independent directors." Id. at 458. A footnote notes that the NYSE has done so. Id. at 458 n.94.

Currently the exchanges, the NASA, and the Nasdaq divide their boards between industry, non-industry, and public directors. Under this construct:

> An *industry* director is generally an individual who is an officer, director or employee of a broker or dealer or an affiliate of a broker or dealer, a consultant or employee of the exchange itself, or an exchange permit holder. *See, e.g.*, NASD Bylaws, Articles I(n) and I(o) and Phlx Bylaws, Article I, Section 1-1(m).
>
> A *non-industry* director may be an individual who has some relationship with the SRO or the financial services industry; thus, a non-industry director could not be considered truly *public*. For example, officers and employees of issuers listed on the exchange are considered non-industry directors. *See, e.g.*, Phlx Bylaws, Article I, Section 1-1(t) and CHX Bylaws, Article III, Section 10(1).
>
> A *public* director is generally an individual who has no material business relationship with a broker or dealer or with the exchange or association. *See, e.g.*, NASD Bylaws, Articles I(ee) and I(ff); Phlx Bylaws, Article I, Section 1-1(y); and CHX Bylaws, Article III, Section 10(2).

Id. at 458. A number of exchanges require that at least 50 percent of the board be composed of public and non-industry directors. Id. at 458–459.

The SEC rule proposals notably alter this allocation to require a majority of each covered securities exchange and securities association be the equivalent to *public* directors. Proposed Rules 6a-5(c)(2) and 15Aa-3(c)(2) provide:

> No director may qualify as an independent director unless the Board affirmatively determines that the director has no material relationship with the national securities exchange or any affiliate of the national securities exchange. The Board must make this determination upon the director's nomination or appointment to the Board and thereafter no less frequently than annually and as often as necessary in light of the director's circumstances.

311

More significantly proposed Rules 6a-5(b)(12) and 15Aa-3(b)(13) elaborately provide:

> The term *independent director* means a director who has no material relationship with the national securities exchange or any affiliate of the national securities exchange, any member of the national securities exchange or any affiliate of such member, or any issuer of securities that are listed or traded on the national securities exchange or a facility of the national securities exchange. A director is not independent if any of the following circumstances exist:
>
> (i) The director, or an immediate family member, is employed by or otherwise has a material relationship with the national securities exchange or any affiliate of the national securities exchange, or within the past three years was employed by or otherwise had a material relationship with the national securities exchange or any affiliate of the national securities exchange.
>
> (ii) The director is a member or is employed by or affiliated with a member or any affiliate of a member or, within the past three years was a member or was employed by or affiliated with a member or any affiliate of a member, or the director has an immediate family member that is, or within the past three years was, an executive officer of a member or any affiliate of a member.
>
> (iii) The director, or an immediate family member, has received during any twelve month period within the past three years more than $60,000 in payments from the national securities exchange or any affiliate of the national securities exchange or from a member or any affiliate of a member, other than the following:
>
>> (A) Compensation for Board or Board committee service;
>> (B) Compensation to an immediate family member who is not an executive officer of the national securities exchange or any affiliate of the national securities exchange or of a member of any affiliate of a member; and
>> (C) Pension and other forms of deferred compensation for prior service, provided such compensation is not contingent in any way on continued service.
>
> (iv) The director, or an immediate family member, is a partner in, or controlling shareholder or executive officer of any organization to which the national securities exchange or any affiliate of the national securities exchange made, or from which the national securities exchange or any affiliate of the national securities

exchange received, payments for property or services in the current or any of the past three full fiscal years that exceed two percent of the recipient's consolidated gross revenues for that year, or $200,000, whichever is more, other than the following:

(A) Payments arising solely from investments in the securities of the national securities exchange or any facility or affiliate of the national securities exchange; or

(B) Payments under non-discretionary charitable contribution matching programs.

(v) The director, or an immediate family member, is, or within the past three years was, an executive officer of an issuer of securities listed or primarily traded on the national securities exchange or a facility of the national securities exchange.

(vi) The director, or an immediate family member, is, or within the past three years was, employed as an executive officer of another entity where any of the national securities exchange's executive officers serves on that entity's compensation committee.

(vii) The director, or an immediate family member, is a current partner of the outside auditor of the national securities exchange or any affiliate of the national securities exchange, or was a partner or employee of the outside auditor of the national securities exchange or any affiliate of the national securities exchange who worked on the national securities exchange's or any affiliate's audit, at any time within the past three years.

(viii) In the case of a director that is a member of the Audit Committee, such director (other than in his or her capacity as a member of the Audit Committee, the Board, or any other Board committee), accepts, directly or indirectly, any consulting, advisory, or other compensatory fee from the national securities exchange, any affiliate of the national securities exchange, any member, or affiliate of a member, other than fixed amounts of pension and other forms of deferred compensation for prior service, provided such compensation is not contingent in any way on continued service.

Other definitions amplify the independent director definition. An *immediate family member*, under proposed Rules 6a-5(b)(11) and 15Aa-3(b)(12) "means a person's spouse, parents, children, and siblings, whether by blood, marriage, or adoption, or anyone residing on such person's home."

P. 739

Compensation, as defined in proposed Rules 6a-5(b)(6) and 15Aa-3(b)(7):

> means any form of compensation and any material perquisites awarded, or that are to be awarded, whether or not set forth in any written documents, to any executive officer of the national securities exchange, including, without limitation, salary, bonus, pension, deferred compensation, compensation awarded pursuant to any incentive plan or equity-based plan, or any other plan, contract, authorization or arrangement pursuant to which cash or securities may be received.

However, "[t]he Commission believes that compensation received as deferred compensation for prior service should not by itself exclude a director from being considered independent." Id. at 460.

Those requirements "are similar to criteria that are contained in SRO listing standards, which recently were approved by the Commission and are designed to address similar governance concerns and the conflicts of interest that can arise between a company's management and its public shareholders." Id. at 461.

There are other independent board requirements. Each covered securities exchange or covered securities association is required to establish policies and procedures that require each director to inform the exchange or association of the existence of any relationship or interest that may reasonably be considered to bear on whether the director is an independent director. Proposed Rules 6a-5(c)(3) and 15Aa-3(c)(3). See also proposed Rules 6a-5(c)(9) and 15Aa-3(c)(9) (covered exchange or association also must establish procedures for interested persons to communicate their concerns regarding any matter within the authority or jurisdiction of a standing committee directly to the independent directors).

At least 20 percent of the total number of directors must be selected by members. Proposed Rules 6a-5(c)(4) and 15Aa-3(c)(4). At least one director must be a representative of the issuers and at least one must be representative of investors. Neither of these directors may be associated with an exchange or association member or a broker-dealer. Proposed Rules 6a-5(c)(5) and 15Aa-3(c)(5). These provisions are intended to be consistent with the requirements of *fair representation* and *issuer and investor representation* requirements of the Securities Exchange Act §§6(b)(3) and 15A(b)(4). The proposal Release further elaborates:

> This requirement is not intended to prohibit exchanges and associations from having boards composed solely of independent directors. If an exchange's or association's board is composed wholly of independent directors, the candidate or candidates selected by members would have to be independent. This *20% standard* for member candidates comports with previously-approved SRO rule changes that raised the issue of fair representation. The Commission preliminarily believes that the proposed 20% requirement strikes a proper balance by giving members a practical voice in the governance of the exchange or association and the administration of its affairs, without jeopardizing the overall independence of the board.

Id. at 462.

When the board of a covered exchange or association considers any matter that is recommended or otherwise within the jurisdiction of a Standing Committee, a majority of the directors who vote on the matter must be independent directors. Proposed Rules 6a-5(c)(6) and 15Aa-3(c)(6). The proposal Release elaborates: "For example, assume an exchange has a board composed of nine independent directors and eight non-independent directors. If two independent directors do not participate in a board meeting but all the non-independent directors participate in such meeting, the matter could be voted upon only by the seven independent directors present and six of the eight non-independent directors present." Id. at 462.

Following the models of the new NYSE and Nasdaq listing requirements and the recent NYSE governance changes, the Commission is proposing that each covered exchange and covered association, at a minimum, have five Standing Committees: Nominating, Governance, Compensation, Audit, and Regulatory

Oversight. Proposed Rules 6a-5(e)(1) and 15Aa-3(e)(1). A footnote, however, somewhat softens this requirement by explaining:

> An SRO would not be precluded from allowing a single committee to carry out the functions of two Standing Committees as long as the committee consisted solely of independent directors, *e.g.*, the functions of the Nominating Committee and the Governance Committee could be carried out by a single committee. Also, to the extent that a Standing Committee of the exchange or association carries out responsibilities on behalf of a regulatory subsidiary, the regulatory subsidiary would not be required to have a Standing Committee that performs the same functions. *See* proposed Rules 6a-5(a) and 15Aa-3(a).

Id. at 463 n.155.

The responsibilities of the Audit and Regulatory Oversight Committees are defined broadly in Rules 6a-5(i)(2), 6a-5(j)(2), 15Aa-3(i)(2), and 15Aa-3(j)(2) and provide in the securities exchange version:

> The Audit Committee must have written a charter that addresses the Audit Committee's purpose and responsibilities, which, at a minimum, must be to assist the Board in oversight of the integrity of the national securities exchange's financial statements; the national securities exchange's compliance with related legal and regulatory requirements; and the qualifications and independence of the national securities exchange's auditor, including direct responsibility for the hiring, firing, and compensation of the auditor; overseeing the auditor's engagement; meeting regularly in executive session with the auditor; reviewing the auditor's reports with respect to the national securities exchange's internal records; pre-approving all audit and nonaudit services performed by the auditor; determining the budget and staffing of the national securities exchange's internal audit department; and establishing procedures for the receipt of complaints regarding accounting, internal accounting controls, or auditing matters of the national securities exchange and the confidential submission by employees of the national securities exchange of concerns regarding questionable accounting or auditing matters....

The Regulatory Oversight Committee must have a written charter that addresses the Regulatory Oversight Committee's purpose and responsibilities, which, at a minimum, must be to assure the adequacy and effectiveness of the regulatory program of the national securities exchange; assess the exchange's regulatory performance; determine the regulatory plan, programs, budget, and staffing for the regulatory functions of the exchange; assess the performance of, and recommend compensation and personnel actions involving, the Chief Regulatory Officer and other senior regulatory personnel to the Compensation Committee; monitor and review regularly with the Chief Regulatory Officer matters relating to the exchange's surveillance, examination, and enforcement units; assure that the exchange's disciplinary and arbitration proceedings are conducted in accordance with the exchange's rules and policies and any other applicable laws or rules, including those of the Commission; prior to the exchange's approval of an affiliated security for listing, certify that such security meets the exchange's rules for listing; and approve reports filed with the Commission as required by Regulation AL....

Each Standing Committee must have the authority to direct and supervise any matter within the scope of its duties and to obtain advice and assistance from independent legal counsel and other advisors as it deems necessary. Proposed Rules 6a-5(e)(2) and 15Aa-3(e)(2). Each covered securities exchange and each covered securities association must provide sufficient resources, "as determined by each Standing Committee" to permit the Standing Committee to fulfill its responsibilities, including retaining independent legal counsel and other advisors. Proposed Rules 6a-5(g)(3) and 15Aa-3(e)(3).

Each Standing Committee, other than the Governance Committee, would be required to conduct an annual performance self-evaluation. Proposed Rules 6a-5(f)(5), 6a-5(h)(3), 6a-5(i)(3), 6a-5(j)(6), 15Aa-3(f)(3), 15Aa-3(h)(3), 15Aa-3(i)(3), and 15A-3(j)(6). The Governance Committee would be required to conduct an evaluation of the exchange or association as a whole. Proposed Rules 6a-5(g)(3) and 15Aa-3(g)(3). Similarly each Standing Committee would be required to have a written charter addressing the Committee's purpose and responsibilities. See Proposed Rules

6a-5(f)(2), 6a-5(g)(2), 6a-5(h)(2), 6a-5(i)(2), 6a-5(j)(2), 15Aa-3(f)(2), 15Aa-3(g)(2), 15Aa-3(h)(2), 15Aa-3(i)(2), and 15Aa-3(j)(2).

In addition, any committee, subcommittee, or panel that is responsible for conducting hearings, rendering decisions, and imposing sanctions with respect to disciplinary matters would be subject to the jurisdiction of the Regulatory Oversight Committee. Although the Regulatory Oversight Committee would be required to be composed solely of independent directors, the Commission believes that, to satisfy the fair representation requirement, the exchange or association must provide for member participation on any committee, subcommittee, or panel that is responsible for conducting hearings, rendering decisions, and imposing sanctions with respect to member disciplinary matters. In order to satisfy this requirement, the proposal would require that at least 20% of the members of any such committee, subcommittee, or panel be members of the exchange or association.

Each covered securities exchange or covered association would be permitted to establish other committees of the board as it determines to be appropriate. If, however, additional Committees, such as an Executive Committee, act on behalf of the board, the Committee would be required to be composed of a majority of independent directors. Proposed Rules 6a-5(k)(i) and 15Aa-3(k)(l). The proposal Release added: "In addition, the Commission is proposing that at least 20% of the persons serving on any committee that is not a Standing Committee and any committee, subcommittee, or panel that is subject to the jurisdiction of a Standing Committee, and that is responsible for providing advice with respect to trading rules or disciplinary rules, be members of the exchange or association." Id. at 466.

Under the proposed Rules, the independent directors are required to meet regularly in executive session, proposed Rules 6a-5(d)(1) and 15Aa-3(d)(1), which is defined by proposed Rules 6a-5(b)(9) and 15Aa-3(b)(10), to mean "a meeting of the independent directors of the Board, without the presence of management...or the directors who are not independent directors." The proposed Rules, however, do not specify a minimum frequency for meetings in executive session. More generally the independent directors, as with the Standing Committees, have authority to

REGULATION OF THE SECURITIES MARKETS P. 739

direct and supervise inquiries brought to their attention within the scope of their duties, to obtain advice and assistance from independent legal counsel and other advisors, and to be provided sufficient funding and other resources, as determined by the independent directors, to fulfill their responsibilities. Proposed Rules 6a-5(d)(2)-(3) and 15Aa-3(d)(2)-(3).

The proposed Rules do not require the separation of the board Chair from the CEO, but do require if an SRO voluntarily chooses separation, that the Chair be an independent director. Proposed Rule 6a-5(m)(1) and 15Aa-3(m)(1). The proposal Release explained:

> The proposed rules, including the provision related to the Chairman and CEO, are designed to foster a greater degree of independent decision-making by the governing body of an exchange or association. However, while recognizing the benefits of independence, the Commission understands that some SROs may perceive efficiencies in having one person serve as Chairman and CEO, and therefore the Commission is not proposing to prohibit this arrangement. In this regard, the Commission notes that both the NYSE and BSE currently have separate individuals serving as the Chairman and as the CEO of the exchange, although the exchanges' governing documents do not expressly require this separation.

Id. at 467. If the Chair and CEO are the same individual, the board would be required to designate an independent director as a *lead director* to preside over executive sessions. Proposed Rules 6a-5(m)(3) and 15Aa-3(m)(3).

While the SEC does not propose to separate the board Chair and CEO, it does propose a more far-reaching separation of regulatory and market operations. Under proposed Rules 6a-5(n) and 15Aa-3(n) each covered securities exchange or covered association is required to establish policies and procedures to assure the independence of its regulatory program from its market operations and other commercial interests. Proposed Rule 6a-5(n)(1) and 15Aa-3(n)(1). This can either be done by (i) structurally separating market operations from other commercial interests by means of separate legal entities or (ii) functional separation

319

within the same legal entity. Proposed Rules 6a-5(n)(3) and 15Aa-3(n)(3). In either case, the proposed Rules would require that the board appoint a Chief Regulatory Officer to administer the regulatory program and that the Chief Regulatory Officer report directly to the Regulatory Oversight Committee. The proposal Release explained:

> The Commission believes that its proposal to require the structural or functional separation of the regulatory functions and the market operations and other commercial interests of the exchange or association, together with the creation of a fully independent Regulatory Oversight Committee and the appointment of a Chief Regulatory Officer who would administer the regulatory program and report directly to the Regulatory Oversight Committee, are designed to manage more effectively the inherent conflicts of interest in our self-regulatory system and a particular structure for this separation — focusing on the ends rather than the means — the proposed rules would provide exchanges and associations with a measure of flexibility in determining how best to achieve the result of functional independence of the regulatory program.

Id. at 468.

In December 2005 the NYSE merged with Archipelago Holdings, Inc. The merger provided the NYSE with an electronic trading platform and was the largest merger in history between securities exchanges.

Two days later the Nasdaq entered into a definitive agreement with Instinet. Big Board, Archipelago Members Approve Merger to Form For-Profit NYSE Group Inc., 37 Sec. Reg. & L. Rep. (BNA) 2026 (2005). See also SEC Approves Rule Changes Needed to Effectuate NYSE/Archipelago Merger, 38 id. 362 (2006); NYSE, Archipelago Merger Complete; New For-Profit Company to Begin Trading, 38 id. 414.

Considerable progress had been made towards a consolidation of NASD and NYSE membership regulation when SEC Chair Cox delivered remarks entitled More Efficient and Effective Regulation in the Era of Global Consolidation of Markets to the first board meeting of the Securities Industry and Financial Markets Association on November 10, 2006 and stated:

The very good news, as we meet here today, is that we're on the verge of historic changes that will simplify the current self regulatory structure. Instead of multiple and often redundant players, we may soon have a single self regulator for all firms in the securities industry. Instead of two rulebooks, two separate and uncoordinated regulatory staffs, and two completely different enforcement systems; instead of a menagerie of potentially conflicting schemes that can actually undermine the effectiveness of regulation and the efficiency of the securities markets — we might soon be able to increase the effectiveness of regulation for the benefit of investors by eliminating the needless and often harmful duplication that interferes with that investor protection mission.

As Chairman of the Securities and Exchange Commission, I strongly support these efforts, which are currently well underway, to fold the member regulation functions of both the NASD and the NYSE into one regulatory body. I'm firmly convinced that, done properly, this can make our self regulatory system more efficient and more robust from an investor protection standpoint.

Before I drill down into exactly what kind of changes we hope to see, it's worth considering the nature of the competitive, technological, and regulatory developments that have already transformed our nation's securities markets, and that have brought us to this point.

First, and most obviously, our U.S. markets are operating in a much more competitive environment. That's true not just domestically, but overseas as well. Both here at home, and abroad as well, our markets are facing increased competition — not just from other exchanges, but also from electronic communications networks. And that, in turn, has prompted significant shifts in market share away from the primary markets. All of this competition has been a catalyst for innovation in a number of areas: in trading systems; in meeting the demands of customers; and in driving down costs, including the fees charged by the trading markets.

Another transformational change that has occurred in U.S. markets is the conversion by a number of exchanges from member-owned organizations to for-profit entities. Some of our exchanges have even attracted investment from major securities firms. There's little doubt that this move toward demutualization — like all the other market developments we've seen — is intended to help our markets to be more nimble and efficient in response to competition.

P. 739

So with everything changing on the competitive landscape to a more responsive, cost-effective, global and customer-driven model, it was inevitable that we would face this question: What is our regulatory system (the design of which is, after all, quite old) doing to be more responsive and cost effective in this new environment? And it has been the intense focus on this question by everyone in this room, by government policy makers, by industry professionals, and by academics, that has led to the current movement toward regulatory consolidation.

In late November 2006 the boards of the NASD and NYSE jointly announced a proposed regulatory consolidation. The term sheet read in part:

> Transaction. On November 28, NASD and NYSE Group announced a plan to consolidate their member regulation operations into a new self-regulatory organization (SRO) that will be the single member regulator for all 5,100 securities firms doing business with the public in the United States. The new SRO will be responsible for all member regulation, arbitration and mediation, and all other current NASD responsibilities, including market regulation by contract for NASDAQ, the American Stock Exchange, the International Securities Exchange and the Chicago Climate Exchange. In addition, the SRO will oversee all member compliance examinations, rule writing, professional training, licensing and registration, and industry utilities like the Alternative Display Facility, the OTC Bulletin Board, and Trade Reporting Facilities. NYSE Regulation will continue to oversee market surveillance and listed company compliance at the New York Stock Exchange and NYSE Arca.
>
> Strategic Rationale and Consolidation Goals. The consolidation plan, which was unanimously approved by the NASD Board of Governors and approved by the Boards of Directors of NYSE Regulation and NYSE Group, will make private-sector regulation more efficient and effective and is designed to accomplish the following goals:
>
> - Help to make U.S. markets more competitive by streamlining regulation.

- Make regulation more sensible, yet more effective, through the creation of a single regulator — which serves to reduce complexity and eliminate potential conflicts.
- Ensure industry participation in the SRO process under a governance structure that guarantees fair and balanced representation.
- Adopt a uniform set of rules that's flexible enough to accommodate securities firms' different business models and sizes.
- Create cost savings for every firm in the industry.
- Ensure the structure we have in place is good for the capital markets and investors.

Consideration.

- The transaction is structured to be financially neutral to NYSE Group shareholders.

Member Benefits.

- The consolidation will reduce the cost of regulation; once approved, NASD will make a one-time payment of $35,000 to all member firms in anticipation of cost savings achieved by the new SRO. The Gross Income Assessment fee — a firm's annual dues to NASD — will be reduced by $1,200 (the minimum payment required) each year for five years.
- The new governance structure guarantees industry participation that ensures fair and balanced member representation on the Board.
- Enhanced Small Firm Advisory Board will be focused on small firm issues.
- Targeted expense reductions beginning in the third year after the transaction, which will result in a more efficient organization and anticipated fee reductions to members.

Management

- Mary Schapiro — CEO of the new organization, member of the Board of Governors
- Rick Ketchum — Non-Executive Chairman of the Board during the three-year transition

Governance Structure. A 23-person interim Board of Governors will oversee the new SRO for a three-year transitional period.

- The CEO and Non-Executive Chairman will serve on the interim Board of Governors.
- Eleven Governors will be appointed from outside the securities industry.
  - The current NASD Board and NYSE Boards each will appoint five Public Governors.
  - One Public Governor will be appointed jointly by both organizations.
- Ten Governors will be from inside the securities industry.
  - 3 representatives (nominated by NASD) to be elected by small firms (1-150 registered representatives); small firms may also present their own slate of nominees.
  - 1 representative (jointly nominated) to be elected by medium-sized firms (151-499 registered representatives); medium-sized firms may also present their own slate of nominees.
  - 3 representatives (nominated by NYSE) to be elected by large firms (500 or more registered representatives); large firms may also present their own slate of nominees.
  - 3 representatives will fill the remaining three seats, including an NYSE-appointed floor member, an NASD-appointed representative of independent dealers/insurance affiliated broker-dealers and a jointly appointed representative of investment companies.

Early in 2007 NASD firms, by a 64 percent majority, approved the bylaw amendments to consolidate NASD and the NYSE into a single SRO, which will initially include the 2400 NASD organization and 470 NYSE regulation, arbitration, and enforcement personnel. NASD Members Overwhelmingly Approve Plan for New SRO for Member Regulation, 39 Sec. Reg. & L. Rep. (BNA) 130 (2007).

The new SRO is known as FINRA (Financial Industry Regulatory Authority). NASD is no more.

2. The Stock Markets

P. 741, end 1st full par. Late in 2005 the SEC approved a NYSE Hybrid Market on a pilot basis. Sec. Ex. Act Rel. 52,954, 86 SEC Dock. 2285 (2005) (adoption). The Phase 1 Pilot Program involved 200 securities out of 3600 listed on the NYSE. "The most substantive change that will apply to trading in Pilot securities will be that Floor brokers will lose their current ability to object to the specialist trading on parity with their orders unless the specialist is manually trading with them in the Crowd.... A Floor broker who does not want to permit the specialist to trade on parity with his or her orders may send the order through SuperDOT, enter a Direct order, or hit a bid/take an offer." Id. at 2288.

In 2006 the Commission approved NYSE rule changes to establish a hybrid automatic extension market. Sec. Ex. Act Rel. 53,539, 87 SEC Dock. 1747 (2006) (approval). "In essence, NYSE has proposed to move from a floor-based auction market with limited automatic order interaction to a more automated market with a limited floor-based auction market availability." Id. at 1751.

In 2007 the Nasdaq acquired the Boston Stock Exchange. Sec. Ex. Act Rel. 58,324, 93 SEC Dock. 2729 (2008) (adopting rule changes).

In 2008 the NYSE acquired the Amex. Sec. Ex. Act Rel. 58,265, 93 SEC Dock. 2483 (2008).

In 2008 the Nasdaq OMX Group, Inc. acquired the Philadelphia Stock Exchange, Sec. Ex. Act Rel. 58,179, 93 SEC Dock. 2157 (2008), and the Boston Stock Exchange. Sec. Ex. Act Rel. 58,183, 93 SEC Dock. 2182 (2008).

In 2008 the Commission approved the registration of the BATS Exchange as a national securities exchange. Sec. Ex. Act Rel. 58,375, 93 SEC Dock. 2905 (2008).

P. 746

c. The Consolidated Reporting System

(iii) *Regulation NMS*

P. 746, new text, end page. In 2004 the Commission proposed a new Regulation NMS to codify its existing national market system rules and to adopt four new rules addressing: (1) Trade Through Transactions; (2) Market Access; (3) Subpenny Quotes; and (4) Market Data. Sec. Ex. Act Rel. 49,325, 82 SEC Dock. 758 (2004) (proposal).

The Commission articulated the rationale for Regulation NMS broadly:

> If adopted, the proposals collectively would constitute a significant upgrade of the NMS regulatory framework and address a variety of issues that have arisen in recent years. The NMS needs to be enhanced and modernized, not because it has failed investors, but because it has been so successful in promoting growth, efficiency, innovation, and competition that many of its old rules now are outdated. Since the NMS was created nearly thirty years ago, trading volume has exploded, competition among market centers has intensified, and investor trading costs have shrunk dramatically. Each of the major milestones in the development of the NMS — including the creation of the consolidated system for disseminating market information in the 1970s, the incorporation of The Nasdaq Stock Market, Inc. ("Nasdaq") securities into the NMS in the 1980s, and the adoption of the Order Handling Rules in the 1990s — has successively generated enormous benefits for investors.
>
> In the 2000s, improvements to the NMS have continued to benefit investors. In particular, the rescission of New York Stock Exchange, Inc. ("NYSE") Rule 390, trading in penny increments, and public disclosure of order execution quality have set the stage for exceptionally vigorous competition among market centers, particularly to provide the best prices for orders of less than block size (10,000 shares). Since November 2001, for example (the first month for which all markets were required to disclose their execution quality), the effective spreads paid by investors seeking liquidity in the NMS have declined steadily across all markets by a cumulative total of more than 40%. In November 2003 alone, these

reduced spreads resulted in cumulative investor savings of more than $340 million, or more than $4.0 billion on an annualized basis. Importantly, small investors seeking direct participation in the U.S. securities markets have shared fully in these savings, and indeed have been the biggest beneficiaries of NMS improvements....

The objectives for the NMS set forth in the Exchange Act are well known — efficiency, competition, price transparency, best execution, and direct interaction of investor orders. Each of these objectives is essential, yet they sometimes conflict with one another in practice and can require delicate balancing. In particular, the objective of market center competition can be difficult to reconcile with the objective of investor order interaction. We want to encourage innovation and competition by the many individual market centers that collectively make up the NMS, while at the same time assuring that each of these parts contributes to a system that, as a whole, generates the greatest benefits for investors — not their market intermediaries.

The Commission therefore has sought to avoid the extremes of, on the one hand, isolated market centers and, on the other hand, a totally centralized system that loses the benefits of vigorous competition and innovation among market centers. To achieve the appropriate degree of integration, the Commission primarily has relied on two tools: (1) transparency of the best prices through the consolidated display of quotes and trades from all NMS market centers; and (2) intermarket "rules of the road" that establish a basic framework within which competition among NMS market centers can flourish on terms that ultimately benefit investors. Today's proposals are intended to continue this strategy.

In particular, the proposals are designed to address a variety of problems that generally fall within three categories:

(1) the need for uniform rules that promote equal regulation of, and free competition among, all types of market centers;
(2) the need to update antiquated rules that no longer reflect current market conditions; and
(3) the need to promote greater order interaction and displayed depth, particularly for the very large orders of institutional investors.

Id. at 762.

In late 2004, the Commission reproposed Regulation NMS. Sec. Ex. Act Rel. 50,870, 84 SEC Dock. 1431 (2004) (proposal). See also In Move Likely to Stall NYSE Plans, SEC Reproposes Market Structure Rules, 36 Sec. Reg. & L. Rep. (BNA) 2221 (2004). By then, the Commission reported: "The NMS encompasses the stocks of more than 5000 listed companies, which collectively represent more than $14 trillion in U.S. market capitalization." 84 SEC Dock. at 1433.

While many of the original regulated NMS proposals were retained in reproposed Regulation NMS, the reproposal did include several significant changes:

(1) The Trade Through Rule (proposed Rule 611): The proposed Rule now focuses on *trading centers*, rather than *order execution facilities*. By definition a *trading center* is defined in reproposed Rule 600(b)(78) to mean a national securities exchange, a national securities association that operates an SRO trading facility, an ATS, an exchange marketmaker, an OTC marketmaker, and a block position ("any other broker or dealer that executes orders internally by trading as principal or crossing orders as agent").

A *trade through* is defined in reproposed Rule 600(b)(77) to mean "the purchase or sale of an NMS stock during regular trading hours, either as principal or agent, at a price that is lower than a protected bid or higher than a protected offer."

The basic goal of preventing trade throughs is retained in reproposed Rule 611(a), unless an exception can be identified in reproposed Rule 611(b). Significantly reproposed Rule 611(b) eliminates the controversial *opt out* exception, but would extend the scope of the reproposed Rule 611 trade through Rule beyond the best limit order on a market's books.

As with the original proposal, the Commission powerfully favors markets with automatic execution over manual markets.

(2) Access Rule (proposed Rule 610): The reproposal was more precise in achieving the three basic goals articulated in the initial proposed Rule 610:

> Rule 610 is designed to promote access to quotations in three ways. First, it would enable the use of private linkages offered by a variety

of connectivity providers, rather than mandating a collective linkage facility such as ITS, to facilitate the necessary access to quotations. The lower cost and increased flexibility of connectivity in recent years has made private linkages a feasible alternative to hard linkages, absent barriers to access. Using private linkages, market participants may obtain indirect access to quotations displayed by a particular trading center through the members, subscribers, or customers of that trading center. To promote this type of indirect access, Rule 610 would prohibit a trading center from imposing unfairly discriminatory terms that would prevent or inhibit the access of any person through members, subscribers, or customers of such trading center.

Second, reproposed Rule 610 would limit the fees that any trading center can charge (or allow to be charged) for accessing its protected quotations to no more than $0.003 per share....

Finally, reproposed Rule 610 would require SROs to establish and enforce rules that, among other things, prohibit their members from engaging in a pattern of displaying quotations that lock or cross the automated quotations of other trading centers. Trading centers would be allowed, however, to display automated quotations that lock or cross the *manual* quotations of other trading centers.

Id. at 1437–1438.

(3) Sub-penny Rule (reproposed Rule 612): Reproposed Rule 612 included only minor changes from the initial proposal. Reproposed Rule 612(a) would prohibit subpenny quotes in NMS stocks over $1.

(4) Market Data Rules and Plan Amendments (reproposed Rules 601 and 603): As with the initial proposal the Commission reproposes a formula for allocating revenues generated by market data fees to SRO participants, but simplifies the initial proposal.

In April 2005, the Commission adopted Regulation NMS. Sec. Ex. Act Rel. 51,808, 85 SEC Dock. 1642 (2005) (adoption). See Norris, SEC Expands Best-Price Rule on Stock Trading, N.Y. Times, Apr. 7, 2005, at C1, quoting the author; Over Dissent of Two Commissioners SEC Adopts Market Structure Regulation, 37 Sec. Reg. & L. Rep. (BNA) 621 (2005). Regulation NMS was adopted by a 3-2 vote over the dissent of Commissioners Atkins and Glassman, prompting a detailed response to the dissent, see id. at 1785–1794, which was unusual, if not a novelty, in an SEC rule adoption.

Three themes dominated the adoption Release. First, the Commission has a strong preference for electronic rather than manual markets. See, e.g., "The new formula eliminates any allocation of revenues for manual quotations." Id. at 1653. This may prove to be the most enduring consequence of Regulation NMS by stimulating an acceleration of new trading technologies and market structures. Second, the Release otherwise expressed a general unwillingness to address fundamental market structure issues such as market linkages. A footnote explained: "Nearly all commenters, both those supporting and opposing the need for an intermarket trade-through rule, agreed that the current ITS trade-through provisions are seriously outdated and in need of reform." Id. at 1656. This significantly understates the long articulated critique that ITS itself is "seriously outdated and in need of reform," which contributed to dissatisfaction with Regulation NMS for tending to side with the New York Stock Exchange (NYSE), which has been the most fervent advocate of ITS. The failure to effectively study or prescribe a new system of linkages is the most fundamental weakness of Regulation NMS. Third, Regulation NMS appropriately did move to equalize standards that applied to traditional stock markets such as the NYSE with those applicable to electronic markets such as the Nasdaq and ECNs.[1] This was an intent of the Securities Act Amendments of 1975, and long overdue.

Regulation NMS largely adopted the December 2004 reproposal Release, with some modifications and a detailed rationale, no doubt designed to withstand potential judicial challenge.

Of primary importance was Rule 611, now called the Order Protection Rule in place of the earlier term, the Trade Through Rule. The adoption Release aptly explained: "Clearly, the Order Protection Rule was most controversial and attracted the most public comment and attention, yet the breadth of support in the record

---

[1] The senior author should note that he was a member of the Board of Governors of the NASD, which owned an equity interest in the Nasdaq. The views stated here are solely those of the author, writing as an independent scholar, and do not articulate the views of the Nasdaq.

for the Rule is compelling." Id. at 1645–1646. The adoption Release, for example, noted that 1689 commenters on the proposal and reproposal favored a uniform trade through rule without an opt out exception, while only 448 opposed a uniform trade through rule. Id. at 1656. The Commission explained:

> Why did a broad spectrum of commenters, many of which have extensive experience and expertise regarding the inner workings of the equity markets, support the Order Protection Rule and its emphasis on the principle of best price? They based their support on two fundamental rationales, with which the Commission fully agrees. First, strengthened assurance that orders will be filled at the best prices will give investors, particularly retail investors, greater confidence that they will be treated fairly when they participate in the equity markets. Maintaining investor confidence is an essential element of well-functioning equity markets. Second, protection of the best displayed and accessible prices will promote deep and stable markets that minimize investor transaction costs. More than 84 million individual Americans participate, directly or indirectly, in the U.S. equity markets. The transaction costs associated with the prices at which their orders are executed represent a continual drain on their long-term savings. Although these costs are difficult to calculate precisely, they are very real and very substantial, with estimates ranging from $30 billion to more than $100 billion per year. Minimizing these investor costs to the greatest extent possible is the hallmark of efficient markets, which is a primary objective of the NMS.

Id. at 1646.

The Order Protection Rule was adopted essentially as reproposed in December 2004 with a new exception for specified *Stopped Orders* added in Rule 611(b)(9). As adopted:

> Rule 611 can be divided into three elements: (1) the provisions that establish the scope of the Rule's coverage, most of which are set forth in the definitions of Rule 600(b); (2) the operative requirements of paragraph (a) of Rule 611, which, among other things, mandate the adoption and enforcement of written policies and procedures that are reasonably designed to prevent trade throughs on that trading center of protected quotations and, if relying on an

P. 746

exception, that are reasonably designed to assure compliance with the terms of the exception; and (3) the exceptions set forth in paragraph (b) of Rule 611....

1. Scope of Rule

...In general, the Rule addresses trade-throughs of protected quotations in NMS stocks by trading centers. A *trading center* is defined in Rule 600(b)(78) as a national securities exchange or national securities association that operates an SRO trading facility, an ATS, an exchange market maker, and OTC market maker, or any other broker or dealer that executes orders internally by trading as principal or crossing orders as agent. This last phrase is intended particularly to cover block petitioners. An *NMS stock* is defined in paragraphs (b)(47) and (b)(46) of Rule 600 as a security, other than an option, for which transaction reports are collected, processed and made available pursuant to an effective national market system plan. This definition effectively covers stocks listed on a national securities exchange and stocks included in either the National Market or SmallCap tiers of Nasdaq. It does not include stocks quoted on the OTC Bulletin Board or elsewhere in the OTC market.

The term *trade-through* is defined in Rule 600(b)(77) as the purchase or sale of an NMS stock during regular trading hours, either as principal or agent, at a price that is lower than a protected bid or higher than a protected offer. Rule 600(b)(57), which defines a *protected bid* or *protected offer*, includes three main elements: (1) an automated quotation; (2) displayed by an automated trading center; and (3) that is the best bid or best offer of an exchange, the NASDAQ Stock Market, or an association other than the NASDAQ Stock Market (currently, the best bid or offer of the NASD's ADF).

As discussed above, an *automated quotation* is defined in Rule 600(b)(3) as a quotation displayed by a trading center that: (1) permits an incoming order to be marked as immediate-or-cancel; (2) immediately and automatically executes an order marked as immediate-or-cancel against the displayed quotation up to its full size; (3) immediately and automatically cancels any unexecuted portion of an order marked as immediate-or-cancel without routing the order elsewhere; (4) immediately and automatically transmits a response to the sender of an order marked as immediate-or-cancel indicating the action taken with respect to such order; and (5) immediately and automatically displays information that updates the displayed quotation to reflect any change to its material terms.

Consequently, a quotation will not qualify as *automated* if any human intervention after the time an order is received is allowed to determine the action taken with respect to the quotation. The term *immediate* precludes any coding of automated systems or other type of intentional device that would delay the action taken with respect to a quotation....

...[A]n *automated trading center* is defined in Rule 600(b)(4) as a trading center that: (1) has implemented such systems, procedures, and rules as are necessary to render it capable of displaying quotations that meet the requirements for an automated quotation set forth in paragraph (b)(3) of this section; (2) identifies all quotations other than automated quotations as manual quotations; (3) immediately identifies its quotations as manual quotations whenever it has reason to believe that it is not capable of displaying automated quotations; and (4) has adopted reasonable standards limiting when its quotations change from automated quotations to manual quotations, and vice versa, to specifically defined circumstances that promote fair and efficient access to its automated quotations and are consistent with the maintenance of fair and orderly markets. The requirement of reasonable standard for switching the automated/manual status of quotations is designed to preclude practices that would cause confusion among market participants concerning the status of a trading center's quotations or that would inappropriately advantage the members or customers of a trading center at the expense of the public.

The third element of the definition of *protected bid* and *protected offer* identifies which automated quotations are protected under the Order Protection Rule. Specifically, Rule 600(b)(57) provides that an automated quotation displayed by an automated trading center that is the BBO [Best Bid or Offer] of an exchange SRO, the BBO of Nasdaq, or the BBO of the NASD (*i.e.*, the ADF) qualifies as a protected quotation. Thus, only a single, accessible best bid and best offer for each of the exchange SROs, Nasdaq, and the NASD is protected under the Order Protection Rule. A best bid and best offer must be accessible by routing an order to a single market

P. 746

destination (*i.e.*, currently, either to a single exchange execution system, a single Nasdaq execution system, or a single ADF participant).

2. Requirement of Reasonable Policies and Procedures

Paragraph (a)(1) of Rule 611 requires a trading center to establish, maintain, and enforce written policies and procedures that are reasonably designed to prevent trade-throughs on that trading center of protected quotations in NMS stocks that do not fall within an exception set forth in paragraph (b) of Rule 611 and, if relying on such an exception, that are reasonably designed to assure compliance with the terms of the exception. In addition, paragraph (a)(2) of Rule 611 requires a trading center to regularly surveil to ascertain the effectiveness of the policies and procedures required by paragraph (a)(1) and to take prompt action to remedy deficiencies in such policies and procedures....

3. Exceptions

Rule 611(b) sets forth a variety of exceptions addressing transactions that may fall within the definition of a trade-through, but which are not subject to the operative requirements of the Rule. The exceptions primarily are designed to achieve workable intermarket price protection and to facilitate certain trading strategies and order types that are useful to investors, but also are consistent with the principle of price protection.

Paragraph (b)(1) excepts a transaction if the trading center displaying the protected quotation that was traded through was experiencing a failure, material delay, or malfunction of its systems or equipment when the trade-through occurred....

Paragraph (b)(8) of Rule 611 sets forth an exception for flickering quotations. It excepts a transaction if the trading center displaying the protected quotation that was traded through had displayed, within one second prior to execution of the trade-through, a best bid or best offer, as applicable, for the NMS stock with a price that was equal or inferior to the price of the trade-through transaction. This exception thereby provides a *window* to address false indications of trade-throughs that in actuality are attributable to rapidly moving quotations. It also potentially will reduce the number of instances in which a trading center must alter its normal trading procedures and route orders to other trading centers to comply with Rule 611. The exception is thereby intended to promote more workable intermarket price protection.

Paragraphs (b)(5) and (b)(6) of Rule 611 set forth exceptions for intermarket sweep orders. An intermarket sweep order is defined in Rule 600(b)(30) as a limit order that meets the following requirements: (1) when routed to a trading center, the limit order is identified as an intermarket sweep order, and (2) simultaneously with the routing of the limit order identified as an intermarket sweep order, one or more additional limit orders, as necessary, are routed to execute against the full displayed size of all protected quotations with a superior price. These additional limit orders must be marked as intermarket sweep orders to allow the receiving market center to execute the order immediately without regard to better-priced quotations displayed at other trading centers (by definition, each of the additional limit orders would meet the requirements for an intermarket sweep order).

Paragraph (b)(5) allows a trading center immediately to execute any order identified as an intermarket sweep order. It therefore need not delay its execution for the updating of the better-priced quotations at other trading centers to which orders were routed simultaneously with the intermarket sweep order. Paragraph (b)(6) allows a trading center itself to route intermarket sweep orders and thereby clear the way for immediate internal executions at the trading center. This exception particularly will facilitate the immediate execution of block orders by dealers on behalf of their institutional clients. Specifically, if a dealer wishes to execute internally a customer order at a price that would trade through one or more protected quotations on other trading centers, the dealer will be able to do so if it simultaneously routes one or more intermarket sweep orders to execute against the full displayed size of each such better-priced protected quotations. If there is only one better-priced protected quotation, then the dealer is only required to route an intermarket sweep order to execute against that protected quotation.

Paragraph (c) of Rule 611 requires that the trading center, broker, or dealer responsible for the routing of an intermarket sweep order take reasonable steps to establish that orders are properly routed in an attempt to execute against all applicable protected quotations. A trading center, broker, or dealer is required to satisfy this requirement regardless whether it routes the order through its own systems or sponsors a customer's access through a third-party vendor's systems....

The exception in paragraph (b)(7) of Rule 611 will facilitate other types of orders that often are useful to investors — benchmark orders. It excepts the execution of an order at a price that was not based, directly or indirectly, on the quoted price of an NMS stock at the time of execution and for which the material terms were not reasonably determinable at the time the commitment to execute the order was made. A common example of a benchmark order is a VWAP order. Assume a broker-dealer's customer decides to buy a stock at 9:00 a.m. before the markets open for normal trading. The customer submits, and the broker-dealer accepts, an order to buy 100,000 shares at the volume-weighted price of the stock from opening until 1:00 p.m. At 1:00 p.m., the national best offer in the stock is $20.00, but the relevant volume-weighted average price (in a rising market) is $19.90. The broker-dealer would be able to rely on the benchmark order exception to execute the order at $19.90 at 1:00 p.m., without regard to better-priced protected quotations at other trading centers. Of course, any transactions effected by the broker-dealer during the course of the day to obtain sufficient stock to fill the benchmark order would remain subject to Rule 611. The benchmark exception also would encompass the execution of an order that is benchmarked to a market's single-priced opening, as the Commission would not interpret such an opening price to be the *quoted price* of the NMS stock at the time of execution.

Paragraph (b)(9) of Rule 611 provides an exception for the execution of certain stopped orders. Specifically, the exception applies to the execution by a trading center of a stopped order where the price of the execution of the order was, for a stopped buy order, lower than the national best bid at the time of execution or, for a stopped sell order, higher than the national best offer at the time of execution....

Finally, paragraph (b) of Rule 611 includes a variety of other exceptions: (1) transactions other than *regular way* contracts; (2) single-price opening, reopening, or closing transactions; and (3) transactions executed at a time when protected quotations were crossed. The crossed quotation exception would not apply when a protected quotation crosses a non-protected (*e.g.*, manual) quotation. The exception for single-priced reopenings will only apply to single-priced reopening transactions after a trading halt conducted pursuant to a trading center rule. To qualify, the reopening process must be transparent and provide for the queuing and ultimate execution of multiple orders at a single equilibrium price.

Id. at 1693–1696.

Given criticism of the proposed Uniform Order Protection Rule as unnecessary to maintain market quality in the Nasdaq, not earlier subject to a trade through rule, the Commission conducted studies to compare trade through rates in the Nasdaq or the NYSE. Specifically stock studies found that overall trade through rates for Nasdaq stocks were 7.9 percent of total volume of traded shares, compared to 7.2 percent for NYSE stocks. Id. at 1658. When NYSE block trades and other noncovered transactions are eliminated, NYSE trade throughs are reduced to approximately 2.3 percent of total share volume. Id. at 1658.

With respect to the argument that the Nasdaq had superior execution quality, the adoption Release responded at length:

> The staff studies indicate that the execution quality statistics submitted by commenters on the original proposal are flawed. The claimed large and systematic disparities between Nasdaq and NYSE effective spreads disappear when an analysis of execution quality more appropriately controls for differences in stocks, order types, and order sizes....
>
> First, the effective spread analyses submitted by commenters do not, in a number of respects, reflect appropriately the comparative costs in Nasdaq and NYSE stocks. They were presented in terms of *cents-per-share* and therefore failed to control for the varying level of stock prices between Nasdaq stocks and NYSE stocks in the S&P 500. Lower priced stocks naturally will tend to have lower spreads in terms of cents-per-share than higher priced stocks, even when such cents-per-share spreads constitute a larger percentage of stock price and therefore represent transaction costs for investors that consume a larger percentage of their investment. By using cents-per-share statistics, commenters did not adjust for the fact that the average prices of Nasdaq stocks are significantly lower than the average prices of NYSE stocks. For example, the average price of Nasdaq stocks in the S&P 500 in January 2004 was $34.14, while the average price of NYSE stocks was $41.32.

P. 746

The effective spread analyses submitted by commenters also were weakened by their failure to address the much lower fill rates of orders in Nasdaq stocks than orders in NYSE stocks. The commenters submitted *blended* statistics that encompassed both market orders and marketable limit orders. The effective spread statistics for these order types are not comparable, however, because market orders do not have a limit price that precludes their execution at prices inferior to the prevailing market price at time of order receipt. In contrast, the limit price of marketable limit orders often precludes an execution, particularly when there is a lack of liquidity and depth at the prevailing market price. For example, the fill rates for marketable limit orders in Nasdaq stocks generally are less than 75%, and often fall below 50% for larger order sizes.

Accordingly, investors must accept trade-offs when deciding whether to submit market orders or marketable limit orders (particularly when the limit price equals the current market price). Use of a limit price generally assures a narrower spread by precluding an execution at an inferior price. By precluding an execution, however, the limit price may cause the investor to *miss the market* if prices move away (for example, if prices rise when an investor is attempting to buy). Effective spreads for marketable limit orders therefore represent transaction costs that are conditional on execution, while effective spreads for market orders much more completely reflect the entire implicit transaction cost for a particular order. Market orders represent only approximately 14% of the blended flow of market and marketable limit orders in Nasdaq stocks (reflecting the fact that ECNs now dominate Nasdaq order flow and limit orders represent the vast majority of ECN order flow). In contrast, market orders represent approximately 36% of the blended order flow in NYSE stocks. Accordingly, the effective spread statistics for marketable limit orders, and particularly for orders in Nasdaq stocks, must be considered in conjunction with the fill rate for such orders—while a narrow spread is good, the benefits are greatly limited if investors are unable to obtain an execution at that spread. The analyses presented by the commenters, however, did not address the respective fill rates for Nasdaq stocks and NYSE stocks or reflect the inherent differences in measuring the transaction costs of market orders and marketable limit orders....

For Nasdaq stocks, the Rule 11Ac1-5 statistics reveal very low fill rates for larger sizes of marketable limit orders (*e.g.*, 2000 shares or more), which generally fall below 50% for most Nasdaq stocks.

> Contrary to the assertion of some commenters, certainty of *execution* for large marketable limit orders clearly is not a strength of the current market for Nasdaq stocks. Certainty of a fast response is a strength, but much of the time the response to large orders will be a *no fill* at any given trading center....
>
> Accordingly, the Commission's concern with fill rates for larger orders in Nasdaq stocks is not that they are lower than those for NYSE stocks, but that they are very low in absolute terms—often falling well below 50%.

Id. at 1665–1667.

To make the Order Protection Rule effective, it is limited to automated quotations. "The Commission agrees with commenters that providing protection to manual quotations...potentially would lead to undue delays in the routing of investor orders, thereby not justifying the benefits of price protection." Id. at 1673. Rule 600(b)(3) adopted the definition of automated quotation as proposed, in essence limiting such quotations to those displayed by a trading center that can (1) act on an incoming order; (2) respond to the send of the order; and (3) update the quotation. See id. at 1674.

In response to commenter concerns that the original trade through rule could not be implemented in a workable manner, particularly for high volume stocks, the Commission made modifications to the original rule:

> First and most importantly, as included in the reproposal and as adopted today, only automated trading centers, as defined in Rule 600(b)(4), that are capable of providing immediate responses to incoming orders are eligible to have their quotations protected. Moreover, an automated trading center is required to identify its quotations as manual (and therefore not protected) whenever it has reason to believe that it is not capable of providing immediate responses to orders. Thus, a trading center that experiences a systems problem, whether because of a flood of orders or otherwise, must immediately identify its quotations as manual....
>
> The adopted Order Protection Rule...provides a *self-help* remedy that will allow trading centers to bypass the quotations of a trading center that fails to meet the immediate response requirement. Rule 611(b(1) sets forth an exception that applies to

quotations displayed by trading centers that are experiencing a failure, material delay, or malfunction of its systems or equipment. To implement this exception consistent with the requirements of Rule 611(a), trading centers will have to adopt policies and procedures reasonably designed to comply with the self-help remedy. Such policies and procedures will need to set forth specific objective parameters for dealing with problem trading centers and for monitoring compliance with the self-help remedy, consistent with Rule 611. Given current industry capabilities, the Commission believes that trading centers should be entitled to bypass another trading center's quotations if it repeatedly fails to respond within one second to incoming orders attempting to access its protected quotations. Accordingly, trading centers will have the necessary flexibility to respond to problems at another trading center as they occur during the trading day.

Id. at 1677.

The Commission declined, however, to create a categorical exemption for actively traded stocks:

> The Commission recognizes that commenters have raised a serious concern regarding implementation of the Order Protection Rule, particularly for many Nasdaq stocks that are very actively traded and whose trading is spread across many different individual trading centers. An exemption for active stocks, however, would be particularly inconsistent with the investor protection objectives of the Order Protection Rule because these also are the stocks that have the highest level of investor participation.

Id. at 1680.

The Commission limited the scope of protected quotations to the Market Best Bid and Offer (BBO) rather than a Voluntary Depth Alternative, which likely would have been more difficult and costly to implement. Id. at 1688.

The Commission characterized the benefits of strengthened order protection in these terms:

> The Commission believes that the benefits of strengthening price protection for exchange-listed stocks (*e.g.*, by eliminating the gaps in ITS coverage of block positioners and 100-share quotes)

and introducing price protection for Nasdaq stocks will be substantial, although the total amount is difficult to quantify. One objective, though quite conservative, estimate of benefits is the dollar amount of quotations that annually are traded through. The Commission staff's analysis of trade-through rates indicates that over 12 billion shares of displayed quotations in Nasdaq and NYSE stocks were traded through in 2003, by an average amount of 2.3 cents for Nasdaq stocks and 2.2 cents for NYSE stocks. These traded-through quotations represent approximately $209 million in Nasdaq stocks and $112 million in NYSE stocks, for a total of $321 million in bypassed limit orders and inferior prices for investors in 2003 that could have been addressed by strong trade-through protection. The Commission believes that this $321 million estimated *annual* benefit, particularly when combined with the benefits of enhanced investor confidence in the fairness and orderliness of the equity markets, justifies the one-time costs of implementation and ongoing annual costs of the Order Protection Rule....

The Order Protection Rule can be expected to generate other categories of benefits that are not quantified in the $321 million estimate, such as the benefits that can be expected to result from increased use of limit orders, increased depth, and increased order interaction.

Id. at 1691–1692.

Buttressing the Order Protection Rule is Rule 610, the Access Rule. Rule 610 was essentially adopted as proposed, with the adoption Release stating:

> All SROs that trade exchange-listed stocks currently are linked through ITS, a collective intermarket linkage facility. ITS provides a means of access to exchanges and Nasdaq by permitting each market to send a *commitment to trade* through the system, with receiving markets generally having up to 30 seconds to respond. ITS also provides access to quotations of participants without fees and establishes uniform rules to govern quoting practices. Although ITS promotes access among participants that is uniform and free, it also is often slow and limited. Moreover, it is governed by a unanimous vote requirement that has at times impeded innovation in the system or its set of rules.

In contrast, there is no collective intermarket linkage system for Nasdaq stocks. Instead, access is achieved primarily through private linkages among individual trading centers. This approach has demonstrated its benefits among electronic markets; it is flexible and can readily incorporate technological advances as they occur. There is no intermarket system, however, that offers free access to quotations in Nasdaq stocks. Nor are the trading centers for Nasdaq stocks subject to uniform intermarket standards governing their quoting and trading practices. The fees for access to ECN quotations in Nasdaq stocks, as well as the absence of standards for quotations that lock and cross markets, have been the source of disputes among participants in the market for Nasdaq stocks for many years. Moreover, access problems have arisen with respect to small market centers operating outside of an SRO trading facility and markets like the Amex that engage in manual trading of Nasdaq stocks. Access problems also have arisen with respect to intentional barriers to access, especially involving fees.

Rule 610 reflects the Commission's determination that fair and efficient access to markets can be achieved without a collective intermarket linkage facility such as ITS, if baseline intermarket rules are established. The rule adopts a private linkage approach for all NMS stocks with modifications to address the most serious problems that have arisen with this approach in the trading of Nasdaq stocks.

Id. at 1700–1701.

Rule 610 first prohibits certain forms of discrimination against nonmembers:

Rules 610(a) and (b) further the goal of fair and efficient access to quotations primarily by prohibiting trading centers from unfairly discriminating against nonmembers or nonsubscribers that attempt to access their quotations through a member or subscriber of the trading center. Market participants can either become members or subscribers of a trading center to obtain direct access to its quotations, or they can obtain indirect access by *piggybacking* on the direct access of members or subscribers. These forms of access are widely used today in the market for Nasdaq stocks (as well as to a lesser extent in the market for exchange-listed stocks). Instead of every market participant establishing separate linkages with every trading center, many different private firms have entered the business of linking with a wide range of trading centers and then offering their customers access to those trading centers through the private firms' linkages. Competitive forces determine the types and costs of these private linkages....

The Commission does not believe that the private linkage approach adopted today will seriously undermine the value of membership in SROs that offer valuable services to their members. First, the fact that markets will not be allowed to impose unfairly discriminatory terms on non-members who obtain indirect access to quotations through members does not mean that non-members will obtain *free* access to quotations. Members who provide piggy-back access to non-members will be providing a useful service and presumably will charge a fee for such service. The fee will be subject to competitive forces and likely will reflect the costs of SRO membership, plus some element of profit to the SRO's members. As a result, non-members that frequently make use of indirect access are likely to contribute to the costs of membership in the SRO market. Moreover, the unfair discrimination standard of Rule 610(a) will apply only to access to quotations, not to the full panoply of services that markets generally provide only to their members. These other services will be subject to the more general fair access provisions applicable to SROs and large ECNs, as well as statutory provisions that govern SRO rules.

On the other hand, any attempt by an SRO to charge differential fees based on the non-member status of the person obtaining indirect access to quotations, such as whether it is a competing market maker, would violate the anti-discrimination standard of Rule 610....

Other types of differential fees, however, would not violate the anti-discrimination standard of Rule 610. Fees with volume-based discounts or fees that are reasonably based on the cost of providing a particular service will be permitted, so long as they do not vary based on the non-member status of a person obtaining indirect access to quotations. For example, a member providing indirect access could be given a volume discount on the full amount of its volume, including the volume accounted for by persons obtaining indirect access to quotations.

Id. at 1701–1703.

The Commission under Rule 610(b)(1) requires ADF participants to bear the costs of providing the necessary connectivity to facilitate access to their quotations. "Specifically, under reproposed Rule 610(b)(1) those ATSs and market makers that choose to display quotations in the ADF would bear the responsibility of providing a level and cost of access to their quotations that is substantially equivalent to the level and cost of access to quotations displayed by SRO trading facilities." Id. at 1704.

Small ADFs will be exempt from this connectivity requirement because Rule 301(b)(3) of Regulation ATS only requires an ATS to display its quotations in a consolidated quotation or stream in those securities for which its trading volume equals 5 percent of total trading volume. Id. at 1705. The NASD as *gatekeeper* for ADF will need to make an affirmative determination that existing ADF participants are in compliance with Rule 610. Id. at 1707.

Separately, in Rule 610(c) the Commission adopted a flat $0.003 per share limitation on access fees:

> The limitation is intended to achieve several objectives. First, Rule 610(c) promotes the NMS objective of equal regulation of markets and broker-dealers by applying equally to all types of trading centers and all types of market participants.... although ECNs and other types of trading centers, including SROs, may currently charge access fees, market makers have not been permitted to charge any fee for counterparties accessing their quotations. The Commission believes, however, that it is consistent with the Quote Rule for market makers to charge fees for access to their quotations, so long as such fees meet the requirements of Rule 610(c). In particular, market makers will be permitted to charge fees for executions of orders against their quotations, irrespective of whether the order executions are effected on an SRO trading facility or directly by a market maker.
>
> Second, the adopted fee limitation is designed to preclude individual trading centers from raising their fees substantially in an attempt to take improper advantage of strengthened protection against trade-throughs and the adoption of a private linkage regime. In particular, the fee limitation is necessary to address *outlier* trading centers that otherwise might charge high fees to other market participants required to access their quotations by the Order Protection Rule. It also precludes a trading center from charging high fees selectively to competitors, practices that have occurred in the market for Nasdaq stocks. In the absence of a fee

limitation, the adoption of the Order Protection Rule and private linkages could significantly boost the viability of the outlier business model....

The $0.003 cap will limit the outlier business model. It will place all markets on a level playing field in terms of the fees they can charge and the rebates they can pass on to liquidity providers. Some markets might choose to charge lower fees, thereby increasing their ranking in the preferences of order routers. Others might charge the full $0.003 and rebate a substantial proportion to liquidity providers. Competition will determine which strategy is most successful....

The Commission notes the $0.003 fee limitation is consistent with current business practices, as very few trading centers currently charge fees that exceed this amount. It appears that only two ECNs currently charge fees that exceed $0.003, charging $0.005 for access through the ADF. These ECNs currently do not account for a large percentage of trading volume. In addition, while a few SROs have large fees on their books for transactions in ETFs that exceed a certain size (*e.g.*, 2100 shares), it is unlikely that these fees generate a large amount of revenues.

Id. at 1709–1710.

The fee limitation cap applies "to manual quotations that are best bids and offers to the same extent it applies to covered automatic quotations." Id. at 1710.

The cap, however, only applies to best bid and offer quotations and will not apply to other trading center quotations, such as depth of book quotations. Id. at 1710.

Rule 610(d) requires each national securities exchange and national securities association to establish written rules that require its members to avoid quotations that lock or cross any covered quotation in an NMS stock. The Commission explained:

> When two market participants are willing to trade at the same quoted price, giving priority to the first-displayed automated quotation will encourage posting of quotations and contribute to fair and orderly markets. The basic principle underlying the NMS is to promote fair competition among markets, but within a system that also promotes interaction between all of the buyers and sellers in a particular NMS stock. Allowing market participants simply to

ignore accessible quotations in other markets and routinely display locking and crossing quotations is inconsistent with this principle. The Rule will, however, not prohibit automated quotations from locking or crossing manual quotations, thereby permitting market participants to reflect information regarding the inaccessibility of a particular trading center's quotations.

Id. at 1712.

Rule 612, the Subpenny Rule, which prohibits subpenny quoting in quotations above $1.00 per share, was adopted in December 2004 with minor amendments. Id. at 1716–1726. The rationale for Rule 612 was articulated succinctly:

> Rule 612 will deter the practice of stepping ahead of exposed trading interest by an economically insignificant amount. Limit orders provide liquidity to the market and perform an important price-setting function. The Commission is concerned that, if orders lose execution priority because competing orders step ahead for an economically insignificant amount, liquidity could diminish.

Id. at 1720.

In adopting Rule 612, the Commission did retain the power by order to exempt any person, security, or quotation, if future circumstances warranted. Id. at 1720.

For trades not subject to the subpenny quote restriction, a provision was adopted limiting a quotation under $1.00 per share to four decimal places. "Thus, under new Rule 612, a quotation of $0.9987 × $1.00 is permitted but a quotation of $0.9987 × $1.0001 is not." Id. at 1723.

Rule 612 does not prohibit subpenny trading, for example, a subpenny execution resulting from a midpoint or volume weighted algorithm, see id. at 1724, nor does Rule 612 apply to options. Id. at 1725.

In adopting Regulation NMS, the Commission wrote that "[t]he Exchange Act rules and joint-SRO Plans for disseminating market information to the public are the heart of NMS." Id. at 1726. In 2004 Market Data Networks collected $434.1 million in revenues derived from market data fees. Id. at 1726. The adoption Release added:

Moreover, the U.S. equity markets are not alone in their reliance on market data revenues as a substantial source of funding. All of the other major world equity markets currently derive large amounts of revenues from selling market information, despite having significantly less trading volume and less market capitalization than the NYSE and Nasdaq. To illustrate, the following table sets forth the respective market information revenues, dollar value of trading, and market capitalization for the largest world equity markets in 2003:

	Data Revenues (millions)	Trading Volume (trillions)	Market Capitalization (trillions)
London	$180	$3.6	$2.5
NYSE	$172	$9.7	$11.3
Nasdaq	$147	$7.1	$2.8
Deutsche Bourse	$146	$1.3	$1.1
Euronext	$109	$1.9	$2.1
Tokyo	$60	$2.1	$3.0

Id. at 1730.

The Commission adopted its Allocation Amendment to each SRO Plan with modifications from both the original proposal and December 2004 reproposal:

> The adopted formula reflects a two-step process. First, a Network's distributable revenues (*e.g.*, $150 million) will be allocated among the many individual securities (*e.g.*, 3000) included in the Network's data stream. Second, the revenues that are allocated to an individual security (*e.g.*, $200,000) will be allocated among the SROs based on measures of the usefulness to investors of the SRO's trades and quotes in the security. The Allocation Amendment provides that, notwithstanding any other provision of a Plan, its SRO participants shall receive an annual payment for each calendar year that is equal to the sum of the SRO's Trading Shares and Quoting Shares in each Network security for the year. These two types of Shares are dollar amounts that are calculated based on SRO trading and quoting activity in each Network security.

Id. at 1739.

P. 746

The Commission elaborated:

> Commenters on the original proposal generally believed that the originally proposed formula was complex and may have been difficult to implement efficiently. They particularly noted that the proposed NBBO Improvement Share was difficult to understand and had the potential to be abused through gaming behavior. The Commission agreed with these commenters and has modified the reproposed formula and adopted formula accordingly. Given that only automated quotations will be entitled to earn an allocation under the adopted formula, the originally proposed NBBO Improvement Share, as well as the proposed cutoff of credits for manual quotations left alone at the NBBO, have been deleted from the reproposed formula and remain deleted in the adopted formula. The elimination of these two elements greatly reduces the complexity of the adopted formula and promotes more efficient implementation of the formula. In addition, the 15% of the Security Income Allocation that was allocated to the NBBO Improvement Share in the proposed formula now has been shifted to the Quoting Share to assign an even allocation of revenues between trading and quoting.

Id. at 1733.

Generalizing the Commission explained:

> The current Plan formulas allocate revenues based on the number of trades (Networks A and B) or on the average number of trades and share volume of trades (Network C) reported by SROs. By focusing solely on trading activity (and particularly by rewarding the reporting of many trades no matter how small their size), these formulas have contributed to a variety of distortive trade reporting practices, including wash sales, shredded trades, and SRO print facilities. To address these practices and to establish a more broad-based measure of an SRO's contribution to the consolidated trade stream, the proposed formula provided that an SRO's Trading Store in a particular stock would be calculated by taking the average of the SRO's percentage of total dollar volume in the stock and the SRO's percentage of qualified trades in the stock. A *qualified trade* was defined as having a dollar volume of $5000 or more....

Several commenters on the original proposal believed that small trades contribute to price discovery and should be entitled to earn at least some credit in the calculation of the number of qualified trades. The Commission agreed and included in the reproposed formula a provision that awards a fractional proportion of a qualified report for trades of less than $5000. The adopted formula also includes this provision. Thus, a $2500 trade will constitute ½ of a qualified transaction report. This approach greatly reduces the potential for large allocations attributable to shredded trades, while recognizing the contribution of small trades to price discovery....

The proposed formula included a Security Income Allocation, pursuant to which a Network's total distributable revenues would be allocated among each of the Network's stocks based on the square root of dollar volume. The square root function was intended to adjust for the highly disproportionate level of trading in the very top tier of Network stocks. A few hundred stocks (*e.g.*, the top 5%) are much more heavily traded than the other thousands of Network stocks....

With one modification, the Commission has retained the square root function in the adopted formula to allocate distributable Network revenues more appropriately among all of the stocks included in a Network. Although the extent to which Network stocks are tiered according to trading volume varies among the three Networks, it is quite pronounced in each of them. The use of the square root function reflects the Commission's judgment that, on average and not necessarily in every particular case, information about a $50,000 trade in a stock with an average daily trading volume of $500,000 is marginally more useful to investors than a $50,000 trade in a stock with an average daily trading volume of $500 million. Markets that provide price discovery in less active stocks serve an extremely important function for investors in those stocks. Price discovery not only benefits those investors who choose to trade on any particular day, but also benefits those who simply need to monitor the status of their investment. Efficient secondary markets support buy-and-hold investors by offering them a ready opportunity to trade at any time at a fair price if they need to buy or sell a stock. Indeed, this enhanced assurance is one of the most important contributions of secondary markets to efficient capital-formation and to reducing the cost of capital for listed companies.

> The square root function allocates revenues to markets that perform this function for less-active stocks by marginally increasing their percentage of market data revenues, while still allocating a much greater dollar amount to more actively traded stocks.
>
> With respect to very inactively traded stocks, however, the adopted formula modifies the reproposed square root allocation by limiting the revenues that can be allocated to a single Network security to an amount that is no greater than $4 per qualified transaction report. The amount that exceeds this $4 limitation will be reallocated among all Network securities in direct proportion to their dollar volume of trading (which is heavily weighted toward the most actively traded stocks). The Commission is adopting this $4 limitation to respond to commenters' concerns about the potential for abusive quoting behavior in extremely inactive stocks by anyone seeking to game the Quoting Share allocation.

Id. at 1736–1737.

The Commission, as in the December 2004 reproposal, followed the Advisory Committee on Market Information, chaired by the author, and limited mandatory quotations in new Rule 603(c) to basic quotation information (price, size, and market center identification of the NBBO). The Commission rescinded the prohibition earlier in former Rule 11Aa3-1 (redesignated as Rule 601) on SROs disseminating their trade reports independently. "Under adopted Rule 601, members of an SRO will continue to be required to transmit trades to the SRO (and the SROs would continue to transmit trades to the Networks pursuant to the Plans), but such members also will be free to distribute their own data independently, with or without fees." Id. at 1741.

The Commission retains the market data consolidation model, see id. at 1742, but substantially revises the consolidated display requirement:

> It incorporates a new definition of *consolidated display* (set forth in adopted Rule 600(b)(13)) that is limited to the prices, sizes, and market center identifications of the NBBO and *consolidated last sale information* (which is defined in Rule 600(b)(14)). The consolidated information on quotations and trades must be provided in an

equivalent manner to any other information on quotations and trades provided by a securities information processor or broker-dealer. Beyond disclosure of this basic information, market forces, rather than regulatory requirements, will be allowed to determine what, if any, additional data from other market centers is displayed. In particular, investors and other information users ultimately will be able to decide whether they need additional information in their displays.

In addition, adopted Rule 603(c) narrows the contexts in which a consolidated display is required to those when it is most needed — a context in which a trading or order-routing decision could be implemented. For example, the consolidated display requirement will continue to cover broker-dealers who provide on-line data to their customers in software programs from which trading decisions can be implemented. Similarly, the requirement will continue to apply to vendors who provide displays that facilitate order routing by broker-dealers. It will not apply, however, when market data is provided on a purely informational website that does not offer any trading or order-routing capability.

Id. at 1742.

The balance of Regulation NMS generally renumbered rules adopted under §11A of the Securities Exchange Act as part of Regulation NMS:

- Rule 600: NMS Security Designation and Definitions (replaces Exchange Act Rule 11Aa2-1, which the Commission is rescinding, and incorporates definitions from the existing NMS rules and the new rules adopted today):
- Rule 601: Dissemination of Transaction Reports and Last Sale Data with Respect to Transactions in NMS Stocks (renumbers and renames Exchange Act Rule 11Aa3-1, the substance of which is being modified);
- Rule 602: Dissemination of Quotations in NMS Securities (renumbers and renames Exchange Act Rule 11Ac1-1 (*Quote Rule*), the substance of which remains largely intact);
- Rule 603: Distribution, Consolidation, and Display of Information with Respect to Quotations for and Transactions in NMS Stocks (renumbers and renames Exchange Act Rule

11Ac1-2 (*Vendor Display Rule*), the substance of which is being modified substantially);
- Rule 604: Display of Customer Limit Orders (renumbers Exchange Act Rule 11Ac1-4 (*Limit Order Display Rule*), the substance of which remains largely intact);
- Rule 605: Disclosure of Order Execution Information (renumbers Exchange Act Rule 11Ac1-5, the substance of which remains largely intact);
- Rule 606: Disclosure of Order Routing Information (renumbers Exchange Act Rule 11Ac1-6, the substance of which remains largely intact);
- Rule 607: Customer Account Statements (renumbers Exchange Act Rule 11Ac1-3, the substance of which remains largely intact);
- Rule 608: Filing and Amendment of National Market System Plans (renumbers Exchange Act Rule 11Aa3-2, the substance of which remains largely intact);
- Rule 609: Registration of Securities Information Processors: Form of Application and Amendments (renumbers Exchange Act Rule 11Ab2-1, the substance of which remains largely intact).

Id. at 1743.

The Commission also made conforming amendments to several other SEC rules, including Securities Act Rule 144; Securities Exchange Act Rules 0-10, 3a51-1, 3b-16, 10a-1, 10b-10, 10b-18, 12a-7, 12f-1, 12f-2, 15b9-1, 15c2-11, 19c-3, 19c-4, and 31; as well as Regulation ATS Rules 300 and 301 and Rule 17a-7 of the Investment Company Act.

3. THE OVER-THE-COUNTER MARKET

a. Nasdaq

P. 758, new text, end carryover par. Earlier in 2006 the SEC approved the application of Nasdaq. SEC approval was conditioned on the satisfaction of several conditions for Nasdaq before commencing operations as an exchange. These included:

- Nasdaq must join the various national market system plans and the Intermarket Surveillance Group.
- The NASD must determine that its control of Nasdaq through its Preferred Class D share is no longer necessary because the NASD can fulfill through other means its obligations with respect to non-Nasdaq exchange-listed securities under the Exchange Act, the rules adopted thereunder, and the various national market system plans.
- The Commission must declare effective certain regulatory plans to be filed by Nasdaq.
- Nasdaq must file, and the Commission must approve, an agreement pursuant to Section 17d-2 of the Exchange Act that allocates to the NASD regulatory responsibility with respect to certain activities of common members.

SEC Rel. 2006-9 (Jan. 13, 2006). See also Sec. Ex. Act Rel. 52,049, 85 SEC Dock. 3069 (2005) (NASD Notice of Proposed Rule Changes to Reflect Nasdaq's Separation Upon Anticipated Approval of Nasdaq's Application to Be a National Securities Exchange).

In 2006 the Nasdaq renamed the Nasdaq National Market as the Nasdaq Global Market and created the Nasdaq Global Select Market, a new tier with higher initial listing standards. Sec. Ex. Act Rels. 53,799, 88 SEC Dock. 17 (2006) (approval); 54,071, 88 SEC Dock. 983 (2006) (approval).

In Sec. Ex. Act Rel. 53,128, 87 SEC Dock. 348 (2006), the Commission issued an Order approving the registration of the Nasdaq Stock Market LLC as a National Securities Exchange on condition that the Nasdaq join the CTA, CQ, Nasdaq UTP, ITS, and Order Execution Quality Disclosure plans. The Nasdaq was also required to join the Intermarket Surveillance Group and file a Minor Rule Violation Plan. The NASD separately was required to represent that control of Nasdaq was no longer necessary because the NASD can fulfill through other means its obligations with respect to non-Nasdaq Exchange listed securities under §15A(b)(11) and Rules 602 and 603 of Regulation NMS.

c. Order Execution

P. 763 n.100, end note. In 2003 the Commission approved a post-trade anonymity feature in SuperMontage. Sec. Ex. Act Rel. 48,527, 81 SEC Dock. 291 (2003) (approval).

In Domestic Sec., Inc. v. SEC, 333 F.3d 239 (D.C. Cir. 2003), the court rejected a petition to review the alternative display facility in SuperMontage because the SEC order was supported by substantial evidence and was not arbitrary or capricious.

4. OPTIONS MARKETS

a. Stock Options

P. 763, new n.101.1, end page. In 2003 the Commission approved a post-trade anonymity feature in SuperMontage. Sec. Ex. Act Rel. 48,527, 81 SEC Dock. 291 (2003) (approval).

In 2008 the Commission approved rules to create the Nasdaq Options Market (NOM), a facility of Nasdaq. Sec. Ex. Act Rel. 57,478, 92 SEC Dock. 2493 (2008).

C. SECURITIES ASSOCIATIONS

2. THE NATIONAL ASSOCIATION OF SECURITIES DEALERS

P. 788 n.4 end note. The Second Circuit has held that the NASD, a private SRO, is not a state actor subject to due process requirements. See Desiderio v. NASD, 191 F.3d 198, 206–207 (2d Cir. 1999), *cert. denied*, 531 U.S. 1069; Perpetual Sec., Inc. v. Tang, 290 F.3d 132, 127–139 (2d Cir. 2002). Cf. D'Alessio v. SEC, 380

F.3d 112, 121–122, n.12 (2d Cir. 2004) (reserving question with respect to NYSE).

The Second Circuit, however, has concluded that the statutory requirement in the Securities Exchange Act of a "fair procedure" will subject SROs to a due process requirement that the decision-maker be impartial. Id. at 121 (concluding that NYSE Hearing Panel could be impartial even if defendants were suing senior Exchange officials).

Similarly the Second Circuit has held that the personal recusals of SEC Commissioners is "sufficient to cure any impropriety in appearance of impropriety with respect to the Commission proceedings." MFS Sec. Corp. v. SEC, 380 F.3d 611, 618–620 (2d Cir. 2004). Unlike an SRO, the Fifth and Fourteenth Amendments do apply to the SEC and do require a tribunal free of personal bias. Ibid.

D. BROKERAGE COMMISSION RATE REGULATION

1. ANTITRUST GENERALLY

P. 797 n.25, end note. In MFS Sec. Corp. v. NYSE, Inc., 142 Fed. Appx. 541 (2d Cir. 2005), the Second Circuit affirmed a dismissal of an antitrust case alleging a group boycott. In the context of a self-regulatory organization operating under the Securities Exchange Act, a plaintiff has to satisfy the rule of reason and allege anticompetitive effects. Here the plaintiff alleged none.

In contrast, in Billing v. Credit Suisse First Boston, 426 F.3d 130 (2d Cir. 2005), the court held that the federal securities laws did not completely repeal the antitrust laws when the plaintiff alleged a conspiracy involving book building in several underwritings.

Subsequently the Supreme Court reversed the Second Circuit in Credit Suisse Sec. (USA) LLC v. Billing, 551 U.S. 264 (2007), citing the text. Justice Breyer writing for the majority stated in part:

P. 797

This Court's prior decisions...make clear that, when a court decides whether securities law precludes antitrust law, it is deciding whether, given context and likely consequences, there is a *clear repugnancy* between the securities law and the antitrust complaint — or as we shall subsequently describe the matter, whether the two are *clearly incompatible*. Moreover *Gordon* and *NASD*, in finding sufficient incompatibility to warrant an implication of preclusion, have treated the following factors as critical: (1) the existence of regulatory authority under the securities law to supervise the activities in question; (2) evidence that the responsible regulatory entities exercise that authority; and (3) a resulting risk that the securities and antitrust laws, if both applicable, would produce conflicting guidance, requirements, duties, privileges, or standards of conduct. We also note (4) that in *Gordon* and *NASD* the possible conflict affected practices that lie squarely within an area of financial market activity that the securities law seeks to regulate....

These principles, applied to the complaints before us, considerably narrow our legal task. For the parties cannot reasonably dispute the existence here of several of the conditions that this Court previously regarded as crucial to finding that the securities law impliedly precludes the application of the antitrust laws.

First, the activities in question here — the underwriters' efforts jointly to promote and to sell newly issued securities — is central to the proper functioning of well-regulated capital markets. The IPO process supports new firms that seek to raise capital; it helps to spread ownership of those firms broadly among investors; it directs capital flows in ways that better correspond to the public's demand for goods and services. Moreover, financial experts, including the securities regulators, consider the general kind of joint underwriting activity at issue in this case, including road shows and book-building efforts essential to the successful marketing of an IPO. [Citations omitted.] Thus, the antitrust complaints before us concern practices that lie at the very heart of the securities marketing enterprise.

Second, the law grants the SEC authority to supervise all of the activities here in question. Indeed, the SEC possesses considerable power to forbid, permit, encourage, discourage, tolerate, limit, and otherwise regulate virtually every aspect of the practices in which underwriters engage. See, e.g., 15 U.S.C. §§77b(a)(3), 77j,

REGULATION OF THE SECURITIES MARKETS P. 797

77z-2 (granting SEC power to regulate the process of book-building, solicitations of "indications of interest," and communications, between underwriting participants and their customers, including those that occur during road shows); §78o(c)(2)(D) (granting SEC power to define and prevent through rules and regulations acts and practices that are fraudulent, deceptive, or manipulative); §78i(a)(6) (similar); §78j(b) (similar). Private individuals who suffer harm as a result of a violation of pertinent statutes and regulations may also recover damages. See §§78bb, 78u-4, 77k.

Third, the SEC has continuously exercised its legal authority to regulate conduct of the general kind now at issue. It has defined in detail, for example, what underwriters may and may not do and say during their road shows. [Citations omitted.] It has brought actions against underwriters who have violated these SEC regulations. [Citations omitted.] And private litigants, too, have brought securities actions complaining of conduct virtually identical to the conduct at issue here; and they have obtained damages. [Citation omitted.]

The preceding considerations show that the first condition (legal regulatory authority), the second condition (exercise of that authority), and the fourth condition (heartland securities activity) that were present in *Gordon* and *NASD* are satisfied in this case as well. Unlike *Silver*, there is here no question of the existence of appropriate regulatory authority, nor is there doubt as to whether the regulators have exercised that authority. Rather, the question before us concerns the third condition: Is there a conflict that rises to the level of incompatibility? Is an antitrust suit such as this likely to prove practically incompatible with the SEC's administration of the Nation's securities laws?...

Given the SEC's comprehensive authority to regulate IPO underwriting syndicates, its active and ongoing exercise of that authority, and the undisputed need for joint IPO underwriter activity, we do not read the complaints as attacking the bare existence of IPO underwriting syndicates or any of the joint activity that the SEC considers a necessary component of IPO-related syndicate activity. [Citations omitted.] Nor do we understand the complaints as questioning underwriter agreements to fix the levels of their commissions, whether or not the resulting price is *excessive*. See *Gordon*, 422 U.S., at 688-689 (securities law conflicts with, and

P. 797

therefore precludes, antitrust attack on the fixing of commissions where SEC has not approved, but later *might* approve, the practice).

We nonetheless can read the complaints as attacking the *manner* in which the underwriters jointly seek to collect *excessive* commissions. The complaints attack underwriter efforts to collect commissions through certain practices (i.e., laddering, tying, collecting excessive commissions in the form of later sales of the issued shares), which according to respondents the SEC itself has already disapproved and, in all likelihood, will not approve in the foreseeable future. In respect to this set of claims, they contend that there is no possible *conflict* since both securities law and antitrust law aim to prohibit the same undesirable activity. Without a conflict, they add, there is no *repugnance* or *incompatibility*, and this Court may not imply that securities law precludes an antitrust suit....

We accept the premises of respondents' argument — that the SEC has full regulatory authority over these practices, that it has actively exercised that authority, but that the SEC has *disapproved* (and, for argument's sake, we assume that it will continue to disapprove) the conduct that the antitrust complaints attack. Nonetheless, we cannot accept respondents' conclusion. Rather, several considerations taken together lead us to find that, even on these prorespondent assumptions, securities law and antitrust law are clearly incompatible.

First, to permit antitrust actions such as the present one *still* threatens serious securities-related harm. For one thing, an unusually serious legal line-drawing problem remains unabated. In the present context only a fine, complex, detailed line separates activity that the SEC permits or encourages (for which respondents must concede antitrust immunity) from activity that the SEC must (and inevitably will) forbid (and which, on respondents' theory, should be open to antitrust attack).

For example, in respect to *laddering* the SEC forbids an underwriter to "solicit customers prior to the completion of the distribution regarding whether and at what price and in what quantity they intend to place immediate aftermarket orders for IPO stock," [citations omitted]. But at the same time the SEC permits, indeed encourages, underwriters (as part of the *book building* process) to "inquir[e] as to a customer's desired future position in the longer term (for example, three to six months), and the price or prices at which the customer might accumulate that position without reference to immediate aftermarket activity." [Citations omitted.]

It will often be difficult for someone who is not familiar with accepted syndicate practices to determine with confidence whether an underwriter has insisted that an investor buy more shares in the immediate aftermarket (forbidden), or has simply allocated more shares of that issue in the long run (permitted). And who but a securities expert could say whether the present SEC rules set forth a virtually permanent line, unlikely to change in ways that would permit the sorts of *laddering-like* conduct that it now seems to forbid? [Citations omitted.]

Similarly, in respect to *tying* and other efforts to obtain an increased commission from future sales, the SEC has sought to prohibit an underwriter "from demanding...an offer from their customers of any payment or other consideration [such as the purchase of a different security] in addition to the security's stated consideration." [Citation omitted.] But the SEC would permit a firm to "allocat[e] IPO shares to a customer because the customer has separately regained the firm for other services, when the customer has not paid excessive compensation in relation to those services." [Citation omitted.] The National Association of Securities Dealers (NASD), over which the SEC exercises supervisory authority, has also proposed a rule that would prohibit a member underwriter from "offering or threatening to withhold" IPO shares "as consideration or inducement for the receipt of compensation that is excessive in relation to the services provided." [Citation omitted.] The NASD would allow, however, a customer legitimately to compete for IPO shares by increasing the level and quantity of compensation it pays to the underwriter. [Citation omitted.]

Under these standards, to distinguish what is forbidden from what is allowed requires an understanding of just when, in relation to services provided, a commission is *excessive*, indeed, so *excessive* that it will remain *permanently* forbidden....And who but the SEC itself could do so with confidence?

For another thing, evidence tending to show unlawful antitrust activity and evidence tending to show lawful securities marketing activity may overlap, or prove identical. Consider, for instance, a conversation between an underwriter and an investor about how long an investor intends to hold the new shares (and at what price), say a conversation that elicits comments concerning both the investor's short and longer term plans. That exchange might, as a plaintiff sees it, provide evidence of an underwriter's insistence upon *laddering* or, as a defendant sees it, provide evidence of a lawful

359

effort to allocate shares to those who will hold them for a longer time. [Citation omitted.]

Similarly, the same somewhat ambiguous conversation might help to establish an effort to collect an unlawfully high commission through atypically high commissions on later sales or through the sales of less popular stocks. Or it might prove only that the underwriter allocates more popular shares to investors who will help stabilize the aftermarket share price. [Citation omitted.]

Further, antitrust plaintiffs may bring lawsuits throughout the Nation in dozens of different courts with different nonexpert judges and different nonexpert juries. In light of the nuanced nature of the evidentiary evaluations necessary to separate the permissible from the impermissible, it will prove difficult for those many different courts to reach consistent results. And, given the fact-related nature of many such evaluations, it will also prove difficult to assure that the different courts evaluate similar fact patterns consistently. The result is an unusually high risk that different courts will evaluate similar factual circumstances differently. [Citation omitted.]

Now consider these factors together — the fine securities-related lines separating the permissible from the impermissible; the need for securities-related expertise (particularly to determine whether an SEC rule is likely permanent); the overlapping evidence from which reasonable but contradictory inferences may be drawn; and the risk of inconsistent court results. Together these factors mean there is no practical way to confine antitrust suits so that they challenge only activity of the kind the investors seek to target, activity that is presently unlawful and will likely remain unlawful under the securities law. Rather, these factors suggest that antitrust courts are likely to make unusually serious mistakes in this respect. And the threat of antitrust mistakes, i.e., results that stray outside the narrow bounds that plaintiffs seek to set, means that underwriters must act in ways that will avoid not simply conduct that the securities law forbids (and will likely continue to forbid), but also a wide range of joint conduct that the securities law permits or encourages (but which they fear could lead to an antitrust lawsuit and the risk of treble damages). And therein lies the problem.

This kind of problem exists to some degree in respect to other antitrust lawsuits. But here the factors we have mentioned make mistakes unusually likely (a matter relevant to Congress' determination of which institution should regulate a particular set of market activities). And the role that joint conduct plays in respect to the marketing of IPOs, along with the important role IPOs themselves play in relation to the effective functioning of capital markets, means that the securities-related costs of mistakes is unusually high. It is no wonder, then, that the SEC told the District Court (consistent with what the Government tells us here) that a "failure to hold that the alleged conduct was immunized would threaten to disrupt the full range of the Commission's ability to exercise its regulatory authority," adding that it would have a "chilling effect" on "lawful joint activities...of tremendous importance to the economy of the country." [Citation omitted.]

We believe it fair to conclude that, where conduct at the core of the marketing of new securities is at issue; where securities regulators proceed with great care to distinguish the encouraged and permissible from the forbidden; where the threat of antitrust lawsuits, through error and disincentive, could seriously alter underwriter conduct in undesirable ways, to allow an antitrust lawsuit would threaten serious harm to the efficient functioning of the securities market.

Second, any enforcement-related need for an antitrust lawsuit is usually small. For one thing, the SEC actively enforces the rules and regulations that forbid the conduct in question. For another, as we have said, investors harmed by underwriters' unlawful practices may bring lawsuits and obtain damages under the securities law.... Finally, the SEC is itself required to take account of competitive considerations when it creates securities-related policy and embodies it in rules and regulations. And that fact makes it somewhat less necessary to rely upon antitrust actions to address anticompetitive behavior. [Citations omitted.]...

In sum, an antitrust action in this context is accompanied by a substantial risk of injury to the securities markets and by a diminished need for antitrust enforcement to address anticompetitive conduct. Together these considerations indicate a serious conflict between, on the one hand, application of the antitrust laws and, on the other, proper enforcement of the securities law....

The upshot is that all four elements present in *Gordon* are present here: (1) an area of conduct squarely within the heartland of securities regulations; (2) clear and adequate SEC authority to regulate; (3) active and ongoing agency regulation; and (4) a serious conflict between the antitrust and regulatory regimes. We therefore conclude that the securities laws are *clearly incompatible* with the application of the antitrust laws in this context.

Id. at 285.

Justice Stevens concurred in the judgment, but not the opinion. Justice Thomas dissented.

2. COMMISSION RATE REGULATION

P. 802 n.39, end note. By 2002 Greenwich Associates estimated that $4.5 billion of the $12.7 billion paid in commissions by mutual funds and other institutional investors was for research and other items purchased with soft dollars. Oster & Lauricella, Mutual Funds' Soft Fees Getting a Hard Look, Wall St. J., Dec. 26, 2003, at C1.

In February 2004 the SEC unanimously voted to outlaw directed brokerage arrangements in which mutual funds use brokerage commissions to pay broker-dealers for selling fund shares. SEC Proposes Directed-Brokerage Ban, Adopts New Fee-Disclosure Requirements, 36 Sec. Reg. & L. Rep. (BNA) 293 (2004).

The Report of the NASD Mutual Fund Task Force on Soft Dollars and Portfolio Transactions (Nov. 11, 2004) unanimously recommended retaining the §28(e) safe harbor, but that the SEC should narrow its interpretation of the scope of §28(e) to better tailor the Section to the type of soft dollar services that benefit the adviser's clients rather than the adviser.

In 2006, after revision of the comments in response to the Proposing Release, the Commission adopted its new interpretation of the scope of *brokerage and research securities* and client commission arrangement under §28(e). Sec. Ex. Act Rels. 52,635, 86 SEC Dock. 1235 (2006) (proposal); 54,165, 88 SEC Dock. 1372 (2006) (adoption). The Release adopted the following interpretation of the §28(e) safe harbor:

> *Research services* are restricted to *advice, analyses,* and *reports* within the meaning of Section 28(e)(3).

Physical items, such as computer hardware, which do not reflect the expression of reasoning or knowledge relating to the subject matter identified in the statute, are outside the safe harbor.

Research related to the market for securities, such as trade analytics (including analytics available through order management systems) and advice on market color and execution strategies, are eligible for the safe harbor.

Market, financial, economic, and similar data could be eligible for the safe harbor.

Mass-marketed publications are not eligible as research under the safe harbor.

Brokerage services within the safe harbor are those products and services that relate to the execution of the trade from the point at which the money manager communicates with the broker-dealer for the purpose of transmitting an order for execution, through the point at which funds or securities are delivered or credited to the advised account.

Eligibility of both brokerage and research services for safe harbor protection is governed by the criteria in Section 28(e)(3), consistent with the Commission's 1986 "lawful and appropriate assistance" standard.

Mixed-use items must be reasonably allocated between eligible and ineligible uses, and the manager must keep adequate books and records concerning allocations so as to enable the manager to make the required good faith determination of the reasonableness of commissions in relation to the value of brokerage and research services.

In order for the safe harbor to be available to the money manager, the following principles apply:

Broker-dealers that are parties to arrangements under Section 28(e) are involved in *effecting* the trade if they execute, clear, or settle the trade, or perform one of four specified functions and allocate the other functions to another broker-dealer.

Broker-dealers *provide* the research if they (i) prepare the research, (ii) are financially obligated to pay for the research, or (iii) are not financially obligated to pay but their arrangements have certain attributes.

Id. at 1374.

Footnote 15 explained:

P. 805

The four functions are: (1) taking financial responsibility for customer trades; (2) maintaining records relating to customer trades; (3) monitoring and responding to customer comments concerning the trading process; and (4) monitoring trades and settlements.

Id. at 1374.

In 2008 the Commission published for comment Guidance Regarding the Duties and Responsibilities of Investment Company Boards of Directors with Respect to Investment Adviser Portfolio Trading Practices, Sec. Ex. Act Rel. 58,264, 93 SEC Dock. 2469 (2008) (proposal). The Release amplified the 2006 Interpretive Release, quoting the text.

E. CLEARANCE AND SETTLEMENT

P. 805, end page. In Whistler Inv. v. Depository Trust & Clearing Corp., 539 F.3d 1159, 1166 (9th Cir. 2008), the court held that "[b]ecause the Commission, in accordance with the congressional directive set forth in Section 17A, has approved [the National Securities Clearing Corporation's] creation of the Stock Borrow Program and the rules it has promulgated to govern Stock Borrow Program operations, we hold that state-law challenges to the existence or the operation of the Stock Borrow Program are federally preempted...."

In Pet Quarters, Inc. v. Depository Trust & Clearing Corp., 559 F.3d 772, 782 (8th Cir. 2009), the court considered a similar complaint and concluded:

In short, all of the damages that Pet Quarters claims to have suffered stem from activities performed or statements made by the defendants in conformity with the program's Commission approved rules. A favorable ruling on any of them would conflict with the Commission's control of the national securities clearing and settlement system and pose an obstacle to the congressional objectives in Section 17A. We conclude that the district court did not err in dismissing the complain on the basis of preemption.

CHAPTER 8

REGULATION OF BROKERS, DEALERS, AND INVESTMENT ADVISERS

A. BROKER-DEALER REGISTRATION

1. THE CHANGING ENVIRONMENT

P. 810, new pars. after 2d par. The 2007–2008 crisis in the housing and credit markets has galvanized Congressional and Department of Treasury initiatives to create a new regulatory structure with proposals for consolidation of regulatory agencies, an agency or agencies unequivocally in charge, and fewer areas of finance such as hedge funds largely outside of regulation altogether. The most powerful case for the need for a new regulatory structure can be based on the sense of surprise and helplessness at the stunningly rapid demise of Bear Stearns and the uncertainty about which financial institution might be next.

Regulatory consolidation already has achieved a conspicuous success with the merger of the former National Association of Securities Dealers and the New York Stock Exchange broker-dealer regulation under a single new self-regulatory organization, the Financial Institutions Regulatory Authority.

Simultaneously, a major initiative of the current SEC has been a move towards harmonizing SEC accounting standards with international standards, a step that potentially could lead to a form of

365

P. 810

international securities regulation. See SEC Weighs Easing Overseas Investing, Wall St. J., Mar. 25, 2008, at A2.

In 2008 the Department of the Treasury published *Blueprint for a Modernized Financial Regulatory Structure*. This Report proposed short-term recommendations, intermediate-term recommendations and an optimal regulatory framework for the United States insurance industry which held assets totaling $6 trillion at the end of 2006, the United States banking sector with total assets of $12.6 trillion, and the United States securities sector worth $12.4 trillion, as well as the United States commodities industry, among other cognate topics. Department of Treasury, Blueprint for a Modernized Financial Regulatory Structure 165 (Mar. 2008), citing the text.

The short-term recommendations most significantly proposed:

- Modernization of the President's Working Group on Financial Markets to enhance its effectiveness as a coordinator of financial regulatory policy, primarily by (1) broadening its focus to include the entire financial sector, rather than financial markets; (2) facilitating better inter-agency coordination and communication in mitigating systemic risk to the financial system, enhancing market integrity, promoting consumer and investor protection, and supporting capital markets efficiency and competitiveness; and (3) expanding the Working Group membership, which now includes the Secretary of the Treasury, who acts as chair of the Group, and the heads of the Federal Reserve Bank, the SEC, and the CFTC, with the proposed addition of the heads of the Office of the Comptroller of the Currency, the FDIC, and the Office of Thrift Supervision. Id. at 5–6, 75–77. This proposal is the most likely to be adopted since it can be effected by a Presidential Executive Order.
- Creation of a new Mortgage Origination Commission to address the high levels of delinquencies, defaults, and foreclosures among subprime borrowers in 2007 and 2008 and develop uniform minimum licensing qualifications for state mortgage market participants. Id. at 6–7, 78–83. Some form of this proposal also is likely to receive serious review since

the greatest *felt need* for a new approach involves the credit crisis that occurred in part because of the meltdown in the mortgage industry. A serious question to be addressed is whether the best approach would be to form a new Commission or simply for the Department of Housing and Urban Development to enforce new standards. The Treasury Department also recommended that appropriate conditions be attached to lending by the Federal Reserve to non-depository institutions.

Within the Report, the intermediate recommendations, in contrast, are most likely to inspire serious debate. These recommendations notably included:

- Within two years, phasing out the federal thrift charter and requiring thrifts to secure a national bank charter and closing the Office of Thrift Supervision. Id. at 8, 89–99.
- Studying who should be the appropriate supervisor for state chartered banks. Id. at 8–9, 99–100.
- Creating a new system of federal regulation administered by the Federal Reserve to address payment and settlement systems. Id. at 9, 100–106.
- Establishing an optional federal charter for insurers that would be subject solely to federal regulation and supervision while continuing state insurance regulation for those insurers that did not elect to be regulated at the national level. Id. at 9–11, 126–133.
- Merging the SEC and CFTC, not only in the sense of a structural merger but a merger of regulatory philosophies. To effectuate this merger, the Report most significantly recommended: (1) tasking the President's Working Group with drafting overarching regulatory principles focusing on investor protection, market integrity, and overall financial system risk reduction; (2) harmonizing securities and commodities rules involving margin, segregation, insider trading, insurance coverage for broker-dealer insolvency, customer suitability, short sales, SRO mergers, implied private rights of

P. 810

action, the SRO rulemaking approval process, and the agency's funding mechanism, with harmonization being achieved by a joint CFTC–SEC staff task force with equal agency representation and a requirement to harmonize specified differences; and (3) harmonizing the regulation of broker-dealers and investment advisers, among other things to create an SRO for investment advisers similar to that of broker-dealers. Id. at 11–13, 106–126.

The SEC, it was recommended, also should use its exemptive authority to adopt core principles to apply to securities clearing agencies and exchanges modeled after the core principles adopted for futures exchanges and clearing agencies under the Commodities Futures Modernization Act.

It was further recommended to permit all clearing agencies and market SROs to self-certify most rulemakings that would become effective upon filing with the SEC retaining its right to abrogate the rulemaking later.

This alone is a breathtaking agenda, but there are even more ambitious proposals for an optimal long-term regulatory structure. This proposed structure was inspired by the objectives-based approach currently used in Australia and the Netherlands, id. at 13–14, 137–146, and ultimately would restructure the financial structure to:

- Transform the Federal Reserve into the Market Stability Regulator, continuing its current role with respect to monetary policy and the provision of liquidity to the financial system and adding new responsibilities to supervise federal insured depository institutions, federal insurance institutions, and federal financial services providers. Id. at 15–17, 146–156.
- Create a new Prudential Financial Regulatory Agency to supervise financial institutions with some type of explicit government guarantees including federal deposit insurance and state-established insurance guarantee funds and assume the role of current federal prudential regulation now conducted

by the Office of the Comptroller of the Currency and the Office of Thrift Supervision. Id. at 17–19, 157–170.
- Create a new Conduct of Business Regulatory Agency to monitor business conduct regulation across all types of financial firms including federal insured depository institutions, federal insurance institutions, and federal financial services providers and be responsible for consumer protection, business practices, standards for entry into the financial services industry, and sales and service practices. The new Agency would also address broker-dealers, hedge funds, private equity funds, venture capital funds, and mutual funds and would develop standards that address such topics as net capital, public disclosures, testing, training, fraud, manipulation, and such duties to customers as best execution and suitability. Id. at 19–21, 170–180. There would remain a role for self-regulatory organizations. The standards developed by the Conduct of Business Regulatory Agency would apply both to nationally chartered and state-chartered firms.
- The SEC would be succeeded both by the new Conduct of Business Regulatory Agency and by a new Corporate Finance Regulator to assume the Commission's current responsibilities with respect to corporate disclosures, corporate governance, accounting, and similar issues. Id. at 21.

The inadequacy of the Commission's consolidated supervised entity program was depicted in brutal detail in a September 2008 Report from the SEC Office of Inspector General., SEC's Oversight of Bear Stearns and Related Entities: The Consolidated Supervised Entity Program (Report No. 446-A 2008). The Report stated in part:

> During the week of March 10, 2008, rumors spread about liquidity problems at The Bear Stearns Companies, Inc. (*Bear Stearns*). As the rumors spread, Bear Stearns was unable to obtain secured financing from counterparties. This caused severe liquidity problems. As a result, on Friday, March 14, 2008, JP Morgan Chase & Co. (*JP Morgan*) provided Bear Stearns with emergency funding from the Federal Reserve Bank of New York (*FRBNY*). According to

Congressional testimony, after the markets closed on March 14, 2008, it became apparent that the FRBNY's funding could not stop Bear Stearns' downward spiral. As a result, Bear Stearns concluded that it would need to file for bankruptcy protection on March 17, 2008, unless another firm purchased it. On Sunday March 16, 2008, (before the Asian markets opened), Bear Stearns' sale to JP Morgan was announced with financing support from the FRBNY. In May 2008, the sale was completed.

. . .

Of the seven original CSE firms, the Commission exercised direct oversight over only five firms (Bear Stearns, Goldman Sachs, Morgan Stanley, Merrill Lynch, and Lehman Brothers), which did not have a principal regulator. The Commission does not directly oversee Citigroup Inc. and JP Morgan because these firms have a principal regulator, the Federal Reserve.

The CSE program is a voluntary program that was created in 2004 by the Commission pursuant to rule amendments under the Securities Exchange Act of 1934. This program allows the Commission to supervise these broker-dealer holding companies on a consolidated basis. In this capacity, Commission supervision extends beyond the registered broker-dealer to the unregulated affiliates of the broker-dealer to the holding company itself. The CSE program was designed to allow the Commission to monitor for financial or operational weakness in a CSE holding company or its unregulated affiliates that might place United States regulated broker-dealers and other regulated entities at risk.

A broker-dealer becomes a CSE by applying to the Commission for an exemption from computing capital using the Commission's standard net capital rule, and the broker-dealer's ultimate holding company consenting to group-wide Commission supervision (if it does not already have a principal regulator). By obtaining an exemption from the standard net capital rule, the CSE firms' broker-dealers are permitted to compute net capital using an alternative method. The Commission designed the CSE program to be broadly consistent with the Federal Reserve's oversight of bank holding companies....

Audit Conclusions and Results. The CSE program's mission (goal) provides in pertinent part as follows:

> The regime is intended to allow the Commission to monitor for, and act quickly in response to, financial or operational

weakness in a CSE holding company or its unregulated affiliates that might place regulated entities, including US and foreign-registered banks and broker-dealers, *or the broader financial system at risk*. [Emphasis added]

Thus, it is undisputable that the CSE program failed to carry out its mission in its oversight of Bear Stearns because under the Commission and the CSE program's watch, Bear Stearns suffered significant financial weaknesses and the FRBNY needed to intervene during the week of March 10, 2008, to prevent significant harm to the broader financial system.

This audit was not intended to be a complete assessment of the multitude of events that led to Bear Stearns' collapse, and accordingly, does not purport to demonstrate any specific or direct connection between the failure of the CSE Program's oversight of Bear Stearns and Bear Stearns' collapse. However, we have identified serious deficiencies in the CSE program that warrant improvements. Overall, we found that there are significant questions about the adequacy of a number of CSE program requirements, as Bear Stearns was compliant with several of these requirements, but nonetheless collapsed. In addition, the audit found that [the Division of Trading and Markets (*TM*)] became aware of numerous potential red flags prior to Bear Stearns' collapse, regarding its concentration of mortgage securities, high leverage, shortcomings of risk management in mortgage-backed securities and lack of compliance with the spirit of certain Basel II standards, but did not take actions to limit these risk factors.

In addition, the audit found that procedures and processes were not strictly adhered to, as for example, the Commission issued an order approving Bear Stearns to become a CSE prior to the completion of the inspection process. Further, the Division of Corporation Finance (*CF*) did not conduct Bear Stearns' most recent 10-K filing review in a timely manner.

The audit also identified numerous specific concerns with the Commission's oversight of the CSE program, some of which are summarized as follows:

    (a) Bear Stearns was compliant with the CSE program's capital and liquidity requirements; however, its collapse raises questions about the adequacy of these requirements;

371

(b) Although TM was aware, prior to Bear Stearns becoming a CSE firm, that Bear Stearns' concentration of mortgage securities was increasing for several years and was beyond its internal limits, and that a portion of Bear Stearns' mortgage securities (e.g., adjustable rate mortgages) represented a significant concentration of market risk, TM did not make any efforts to limit Bear Stearns' mortgage securities concentration;

(c) Prior to the adoption of the rule amendments which created the CSE program, the broker-dealers affiliated with the CSE firms were required to either maintain:

- A debt-to-net capital ratio of less than 15 to 1 (after their first year of operation); or
- Have net capital not less than the greater of $250,000 or two percent of aggregate debit items computed in accordance with the *Formula for Determination* of *Reserve Requirements for Broker-Dealers*.

However, the CSE program did not require a leverage ratio limit for the CSE firms. Furthermore, despite TM being aware that Bear Stearns' leverage was high, TM made no efforts to require Bear Stearns to reduce its leverage, despite some authoritative sources describing a linkage between leverage and liquidity risk;

(d) TM became aware that risk management of mortgages at Bear Stearns had numerous shortcomings, including lack of expertise by risk managers in mortgage-backed securities at various times; lack of timely formal review of mortgage models; persistent understaffing; a proximity of risk managers to traders suggesting a lack of independence; turnover of key personnel during times of crisis; and the inability or unwillingness to update models to reflect changing circumstances. Notwithstanding this knowledge, TM missed opportunities to push Bear Stearns aggressively to address these identified concerns;

(e) There was no documentation of discussions between TM and Bear Stearns of scenarios involving a meltdown of mortgage market liquidity, accompanied by a fundamental deterioration of the mortgages themselves. TM appeared to identify the types of risks associated with these mortgages that evolved into the subprime mortgage

crisis yet did not require Bear Stearns to reduce its exposure to subprime loans;
(f) Bear Stearns was not compliant with the spirit of certain Basel II standards and we did not find sufficient evidence that TM required Bear Stearns to comply with these standards;
(g) TM took no actions to assess Bear Stearns' Board of Directors' and senior officials' (e.g., the Chief Executive Officer) tolerance for risk although we found that this is a prudent and necessary oversight procedure;
(h) TM authorized (without an appropriate delegation of authority) the CSE firm's internal audit staff to perform critical audit work involving the risk management systems instead of the firms' external auditors as required by the rule that created the CSE program;
(i) In June 2007, two of Bear Stearns' managed hedge funds collapsed. Subsequent to this collapse, significant questions were raised about some of Bear Stearns' senior managements' lack of involvement in handling the crisis. However, TM did not reassess the communication strategy component of Bear Stearns' Contingency Funding Plan (*CFP*) after the collapse of the hedge funds, and very significant questions were once again raised about some of Bear Stearns' managements' handling of the crisis during the week of March 10, 2008;
(j) The Commission issued four of the five Orders approving firms to use the alternative capital method, and thus become CSEs (including Bear Stearns) before the inspection process was completed; and
(k) CF did not conduct Bear Stearns' most recent 10-K filing review in a timely manner. The effect of this untimely review was that CF deprived investors of material information that they could have used to make well-informed investment decisions (i.e., whether to buy/sell Bear Stearns' securities). In addition, the information (e.g., Bear Stearns' exposure to subprime mortgages) could have been potentially beneficial to dispel the rumors that led to Bear Stearns' collapse.

Id. at iv-xi.

Simultaneous with the release of the damning SEC Inspector General report, the Commission terminated the CSE program. See Chairman Cox Announces End of Consolidated Supervised Entities Program, SEC Press Rel. 2008-230 (Sept. 26, 2008). The Release stated in part:

> Chairman Cox made the following statement:
>
> The last six months have made it abundantly clear that voluntary regulation does not work. When Congress passed the Gramm-Leach-Bliley Act, it created a significant regulatory gap by failing to give to the SEC or any agency the authority to regulate large investment bank holding companies, like Goldman Sachs, Morgan Stanley, Merrill Lynch, Lehman Brothers, and Bear Stearns....
>
> As I have reported to the Congress multiple times in recent months, the CSE program was fundamentally flawed from the beginning, because investment banks could opt in or out of supervision voluntarily. The fact that investment bank holding companies could withdraw from this voluntary supervision at their discretion diminished the perceived mandate of the CSE program, and weakened its effectiveness.
>
> The Inspector General of the SEC today released a report on the CSE program's supervision of Bear Stearns, and that report validates and echoes the concerns I have expressed to Congress. The report's major findings are ultimately derivative of the lack of specific legal authority for the SEC or any other agency to act as the regulator of these large investment bank holding companies.
>
> With each of the major investment banks that had been part of the CSE program being reconstituted within a bank holding company, they will all be subject to statutory supervision by the Federal Reserve. Under the Bank Holding Company Act, the Federal Reserve has robust statutory authority to impose and enforce supervisory requirements on those entities. Thus, there is not currently a regulatory gap in this area.
>
> The CSE program within the Division of Trading and Markets will now be ending.
>
> Under the Memorandum of Understanding between the SEC and the Federal Reserve that was executed in July of this year, we will continue to work closely with the Fed, but focused even more clearly on our statutory obligation to regulate the broker-dealer subsidiaries of the banking conglomerates. The information from

the bank holding company level that the SEC will continue to receive under the MOU will strengthen our ability to protect the customers of the broker-dealers and the integrity of the broker-dealer firms....

As we learned from the CSE experience, it is critical that Congress ensure there are no similar major gaps in our regulatory framework. Unfortunately, as I reported to Congress this week, a massive hole remains; the approximately $60 trillion credit default swap (CDS) market, which is regulated by no agency of government. Neither the SEC nor any regulator has authority even to require minimum disclosure. I urge Congress to take swift action to address this.

On September 15, 2008, Lehman Brothers filed for Chapter 11 bankruptcy protection after the Department of Treasury indicated that emergency funding would not be available to stabilize the firm. Lehman Brothers Holdings Files Ch. 11 Petition after Gov't Denies Funding, 40 Sec. Reg. & L. Rep. (BNA) 1476 (2008). At the time Lehman was the fourth largest investment bank in the United States, with more than 25,000 employees. Three days later SIPC placed Lehman in SIPA liquidation. To Ease Accounts Transfer to Barclays, SIPC to Place Lehman in SIPA Liquidation, 40 id. 1477.

The turmoil accelerated. The day after Lehman Brothers was allowed to fail the Department of Treasury orchestrated an $85 billion rescue package for insurance giant AIG. 40 id. 1476. See also Fed Again Invokes Emergency Powers with $37.8 Billion in New Loans to AIG, 40 id. 1643.

On the same day Lehman Brothers failed Bank of America acquired Merrill Lynch for $50 billion in an all stock deal. Bank of America Buys Merrill Lynch; Experts See More Concentrated Section, 40 id. 1480.

Breathtakingly in six months, three of the five largest independent investment banks (Bear Stearns, Lehman, Merrill) were gone as independent entities. Within a few days, Goldman Sachs and Morgan Stanley converted from investment banks to commercial bank holding companies. Among other things, this meant that the Federal Reserve Bank of New York could extend credit "to provide increased liquidity support." Goldman, Morgan Become Banks in Radical Change to Face of Wall Street, 40 id. 1534.

Most significantly, on October 3, 2008, Congress adopted a $700 billion financial bill, the Emergency Economic Stabilization Act of 2008, 122 Stat. 3765, 110th Cong., 2d Sess., a few days after the House of Representatives had initially defeated a similar bill. Financial Bailout Package Signed into Law, Though Doubts Remain about Effectiveness, 40 id. 1581.

The Emergency Economic Stabilization Act of 2008 was most notable for its Troubled Assets Relief Program, which can provide up to $700 billion "to restore liquidity and stability to the financial system of the United States." §2(1).

By 2008, there was an urgent need for a fundamental restructuring of federal financial regulation primarily based on three overlapping causes:

First, an ongoing economic emergency, initially rooted in our housing and credit markets, which has been succeeded by the collapse of several leading investment and commercial banks and insurance companies, dramatic deterioration of our stock market indices, and now a rapidly deepening recession.

Second, serious breakdowns in the enforcement and fraud deterrence missions of federal financial regulation, notably in recent months as illustrated by matters involving Bear Stearns and the other four then independent investment banks subject to the Securities and Exchange Commission's former Consolidated Supervised Entities program, the government creation of conservatorships for Fannie Mae and Freddie Mac, the Bernard Madoff case, and more generally a significant decline in the number of prosecutions for securities fraud at least in 2008.

Third, a misalignment between federal financial regulation and financial firms and intermediaries. The structure of financial regulation that was developed during the 1930s has not kept pace with fundamental changes in finance:

- In the New Deal period, most finance was atomized into separate investment banking, commercial banking, or insurance firms. Today finance is dominated by financial holding

- companies that operate in each of these and cognate areas such as commodities.
- In the New Deal period, the challenge of regulating finance was domestic. Now, when our credit markets are increasingly reliant on trades originating from abroad; our major financial institutions trade simultaneously throughout the world; and information technology has made international money transfers virtually instantaneous, the fundamental challenge is increasingly international.
- In 1930, approximately 1.5 percent of the American public directly owned stock on the New York Stock Exchange. A recent report estimates that in the first quarter of 2008 approximately 47 percent of U.S. households owned equities or bonds. A dramatic deterioration in stock prices affects the retirement plans and sometimes the livelihood of millions of Americans.
- In the New Deal period, the choice of financial investments was largely limited to stocks, debt, and bank accounts. Today we live in an age of complex derivative instruments, some of which recent experience has painfully shown are not well understood by investors and on some occasions by issuers or counterparties.
- Most significantly, we have learned that our system of finance is more fragile than we earlier had believed. The web of interdependency that is the hallmark of sophisticated trading today means when a major firm such as Lehman Brothers is bankrupt, cascading impacts can have powerful effects on an entire economy.

It was difficult to rationalize our current federal system of regulation that includes five separate federal depository institutions, specifically including the Federal Reserve System, the Office of the Comptroller of the Currency, the Federal Deposit Insurance Corporation, the Office of Thrift Supervision, and the National Credit Union Administration as well as state banking regulation

P. 810   2010 SUPPLEMENT

in each state. We are one of the few countries that separately regulate securities and commodities. Securities regulation, like banking, occurs both at the national and state level. Insurance regulation, in contrast, occurs solely at the state level.

On June 17, 2009 the Obama Administration Department of Treasury formally proposed its own approach, Financial Regulatory Reform: A New Foundation: Rebuilding Financial Supervision and Regulation.

The key recommendations were summarized at 10-18:

> I. Promote Robust Supervision and Regulation of Financial Firms
>
>> A. Create a Financial Services Oversight Council
>>
>>> 1. We propose the creation of a Financial Services Oversight Council to facilitate information sharing and coordination, identify emerging risks, advise the Federal Reserve on the identification of firms whose failure could pose a threat to financial stability due to their combination of size, leverage, and interconnectedness (hereafter referred to as a *Tier 1 FHC* [that is, Tier 1 Financial Holding Companies], and provide a forum for resolving jurisdictional disputes between regulators.
>>>
>>>> a. The membership of the Council should include (i) the Secretary of the Treasury, who shall serve as the Chairman; (ii) the Chairman of the Board of Governors of the Federal Reserve System; (iii) the Director of the National Bank Supervisor; (iv) the Director of the Consumer Financial Protection Agency; (v) the Chairman of the SEC; (vi) the Chairman of the CFTC; (vii) the Chairman of the FDIC; and (viii) the Director of the Federal Housing Finance Agency (*FHFA*).
>>>>
>>>> b. The Council should be supported by a permanent, full-time expert staff at Treasury. The staff should be responsible for providing the Council with the information and resources it needs to fulfill its responsibilities.

2. Our legislation will propose to give the Council the authority to gather information from any financial firm and the responsibility for referring emerging risks to the attention of regulators with the authority to respond.

B. Implement Heightened Consolidated Supervision and Regulation of All Large, Interconnected Financial Firms

1. Any financial firm whose combination of size, leverage, and interconnectedness could pose a threat to financial stability if it failed (Tier 1 FHC) should be subject to robust consolidated supervision and regulation, regardless of whether the firm owns an insured depository institution.
2. The Federal Reserve Board should have the authority and accountability for consolidated supervision and regulation of Tier 1 FHCs.
3. Our legislation will propose criteria that the Federal Reserve must consider in identifying Tier 1 FHCs.
4. The prudential standards for Tier 1 FHCs — including capital, liquidity and risk management standards — should be stricter and more conservative than those applicable to other financial firms to account for the greater risks that their potential failure would impose on the financial system.
5. Consolidated supervision of a Tier 1 FHC should extend to the parent company and to all of its subsidiaries — regulated and unregulated, U.S. and foreign. Functionally regulated and depository institution subsidiaries of a Tier 1 FHC should continue to be supervised and regulated primarily by their functional or bank regulator, as the case may be. The constraints that the Gramm-Leach-Bliley Act (*GLB Act*) introduced on the Federal Reserve's ability to require reports from, examine, or impose higher prudential requirements or more stringent activity restrictions on the functionally regulated or depository institution subsidiaries of FHCs should be removed.
6. Consolidated supervision of a Tier 1 FHC should be macroprudential in focus. That is, it should consider risk to the system as a whole.

7. The Federal Reserve, in consultation with Treasury and external experts, should propose recommendations by October 1, 2009 to better align its structure and governance with its authorities and responsibilities.

C. Strengthen Capital and Other Prudential Standards For All Banks and BHCs

1. Treasury will lead a working group, with participation by federal financial regulatory agencies and outside experts that will conduct a fundamental reassessment of existing regulatory capital requirements for banks and BHCs, including new Tier 1 FHCs. The working group will issue a report with its conclusions by December 31, 2009.
2. Treasury will lead a working group, with participation by federal financial regulatory agencies and outside experts, that will conduct a fundamental reassessment of the supervision of banks and BHCs. The working group will issue a report with its conclusions by October 1, 2009.
3. Federal regulators should issue standards and guidelines to better align executive compensation practices of financial firms with long-term shareholder value and to prevent compensation practices from providing incentives that could threaten the safety and soundness of supervised institutions. In addition, we will support legislation requiring all public companies to hold non-binding shareholder resolutions on the compensation packages of senior executive officers, as well as new requirements to make compensation committees more independent.
4. Capital and management requirements for FHC status should not be limited to the subsidiary depository institution. All FHCs should be required to meet the capital and management requirements on a consolidated basis as well.
5. The accounting standard setters (the FASB, the IASB, and the SEC) should review accounting standards to determine how financial firms should be required to employ more forward-looking loan loss

provisioning practices that incorporate a broader range of available credit information. Fair value accounting rules also should be reviewed with the goal of identifying changes that could provide users of financial reports with both fair value information and greater transparency regarding the cash flows management expects to receive by holding investments.

6. Firewalls between banks and their affiliates should be strengthened to protect the federal safety net that supports banks and to better prevent spread of the subsidy inherent in the federal safety net to bank affiliates.

D. Close Loopholes in Bank Regulation

1. We propose the creation of a new federal government agency, the National Bank Supervisor (*NBS*), to conduct prudential supervision and regulation of all federally chartered depository institutions, and all federal branches and agencies of foreign banks.
2. We propose to eliminate the federal thrift charter, but to preserve its interstate branching rules and apply them to state and national banks.
3. All companies that control an insured depository institution, however organized, should be subject to robust consolidated supervision and regulation at the federal level by the Federal Reserve and should be subject to the nonbanking activity restrictions of the BHC Act. The policy of separating banking from commerce should be re-affirmed and strengthened. We must close loopholes in the BHC Act for thrift holding companies, industrial loan companies, credit card banks, trust companies, and grandfathered *nonbank* banks.

E. Eliminate the SEC's Programs for Consolidated Supervision

The SEC has ended its Consolidated Supervised Entity Program, under which it had been the holding company supervisor for companies such as Lehman Brothers and Bear Stearns. We propose also eliminating the SEC's Supervised Investment Bank Holding

Company program. Investment banking firms that seek consolidated supervision by a U.S. regulator should be subject to supervision and regulation by the Federal Reserve.

F. Require Hedge Funds and Other Private Pools of Capital to Register

All advisers to hedge funds (and other private pools of capital, including private equity funds and venture capital funds) whose assets under management exceed some modest threshold should be required to register with the SEC under the Investment Advisers Act. The advisers should be required to report information on the funds they manage that is sufficient to assess whether any fund poses a threat to financial stability.

G. Reduce the Susceptibility of Money Market Mutual Funds (*MMFs*) to Runs

The SEC should move forward with its plans to strengthen the regulatory framework around MMFs to reduce the credit and liquidity risk profile of individual MMFs and to make the MMF industry as a whole less susceptible to runs. The President's Working Group on Financial Markets should prepare a report assessing whether more fundamental changes are necessary to further reduce the MMF industry's susceptibility to runs, such as eliminating the ability of a MMF to use a stable net asset value or requiring MMFs to obtain access to reliable emergency liquidity facilities from private sources.

H. Enhance Oversight of the Insurance Sector

Our legislation will propose the establishment of the Office of National Insurance within Treasury to gather information, develop expertise, negotiate international agreements, and coordinate policy in the insurance sector. Treasury will support proposals to modernize and improve our system of insurance regulation in accordance with six principles outlined in the body of the report.

I. Determine the Future Role of the Government Sponsored Enterprises (*GSEs*)

Treasury and the Department of Housing and Urban Development, in consultation with other government agencies, will engage in a wide-ranging initiative to develop recommendations on the future of Fannie Mae and Freddie Mac, and the Federal Home Loan Bank system. We need to maintain the continued stability and strength of the GSEs during these difficult financial times. We will report to the Congress and the American public at the time of the President's 2011 Budget release.

II. Establish Comprehensive Regulation of Financial Markets

  A. Strengthen Supervision and Regulation of Securitization Markets

    1. Federal banking agencies should promulgate regulations that require originators or sponsors to retain an economic interest in a material portion of the credit risk of securitized credit exposures.

    2. Regulators should promulgate additional regulations to align compensation of market participants with longer term performance of the underlying loans.

    3. The SEC should continue its efforts to increase the transparency and standardization of securitization markets and be given clear authority to require robust reporting by issuers of asset backed securities (*ABS*).

    4. The SEC should continue its efforts to strengthen the regulation of credit rating agencies, including measures to promote robust policies and procedures that manage and disclose conflicts of interest, differentiate between structured and other products, and otherwise strengthen the integrity of the ratings process.

    5. Regulators should reduce their use of credit ratings in regulations and supervisory practices, wherever possible.

  B. Create Comprehensive Regulation of All OTC Derivatives, Including Credit Default Swaps (*CDS*)

    All OTC derivatives markets, including CDS markets, should be subject to comprehensive regulation that

P. 810

addresses relevant public policy objectives: (1) preventing activities in those markets from posing risk to the financial system; (2) promoting the efficiency and transparency of those markets; (3) preventing market manipulation, fraud, and other market abuses; and (4) ensuring that OTC derivatives are not marketed inappropriately to unsophisticated parties.

C. Harmonize Futures and Securities Regulation

The CFTC and the SEC should make recommendations to Congress for changes to statutes and regulations that would harmonize regulation of futures and securities.

D. Strengthen Oversight of Systemically Important Payment, Clearing and Settlement Systems and Related Activities

We propose that the Federal Reserve have the responsibility and authority to conduct oversight of systemically important payment, clearing and settlement systems, and activities of financial firms.

E. Strengthen Settlement Capabilities and Liquidity Resources of Systemically Important Payment, Clearing, and Settlement Systems

We propose that the Federal Reserve have authority to provide systemically important payment, clearing, and settlement systems access to Reserve Bank accounts, financial services, and the discount window.

III. Protect Consumers and Investors From Financial Abuse

A. Create a New Consumer Financial Protection Agency

1. We propose to create a single primary federal consumer protection supervisor to protect consumers of credit, savings, payment, and other consumer financial products and services, and to regulate providers of such products and services.
2. The CFPA should have broad jurisdiction to protect consumers in consumer financial products and services such as credit, savings, and payment products.
3. The CFPA should be an independent agency with stable, robust funding.

4. The CFPA should have sole rule-making authority for consumer financial protection statutes, as well as the ability to fill gaps through rule-making.
5. The CFPA should have supervisory and enforcement authority and jurisdiction over all persons covered by the statutes that it implements, including both insured depositories and the range of other firms not previously subject to comprehensive federal supervision, and it should work with the Department of Justice to enforce the statutes under its jurisdiction in federal court.
6. The CFPA should pursue measures to promote effective regulation, including conducting periodic reviews of regulations, an outside advisory council, and coordination with the Council.
7. The CFPA's strong rules would serve as a floor, not a ceiling. The states should have the ability to adopt and enforce stricter laws for institutions of all types, regardless of charter, and to enforce federal law concurrently with respect to institutions of all types, also regardless of charter.
8. The CFPA should coordinate enforcement efforts with the states.
9. The CFPA should have a wide variety of tools to enable it to perform its functions effectively.
10. The Federal Trade Commission should also be given better tools and additional resources to protect consumers.

B. Reform Consumer Protection

1. Transparency. We propose a new proactive approach to disclosure. The CFPA will be authorized to require that all disclosures and other communications with consumers be reasonable: balanced in their presentation of benefits, and clear and conspicuous in their identification of costs, penalties, and risks.
2. Simplicity. We propose that the regulator be authorized to define standards for *plain vanilla* products that are simpler and have straightforward pricing. The CFPA should be authorized to require all providers and intermediaries to offer these products

prominently, alongside whatever other lawful products they choose to offer.
3. Fairness. Where efforts to improve transparency and simplicity prove inadequate to prevent unfair treatment and abuse, we propose that the CFPA be authorized to place tailored restrictions on product terms and provider practices, if the benefits outweigh the costs. Moreover, we propose to authorize the Agency to impose appropriate duties of care on financial intermediaries.
4. Access. The Agency should enforce fair lending laws and the Community Reinvestment Act and otherwise seek to ensure that underserved consumers and communities have access to prudent financial services, lending, and investment.

C. Strengthen Investor Protection

1. The SEC should be given expanded authority to promote transparency in investor disclosures.
2. The SEC should be given new tools to increase fairness for investors by establishing a fiduciary duty for broker-dealers offering investment advice and harmonizing the regulation of investment advisers and broker-dealers.
3. Financial firms and public companies should be accountable to their clients and investors by expanding protections for whistleblowers, expanding sanctions available for enforcement, and requiring non-binding shareholder votes on executive pay plans.
4. Under the leadership of the Financial Services Oversight Council, we propose the establishment of a Financial Consumer Coordinating Council with a broad membership of federal and state consumer protection agencies, and a permanent role for the SEC's Investor Advisory Committee.
5. Promote retirement security for all Americans by strengthening employment-based and private retirement plans and encouraging adequate savings.

IV. Provide The Government With The Tools It Needs To Manage Financial Crises

A. Create a Resolution Regime for Failing BHCs, Including Tier 1 FHCs

We recommend the creation of a resolution regime to avoid the disorderly resolution of failing BHCs, including Tier 1 FHCs, if a disorderly resolution would have serious adverse effects on the financial system or the economy. The regime would supplement (rather than replace) and be modeled on to the existing resolution regime for inspired depository institutions under the Federal Deposit Insurance Act.

B. Amend the Federal Reserve's Emergency Lending Authority

We will propose legislation to amend Section 13(3) of the Federal Reserve Act to require the prior written approval of the Secretary of the Treasury for any extensions of credit by the Federal Reserve to individuals, partnerships, or corporations in "unusual and exigent circumstances."

V. Raise International Regulatory Standards and Improve International Cooperation

A. Strengthen the International Capital Framework

We recommend that the Basel Committee on Banking Supervision (*BCBS*) continue to modify and improve Basel II by refining the risk weights applicable to the trading book and securitized products, introducing a supplemental leverage ratio, and improving the definition of capital by the end of 2009. We also urge the BCBS to complete an in-depth review of the Basel II framework to mitigate its procyclical effects.

B. Improve the Oversight of Global Financial Markets

We urge national authorities to promote the standardization and improved oversight of credit derivatives and other OTC derivative markets, in particular through the use of central counterparties, along the lines of the G-20 commitment, and to advance these goals through international coordination and cooperation.

C. Enhance Supervision of Internationally Active Financial Firms

We recommend that the Financial Stability Board (*FSB*) and national authorities implement G-20 commitments to strengthen arrangements for international cooperation on supervision of global financial firms through establishment and continued operational development of supervisory colleges.

D. Reform Crisis Prevention and Management Authorities and Procedures

We recommend that the BCBS expedite its work to improve cross-border resolution of global financial firms and develop recommendations by the end of 2009. We further urge national authorities to improve information-sharing arrangements and implement the FSB principles for cross-border crisis management.

E. Strengthen the Financial Stability Board

We recommend that the FSB complete its restructuring and institutionalize its new mandate to promote global financial stability by September 2009.

F. Strengthen Prudential Regulations

We recommend that the BCBS take steps to improve liquidity risk management standards for financial firms and that the FSB work with the Bank for International Settlements (*BIS*) and standard setters to develop macroprudential tools.

G. Expand the Scope of Regulation

1. Determine the appropriate Tier 1 FHC definition and application of requirements for foreign financial firms.
2. We urge national authorities to implement by the end of 2009 the G-20 commitment to require hedge funds or their managers to register and disclose appropriate information necessary to assess the systemic risk they pose individually or collectively.

H. Introduce Better Compensation Practices

In line with G-20 commitments, we urge each national authority to put guidelines in place to align compensation with long-term shareholder value and to promote compensation structures that do not provide incentives for excessive risk taking. We recommend that the BCBS expediently integrate the FSB principles on compensation into its risk management guidance by the end of 2009.

I. Promote Stronger Standards in the Prudential Regulation, Money Laundering/Terrorist Financing, and Tax Information Exchange Areas

1. We urge the FSB to expeditiously establish and coordinate peer reviews to assess compliance and implementation of international regulatory standards, with priority attention on the international cooperation elements of prudential regulatory standards.
2. The United States will work to implement the updated International Cooperation Review Group (*ICRG*) peer review process and work with partners in the Financial Action Task Force (*FATF*) to address jurisdictions not complying with international anti-money laundering/terrorist financing (*AML/CFT*) standards.

J. Improve Accounting Standards

1. We recommend that the accounting standard setters clarify and make consistent the application of fair value accounting standards, including the impairment of financial instruments, by the end of 2009.
2. We recommend that the accounting standard setters improve accounting standards for loan loss provisioning by the end of 2009 that would make it more forward looking, as long as the transparency of financial statements is not compromised.
3. We recommend that the accounting standard setters make substantial progress by the end of 2009 toward development of a single set of high quality global accounting standards.

K. Tighten Oversight of Credit Rating Agencies
   We urge national authorities to enhance their regulatory regimes to effectively oversee credit rating agencies (*CRAs*), consistent with international standards and the G-20 Leaders' recommendations.

Notably the Financial Services Oversight Council: should replace the President's Working Group on Financial Markets and have

P. 810   2010 SUPPLEMENT

additional authorities and responsibilities with respect to systemic risk and coordination of financial regulation. We propose that the council should:

- facilitate information sharing and coordination among the principal federal financial regulatory agencies regarding policy development, rulemakings, examinations, reporting requirements, and enforcement actions;
- provide a forum for discussion of cross-cutting issues among the principal federal financial regulatory agencies; and
- identify gaps in regulation and prepare an annual report to Congress on market developments and potential emerging risks.

Id. at 20-21.

The Federal Reserve Board would become the sole regulator responsible for consolidated supervision and regulation of the largest financial holding companies:

We propose that authority for supervision and regulation of Tier 1 FHCs be vested in the Federal Reserve Board, which is by statute the consolidated supervisor and regulator of all bank holding companies today. As a result of changes in corporate structure during the current crisis, the Federal Reserve already supervises and regulates all major U.S. commercial and investment banks on a firm-wide basis. The Federal Reserve has by far the most experience and resources to handle consolidated supervision and regulation of Tier 1 FHCs....

The ultimate responsibility for prudential standard-setting and supervision for Tier 1 FHCs must rest with a single regulator. The public has a right to expect that a clearly identifiable entity, not a committee of multiple agencies, will be answerable for setting standards that will protect the financial system and the public from risks posed by the potential failure of Tier 1 FHCs. Moreover, a committee that included regulators of specific types of financial institutions such as commercial banks or broker-dealers (functional regulators) may be less focused on systemic needs and more focused on the needs of the financial firms they regulate....

Diffusing responsibility among several regulators would weaken incentives for effective regulation in other ways. For example, it would weaken both the incentive for and the ability of the relevant agencies to act in a timely fashion — creating the risk that clearly ineffective standards remain in place for long periods.

The Federal Reserve should fundamentally adjust its current framework for supervising all BHCs in order to carry out its new responsibilities effectively with respect to Tier 1 FHCs. For example, the focus of BHC regulation would need to expand beyond the safety and soundness of the bank subsidiary to include the activities of the firm as a whole and the risks the firm might pose to the financial system. The Federal Reserve would also need to develop new supervisory approaches for activities that to date have not been significant activities for most BHCs.

Id. at 22.

The approach to regulation of Tier I FHCs would significantly change. Where earlier their diversification was seen as a justification for looser capital, liquidity, and risk management standards, the Report stressed:

> Tier I FHCs should be subject to heightened supervision and regulation because of the greater risks their potential failure would pose to the financial system....
>
> Capital Requirements. Capital requirements for Tier I FHCs should reflect the large negative externalities associated with the financial distress, rapid deleveraging, or disorderly failure of each firm and should, therefore, be strict enough to be effective under extremely stressful economic and financial conditions. Tier I FHCs should be required to have enough high-quality capital during good economic times to keep them above prudential minimum capital requirements during stressed economic times. In addition to regulatory capital ratios, the Federal Reserve should evaluate a Tier 1 FHC's capital strength using supervisory assessments, including assessments of capital adequacy under severe stress scenarios and assessments of the firm's capital planning practices, and market-based indicators of the firm's credit quality.
>
> Prompt Corrective Action. Tier 1 FHCs should be subject to a prompt corrective action regime that would require the firm or its supervisor to take corrective actions as the firm's regulatory capital levels decline, similar to the existing prompt corrective action

regime for insured depository institutions established under the Federal Deposit Insurance Corporation Improvement Act (*FDICIA*).

Liquidity Standards. The Federal Reserve should impose rigorous liquidity risk requirements on Tier 1 FHCs that recognize the potential negative impact that the financial distress, rapid deleveraging, or disorderly failure of each firm would have on the financial system. The Federal Reserve should put in place a robust process for continuously monitoring the liquidity risk profiles of these institutions and their liquidity risk management processes....

Overall Risk Management. Supervisory expectations regarding Tier 1 FHCs' risk-management practices must be in proportion to the risk, complexity, and scope of their operations. These firms should be able to identify firm-wide risk concentrations (credit, business lines, liquidity, and other) and establish appropriate limits and controls around these concentrations. In order to credibly measure and monitor risk concentrations, Tier 1 FHCs must be able to identify aggregate exposures quickly on a firm-wide basis.

Market Discipline and Disclosure. To support market evaluation of a Tier 1 FHC's risk profile, capital adequacy, and risk management capabilities, such firms should be required to make enhanced public disclosures.

Restrictions on Nonfinancial Activities. Tier 1 FHCs that do not control insured depository institutions should be subject to the full range of prudential regulations and supervisory guidance applicable to BHCs. In addition, the long-standing wall between banking and commerce — which has served our economy well — should be extended to apply to this new class of financial firm. Accordingly, each Tier 1 FHC also should be required to comply with the nonfinancial activity restrictions of the BHC Act, regardless of whether it controls an insured depository institution. We propose that a Tier 1 FHC that has not been previously subject to the BHC Act should be given five years to conform to the existing activity restrictions imposed on FHCs by the BHC Act.

Rapid Resolution Plans. The Federal Reserve also should require each Tier 1 FHC to prepare and continuously update a credible plan for the rapid resolution of the firm in the event of severe financial distress. Such a requirement would create incentives for the firm to better monitor and simplify its organizational structure and would better prepare the government, as well as the firm's investors, creditors, and counterparties, in the event that the firm collapsed. The Federal Reserve should review the adequacy of each firm's plan regularly.

Id. at 24-25.

Under the proposal, hedge funds and other private pools of capital would be required to register.

OTC derivatives would be subject to new regulation:

> To contain systemic risks, the Commodities Exchange Act (*CEA*) and the securities laws should be amended to require clearing of all standardized OTC derivatives through regulated central counterparties (*CCPs*). To make these measures effective, regulators will need to require that CCPs impose robust margin requirements as well as other necessary risk controls and that customized OTC derivatives are not used solely as a means to avoid using a CCP. For example, if an OTC derivative is accepted for clearing by one or more fully regulated CCPs, it should create a presumption that it is a standardized contract and thus required to be cleared.
>
> All OTC derivatives dealers and all other firms whose activities in those markets create large exposures to counterparties should be subject to a robust and appropriate regime of prudential supervision and regulation. Key elements of that robust regulatory regime must include conservative capital requirements (more conservative than the existing bank regulatory capital requirements for OTC derivatives), business conduct standards, reporting requirements, and conservative requirements relating to initial margins on counterparty credit exposures. Counterparty risks associated with customized bilateral OTC derivatives transactions that should not be accepted by a CCP would be addressed by this robust regime covering derivative dealers. As noted above, regulatory capital requirements on OTC derivatives that are not centrally cleared also should be increased for all banks and BHCs.
>
> The OTC derivatives markets should be made more transparent by amending the CEA and the securities laws to authorize the CFTC and the SEC, consistent with their respective missions, to impose recordkeeping and reporting requirements (including an audit trail) on all OTC derivatives. Certain of those requirements should be deemed to be satisfied by either clearing standardized transactions through a CCP or by reporting customized transactions to a regulated trade repository. CCPs and trade repositories

P. 810

should be required to, among other things, make aggregate data on open positions and trading volumes available to the public and make data on any individual counterparty's trades and positions available on a confidential basis to the CFTC, SEC, and the institution's primary regulators.

Market efficiency and price transparency should be improved in derivatives markets by requiring the clearing of standardized contracts through regulated CCPs as discussed earlier and by moving the standardized part of these markets onto regulated exchanges and regulated transparent electronic trade execution systems for OTC derivatives and by requiring development of a system for timely reporting of trades and prompt dissemination of prices and other trade information. Furthermore, regulated financial institutions should be encouraged to make greater use of regulated exchange-traded derivatives. Competition between appropriately regulated OCT derivatives markets and regulated exchanges would make both sets of markets more efficient and thereby better serve end-users of derivatives.

Market integrity concerns should be addressed by making whatever amendments to the CEA and the securities laws which are necessary to ensure that the CFTC and the SEC, consistent with their respective missions, have clear, unimpeded authority to police and prevent fraud, market manipulation, and other market abuses involving all OTC derivatives. The CFTC also should have authority to set position limits on OTC derivatives that perform or affect a significant price discovery function with respect to regulated markets.

Id. at 47-48.

The proposed new Consumer Financial Protection Agency explicitly would not have authority for investment products and services already regulated by the SEC or CFTC. Id. at 55-56.

Notably within its scope, the new agency would have authority to ban mandatory arbitration clauses. Id. at 62-63.

The Report did seek to harmonize broker-dealer and investment adviser regulation:

> ...[I]nvestment advisers and broker-dealers are regulated under different statutory and regulatory frameworks, even though the

services they provide often are virtually identical from a retail investor's perspective.

Retail investors are often confused about the differences between investment advisers and broker-dealers. Meanwhile, the distinction is no longer meaningful between a disinterested investment advisor and a broker who acts as an agent for an investor; the current laws and regulations are based on antiquated distinctions between the two types of financial professionals that date back to the early 20th century. Brokers are allowed to give *incidental advice* in the course of their business, and yet retail investors rely on a trusted relationship that is often not matched by the legal responsibility of the securities broker. In general, a broker-dealer's relationship with a customer is not legally a fiduciary relationship, while an investment adviser is legally its customer's fiduciary.

From the vantage point of the retail customer, however, an investment adviser and a broker-dealer providing *incidental advice* appear in all respects identical. In the retail context, the legal distinction between the two is no longer meaningful. Retail customers repose the same degree of trust in their brokers as they do in investment advisers, but the legal responsibilities of the intermediaries may not be the same.

The SEC should be permitted to align duties for intermediaries across financial products. Standards of care for all broker-dealers when providing investment advice about securities to retail investors should be raised to the fiduciary standard to align the legal framework with investment advisers. In addition, the SEC should be empowered to examine and ban forms of compensation that encourage intermediaries to put investors into products that are profitable to the intermediary, but are not in the investors' best interest.

New legislation should bolster investor protections and bring important consistency to the regulation of these two types of financial professionals by:

- requiring that broker-dealers who provide investment advice about securities to investors have the same fiduciary obligations as registered investment advisers;
- providing simple and clear disclosure to investors regarding the scope of the terms of their relationships with investment professionals; and

- prohibiting certain conflict of interests and sales practices that are contrary to the interest of investors.

The SEC should study the use of mandatory arbitration clauses in investor contracts.

Broker-dealers generally require their customers to contract at account opening to arbitrate all disputes. Although arbitration may be a reasonable option for many consumers to accept after a dispute arises, mandating a particular venue and up-front method of adjudicating disputes — and eliminating access to courts — may unjustifiably undermine investor interests. We recommend legislation that would give the SEC clear authority to prohibit mandatory arbitration clauses in broker-dealer and investment advisory accounts with retail customers. The legislation should also provide that, before using such authority, the SEC would need to conduct a study on the use of mandatory arbitration clauses in these contracts. The study shall consider whether investors are harmed by being unable to obtain effective redress of legitimate grievances, as well as whether changes to arbitration are appropriate.

Id. at 71-73.

3. Definitions of *Broker* and *Dealer* [§§3(a)(4), 3(a)(5)]

d. Banks and Other Depository Institutions

P. 818 n.30, end note. In 2007 the SEC and Federal Reserve Board adopted final rules to implement the broker exceptions for banks relating to third-party networking arrangements, trust and fiduciary activities, sweet activities, and custody and safekeeping activities. Sec. Ex. Act Rels. 54,946, 89 SEC Dock. 1682 (2006) (proposal); 56,501, 91 SEC Dock. 1699 (2007) (adoption).

Simultaneously, the Commission and the Federal Reserve Board withdrew proposed Regulation B and removed Interim Rules 3a4-2 to 3a4-6 and 3b-17, which were superseded by these final Rules. Id. at 1744.

In 2007 the Commission: (1) adopted Rule 3a5-2 to provide a conditional exemption from the definition of *dealer* to allow banks to engage in specified transactions involving securities exempted from the registration by Regulation S; (2) adopted a clarifying amendment to Rule 15a-6 to provide a conditional exemption from United States registration requirements for covered foreign broker-dealers; (3) redesignated as Rule 3a5-3 the dealer provisions of former Rule 15a-11; and (4) withdrew former Rules 3b-9, 15a-8, and 15a-9. Sec. Ex. Act Rel. 56,502, 91 SEC Dock. 1766 (2007) (adoption).

5. Qualifications and Discipline

a. Grounds for Proceeding

(iv) *Willful Violations*

P. 826 n.64, end note. Under NASD Membership Rule 1022(b) a person such as an accountant who caused a NASD member to violate an SEC rule may also be held responsible for the violation of the SEC rule even if by its terms the SEC rule only applied to a broker-dealer. Avello v. SEC, 454 F.3d 619, 624-625 (7th Cir. 2006).

8. Research Analysts

a. The Global Settlement

P. 841, new n.109.1, end 2d par. In Merrill Lynch & Co., Inc. Research Reports, 272 F. Supp. 2d 243 (S.D.N.Y. 2003), the late Judge Milton Pollack dismissed with prejudice an action against a proprietary mutual fund that invested in the common stock of companies covered by Merrill Lynch analyst researches, in part,

P. 841

because the court did not find that the defendants had a duty to disclose specified omitted information.

In affirming Judge Pollack's decision, the Second Circuit in Lentell v. Merrill Lynch & Co., Inc., 396 F.3d 161 (2d Cir. 2005), *cert. denied*, 546 U.S. 935, assumed a less vituperative tone and relied upon the plaintiff's failure to adequately plead loss causation:

> Plaintiffs allege that when they invested, there were relying on the integrity of the market (including the fraudulent recommendations and omissions made by Merrill Lynch during the putative class periods), that the shares plummeted, and that their investments became virtually worthless. To plead loss causation, the complaints must allege facts that support an inference that Merrill's misstatements and omissions concealed the circumstances that bear upon the loss suffered such that plaintiffs would have been spared all or an ascertainable portion of that loss absent the fraud. As the district court found, no such allegations are made. *Merrill Lynch*, 273 F. Supp. 2d at 367-68. There is no allegation that the market reacted negatively to a corrective disclosure regarding the falsity of Merrill's *buy* and *accumulate* recommendations and no allegation that Merrill misstated or omitted risks that did lead to the loss. This is fatal under Second Circuit precedent....
>
> As noted, to establish loss causation, "a plaintiff must allege...that the *subject* of the fraudulent statement or omission was the cause of the actual loss suffered." *Suez Equity*, 250 F.3d at 95 (emphasis added). It is alleged that Merrill's *buy* and *accumulate* recommendations were false and misleading with respect to 24/7 Media and Interliant, and that those recommendations artificially inflated the value of 24/7 Media and Interliant stock. However, plaintiffs do not allege that the subject of those false recommendations (that investors should buy or accumulate 24/7 Media and Interliant stock), or any corrective disclosure regarding the falsity of those recommendations, is the cause of the *decline* in stock value that plaintiffs claim as their loss. Nor do plaintiffs allege that Merrill Lynch concealed or misstated any risks associated with an investment in 24/7 Media or Interliant, some of which presumably

caused plaintiffs' loss. Plaintiffs therefore failed to allege loss causation, as that requirement is set out in *Emergent Capital, Castellano,* and *Suez Equity.*

Id. at 175.

In Merrill Lynch & Co., Inc., 273 F. Supp. 2d 351 (S.D.N.Y. 2003), Judge Pollack also dismissed claims against Merrill Lynch for the opinions expressed by its Internet research group. This case was striking for its tone. Judge Pollack wrote in part:

> The record clearly reveals that plaintiffs were among the high-risk speculators who, knowing full well or being properly chargeable with appreciation of the unjustifiable risks they were undertaking in the extremely volatile and highly untested stocks at issue, now hope to twist the federal securities laws into a scheme of cost-free speculators' insurance. Seeking to lay the blame for the enormous Internet Bubble solely at the feet of a single actor, Merrill Lynch, plaintiffs would have this court conclude that the federal securities laws were meant to underwrite, subsidize, and encourage their rash speculation in joining a freewheeling casino that lured thousands obsessed with the fantasy of Olympian riches, but which delivered such riches to only a scant handful of lucky winners. Those few lucky winners, who are not before the court, now hold the monies that the unlucky plaintiffs have lost — fair and square — and they will never return those monies to plaintiffs. Had plaintiffs themselves won the game instead of losing, they would have owed not a single penny of their winnings to those they left to hold the bag (or to defendants).
>
> Notwithstanding this — the federal securities laws at issue here only fault those who, *with intent to defraud,* make a *material* misrepresentation or omission of *fact* (not opinion) in connection with the purchase or sale of securities that *causes* a plaintiff's losses. Considering all of the facts and circumstances of the cases at bar, and accepting all of plaintiffs' voluminous inflammatory and improperly generalized allegations as true, this court is utterly unconvinced that the misrepresentations and omissions alleged in the complaints have been sufficiently alleged to be cognizable misrepresentations and omissions made with the intent to defraud. Plaintiffs have failed to adequately plead that defendant and its former

P. 843 2010 SUPPLEMENT

chief internet analyst *caused* their losses. The facts and circumstances fully within this court's proper province to consider on a motion to dismiss show beyond doubt that plaintiffs brought their own losses upon themselves when they knowingly spun an extremely high-risk, high-stakes wheel of fortune.

Id. at 358. See also Merrill Lynch & Co., Inc. Research Reports, 289 F. Supp. 2d 416 (S.D.N.Y. 2003) (dismissal of similar complaints); Merrill Lynch & Co., Inc. Research Reports, 289 F. Supp. 2d 429 (S.D.N.Y. 2003).

In July 2003 Citigroup, Inc. and J. P. Morgan Chase & Co. agreed to pay approximately $305 million to settle federal and state charges that they structured transactions by Enron in a way that allowed Enron to falsely characterize loan proceeds as cash from operations. Citigroup, J. P. Morgan Chase Settle Charges They Helped Enron Commit Fraud, 35 Sec. Reg. & L. Rep. (CCH) 1285 (2003).

b. NASD and NYSE Rules

P. 843 n.111, end note. In 2003 the SEC approved the NYSE and NASD rules. Sec. Ex. Act Rel. 48,252, 80 SEC Dock. 2179 (2003) (approval). See also Responses to Frequently Asked Questions Concerning Regulation Analyst Certification, 2003 Fed. Sec. L. Rep. (CCH) ¶86,955 (Aug. 6, 2003).

Early in 2005, the Commission approved further amendments to the NYSE and NASD rules that restrict research analyst activities. Sec. Ex. Act Rels. 51,358, 84 SEC Dock. 3571 (2005) (proposed NYSE Rule 472(b) and NASD Rule 2711(c)); 51,593, 85 SEC Dock. 739 (2005) (approval). The new restrictions, which were inspired by the global settlement, prohibit research analyst participation in road shows; three way conversations with research analysts, investors, *and* investment bankers or executives of a corporate issuer; research analyst sales or marketing activities; and require fair, balanced, and not misleading research analyst written or oral communications.

In Sec. Ex. Act Rel. 54,686, 89 SEC Dock. 338 (2006) (approval), the Commission approved amendments of NYSE Rule 472 and NASD Rule 2711 to codify existing interpretive guidance concerning investment research.

In Sec. Ex. Act Rel. 55,072, 89 SEC Dock. 2252 (2007) (proposal), the NYSE and NASD proposed amendments to their research analyst conflict of interest rules. The proposal Release summarized these amendments:

> The Exchange proposes to amend certain provisions of NYSE Rules 472 and 344. These amendments eliminate the exception for pre-publication factual verification review of research reports by non-research personnel; change the quiet periods surrounding securities offerings and the release of lock-up agreements; allow member organizations to develop policies and procedures if they choose to prohibit research analysts from holding securities for companies they cover; alter the format for certain disclosures in research reports; and extend the anti-retaliation prohibitions to all employees of a member organization, not just investment banking.
>
> NASD is proposing to amend NASD Rules 1050 and 2711 to implement certain recommendations contained in the December 2005 *Joint Report by NASD and the NYSE on the Operation and Effectiveness of the Research Analyst Conflict of Interest Rules*. NASD believes that the proposed rule changes are intended to improve the effectiveness of the research analyst conflict of interest rules and registration requirements by making certain changes to the existing provisions regarding, among other things: disclosure of conflicts; quiet periods; restrictions on review of research reports by non-research personnel; and restrictions on personal trading by research analysts.

Id. at 2253.

B. BROKER-DEALER SUBSTANTIVE REGULATION

2. INSPECTIONS

P. 860, add new par. at end of text. In Sec. Ex. Act Rel. 55,145, 89 SEC Dock. 2482 (2007) (approval), the Commission approved amendments to an SRO participants' plan for allocating regulatory responsibilities under Rule 17d-2 to provide that the NASD (now FINRA) and NYSE will be the Designated Options Examining Authority (*DOEA*) for the other SROs (Amex, CBOE, and the Boston, International, and Philadelphia securities exchanges).

3. SHORT SALES

b. SEC Short Sale Rules

P. 866, new par. after 1st full par. In 2007 the Commission rescinded Rule 10a-1 and added Rule 201 to Regulation SHO to eliminate the possibility that any price test, including any SRO price test, apply to short selling in any security. A related amendment was made to Rule 200(g) of Regulation SHO to remove the requirement that a broker-dealer mark a sell order of an equity security as *short exempt* if the seller is relying on an exemption from the price test of the former Rule 10a-1 or any SRO price test. Sec. Ex. Act Rels. 54,891, 89 SEC Dock. 1364 (2006) (proposal); 55,970, 90 SEC Dock. 2604 (2007) (adoption).

In Sec. Ex. Act Rel. 56,212, 91 SEC Dock. 814 (2007) (adoption), the Commission adopted the amendments to Regulation SHO to reduce the number of persistent fails to deliver attributable to the grandfather provision and to the options market maker exception in Rule 203(b).

In October 2008 the Commission adopted amendments to Regulation SHO to eliminate the options market maker exception to the close-out requirement of Regulation SHO. Sec. Ex. Act Rel. 58,775, 94 SEC Dock. 1110 (2008) (adoption).

In October 2008 the Commission adopted Rule 10b-21 substantially as proposed to address fails to deliver that had been associated with *naked* short selling. Sec. Ex. Act Rel. 58,774, 94 SEC Dock. 1095 (2008) (adoption). In adopting Rule 10b-21, the Commission clarified that the rule applies only to equity securities.

The Commission also adopted an interim final Temporary Rule 204T of Regulation SHO to address abusive *naked* short selling in all equity securities by requiring that participants of a registered clearing agency deliver securities by the settlement date, or if the participants have not delivered by that date, immediately purchase or borrow securities to close out the fail to deliver position by no later than the beginning of regular trading hours on the following settlement day. A participant that does not comply with this close out requirement and any broker-dealer from which it receives trades by clearance and settlement will not be able to short sell the security either for itself or for the accounts of others, unless it has previously arranged to borrow the security until the fail to deliver position is closed out. Sec. Ex. Act Rel. 58,773, 94 SEC Dock. 1001 (2008) (interim final Temporary Rule).

In May 2009 the Commission proposed further amendments to Regulation SHO with alternative short sale price tests (that is, the uptick rule) and with alternative SEC circuit breakers that would apply to a particular security, rather than the entire market. Sec. Ex. Act Rel. 59,748, __ SEC Dock. __ (2009) (proposal).

On September 17, 2008, at the height of what was widely viewed as a near financial system meltdown, the Commission invoked its emergency power under §12(k)(2) to issue an Order Taking Temporary Action to Respond to Market Developments. Sec. Ex. Act Rels. 58,572, 94 SEC Dock. 293 (2008); 58,591, 94 SEC Dock. 312 (2008); 58,591A, 94 SEC Dock. 445 (2008) (amendment to emergency order); 58,711, 94 SEC Dock. 795 (2008) (extension of emergency order until October 17, 2008). The initial adoption Release stated in part:

The Commission continues to be concerned that there is a substantial threat of sudden and excessive fluctuations of securities prices and disruption in the functioning of the securities markets that could threaten fair and orderly markets. As evidenced by our recent publication of an emergency order under Section 12(k) of the Securities Exchange Act of 1934 (the *July Emergency Order*), we are concerned about the possible unnecessary or artificial price movements based on unfounded rumors regarding the stability of financial institutions and other issuers exacerbated by *naked* short selling....

Given the importance of confidence in our financial markets as a whole, we have become concerned about sudden and unexplained declines in the prices of securities. Such price declines can give rise to questions about the underlying financial condition of an issuer, which in turn can create a crisis of confidence without a fundamental underlying basis. This crisis of confidence can impair the liquidity and ultimate viability of an issuer, with potentially broad market consequences....

We have concluded that it is necessary to impose enhanced delivery requirements on sales of all equity securities, by adding and making immediately effective a temporary rule to Regulation SHO, Rule 204T. The temporary rule imposes a penalty on any participant of a registered clearing agency, and any broker-dealer from which it receives trades for clearance and settlement, for having a fail to deliver position at a registered clearing agency in any equity security. In addition, we have concluded it is necessary to make immediately effective amendments to Rule 203(b)(3) of Regulation SHO that eliminate the options market maker exception from Regulation SHO's close-out requirement. We are also making immediately effective Rule 10b-21, a *naked* short selling antifraud rule. We intend these enhanced delivery requirements and the antifraud rule to impose powerful disincentives to those who might otherwise exacerbate artificial price movements through *naked* short selling....

This emergency requirement should significantly reduce any possibility that *naked* short selling may contribute to the disruption of markets in these securities. We believe, however, that the unusual circumstances we now confront require the enhanced requirements we are imposing today.

Subsequently in October 15, 2008, the Commission adopted Rule 10a-3T requiring specified institutional investment managers to file information on Form SH concerning short sales and positions of §13(f) securities, other than options. The temporary Rule requires managers that exercise investment discretion with respect to accounts holding §13(f) securities having an aggregate fair market value of at least $100 million to file Form SH on the last business day of following a calendar week in which it effected a short sale in a §13(f) security. Sec. Ex. Act Rel. 58,785, 94 SEC Dock. 1145 (2008) (interim temporary final Rule).

C. INVESTMENT ADVISERS

2. DEFINITION OF *INVESTMENT ADVISER*

b. Exclusions

(iv) *Brokers and Dealers*

P. 894, new par. after carryover par. In 2005, the Commission adopted Rule 202(a)(11)-1 after earlier having adopted most of the proposed Rule on a temporary basis in Rule 202(a)(11)T. Inv. Adv. Act Rels. 2340, 84 SEC Dock. 2208 (2005) (proposed Rule 202(a)(11)-1); 2339, 84 SEC Dock. 2204 (2005) (adoption of Rule 202(a)(11)T); 2376, 85 SEC Dock. 474 (2005) (adoption of Rule 202(a)(11)-1).

In 2007 the Court of Appeals for the District of Columbia held that Rule 202(a)(11)-1 exceeded the Commission's authority and vacated the Rule. Financial Planning Ass'n v. SEC, 482 F.3d 481 (D.C. Cir. 2007).

In 1999, the Commission had proposed a rule under §202(a)(11) to respond to the introduction of fee-based brokerage and discount brokerage programs by full service brokers. Inv. Adv. Rel. 1841, 70 SEC Dock. 2486 (1999) (proposed Rule). The 2005 proposal Release explained:

405

P. 894

> Fee-based brokerage programs provide customers a package of brokerage services — including execution, investment advice, custodial and recordkeeping services — for a fee based on the amount of assets on account with the broker-dealer (*i.e.*, an asset-based fee) or a fixed fee. Asset-based fees generally range from 1.10 percent to 1.50 percent of assets. A broker-dealer may be deemed to have received special compensation solely because the broker or dealer would not be deemed to have received special compensation solely because the broker or dealer charges a commission, mark-up, mark-down, or similar fee for brokerage services that is greater than or less than one it charges another customer. This provision was designed to permit full-service broker-dealers to offer discounted brokerage, including electronic trading, without having to treat full-price, full-service brokerage customers as advisory clients.

Inv. Adv. Rel. 2340, 84 SEC Dock. at 2210–2211.

The Commission received over 1700 comment letters on the proposal, with broker-dealers strongly supporting the new approach and investment advisers fervently opposing it:

> Broker-dealers commenting on the rule strongly supported it. They asserted that fee-based brokerage programs benefitted customers by aligning the interests of representatives with those of their customers. According to some of these broker-dealers, the application of the Advisers Act would discourage the introduction of fee-based programs by imposing what these brokerage firms viewed to be a duplicative and unnecessary regulatory regime....

Id. 85 SEC Dock. at 478–479.

After several years of reconsideration, the Commission proposal largely sided with the broker-dealers:

> We continue, however, to believe that fee-based brokerage has the potential to provide significant benefits to brokerage customers. Our reproposal therefore reflects our belief that when broker-dealers offer advisory services as part of the traditional package of brokerage services, broker-dealers ought not to be subject to the Advisers Act merely because they re-price those services. The reproposal also reflects our belief that broker-dealers should be

permitted to offer both full-service brokerage and discount brokerage services without triggering application of the Advisers Act. The reproprosal also reflects our belief that a broker-dealer providing discretionary advice would be deemed to be an investment adviser under the Advisers Act.

Id. 84 SEC Dock. at 2213.

The Commission also acknowledged that fee-based brokerage programs were now offered by most large broker-dealers and held over $254 billion in customer assets, meaning that there had been a significant growth in the number of broker-dealers that were now covered by both the Securities Exchange and Investment Advisers acts. Id. at 2215.

The Commission acknowledged that there was an open question as to whether the legislative history of §202(a)(11)(c) supported proposed Rule 202(a)(11)-1(b). Id. at 2222.

A majority of the Court of Appeals for the District of Columbia disagreed with the Commission's analysis in Financial Planning Ass'n v. SEC, 482 F.3d 481 (D.C. Cir. 2007), citing the text:

> In the final rule, the SEC purports to use its authority under subsection (F) to broaden the exemption for broker-dealers provided under subsection (C). The rule is inconsistent with the IAA, however, because it fails to meet either of the two requirements for an exemption under subsection (F). First, the legislative *intent* does not support an exemption for broker-dealers broader than the exemption set forth in the text of subsection (C); therefore, the final rule does not meet the statutory requirement that exemptions under subsection (F) be consistent with the *intent* of paragraph 11 of section 202(a). Second, because broker-dealers are already expressly addressed in subsection (C), they are not *other persons* under subsection (F); therefore the SEC cannot use its authority under subsection (F) to establish new, broader exemptions for broker-dealers.
>
> The final rule's exemption for broker-dealers is broader than the statutory exemption for broker-dealers under subsection (C). Although the SEC maintains that the intent of paragraph 11 is to exempt broker-dealers who receive special compensation for

407

investment advice, the plain text of subsection (C) exempts only broker-dealers who do not receive special compensation for investment advice.

Id. at 488.

The majority decision written by Judge Rogers added:

> While the SEC's failure to respect the unambiguous textual limitations marked by the phrase *intent of this paragraph* and *other persons* is fatal to the final rule, an additional weakness exists in the SEC's interpretation: it flouts six decades of consistent SEC understanding of its authority under subsection (F). [Citing cases.] Subsection (F) is not a catch-all that authorizes the SEC to rewrite the statute. Rather, as subsection (F)'s terms provide, the authority conferred must be exercised consistent with the *intent of this paragraph* and apply to *other persons*. The SEC cannot point to any instance between the 1940 enactment of the IAA and the commencement of the rulemaking proceedings that resulted in the final rule in 2005, when it attempted to invoke subsection (F) to alter or rewrite the exemptions for persons qualifying for exemptions under subsections (A)-(E). Rather, the SEC has historically invoked subsection (F) to exempt persons not otherwise addressed in the five exemptions established by Congress: For example, the adviser to a family trust who was otherwise subject to fiduciary duties, Oral Arg. Tape at 39:20-43:24; or new groups, such as thrift institutions acting in a fiduciary capacity, 69 Fed. Reg. 25,777-90 (May 7, 2004), and WorldBank instrumentalities that provide advice only to sovereigns, *In re Int'l Bank for Reconstr. & Dev.*, 2001 SEC LEXIS 1782 (Sept. 4, 2001). As the SEC's own actions for the last 65 years suggest, subsection (F) serves the clear purpose of authorizing the SEC to address persons or classes involving situations that Congress had not foreseen in the statutory text—not to broaden the exemptions of the classes of persons (such as broker-dealers) Congress had expressly addressed....
>
> The SEC's invocation of its general rulemaking authority under IAA section 211(a), is likewise to no avail because it suggests no intention by Congress that the SEC could ignore either of the two requirements in subsection (C) for broker-dealers to be exempt from the IAA. [Citing case.] Paraphrasing an apt observation, while, in the SEC's view, "[t]he statute may be imperfect,...the [SEC] has no power to correct flaws that it perceives in the statute it

is empowered to administer. Its [subsection (F) authority and its] rulemaking power[s] [are] limited to adopting regulations to carry into effect the will of Congress as expressed in the statute." *Bd. of Governors v. Dimension Fin. Corp.*, 474 U.S. 361, 374 (1986).

Id. at 490-493.

Judge Garland dissented, stating in part:

> The Investment Advisers Act contains five specific exceptions, and further authorizes the SEC to exempt "such other persons not within the intent of this paragraph, as the Commission may designate by rules." 15 U.S.C. §80b-2(a)(11). Unlike my colleagues, I cannot derive an unambiguous meaning from the terms "such other persons" and "within the intent of this paragraph." As required by *Chevron*, I would therefore defer to the SEC's reasonable interpretation of the statute it administers and uphold the Commission's fee-based brokerage rule.

Id. at 493.

The LRN-Rand Center for Corporate Ethics, Law and Governance (2008) study was published to provide a factual description of the current state of the investment advisor and brokerage industries for the SEC to use in evaluating the legal and regulatory environment concerning investment professionals.

After the *Financial Planning Ass'n* decision the Commission received requests from broker-dealers to clarify the status of its interpretative positions. See Inv. Adv. Act Rel. 2652, 91 SEC Dock. 1908, 1909 (2007) (proposal). "Though the Court did not question the validity of our interpretive positions, it vacated the entire rule, leaving our interpretations potentially in doubt." Ibid. In Inv. Adv. Act Rel. 2652, the Commission reproposed the interpretive positions:

> Because of the significance of the interpretations, and in order to provide the public with an opportunity for meaningful comment on them in light of the *FPA* decision, we are re-proposing the interpretive positions. Proposed rule 202(a)(11)-1 would clarify that (i) a broker-dealer provides investment advice that is not *solely incidental to* the conduct of its business as a broker-dealer if it exercises

P. 894

investment discretion (other than on a temporary or limited basis) with respect to an account or charges a separate fee, or separately contracts, for advisory services, (ii) a broker-dealer does not receive *special compensation* solely because it charges different rates for its full-service brokerage services and discount brokerage services, and (iii) a registered broker-dealer is an investment adviser solely with respect to accounts for which it provides services that subject it to the Advisers Act.

Id. at 1909.

With respect to proposed Rule 202(a)(1)(11)-1(a), the proposal Release explained:

> Many commenters responding to the 2005 Proposing Release urged us to clarify that certain practices are not solely incidental to brokerage services. Proposed rule 202(a)(11)-1(a) would re-codify two of the interpretations we announced in 2005 regarding activity that is not *solely incidental* to brokerage services for purposes of section 202(a)(11)(C). The situations addressed by these interpretations are not the only ones in which a broker-dealer provides advice that is not solely incidental to its business as a broker-dealer....
>
> 1. *Separate Contract or Fee for Advisory Services.* Proposed rule 202(a)(11)-1(a)(1) would provide that a broker-dealer that separately contracts with a customer for, or separately charges a fee for, investment advisory services cannot be considered to be providing advice that is solely incidental to its brokerage. We view a separate contract specifically providing for the provision of investment advisory services to reflect a recognition that the advisory services are provided independent of brokerage services and, therefore, cannot be considered solely incidental to the brokerage services. Similarly, we have long held the view that when a broker-dealer charges its customers a separate fee for investment advice, it clearly is providing advisory services and is subject to the Advisers Act. In light of the *FPA* decision, brokerage firms and other interested parties may be unsure about whether we continue to hold these views. In order to provide certainty to those parties, the proposed rule would codify our interpretations....
>
> 2. *Discretionary Investment Advice.* We have long acknowledged that a broker-dealer's exercise of investment discretion over customer accounts raises serious questions about whether those

accounts must be treated as subject to the Advisers Act — even where no special compensation is received. In 2005, we adopted, and today we are re-proposing, a rule that would clarify that any account over which a broker-dealer exercises investment discretion is subject to the Advisers Act. Specifically, rule 202(a)(11)-1(a) would clarify that discretionary investment advice is not *solely incidental to* the business of a broker-dealer within the meaning of section 202(a)(11)(C) and, accordingly, brokers and dealers are not excepted from the Act for any accounts over which they exercise investment discretion as that term is defined in section 3(a)(35) of the Exchange Act (except that investment discretion granted by a customer on a temporary or limited basis is excluded).

We believe that a broker-dealer's authority to effect a trade without first consulting a customer is qualitatively distinct from simply providing advice as part of a package of brokerage services. When a broker-dealer exercises investment discretion, it is not only the source of investment *advice*, it also has the authority to make the investment *decision* relating to the purchase or sale of securities on behalf of its client. This, in our view, warrants the protection of the Advisers Act because of the *special trust and confidence inherent* in such a relationship. Most commenters who addressed this aspect of our 2005 proposal, including those representing investors, advisers, and broker-dealers, generally agreed with us.

Under the proposed rule, the exception provided by section 202(a)(11)(C) of the Act is unavailable for any account over which a broker-dealer exercises investment discretion, regardless of the form of compensation and without regard to how the broker-dealer handles other accounts. We believe our interpretation is appropriate for several reasons. First, we believe it would apply the Advisers Act to the sort of relationship with a broker-dealer that the Act was intended to reach. Second, we believe the proposed rule is consistent with the interpretation that a broker-dealer is an investment adviser only with respect to those accounts for which the broker-dealer provides services or receives compensation that subject the broker-dealer to the Advisers Act. Finally, we believe the proposed rule would provide a workable, bright-line test for the availability of the section 202(a)(11)(C) exception.

Id. at 1910–1911.

P. 894   2010 SUPPLEMENT

The Commission did not repropose the financial planning provision "which many financial service firms found difficult to apply." Id. at 1912.

The Commission did repropose the *special compensation* provision:

> As part of our 2005 rulemaking, we adopted an interpretive provision which clarified that a broker-dealer will not be considered to have received *special compensation* for purposes of section 202(a)(11)(C) of the Advisers Act (and therefore will not be subject to the Act) *solely* because the broker-dealer charges a commission, mark-up, mark-down or similar fee for brokerage services that is greater or less than one it charges another customer. We are reproposing that interpretive position today as proposed rule 202(a)(11)-1(b).
>
> This interpretive position reflects the longstanding view that, with respect to brokerage commissions or other transaction-based compensation, broker-dealers receive *special compensation* where there is a clearly definable charge for investment advice. But, if a firm negotiates different fees with its customers for similar transactions, the Commission would not conclude that the customer being charged the higher fee is paying *special compensation* for investment advice based solely on differences in charges, because whether the pricing difference is based on the presence or absence of investment advice is *too hypothetical*. Similarly, if, for example, a broker-dealer had a general fee schedule for full service brokerage that included access to brokerage personnel, and had a separate fee schedule for automated transactions using an Internet Web site, we would not, absent other factors, view the difference as *special compensation*. As one commenter to our 2005 proposal noted, electronic brokerage programs offer "lower expenses and less overhead, [and it is] entirely appropriate, and necessarily competitive, for firms to have reduced their fees for such services, and this reduction is obviously in clients' best interests."
>
> The Commission would not look outside the fee structure of a given firm to determine whether special compensation exists. That is, just because a *discount* firm offered lower rates than a *full-service* firm, we would not consider the *full-service* firm's charges *special compensation*.

Id. at 1912.

The Commission also reproposed Rule 202(a)(11)-1(c) that would provide that a broker-dealer that is registered under both the Securities Exchange and Investment Advisers Acts is an investment adviser solely with respect to those accounts for which it provided advice or receives compensation that subject the broker-dealer to the Investment Advisers Act. Id. at 1912–1913.

The Commission also adopted Interim Rule 206(3)-3T in response to the *Financial Planning Association* decision. Inv. Adv. Act Rel. 2653, 91 SEC Dock. 1915 (2007) (adoption). Rule 206(3)-3T has a sunset provision of December 31, 2009. The adoption Release explained in part:

> As a result of the *FPA* decision, customers must elect on or before October 1, 2007, to convert their fee-based brokerage accounts to advisory accounts or to traditional commission-based brokerage accounts. Several firms emphasized to our staff that the inability of a client to access certain securities held in the firm's principal accounts — particularly municipal securities and other fixed income securities that they contend have limited availability and are dealt through a firm's account using electronic communications networks — may be a determinative factor in whether the client selects (or the firm makes available) a non-discretionary advisory account to replace the client's fee-based brokerage account. As discussed in this Release, many firms informed us that, because of the practical difficulties with complying with the trade-by-trade written disclosure requirements of section 206(3)..., they simply refrain from engaging in principal trading with their advisory clients. Accordingly, customers who wish to access firms' principal inventories may, as a practical matter, have no choice but to open a traditional brokerage account in which they will pay transaction-based compensation, rather than convert their fee-based brokerage account to an advisory account....
>
> To address the concerns described above and to protect the interests of customers who previously held fee-based brokerage accounts, we are adopting a temporary rule, on an interim final basis, that provides an alternative method for advisers who also are registered as broker-dealers to comply with section 206(3) of the Act. We believe this rule both protects investors' choice—fee-based brokerage customers would be able to choose an account that offers a similar set of services (including access to the same securities) that

> were available to them in fee-based brokerage accounts—and avoids disruption to, and confusion among, investors who may wish to access and sell securities only available through a firm acting in a principal capacity and who, as a result, may no longer be offered any fee-based account. We believe the temporary rule will allow fee-based brokerage customers to maintain their existing relationships with, and receive roughly the same services from, their broker-dealers. We believe further that making a rule temporary allows us an opportunity to observe how those firms use the alternative means of compliance provided by the rule, and whether those firms serve their clients' best interests.

Id. at 1919–1920.

Specifically Rule 206(3)-3T:

> permits an adviser, with respect to a non-discretionary advisory account, to comply with section 206(3) of the Advisers Act by, among other things: (i) providing written prospective disclosure regarding the conflicts arising from principal trades; (ii) obtaining written, revocable consent from the client prospectively authorizing the adviser to enter into principal transactions; (iii) making certain disclosures, either orally or in writing, and obtaining the client's consent before each principal transaction; (iv) sending to the client confirmation statements disclosing the capacity in which the adviser has acted and disclosing that the adviser informed the client that it may act in a principal capacity and that the client authorized the transaction; and (v) delivering to the client an annual report itemizing the principal transactions. The rule also requires that the investment adviser be registered as a broker-dealer under section 15 of the Exchange Act and that each account for which the adviser relies on this rule be a brokerage account subject to the Exchange Act, and the rules thereunder, and the rules of the self-regulatory organization(s) of which it is a member.
>
> These conditions...are designed to prevent overreaching by advisers by requiring an adviser to disclose to the client the conflicts of interest involved in these transactions, inform the client of the circumstances in which the adviser may effect a trade on a principal basis, and provide the client with meaningful opportunities to refuse to consent to a particular transaction or revoke the prospective general consent to these transactions.

Id. at 1920.

CHAPTER 9

FRAUD

A. COMMON LAW AND SEC *FRAUD*

2. The Relation between SEC *Fraud* Concepts and Common Law Deceit

P. 913 n.32, end note. Then Judge Alito phrased matters succinctly: "It is well known that the federal securities laws provide broader fraud protection than the common law, having been enacted in response to the common law's perceived failure at stamping out fraud in the securities markets." MBIA Ins. Corp. v. Royal Indem. Co., 426 F.3d 204, 218 (3d Cir. 2005).

"The principle is well settled that federal law, rather than state law, governs the construction of all aspects of Rule 10b-5." Thompson v. Paul, 547 F.3d 1055, 1061 (9th Cir. 2008), citing cases.

P. 918 n.62, end note. In SEC v. Tambone, 550 F.3d 106, 125-128 (1st Cir. 2008), the court read §17(a)(2) to be broader in scope than Rule 10b-5 and to not require a seller of a security solely to be liable when the seller makes a false statement, but also to impose liability based on a false statement made by another individual.

415

B. ISSUERS AND *INSIDERS*

4. THE FRAUD ELEMENT

a. The *Disclose or Abstain* Rule

P. 943 n.69, end note. In United States v. Royer, 549 F.3d 886, 897 (2d Cir. 2008), the court upheld a conviction for insider trading by construing the term *public* for trading purposes to mean "readily available, broadly disseminated, or the like."

b. Issuers' Activities

(ii) *Regulation FD*

P. 957, end text. Twenty-two law professors, including the author, signed a brief defending Regulation FD when a defendant, Siebel Systems, Inc., as well as the Chamber of Commerce, challenged the SEC authority to adopt the Regulation. SEC v. Siebel Sys., Inc., No. 04 (CV 5130m (GBD)) (S.D.N.Y. Mar. 10, 2005) (Law Professors Brief as *Amicus Curiae* in Opposition to Motion to Dismiss); Plitch, Law Professors Back Reg. FD, Take SEC Side vs. Challenge, Dow Jones Newswire, Mar. 11, 2005.

Subsequently, without addressing the Commission's authority to adopt Regulation FD or its constitutionality, the court granted the defendant's motion to dismiss on the ground that the statements that the SEC alleged violated Regulation FD did not support the Commission's claim that Siebel, or its senior officers, privately disclosed material nonpublic information. SEC v. Siebel Sys., Inc., 384 F. Supp. 2d 694 (S.D.N.Y. 2005).

In United States v. Royer, 549 F.3d 886, 899 (2d Cir. 2008), the court followed the *knowing possession* test in United States v. Teicher, 987 F.2d 112, 119-121 (2d Cir. 1993). The court further stated "[T]he SEC subsequently enacted Rule 10b5-1, adopting a knowing possession standard, and that determination is itself entitled to deference." [Citing *Chevron*.]

(iii) *The Duty to Update and the Duty to Correct*

P. 958 n.119, end note. In Overton v. Todman & Co., CPAs, P.C., 478 F.3d 479 (2d Cir. 2007), the court held that an auditor will incur primary liability under the duty to correct when he provides a certified opinion that is false or misleading when issued, subsequently learns or was reckless in not learning that the earlier statement was false or misleading, knows or should know that the potential investors are relying on the opinion, but fails to correct or withdraw the opinion and/or underlying financial statements.

Cf. Lattanzio v. Deloitte & Touche LLP, 476 F.3d 147 (2d Cir. 2007) (limiting the duty to correct to the class period).

5. THE DUTY ELEMENT

c. Tippers and Tippees

(i) The *Dirks* Standard

P. 1002 n.229, end note. In United States v. Evans, 486 F.3d 315 (7th Cir. 2007), *cert. denied*, 128 S. Ct. 876, the Seventh Circuit affirmed that a tippee can be criminally convicted even if a tipper is acquitted.

In SEC v. Talbot, 530 F.3d 1085 (9th Cir. 2008), the Ninth Circuit reversed the District Court's misappropriation analysis:

> Neither party challenges the district court's findings that (1) the SEC failed to carry its burden of showing that Fidelity owed a fiduciary duty to LendingTree; (2) the information was nonpublic; or (3) Talbot knowingly used the LendingTree information to trade in LendingTree securities. Thus, for the SEC to prevail on appeal, it must demonstrate that (1) Talbot breached a fiduciary duty arising

from a relationship of trust and confidence owed to the source of the information on which he traded; and (2) the information on which Talbot traded was material....

Id. at 1092.

The Ninth Circuit rejected the District Court premise that for misappropriation liability to be imposed, "the trader and the originating source of the nonpublic information [be] linked through a continuous chain of fiduciary relationships: The employee [must owe] a duty to his employer to refrain from exploiting the information, and the employer in turn [must owe] the same duty to the corporate client." Id. at 1093. The District Court confused Tipper-Tippee liability with misappropriation. See id. at 1093-1094.

Misappropriation and tipping cases can be proven from the same underlying facts. See, e.g., SEC v. Michel, 521 F. Supp. 2d 795, 822–829 (N.D. Ill. 2007).

6. SCIENTER

P. 1019 n.315, end note. See also Dolphin & Bradbury, Inc. v. SEC, 512 F.3d 634, 642 (D.C. Cir. 2008) (reliance on counsel defense substantially undercut when party failed to disclose facts to counsel).

P. 1025 n.327, end note. In Ottmann v. Hanger Orthopedic Group, Inc., 353 F.3d 338, 344 (4th Cir. 2003), the Fourth Circuit definitively stated: "[W]e therefore agree with our sister circuits that a securities fraud plaintiff may allege scienter by pleading not only intentional misconduct, but also recklessness."

In Brown v. Earthboard Sports USA, Inc., 481 F.3d 901, 917 (6th Cir. 2007), the court followed the City of Monroe Employees Ret. Sys. v. Bridgestone Corp., 399 F.3d 651, 683 (6th Cir. 2005), *cert. denied,* 546 U.S. 936, *totality of circumstances* test to assess whether the plaintiff had adequately alleged scienter, considering "among the factors that we have considered in the past" are:

(1) insider trading at a suspicious time or in an unusual amount; (2) divergence between internal reports and external statements on the same subject; (3) closeness in time of an allegedly fraudulent statement or omission and the later disclosure of inconsistent information; (4) evidence of bribery by a top company official; (5) existence of an ancillary lawsuit charging fraud by a company and the company's quick settlement of that suit; (6) disregard of the most current factual information before making statements; (7) disclosure of accounting information in such a way that its negative implications could only be understood by someone with a high degree of sophistication; (8) the personal interest of certain directors in not informing disinterested directors of an impending sale of stock; and (9) the self-interested motivation of defendants in the form of saving their salaries or jobs.

In Ezra Charitable Trust v. Tyco Int'l, Ltd., 466 F.3d 1, 12 (1st Cir. 2006), the court quoted *Cabletron*, 311 F.3d at 34: "Merely stating in conclusory fashion that a company's books are out of compliance with GAAP would not itself demonstrate liability under section 10(b) or Rule 10b-5."

Nor is scienter required for the Commission to plead a Rule 13b2-1 or 13b2-2 claim. McConville v. SEC, 465 F.3d 780, 789-790 (7th Cir. 2006), *cert. denied*, 128 S. Ct. 48.

In Garfield v. NDC Health Corp., 466 F.3d 1255, 1266 (11th Cir. 2006), the court held that: "The plain meaning of the language contained in Sarbanes-Oxley, 18 U.S.C. §1350, does not indicate any intent to change the requirements for pleading scienter set forth in the PSLRA.... Instead, we hold that a Sarbanes-Oxley certification is only probative of scienter if the person signing the certification was severely reckless in certifying the accuracy of the financial statements." Ibid.

Cf. Central Laborers' Pension Fund v. Integrated Elec. Serv., Inc., 497 F.3d 546, 552 (5th Cir. 2007) ("GAAP violations, without more, do not establish scienter").

In Rodriguez-Ortiz v. Margo Caribe, Inc., 490 F.3d 92 (5th Cir. 2007), the court held that "the requisite scienter is an intent to deceive at the time the promise was made, not a later intent to break a promise already made." Id. at 97.

P. 1025

In Indiana Elec. Workers' Pension Trust Fund IBEW v. Shaw Group, Inc., 537 F.3d 527 (5th Cir. 2008), the plaintiffs failed to allege scienter when they did not allege specific events that officers knew and concealed from the public.

In New Jersey Carpenters Pension & Annuity Funds v. Biogen Idec, Inc., 537 F.3d 35 (1st Cir. 2008), the court affirmed dismissal of a complaint in part because "[a] statement cannot be intentionally misleading if the defendant did not have sufficient information at the relevant time to form an evaluation that there was a need to disclose certain information and to form an intent not to disclose it." Id. at 45.

In Teamsters Local 445 Freight Div. Pension Fund v. Dynex Capital Inc., 531 F.3d 190, 196 (2d Cir. 2008), the court held that a plaintiff can plead scienter against a corporation without pleading scienter against an expressly named officer.

After *Tellabs*, the Sixth Circuit reversed a District Court decision following earlier Sixth Circuit precedent in Helwig v. Vencor, Inc., 251 F.3d 540, 548 (6th Cir. 2001), which had held that the plaintiff must establish an inference of scienter if that is "more plausible" in favor of the *Tellabs* "at least as compelling" standard. Frank v. Dana Corp., 547 F.3d 564, 571 (6th Cir. 2008).

In Glazer Capital Mgmt., LP v. Magistri, 549 F.3d 736 (9th Cir. 2008), the court required that the plaintiff plead individual scienter in the context of this case but did not preclude the possibility that scienter could be pled under a collective theory in other circumstances.

In Katz v. Image Innovations Holdings, Inc., 542 F. Supp. 2d 269 (S.D.N.Y. 2008), the court held that the fact that a defendant officer or director was not trained as an accountant was insufficient to negate scienter as to the alleged booking of fictitious sales.

In SEC v. Lyttle, 538 F.3d 601 (7th Cir. 2008), Judge Posner affirmed a summary judgment on the basis of substantial uncontradicted circumstantial evidence concerning scienter when defendants declined to testify.

7. SCOPE OF RULE 10b-5

b. In Connection with a Purchase or Sale

P. 1045 n.401, end note. An issuer of municipal bonds that becomes the owner upon default has standing under Rule 10b-5 even when the bonds continue to be held by the bondholders. Financial Sec. Assur., Inc. v. Stephens, Inc., 450 F.3d 1257 (11th Cir. 2006). The court analogized the contractual arrangement to the pledge in Rubin v. United States, 449 U.S. 424, 429–431 (1981). Id. at 1266.

P. 1047 n.418, end note. In Smith v. Pennington, 352 F.3d 884 (4th Cir. 2003), a de facto beneficiary or plan participant, who had no control over trust investments, was denied standing to sue.

In Mutual Funds Inv. Litig., 384 F. Supp. 2d 845, 854–855 (D. Md. 2005), Judge Motz questioned whether *Blue Chip Stamps* should ban holders of mutual fund shares who suffered dilution because of market timing and late trades.

P. 1047 n.420, end note. In Financial Sec. Assur., Inc. v. Stephens, Inc., 500 F.3d 1276 (11th Cir. 2007), the court granted a petition for panel rehearing and vacated the prior decision, 450 F.3d 1257 (11th Cir. 2006), and in its place substituted a decision that held that a guarantor does not have standing as a purchaser of securities.

P. 1049 n.430, end note. In Johnson v. Alijan, 490 F.3d 778 (9th Cir. 2008), *cert. denied*, 128 S. Ct. 1650, the court held that a predicate Rule 10b-5 claim need not be filed within its period of limitations. It is sufficient if the §20A claim is filed within its five-year statute of limitations.

8. Rule 14e-3

P. 1051 n.442, end note. In SEC v. Ginsburg, 362 F.3d 1292, 1304 (11th Cir. 2004), the court held:

> In this case there was a meeting between executives, which was followed by due diligence procedures, a confidentiality agreement, and by a meeting between Ginsburg and Olds — from which Ginsburg realized that the deal had to go down fast. These activities, which did result in a tender offer, were substantial steps for purposes of Rule 14e-3. Were it otherwise, liability could be avoided by taking care to tip only before the formal steps finalizing the acquisition are completed, leaving a substantial gap between the acquisition of inside information and the regulation of its disbursement.

9. Special *Insider Trading* Sanctions

a. Disgorgement

P. 1054 n.464, end note. In SEC v. JT Wallenbrock & Assocs., 440 F.3d 1109, 1114 (9th Cir. 2006), the court held that "it would be unjust to permit the defendants to offset against the investor dollars they received the expenses of running the very business they created to defraud those investors into giving the defendants the money in the first place."

In SEC v. Great White Marine & Recreation, Inc., 428 F.3d 553 (5th Cir. 2005), the court proceeded with a disgorgement proceeding and dismissed a subsequently initiated involuntary bankruptcy proceeding.

In SEC v. Smyth, 420 F.3d 1225 (11th Cir. 2005), the Eleventh Circuit reversed the District Court's denial of an evidentiary hearing concerning the appropriate disgorgement amount and remanded for further proceedings.

C. BROKERS AND DEALERS

1. Unreasonable Spreads

a. The *Shingle* Theory and Markups

P. 1071 n.34, end note. Excessive markups have been found in municipal cases when markups ranged from 1.42 to 5.64 percent in challenged transactions. Mark D. Anderson, Sec. Ex. Act Rel. 48,352, 80 SEC Dock. 2567, 2568 (2003). Excessive markups were also found with respect to treasury notes (in amounts of 2.75–3.87 percent); Treasury strips (2.99–4.01 percent; agency specified pool securities (2.29–4.01 percent); collateralized mortgage obligations (1.42–4.02 percent). Id. at 2570–2571.

In SEC v. Zwick, 2008 Fed. Sec. L. Rep. (CCH) ¶94,818 (2d Cir. 2008), the Second Circuit emphasized that whether markups are excessive "does not rely on any sort of bright-line rule, but rather considers each situation on a fact-specific basis as those facts are presented in the particular case. See Press v. Chem. Inv. Servs. Corp., 166 F.3d 529, 535 (2d Cir. 1999).

P. 1071 n.35, end note. In 2007 the NASD extended its markup policy to debt securities transactions, other than municipal securities. Sec. Ex. Act Rel. 55,638, 90 SEC Dock. 1220 (2007) (approval).

2. Broker-Dealer Fiduciary Duties

b. Determination of Fiduciary Status

P. 1084 n.70, end note. In 2007 the Commission approved an NASD rule change to extend the *Manning Rule* to include all OTC equity securities. Sec. Ex. Act Rel. 55,351, 90 SEC Dock. 159 (2007) (approval).

P. 1093

3. DUTY TO INVESTIGATE AND THE SUITABILITY DOCTRINE

   a. Penny Stock Suitability Requirements [Rule 15g-9]

P. 1093, end carryover par. In 2005 the Commission adopted amendments to the *penny stock* Rules. Sec. Ex. Act Rel. 51,983, 85 SEC Dock. 2605 (2005) (adoption). Rule 3a51-1(a) was amended to address exclusions from the initial concept that a penny stock involves any equity security. Under Rule 3a51-1(a)(1) a security is excluded from the definition of a *penny stock* if it is registered or approved for registration upon notice of issuance on a national securities exchange that has been continuously registered since April 20, 1992 (when Rule 3a51-1 was adopted) and the exchange has maintained quantitative listing standards that are substantially similar to or stricter than the listing standards that were in place on that exchange on January 8, 2004. Alternatively, under Rule 3a51-1(a)(2) a security would be excluded from the definition of a *penny stock* if the security is registered or approved for registration upon notice of issuance on an exchange or listed or approved for listing on an automated quotation system sponsored by a registered national association that:

   (i) Has established initial listing standards that meet or exceed the following criteria:
      (A) The issuer shall have:
         (1) Stockholders' equity of $5 million;
         (2) Market value of listed securities of $50 million for 90 consecutive days prior to applying for the listing (market value means the closing bid price multiplied by the number of securities listed); or
         (3) Net income of $750,000 (excluding extraordinary or non-recurring items) in the most recently completed fiscal year or in two of the last three most recently completed fiscal years;
      (B) The issuer shall have an operating history of at least one year or a market value of listed securities of $50 million (market value means the closing bid price multiplied by the number of securities listed);

(C) The issuer's stock, common or preferred, shall have a minimum bid price of $4 per share;

(D) In the case of common stock, there shall be at least 300 round lot holders of the security (a round lot holder means a holder of a normal unit of trading);

(E) In the case of common stock, there shall be at least 1 million publicly held shares and such shares shall have a market value of at least $5 million (market value means the closing bid price multiplied by the number of publicly held shares, and shares held directly or indirectly by an officer or director of the issuer and by any person who is the beneficial owner of more than 10 percent of the total shares outstanding are not considered to be publicly held);

(F) In the case of a convertible debt security, there shall be a principal amount outstanding of at least $10 million;

(G) In the case of rights and warrants, there shall be at least 100,000 issued and the underlying security shall be registered on a national securities exchange or listed on an automated quotation system sponsored by a registered national securities association and shall satisfy the requirements of paragraph (a) or (e) of this section;

(H) In the case of put warrants (that is, instruments that grant the holder the right to sell to the issuing company a specified number of shares of the company's common stock, at a specified price until a specified date), there shall be at least 100,000 issued and the underlying security shall be registered on a national securities exchange or listed on an automated quotation system sponsored by a registered national securities association and shall satisfy the requirements of paragraph (a) or (e) of this section;

(I) In the case of units (that is, two or more securities traded together), all component parts shall be registered on a national securities exchange or listed on an automated quotation system sponsored by a registered national securities association and shall satisfy the requirements of paragraph (a) or (e) of this section; and

(J) In the case of equity securities (other than common and preferred stock, convertible debt securities, rights and warrants, put warrants, or units), including hybrid products and derivative securities products, the national securities exchange or registered national securities association shall

P. 1093

establish quantitative listing standards that are substantially similar to those found in paragraphs (a)(2)(i)(A) through (a)(2)(i)(I) of this section; and

(ii) Has established quantitative continued listing standards that are reasonably related to the initial listing standards set forth in paragraph (a)(2)(i) of this section, and that are consistent with the maintenance of fair and orderly markets.

This represents an attempt to preserve the *status quo* for existing markets, 85 SEC Dock. at 2608, rather than an attempt to require uniform standards across all markets and exchanges, which the adoption Release characterized as "inappropriate because it would require the Commission, as opposed to the markets, to establish listing standards." Id. at 2608.

The Commission also eliminated the former Rule 3a51-1(f), which excluded specified securities quoted or authorized for quotation on Nasdaq "because we believe it no longer serves any purpose." Id. at 2608.

A new Rule 3a51-1(f) excluded penny stock futures products listed on a national securities exchange or an automated quotation system sponsored by a registered national securities association. This approach is consistent with the treatment of options under Rule 3a51-1(c).

The Commission eliminated the exclusion in Rule 3a51-1(a) for Amex's Emerging Company Marketplace for the straightforward reason that the market no longer exists.

Rule 15g-2(a) was modestly amended. The Rule earlier required a customer before effecting a penny stock transaction to be furnished a document containing information delineated in Schedule 15G. As amended Rule 15g-2(a) no longer requires that the customer manually sign and date an acknowledgment of receipt of the disclosure document, but merely sign and date the acknowledgment. More significantly Rule 15g-2(b) now requires a two business day waiting period after a penny stock disclosure document has been sent either electronically or by mail or by other means before a penny stock transaction can be effected. Id. at 3194.

A corresponding amendment was made to Rule 15g-9 to prohibit a broker-dealer from executing a penny stock transaction until at least two business days after the broker-dealer has sent the suitability statement required by Rule 15g-9(b) and the agreement to a penny stock transaction required by Rule 15g-9(a)(2)(ii). Id. at 3194–3197.

The Commission also adopted amendments to the Schedule 15G penny stock disclosure document, largely to modernize the document and make it easier to read. Id. at 3197–3200.

In 2007 the Commission adopted suitability requirements as well as principal review and approval, supervisory, and training requirements for deferred variable annuities. Sec. Ex. Act Rel. 56,375, 91 SEC Dock. 1386 (2007).

D. FRAUD BY INVESTMENT ADVISERS

P. 1108, new par. of text after carryover indented quotation. In 2003 the Commission adopted Rule 206(4)-7 to require each investment adviser to adopt and implement written policies and procedures reasonably designed to prevent violation of the Investment Adviser Act by the adviser or any of its supervised persons. Inv. Adv. Rel. 2204, 81 SEC Dock. 2775 (2003) (adoption). Investment Company Act Rule 38a-1 requires fund boards to take a similar approach with respect to violations of the federal securities laws.

After the District of Columbia Court of Appeals in 2004 vacated a rule requiring hedge fund advisers to register under the Investment Advisers Act, see *Goldstein v. SEC*, 451 F.3d 873 (D.C. Cir. 2006), the Commission adopted Investment Advisers Act Rule 206(4)-8 to prohibit fraud by an investment adviser to a pooled investment vehicle. Inv. Adv. Act Rels. 2576, 89 SEC Dock. 1938 (2006) (proposal); 2628, 90 SEC Dock. 938 (2007) (adoption).

Rule 206(4)-8(b) defined *pooled investment vehicle* to mean "any investment company as defined in section 3(a) of the Investment Company Act of 1940 or any company that would be an investment company under section 3(a) of that Act but for the exclusion

P. 1108

provided from that definition by either section 3(c)(1) or section 3(c)(7) of that Act."

The proposal Release explained in part with respect to the proposed Rule:

> Recently, an opinion by the Court of Appeals for the D.C. Circuit created uncertainties regarding obligations that investment advisers to pools have to the pools' investors. The court, in *Goldstein v. SEC*, vacated a rule we adopted in 2004 that required certain hedge fund advisers to register under the Advisers Act. In addressing the scope of the exemption from registration in section 203(b)(3) of the Advisers Act and the meaning of *client* as used in that section, the court expressed the view that, for purposes of sections 206(1) and (2), the *client* of an investment adviser managing a pool is the pool itself, not the investors in the pool. As a result, the opinion created some uncertainty regarding the application of sections 206(1) and 206(2) of the Advisers Act in certain cases where investors in a pool are defrauded by an investment adviser.
>
> The *Goldstein* decision did not, however, call into question the Commission's authority to adopt rules under section 206(4) of the Advisers Act to protect investors in pooled investment vehicles. Section 206(4) is broader in scope and not limited to conduct aimed at clients or prospective clients. This section permits us to adopt rules proscribing fraudulent conduct that is potentially harmful to the growing number of investors who directly or indirectly invest in hedge funds and other types of pooled investment vehicles. Our commitment to protect the interests of those investors is no less than those to whom the adviser directly provides investment advice.
>
> Accordingly, today we are using our authority under section 206(4) to propose, as a means reasonably designed to prevent fraud, a new rule under the Advisers Act that would prohibit advisers to investment companies and other pooled investment vehicles from (i) making false or misleading statements to investors in those pools, or (ii) otherwise defrauding them. We would enforce the rule through administrative and civil actions against advisers under section 206(4) of the Advisers Act....
>
> The proposed rule would apply to any investment adviser to a pooled investment vehicle, including advisers that are not registered or required to be registered under the Advisers Act. Many of our enforcement cases against advisers to pools have been against

advisers that are not registered under the Advisers Act, and we believe it is critical that we continue to be in a position to bring actions against unregistered advisers that manage pools and that defraud investors in those pools....

The proposed rule would not distinguish among types of pooled investment vehicles and is designed to protect investors both in investment companies and in pools that are excluded from the definition of investment company under section 3(a) of the Investment Company Act of 1940 (*Company Act*) by reason of either section 3(c)(1) or 3(c)(7) of the Company Act. We believe that most of the pooled investment vehicles privately offered to investors are organized under one or the other of these two provisions.

Like section 206, the new antifraud rule would apply to all advisers regardless of the investment strategy they employ, or the structure of the type of pooled investment vehicle they manage. As a result, the rule would apply to investment advisers subject to section 206 of the Advisers Act with respect to all pooled investment vehicles that they advise, such as hedge funds, private equity funds, venture capital funds, and other types of privately offered pools that invest in securities, as well as investment companies that are offered to the public. Defrauding investors in any of these pools is equally unacceptable....

Unlike rule 10b-5 under the Exchange Act and other rules that focus on securities transactions, rule 206(4)-8 would not be limited to fraud in connection with the purchase and sale of a security. Accordingly, proposed rule 206(4)-8(a)(1) would prohibit advisers to pooled investment vehicles from making any materially false or misleading statements to investors in the pool regardless of whether the pool is offering, selling, or redeeming securities. Unlike violations of rule 10b-5, the Commission would not need to demonstrate that an adviser violating rule 206(4)-8 acted with scienter. There would be no private cause of action against an adviser under the proposed rule....

Proposed rule 206(4)-8 would not create a fiduciary duty to investors or prospective investors in the pooled investment vehicle not otherwise imposed by law. Nor would the rule alter any duty or obligation an adviser has under the Advisers Act, any other federal law or regulation, or any state law or regulation (including state securities laws) to investors in a pooled investment vehicle it advises.

Id. at 1941–1942.

P. 1108   2010 SUPPLEMENT

The proposal Release also proposed new Securities Act Rules 509 and 218 to define a new category of *accredited natural persons* that would apply to offers and sales issued by Investment Company Act §3(c)(1) pools to accredited persons under Regulation D and §4(6). In this context *accredited natural person* would mean any natural person who owns at least $2.5 million in investments and otherwise satisfies the net worth or income test specified in Securities Act Rules 501(a) or 215. As proposed this dollar amount would be adjusted for inflation on April 1, 2012 and every five years after that. See proposed Rules 216(c)(6) and 509(c)(6). As proposed these amendments and rules would not otherwise alter the criteria for investments by natural persons in Rules 501(a)(4) and 215(d).

With respect to the scope of these *accredited natural person* provisions, the proposal Release explained:

> The proposed rules would apply solely to the offer and sale of securities issued by private investment vehicles, as defined in the proposed rules. The proposed rules would not apply to offers and sales of securities issued by private funds not meeting the proposed definition of the term private investment vehicle, including venture capital funds....
>
> The proposed rules would define the term private investment vehicle to mean an issuer that would be an investment company (as defined in section 3(a) of the Company Act) but for the exclusion provided by section 3(c)(1) of that Act. The proposed rules would apply to private investment vehicles that rely on the safe harbor provisions of Regulation D in connection with the offer and sale of their securities. The proposed rules would also apply to offerings of private investment vehicles made in reliance on section 4(6) of the Securities Act.
>
> We are not including 3(c)(7) Pools within the definition of private investment vehicle because offers and sales of securities issued by 3(c)(7) Pools must be made to qualified purchasers (as that term is defined by section 2(a)(51)(A) of the company Act) who are also accredited investors under Regulation D. As noted, 3(c)(7) Pools already are subject to investor protections with higher thresholds than the ones that we propose today.

Id. at 1946.

Cf. United States v. Lay, 566 F. Supp. 2d 652 (N.D. Ohio 2008), distinguishing *Goldstein* and sustaining conviction when there was evidence in the record that an investor did not have a passive role and the characteristics of an adviser-client relationship were present.

CHAPTER 10

MANIPULATION

D. MANIPULATION OF THE OVER-THE-COUNTER MARKET UNDER THE SEC STATUTES

P. 1137, end carryover par. In Rockies Fund v. SEC, 428 F.3d 1088 (D.C. Cir. 2005), the court held that the Commission failed to show requisite scienter in a manipulation case under either §9(a)(1) or Rule 10b-5. With respect to the different scienter standards, the court explained:

> Whereas Section 9(a)(1) requires a showing of specific intent, Rule 10b-5 generally requires only "extreme recklessness." SEC v. Steadman, 967 F.2d 636, 641 (D.C. Cir. 1992). Extreme recklessness is an "extreme departure from the standards of ordinary care, ...which presents a danger of misleading buyers or sellers that is either known to the defendant or is so obvious that the actor must have been aware of it." Id. at 642 (internal quotations omitted) (alteration in original). In other words, extreme recklessness requires a stronger showing than simple recklessness but does not rise to the level of specific intent. The difference between the standards could potentially have significant effects on the interplay between Section 10(b) and Section 9(a)(1) and SEC actions under each provision. Because we conclude that the SEC has not met its burden of proving scienter under either standard, we need not reach the question of what standard of intent should be applied to matched orders and wash sales under Section 10(b) and Rule 10b-5.

Id. at 1093.

P. 1137

In ATSI Communications, Inc. v. Shaar Fund, Ltd., 493 F.3d 87, 101 (2d Cir. 2007), the court held:

> Market manipulation requires a plaintiff to allege (1) manipulative acts; (2) damage; (3) caused by reliance on an assumption of an efficient market free of manipulation; (4) scienter; (5) in connection with the purchase or sale of securities; (6) furthered by the defendant's use of the mails or any facility of a national security exchange. [Citing cases.]
> Because a claim for market manipulation is a claim for fraud, it must be pled with particularity under Rule 9(b).

The court notably added: "A claim of manipulation, however, can involve facts solely within the defendant's knowledge; therefore, in the early stages of litigation, the plaintiff need not plead manipulation to the same degree of specificity as a plain misrepresentation claim." Id. at 102.

"[A] manipulation complaint must plead with particularity the nature, purpose, and effect of the fraudulent conduct and the roles of the defendants." Ibid. [Citing cases.] "This test will be satisfied if the complaint sets forth, to the extent possible, 'what manipulative acts were performed, which defendants performed them, when the manipulative acts were performed, and what effect the scheme had on the market for the securities at issue'." Ibid. [Citing cases.]

"Because a claim for market manipulation requires a showing of scienter, the PSLRA's heightened standards for pleading scienter also apply." Ibid.

In the Second Circuit, "[a] market manipulation claim...cannot be based solely upon misrepresentations or omissions. Lentell v. Merrill Lynch & Co., 396 F.3d 161, 177 (2d Cir. 2005), *cert. denied*, 546 U.S. 935. There must be some market activity, such as 'wash sales, matched orders, or rigged prices'." ATSI Communications, Inc. v. Shaar Fund, Ltd., 493 F.3d at 101. There need not be a fiduciary relationship between the transaction participants. Ibid.

Moreover, "short selling—even in high volumes—is not, by itself, manipulative." Ibid. "To be actionable as a manipulative act, short selling must be willfully combined with something more to create a false impression of how market participants value a security." Ibid.

E. STABILIZATION

2. Activities by Distribution Participants [Rule 101]

a. Basic Prohibitions

P. 1141 n.17, end note. After bringing three enforcement actions alleging abuses in the offering process under Regulation M, the Commission in 2005 issued an interpretative Release with respect to book building and the process for allocating IPO shares. Sec. Act Rel. 8565, 85 SEC Dock. 266 (2005). The Release highlighted prohibited activities that underwriters should avoid during restricted periods, including:

- Inducements to purchase in the form of tie-in agreements or other solicitations of aftermarket bids or purchases prior to the completion of the distribution.
- Communicating to customers that expressing an interest in buying shares in the immediate aftermarket (aftermarket interest) or immediate aftermarket buying would help them obtain allocations of hot IPOs.
- Soliciting customers prior to the completion of the distribution regarding whether and at what price and in what quantity they intend to place immediate aftermarket orders for IPO stock.
- Proposing aftermarket prices to customers or encouraging customers who provide aftermarket interest to increase the prices that they are willing to place orders in the immediate aftermarket.
- Accepting or seeking expressions of interest from customers that they intend to purchase an amount of shares in the

aftermarket equal to the size of their IPO allocation ("1 for 1") or intend to bid for or purchase specific amounts of shares in the aftermarket that are pegged to the allocation amount without any reference to a fixed total position size.
- Soliciting aftermarket orders from customers before all IPO shares are distributed or rewarding customers for aftermarket orders by allocating additional IPO shares to such customers.
- Communicating to customers in connection with one offering that expressing an interest in the aftermarket or buying in the aftermarket would help them obtain IPO allocations of other hot IPOs.

Id. at 267.

With respect to book building, the interpretative Release elaborated:

Book-building refers to the process by which underwriters gather and assess potential investor demand for an offering of securities and seek information important to their determination as to the size and pricing of an issue. When used, the IPO book-building process begins with the filing of a registration statement with an initial estimated price range. Underwriters and the issuer then conduct road shows to market the offering to potential investors, generally institutions. The road shows provide investors, the issuer, and underwriters the opportunity to gather important information from each other. Investors seek information about a company, its management and its prospects, and underwriters seek information from investors that will assist them in determining particular investors' interest in the company, assessing demand for the offering, and improving pricing accuracy for the offering. Investors' demand for an offering necessarily depends on the value they place, and the value they expect the market to place, on the stock, both initially and in the future. In conjunction with the road shows, there are discussions between the underwriter's sales representatives and prospective investors to obtain investors' views about the issuer and the offered securities, and to obtain indications of the investors' interest in purchasing quantities of the underwritten securities in the offering at particular prices. As the IPO Advisory Committee Report stated: "[C]ollecting information about investors' long-term interest in, and valuation of, a prospective issuer is an essential part of the book-building process. By aggregating information obtained during this period from investors with other information, the underwriters and the issuer will agree on the size and pricing of the offering, and the underwriters will decide how to allocate the IPO shares to purchasers...."

While we recognize the importance of the book-building process in obtaining and assessing demand for an offering and in pricing the securities, we remind market participants that there is no "book-building exception" to Regulation M for inducing or attempting to induce aftermarket bids or purchases. Although a distribution participant's obtaining and assessing information about demand for an offering during the book-building process would not, by itself, constitute an inducement or attempt to induce, accompanying conduct or communications, including one or more of the activities described below, may cause the collection of information to be part of conduct that violates Regulation M.

Id. at 271.

6. SHORT SALES IN CONNECTION WITH AN OFFERING [RULE 105]

P. 1168, new text after 2d full par. In 2004, the Commission proposed amendments to Regulation M. Sec. Ex. Act Rel. 50,831, 84 SEC Dock. 1118 (2004) (proposal), citing the text. The proposal Release summarized the proposed amendments:

- Amend Rule 100's definition of restricted period with respect to IPOs and to expressly reflect the Commission's long-standing application of the definition in the context of mergers, acquisitions, and exchange offers;
- Amend Rule 101's "*de minimis* exception" to require recordkeeping;
- Amend Rules 100, 101, and 102 to update the average daily trading volume (ADTV) value and public float value qualifying thresholds for purposes of the *restricted period* definition and the *actively-traded* securities and *actively-traded* reference securities exceptions;

437

P. 1168

- Amend Rule 104 to require disclosure of syndicate covering bids and to prohibit penalty bids;
- Amend Rule 104(j)(2) to include reference securities in the exception for transactions in securities eligible for resale under Rule 144A; and
- Adopt new Rule 106 to expressly prohibit conditioning the award of allocations of offered securities on the receipt of consideration in addition to the stated offering consideration.

As a consequence of these proposals, we are also recommending amendments to Rule 481 and Item 508 of Regulations S-K and S-B under the Securities Act concerning disclosure, and Rules 17a-2 and 17a-4 with respect to recordkeeping.

Id. at 1121.

The proposals were intended to address misconduct in connection with IPOs identified in recent SEC, SRO, and private actions. Id. at 1120.

New proposed Rule 106 was intended to explicitly prohibit distribution participants, including underwriters, and issuers and their affiliates, directly or indirectly, from demanding, soliciting, or attempting to induce, or accepting an offer from their customers of any payment or other consideration in addition to the security's stated consideration. For example, this rule would prohibit distribution participants, issuers and their affiliated persons, in connection with allocating an offered security, from inducing, soliciting, requiring or otherwise accepting an offer from a potential purchaser to purchase any other security to be sold or proposed to be offered or sold by such person. Similarly, Rule 106 would also prohibit distribution participants, issuers and their affiliated persons, in connection with allocating an offered security, from inducing, soliciting, requiring (or accepting an offer from) prospective customers to effect any other transaction or refrain from any of the foregoing, other than as stated in the registration statement or applicable offering document for the offer and sale of such offered security. Rule 106 would apply to any distribution of securities, whether a public offering or private placement of securities, and would apply to initial as well as secondary offerings.

Id. at 1133.

In 2007 the Commission adopted amendments to Rule 105 of Regulation M to prohibit any person from effecting a restricted period short sale and then purchasing the security in the offering, including purchases made by entering into a contract of sale for the security in the offering. Sec. Ex. Act Rels. 54,888, 89 SEC Dock. 1346 (2006) (proposal); 56,206, 91 SEC Dock. 781(2007) (adoption).

CHAPTER 11

CIVIL LIABILITY

B. BLUE SKY LAWS AND THE SECURITIES LITIGATION UNIFORM STANDARDS ACT OF 1998

P. 1192 n.13, end note. In Enron Corp. Sec., Deriv. & ERISA Litig., 284 F. Supp. 2d 511 (S.D. Tex. 2003), the court held that SLUSA preempts cases based on the purchase or sale of a security, but does not apply to claims that solely address the retention of securities, id. at 632–642, and state claims including negligence that do not meet the §10(b) scienter requirement, id. at 642–644, 682–683.

An appeals court concluded it lacked jurisdiction to review a District Court order remanding a case to a state court. 28 U.S.C. §1447(d) has been interpreted to preclude appellate review based on lack of subject matter jurisdiction or to remove procedural irregularities. The Ninth Circuit concluded that the District Court reached its decision on the basis of lack of subject matter jurisdiction. United Investors Life Ins. Co. v. Waddell & Reed, Inc., 360 F.3d 960 (9th Cir. 2004).

After Spielman v. Merrill Lynch, Pierce, Fenner & Smith, Inc., 332 F.3d 116 (2d Cir. 2003), "it is now clear that the courts must probe the plaintiff's pleading to determine whether SLUSA preemption applies." Xpedior Creditor Trust v. Credit Suisse First Boston (USA) Inc., 341 F. Supp. 2d 258, 265–266 (S.D.N.Y. 2004) (discussing other cases, and adopting *necessary component* test:

P. 1192　　　2010 SUPPLEMENT

whether the state law claim relies on misstatements or omissions as a *necessary component* of a claim). Id. at 266-269. In the immediate case none of the plaintiff's claims were banned by SLUSA:

> None of the state law claims asserted by Xpedior — breach of contract, breach of the implied covenants of good faith and fair dealing, breach of fiduciary duty, or unjust enrichment — require misrepresentations or omissions as a necessary element.

Id. at 269. See also Breakaway Solutions, Inc. v. Morgan Stanley & Co., Inc., 2004 Del. Ch. LEXIS 125 (Del. Ch. 2004) (citing *Spielman* and *Xpedior* and similarly declining to preempt after applying *necessary component* test to state contract case); Finance & Trading LTD v. Rhodia S.A., 2004 Fed. Sec. L. Rep. (CCH) ¶93,046 (S.D.N.Y. 2004) (declining to remove state case to federal court when no substantial federal question was presented).

In Kircher v. Putnam Funds Trust, 373 F.3d 847 (7th Cir. 2004), the court held that suits that a district court finds to have been properly removed are unaffected by 28 U.S.C. §1447(d) and can be appealed. In a later decision in this case, the court held: "Every court of appeals to encounter SLUSA has held that its language has the same scope as its antecedent in Rule 10b-5." Kircher v. Putnam Funds Trust, 403 F.3d 478, 482 (7th Cir. 2005), *cert. denied*, 546 U.S. 1285, citing cases.

In Dabit v. Merrill Lynch, Pierce, Fenner & Smith, Inc., 395 F.3d 25, 28 (2d Cir. 2005), the court held:

> (i) the meaning of "in connection with" under SLUSA is coterminous with the meaning of the nearly identical language of §10(b) of the Securities Exchange Act of 1934..., and its corresponding Rule 10b-5...and (ii) the purchaser-seller rule of *Blue Chip Stamps v. Manor Drug Stores*, 421 U.S. 723, 95 S. Ct. 1917, 44 L. Ed. 2d 539 (1975), applies as a limit on SLUSA's "in connection with" requirement such that SLUSA does not preempt claims that do not allege purchases or sales made by the plaintiff or the alleged class members.

In Merrill Lynch, Pierce, Fenner & Smith, Inc. v. Dabit, 547 U.S. 71 (2006), the Supreme Court rejected the Second Circuit decision and adopted language in Kircher v. Putnam Funds Trust, 403 F.3d 478 (7th Cir. 2005), which held that SLUSA also preempts state law class actions for which the federal securities law provides no remedy. The Court explained in part:

> Respondent urges that the operative language must be read narrowly to encompass (and therefore preempt) only those actions in which the purchaser-seller requirement of *Blue Chip Stamps* is met. Such, too, was the Second Circuit's view. But insofar as the argument assumes that the rule adopted in *Blue Chip Stamps* stems from the text of Rule 10b-5 — specifically, the "in connection with" language, it must be rejected. Unlike the *Birnbaum* court, which relied on Rule 10b-5's text in crafting its purchaser-seller limitation, this Court in *Blue Chip Stamps* relied chiefly, and candidly, on "policy considerations" in adopting that limitation. 421 U.S., at 737. The *Blue Chip Stamps* Court purported to define the scope of a private right of action under Rule 10b-5 — not to define the words "in connection with the purchase or sale." *Id.* at 749....Any ambiguity on that score had long been resolved by the time Congress enacted SLUSA....
>
> Moreover, when this Court *has* sought to give meaning to the phrase in the context of §10(b) and Rule 10b-5, it has espoused a broad interpretation. A narrow construction would not, as a matter of first impression, have been unreasonable; one might have concluded that an alleged fraud is "in connection with" a purchase or sale of securities only when the plaintiff himself was defrauded into purchasing or selling particular securities. After all, that was the interpretation adopted by the panel in the *Birnbaum* case. See 193 F.2d at 464. But this Court, in early cases like *Superintendent of Ins. of N.Y. v. Bankers Life & Casualty Co.*, 404 U.S. 6 (1971), and most recently in *SEC v. Zandford*, 535 U.S. 813, 820, 822 (2002), has rejected that view. Under our precedents, it is enough that the fraud alleged "coincide" with a securities transaction — whether by the plaintiff or by someone else. See *O'Hagan*, 521 U.S., at 651. The requisite showing, in other words, is "deception 'in connection with the purchase or sale of any security,' not deception of an identifiable purchaser or seller." *Id.*, at 658. Notably, this broader interpretation of the statutory language comports with the longstanding views of the SEC. See *Zandford*, 535 U.S., at 819–820.
>
> Congress can hardly have been unaware of the broad construction adopted by both this Court and the SEC when it imported the

key phrase — "in connection with the purchase or sale" — into SLUSA's core provision. And when "judicial interpretations have settled the meaning of an existing statutory provision, repetition of the same language in a new statute indicates, as a general matter, the intent to incorporate its...judicial interpretations as well." *Bragdon v. Abbott*, 524 U.S. 624, 645 (1998); see *Cannon v. University of Chicago*, 441 U.S. 677, 696–699 (1979). Application of that presumption is particularly apt here; not only did Congress use the same words as are used in §10(b) and Rule 10b-5, but it used them in a provision that appears in the same statute as §10(b). Generally, "identical words used in different parts of the same statute are...presumed to have the same meaning." *IBP, Inc. v. Alvarez*, [126 S. Ct. 514] (2005) (slip op., at 11).

The presumption that Congress envisioned a broad construction follows not only from ordinary principles of statutory construction but also from the particular concerns that culminated in SLUSA's enactment. A narrow reading of the statute would undercut the effectiveness of the 1995 Reform Act and thus run contrary to SLUSA's stated purpose, viz., "to prevent certain State private securities class action lawsuits alleging fraud from being used to frustrate the objectives" of the 1995 Act. SLUSA §2(5), 112 Stat. 3227. As the *Blue Chip Stamps* Court observed, class actions brought by holders pose a special risk of vexatious litigation. 421 U.S., at 739. It would be odd, to say the least, if SLUSA exempted that particularly troublesome subset of class actions from its preemptive sweep. See *Kircher*, 403 F.3d at 484.

Respondent's preferred construction also would give rise to wasteful, duplicative litigation. Facts supporting an action by purchasers under Rule 10b-5 (which must proceed in federal court if at all) typically support an action by holders as well, at least in those States that recognize holder claims. The prospect is raised, then, of parallel class actions proceeding in state and federal court, with different standards governing claims asserted on identical facts. That prospect, which exists to some extent in this very case, squarely conflicts with the congressional preference for "national standards for securities class action lawsuits involving nationally traded securities." SLUSA §2(5), 112 Stat. 3227.

In concluding that SLUSA preempts state-law holder class-action claims of the kind alleged in Dabit's complaint, we do not lose sight of the general "presum[ption] that Congress does not cavalierly preempt state-law causes of action." *Medtronic, Inc. v.*

Lohr, 518 U.S. 470, 485 (1996). But that presumption carries less force here than in other contexts because SLUSA does not actually preempt any state cause of action. It simply denies plaintiffs the right to use the class action device to vindicate certain claims. The Act does not deny any individual plaintiff, or indeed any group of fewer than 50 plaintiffs, the right to enforce any state-law cause of action that may exist....

Finally, federal law, not state law, has long been the principal vehicle for asserting class-action securities fraud claims....More importantly, while state-law holder claims were theoretically available both before and after the decision in *Blue Chip Stamps*, the actual assertion of such claims by way of class action was virtually unheard of before SLUSA was enacted; respondent and his *amici* have identified only *one* pre-SLUSA case involving a state-law class action asserting holder claims. This is hardly a situation, then, in which a federal statute has eliminated a historically entrenched state-law remedy.

Id. at 1512–1515.

In Kircher v. Putnam Funds Trust, 547 U.S. 633 (2006), the Supreme Court subsequently held that an order remanding a case removed under SLUSA is not appealable.

Cf. Rowinski v. Salomon Smith Barney, Inc., 398 F.3d 294 (3d Cir. 2005), in which the court concluded at 299–300:

> The misrepresentation issue is straightforward. Plaintiff's complaint is replete with allegations that Salomon Smith Barney disseminated biased and materially misleading investment research. Plaintiff alleges Salomon Smith Barney "provides customers with biased investment research and analysis"; "artificially inflates the ratings and analysis of its investment banking clients"; was fined by the NASD "for issuing materially misleading research reports"; and "provided biased and misleading analysis that was intended to curry favor with Defendant's existing and potential investment banking clients." These allegations, which are incorporated by reference in every count in the complaint, readily satisfy the misrepresentation requirement under SLUSA.
>
> Plaintiff responds that the "breach of contract claim does not involve a misrepresentation or omission." In other words, plaintiff contends that because "misrepresentation" is not an essential legal

P. 1192

element of his claim under Pennsylvania contract law, the factual allegations of misrepresentation included in the complaint are irrelevant to the SLUSA inquiry.

We disagree. Plaintiff's suggested distinction — between the legal and factual allegations in a complaint — is immaterial under the statute. SLUSA preempts any covered class action "alleging" a material misrepresentation or omission in connection with the purchase or sale of securities. 15 U.S.C. §78bb(f)(1). Under this provision, preemption does not turn on whether allegations are characterized as facts or as essential legal elements of a claim, but rather on whether the SLUSA prerequisites are "alleged" in one form or another. A contrary approach, under which only essential legal elements of a state law claim trigger preemption, is inconsistent with the plain meaning of the statute. Furthermore, it would allow artful pleading to undermine SLUSA's goal of uniformity — a result manifestly contrary to congressional intent.

The court relied on *Zandford* for a broad reading of the *in connection with* element of §10(b) and Rule 10b-5. Id. at 300–305.

But see Blaz v. Belfer, 368 F.3d 501 (5th Cir. 2004), *cert. denied*, 543 U.S. 874, where the Court applied SLUSA retroactively to preenactment conduct. "The application is permitted because SLUSA governs why secondary conduct — procedural requirements for filing certain state law securities claims — and not the primary conduct that is the subject of these claims." Id. at 502.

In Ring v. AXA Fin., Inc., 483 F.3d 95 (2d Cir. 2007), a children's term rider to a variable life insurance policy was held not to be a *covered security* although the plaintiff conceded that the variable life insurance policy was a *covered security*.

Common stock received during an insurance demutualization case was a covered security under SLUSA. Sofonia v. Principal Life Ins. Co., 465 F.3d 873, 877 (8th Cir. 2006). The exchange of mutual insurance membership interests for the stock conditioned a *purchase or sale* under the 1934 Act. Id. at 878-880. Nor does the McCarron-Ferguson Act preclude application of SLUSA. Id. at 880.

In Gavin v. AT&T Corp., 464 F.3d 634 (7th Cir. 2006), Judge Posner declined to permit removal under SLUSA when the court concluded that the alleged fraud was not "in connection with the purchase or sale of a covered stock" but occurred after the relevant securities transaction. "The plaintiffs are not trying to litigate a securities fraud case, but instead a consumer fraud case against companies that have made no effort to influence the purchase or sale of a covered security." Id. at 640. See also Instituto de Prevision Militar v. Merrill Lynch & Co., 546 F.3d 1340 (11th Cir. 2008) (defendant established all four elements of SLUSA preclusions); SEC v. Wolfson, 539 F.3d 1249, 1262-1263 (10th Cir. 2008) (following *Dabit* and *Zandford*).

Following *Dabit*, the Eighth Circuit held that SLUSA preempts state law claims that a trustee breached its fiduciary duty by failing to disclose conflicts of interest in its selection of investment securities. Siepel v. Bank of Am., N.A., 526 F.3d 1122 (8th Cir. 2008).

In Enron Corp. Sec., Deriv. & ERISA Litig., 535 F.3d 325 (5th Cir. 2008), the court held that several separate actions should be treated as "proceeding as a single action" and accordingly then involved a *covered class action* within the meaning of SLUSA.

In Kurz v. Fidelity Mgmt. & Research Co., 556 F.3d 639 (7th Cir. 2009), the court held that SLUSA preempted a claim that involved allegations that a broker-dealer had bribed a mutual fund complex's employees to send trades its way in violation of the NASD best execution rule.

In Kutten v. Bank of Am., 530 F.3d 669 (8th Cir. 2008), in a case which sought remedy for the same alleged injuries as in Siepel v. Bank of Am., 526 F.3d 1122, 1125 (8th Cir. 2008), the court dismissed a complaint as preempted by SLUSA that included allegations that the bank misrepresented or omitted material facts.

In Lord Abbett Mut. Funds Fee Litig., 553 F.3d 248 (3d Cir. 2009), the court held that a District Court should not dismiss an entire action that both included claims precluded by SLUSA's prohibition on state law securities claims and those that do not.

Cf. Madden v. Cowen & Co., 556 F.3d 786 (9th Cir. 2009) (Delaware carve out applies to action by 63 shareholders against an investment bank for misleading them in connection with a sale of their closely held corporation to a publicly traded acquiror).

But see also LaSala v. Bordier et Cie, 519 F.3d 121, 137 (3d Cir. 2008) (concluding that the text of §78(f) and Congress's intent

447

sought "not to preempt corporate claims, and to leave the bankruptcy process undisturbed").

The Class Action Fairness Act of 2005 precludes a federal district court from exercising original jurisdiction over any class action that solely involves a claim concerning a covered security as defined under §16(f)(7) of the Securities Act or §28(f)(5)(b) of the Securities Exchange Act. 28 U.S.C. §1332(d)(9)(A).

C. SEC STATUTES

2. SECURITIES ACT OF 1933

b. Section 12(a)(2)

(iv) *Secondary Trading*

P. 1216 n.51, end note.   See also Yung v. Lee, 432 F.3d 142, 149 (2d Cir. 2005) ("We now join...courts in holding that *Gustafson*'s definition of a prospectus...compels the conclusion that a Section 12(a)(2) action cannot be maintained by a plaintiff who acquires securities through a private transaction, whether primary or secondary"); Faye L. Roth Revocable Trust v. UBS PaineWebber, Inc., 323 F. Supp. 2d 1279, 1290, n.1 (S.D. Fla. 2004), quoting the text. On the other hand, several courts have now held that whether a claimed §4(2) private offering, Rule 144A or Regulation S is subject to §12(a)(2) involves a fact question whether the claimed exemption, in fact, involved a public offering. Enron Corp., Sec., Deriv. & ERISA Litig., 310 F. Supp. 2d 819, 859–866 (S.D. Tex. 2004) (declining to resolve issue on pretrial motion before discovery). See also Fisk v. Superannuities, Inc., 927 F. Supp. 718, 729–731 (S.D.N.Y. 1996) (§12(a)(2) claim can be successfully pled if defendants could not establish entitlement to §4(2) private placement exemption); Steed Fin. LDC v. Nomura Sec. Int'l, Inc., 2001 Fed. Sec. L. Rep. (CCH) ¶91,552 (S.D.N.Y. 2001) (declining to dismiss §12(a)(2) claim when defendants claimed §4(2) private placement and plaintiff pled that securities were offered to the public), citing cases.

d. Section 11: Misstatements or Omissions in Registration Statement

(i) *Elements of the Action*

P. 1228 n.84, end note. In Krim v. PC Order.Com, Inc., 402 F.3d 489 (5th Cir. 2005), the Fifth Circuit addressed statistical methodology in a tracing case, explaining in part:

> In *Rosenzweig*, we further held that this traceability requirement is satisfied, as a matter of logic, when stock has only entered the market via a single offering. We did not speculate on what other methods might be available to satisfy the traceability requirement for aftermarket purchases, but we were careful to note the Supreme Court's concern "that the Securities Act remain anchored to its original purpose of regulating only public offerings."
>
> Appellants, as aftermarket purchasers, assert that they can also demonstrate standing by showing a very high probability that they each have at least one PO share. Appellants argue that their statistical determinations, being over 50%, demonstrate by a preponderance of the evidence, that it is "more likely than not," that their shares are traceable to the public offerings in question.
>
> We are persuaded that accepting such "statistical tracing" would impermissibly expand the statute's standing requirement. Because any share of pcOrder.com stock chosen at random in the aftermarket has at least a 90% chance of being tainted, its holder, according to Appellants' view, would have Section 11 standing. In other words, *every* aftermarket purchaser would have standing for every share, despite the language of Section 11, limiting suit to "any person acquiring *such* security." As the district court found, it is "likely that any street name shareholder can make a similar claim with regard to *one* share." This cannot be squared with the statutory language—that is, with what Congress intended. We decline the invitation to reach further than the statute....
>
> However, as we have explained, Section 11 *is* available for anyone who purchased directly in the offering and any aftermarket

purchasers who can demonstrate that their shares are traceable to the registration statement in question — *e.g.*, when, as with Beebe, there had only been one offering at the time of purchase. When Congress enacted the Securities Act of 1933 it was not confronted with the widespread practice of holding stock in street name that Appellants describe as an impediment, absent our acceptance of statistical tracing, to invoking Section 11. That present market realities, given the fungibility of stock held in street name, may render Section 11 ineffective as a practical matter in some aftermarket scenarios is an issue properly addressed by Congress. It is not within our purview to rewrite the statute to take account of changed conditions. In the words of one court, Appellants' arguments may "have the sound ring of economic reality but unfortunately they merely point up the problems involved in the present scheme of statutory regulation."

It is, therefore, perhaps not surprising that we failed to locate any court, nor did Appellants point to any, that found Section 11 standing based solely on the statistical tracing theory espoused today. Given that the statute has been in existence for over 70 years and such elementary statistical calculations have been around for centuries, it is difficult to conclude that this is a coincidence. We note that a handful of lower courts have rebuffed similar attempts by plaintiffs. [Citing cases.]

Id. at 495-498.

In APA Excelsior III, L.P. v. Premiere Tech., 476 F.3d 1261 (11th Cir. 2007), the court held that a purchaser of a security falls outside the scope of §11 when the purchase decision was made in a preregistration commitment.

In Stark Trading v. Falconbridge Ltd., 552 F.3d 568 (7th Cir. 2008), plaintiffs failed to establish damages under §11 when they exchanged shares in a tender offer and received a significant premium in the shares received.

P. 1232 n.105, end note. In WorldCom, Inc. Sec. Litig., 346 F. Supp. 2d 628 (S.D.N.Y. 2004), quoting the text, Judge Cote addressed the underwriters' due diligence obligations with respect to the financial statements that were incorporated into two WorldCom bond offerings. Both were prepared by Arthur Andersen.

CIVIL LIABILITY P. 1232

First, with respect to accountants as expert, the court wrote:

Not every auditor's opinion, however, qualifies as an expert's opinion for purposes of the Section 11 reliance defense. To distinguish among auditor's opinions, some background is in order. While financial statements are prepared by the management of a company, an accountant serving as the company's auditor may give an opinion as to whether the financial statements have been presented in conformity with GAAP. This opinion is given after the accountant has performed an audit of the company's books and records. Audits are generally completed once a year, in connection with a company's year-end financial statements. There are ten audit standards with which an auditor must comply in performing its annual audit. They are known as Generally Accepted Auditing Standards ("GAAS"). If an auditor signs a consent to have its opinion on financial statements incorporated into a company's public filings, the opinion may be shared with the public through incorporation.

Public companies are also required under the Exchange Act to file quarterly financial statements, which are referred to as interim financial statements. While not subject to an audit, interim financial statements included in Form 10-Q quarterly reports are reviewed by an independent public accountant using professional standards and procedures for conducting such reviews, as established by GAAS. The standards for the review of interim financial statements are set forth in Statement of Auditing Standards No. 71, Interim Financial Information ("SAS 71"). When a public company files a registration statement for a sale of securities, the auditor is customarily asked by underwriters to provide a comfort letter. The comfort letter will contain representations about the auditor's review of the interim financial statements. Guidance about the content of comfort letters is contained in the Statement on Auditing Standards No. 72, Letters for Underwriters and Certain Other Requesting Parties ("SAS 72"). There is frequently more than one comfort letter for a transaction: an initial comfort letter, and a second or "bringdown" comfort letter issued closer to the time of closing.

In order for an accountant's opinion to qualify as an expert opinion under Section 11(b)(3)(C), there are three prerequisites. First, it must be reported in the Registration Statement. Second, it must

451

P. 1232   2010 SUPPLEMENT

be an audit opinion. Finally, the accountant must consent to inclusion of the audit opinion in the registration statement.

In an effort to encourage auditor reviews of interim financial statements, the SEC acted in 1979 to assure auditors that their review of unaudited interim financial information would not subject them to liability under Section 11. [Citation omitted.] The SEC addressed the circumstances in which an accountant's opinion can be considered an expert's opinion for purposes of Section 11(b) and made it clear that reviews of unaudited interim financial statements do not constitute such an opinion. Under Rule 436, where the opinion of an expert is quoted or summarized in a registration statement, or where any information contained in a registration statement "has been reviewed or passed upon" by an expert, the written consent of the expert must be filed as an exhibit to the registration statement. [Rule] 436(a), (b). Yet written consent is not sufficient to convert an opinion or review into an expertised statement. Rule 436 provides that notwithstanding written consent, "*a report on unaudited interim financial information*...by an independent accountant who has conducted a review of such interim financial information *shall not be considered a part of a registration statement prepared or certified by an accountant* or a report prepared or certified by an accountant within the meaning of sections 7 and 11" of the Securities Act. [Rule] 436(c) (emphasis supplied).

Rule 436 also defined the term "report on unaudited interim financial information." It consists of a report that contains the following five items:

(1) A statement that the review of interim financial information was made in accordance with established professional standards for such reviews;
(2) An identification of the interim financial information reviewed;
(3) A description of the procedures for a review of interim financial information;
(4) A statement that a review of interim financial information is substantially less in scope than an examination in accordance with generally accepted auditing standards, the objective of which is an expression of opinion regarding the financial statements taken as a whole, and, accordingly, no such opinion is expressed; and

(5) A statement about whether the accountant is aware of any material modifications that should be made to the accompanying financial information so that it conforms with generally accepted accounting principles.

Rule 436(d).

In promulgating Rule 436, the SEC contrasted accountants' review of year-end financial statements with those of interim financial data, remarking that

> *The objective of a review of interim financial information differs significantly from the objective of an examination of financial statements in accordance with generally accepted auditing standards.* The objective of an audit is to provide a reasonable basis for expressing an opinion regarding the financial statements taken as a whole. A review of interim financial information does not provide a basis for the expression of such an opinion, because the review does not contemplate a study and evaluation of internal accounting control; tests of accounting records and of responses to inquiries by obtaining corroborating evidential matter through inspection, observation, or confirmation; and certain other procedures ordinarily performed during an audit. A review may bring to the accountant's attention significant matters affecting the interim financial information, but it does not provide assurance that the accountant will become aware of all significant matters that would be disclosed in an audit.

Id. at 664–666.

Second, the court highlighted that underwriters ability to rely on accountants as experts is correlatively limited:

> Rule 436 underscores that SAS 71 reports and SAS 72 letters are not expertised statements within the meaning of the Section 11 reliance defense. Specifically, in finalizing Rule 436, the SEC directed that
>
> > [i]n any suit for damages under Section 11(a), the directors and *underwriters should not be able to rely on SAS No. [71] reports on interim financial data included in a registration statement* as statements "purporting to be made on the authority of an expert...which they had no ground to believe...were

untrue..." under Section 11(b)(3)(C). Rather, *underwriters and directors should be required*, as has previously been the case whenever unaudited financials are included in a registration statement, *to demonstrate affirmatively* under Section 11(b)(3)(A) *that, after conducting a reasonable investigation, they had reasonable ground to believe, and did believe, that the interim financial data was true....*

Given this, the SEC expects that "underwriters will continue to exercise due diligence in a vigorous manner with respect to SAS No. [71] reports."...

In sum, underwriters can rely on an accountant's audit opinion incorporated into a registration statement in presenting a defense under Section 11(b)(3)(C). Underwriters may not rely on an accountant's comfort letters for interim financial statements in presenting such a defense. Comfort letters do not "expertise any portion of the registration statement that is otherwise non-expertised."

Id. at 666.

Third, the court reiterated that in spite of Rule 176 "current law continues to place a burden upon an underwriter to conduct a reasonable investigation of non-expertised statements in a registration, including an issuer's interim financial statements." Id. at 671. See generally id at 674–678.

Fourth, an underwriter's reliance on audited financial statements may not be blind, but must respond to red flags. Id. at 672–673, citing cases.

In Bradbury v. SEC, 512 F.3d 634, 641–642 (D.C. Cir. 2008), the court generalized:

> An underwriter must investigate and disclose material facts that are known or *reasonably ascertainable*." *Municipal Securities Disclosure*, 1988 WL 999989, at *20 (quoting *Hanly*, 415 F.2d at 597); cf. *SEC v. Dain Rauscher, Inc.*, 254 F.3d 852, 858 (9th Cir. 2001) (holding an underwriter "had a duty to make an investigation that would provide him with a reasonable basis for a belief that the key representations in the statements...were truthful and complete"). Although other broker-dealers may have the same responsibilities in certain contexts, underwriters have a *heightened obligation* to ensure

adequate disclosure. *Municipal Securities Disclosure,* 1988 WL 999989, at *21 & n.74. Moreover, these duties do not disappear simply because "customers may be sophisticated and knowledgeable." See *Hanly,* 415 F.2d at 596. Indeed, the doctrine of caveat emptor has little application in this context. *SEC v. Capital Gains Research Bureau, Inc.*, 375 U.S. 180, 186 (1963).

In EBC I v. Goldman Sachs & Co., 832 N.E.2d 26 (N.Y. 2005), citing the text, the highest court in New York held that a cause of action for breach of fiduciary duty may survive when the plaintiff alleges that the underwriter and issuer created a relationship of higher trust than would arise from the underwriting agreement itself. The underwriting agreement itself normally would not create a fiduciary relationship, but an advisory relationship independent of the underwriting agreement could create a fiduciary relationship.

(iii) *Comparison with Common Law Actions and §12(a)(2)*

P. 1237 n.121, end note. In Tricontinental Indus. v. PricewaterhouseCoopers, 475 F.3d 824 (7th Cir. 2007), *cert. denied*, 128 S. Ct. 357, applying Illinois law to public accountants as articulated in the Illinois Public Accounting Act, 225 ILCS *450/30.1*: "The plaintiff must show that a primary purpose and intent of the accountant-client relationship was to benefit or influence the third-party plaintiff." Id. at 836, also following Brumley v. Touche Ross & Co., 487 N.E.2d 641 (Ill. 1985). "This 'primary intent' may be demonstrated by 'independent verification' or by other affirmative actions taken by the accountant and directed to the third party." Id. at 838.

3. SECURITIES EXCHANGE ACT OF 1934: EXPRESS LIABILITIES

P. 1240 n.125, end note. In Suprema Specialties, Inc. Sec. Litig., 438 F.3d 256, 283 (3d Cir. 2006), the Court held that plaintiffs must prove actual reliance on specific statements in SEC filings in a §18 case.

Under §18(a), a plaintiff is required to plead that a defendant made or caused to be made a false or misleading statement of material fact that was false or misleading at the time and under the circumstances under which it was made. To determine whether a statement is false or misleading, the court in Deephaven Private Placement Trading Ltd. v. Grant Thornton & Co., 454 F.3d 1168, 1173–1174 (10th Cir. 2006), articulated three pleading requirements under the PSLRA. The Complaint must specify: (1) each statement alleged to be misleading, (2) the reason why the statement is misleading, and (3) if an allegation is made on information or belief, all facts on which the complaint is based.

Under §29(b) for a person to void an agreement, the Plaintiff must establish that: (1) the contract involved a prohibited transaction; (2) the plaintiff is in contractual privity with the defendant; and (3) the plaintiff is in the class of persons that the securities acts were designed to protect. Berckeley Inv. Group, Ltd. v. Colkitt, 455 F.3d 195, 205 (3d Cir. 2006). The securities violations must be inseparable from the agreement under §29(b), rather than "downstream" or subsequent to entering into the agreement. Id. at 205–206.

4. Securities Exchange Act of 1934: Implied Liabilities

a. Theory and Scope

P. 1264, new text, end page. In Alexander v. Sandoval, 532 U.S. 275 (2001), Justice Scalia, writing for the Supreme Court majority, addressed a private right of action to enforce regulations issued under Title VI of the Civil Rights Act of 1964:

> Respondents would have us revert in this case to the understanding of private causes of action that held sway 40 years ago when Title VI was enacted. That understanding is captured by the

CIVIL LIABILITY P. 1264

Court's statement in *J. I. Case Co. v. Borak*, 377 U.S. 426, 433 (1964), that "it is the duty of the courts to be alert to provide such remedies as are necessary to make [effectuate] the congressional purpose" expressed by a statute. We abandoned that understanding in *Cort v. Ash*, 422 U.S. 66, 78 (1975) — which itself interpreted a statute enacted under the *ancien regime* — and have not returned to it since. Not even when interpreting the same Securities Exchange Act of 1934 that was at issue in *Borak* have we applied *Borak's* method for discerning and defining causes of action. See *Central Bank of Denver, N.A. v. First Interstate Bank of Denver, N.A., supra*, at 188; *Musick, Peeler & Garrett v. Employers Ins. of Wausau*, 508 U.S. 286, 291–293 (1993); *Virginia Bankshares, Inc. v. Sandberg, supra*, at 1102–1103; *Touche Ross & Co. v. Redington, supra*, at 576–1578. Having sworn off the habit of venturing beyond Congress's intent, we will not accept respondents' invitation to have one last drink.

Nor do we agree with the Government that our cases interpreting statutes enacted prior to *Cort v. Ash* have given "dispositive weight" to the "expectations" that the enacting Congress had formed "in light of the 'contemporary legal context.'" Brief for United States 14. Only three of our legion implied-right-of-action cases have found this sort of "contemporary legal context" relevant, and two of those involved in Congress's enactment (or reenactment) of the verbatim statutory text that courts had previously interpreted to create a private right of action. See *Merrill Lynch, Pierce, Fenner & Smith, Inc. v. Curran*, 456 U.S. 353, 378–379 (1982); *Cannon v. University of Chicago*, 441 U.S. at 698–699. In the third case, this sort of "contemporary legal context" simply buttressed a conclusion independently supported by the text of the statute. See *Thompson v. Thompson*, 484 U.S. 174 (1988). We have never accorded dispositive weight to context shorn of text. In determining whether statutes create private rights of action, as in interpreting statutes generally, see *Blatchford v. Native Village of Noatak*, 501 U.S. 775, 784 (1991), legal context matters only to the extent it clarifies text.

We therefore begin (and find we can end) our search for Congress's intent with the text and structure of Title VI.

Id. at 287–288.

P. 1264

In Stoneridge Inv. Partners, LLC v. Scientific-Atlanta, Inc., 552 U.S. 148, the Court followed *Sandoval* in a §10(b) case, adding:

> The history of the §10(b) private right and the careful approach the Court has taken before proceeding without congressional direction provide further reasons to find no liability here. The §10(b) private cause of action is a judicial construct that Congress did not enact in the text of the relevant statutes. See *Lampf, Pleva, Lipkind, Prupis & Petigrow v. Gilbertson*, 501 U.S. 350, 358–359 (1991); *Blue Chip*, supra, at 729. Though the rule once may have been otherwise, see *J. I. Case Co. v. Borak*, 377 U.S. 426, 432–433 (1964), it is settled that there is an implied cause of action only if the underlying statute can be interpreted to disclose the intent to create one, see, e.g., *Alexander*, supra, at 286–287; *Virginia Bankshares*, supra, at 1102; *Touche Ross & Co. v. Redington*, 442 U.S. 560, 575 (1979). This is for good reason. In the absence of congressional intent the Judiciary's recognition of an implied private right of action "necessarily extends its authority to embrace a dispute Congress has not assigned it to resolve. This runs contrary to the established principle that 'the jurisdiction of the federal courts is carefully guarded against expansion by judicial interpretation…,' *American Fire & Casualty Co. v. Finn*, 341 U.S. 6, 17 (1951), and conflicts with the authority of Congress under Art. III to set the limits of federal jurisdiction." *Cannon v. University of Chicago*, 441 U.S. 677, 746 (1979) (Powell, J., dissenting) (citations and footnote omitted). The determination of who can seek a remedy has significant consequences for the reach of federal power. [Citation omitted.]
>
> Concerns with the judicial creation of a private cause of action caution against its expansion. The decision to extend the cause of action is for Congress, not for us. Though it remains the law, the §10(b) private right should not be extended beyond its present boundaries. See *Virginia Bankshares*, supra, at 1102 ("The breadth of the [private right of action] once recognized should not, as a general matter, grow beyond the scope congressionally intended"); see also *Central Bank*, supra, at 173 (determining that the scope of conduct prohibited is limited by the text of §10(b)).
>
> This restraint is appropriate in light of the PSLRA, which imposed heightened pleading requirements and a loss causation requirement upon *any private action* arising from the Securities

Exchange Act. See 15 U.S.C. §78u-4(b). It is clear these requirements touch upon the implied right of action, which is now a prominent feature of federal securities regulation. [Citations omitted.] Congress thus ratified the implied right of action after the Court moved away from a broad willingness to imply private rights of action. See *Merrill Lynch, Pierce, Fenner & Smith, Inc. v. Curran*, 456 U.S. 353, 381–382, and n.66 (1982); cf. *Borak*, supra, at 433. It is appropriate for us to assume that when §78u-4 was enacted, Congress accepted the §10(b) private cause of action as then defined but chose to extend it no further.

c. Tender Offers

(i) *Standing*

P. 1272 n.232, end note. Edelson v. Ch'ien, 405 F.3d 620 (7th Cir. 2005), *cert. denied sub nom.* Edelson v. CDC Corp., 546 U.S. 1169, the court concluded that Congress intended to recognize a private cause of action under §13(d) but "only in the context of a tender offer or other contest for control." Id. at 634.

In Motient Corp. v. Dondero, 529 F.3d 532 (5th Cir. 2008), the court concluded that there was no private cause of action for money damages under §13(d).

d. Rule 10b-5

(i) *Reliance and Causation*

P. 1281 n.265, end note. In a fraud on the market case when a plaintiff made both statements that suggested he did not rely on a market price and other statements that suggested he did rely, a reasonable jury could find that the defendant has not established that the plaintiff did not rely on the market price. The Second Circuit accordingly reversed a District Court judgment as a matter of law that has overturned a jury verdict for the plaintiff. Black v. Finantra Capital, Inc., 418 F.3d 203 (2d Cir. 2005).

P. 1283

The Fifth Circuit joined several other circuits in requiring a rigorous, though preliminary, standard of proof to the market efficiency determinations. See Bell v. Ascendant Solutions, Inc., 422 F.3d 307 (5th Cir. 2005). The Court set forth specific rules to determine whether a stock trades in an efficient market. Cf. n.10:

(1) the average weekly trading volume expressed as a percentage of total outstanding shares;
(2) the number of securities analysts following and reporting on the stock;
(3) the extent to which market makers and arbitrageurs trade in the stock;
(4) the company's eligibility to file SEC registration Form S-3 (as opposed to Form S-1 or S-2);
(5) the existence of empirical facts "showing a cause and effect relationship between unexpected corporate events or financial releases and an immediate response in the stock price";
(6) the company's market capitalization;
(7) the bid-ask spread for stock sales; and
(8) float, the stock's trading volume without counting insider-owned stock.

Cf. Teamsters Local 445 Freight Div. Pension Fund v. Bombardier, Inc., 546 F.3d 196 (2d Cir. 2008) (following *Cammer* factors and concluding by a preponderance of evidence that the District Court made no clear error in concluding certificates did not trade in an efficient market).

P. 1283 n.271, end note. On the other hand, for there to be liability under *Affiliated Ute*, the plaintiff must demonstrate that the defendant had a duty to disclose. See, e.g., Regents of Univ. of Cal. v. Credit Suisse First Boston, 482 F.3d 372, 383–385 (5th Cir. 2007), *cert. denied*, 128 S. Ct. 1120.

In *Regents of Univ. of Cal.*, the court reversed class certification in 2006 U.S. Dist. LEXIS 43,146 applicable to two banks in the *Enron* litigation because they "were not fiduciaries and were not otherwise obligated to the plaintiffs," id. at 384, and specifically because "[m]erely pleading that defendants failed to fulfill that duty by means of a scheme or act, rather than by a misleading statement, does not entitle the plaintiff to employ the *Affiliated Ute* presumption." Ibid.

P. 1285, new text after carryover par. In Broudo v. Dura Pharmaceuticals, Inc., 339 F.3d 933 (9th Cir. 2003), the court quoted earlier Ninth Circuit cases for the proposition that "loss causation is satisfied where 'the plaintiff shows that the misrepresentation touches upon the reasons for the investment decline in value.'" Id. at 937–938. While acknowledging that the "touches upon language is admittedly ambiguous," id. at 938, the court held: "loss causation does not require pleading a stock price drop following a corrective disclosure or otherwise. It merely requires pleading that the price at the time of purchase was overstated and sufficient identification of the cause." Ibid. See also Gebhardt v. ConAgra Foods, Inc., 335 F.3d 824, 831 (8th Cir. 2003) (similar loss causation standard).

The Eleventh Circuit, in contrast, did require "proof of a causal connection between the misrepresentation and the investment's subsequent decline in value." Robbins v. Koger Prop., Inc., 116 F.3d 1441, 1448 (11th Cir. 1997). *Robbins* was explicitly followed by the Third Circuit, Semerenko v. Cendant Corp., 223 F.3d 165, 185 (3d Cir. 2000), *cert. denied*, 531 U.S. 1149; similar holdings also have been reached in the Second and Seventh Circuits, Emergent Capital Inv. Mgmt., LLC v. Stonepath Group, Inc., 343 F.3d 189, 198–199 (2d Cir. 2003) (plaintiff must demonstrate a causal connection between the alleged misstatements or omissions and "the harm actually suffered"); Bastian v. Petren Resources Corp., 892 F.2d 680, 682–683 (7th Cir. 1990) *cert. denied*, 496 U.S. 906 (similar).

The United States Solicitor General and SEC filed an amicus brief with the United States Supreme Court in Dura Pharmaceuticals, Inc. v. Broudo, No. 03-932 (May 2004), urging the Court to grant certiorari and reverse the Ninth Circuit. The SEC brief stated in part:

> 1. In a Rule 10b-5 action brought by a private party, the plaintiff must prove that he suffered an injury that was caused by the

P. 1285

defendant's misrepresentations. As the court of appeals correctly recognized, the causation requirement encompasses both transaction causation — "that the violations in question caused the plaintiff to engage in the transaction" — and loss causation — "that the misrepresentations or omissions caused the harm." [citation omitted.] Loss causation had long been a judicially inferred element of a Rule 10b-5 claim, see *Bastian*, 892 F.2d at 683–685, and for nearly a decade it has been a statutory element by virtue of the Private Securities Litigation Reform Act of 1995 (PSLRA), Pub. L. No. 104-67, 109 State. 737. As amended by the PSLRA, the Exchange Act, in a provision titled "Loss causation," requires a plaintiff in a private action to prove that "the [challenged] act or omission of the defendant... caused the loss for which the plaintiff seeks to recover damages." 15 U.S.C. 78u-4(b)(4). Under the court of appeals' view of loss causation, an investor's loss in a fraud-on-the-market case "occurs at the time of the transaction," when he is harmed by paying too much for the security, and a causal link exists because the defendant's misrepresentation inflated the price. [citation omitted.] That holding is incorrect.

A material misrepresentation that reflects an unduly favorable view of a company, when disseminated to the investing public, will typically raise the price of the company's stock, because the price of a security traded in an efficient market ordinarily reflects all publicly available information. See *Basic Inc. v. Levinson*, 485 U.S. at 241–249. The artificial inflation will not be reduced or eliminated until the market price reflects the true facts that had been concealed by the fraud. This will most commonly occur when the truth is revealed in whole or in part through a corrective disclosure. That, however, is not the only way the fraud may be revealed. Events may also effectively disclose the truth. [Citation omitted.]

Because "the cost of the alleged misrepresentation" will be "incorporated into the value of the security" until that time, the investor who purchased the security will be able to recoup part or all of his overpayment "by reselling the security at the inflated price." *Semerenko*, 223 F.3d at 185. For that reason, it cannot be said that an investor in a fraud-on-the-market case who purchases a security at an inflated price has suffered *any* loss at the time of purchase, much less one caused by the defendant's misrepresentation. See *Robbins*, 116 F.3d at 1448. Measuring the loss in such a case as of the time of purchase, and not requiring any allegation of a subsequent loss of value attributable to the fraud, would grant a

CIVIL LIABILITY P. 1285

windfall to investors who sold before the reduction of elimination of the artificial inflation, because they would recover the portion of the purchase price attributable to the fraud on resale, and then would be entitled to recover that same amount again in damages.

Id. at 9–11.

The Supreme Court adopted the logic of the SEC-Solicitor General brief in Dura Pharmaceuticals, Inc. v. Broudo, 544 U.S. 336 (2005), citing this text and stating in part:

> Private federal securities fraud actions are based upon federal securities statutes and their implementing regulations. Section 10(b) of the Securities Exchange Act of 1934 forbids (1) the "use or employ[ment...of any...deceptive device,"] "in connection with the purchase or sale of any security," and (3) "in contravention of" Securities and Exchange Commission "rules and regulations." [Citation omitted.] Commission Rule 10b-5 forbids, among other things, the making of any "untrue statement of material fact" or the omission of any material fact "necessary in order to make the statements made...not misleading." [Citation omitted.]
>
> The courts have implied from these statutes and Rule a private damages action, which resembles, but is not identical to, common law tort actions for deceit and misrepresentation. [Citations omitted.] And Congress has imposed statutory requirements on that private action. [Citation omitted.]
>
> In cases involving publicly traded securities and purchases or sales in public securities markets, the action's basic elements include:
>
> (1) *a material misrepresentation (or omission),* see *Basic Inc. v. Levinson,* 485 U.S. 224, 231–232 (1988);
> (2) *scienter, i.e.,* a wrongful state of mind, see *Ernst & Ernst, supra,* at 197, 199;
> (3) *a connection with the purchase or sale of a securities,* see *Blue Chip Stamps, supra,* at 730–731;
> (4) *reliance,* often referred to in cases involving public securities markets (fraud-on-the-market cases) as "transaction causation," see *Basic, supra,* at 248–249 (nonconclusively presuming that the price of a publicly traded share reflects a material misrepresentation as long as they would not have bought the share in its absence);

463

P. 1285

(5) *economic loss*, 15 U.S.C. §78u–4(b)(4); and
(6) *"loss causation,"* *i.e.*, a causal connection between the material misrepresentation and the loss, *ibid.*;...

Dura argues that the complaint's allegations are inadequate in respect to these last two elements....

We begin with the Ninth Circuit's basic reason for finding the complaint adequate, namely, that at the end of the day plaintiffs need only "establish," *i.e.*, prove, that "the price *on the date of purchase* was inflated because of the misrepresentation." 339 F.3d at 938 (internal quotation marks omitted). In our view, this statement of the law is wrong. Normally, in cases such as this one (*i.e.*, fraud-on-the-market cases), and inflated purchase price will not itself constitute or proximately cause the relevant economic loss.

For one thing, as a matter of pure logic, at the moment the transaction takes place, the plaintiff has suffered no loss; the inflated purchase payment is offset by ownership of a share that *at that instant* possesses equivalent value. Moreover, the logical link between the inflated share purchase price and any later economic loss is not invariably strong. Shares are normally purchased with an eye toward a later sale. But if, say, the purchaser sells the shares quickly before the relevant truth begins to leak out, the misrepresentation will not have led to any loss. If the purchaser sells later after the truth makes its way into the marketplace, an initially inflated purchase price *might* mean a later loss. But that is far from inevitably so. When the purchaser subsequently resells such shares, even at a lower price, that lower price may reflect, not the earlier misrepresentation, but changed economic circumstances, changed investor expectations, new industry-specific or firm-specific facts, conditions, or other events, which taken separately or together account for some or all of that lower price. (The same is true in respect to a claim that a share's higher price is lower than it would otherwise have been—a claim we do not consider here.) Other things being equal, the longer the time between purchase and sale, the more likely that this is so, *i.e.*, the more likely that other factors caused the loss.

Given the tangle of factors affecting price, the most logic alone permits us to say is that the higher purchase price will *sometimes* play a role in bringing about a future loss. It may prove to be a necessary condition of any such loss, and in that sense one might say that the inflated purchase price suggests that the misrepresentation (using language the Ninth Circuit used) "touches upon" a later economic loss. *Ibid.* But, even if that is so, it is insufficient. To "touch upon" a loss is not to *cause* a loss, and it is the latter that the law requires. 15 U.S.C. §78u-4(b)(4).

For another thing, the Ninth Circuit's holding lacks support in precedent. Judicially implied private securities-fraud actions resemble in many (but not all) respects common-law deceit and misrepresentation actions. See *Blue Chip Stamps, supra,* at 744; see also L. Loss & J. Seligman, Fundamentals of Securities Regulation, 910–918 (5th ed. 2004) (describing relationship to common-law deceit). The common law of deceit subjects a person who "fraudulently" makes a "misrepresentation" to liability "for pecuniary loss caused" to one who justifiably relies upon that misrepresentation. Restatement (Second) of Torts §525, p. 55 (1977) (hereinafter Restatement of Torts); see also *Southern Development Co. v. Silva,* 125 U.S. 247, 250 (1988) (setting forth elements of fraudulent misrepresentation). And the common law has long insisted that a plaintiff in such a case show not only that had he known the truth he would not have acted but also that he suffered actual economic loss. See, *e.g., Pasley v. Freeman,* 3 T.R. 5:1, 100 Eng. Rep. 450, 457 (1789) (if "no injury is occasioned by the lie, it is not actionable; but if it be attended with a damage, it then becomes the subject of an action"); *Freeman v. Venner,* 120 Mass. 424, 426 (1876) (a mortgagee cannot bring a tort action for damages stemming from a fraudulent note that a misrepresentation led him to execute unless and until the note has to be paid); see also M. Bigelow, Law of Torts 101 (8th ed. 1907) (damage "must already have been suffered before the bringing of the suit"); 2 T. Cooley, Law of Torts §348, p. 551 (4th ed. 1932) (plaintiff must show that he "suffered damage" and that the "damage followed proximately the deception"); W. Keeton, D. Dobbs, R. Keeton, & D. Owen, Prosser and Keeton on Law of Torts §110, p. 765 (5th ed. 1984) (hereinafter Prosser and Keeton) (plaintiff "must have suffered substantial damage" not simply nominal damages, before "the cause of action can arise").

Given the common-law roots of the securities fraud action (and the common-law requirement that a plaintiff show actual damages), it is not surprising that other courts of appeals have rejected the Ninth Circuit's "inflated purchase price" approach to proving causation and loss. See, *e.g., Emergent Capital,* 343 F.3d at 198 (inflation of purchase price alone cannot satisfy loss causation); *Semerenko,* 223 F.3d, at 185 (same); *Robbins,* 116 F.3d, at 1448 (same); cf.

P. 1285

Bastian, 892 F.2d, at 685. Indeed, the Restatement of Torts, in setting forth the judicial consensus, says that a person who "misrepresents the financial condition of a corporation in order to sell its stock" becomes liable to a relying purchase "for the loss" the purchaser sustains "when the facts...become generally known" and "as a result" share value "depreciate[s]." §548A, Comment b, at 107. Treatise writers, too, have emphasized the need to prove proximate causation. Prosser and Keeton §110, at 767 (losses do "not afford any basis for recovery" if "brought about by business conditions or other factors").

We cannot reconcile the Ninth Circuit's "inflated purchase price" approach with these views of other courts. And the uniqueness of its perspective argues against the validity of its approach in a case like this one where we consider the contours of a judicially implied cause of action with roots in the common law.

Finally, the Ninth Circuit's approach overlooks an important securities law objective. The securities statutes seek to maintain public confidence in the marketplace. See *United States v. O'Hagan,* 521 U.S. 642, 658 (1997). They do so by deterring fraud actions. *Randall v. Loftsgaarden,* 478 U.S. 647, 664 (1986). But the statutes make these latter actions available, not to provide investors with broad insurance against market losses, but to protect them against those economic losses that misrepresentations actually cause. Cf. *Basic,* 485 U.S., at 252 (White, J., joined by O'CONNOR, J., concurring in part and dissenting in part) ("[A]llowing recovery in the face of affirmative evidence of nonreliance — would effectively convert Rule 10b-5 into a scheme of investor's insurance. There is no support in the Securities Exchange Act, the Rule, or our cases for such a result" (internal quotation marks and citations omitted)).

The statutory provision at issue here and the paragraphs that precede it emphasize this last mentioned objective. Private Securities Litigation Reform Act of 1995, 109 Stat. 737. The statute insists that securities fraud complaints "specify" each misleading statement; that they set forth the facts "on which [a] belief" that a statement is misleading was "formed"; and that they "state with particularity facts giving rise to a strong inference that the defendant acted with the required state of mind." 15 U.S.C. §§78u-4(b)(1), (2). And the statute expressly imposes on plaintiffs "the burden of proving" that the defendant's misrepresentations "caused the loss for which the plaintiff seeks to recover." §78u-4(b)(4).

The statute thereby makes clear Congress' intent to permit private securities fraud actions for recovery where, but only where, plaintiffs adequately allege and prove the traditional elements of causation and loss. We need not, and do not, consider other proximate cause or loss-related questions.

Id. at 339–346.

The Supreme Court decision in *Dura* was notable for its close reliance on common law concepts and for how limited its impact is likely to be on future securities class actions. While the courts rarely, if ever, have so linked the federal securities laws to common law precedents, the result here is unexceptional. The question is not must the plaintiff plead and prove that the defendant was responsible for the plaintiff's loss. But rather, how, does the plaintiff plead and prove such responsibility. Here *Dura* is strikingly limited in its significance.

At its core *Dura* is largely a case about pleading. The Court concluded its analysis by highlighting how little would have been necessary by the plaintiffs to have effectively pled this cause of action:

> Our holding about plaintiffs' need to *prove* proximate causation and economic loss leads us also to conclude that the plaintiffs' complaint here failed adequately to *allege* these requirements. We concede that the Federal Rules of Civil Procedure require only "a short and plain statement of the claim showing that the pleader is entitled to relief." Fed. Rule Civ. Proc. 8(a)(2). And we assume, at least for argument's sake, that neither the Rules nor the securities statutes impose any special further requirement in respect to the pleading of proximate causation or economic loss. But, even so, the "short and plain statement" must provide the defendant with "fair notice of what the plaintiff's claim is and the grounds upon which it rests." *Conley v. Gibson*, 355 U.S. 41, 47 (1957). The complaint before us fails this simple test.
>
> As we have pointed out, the plaintiffs' lengthy complaint contains only one statement that we can fairly read as describing the loss caused by the defendants' "spray device" misrepresentations. That statement says that the plaintiffs "paid artificially inflated prices for Dura's securities" and suffered "damage[s]." App. 139a. The statement implies that the plaintiffs' loss consisted of the "artificially inflated" purchase "prices." The complaint's failure to

claim that Dura's share price fell significantly after the truth became known suggests that the plaintiffs considered the allegation of purchase price inflation alone sufficient. The complaint contains nothing that suggests otherwise.

For reasons set forth in Part II-A, *supra*, however, the "artificially inflated purchase price" is not a relevant economic loss. And the complaint nowhere else provides the defendants with notice of what the relevant economic loss might be or of what the causal connection might be between that loss and the misrepresentation concerning Dura's "spray device."

We concede that ordinary pleading rules are not meant to impose a great burden upon a plaintiff. *Swierkiewicz v. Sorema N.A.*, 534 U.S. 506, 513–515 (2002). But it should not prove burdensome for a plaintiff who has suffered an economic loss to provide a defendant with some indication of the loss and the causal connection that the plaintiff has in mind. At the same time, allowing a plaintiff to forgo giving any indication of the economic loss and proximate cause that the plaintiff has in mind would bring about harm of the very sort the statutes seek to avoid. Cf. H.R. Conf. Rep. No. 104-369, p. 31 (1995) (criticizing "abusive" practices including "the routine filing of lawsuits...with only a faint hope that the discovery process might lead eventually to some plausible cause of action"). It would permit a plaintiff "with a largely groundless claim to simply take up the time of a number of other people, with the right to do so representing an *in terrorem* the settlement value, rather than a reasonably founded hope that the [discovery] process will reveal relevant evidence." *Blue Chip Stamps*, 421 U.S., at 741. Such a rule would tend to transform a private securities action into a partial downside insurance policy.

Id. at 346–348.

In Brown v. Earthboard Sports USA, Inc., 481 F.3d 901, 920 (6th Cir. 2007), the plaintiff satisfied *Dura* in a small private offering by showing that an offering was "wholly fictitious."

In Lattanzio v. Deloitte & Touche, 476 F.3d 147 (2d Cir. 2007), the court held that the plaintiff failed to allege a sufficient connection between an accountant's misstatements and the losses suffered as a result of a bankruptcy when it failed to allege that the misstatement concealed the risk of bankruptcy.

In Ray v. Citigroup Global Mkt., Inc., 482 F.3d 991 (7th Cir. 2007), loss causation could not be established when there was no evidence that a drop in share prices could be attributed to defendants' alleged misrepresentation.

Cf. Glaser v. Enzo Biochem, Inc., 464 F.3d 474 (4th Cir. 2006), *cert. denied*, 549 U.S. 1304 (2007) (dismissing common law fraud claims in reliance on *Dura* causation analysis); Tricontinental Indus. v. PricewaterhouseCoopers, 475 F.3d 824, 842-844 (7th Cir. 2007), *cert. denied*, 128 S. Ct. 357 (similar); Intelligroup Sec. Litig., 488 F. Supp. 2d 670, 681-691 (D.N.J. 2006) (investors failed to plead *Dura* cost causation element), citing the text.

In Teachers' Retirement Sys. of La. v. Hunter, 477 F.3d 162, 186 (4th Cir. 2007), after observing *Dura*'s silence on the issue, the Fourth Circuit held that a plaintiff must plead loss causation with sufficient specificity to enable the court to evaluate whether a necessary causal link exists.

After *Dura*, the Fifth Circuit requires loss causation in order to trigger the fraud-on-the-market presumption. Oscar Private Equity Inv. v. Allegiance Telecom, Inc., 487 F.3d 261, 265 (5th Cir. 2007), held: "[T]he plaintiff [may] recover under the fraud on the market theory if he [can] prove that the defendant's nondisclosure materially affected the market price of the security." In effect this takes the rebuttal of the *Basic v. Levinson* presumption of reliance ("any showing that severs the link between alleged misrepresentation...and the price received (or paid) by the plaintiff") and transforms this into part of the plaintiff's prima facie case.

Judge Dennis dissented: "The majority's decision is, in effect, a breathtaking revision of a securities class action procedure that eviscerates *Basic's* fraud-on-the-market presumption, creates a split from other circuits by requiring mini-trials on the merits of cases of the class certification stage, and effectively overrules legitimately binding circuit precedents." Id. at 272.

Several courts have rejected the reasoning of *Oscar* as a misinterpretation of *Basic*. Lapin v. Goldman Sachs & Co., 2008 Fed. Sec. L. Rep. (CCH) ¶94,842 at 95,516-95,517 (S.D.N.Y. 2008).

In Stark Trading v. Falconbridge Ltd., 552 F.3d 568 (7th Cir. 2009), the court rejected an attempt to assert fraud on the market by plaintiffs who saw through a fraud even if other shareholders were deceived.

In Salomon Analyst Metromedia Litig., 544 F.3d 474 (2d Cir. 2008), the court was unwilling to apply a bright line rule prohibiting application of the *Basic* fraud-on-the-market presumption in a suit against research analysts. The court also held that "no heightened test is needed in the case of research analysts." Id. at 484.

In McCabe v. Ernst & Young, LLP, 494 F.3d 418, 426 (3d Cir. 2007), quoting the text, the court analyzed an atypical §10(b) action:

> [W]here the plaintiff does not simply allege that the price of a publicly-traded security has been affected, the factual predicates of loss causation fall into less of a rigid pattern. For example, the plaintiff corporation in *EP MedSystems* alleged the defendant corporation had violated §10(b) by inducing plaintiff to buy shares in defendant through misrepresentations about *imminent* business opportunities that were actually non-existent....We held the plaintiff's argument it had been "induced to make an investment of $1.4 million which turned out to be worthless" was a sufficient allegation of loss causation to survive a motion to dismiss....And in *Newton*, a putative class of investors sued defendant broker for violating §10(b) by executing trades at stock prices established by an industry-wide system rather than on the reasonably available terms most favorable to plaintiffs.
>
> ...We stated that the difference between (1) the price at which a trade had been executed and (2) the price at which it could reasonably have been executed could be a sufficient showing of loss causation....The ATS Plaintiffs' §10(b) claim is clearly a non-typical one. In return for selling their ATS shares in a private transaction, they received consideration that included unregistered shares of and options for Vertex stock. That the ATS Plaintiffs could not re-sell those shares for a year unless Vertex registered them further distinguished the ATS Plaintiffs from the typical purchaser of publicly-traded securities who claims to have been misled into making the purchase by fraud on the market.

In Merrill Lynch & Co., Inc. v. Allegheny Energy, Inc., 500 F.3d 171, 184 (2d Cir. 2007), the court cited *Dura* in a New York State law case: "[A]ctual loss cannot be shown in the securities context by mere allegation that a plaintiff purchased shares at a price that exceeded their true value."

See also Gilead Sciences Sec. Litig., 536 F.3d 1049 (9th Cir. 2008), *cert. denied*, 129 S. Ct. 1993 (satisfying *Dura* loss causation standard when the complaint sufficiently alleged a causal relationship between (1) the increase in sales resulting from the off-label marketing, (2) a warning letter's effect on orders, and (3) the warning letter's effect on the defendant's stock price).

In Metzler Inv. GMBH v. Corinthian Colleges, Inc., 540 F.3d 1049, 1062-1065 (9th Cir. 2008), the court applied *Dura* and held that a plaintiff's complaint must set forth allegations that, if assumed true, are sufficient to provide the defendant with some indication that the drop in the defendant's stock price was causally related to the defendant's misstatements. A drop in stock price before a misstatement will not suffice.

In Williams Sec. Litig. — WCG Subclass, 558 F.3d 1130 (10th Cir. 2009), following *Dura*: "The plaintiff bears the burden of showing that his losses were attributable to the revelation of the fraud and not the myriad other factors that affect a company's stock price. Without showing a causal connection that specifically links losses to misrepresentations, he cannot succeed." Id. at 1137.

(ii) *Damages and Rescission*

P. 1286 n.289, end note. A finding of liability can be found without an award of damages. Miller v. Asensio & Co., Inc., 364 F.3d 223 (4th Cir. 2004).

See also Media Gen., Inc. v. Tomlin, 532 F.3d 854, 859-860 (D.C. Cir. 2008), rejecting damages theory as speculative.

5. INVESTMENT COMPANY ACT OF 1940

P. 1303 n.366, end note. In Bellikoff v. Eaton Vance, 481 F.3d 110 (2d Cir. 2007), the court held that (1) no private rights of action exist under §§34(b), 36(a), and 48(a) of the 1940 Act and (2) claims brought under §§36(a) and 48(a) must be brought derivatively.

Cf. Amron v. Morgan Stanley Inv. Advisors, Inc., 464 F.3d 338, 344 (2d Cir. 2006) (Section 36(b) claim dismissed when plaintiffs failed to plead that defendants' fund's performance "is appreciably worse than comparable funds").

In Jones v. Harris Assoc., L.P., 527 F.3d 627 (7th Cir. 2008), *cert. granted*, 129 S. Ct. 1579, Judge Easterbrook, writing for a unanimous panel in the Seventh Circuit, rejected the *Gartenberg* factors and propounded a strikingly different approach to 36(b):

> ...[W]e are skeptical about *Gartenberg* because it relies too little on markets. And this is not the first time we have suggested that *Gartenberg* is wanting. See Green v. Nuveen Advisory Corp., 295 F.3d 738, 743 n.8 (7th Cir. 2002)....
>
> Having had another chance to study this question, we now disapprove the *Gartenberg* approach. A fiduciary duty differs from rate regulation. A fiduciary must make full disclosure and play no tricks but is not subject to a cap on compensation. The trustees (and in the end investors, who vote with their feet and dollars), rather than a judge or jury, determine how much advisory services are worth.
>
> Second 36(b) does not say that fees must be *reasonable* in relation to a judicially created standard. It says instead that the adviser has a fiduciary duty. That is a familiar word; to use it is to summon up the law of trusts. Cf. Firestone Tire & Rubber Co. v. Bruch, 489 U.S. 101...(1989). And the rule in trust law is straightforward: A trustee owes an obligation of candor in negotiation, and honesty in performance, but may negotiate in his own interest and accept what the settlor or governance institution agrees to pay. Restatement (Second) of Trusts §242 & comment f. When the trust instrument is silent about compensation, the trustee may petition a court for an award, and then the court will ask what is *reasonable*; but when the settlor or the persons charged with the trust's administration make a decision, it is conclusive. John H. Langbein, The Contractarian Basis of the Law of Trusts, 105 Yale L.J. 625 (1995)....
>
> ...Judicial price-setting does not accompany fiduciary duties. Section 36(b) does not call for a departure from this norm....
>
> Federal securities laws, of which the Investment Company Act is one component, work largely by requiring disclosure and then

CIVIL LIABILITY   P. 1310

allowing price to be set by competition in which investors make their own choices. Plaintiffs do not contend that Harris Associates pulled the wool over the eyes of the disinterested trustees or otherwise hindered their ability to negotiate a favorable price for advisory services. The fees are not hidden from investors — and the Oakmark funds' net return has attracted new investment rather than driving investors away. As §36(b) does not make the federal judiciary a rate regulator, after the fashion of the Federal Energy Regulatory Commission, the judgment of the district court is affirmed.

Id. at 632–635.

The Supreme Court subsequently granted *certiorari* in Jones v. Harris Assoc., 129 S. Ct. 1579 (2009).

Cf. Gallus v. Ameriprise Fin., Inc., 561 F.3d 816 (8th Cir. 2009), generally following *Gartenberg* and rejecting *Jones*, but highlighting at 823:

> At the same time, however, we think that *Jones* highlights a flaw in the way many courts have applied *Gartenberg*. The *Gartenberg* case demonstrates one way in which a fund adviser can breach its fiduciary duty; but it is not the only way...
>
> We believe that the proper approach to §36(b) is one that looks to both the adviser's conduct during negotiation and the end result.

The purpose of the dual look, as applied in *Gallus*, is to avoid creating a "safe harbor of exorbitance" when a fee was not egregiously out of line with industry norms.

D. GENERAL PROVISIONS

1. SECONDARY LIABILITY

a. Controlling Persons

P. 1310 n.16, end note. In Suprema Specialties, Inc. Sec. Litig., 438 F.3d 256, 284–286 (3d Cir. 2006), the court held that in

P. 1310

a §15 or §20 case there is no requirement that the controlled person be named as a defendant to impose liability upon the controlling persons. The plaintiff need only establish the controlled person's liability in order to bring suit against the controlled person.

In SEC v. J.W. Barclay & Co., Inc., 442 F.3d 834, 841 (3d Cir. 2006), the court ruled:

> The plain language of §20(a) supports our holding that the SEC had a claim for payment from Bruno under §20(a) because Bruno was jointly and severally liable to the SEC for a debt in the amount of Barclay's unpaid penalty. In order for Bruno to be jointly and severally liable to the SEC under §20(a): (1) the SEC has to be a person; (2) to whom the controlled person, Barclay, was liable; (3) as a result of some act or acts constituting a violation or cause of action under any provision of the Exchange Act or any rule or regulation thereunder.

Cf. Brown v. Earthboard Sports, USA, Inc., 481 F.3d 901, 921–922 (6th Cir. 2007), where the defendant satisfied the §20(b) safe harbor by claiming it had no actual knowledge of, nor any reason to suspect, his controlled person's alleged fraud. "No evidence to the contrary has been adduced." Id. at 922.

In SEC v. Hawk, 2007 Fed. Sec. L. Rep. (CCH) ¶94,461 (D. Nev. 2007), the court correctly concluded that the SEC can bring an enforcement action under §20(a), rejecting SEC v. Stringer, 2003 U.S. Dist. LEXIS 25,523 (D. Or. 2003). The court also correctly concluded that the Commission is not required to join the allegedly controlled entity to initiate a suit.

In Johnson v. Alijan, 490 F.3d 778, 781 (9th Cir. 2007), *cert. denied*, 128 S. Ct. 1650, the court held: "Claims under Section 20A are derivative and therefore require an independent violation of the Exchange Act." By this the court reasoned, "the term *violates* ordinarily is understood to mean that a person has satisfied the essential elements of the proscribed action regardless of whether an action is commenced within the applicable statute of limitations." Id. at 781–782. "Accordingly, we are persuaded that the plain meaning of the term *violates* does not require that the predicate claim be filed within its own period of limitations." Id. at 783.

b. *Respondeat Superior*

P. 1313, after 1st full par. In Makor Issues & Rights, Ltd. v. Tellabs, 513 F.3d 702, 708 (7th Cir. 2008), Judge Posner ruled that even after *Central Bank*, "the doctrines of *respondeat superior* and apparent authority remain applicable to [Rule 10b-5] suits for securities fraud."

c. Aiding and Abetting

P. 1332 n.43, end note. In Stoneridge Inv. Partners, LLC v. Scientific-Atlanta, Inc., 552 U.S. 148 (2008), a 5–3 majority of the Supreme Court definitively concluded that the implied private right of action under §10(b) and Rule 10b-5 does not reach customer and supplier companies when investors did not rely upon their statements or representations. As he had in *Central Bank*, Justice Kennedy wrote for the majority, stating in part:

> This class action suit by investors was filed against Charter Communications, Inc....
>
> Charter issued the financial statements and the securities in question. It was a named defendant along with some of its executives and Arthur Andersen LLP, Charter's independent auditor during the period in question. We are concerned, though, with two other defendants, respondents here. Respondents are Scientific-Atlanta, Inc., and Motorola, Inc. They were suppliers, and later customers, of Charter.
>
> For purposes of this proceeding, we take these facts, alleged by petitioner, to be true. Charter, a cable operator, engaged in a variety of fraudulent practices so its quarterly reports would meet Wall Street expectations for cable subscriber growth and operating cash flow. The fraud included misclassification of its customer base; delayed reporting of terminated customers; improper capitalization of costs that should have been shown as expenses; and manipulation of the company's billing cutoff dates to inflate reported revenues. In late 2000, Charter executives realized that, despite these efforts, the company would miss projected operating

cash flow numbers by $15 to $20 million. To help meet the shortfall, Charter decided to alter its existing arrangements with respondents, Scientific-Atlanta and Motorola....

Respondents supplied Charter with the digital cable converter (set top) boxes that Charter furnished to its customers. Charter arranged to overpay respondents $20 for each set top box it purchased until the end of the year, with the understanding that respondents would return the overpayment by purchasing advertising from Charter. The transactions, it is alleged, had no economic substance; but, because Charter would then record the advertising purchases as revenue and capitalize its purchase of the set top boxes, in violation of generally accepted accounting principles, the transactions would enable Charter to fool its auditor into approving a financial statement showing it met projected revenue and operating cash flow numbers. Respondents agreed to the arrangement.

So that Arthur Andersen would not discover the link between Charter's increased payments for the boxes and the advertising purchases, the companies drafted documents to make it appear the transactions were unrelated and conducted in the ordinary course of business. Following a request from Charter, Scientific-Atlanta sent documents to Charter stating — falsely — that it had increased production costs. It raised the price for set top boxes for the rest of 2000 by $20 per box. As for Motorola, in a written contract Charter agreed to purchase from Motorola a specific number of set top boxes and pay liquidated damages of $20 for each unit it did not take. The contract was made with the expectation Charter would fail to purchase all the units and pay Motorola the liquidated damages.

To return the additional money from the set top box sales, Scientific-Atlanta and Motorola signed contracts with Charter to purchase advertising time for a price higher than fair value. The new set top box agreements were backdated to make it appear that they were negotiated a month before the advertising agreements. The backdating was important to convey the impression that the negotiations were unconnected, a point Arthur Andersen considered necessary for separate treatment of the transactions. Charter recorded the advertising payments to inflate revenue and operating cash flow by approximately $17 million. The inflated number was shown on financial statements filed with the Securities and Exchange Commission (SEC) and reported to the public.

CIVIL LIABILITY   P. 1332

Respondents had no role in preparing or disseminating Charter's financial statements. And their own financial statements booked the transactions as a wash, under generally accepted accounting principles. It is alleged respondents knew or were in reckless disregard of Charter's intention to use the transactions to inflate its revenues and knew the resulting financial statements issued by Charter would be relied upon by research analysts and investors.

Petitioner filed a securities fraud class action on behalf of purchasers of Charter stock alleging that, by participating in the transactions, respondents violated §10(b) of the Securities Exchange Act of 1934 and SEC Rule 10b-5.

Id. at 766–767.

The Court granted *certiorari* to resolve a conflict among the circuits as to whether an injured investor may rely upon §10(b) to recover from a party that neither makes a public misstatement nor violates a duty to disclose but does participate in a scheme to violate §10(b). Cf. the decision below, Charter Communications, Inc., Sec. Litig., 443 F.3d 987 (8th Cir. 2006) (dismissing the complaint when at most respondents aided and abetted a misstatement), with Simpson v. AOL Time Warner Inc., 452 F.3d 1040 (9th Cir. 2006) and Regents of Univ. of Cal. v. Credit Suisse First Boston (USA), Inc., 482 F.3d 372 (5th Cir. 2007). In rejecting scheme liability, Justice Kennedy explained:

> In *Central Bank*, the Court determined that §10(b) liability did not extend to aiders and abettors. The Court found the scope of §10(b) to be delimited by the text, which makes no mention of aiding and abetting liability. 511 U.S., at 177. The Court doubted the implied §10(b) action should extend to aiders and abettors when none of the express causes of action in the securities Acts included that liability. Id., at 180. It added the following:
>
>> Were we to allow the aiding and abetting action proposed in this case, the defendant could be liable without any showing that the plaintiff relied upon the aider and abettor's statements or actions. See also *Chiarella* [*v. United States*, 445 U.S. 222, 228 (1980)]. Allowing plaintiffs to circumvent the

477

P. 1332 2010 SUPPLEMENT

reliance requirement would disregard the careful limits on 10b-5 recovery mandated by our earlier cases. Ibid.

The decision in *Central Bank* led to calls for Congress to create an express cause of action for aiding and abetting within the Securities Exchange Act. Then-SEC Chairman Arthur Levitt, testifying before the Senate Securities Subcommittee, cited *Central Bank* and recommended that aiding and abetting liability in private claims be established. S. Hearing No. 103-759, p. 13–14 (1994). Congress did not follow this course. Instead, in §104 of the Private Securities Litigation Reform Act of 1995 (*PSLRA*), 109 Stat. 757, it directed prosecution of aiders and abettors by the SEC. 15 U.S.C. §78t(e).

The §10(b) implied private right of action does not extend to aiders and abettors. The conduct of a secondary actor must satisfy each of the elements or preconditions for liability; and we consider whether the allegations here are sufficient to do so....

The Court of Appeals concluded petitioner had not alleged that respondents engaged in a deceptive act within the reach of the §10(b) private right of action, noting that only misstatements, omissions by one who has a duty to disclose, and manipulative trading practices (where *manipulative* is a term of art, see, e.g., *Santa Fe Industries, Inc. v. Green*, 430 U.S. 462, 476–477 (1977)) are deceptive within the meaning of the rule. 443 F.3d at 992. If this conclusion were read to suggest there must be a specific oral or written statement before there could be liability under §10(b) or Rule 10b-5, it would be erroneous. Conduct itself can be deceptive, as respondents concede. In this case, moreover, respondents' course of conduct included both oral and written statements, such as the backdated contracts agreed to by Charter and respondents.

A different interpretation of the holding from the Court of Appeals opinion is that the court was stating only that any deceptive statement or act respondents made was not actionable because it did not have the requisite proximate relation to the investors' harm. That conclusion is consistent with our own determination that respondents' acts or statements were not relied upon by the investors and that, as a result, liability cannot be imposed upon respondents....

Reliance by the plaintiff upon the defendants' deceptive acts is an essential element of the §10(b) private cause of action. It ensures that, for liability to arise, the "requisite causal connection between a defendant's misrepresentation and a plaintiff's injury" exists as a predicate for liability. *Basic Inc. v. Levinson*, 485 U.S. 224, 243

(1988); see also *Affiliated Ute Citizens of Utah v. United States*, 406 U.S. 128, 154 (1972) (requiring *causation in fact*). We have found a rebuttable presumption of reliance in two different circumstances. First, if there is an omission of a material fact by one with a duty to disclose, the investor to whom the duty was owed need not provide specific proof of reliance. Id., at 153–154. Second, under the fraud-on-the-market doctrine, reliance is presumed when the statements at issue become public. The public information is reflected in the market price of the security. Then it can be assumed that an investor who buys or sells stock at the market price relies upon the statement. *Basic*, supra, at 247.

Neither presumption applies here. Respondents had no duty to disclose; and their deceptive acts were not communicated to the public. No members of the investing public had knowledge, either actual or presumed, of respondents' deceptive acts during the relevant times. Petitioner, as a result, cannot show reliance upon any of the respondents' actions except in an indirect chain that we find too remote for liability....

Invoking what some courts call *scheme liability*, see, e.g., *In re Enron Corp. Sec. v. Enron Corp.*, 439 F. Supp. 2d 692, 723 (S.D. Tex. 2006), petitioner nonetheless seeks to impose liability on respondents even absent a public statement. In our view this approach does not answer the objection that petitioner did not in fact rely upon respondents' own deceptive conduct.

Liability is appropriate, petitioner contends, because respondents engaged in conduct with the purpose and effect of creating a false appearance of material fact to further a scheme to misrepresent Charter revenue. The argument is that the financial statement Charter released to the public was a natural and expected consequence of respondents' deceptive acts; had respondents not assisted Charter, Charter's auditor would not have been fooled, and the financial statement would have been a more accurate reflection of Charter's financial condition. That causal link is sufficient, petitioner argues, to apply *Basic's* presumption of reliance to respondents' acts. See, e.g., *Simpson*, 452 F.3d, at 1051–1052; *In re Parmalat Securities Litigation*, 376 F. Supp. 2d 472, 509 (S.D.N.Y. 2005).

In effect petitioner contends that in an efficient market investors rely not only upon the public statements relating to a security but also upon the transactions those statements reflect. Were this concept of reliance to be adopted, the implied cause of action would

P. 1332

reach the whole marketplace in which the issuing company does business; and there is no authority for this rule.

As stated above, reliance is tied to causation, leading to the inquiry whether respondents' acts were immediate or remote to the injury. In considering petitioner's arguments, we note §10(b) provides that the deceptive act must be "in connection with the purchase or sale of any security." 15 U.S.C. §78j(b). Though this phrase in part defines the statute's coverage rather than causation (and so we do not evaluate the *in connection with* requirement of §10(b) in this case), the emphasis on a purchase or sale of securities does provide some insight into the deceptive acts that concerned the enacting Congress....In all events we conclude respondents' deceptive acts, which were not disclosed to the investing public, are too remote to satisfy the requirement of reliance. It was Charter, not respondents, that misled its auditor and filed fraudulent financial statements; nothing respondents did made it necessary or inevitable for Charter to record the transactions as it did.

The petitioner invokes the private cause of action under §10(b) and seeks to apply it beyond the securities markets — the realm of financing business — to purchase and supply contracts — the realm or ordinary business operations. The latter realm is governed, for the most part, by state law. It is true that if business operations are used, as alleged here, to affect securities markets, the SEC enforcement power may reach the culpable actors. It is true as well that a dynamic, free economy presupposes a high degree of integrity in all of its parts, an integrity that must be underwritten by rules enforceable in fair, independent, accessible courts. Were the implied cause of action to be extended to the practices described here, however, there would be a risk that the federal power would be used to invite litigation beyond the immediate sphere of securities litigation and in areas already governed by functioning and effective state-law guarantees....Though §10(b) is "not 'limited to preserving the integrity of the securities markets,'" *Bankers Life*, 404 U.S., at 12, it does not reach all commercial transactions that are fraudulent and affect the price of a security in some attenuated way.

These considerations answer as well the argument that if this were a common-law action for fraud there could be a finding of reliance. Even if the assumption is correct, it is not controlling. Section 10(b) does not incorporate common-law fraud into federal law. See, e.g., *SEC v. Zandford*, 535 U.S. 813, 820 (2002) ("[Section

10(b)] must not be construed so broadly as to convert every common-law fraud that happens to involve securities into a violation"); *Central Bank,* 511 U.S., at 184 ("Even assuming...a deeply rooted background of aiding and abetting tort liability, it does not follow that Congress intended to apply that kind of liability to the private causes of action in the securities Acts"); see also *Dura,* 544 U.S., at 341. Just as §10(b) "is surely badly strained when construed to provide a cause of action...to the world at large," *Blue Chip Stamps v. Manor Drug Stores,* 421 U.S. 723, 733, n.5 (1975), it should not be interpreted to provide a private cause of action against the entire marketplace in which the issuing company operates.

Petitioner's theory, moreover, would put an unsupportable interpretation on Congress' specific response to *Central Bank* in §104 of the PSLRA. Congress amended the securities laws to provide for limited coverage of aiders and abettors. Aiding and abetting liability is authorized in actions brought by the SEC but not by private parties. See 15 U.S.C. §78t(e). Petitioner's view of primary liability makes any aider and abettor liable under §10(b) if he or she committed a deceptive act in the process of providing assistance. Reply Brief for Petitioner 6, n.2; Tr. of Oral Arg. 24. Were we to adopt this construction of §10(b), it would revive in substance the implied cause of action against all aiders and abettors except those who committed no deceptive act in the process of facilitating the fraud; and we would undermine Congress' determination that this class of defendants should be pursued by the SEC and not by private litigants....

This is not a case in which Congress has enacted a regulatory statute and then has accepted, over a long period of time, broad judicial authority to define substantive standards of conduct and liability. Cf. *Leegin Creative Leather Products v. PSKS, Inc.,* 551 U.S. 877 (2007) (slip op., at 19–20). And in accord with the nature of the cause of action at issue here, we give weight to Congress' amendment to the Act restoring aiding and abetting liability in certain cases but not others. The amendment, in our view, supports the conclusion that there is no liability.

The practical consequences of an expansion, which the Court has considered appropriate to examine in circumstances like these, see *Virginia Bankshares, Inc. v. Sandberg,* 501 U.S. 1083, 1104–1105 (1991); *Blue Chip,* 421 U.S., at 737, provide a further reason to reject petitioner's approach. In *Blue Chip,* the Court noted that extensive discovery and the potential for uncertainty and disruption in a lawsuit allow plaintiffs with weak claims to extort settlements from innocent companies. Id., at 740–741. Adoption of petitioner's approach would expose a new class of defendants to these risks. As noted in *Central Bank*, contracting parties might find it necessary to protect against these threats, raising the costs of doing business. See 511 U.S., at 189. Overseas firms with no other exposure to our securities laws could be deterred from doing business here. See Brief for Organization for International Investment et al. as Amici Curiae 17–20. This, in turn, may raise the cost of being a publicly traded company under our law and shift securities offerings away from domestic capital market. Brief for NASDAQ Stock Market, Inc., et al. as Amici Curiae 12–14....

Secondary actors are subject to criminal penalties, see, e.g., 15 U.S.C. §78ff and civil enforcement by the SEC, see, e.g., §78t(e). The enforcement power is not toothless. Since September 30, 2002, SEC enforcement actions have collected over $10 billion in disgorgement and penalties, much of it for distribution to injured investors. See SEC, 2007 Performance and Accountability Report, p. 26, http://www.sec.gov/about/secpar2007.shtml (as visited Jan. 2, 2008, and available in Clerk of Court's case file). And in this case both parties agree that criminal penalties are a strong deterrent. See Brief for Respondents 48; Reply Brief for Petitioner 17. In addition some state securities laws permit state authorities to seek fines and restitution from aiders and abettors. See, e.g., Del. Code Ann., Tit. 6, §7325 (2005). All secondary actors, furthermore, are not necessarily immune from private suit. The securities statutes provide an express private right of action against accountants and underwriters in certain circumstances, see 15 U.S.C. §77k, and the implied right of action in §10(b) continues to cover secondary actors who commit primary violations. *Central Bank*, supra, at 191.

Here respondents were acting in concert with Charter in the ordinary course as suppliers and, as matters then evolved in the not so ordinary course, as customers. Unconventional as the arrangement was, it took place in the marketplace for goods and services, not in the investment sphere. Charter was free to do as it chose in preparing its books, conferring with its auditor, and preparing and then issuing its financial statements. In these circumstances the investors cannot be said to have relied upon any of respondents' deceptive acts in the decision to purchase or sell securities; and as the requisite reliance cannot be shown, respondents have no liability to petitioner under the implied right of action. This conclusion is consistent with the narrow dimensions we must give to a right of action Congress did not authorize when it first enacted the statute and did not expand when it revisited the law.

The judgment of the Court of Appeals is affirmed, and the case is remanded for further proceedings consistent with this opinion.

Id. at 768–774.

Justice Stevens, joined by Justices Souter and Ginsburg, dissented:

> The Court seems to assume that respondents' alleged conduct could subject them to liability in an enforcement proceeding initiated by the Government, *ante*, at 15, but nevertheless concludes that they are not subject to liability in a private action brought by injured investors because they are, at most, guilty of aiding and abetting a violation of §10(b), rather than an actual violation of the statute. While that conclusion results in an affirmance of the judgment of the Court of Appeals, it rests on a rejection of that court's reasoning. Furthermore, while the Court frequently refers to petitioner's attempt to *expand* the implied cause of action — a conclusion that begs the question of the contours of that cause of action — it is today's decision that results in a significant departure from *Central Bank*.
>
> The Court's conclusion that no violation of §10(b) giving rise to a private right of action has been alleged in this case rests on two faulty premises: (1) the Court's overly broad reading of *Central Bank*, and (2) the view that reliance requires a kind of super-causation — a view contrary to both the Securities and Exchange Commission's (SEC) position in a recent Ninth Circuit case *Simpson v. AOL Time Warner, Inc.* and our holding in *Basic Inc. v. Levinson*, 485 U.S. 224 (1988). These two points merit separate discussion.
>
> The Court of Appeals incorrectly based its decision on the view that "[a] device or contrivance is not *deceptive*, within the meaning of §10(b), absent some misstatement or a failure to disclose by one who has a duty to disclose." *In re Charter Communications, Inc., Securities Litigation*, 443 F.3d 987, 992 (CA8 2006). The Court correctly explains why the statute covers nonverbal as well as verbal deceptive conduct. *Ante*, at 7. The allegations in this case—that respondents produced documents falsely claiming costs had risen and signed contracts they knew to be backdated in order to disguise the connection between the increase in costs and the purchase of

advertising — plainly describe *deceptive devices* under any standard reading of the phrase.

What the Court fails to recognize is that this case is critically different from *Central Bank* because the bank in that case did not engage in any deceptive act and, therefore, did not *itself* violate §10(b). The Court sweeps aside any distinction, remarking that holding respondents liable would "revive the implied cause of action against all aiders and abettors except those who committed no deceptive act in the process of facilitating the fraud." *Ante*, at 12. But the fact that Central Bank engaged in no deceptive conduct whatsoever — in other words, that it was at most an aider and abettor — sharply distinguishes *Central Bank* from cases that do involve allegations of such conduct....

The Court's next faulty premise is that petitioner is required to allege that Scientific-Atlanta and Motorola made it "necessary or inevitable for Charter to record the transactions in the way it did," *ante*, at 10, in order to demonstrate reliance. Because the Court of Appeals did not base its holding on reliance grounds, see 443 F.3d at 992, the fairest course to petitioner would be for the majority to remand to the Court of Appeals to determine whether petitioner properly alleged reliance, under a correct view of what §10(b) covers. Because the Court chooses to rest its holding on an absence of reliance, a response is required.

In *Basic Inc.*, 485 U.S., at 243, we stated that "reliance provides the requisite causal connection between a defendant's misrepresentation and a plaintiff's injury." The Court's view of the causation required to demonstrate reliance is unwarranted and without precedent.

In *Basic Inc.*, we held that the *fraud-on-the-market* theory provides adequate support for a presumption in private securities actions that shareholders (or former shareholders) in publicly traded companies rely on public material misstatements that affect the price of the company's stock. Id. at 248. The holding in *Basic* is surely a sufficient response to the argument that a complaint alleging that deceptive acts which had a material effect on the price of a listed stock should be dismissed because the plaintiffs were not subjectively aware of the deception at the time of the securities' purchase or sale. This Court has not held that investors must be aware of the specific deceptive act which violates §10b to demonstrate reliance.

The Court is right that a fraud-on-the-market presumption coupled with its view on causation would not support petitioner's view of reliance. The fraud-on-the-market presumption helps investors who cannot demonstrate that they, *themselves,* relied on fraud that reached the market. But that presumption says nothing about causation from the other side: what an individual or corporation must do in order to have *caused* the misleading information that reached the market. The Court thus has it backwards when it first addresses the fraud-on-the-market presumption, rather than the causation required. See, *ante,* at 8. The argument is not that the fraud-on-the-market presumption is enough standing alone, but that a correct view of causation coupled with the presumption would allow petitioner to plead reliance.

Lower courts have correctly stated that the causation necessary to demonstrate reliance is not a difficult hurdle to clear in a private right of action under §10(b). Reliance is often equated with *"transaction causation." Dura Pharmaceuticals, Inc. v. Broudo,* 544 U.S. 336, 341, 342 (2005). Transaction causation, in turn, is often defined as requiring an allegation that but for the deceptive act, the plaintiff would not have entered into the securities transaction. See, e.g., *Lentell v. Merrill Lynch & Co.,* 396 F.3d 161, 172 (CA2 2005); *Binder v. Gillespie,* 184 F.3d 1059, 1065–1066 (CA9 1999).

Even if but-for causation, standing alone, is too weak to establish reliance, petitioner has also alleged that respondents proximately caused Charter's misstatement of income; petitioner has alleged that respondents knew their deceptive acts would be the basis for statements that would influence the market price of Charter stock on which shareholders would rely. Second Amended Consolidated Class Action Complaint Pp. 8, 98, 100, 109, App. 19a, 55a–56a, 59a. Thus, respondents' acts had the foreseeable effect of causing petitioner to engage in the relevant securities transactions. The Restatement (Second) of Torts §533, pp. 72–73 (1977), provides that "the maker of a fraudulent misrepresentation is subject to liability... if the misrepresentation, although not made directly to the other, is made to a third person and the maker intends or has reason to expect that its terms will be repeated or its substance communicated to the other." The sham transactions described in the complaint in this case had the same effect on Charter's profit and loss statement as a false entry directly on its books that included $17 million of gross revenues that had not been received. And respondents are alleged to have known that the outcome of their fraudulent transactions would be communicated to investors.

P. 1332

The Court's view of reliance is unduly stringent and unmoored from authority. The Court first says that if the petitioner's concept of reliance is adopted the implied cause of action "would reach the whole marketplace in which the issuing company does business." *Ante*, at 9. The answer to that objection is, of course, that liability only attaches when the company doing business with the issuing company has *itself* violated §10(b). The Court next relies on what it views as a strict division between the *realm of financing business* and the *ordinary business operations*. *Ante*, at 10. But petitioner's position does not merge the two: A corporation engaging in a business transaction with a partner who transmits false information to the market is only liable where the corporation *itself* violates §10(b). Such a rule does not invade the province of *ordinary* business transactions.

The majority states that "section 10(b) does not incorporate common-law fraud into federal law," citing *SEC v. Zandford*, 535 U.S. 813 (2002). *Ante*, at 11. Of course, not every common-law fraud action that happens to touch upon securities is an action under §10(b), but the Court's opinion in *Zandford* did not purport to jettison all reference to common-law fraud doctrines from §10(b) cases. In fact, our prior cases explained that to the extent that "the antifraud provisions of the securities laws are not coextensive with common-law doctrines of fraud," it is because common-law fraud doctrines might be too restrictive. *Herman & MacLean v. Huddleston*, 459 U.S. 375, 388–389 (1983). "Indeed, an important purpose of the federal securities statutes was to rectify perceived deficiencies in the available common-law protections by establishing higher standards of conduct in the securities industry." *Id.*, at 389. I, thus, see no reason to abandon common-law approaches to causation in §10(b) cases.

Finally, the Court relies on the course of action Congress adopted after our decision in *Central Bank* to argue that siding with petitioner on reliance would run contrary to congressional intent. Senate hearings on *Central Bank* were held within one month of our decision. Less than one year later, Senators Dodd and Domenici introduced S.240, which became the Private Securities Litigation Reform Act of 1995 (*PSLRA*), 109 Stat. 737. Congress stopped short of undoing *Central Bank* entirely, instead adopting a compromise which restored the authority of the SEC to enforce aiding and abetting liability. A private right of action based on aiding and abetting violations of §10(b) was not, however, included in the PSLRA, despite support from Senator Dodd and members of the Senate Subcommittee on Securities. This compromise surely provides no support for extending *Central Bank* in order to immunize an undefined class of actual violators of §10(b) from liability in private litigation. Indeed, as Members of Congress — including those who rejected restoring a private cause of action against aiders and abettors — made clear, private litigation under §10(b) continues to play a vital role in protecting the integrity of our securities markets. That Congress chose not to restore the aiding and abetting liability removed by *Central Bank* does not mean that Congress wanted to exempt from liability the broader range of conduct that today's opinion excludes.

The Court is concerned that such liability would deter overseas firms from doing business in the United States or "shift securities offerings away from domestic capital markets." *Ante*, at 13. But liability for those who violate §10(b) "will not harm American competitiveness; in fact, investor faith in the safety and integrity of our markets *is* their strength. The fact that our markets are the safest in the world has helped make them the strongest in the world." Brief for Former SEC Commissioners as Amici Curiae 9.

Id. at 774–779.

Stoneridge establishes some very firm limits to §10(b) litigation. First, secondary defendants can only be reached when there is reliance upon their statements or representations. Cf. SEC v. Thielbar, 2007 Fed. Sec. L. Rep. (CCH) ¶94,436 at 93,075 (S.D.N.Y. 2007) (distinguishing *Charter*, 443 F.3d at 990–992, when defendant was alleged to have provided false information which he knew would be incorporated into SEC filings). While the majority does agree that "conduct itself can be deceptive" and can include oral as well as written statements such as Charter's background contracts, see id. at 769, there is a requirement that the alleged misconduct be communicated or required to be communicated to the public. While this is a clear limit to §10(b), it is a questionable one. The misconduct here involved the deliberate falsification of records by two suppliers to facilitate a financial fraud that otherwise presumably could not have occurred. There seems little risk in such circumstances that Rule 10b-5 "would reach the whole marketplace in which the issuing company does business" and a reasonable probability that fewer financial frauds would occur.

P. 1332

Second, not just scheme liability, but private cases involving conspiracy and *respondeat superior*, to the extent they had life after *Central Bank*, see supra ch. 11.D.1.b and infra ch. 11.D.1.d, now appear to be dead.

Third, while the Court's confidence in SEC enforcement actions as a policy matter is not begging the question, it is troublesome to see the Court base its decision in part on needs as frail as: "Overseas firms with no other exposure to our securities laws could be deterred from doing business here," citing an *amicus* brief of the Organization for International Investment, with no further discussion of evidence either way. Cf. Seligman, The Implications of *Central Bank*, 49 Bus. Law. 1429, 1433 (1994) (criticizing policy discussion in the case as more "an articulation of a judicial mood than legal analysis"). It is also plausible that overseas firms could find the United States more attractive because of the integrity of our markets.

In United States v. Finnerty, 533 F.3d 143, 148-149 (2d Cir. 2008), the court followed *Stoneridge's* holding: "Conduct itself can be deceptive" and liability under Rule 10b-5 does not require "a specific oral or written statement." But the court declined to extend Rule 10b-5 to a specialist's interpositioning when there was no evidence that the defendant "communicated anything to his customers, let alone anything false."

In SEC v. Wolfson, 539 F.3d 1249, 1258-1260 (10th Cir. 2008), the court declined to adopt a requirement that a relevant misrepresentation be attributed to the secondary actor at the time it is disseminated to investors. The court followed Anixter v. HomeStake Prod. Co., 77 F.3d 1215, 1226 (10th Cir. 1996): "[I]n order for accountants to [be primarily liable under §10(b)], they must themselves make a false or misleading statement (or omission) that they know or should know will reach potential investors."

In SEC v. Tambone, 550 F.3d 106 (1st Cir. 2008), the court enumerated the *Stoneridge* elements of a private Rule 10b-5 action, by explaining that the SEC "need not allege any of the elements required to establish a direct link between a defendant's misrepresentation and an investor's injury — including reliance by the investor on an explicit misstatement, economic loss and loss causation." Id. at 130.

CIVIL LIABILITY P. 1335

In *Tambone*, the court also followed Dolphin & Bradbury, Inc. v. SEC, 512 F.3d 634, 640-641 (D.C. Cir. 2008), and held under Rule 10b-5 that an underwriter could be held primarily liable when "an underwriter impliedly makes a statement of its own to potential investors that it has a reasonable basis to believe that the information contained in the prospectus it uses to offer or sell securities is truthful and complete."

In J&R Mrkt. SEP v. General Motors Corp., 549 F.3d 384 (6th Cir. 2008), the court declined to extend the Item 303(a) requirement to GMAC to disclose known trends regarding a registrant's liquidity to reach a multibillion dollar pension liability of a GM subsidiary when the complaint did not contend that GMAC had any knowledge about this liability.

In United States v. Royer, 549 F.3d 886, 899-900 (2d Cir. 2008), the court followed *Stoneridge* and construed Rule 10b-5 as extending to so-called constructive frauds, including manipulation, whether by making false statements or otherwise. Here Rule 10b-5 was held to reach front running by an investment adviser who had created a relationship that included a specific warranty he would not front run.

2. DEFENSES

a. Statutes of Limitations

(i) *Express Liabilities*

P. 1335 n.49, end note. In BP Am. Prod. Co. v. Burton, 549 U.S 84 (2006), the Supreme Court held that 28 U.S.C.S. §2415(a), which sets out a six-year statute of limitations for government contract actions, did not apply to administrative payment orders issued by the Department of Interior's Minerals Management Service. "To the extent that any doubts remain regarding the meaning of §2415(a), they are erased by the rule that statutes of limitations are construed narrowly against the government." Id. at 646.

P. 1335 n.50, end note. In P. Stolz Family Partnership L.P. v. Daum, 355 F.3d 92 (2d Cir. 2004), quoting and citing the text, the court followed the vast majority of courts and concluded that the §13 three year statute of limitations begins when a security is first bona fide offered. Id. at 100–106.

P. 1338 n.63, end note. In Litzler v. CC Inv., L.D.C., 362 F.3d 203 (2d Cir. 2004), the court concluded "that the two-year limitations period of Section 16(b) is subject to equitable tolling when a covered party fails to comply with Section 16(a) and that such tolling ends when a potential claimant otherwise receives sufficient notice that short-swing profits were realized by the party covered by Section 16(a)." Id. at 205.

(ii) *Implied Liabilities*

P. 1346 n.92, end note. See also New Eng. Health Care Employees Pension Fund v. Ernst & Young, LLP, 336 F.3d 495 (6th Cir. 2003), *cert. denied*, 540 U.S. 1183 (joining at least seven other circuits in adoption of inquiry notice standard); Newman v. Warnaco Group, Inc., 335 F.3d 187 (2d Cir. 2003) (earnings restatements did not place plaintiff on inquiry notice of fraud); Caprin v. Simon Transp. Serv., Inc., 2003–2004 Fed. Sec. L. Rep. (CCH) ¶92,692 (10th Cir. 2004) (following *Sterlin*); Grippo v. Perazzo, 357 F.3d 1218 (11th Cir. 2004) (inquiry notice required); LaGrasta v. First Union Sec., Inc., 358 F.3d 840 (11th Cir. 2004) (disagreeing that investor put on inquiry notice when article on Smart Money was published); Lentell v. Merrill Lynch & Co., Inc. 396 F.3d 161 (2d Cir. 2005), *cert. denied*, 546 U.S. 935 (declining to dismiss on inquiry notice grounds when there was no "manifest indication that plaintiffs 'could have learned' the facts underpinning their allegations more than a year prior to filing"); Benak v. Alliance Capital Mgmt. L.P., 435 F.3d 396 (3d Cir. 2006) (comparing mutual fund investing to direct investing for purposes of inquiry notice and concluding on facts in this case that even mutual fund investor was on inquiry notice).

For a definitive judgment that inquiry notice began when a specific *Fortune* magazine article was published, see Shah v. Meeker, 435 F.3d 244 (2d Cir. 2006).

Inquiry notice is also relevant to the question of whether a claim filed after November 15, 2002, will be barred because the class was sufficiently on notice before the effective date of the Sarbanes-Oxley Act. Tello v. Dean Witter Reynolds, 410 F.3d 1275 (11th Cir. 2005). The Act does not apply retroactively to revive stale claims. See, e.g., ADC Telecomms., Inc. Sec. Litig., 409 F.3d 974 (8th Cir. 2005).

In WorldCom Sec. Litig., 496 F.3d 245 (2d Cir. 2007), the court held that "the filing of a class action tolls the statute of limitations for all members of the asserted class, regardless of whether they file an individual action before resolution of the question whether the purported class will be certified." Id. at 247. The court relied on American Pipe & Constr. Co. v. Utah, 414 U.S. 538, 514 (1974) ("The commencement of a class action suspends the applicable statute of limitations as to all asserted members of the class").

The *WorldCom* court further held that the tolling required on *American Pipe* not only applies to members of a class on whose behalf a class action is filed but also to class members who file individual suits before class certification is resolved.

In Betz v. Trainer Wortham & Co., Inc., 486 F.3d 590 (9th Cir. 2007), the court held that either actual or inquiry notice are sufficient to invoke the statute of limitations under §10(b). This was the first such holding by the Ninth Circuit in contrast to its District Courts. The Ninth Circuit adopted the inquiry–plus–reasonable diligence test for inquiry notice used in the Tenth Circuit, see Berry v. Valence Tech., Inc., 175 F.3d 699, 704 (9th Cir. 1999), *cert. denied*, 528 U.S. 1019; see also Livid Holdings Ltd. v. Salomon Smith Barney, Inc., 416 F.3d 940, 951 (9th Cir. 2005). In this case, on a summary judgment motion, the court declined to apply the statute of limitations when the plaintiff had received account statements indicating a declining account balance. This alone was insufficient to put the plaintiff on inquiry notice that she had been defrauded. Id. at 593–599.

See also Betz v. Trainer Wortham & Co., Inc., 519 F.3d 863, 870 (9th Cir. 2008), when the court again adopted an inquiry notice standard for §10(b) suits similar to that applied by the Tenth Circuit.

Cf. DeBenedictis v. Merrill Lynch & Co., Inc., 492 F.3d 209, 216 (3d Cir. 2007). A plaintiff in a securities fraud action is put on inquiry notice when a "'reasonable investor of ordinary intelligence would have discovered the information and recognized it as a storm warning.'" [Citing cases.] See also Sudo Properties, Inc. v. Terrebonne Parish, 503 F.3d 371, 376 (5th Cir. 2007) (following *DeBenedictis*).

Judge Easterbrook generalized with respect to equitable tolling or fraudulent concealment in SEC v. Koenig, 557 F.3d 736 (7th Cir. 2009):

> We need not decide when a "claim accrues" for the purpose of §2462 generally, because the nineteenth century recognized a special rule for fraud, a concealed wrong. See, e.g., Bailey v. Glover, 88 U.S. (21 Wall.) 342 (1875); Holmberg v. Armbrecht, 327 U.S. 392 (1946). These days the doctrine is apt to be called equitable tolling, see Cada v. Baxter Healthcare Corp., 920 F.2d 446 (7th Cir. 1990). Whether a court says that a claim for fraud accrues only on its discovery (more precisely, when it *could have been* discovered by a person exercising reasonable diligence) or instead says that the claim accrues with the wrong, but that the statute of limitations is tolled until the fraud's discovery, is unimportant in practice. Either way, a victim of fraud has the full time from the date that the wrong came to light, or would have done had diligence been employed. And the United States is entitled to the benefit of this rule even when it sues to enforce laws that protect the citizenry from fraud, but is not itself a victim. Exploration Co. v. United States, 247 U.S. 435 (1918).

Id. at 739.

In Staehr v. Hartford Fin. Serv. Group, Inc., 547 F.3d 406 (2d Cir. 2008), the court reviewed the development of the *storm warnings* concept under the inquiry notice doctrine beginning with Dodd v. Cigna, 12 F.3d 346, 350 (2d Cir. 1993) and five subsequent published opinions.

In Alaska Elec. Pension Fund v. Pharmacia Corp., 554 F.3d 342 (3d Cir. 2009), the court followed Merck & Co., i.e., Sec., Deriv. & ERISA Litig., 543 F.3d 150 (3d Cir. 2008), *cert. gr.*, 2009 U.S.

LEXIS 3913, and held that for investors to be on inquiry notice "there must be some indication that defendants did not, in fact, hold the views expressed. Inquiry notice requires storm warnings of *culpable activity*. [Citation omitted.] Under §10(b), a corporation does not engage in culpable activity unless it acted with scienter. Scienter is not incidental to §10(b). It is elemental." Id. at 348.

(iii) *Sarbanes–Oxley Act Amendments*

P. 1347, new n.92.1, after indented quotation. The new statute of limitations, however, has been held not to apply to §§11 and 12 of the Securities Act since these provisions do not sound in "fraud, deceit manipulation or contrivance" as is required under §804. See WorldCom, Inc. Sec. Litig., 294 F. Supp. 2d 431, 443 (S.D.N.Y. 2003); Global Crossing, Ltd. Sec. Litig., 2003–2004 Fed. Sec. L. Rep. (CCH) ¶92,654 (S.D.N.Y. 2003).

In Enterprise Mortgage Acceptance Co., LLC, Sec. Litig., 391 F.3d 401 (2d Cir. 2004), the Second Circuit held that §804 of the Sarbanes-Oxley Act did not revive plaintiffs' expired securities fraud cases. Enterprise relied on Landgraf v. USI Film Prod., 511 U.S. 244 (1994) and declined to apply §804 retroactively. *Accord*: Foss v. Bear, Stearns & Co., Inc., 394 F.3d 540, 542 (7th Cir. 2005) (§804 does not apply retroactively).

In Margolies v. Deason, 464 F.3d 547 (5th Cir. 2006), the Fifth Circuit followed decisions in the Second, Third, Fourth, Seventh, and Eighth Circuits and held that §804 did not revive previously extinguished causes of action.

In Tello v. Dean Witter Reynolds, Inc., 494 F.3d 956, 974–975 (11th Cir. 2007), after an interlocutory appeal from denial of Dean Witter's motion to dismiss, the court determined that when the class action was filed, it was time-barred by both the former statute of limitations and the Sarbanes-Oxley Act statute of limitations. Both employ inquiry notice.

In Exxon Mobil Corp. Sec. Litig., 500 F.3d 189 (3d Cir. 2007), the court reasoned:

P. 1347

To repeat,...we held that the lengthier limitations periods provided by Sarbanes-Oxley did not apply to claims that had expired under the limitation periods in place prior to the passage of that legislation, even if the claims were filed after its enactment and would be timely under its provisions. [Citation omitted.] We explicitly reserved the question, however, whether that Act lengthened the limitations periods for claims on which the periods were already running but had not yet expired. [Citation omitted.]

...As noted above, in §804(b) of Sarbanes-Oxley, Congress explicitly stated that "[t]he limitations period[s] provided by section 1658(b) of title 28, United States Code, as added by this section, shall apply to all proceedings addressed by this section that are commenced on or after the date of enactment of this Act." 116 Stat. 801. Congress used the terms *proceedings...that are commenced* instead of *claims that accrue* or similar such language. The plain meaning of these words directs that claims filed after July 30, 2002, receive the benefit of the extended limitations periods, even if the shorter periods had already begun (but had not expired) on the underlying causes of action. Hence, the types of claims listed in 28 U.S.C. §1658(b) and raised in suits with timing like this one — filed in 2004 but complaining of events in 1999 — get the benefit of Sarbanes-Oxley's two-year statute of limitations and five-year statute of repose. The lingering question, though, is whether each of plaintiffs' claims here is in fact within the scope of 28 U.S.C. §1658(b)....

There can be no question that 28 U.S.C. §1658(b) covers claims based on §10(b) of the Securities Exchange Act. The statute refers explicitly to "private right[s] of action that involve[ ] a claim of fraud...in contravention of...the securities laws." 28 U.S.C. §1658(b). Indeed, the implied cause of action recognized under §10(b) is widely known and referred to as *securities fraud*. [Citations omitted.] To conclude that §1658(b) does not apply to 10(b) claims would be absurd.

But does §1658(b) also apply to plaintiffs' §14(a) claim? Section 1658(b), by its terms, applies to claims that *involve[ ]...fraud, deceit, manipulation, or contrivance*. This wording closely tracks the language of §10(b), which prohibits employing *any manipulative or deceptive device or contrivance*. Violations of §14(a), on the other hand, may be committed without scienter; in other words, no culpable intent is required....

CIVIL LIABILITY P. 1353

Given this material distinction, we conclude that Congress did not intend to include §14(a) claims within the scope of §1658(b), but rather intended that provision to apply to §10(b) claims and other claims requiring proof of fraudulent intent. Several district courts have done the same analysis and reached the same conclusion when deciding §1658(b)'s relevant to §14(a) and other securities-related claims. [Citations omitted.]

Id. at 196–197.

Section 804 does not apply to §11, Metropolitan Sec. Litig., 532 F. Supp. 2d 1260, 1283–1284 (E.D. Wash. 2007), or §18. Able Lab. Sec. Litig., 2007–2008 Fed. Sec. L. Rep. (CCH) ¶94,618 (D.N.J. 2008).

c.   Failure to Plead Fraud with Particularity

P. 1353 n.115, end note. During the same term as *Tellabs*, the Supreme Court also decided Bell Atl. Corp. v. Twombly, 550 U.S. 544 (2007), which further tightened Rule 8's notice pleading requirements by rejecting the *pure notice* approach of Conley v. Gibson, 355 U.S. 41, 45–46 (1957). Conley's oft-quoted language that a "complaint should not be dismissed for failure to state a claim unless it appears beyond doubt that the plaintiff can prove no set of facts in support of his claim which would entitle him to relief" was characterized by *Bell Atlantic* as "best forgotten." 550 U.S. at 562–563. Under *Bell Atlantic* Rule 8 requires "enough factual material" to suggest that the alleged event took place. Id. at 556. Cf. Intelligroup Sec. Litig., 527 F. Supp. 2d 262, 276–279 (D.N.J. 2007) (discussing *Tellabs* and *Bell Atlantic*). The elevation in *Bell Atlantic* was not intended to be insurmountable: "[W]e do not require heightened fact pleading of specifics, but only enough facts to state a claim that is plausible on its face." 550 U.S. at 570. The complaint must "raise a right to relief above a speculative level." Id. at 1965. Cf. Schaaf v. Residential Funding Corp., 517 F.3d 544, 549 (8th Cir. 2008), *cert. denied*, 129 S. Ct. 222 ("otherwise, a plaintiff with no hope of showing proximate causation could require inefficient expenditure of resources and potentially induce a defendant to settle a meritless claim").

495

P. 1353   2010 SUPPLEMENT

In Ashcroft v. Iqbal, 129 S. Ct. 1937 (2009), the Supreme Court, on a 5-4 vote, amplified its decision in *Twombly*:

> ...Under Federal Rule of Civil Procedure 8(a)(2), a pleading must contain "a short and plain statement of the claim showing that the pleader is entitled to relief." As the Court held in *Twombly*, 550 U.S. 544, 127 S. Ct. 1955, 167 L.Ed. 2d 929, the pleading standard Rule 8 announces does not require *detailed factual allegations*, but it demands more than an unadorned, the-defend-unlawfully-harmed-me accusation. [Citation omitted] A pleading that offers "labels and conclusions" or "a formulaic recitation of the elements of a cause of action will not do." [Citation omitted] Nor does a complaint suffice if it tenders "naked assertion[s]" devoid of "further factual enhancement." [Citation omitted]
>
> To survive a motion to dismiss, a complaint must contain sufficient factual matter, accepted as true, to "state a claim to relief that is plausible on its face." [Citation omitted] A claim has facial plausibility when the plaintiff pleads factual content that allows the court to draw the reasonable inference that the defendant is liable for the misconduct alleged. [Citation omitted] The plausibility standard is not akin to a "probability requirement," but it asks for more than a sheer possibility that a defendant has acted unlawfully. [Citation omitted.] Where a complaint pleads facts that are "merely consistent with" a defendant's liability, it "stops short of the line between possibility and plausibility of 'entitlement to relief.'" [Citation omitted]
>
> Two working principles underlie our decision in *Twombly*. First, the tenet that a court must accept as true all of the allegations contained in a complaint is inapplicable to legal conclusions. Threadbare recitals of the elements of a cause of action, supported by mere conclusory statements, do not suffice. [Citation omitted] Rule 8 marks a notable and generous departure from the hyper-technical, code-pleading regime of a prior era, but it does not unlock the doors of discovery for a plaintiff armed with nothing more than conclusions. Second, only a complaint that states a plausible claim for relief survives a motion to dismiss. [Citation omitted] Determining whether a complaint states a plausible claim for relief will, as the Court of Appeals observed, be a context-specific task that requires the reviewing court to draw on its judicial experience and common sense. [Citation omitted.] But where the well-pleaded facts do not permit the court to infer more than the mere possibility

of misconduct, the complaint has alleged — but it has not "show[n]" — "that the pleader is entitled to relief." Fed. Rule Civ. Proc. 8(a)(2).

In keeping with these principles a court considering a motion to dismiss can choose to begin by identifying pleadings that, because they are not more than conclusions, are not entitled to the assumption of truth. While legal conclusions can provide the framework of a complaint, they must be supported by factual allegations. When there are well-pleaded factual allegations, a court should assume their veracity and then determine whether they plausibly give rise to an entitlement to relief.

P. 1357 n.120, new par., next to last par. See also Ottmann v. Hanger Orthopedic Group, Inc., 353 F.3d 338, 345 (4th Cir. 2003), the court adopted "a flexible, case-specific analysis":

> We agree that a flexible, case-specific analysis is appropriate in examining scienter pleadings. Both the absence of any statutory language addressing particular methods of pleading and the inconclusive legislative history regarding the adoption of Second Circuit pleading standards indicate that Congress ultimately chose not to specify particular types of facts that would or would not show a strong inference of scienter. [Citations omitted.] We therefore conclude that courts should not restrict their scienter inquiry by focusing on specific categories of facts, such as those relating to motive and opportunity, but instead should examine all of the allegations in each case to determine whether they collectively establish a strong inference of scienter. And, while particular facts demonstrating a motive and opportunity to commit fraud (or lack of such facts) may be relevant to the scienter inquiry, the weight accorded to those facts should depend on the circumstances of each case.

P. 1359 n.120, end note. In Tellabs, Inc. v. Makor Issues & Rights, Ltd., 551 U.S. 308 (2007), Justice Ginsburg wrote for an 8-1 majority in articulating the Supreme Court's approach to pleading standards under the Private Securities Litigation Reform Act. While her decision recognized that "meritorious private actions to enforce federal antifraud securities laws are an essential supplement to criminal and civil enforcement actions,"

P. 1359   2010 SUPPLEMENT

id. at 313, the gravamen of the decision focused on exacting pleading standards "[a]s a check against abusive litigation by private parties." Id. at 313.

Justice Ginsburg's decision explained in relevant part:

> Exacting pleading requirements are among the control measures Congress included in the PSLRA. The Act requires plaintiffs to state with particularity both the facts constituting the alleged violation, and the facts evidencing scienter, i.e., the defendant's intention "to deceive, manipulate, or defraud." Ernst & Ernst v. Hochfelder, 425 U.S. 185, 194, and n.12 (1976); see 15 U.S.C. §78u-4(b)(1), (2). This case concerns the latter requirement. As set out in §21D(b)(2) of the PSLRA, plaintiffs must "state with particularity facts giving rise to a strong inference that the defendant acted with the required state of mind." 15 U.S.C. §78u-4(b)(2).
>
> Congress left the key term *strong inference* undefined, and Courts of Appeals have divided on its meaning. In the case before us, the Court of Appeals for the Seventh Circuit held that the *strong inference* standard would be met if the complaint "allege[d] facts from which, if true, a reasonable person could infer that the defendant acted with the required intent." 437 F.3d 588, 602 (2006). That formulation, we conclude, does not capture the stricter demand Congress sought to convey in §21D(b)(2). It does not suffice that a reasonable factfinder plausibly could infer from the complaint's allegations the requisite state of mind. Rather, to determine whether a complaint's scienter allegations can survive threshold inspection for sufficiency, a court governed by §21D(b)(2) must engage in a comparative evaluation; it must consider, not only inferences urged by the plaintiff, as the Seventh Circuit did, but also competing inferences rationally drawn from the facts alleged. An inference of fraudulent intent may be plausible, yet less cogent than other, nonculpable explanations for the defendant's conduct. To quality as *strong* within the intendment of §21D(b)(2), we hold, an inference of scienter must be more than merely plausible or reasonable — it must be cogent and at least as compelling as any opposing inference of nonfraudulent intent....
>
> In an ordinary civil action, the Federal Rules of Civil Procedure require only "a short and plain statement of the claim showing that the pleader is entitled to relief." Fed. Rule Civ. Proc. 8(a)(2). Although the rule encourages brevity, the complaint must say

enough to give the defendant "fair notice of what the plaintiff's claim is and the grounds upon which it rests." *Dura Pharmaceuticals*, 544 U.S., at 346 (internal quotation marks omitted). Prior to the enactment of the PSLRA, the sufficiency of a complaint for securities fraud was governed not by Rule 8, but by the heightened pleading standard set forth in Rule 9(b)....Rule 9(b) applies to "all averments of fraud or mistake"; it requires that "the circumstances constituting fraud...be stated with particularity" but provides that "[m]alice, intent, knowledge, and other condition of mind of a person, may be averred generally."

Courts of Appeals diverged on the character of the Rule 9(b) inquiry in §10(b) cases: Could securities fraud plaintiffs allege the requisite mental state "simply by stating that scienter existed." [Citations omitted.] Circuits requiring plaintiffs to allege specific facts indicating scienter expressed that requirement variously. [Citation omitted.] The Second Circuit's formulation was the most stringent. Securities fraud plaintiffs in that Circuit were required to "specifically plead those [facts] which they assert give rise to a *strong inference* that the defendants had" the requisite state of mind. [Citation omitted.] The *strong inference* formulation was appropriate, the Second Circuit said, to ward off allegations of *fraud by hindsight*. [Citations omitted.]

Setting a uniform pleading standard for §10(b) actions was among Congress' objectives when it enacted the PSLRA....

Under the PSLRA's heightened pleading instructions, any private securities complaint alleging that the defendant made a false or misleading statement must: (1) "specify each statement alleged to have been misleading [and] the reason or reasons why the statement is misleading," 15 U.S.C. §78u-4(b)(1); and (2) "state with particularity facts giving rise to a strong inference that the defendant acted with the required state of mind," §78u-4(b)(2). In the instant case,...District Court and the Seventh Circuit agreed that the Shareholders met the first of the two requirements: The complaint sufficiently specified Notebaert's alleged misleading statements and the reasons why the statements were misleading. ....But those courts disagreed on whether the Shareholders, as required by §21D(b)(2), "state[d] with particularity facts giving rise to a strong inference that [Notebaert] acted with [scienter]."...

The *strong inference* standard "unequivocally raise[d] the bar for pleading scienter," 437 F.3d, at 601, and signaled Congress' purpose to promote greater uniformity among the Circuits, see H.R.

499

P. 1359

Conf. Rep., p. 41. But "Congress did not...throw much light on what facts...suffice to create [a strong] inference," or on what "degree of imagination courts can use in divining whether" the requisite inference exists. 437 F.3d at 601. While adopting the Second Circuit's *strong inference* standard, Congress did not codify that Circuit's case law interpreting the standard. See §78u-4(b)(2). See also Brief for United States as Amicus Curiae 18. With no clear guide from Congress other than its "inten[tion] to strengthen existing pleading requirements," H.R. Conf. Rep., p. 41, Courts of Appeals have diverged again, this time in construing the term *strong inference*. Among the uncertainties, should courts consider competing inferences in determining whether an inference of scienter is *strong*? See 437 F.3d at 601-602 (collecting cases). Our task is to prescribe a workable construction of the *strong inference* standard, a reading geared to the PSLRA's twin goals: to curb frivolous, lawyer-driven litigation, while preserving investors' ability to recover on meritorious claims.

We establish the following prescriptions: First, faced with a Rule 12(b)(6) motion to dismiss a §10(b) action, courts must, as with any motion to dismiss for failure to plead a claim on which relief can be granted, accept all factual allegations in the complaint as true. [Citation omitted.] On this point, the parties agree. [Citation omitted.]

Second, courts must consider the complaint in its entirety, as well as other sources courts ordinarily examine when ruling on Rule 12(b)(6) motions to dismiss, in particular, documents incorporated into the complaint by reference, and matters by which a court may take judicial notice. [Citation omitted.] The inquiry, as several Courts of Appeals have recognized, is whether *all* of the facts alleged, taken collectively, give rise to a strong inference of scienter, not whether any individual allegation, scrutinized in isolation, meets that standard. [Citations omitted.]

Third, in determining whether the pleaded facts give rise to a *strong* inference of scienter, the court must take into account plausible opposing inferences. The Seventh Circuit expressly declined to engage in such a comparative inquiry. A complaint could survive, that court said, as long as it "alleges facts from which, if true, a reasonable person could infer that the defendant acted with the required intent"; in other words, only "[i]f a reasonable person could not draw such an inference from the alleged facts" would the defendant prevail on a motion to dismiss. 437 F.3d at 602. But in

§21D(b)(2), Congress did not merely require plaintiffs to "provide a factual basis for [their] scienter allegations,"...i.e., to allege facts from which an inference of scienter rationally *could* be drawn. Instead, Congress required plaintiffs to plead with particularity facts that give rise to a *strong* — i.e., a powerful or cogent — inference....

The strength of an inference cannot be decided in a vacuum. The inquiry is inherently comparative: How likely is it that one conclusion, as compared to others, follows from the underlying facts? To determine whether the plaintiff has alleged facts that give rise to the requisite *strong inference* of scienter, a court must consider plausible nonculpable explanations for the defendant's conduct, as well as inferences favoring the plaintiff. The inference that the defendant acted with scienter need not be irrefutable, i.e., of the *smoking-gun* genre, or even the "most plausible of competing inferences." [Citations omitted.] Recall in this regard that §21D(b)'s pleading requirements are but one constraint among many the PSLRA installed to screen out frivolous suits, while allowing meritorious actions to move forward....Yet the inference of scienter must be more than merely *reasonable* or *permissible* — it must be cogent and compelling, thus strong in light of other explanations. A complaint will survive, we hold, only if a reasonable person would deem the inference of scienter cogent and at least as compelling as any opposing inference one could draw from the facts alleged....

Tellabs contends that when competing inferences are considered, Notebaert's evident lack of pecuniary motive will be dispositive. The Shareholders, Tellabs stresses, did not allege that Notebaert sold any shares during the class period. See Brief for Petitioners 50 ("The absence of any allegations of motive color all the other allegations putatively giving rise to an inference of scienter."). While it is true that motive can be a relevant consideration, and personal financial gain may weigh heavily in favor of a scienter inference, we agree with the Seventh Circuit that the absence of a motive allegation is not fatal....

Tellabs also maintains that several of the Shareholders' allegations are too vague or ambiguous to contribute to a strong inference of scienter. For example, the Shareholders alleged that Tellabs flooded its customers with unwanted products, a practice known as *channel stuffing*....But they failed, Tellabs argues, to specify whether the channel stuffing allegedly known to Notebaert was the illegitimate kind (e.g., writing orders for products customers had not requested) or the legitimate kind (e.g., offering customers discounts as an incentive to buy)....But see 437 F.3d at 598, 603-604 (pointing to multiple particulars alleged by the Shareholders, including specifications as to timing). We agree that omissions and ambiguities count against inferring scienter, for plaintiffs must "state with particularity facts giving rise to a strong inference that the defendant acted with the required state of mind." §78u-4(b)(2). We reiterate, however, that the court's job is not to scrutinize each allegation in isolation but to assess all the allegations holistically....In sum, the reviewing court must ask: When the allegations are accepted as true and taken collectively, would a reasonable person deem the inference of scienter at least as strong as any opposing inference?...

While we reject the Seventh Circuit's approach to §21D(b)(2), we do not decide whether, under the standard we have described, ...the Shareholders' allegations warrant "a strong inference that [Notebaert] and [Tellabs] acted with the required state of mind," 15 U.S.C. §78u-4(b)(2). Neither the District Court nor the Court of Appeals had the opportunity to consider the matter in light of the prescriptions we announce today. We therefore vacate the Seventh Circuit's judgment so that the case may be reexamined in accord with our construction of §21D(b)(2).

The judgment of the Court of Appeals is vacated, and the case is remanded for further proceeding consistent with this opinion.

Justices Scalia and Alito concurred in judgment.
Justice Stevens dissented.

In Rombach v. Chang, 355 F.3d 164 (2d Cir. 2004), the Second Circuit, following several circuits, held that the heightened pleading standards of Rule 9(b) apply to §§11 and 12(a)(2) when they are premised on claims of fraud.

Following Shapiro v. UJB Fin. Corp., 964 F.2d 272, 288 (3d Cir. 1992), *cert. denied*, 506 U.S. 934, the court in California Pub. Employees Retirement Sys. v. Chubb Corp., 394 F.3d 126, 160–163 (3d Cir. 2004) dismissed §11 claims under Rule 9(b) when the claims "sounded in fraud." Judge Sloviter dissented on this point. Id. at 166.

See also Knollenberg v. Harmonic, Inc., 2005–2006 Fed. Sec. L. Rep. (CCH) ¶93,554, at 97,342–97,343 (9th Cir. 2005) ("Claims brought under Sections 11 and 12 of the 1933 Act are *not* subject to the heightened pleading requirements of the PSLRA"); Suprema Specialties, Inc., Sec. Litig., 438 F.3d 256, 269–270 (3d Cir. 2006) (following *CALPERS*).

A subsequent circuit split has concerned the endurance of group pleading after the 1995 Act. See Financial Acquisition Partners LP v. Blackwell, 440 F.3d 278, 281 (5th Cir. 2006) (the PSLRA abolished the group pleading doctrine, following Southland Sec. Corp. v. INSpire Ins. Solutions, Inc., 365 F.3d 353, 364–365 (5th Cir. 2004)).

In Winer Family Trust v. Queen, 503 F.3d 319, 334–337 (3d Cir. 2007), the court followed post-PSLRA decisions in the Fifth and Seventh Circuits and held that the group pleading doctrine is no longer viable in private securities actions after the enactment of the PSLRA.

In Makor Issuers & Rights, Ltd. v. Tellabs, 437 F.3d 588, 602–603 (7th Cir. 2006), *rev'd on other grounds*, 551 U.S. 308, the Seventh Circuit held that group pleading did not survive the enactment of the PSLRA. The Supreme Court noted the split among circuits on this issue, but did not address this conflict when it reviewed *Tellabs*. 551 U.S. at 325 n.6.

Insider trading will only support an inference of scienter by revealing a motive and opportunity for profiting from a fraud if the timing and amount are "unusual or suspicious." PEC Solutions, Inc., Sec. Litig., 418 F.3d 379, 390 (4th Cir. 2005). Here sales between 1.17 and 13 percent of defendant's holdings were characterized as *de minimis*. The court further noted that some of the individual defendants simultaneously exercised and did not sell stock options and lost money on their stock sales. Ibid.

In Makor Issues & Rights Ltd. v. Tellabs, Inc., 437 F.3d 588 (7th Cir. 2006), *rev'd on other grounds*, 551 U.S. 308 (2007), the Seventh Circuit agreed with several other circuits that a complaint could proceed under the Private Securities Litigation Reform Act relying on confidential sources, but a complaint must describe its sources with sufficient particularity "to support the probability that a person in the position occupied by the source would possess the information alleged." Id. at 596.

Plaintiffs are not required to name witnesses, but can rely on confidential witnesses if appropriate in the circumstance of a case.

P. 1359

Metawave Communications Corp. Sec. Litig., 298 F. Supp. 2d 1056, 1068 (W.D. Wash. 2003), citing Novak v. Kasaks, 216 F.3d 300, 314 (2d Cir. 2000), *cert. denied*, 531 U.S. 1012. The court in *Metawave amplified*:

> "To contribute meaningfully toward a 'strong inference' of scienter, however, allegations attributed to unnamed sources must be accompanied by enough particularized detail to support a reasonable conviction in the informant's basis of knowledge." [Citations omitted.] Plaintiffs must plead "with substantial specificity" how confidential witnesses "came to learn of the information they provide in the complaint." [Citation omitted.] The court must be able to tell whether a confidential witness is speaking from personal knowledge, or "merely regurgitating gossip and innuendo." [Citation omitted.] The court can look to "the level of the detail provided by the confidential witnesses, the corroborative nature of the other facts alleged (including from other sources), the coherence and plausibility of the allegations, the number of sources, the reliability of the sources, and similar indicia." [Citation omitted.]

The Third Circuit, in California Pub. Employees Retirement Sys. v. Chubb Corp., 394 F.3d 126 (3d Cir. 2004), followed Novak v. Kasaks, 216 F.3d 300, 314 (2d Cir. 2000), *cert. denied*, 531 U.S. 1012, as well as ABC Arbitrage Plaintiffs Group v. Tchuruk, 291 F.3d 336, 351–354 (5th Cir. 2002); and Cabletron Sys., Inc., 311 F.3d 11, 29–31 (1st Cir. 2002) in not requiring disclosure of confidential sources as a general matter. Plaintiffs are only required to "plead with particularly *sufficient* facts to support those beliefs." *Chubb* at 146. However, in this case when confidential sources were not described with sufficient particularity, plaintiffs failed to state a claim. Id. at 156. See also Daou Sys., Inc. Sec. Litig., 411 F.3d 1006, 1015–1016 (9th Cir. 2005), *cert. denied*, 546 U.S. 1772 (plaintiffs description of confidential witnesses pled with sufficient particularity).

In Berson v. Applied Signal Tech., Inc., 527 F.3d 982, 985 (9th Cir. 2008), four confidential witnesses, who were engineers or technical editors, were sufficient to infer the issuance of stop-work orders. The court rejected the argument that only managers would see the stop-work orders first hand.

In New Jersey Carpenters' Pension & Annuity Funds v. Biogen Idec, Inc., 537 F.3d 35, 52 (1st Cir. 2008), the court held: "We decline to adopt a rule which would exclude confidential source allegations which have every indication both that the source had access to information and that the information has the earmarks of credibility, simply because the identity of the source is not initially revealed. And we see no reason to exclude consideration of such information from the evaluation of whether plaintiffs' strong inferences of scienter are at least as plausible as defendants' inferences."

In Mizzaro v. Home Depot, Inc., 544 F.3d 1230 (11th Cir. 2008), after *Tellabs*, the Eleventh Circuit held: "[w]e see no reason to adopt a *per se* rule that always requires a securities fraud complaint to name the confidential source, so long as the complaint unambiguously provides in a cognizable and detailed way the basis of the whistleblower's knowledge." Id. at 1239-1240, citing cases.

In Zucco Partners, LLC v. Digimarc, 552 F.3d 981, 995 (9th Cir. 2009), the court adumbrated a two-prong test to satisfy the PSLRA with respect to confidential witness pleading requirements:

> First, the confidential witnesses whose statements are introduced to establish scienter must be described with sufficient particularity to establish their reliability and personal knowledge. [Citing cases] Second, those statements, which are reported by confidential witnesses with sufficient reliability and personal knowledge must themselves be indicative of scienter.

Here, a majority of the confidential witnesses based their knowledge on vague hearsay, which was not enough to satisfy the reliability standard. Id. at 997.

See also McMulen v. Fluor Corp., 2003–2004 Fed. Sec. L. Rep. (CCH) ¶92,665 (9th Cir. 2004) (allowing leave to amend when court concluded that further amendment would not be futile); Miller v. Champion Enter., Inc., 346 F.3d 660, 689–692 (6th Cir. 2003) (denying motion to amend pleadings as futile).

Cf. ATSI Communications, Inc. v. Shaar Fund, Ltd., 493 F.3d 87, 99 (2d Cir. 2007) (following *Tellabs*: "[I]n determining whether the pleaded facts give rise to a *strong* inference of scienter, the court must take into account plausible opposing inferences").

P. 1359

In Winer Family Trust v. Queen, 503 F.3d 319 (3d Cir. 2007), following *Tellabs*, "courts may find it necessary to probe the documents integral to the complaint." Id. at 329.

On remand, the Seventh Circuit adhered to its decision in Makor Issues & Rights, Ltd. v. Tellabs, Inc., 513 F.3d 702 (7th Cir. 2008), that the plaintiff had adequately pled a complaint with respect to falsity, materiality, and scienter and reversed the judgment of the district court dismissing the suit. Judge Posner wrote in part:

> The critical question, therefore, is how likely it is that the allegedly false statements that we quoted earlier in this opinion were the result of merely careless mistakes at the management level based on false information fed it from below, rather than of an intent to deceive or a reckless indifference to whether the statements were misleading. It is exceedingly unlikely. The 5500 and the 6500 were Tellabs's most important products. The 5500 was described by the company as its *flagship* product and the 6500 was the 5500's heralded successor. They were to Tellabs as Windows XP and Vista are to Microsoft. That no member of the company's senior management who was involved in authorizing or making public statements about the demand for the 5500 and 6500 knew that they were false is very hard to credit, and no plausible story has yet been told by the defendants that might dispel our incredulity. The closest is the suggestion that while *available* no doubt meant to most investors that the 6500 was ready to be shipped to customers rather than that the new product was having teething troubles that would keep it off the market for many months, this may have been a bit of corporate jargon innocently intended to indicate that the company was ready to take orders. If so, then while it was false as reasonably understood by investors the false impression was a result of mutual misunderstanding rather than of fraud. See *Banque Arabe et Internationale D'Investissement v. Maryland National Bank*, 57 F.3d 146, 153-54 (2d Cir. 1995). But this is highly implausible when *available* is set among the company's alleged lies about the 6500 — that "customers are embracing" the 6500, that "interest in and demand for the 6500 continues to grow," that "we are satisfying very strong demand and growing customer demand [for the 6500 and] as we are as confident as ever — that may be an understatement — about the 6500," and that "we should hit our full manufacturing capacity

in May or June to accommodate the demand [for the 6500] we are seeing. Everything we can build, we are building and shipping. The demand is very strong."

Id. at 709. Cf. Cornelia I. Crowell GST Trust v. Possis Med., Inc., 519 F.3d 778, 782 (8th Cir. 2008) (pleading did not provide the level of detail necessary to supports its allegations).

In Higginbotham v. Baxter Int'l, Inc., 495 F.3d 753, 756–757 (7th Cir. 2007), Judge Easterbrook elaborated on the implications of *Tellabs* for anonymous sources in a complaint:

> One upshot of the approach that *Tellabs* announced is that we must discount allegations that the complaint attributes to five *confidential witnesses* — one ex-employee of the Brazilian subsidiary, two ex-employees of Baxter's headquarters, and two consultants. It is hard to see how information from anonymous sources could be deemed *compelling* or how we could take account of plausible opposing inferences. Perhaps these confidential sources have axes to grind. Perhaps they are lying. Perhaps they don't even exist.
>
> At oral argument, we asked when the identity of these five persons would be revealed and how their stories could be tested. The answer we received was that the sources' identity would never be revealed, which means that their stories can't be checked. Yet *Tellabs* requires judges to weight the strength of plaintiffs' favored inference in comparison to other possible inferences; anonymity frustrates that process.
>
> Not that anonymity is possible in the long run. There is no *informer's privilege* in civil litigation. Defendants are entitled to learn in discovery who has relevant evidence, and to obtain that evidence. Indeed, plaintiffs are obliged by Fed. R. Civ. P. 26(a)(1)(A) to provide defendants with the names and addresses of all persons "likely to have discoverable information that the disclosing party may use to support its claims or defenses." Concealing names at the complaint stage thus does not protect informers from disclosure (and the risk of retaliation); it does nothing but obstruct the judiciary's ability to implement the PSLRA.
>
> This does not mean that plaintiffs must reveal all of their sources, as one circuit has required. See *In re Silicon Graphics Inc. Securities Litigation*, 183 F.3d 970, 985 (9th Cir. 1999). A complaint is not a discovery device. Our point, rather, is that anonymity conceals

information that is essential to the sort of comparative evaluation required by *Tellabs*. To determine whether a *strong* inference of scienter has been established, the judiciary must evaluate what the complaint reveals and disregard what it conceals....

It is possible to imagine situations in which statements by anonymous sources may corroborate or disambiguate evidence from disclosed sources. Informants sometimes play this role in applications for search warrants. Because it is impossible to anticipate all combinations of information that may be presented in the future, and because *Tellabs* instructs courts to evaluate the allegations in their entirety, we said above that allegations from *confidential witnesses* must be *discounted* rather than ignored. Usually that discount will be steep. It is unnecessary to say more today.

In Makor Issues & Rights, Ltd. v. Tellabs, Inc., 513 F.3d at 711–712, the court distinguished *Higginbotham*:

...allegations based on anonymous informants are very difficult to assess. This concern led us to suggest in *Higginbotham v. Baxter International, Inc., supra*, 495 F.3d at 756–57, that such allegations must be steeply discounted. But that was a very different case from this one. The misconduct alleged consisted of frauds committed by Baxter's Brazilian subsidiary, but because the suit was against the parent, the plaintiffs had to show that the parent knew about the Brazilian fraud. The subsidiary had tried to conceal it from its parent as well as from the Brazilian government. There was no basis other than the confidential sources, described merely as three ex-employees of Baxter and two consultants, for a strong inference that the subsidiary had failed to conceal the fraud from its parent and thus that the management of the parent had been aware of the fraud during the period covered by the complaint.

The confidential sources listed in the complaint in this case, in contrast, are numerous and consist of persons who from the description of their jobs were in a position to know at first hand the facts to which they are prepared to testify, such as the returns of the 5500s, that sales of the 5500 were dropping off a cliff while the company pretended that demand was strong, that the 6500 was not approved by the Regional Bell Operating Companies, that it was still in the beta stage and failing performance tests conducted by prospective customers, and that it was too bulky for customers' premises. The information that the confidential informants are reported to have obtained is set forth in convincing detail, with some of the information, moreover, corroborated by multiple sources. It would be better were the informants named in the complaint, because it would be easier to determine whether they had been in a good position to know the facts that the complaint says they learned. But the absence of proper names does not invalidate the drawing of a strong inference from informants' assertions.

In Belizan v. Hershon, 495 F.3d 686 (D.C. Cir. 2007), on the second appeal, each time after the District Court had twice dismissed a complaint with prejudice, the court of appeals again reversed and remanded. In this instance the specific allegations appeared to satisfy §10(b) but the appeals court remanded to determine whether the inference that the defendants acted recklessly is, as required by *Tellabs* "at least as compelling as any opposing inference of nonfraudulent intent." Id. at 692. Cf. Foster v. Wilson, 504 F.3d 1046 (9th Cir. 2007) (following *Tellabs* and dismissing complaint).

Cf. Berson v. Applied Signal Tech., Inc., 527 F.3d 982, 987 (9th Cir. 2008):

> Plaintiffs must "state with particularity facts giving rise to a strong inference" that defendants acted with the intent to deceive or with deliberate recklessness as to the possibility of misleading investors. 15 U.S.C. §78u-4(b)(2); In re Silicon Graphics, Inc. Sec. Litig., 183 F.3d 970, 983 (9th Cir. 1999). Plaintiffs have done so by alleging that defendants Gary Yancey and James Doyle (Applied Signal's CEO and CFO) were aware that stop-work orders had halted significant amounts of work, yet counted the stopped work as backlog anyway.

In Rosenberg v. Gould, 554 F.3d 962, 965 (11th Cir. 2009), following *Tellabs*, the court dismissed an options backdating complaint when allegations of intent to defraud were insufficient to establish an inference "at least as compelling as any opposing inference of nonfraudulent intent."

In Teamsters Local 445 Freight v. Dynex Capital, Inc., 531 F.3d 190, 196 (2d Cir. 2008), following *Makor*, the court held:

...Congress has imposed strict requirements on securities fraud pleadings, but we do not believe they have imposed the rule urged by defendants, that in no case can corporate scienter be pleaded in the absence of successfully pleading scienter as to an expressly named officer.

In Ceridian Corp. Sec. Litig., 542 F.3d 240 (8th Cir. 2008), the court followed *Tellabs* and applied the Supreme Court application of a strong inference…"at least as compelling as any opposing inference" and concluded here that "[t]he allegations in the complaint reek of incompetence, not fraud." Id. at 249.

In South Ferry LP, #2 v. Killinger, 542 F.3d 776 (9th Cir. 2008), the court followed *Tellabs* and adopted the argument that "facts critical to a business's *core operations* or an important transaction generally are so apparent that their knowledge may be attributed to the company and its key officers" can be one relevant part of a plaintiff's complaint. Id. at 783. Indeed, "in some unusual circumstances, the core operations inference, without more, may raise the strong inference required by the PSLRA." Id. at 785. See also Brodsky v. Yahoo! Inc., 592 F. Supp. 2d 1192, 1204 (N.D. Cal. 2008) (following *South Ferry*).

In Frank v. Dana Corp., 547 F.3d 564, 571 (6th Cir. 2008), the court followed *Tellabs* and recognized that the earlier Sixth Circuit standard in *Helwig* ("the *strong inference* requirement means that plaintiffs are entitled only to the most plausible of competing inferences") was no longer good law.

In ECA, Local 134 IBEW Joint Pens. Trust v. JP Morgan Chase, 553 F.3d 187, 199 (2d Cir. 2009), the court cited cases and identified four circumstances in a complaint that may give rise to a strong inference of fraud: "…[t]he defendants (1) 'benefitted in a concrete and personal way from the purported fraud'; (2) 'engaged in deliberately illegal behavior'; (3) 'knew facts or had access to information suggesting that their public statements were not accurate'; or (4) 'failed to check information they had a duty to monitor.'"

In Zucco Partners, LLC v. Digimarc Corp., 552 F.3d 981, 1005 (9th Cir. 2009), the court, citing *Silicon Graphics*, characterized "three factors that must be considered to determine whether stock sales raise a strong inference of deliberate recklessness are: '(1) the amount and percentage of shares sold by insiders; (2) the timing of the sales; and (3) whether the sales were consistent with the insider's prior trading history.'" Cf. Bausch & Lomb, Inc. Sec. Litig., 592 F. Supp. 2d 323, 345 (W.D.N.Y. 2008):

> ...The Court concludes that the stock sales at issue, being remote in time from any misstatements and in amounts that do not necessarily support a claim of fraud, were not unusual or suspicious and therefore do not demonstrate that defendants had a motive to commit fraud.

Zucco Partners, 552 F.3d at 991-992 (9th Cir. 2009), also revised the Ninth Circuit's approach to reviewing scienter allegations after *Tellabs* to conduct a dual inquiry:

> [F]irst, we will determine whether any of the plaintiff's allegations, standing alone, are sufficient to create a strong inference of scienter; second, if no individual allegations are sufficient, we will conduct a *holistic* review of the same allegations to determine whether the insufficient allegations combine to create a strong inference of intentional conduct or deliberate recklessness.

The court added: "In general, the mere publication of a restatement is not enough to create a strong inference of scienter." Id. at 1000.

Zucco, however, revised the Ninth Circuit approach to core operations and their relevant to scienter pleadings:

> [W]e have previously found inadequate complaints alleging that "facts critical to a business core operations or an important transaction generally are so apparent that their knowledge may be attributed to the company and its key officers." [Citations omitted.]
>
> Recently, however, we have recognized two exceptions to this general rule, and have found bare allegations of falsely reported information probative under certain narrow conditions....Specifically, falsity may itself be indicative of scienter where it is combined with "allegations regarding a management's role in the company"

that are "particular and suggest that the defendant had actual access to the disputed information," and where "the nature of the relevant fact is of such prominence that it would be 'absurd' to suggest that management was without knowledge of the matter." [Citation omitted.]

The first exception permits general allegations about "management's role in a corporate structure and the importance of the corporate information about which management made false or misleading statements" to create a strong inference of scienter when these allegations are buttressed with "detailed and specific allegations about management's exposure to factual information within the company." [Citation omitted.] To satisfy this standard, plaintiffs might include in their complaint "specific admissions from top executives that they are involved in every detail of the company and that they monitored portions of the company's database" ....

The second exception...permits an inference of scienter where the information misrepresented is readily apparent to the defendant corporation's senior management. Where the defendants "must have known" about the falsity of the information they were providing to the public because the falsity of the information was obvious from the operations of the company, the defendants' awareness of the information's falsity can be assumed.

Id. at 1000-1001.

d. *In Pari Delicto* and Unclean Hands

P. 1362 n.134, end note. In Brandaid Mktg. Corp. v. Biss, 462 F.3d 216 (2d Cir. 2006), the court vacated a district court decision in favor of the defendants based on the *in pari delicto* defense. Specifically the court found that the "plaintiff's wrongdoing was far less culpable than defendants' and because, in any event, plaintiff's wrongdoing was not in any meaningful respect the cause of defendants' fraud and misconduct...". Id. at 219.

In Nisselson v. Lernout, 469 F.3d 143, 151-152 (1st Cir. 2006), *cert. denied*, 550 U.S. 918, Judge Selya generalized about the *in pari delicto* defense:

The in pari delicto defense has long been woven into the fabric of federal law. [Citations omitted.] It does not make a difference that some of the trustee's claims are premised on state law. Those claims invoke the law of Massachusetts — and the Massachusetts courts, like the federal courts, have warmly embraced the in pari delicto defense. [Citations omitted.]

As originally conceived, the in pari delicto doctrine forged a defense of limited utility. Over time, however, courts expanded the doctrine's sweep, deploying it as a basis for dismissing suits whenever a plaintiff had played any role — no matter how modest — in the harm-producing activity. See Bateman Eichler, 472 U.S. at 307, 105 S.Ct. 2622. Deploring this overly commodious construction, the Supreme Court later reined in the doctrine and returned it to its classic contours. See Pinter v. Dahl, 486 U.S. 622, 635, 108 S.Ct. 2063, 100 L.Ed.2d 658 (1988); Bateman Eichler, 472 U.S. at 310-11, 105 S.Ct. 2622. This retrenchment, which governs here, restricts the application of the in pari delicto doctrine to those situations in which (i) the plaintiff, as compared to the defendant, bears at least substantially equal responsibility for the wrong he seeks to redress and (ii) preclusion of the suit would not interfere with the purposes of the underlying law or otherwise contravene the public interest.

3. ARBITRATION AND NONWAIVER PROVISIONS

P. 1376 n.198, end note. In Credit Suisse First Boston Corp. v. Grunwald, 400 F.3d 1119 (9th Cir. 2005), the court held that the Securities Exchange Act of 1934 preempted application of California's Ethics Standards to NASD appointed arbitrators. The court relied on Merrill Lynch, Pierce, Fenner & Smith v. Ware, 414 U.S. 117, 125, 130–131 (1973) to determine when SRO rules would preempt state law. The court also noted that the 1975 Securities Acts Amendments requires the SEC to determine that proposed SRO rule changes must be consistent with the purposes of the Securities Exchange Act. Id. at 1128–1130.

In Buckeye Check Cashing v. Cardegna, 546 U.S. 440 (2006), the Supreme Court held that the arbitrator, rather than the court, should consider the claim that a contract containing an arbitration provision is void for illegality. The Court relied on

P. 1384

Southland Corp. v. Keating, 465 U.S. 1 (1984), and Prima Paint Corp. v. Flood & Conklin Mfg. Co., 388 U.S. 395 (1967), to generalize:

> *Prima Paint* and *Southland* answer the question presented here by establishing three propositions. First, as a matter of substantive federal arbitration law, an arbitration provision is severable from the remainder of the contract. Second, unless the challenge is to the arbitration clause itself, the issue of the contract's validity is considered by the arbitrator in the first instance. Third, this arbitration law applies in state as well as federal courts. The parties have not requested, and we do not undertake, reconsideration of those holdings. Applying them to this case, we conclude that because respondents challenge the Agreement, but not specifically its arbitration provisions, those provisions are enforceable apart from the remainder of the contract. The challenge should therefore be considered by an arbitrator, not a court.

546 U.S. at 445–446.

In Alliance Bernstein Inv. Research & Mgmt., Inc. v. Schaffran, 445 F.3d 121 (2d Cir. 2006), the court held that an arbitration panel, not the court, decides whether a Sarbanes-Oxley claim falls within the exception for employment discrimination set forth in NASD Rule 10,201(b).

In Sec. Ex. Act Rel. 55,158, 89 SEC Dock. 2562 (2007), the SEC approved a new NASD Code of Arbitration. The Code is divided into three parts: the Customer Code, the Industry Code, and the Mediation Code. The broad reorganization was intended to simplify rule language into plain English, reorganize the rules, and implement specific substantive changes.

As approved the final texts of the codes are available on the NASD Web site at http://www.nasd.com/web/groups/med_arb/documents/mediation_arbitration/nasdw_018335.pdf.

4. CLASS ACTIONS

P. 1384 n.222, end note. In Merck & Co. Sec. Litig., 432 F.3d 261 (3d Cir. 2005), lead plaintiff retained appellate counsel without court approval. The Third Circuit permitted this counsel to prosecute this appeal but held that future lead plaintiffs must obtain court approval for any new counsel, including appellate counsel.

Cf. Koehler v. Brody, 483 F.3d 590, 594 (8th Cir. 2007), holding, as had other cited cases, that the PSLRA "did not explicitly [grant] a veto power [over settlements] to lead plaintiffs."

P. 1391, 3d full par. & nn.242–243. Substitute: §21D(f) for §21D(g). [In 1998 §21D(g) was renumbered §21D(f).]

The Class Action Fairness Act of 2005 generally enables defendants to remove class actions when (1) the aggregate claims of all plaintiffs exceed $5 million and (2) at least one plaintiff is diverse from at least one defendant. 28 U.S.C. §1332(d).

7. INDEMNIFICATION, CONTRIBUTION, AND INSURANCE

PP. 1397–1398. Substitute: §21D(f) for §21D(g). [In 1998 §21D(g) was renumbered §21D(f).]

P. 1398 n.281, end note. In Gerber v. MTC Elec. Tech., 329 F.3d 297 (2d Cir. 2003), *cert. denied sub nom.* Daiwa Sec. Am., Inc. v. Kayne, 540 U.S. 966, the trial court followed a "capped proportionate rule" under which the credit given for a settlement will be the greater of the settlement amount for common damages (a "pro tanto" rule) or the "proportionate share" of the settling defendants as proven at fault. Id. at 302–303. On appeal the Court of Appeals generally approved this approach for limiting its application to common damages. Id. at 304. This was a pre-PSLRA Act case, but the court remanded the District order approving a nonmutual bar order for further consideration and balancing of competing fairness issues. Id. at 307–309. See also BankAmerica Sec. Litig., 350 F.3d 747 (8th Cir. 2003) (affirming approval of global settlement over objections after fairness hearing).

In Heritage Bond Litig., 546 F.3d 667 (9th Cir. 2008), the court followed Gerber v. MTC Elec. Tech. Co., 329 F.3d 297 (2d Cir. 2003), and held that bar orders under the PSLRA may bar claims for contribution and indemnity or disguised claims for such relief. "Independent claims — those where the injury is not the non-settling defendant's liability to the plaintiff — may not be barred." Id. at 671.

P. 1403 n.300, end note. Cf. AAL High Yield Bond Fund v. Deloitte & Touche LLP, 361 F.3d 1305 (11th Cir. 2004), in which the court vacated a ban of all related present and future claims by Deloitte and a nonsettling defendant, and also banned claims against officers and agents of a nonparty. The lower court made no findings of fact and expressed no rationale or authority for barring claims without a settlement credit or set off.

8. Attorneys' Fees and Security for Costs

P. 1405 n.305, end note. See also Bristol-Myers Sec. Litig., 2007 Fed. Sec. L. Rep. (CCH) ¶94,447 (3d Cir. 2007) (declining to reverse district court fee approval when Notice accurately described fee amount sought but amount was different than the original agreement with lead plaintiff).

P. 1408 n.318, end note. In Professional Mgmt. Assoc. Inc. Employees' Profit Sharing Plan v. KPMG LLP, 345 F.3d 1030 (8th Cir. 2003), the court of Appeals reversed and remanded a District Court opinion declining to award Rule 11 sanctions when the well settled law of res judicata establishes the frivolousness of a plaintiff seeking to relitigate a claim he has been denied leave to serve against the same party in an earlier lawsuit.

In Morris v. Wachovia Sec., Inc., 448 F.3d 268 (4th Cir. 2006), the court held that a district court must impose a sanction when it finds a violation of Rule 11.

In Tracinda Corp. v. DaimlerChrysler, 502 F.3d 212 (3d Cir. 2007), the court awarded expense sanctions under FRCP Rule 16(f) when a party was wholly responsible for late document production that caused the other party to incur substantial expense.

Judge Rendell dissented because a Special Master had heard no evidence of intentional or bad faith conduct.

CIVIL LIABILITY P. 1409

In De la Fuente v. OCI DCI Telecommunications, Inc., 2003–2004 Fed. Sec. L. Rep. (CCH) ¶92,646 (2d Cir. 2003), the court affirmed sanctions when all arguments made by a plaintiff in response to a motion to dismiss were considered frivolous.

In Brunig v. Clark, 560 F.3d 292 (5th Cir. 2009), the court held that a magistrate's report can satisfy a district court's Rule 11 procedural requirement to issue a show cause order, but noted that the appellees' sanction motion did not comply with the Rule 11 safe harbor. Accordingly, the district court sanctions order was reversed and remanded for reconsideration.

P. 1409, 1st full par., 1st line. *Substitute*: Securities Act §20(f) [not §21(f)].

CHAPTER 12

GOVERNMENT LITIGATION

B. CRIMINAL PROSECUTION

1. SEC PENAL PROVISIONS

P. 1420, end 3d full par. In SEC v. Gemstar-TV Guide Int'l Inc., 401 F.3d 1031 (9th Cir. *en banc* 2005), *cert. denied sub nom.* Yuen v. SEC, 546 U.S. 933, the court reversed and concluded that the $37.4 million paid to Yuen and Levy were extraordinary payments under §1103. The court explained:

> "Extraordinary" means, in plain language, out of the ordinary. In the context of a statute aimed at preventing the raiding of corporate assets, "out of the ordinary" means a payment that would not typically be made by a company in its customary course of business. The standard of comparison is the company's common or regular behavior. Thus, the determination of whether a payment is extraordinary will be a fact-based and flexible inquiry. Context-specific factors such as the circumstances under which the payment is contemplated or made the purpose of the payment, and the size of the payment may inform whether a payment is extraordinary, as the district court properly noted in this case. For example, a payment made by a company that would otherwise be unremarkable may be rendered extraordinary by unusual circumstances....
>
> A nexus between the suspected wrongdoing and the payment itself may further demonstrate that the payment is extraordinary, although such a connection is not required. Evidence of the company's deviation from an "industry standard"—or the practice of

P. 1422

similarly situated businesses — also might reveal whether a payment is extraordinary.

Id. at 1045.

2. WILLFULLY AND KNOWINGLY

P. 1422 n.18, end note. Under §32(a), a court should apply the reasonable investor materiality standard and not analyze materiality from the perspective of the SEC. United States v. Berger, 473 F.3d 1080, 1097-1100 (9th Cir. 2007), *cert. denied*, 128 S. Ct. 574. The court further held that proof of a materially false statement under §24 of the 1933 Act was equivalent to proof of a materially false statement under §32(a) of the 1934 Act. Id. at 1100-1102.

3. RELEVANT PROVISIONS OF THE CRIMINAL CODE

P. 1423, end carryover par. In May 2005 the United States Supreme Court reversed and remanded the conviction of Arthur Andersen because "the jury instructions failed to convey properly the elements of a 'corrupt persuas[ion]' conviction under [18 U.S.C.] §1512(b)." Arthur Andersen LLP v. United States, 544 U.S. 696 (2005).

In United States v. Skilling, 554 F.3d 529 (5th Cir. 2009), the Fifth Circuit affirmed Jeffrey Skilling's convictions in all respects, but remanded his sentencing because the District Court improperly had enhanced his sentence under the Sentencing Guidelines by wrongly characterizing an ERISA plan as a financial institution.

C. JUDICIAL REVIEW OF SEC ORDERS

P. 1430 n.11, end note. In McConville v. SEC, 465 F.3d 780 (7th Cir. 2006), *cert. denied*, 128 S. Ct. 48, the court declined to review an SEC administrative action that a corporate CFO had violated

§§10(b), 13(b)(2), and 13(b)(5) and Rules 13b2-1 and 13b2-2 and should be subject to a cease and desist order. The court reasoned that the 1934 Act "requires us to give highly deferential, conclusive effect to the Commission's factual findings, so long as they are supported by substantial evidence in the record." The court cited Monetta Fin. Serv., Inc. v. SEC, 390 F.3d 952, 955 (7th Cir. 2004).

In Lipkin v. SEC, 468 F. Supp. 2d 614 (S.D.N.Y. 2006), two SEC attorneys were entitled to absolute immunity from common law tort claims and held not to have violated a constitutional right.

Similarly, in Rosenberg v. MetLife, Inc., 8 N.Y.3d 359 (2007), in response to a certified question articulated by the Second Circuit in Rosenberg v. MetLife, Inc., 453 F.3d 122 (2d Cir. 2006), the New York Court of Appeals held that statements made by an employer in a Form U-5 are subject to an absolute privilege in a suit for defamation. Judge Pigott dissented and would have answered the certified question by stating that such statements are protected by a qualified privilege.

P. 1436 n.33, end note. In NYSE Specialists Sec. Litig., 503 F.3d 89 (2d Cir. 2007), *cert. denied*, 128 S. Ct. 1707, the court elaborated:

> Absolute immunity affords "complete protection from suit," *Harlow v. Fitzgerald*, 457 U.S. 800, 807 (1982), because it gives "public officials entrusted with sensitive tasks a protected area of discretion within which to carry out their responsibilities," *Barr v. Abrams*, 810 F.2d 358, 361 (2d Cir. 1987), so that they will not feel "constrained in making every decision by the consequences in terms of [their] own potential liability in a suit for damages." *Imbler v. Pachtman*, 424 U.S. 409, 424–25 (1976). The doctrine's nature "is such that it 'accords protection from ... any judicial scrutiny of the motive for and reasonableness of official action,'" *Shmueli v. City of New York*, 424 F.3d 231, 237 (2d Cir. 2005) (quoting *Robison v. Via*, 821 F.2d, 913, 918 (2d Cir. 1987)), even where the challenged conduct was motivated by a wrongful motive or even malice, *Bernard v. County of Suffolk*, 356 F.3d 495, 503 (2d Cir. 2004) (citing *Cleavinger v. Saxner*, 474 U.S. 193, 199–200 (1985)). Given this significant protection, we have cautioned that the doctrine "is of a rare and exceptional character." *Barrett v. United States*, 798 F.2d 565, 571 (2d Cir. 1986) (internal quotation marks omitted). As such, courts must examine

P. 1436

the invocation of absolute immunity on a case-by-case basis, *DL Capital Group v. NASDAQ Stock Mkt. Inc.*, 409 F.3d 93, 97 (2d Cir. 2005), and the party asserting immunity bears the burden of demonstrating its entitlement to it, *D'Alessio v. N.Y. Stock Exch., Inc.*, 258 F.3d 93, 104 (2d Cir. 2001).

Although the NYSE is not a government entity, we have recognized that in certain circumstances, it is entitled to absolute immunity for actions it takes pursuant to its quasi-governmental role in the regulation of the securities market. [Citation omitted.] Indeed, as in other absolute immunity contexts, we focus on "the nature of the function performed, not the identity of the actor who performed it," *Forrester v. White*, 484 U.S. 219, 229 (1988), in order to determine whether an SRO, such as the Exchange, is entitled to immunity, see *D'Alessio*, 258 F.3d at 104–06 (applying functional approach to determine whether the NYSE was entitled to immunity). Applying this analysis, we have found stock exchange SROs absolutely immune from suit where the alleged misconduct concerned (1) disciplinary proceedings against exchange members, *Barbara*, 99 F.3d at 59; (2) the enforcement of security rules and regulations and general regulatory oversight over exchange members. *D'Alessio*, 258 F.3d at 106; (3) the interpretation of the securities laws and regulations as applied to the exchange or its members, id.; (4) the referral of exchange members to the SEC and other government agencies for civil enforcement or criminal prosecution under the securities laws, id.; and (5) the public announcement of regulatory decisions, *DL Capital Group*, 409 F.3d at 98. The common thread in these cases is that absolute immunity attaches where the activity "relate[s] to the proper functioning of the regulatory system." *D'Alessio*, 258 F.3d at 106 (internal quotation marks omitted). Indeed, because:

> [t]he NYSE, as a[n] SRO, stands in the shoes of the SEC in interpreting the securities laws for its members and in monitoring compliance with those laws...[i]t follows that the NYSE should be entitled to the same immunity enjoyed by the SEC when it is performing functions delegated to it under the SEC's broad oversight authority.

Id. at 105. Thus, so long as the "alleged misconduct falls within the scope of the quasi-governmental powers delegated to the NYSE," absolute immunity attaches. Id. at 106.

Id. at 95.
In the *en banc* decision, Weissman v. NASD, Inc., 500 F.3d 1293 (11th Cir. 2007), the Eleventh Circuit reached similar conclusions:

> Under the Securities Exchange Act of 1934, Congress established a system of regulation over the securities industry, which relies on private, self-regulatory organizations to conduct the day-to-day regulation and administration of the United States' stock markets, under the close supervision of the United States Securities and Exchange Commission (*SEC*). The SEC authorized NASD to delegate its SRO functions to NASDAQ for operating and maintaining the NASDAQ stock market. [Citations omitted.] Thus, NASDAQ serves as an SRO within the meaning of the Securities Exchange Act, 15 U.S.C. §78c(a)(26), which vests it with a variety of adjudicatory, regulatory, and prosecutorial functions, including implementing and effectuating compliance with securities laws; promulgating and enforcing rules governing the conduct of its members; and listing and de-listing stock offerings. [Citations omitted.] At the same time, as a private corporation, NASDAQ may engage in a variety of non-governmental activities that serve its private business interests, such as its efforts to increase trading volume and company profit, as well as its daily administration and management of other business affairs. Indeed, even though the SEC has explicitly delegated regulatory functions to SROs, the SEC itself is mindful that SROs have dual status as both quasi-regulators and private businesses.
>
> Because they perform a variety of vital governmental functions, but lack the sovereign immunity that governmental agencies enjoy, SROs are protected by absolute immunity when they perform their statutorily delegated adjudicatory, regulatory, and prosecutorial functions. [Citations omitted.] However, entities that enjoy absolute immunity when performing governmental functions cannot claim that immunity when they perform non-governmental functions....The dual nature of SROs as private companies that carry out governmental functions is similar to that of municipal corporations.

Thus, "[t]o be sure, self-regulatory organizations do not enjoy complete immunity from suits." *Sparta*, 159 F.3d at 1214. Only when an SRO is *acting under the aegis of the Exchange Act's delegated authority* does it enjoy that privilege. Id. Absolute immunity is not appropriate unless the relevant conduct constitutes a delegated quasi-governmental prosecutorial, regulatory, or disciplinary function. [Citations omitted.]

Furthermore, because the law favors providing legal remedy to injured parties, grants of immunity must be narrowly construed; that is, courts must be "careful not to extend the scope of the protection further than its purposes require." *Forrester v. White*, 484 U.S. 219, 224 (1988); see also *Owen*, 445 U.S. at 645 n.28 (1980) (citations omitted). Thus, because immunity is appropriate only when an SRO is performing regulatory, adjudicatory, or prosecutorial functions that would otherwise be performed by a government agency, it follows that absolute immunity must be coterminous with an SRO's performance of a governmental function. When an SRO is not performing a purely regulatory, adjudicatory, or prosecutorial function, but rather acting in its own interest as a private entity, absolute immunity from suit ceases to obtain. To determine whether an SRO's conduct is quasi-governmental, we look to the objective nature and function of the activity for which the SRO seeks to claim immunity. The test is not an SRO's subjective intent or motivation [citations omitted], although there may be some correlation between motive and intent and the function being performed.

Id. at 1296–1297.

In this case because the court concluded that Nasdaq's advertisements did not serve an adjudicatory, regulatory, or prosecutorial function, the district court's denial of absolute immunity was affirmed.

In Series 7 Broker Qualification Exam Scoring Litig., 548 F.3d 110 (D.C. Cir. 2008), the court held that a common law negligence claim against the NASD for its administration of the Series 7 qualification examination was preempted by the Securities Exchange Act. Id. at 114-115. The court stated in part:

Turning to an immunity analysis, the Exchange Act reveals a deliberate and careful design for regulation of the securities industry. This regulatory model depends on the SEC's delegation of certain governmental functions to private SROs, such as NASD's administration and scoring of the Series 7 exam. Absent the unique self-regulatory framework of the securities industry, these responsibilities would be handled by the SEC — "an agency which is accorded sovereign immunity from all suits for money damages." DL Capital Group, LLC v. Nasdaq Stock Mkt., 409 F.3d 93, 97 (2d Cir. 2005). When an SRO acts under the aegis of the Exchange Act's delegated authority, it is absolutely immune from suit for the improper performance of regulatory, adjudicatory, or prosecutorial duties delegated by the SEC. See Weissman v. NASD, 500 F.3d 1293, 1298-99 (11th Cir. 2007).

The comprehensive structure set up by Congress is suggestive both of an intent to create immunity for such duties and of an intent to preempt state common law causes of action. The elaboration of duties, allowance of delegation and oversight by the SEC, and multi-layered system of review show Congress's desire to protect SROs from liability for common law suits. "The presumption that a remedy was deliberately omitted from a statute is strongest when Congress has enacted a comprehensive legislative scheme including an integrated system of procedures for enforcement." Feins v. Am. Stock Exch., Inc., 81 F.3d 1215, 1221 (2d Cir. 1996) (quoting Nw. Airlines v. Transp. Workers Union of Am., 451 U.S. 77, 97 (1981))....

Where courts accord immunity to SROs, the protection has been absolute. Courts have declined to craft exceptions for bad faith (*Desiderio*, 191 F.3d at 208), fraud (*DL Capital Group*, 409 F.3d at 98), negligence, or even gross negligence (*Sparta*, 159 F.3d at 1215)....

CHAPTER 13

SEC ADMINISTRATIVE LAW

A. SECURITIES LAWYERS

1. Requirements for Practicing

P. 1449 n.1, end note. In developments for the plaintiffs bar comparable to the significance of Enron, leading class action attorney Bill Lerach pled guilty to a secret kickback scheme at his former law firm, Milberg Weiss, shortly after another named partner, David Bershad, had similarly pled. Class Action Attorney Lerach Agrees to Plead Guilty over Kickback Scheme, 39 Sec. Reg. & L. Rep. (BNA) 1433 (2007); Lerach Given Two Years over Role in Milberg, Weiss Scheme, 40 id. 241 (2008). Subsequently, another former named partner, Steven Schulman, also pled guilty to related charges and Melvyn Weiss, who along with Lerach was the leader of the plaintiff's bar, was indicted. Milberg, Weiss Founder Indicted in Widening Kickback Probate, 39 id. 1432; Weiss of Milberg, Weiss Law Firm Agrees to Plead Guilty in Kickback Case, 40 id. 447.

2. The Securities Lawyer in General

P. 1458 n.29, end note. In August 2003 the ABA House of Delegates approved both the Task Force proposed amendments to Rule 1.13 and to Rule 1.6. ABA Amends Rule on Client Confidentiality to Allow Lawyers to Disclose Financial Fraud,

P. 1484

35 Sec. Reg. L. Rep. (BNA) 1357 (2003); ABA Amends Model Ethics Rules to Permit Up the Ladder Reports of Corporate Wrongs, 35 id. 1358.

B. INVESTIGATION

1. THE STATUTORY PROVISIONS AND THE COMMISSION'S PROCEDURES

P. 1484 n.21, end note. In 2003 the Commission announced that it would no longer permit defendants who settle civil injunctive cases to subsequently contest the factual allegations in later administrative proceedings. SEC Outlines New Enforcement Policy Based on Use of Facts in Settled Cases, 35 Sec. Reg. & L. Rep. (BNA) 1322 (2003).

In April 2004 Stephen Cutler, Director of the SEC Division of Enforcement, noted that "all but three of the 12 penalties of $50 million or more obtained in Commission settlements since 1986 were obtained in the last twelve months." Speech, 24th Ann. Ray Garrett Jr. Corporate and Securities Law Inst., Apr. 29, 2004, Chicago, Ill.

In February 2006, SEC Chair Cox reacted swiftly to media reports that the Commissioner had ordered two journalists to provide information to the SEC about conversations they had with stock traders and analysts, stating:

> The issuance of a subpoena to a journalist which seeks to compel production of his or her notes and records of conversations with sources is highly unusual. Until the appearance of media reports this weekend, neither the Chairman of the SEC, the General Counsel, the Office of Public Affairs, nor any Commissioner was apprised of or consulted in connection with a decision to take such an extraordinary step. The sensitive issues that such a subpoena raises are of sufficient importance that they should, and will be, considered and decided by the Commission before this matter proceeds further.

SEC Press Rel. 2006-24 (Feb. 27, 2006). See also Labaton & Norris, Crime and Consequences Still Weigh on Corporate World, N.Y. Times, Jan. 5, 2006, at C1; Ferrara, Clark, & Chang, The SEC's Newly Announced Standards for the Imposition of Corporate Monetary Penalties: An Overdue Step Toward Predictability, 38 Sec. Reg. & L. Rep. (BNA) 170 (2006).

In 2006 the Commission issued a Statement Concerning Financial Penalties in the context of an announcement of the settled actions against corporate issuers, SEC v. McAfee, Inc., and Applix, Inc. The Statement explained in part:

> The question of whether, and if so to what extent, to impose civil penalties against a corporation raises significant questions for our mission of investor protection. The authority to impose such penalties is relatively recent in the Commission's history, and the use of very large corporate penalties is more recent still. Recent cases have not produced a clear public view of when and how the Commission will use corporate penalties, and within the Commission itself a variety of views have heretofore been expressed, but not reconciled....
>
> In 1990, Congress passed the Securities Enforcement Remedies and Penny Stock Reform Act (the "Remedies Act"), which gave the Commission authority generally to seek civil money penalties in enforcement cases. The penalty provisions added by the Remedies Act expressly authorize the Commission to obtain money penalties from entities, including corporate issuers....
>
> ...[A] key question for the Commission is whether the issuer's violation has provided an improper benefit to the shareholders, or conversely whether the violation has resulted in harm to the shareholders. Where shareholders have been victimized by the violative conduct, or by the resulting negative effect on the entity following its discovery, the Commission is expected to seek penalties from culpable individual offenders acting for a corporation....
>
> In addition to the benefit or harm to shareholders, the statute and its legislative history suggest several other factors that may be pertinent to the analysis of corporate issuer penalties. For example, the need for effective deterrence is discussed throughout the legislative history of the Remedies Act. The Senate Report also notes the importance of good compliance programs and observes that the availability of penalties may encourage development of

such programs. The Senate Report also observes that penalties may serve to decrease the temptation to violate the law in areas where the perceived risk of detection of wrongdoing is small. Other factors discussed in the legislative history include whether there was fraudulent intent, harm to innocent third parties, and the possibility of unjust enrichment to the wrongdoer.

The Sarbanes-Oxley Act of 2002 changed the ultimate disposition of penalties. Section 308 of Sarbanes-Oxley (the Fair Funds provision) allows the Commission to take penalties paid by individuals and entities in enforcement actions and add them to disgorgement funds for the benefit of victims. Penalty moneys no longer always go to the Treasury. Under Fair Funds, penalty moneys instead can be used to compensate the victims for the losses they experienced from the wrongdoing. If the victims are shareholders of the corporation being penalized, they will still bear the cost of issuer penalty payments (which is the case with any penalty against a corporate entity). When penalty moneys are ultimately returned to all or some of the investors who were victims of the violation, the amounts returned are less the administrative costs of the distribution. While the legislative history of the Fair Funds provision is scant, there are two general points that can be discerned. First, the purpose of the provision is to provide an additional source of compensation to victims of securities law violations. Second, the provision applies to all penalties and makes no distinction between penalties against individuals or entities....

We proceed from the fundamental principle that corporate penalties are an essential part of an aggressive and comprehensive program to enforce the federal securities laws, and that the availability of a corporate penalty, as one of a range of remedies, contributes to the Commission's ability to achieve an appropriate level of deterrence through its decision in a particular case.

With this principle in mind, our view of the appropriateness of a penalty on the corporation in a particular case, as distinct from the individuals who commit a securities law violation, turns principally on two considerations:

The presence or absence of a direct benefit to the corporation as a result of the violation. The fact that a corporation itself has received a direct and material benefit from the offense, for example through reduced expenses or increased revenues, weighs in support of the imposition of a corporate penalty. If the corporation is in any other way unjustly enriched, this similarly weighs in support of the imposition of a corporate penalty. Within this parameter, the strongest case for the imposition of a corporate penalty is one in which the shareholders of the corporation have received an improper benefit as a result of the violation; the weakest case is one in which the current shareholders of the corporation are the principal victims of the securities law violation.

The degree to which the penalty will recompense or further harm the injured shareholders. Because the protection of innocent investors is a principal objective of the securities laws, the imposition of a penalty on the corporation itself carries with it the risk that shareholders who are innocent of the violation will nonetheless bear the burden of the penalty. In some cases, however, the penalty itself may be used as a source of funds to recompense the injury suffered by victims of the securities law violations. The presence of an opportunity to use the penalty as a meaningful source of compensation to injured shareholders is a factor in support of its imposition. The likelihood a corporate penalty will unfairly injure investors, the corporation, or third parties weighs against its use as a sanction.

In addition to these two principal considerations, there are several additional factors that are properly considered in determining whether to impose a penalty on the corporation. These are:

The need to deter the particular type of offense. The likelihood that a corporate penalty will serve as a strong deterrent to others similarly situated weighs in favor of the imposition of a corporate penalty. Conversely, the prevalence of unique circumstances that render the particular offense unlikely to be repeated in other contexts is a factor weighing against the need for a penalty on the corporation rather than on the responsible individuals.

The extent of the injury to innocent parties. The egregiousness of the harm done, the number of investors injured, and the extent of societal harm if the corporation's infliction of such injury on innocent parties goes unpunished, are significant determinants of the propriety of a corporate penalty.

Whether complicity in the violation is widespread throughout the corporation. The more pervasive the participation in the offense by responsible persons within the corporation, the more appropriate is the use of a corporate penalty. Conversely, within this parameter, isolated conduct by only a few individuals would tend not to support the imposition of a corporate penalty. Whether the corporation has replaced those persons responsible for the violation will also be considered in weighing this factor.

The level of intent on the part of the perpetrators. Within this parameter, the imposition of a corporate penalty is most appropriate in egregious circumstances, where the culpability and fraudulent intent of the perpetrators are manifest. A corporate penalty is less likely to be imposed if the violation is not the result of deliberate, intentionally fraudulent conduct.

The degree of difficulty in detecting the particular type of offense. Because offenses that are particularly difficult to detect call for an especially high level of deterrence, this factor weighs in support of the imposition of a corporate penalty.

Presence or lack of remedial steps by the corporation. Because the aim of the securities laws is to protect investors, the prevention of future harm, as well as the punishment of past offenses, is a high priority. The Commission's decisions in particular cases are intended to encourage the management of corporations accused of securities law violations to do everything within their power to take remedial steps, from the first moment that the violation is brought to their attention. Exemplary conduct by management in this respect weighs against the use of a corporate penalty; failure of management to take remedial steps is a factor supporting the imposition of a corporate penalty.

Extent of cooperation with Commission and other law enforcement. Effective compliance with the securities laws depends upon vigilant supervision, monitoring, and reporting of violations. When securities law violations are discovered, it is incumbent upon management to report them to the Commission and to other appropriate law enforcement authorities. The degree to which a corporation has self reported an offense, or otherwise cooperated with the investigation and remediation of the offense, is a factor that the Commission will consider in determining the propriety of a corporate penalty.

In April 2006 the Commission codified a policy statement concerning subpoenas to members of the news media. Sec. Ex. Act Rel. 53,638, 87 SEC Dock. 2251 (2006) (adding 17 C.F.R. §202.10).

In December 2008 former Nasdaq stock market chair Bernard Madoff was charged by both the SEC and the United States Attorney with perpetrating a massive fraud on his investors. SEC v. Madoff Complaint, 08 Civ. 10,791 (S.D.N.Y. Dec. 11, 2008) (alleging $50 billion Ponzi scheme).

The Madoff case proved a major embarrassment to the SEC. Later in December 2008 SEC Chair Christopher Cox issued a release that stated in part:

> I am gravely concerned by the apparent multiple failures over at least a decade to thoroughly investigate these allegations or at any point to seek formal authority to pursue them. Moreover, a consequence of the failure to seek a formal order of investigation from the Commission is that subpoena power was not used to obtain information, but rather the staff relied upon information voluntarily produced by Mr. Madoff and his firm.
>
> In response, after consultation with the Commission, I have directed a full and immediate review of the past allegations regarding Mr. Madoff and his firm and the reasons they were not found credible, to be led by the SEC's Inspector General. The review will also cover the internal policies at the SEC governing when allegations such as those in this case should be raised to the Commission level, whether those policies were followed, and whether improvements to those policies are necessary. The investigation should also include all staff contact and relationships with the Madoff family and firm, and their impact, if any, on decisions by staff regarding the firm.

Statement Regarding Madoff Investigation, SEC Press Rel. 2008-297 (Dec. 16, 2008); see also Labaton, SEC Image Suffers in a String of Setbacks, N.Y. Times, Dec. 15, 2008 at B6, quoting the senior author.

Subsequently the *New York Times* reported:

> There were 133 prosecutions for securities fraud in the first 11 months of this fiscal year. That is down from 437 cases in 2000 and from a high of 513 cases in 2002, when Wall Street scandals from Enron to WorldCom led to a crackdown on corporate crime, the data showed.

P. 1484 2010 SUPPLEMENT

At the SEC, agency investigations that led to Justice Department prosecutions for securities fraud dropped from 69 in 2000 to just 9 in 2007, a decline of 87 percent, the data showed.

Lichtblau, Wall St. Fraud Prosecutions Fall Sharply, New York Times, Dec. 25, 2008, at A1.

See also Cox Says Staff Ignored Red Flags, Seeks Investigation by SEC IG Kotz [in Madoff Case], 40 Sec. Reg. & L. Rep. (BNA) 2104 (2008); First Lawsuits Filed against Madoff, His Firm, Others; More Likely to Follow, 40 id. 2107; Suits from Madoff Fraud Will Be Massive, Will Involve Family Members, Attorneys Say, 40 id. 2107; Madoff Case Likely to Prompt Closer Look at Funds, Advisers, Brokers, and Regulators, 40 id. 2108.

Soon after being confirmed as Chair of the SEC, Mary Schapiro announced that the Commission was suspending its two year penalty pilot experiment "which had required the Enforcement Staff to obtain a special set of approvals from the Commission in cases involving civil monetary penalties for public companies as punishment for securities fraud" and "putting in place [another immediate change] to bolster the SEC's enforcement program...to provide for more rapid approval of formal orders of investigation." Mary L. Schapiro, Address to PLI SEC Speaks in 2009 Program, Ronald Reagan Int'l Trade Center (Feb. 6, 2009) at 3. She sought to bring back the procedure that had operated when she earlier had been a Commissioner and "formal orders were routinely reviewed and approved within a couple of days by written approval of the Commission or by [a] *duty officer* — a single Commissioner acting promptly and on behalf of the entire Commission." Ibid.

Approximately the same time SEC Enforcement Director Linda Thomsen resigned, after being berated in Congressional hearings for failing to uncover the Madoff Ponzi scheme, and was succeeded by Robert Khuzami, a former federal prosecutor. Enforcement Chief Thomsen Leaving SEC; Deutsche Bank Lawyer Seen as Successor, 41 Sec. Reg. & L. Rep. (BNA) 245 (2009).

In March 2009 the SEC Office of Inspector General Report, Practices Related to Naked Short Selling Complaints and Referrals (Report No. 450, Mar. 18, 2009) generalized about the Enforcement Division's Enforcement Complaint Center (*ECC*) at 3-4, 6:

> According to ECC information available as of 2007, the ECC typically received between 5,000 and 7,000 e-mail complaints per day. The number of complaints received in the ECC greatly increased beginning with the Enron accounting scandal in the fall of 2001. While the number of complaints per day subsequently began to level off, the "fluctuations in complaint volume typically depend on the SEC's profile in the news." Based on information the Office of Inspector General (*OIG*) obtained from Enforcement, we found that the ECC received approximately 1.38 million complaints via e-mail from January 1, 2007 to June 1, 2008, which were handled by a staff of four persons.
>
> After complaints are received in the ECC, they go through a three-step process. First, an initial coordinator review is conducted on the morning of each business day "to cull out a) extraneous e-mails not involving securities matters; and b) large-scale spam (10, 20, 50 or more) involving pending investigations of which the coordinator is aware." Also, at this initial stage, to the extent possible, certain *consumer* matters, i.e., investors' private disputes with brokers — are sent to the Office of Investor Education and Advocacy (*OIEA*) for review.
>
> Second, a second-level coordinator review is conducted on the remaining complaints to determine if they:
>
> - Relate to pending investigations;
> - Describe conduct better handled by OIEA;
> - Relate to situations more appropriately handled by other agencies; or
> - Should be sent to state regulators.
>
> Third, complaints that remain after the first and second level reviews are forwarded to OIE staff every ten days to conduct a *triage*. Triage is "the process of research and analysis used to determine if an incoming investor complaint is likely to trigger sufficient staff interest to entail the opening of" a MUI or formal investigation. Essentially, "it is a series of steps designed to assess what type

of wrongdoing is being alleged, what the market impact of that wrongdoing is, who may be involved in the conduct, and who the most appropriate persons are to look into that conduct."

In March 2009, the GAO published Securities and Exchange Commission: Greater Attention Is Needed to Enhance Communication and Utilization of Resources in the Division of Enforcement (GAO-09-358). The GAO Report explained, among other things:

> While overall Enforcement resources and activities have remained relatively level in recent years, the number of non-supervisory investigative attorneys, who have primary responsibility for developing enforcement cases, decreased by 11.5 percent, from a peak of 566 in fiscal year 2004 to 501 for fiscal year 2008. At the same time, staff turnover has decreased and staff tenure has increased. Measured by the number of enforcement cases opened annually, and number of enforcement actions brought annually, Enforcement activity has been relatively level in recent years. Case backlogs have declined as the division has made case closings a greater priority. Nevertheless, Enforcement management and investigative attorneys agreed that resource challenges have affected their ability to bring enforcement actions effectively and efficiently. Although Enforcement management told us that the current level of resources has not prevented the division from continuing to bring cases across a range of violations, management and staff acknowledged that current staffing levels mean some worthwhile leads cannot be pursued, and some cases are closed without action earlier than they otherwise would have been. More specifically, investigative attorneys cited the low level of administrative, paralegal, and information technology support, unavailability of specialized services and expertise, and a burdensome system for internal case review as causing significant delays in bringing cases, reducing the number of cases that can be brought, and potentially undermining the quality of cases. Effective and efficient use of resources is important to accomplishing Enforcement's mission. SEC's strategic plan calls for targeting resources strategically, examining whether positions are deployed effectively, and exploring how to improve program design and organizational

structure. Recently, Enforcement management has begun an initiative that seeks to streamline the case review process. This effort is focused on process, but our review suggests that organizational culture issues, such as risk aversion and incentives to drop cases or narrow their scope, are also present. If the division does not consider such issues in its initiative, the effort may not be as successful as it otherwise could be.

Enforcement staff consider multiple factors when determining the dollar amounts of penalties and disgorgements, which in total have declined in recent years. To determine a penalty in an individual case, Enforcement staff consider factors such as nature of the violation, egregiousness of conduct, cooperation by the defendant, remedial actions taken, and ability to pay. Disgorgement is intended to recover gains made, or losses avoided, through a defendant's actions. In 2006 and 2007, the Commission articulated certain policies for determining the appropriateness and size of corporate penalties. The 2006 policy focuses on the direct benefit a corporation has gained through its conduct and whether a penalty stands to cause additional harm to shareholders. The 2007 policy required Enforcement staff, when contemplating a corporate penalty, to obtain Commission approval of a penalty range before settlement discussions can begin. Setting aside the effect of the implementation of any policy, the total amount of penalties and disgorgement ordered on an annual basis can vary according to the type and magnitude of cases concluded in a given period. Since fiscal years 2005 and 2006, total annual penalty and disgorgement amounts have declined. While both have fallen, penalties have been declining at an accelerating rate, falling 39 percent in fiscal year 2006, another 48 percent in fiscal year 2007, and then 49 percent in fiscal year 2008. Although there were more corporate penalty cases in fiscal year 2007 than in fiscal year 2006, penalty amounts were larger in the fiscal year 2006 cases. Four of the six cases in 2006 resulted in penalties of $50 million or more, with the two largest, American International Group (AIG) and Fannie Mae, totaling $100 million and $400 million, respectively. By contrast, 2 of the 10 cases in fiscal year 2007, against MBIA, Inc., and Freddie Mac, assessed penalties of at least $50 million.

We found that Enforcement management, investigative attorneys, and others concurred that the 2006 and 2007 penalty policies, as applied, have had the effect of delaying cases and producing fewer and smaller corporate penalties. Our review also identified several other concerns:

- That the policies have had the effect of making penalties less punitive in nature — by conditioning corporate penalties in large part on whether a corporation has benefited from improper practices, penalties effectively become more like disgorgement.
- That the 2007 policy (Commission pre-approval of a settlement range; also known as the *pilot program*) could have led to less-informed decisions about corporate penalties. This is because settlement discussions can further reveal relevant information about conduct of the wrongdoer, and the Commission would have decided upon a penalty range without having received such information.
- That the policies have reduced incentives for subjects of enforcement actions to cooperate with the agency, because of the perception that SEC has retreated on penalties.
- That it became more difficult to obtain *formal orders of investigation*, which allow issuance of subpoenas to compel testimony and produce books, records, and other documents. Since fiscal year 2005, the number of formal orders approved by the Commission has decreased 14 percent.

Our review also showed that in adopting and implementing the policies, the Commission did not act in concert with agency strategic goals calling for broad communication with, and involvement of, the staff. In particular, Enforcement, which is responsible for implementing the policies, had only limited input into their development. As a result, Enforcement attorneys say there has been frustration and uncertainty in application of the penalty policies.

This report makes four recommendations designed to strengthen Enforcement's ability to achieve its objectives. In summary, we recommend that the SEC Chairman:

1. Consider an alternative organizational structure and reporting relationship for OCD;
2. Further review the level and mix of resources dedicated to Enforcement, and assess the impact that the division's current review and approval process for investigative staff

work has on organizational culture and the ability to bring timely enforcement actions;

3. Examine the effects of the 2006 corporate penalty policy to determine whether the policy is achieving its stated goals, and any other effects the policy may have had in adoption or implementation; and

4. Take steps to ensure that the Commission, in creating, monitoring, and evaluating its policies, follows the agency strategic goal and other best practices for communication with, and involvement of, the staff affected by such changes.

Id. at 4-8.

C. QUASIJUDICIAL PROCEEDINGS

P. 1499 n.39, end note. In Rule 161(b) the Commission adopted a policy to strongly disfavor requests to extend time limits or grant postponements, adjournments, and extensions, but the Commission or the hearing officer can extend the time limits. Rule 161(c)(2) permits an extension to consider an offer of settlement. Under Rule 360 the deadlines will be 120, 210, and 300 days. Other temporal amendments were made to Rules 230(d) and 450. Sec. Ex. Act Rel. 48,018, 80 SEC Dock. 1266 (2003) (adoption).

D. STATUTORY REMEDIES

2. CEASE AND DESIST ORDERS

P. 1510 n.18, end note. See also WHX Corp. v. SEC, 362 F.3d 854 (D.C. Cir. 2004), citing *KPMG* standard, but reversing cease and desist order; Geiger v. SEC, 363 F.3d 481 (D.C. Cir. 2004), affirming cease and desist order, and observing, "under Commission precedent, the existence of a violation raises an inference that it will be repeated." Id. at 489.

3. CORPORATE BAR ORDERS

P. 1511 n.24, end note. In Vernazza v. SEC, 327 F.3d 851, 862–863 (9th Cir. 2003), the court agreed with the SEC that a six month bar from association with other investment advisers was reasonable after the investment adviser was deceived by a fraudulent scheme that spanned several years. See also Lowry v. SEC, 340 F.3d 501 (5th Cir. 2003) (similar).

In Gibson v. SEC, 561 F.3d 548 (6th Cir. 2009), the court followed Steadman v. SEC, 603 F.2d 1126, 1140 (5th Cir. 1979), and its articulation of six factors to consider when imposing a disciplinary sanction and imposed a lifetime bar on a certified financial planner.

P. 1511, new text, end page. In SEC v. Smyth, 420 F.3d 1225 (11th Cir. 2005), the court vacated a disgorgement order when the District Court refused to hold an evidentiary hearing to determine the amount that should have been disgorged. The amount was in dispute. The case was remanded for further proceedings.

CHAPTER 14

CONFLICT OF LAWS, PROCEDURAL ASPECTS, AND *GLOBALIZATION*

A. JURISDICTION AND VENUE

1. Subject Matter Jurisdiction

P. 1534, end 3d par. In Katz v. Gerardi, 552 F.3d 558 (7th Cir. 2009), the Seventh Circuit disagreed with the Ninth Circuit in Luther v. Countrywide Home Loans Serv., L.P., 533 F.3d 1031 (9th Cir. 2008), and held that securities class actions covered by the Class Action Fairness Act of 2005 are removeable to federal court despite §22(a) of the 1933 Act, subject to exceptions specified in §§1332(d)(9) and 1453(d).

5. Criminal Actions

P. 1545 n.55, end note. In United States v. Johnson, 510 F.3d 521, 525 (4th Cir. 2007), the court held with respect to venue:

We therefore hold that causing the transmission of the Form 10-Q to the Eastern District of Virginia will suffice to sustain venue in that district. The notion that venue in securities prosecutions must be limited to where the *essence* of the offense exists finds no basis in the text of §78aa. To the contrary, this provision, whose language is *manifestly broad,* [citation omitted] simply requires that *"any* act or transaction constituting the violation" have taken place in the pertinent district, [citation omitted]. As a result, the "venue-sustaining act need not constitute the core of the alleged violation," but merely one that is material to the charged offense. [Citation omitted.]

C. INTERNATIONAL ASPECTS

1. CHOICE OF LAW

P. 1563, end 1st full par.   In Morrison v. National Aust. Bank, Ltd., 547 F.3d 167 (2d Cir. 2008), the court applied the conduct and effects test to a *foreign-cubed* class action in which (1) *foreign* plaintiffs sued (2) a *foreign* issuer in a United States court for violations of United States securities laws based on securities transactions in (3) *foreign* countries. The court ultimately concluded given the facts of the case that it did not have subject matter jurisdiction, but it declined to articulate a *per se* rule that in no *foreign cubed* case would subject matter jurisdiction be possible.

TABLE OF CASES

References are to page numbers of main volume.

AAL High Yield Bond Fund v. Deloitte & Touche LLP (361 F.3d 1305), 1403
ABC Arbitrage Plaintiffs Group v. Tchuruk (291 F.3d 336), 1359
ADC Telecomm., Inc. Sec. Litig. (409 F.3d 974), 1346
APA Excelsior III, L.P. v. Premiere Tech. (476 F.3d 1261), 1228
ATSI Communications, Inc. v. Shaar Fund, Ltd. (493 F.3d 87), 1137, 1359
Able Lab. Sec. Litig. (2007–2008 Fed. Sec. L. Rep. (CCH) ¶94,618), 1347
Affiliated Ute Citizens v. United States (406 U.S. 128), 1283, 1332
Alaska Elec. Pension Fund v. Pharmacia Corp. (554 F.3d 342), 1346
Alexander v. Sandoval (532 U.S. 275), 1264
Alliance Bernstein Inv. Research & Mgmt., Inc. v. Schaffran (445 F.3d 121), 1376
American Fed. of State, County & Mun. Employees v. American Int'l Group, Inc. (462 F.3d 121), 539, 573
American Fire & Casualty Co. v. Finn (341 U.S. 6), 1264

American High-Income Trust v. AlliedSignal (329 F. Supp. 2d 534), 438
American Pipe & Constr. Co. v. Utah (414 U.S. 538), 1346
Amron v. Morgan Stanley Inv. Advisors, Inc. (464 F.3d 338), 1303
Anderson, Mark D. (Sec. Ex. Act Rel. 48,352), 1071
Andresen, State v. (773 A.2d 328), 344
Anixter v. Home-Stake Prod. Co. (77 F.3d 1215), 1332
Arthur Andersen LLP v. United States (544 U.S. 696), 1423
Ashcroft v. Iqbal (129 S. Ct. 1937), 1353
Asher v. Baxter Int'l, Inc. (377 F.3d 727), 165
At Home Corp. v. Cox Communications, Inc. (446 F.3d 403), 687
Autocorp Equities, Inc., SEC v. (292 F. Supp. 2d 1310), 227
Avello v. SEC (454 F.3d 619), 826

BP Am. Prod. Co. v. Burton (549 U.S. 84), 1335
Bailey v. Glover (88 U.S. (21 Wall.) 342), 1346
BankAmerica Sec. Litig. (350 F.3d 747), 1398

543

Banque Arabe et Internationale D'Investissement v. Maryland National Bank (57 F.3d 146), 1359
Barbara v. New York Stock Exch. (99 F.3d 49), 1430
Baron v. Smith (380 F.3d 49), 165
Barr v. Abrams (810 F.2d 358), 1436
Barrett v. United States (798 F.2d 565), 1436
Basic Inc. v. Levinson (485 U.S. 224), 590, 1285, 1332
Bastian v. Petren Resources Corp. (892 F.2d 680), 1285
Bateman Eichler, Hill Richards, Inc. v. Berner (472 U.S. 299), 1362
Bausch & Lomb., Inc. Sec. Litig. (592 F. Supp. 2d 323), 1359
Belizan v. Hershon (495 F.3d 686), 1359
Bell v. Ascendant Solutions, Inc. (422 F.3d 307), 1281
Bell Atl. Corp. v. Twombly (550 U.S. 544), 1353
Bellikoff v. Eaton Vance (481 F.3d 110), 1303
Benak v. Alliance Capital Mgmt. L.P. (435 F.3d 396), 1346
Benzon v. Morgan Stanley Distrib., Inc. (420 F.3d 598), 576
Berckeley Inv. Group, Ltd. v. Colkitt (455 F.3d 195), 327, 413, 429, 1240
Berger, United States v. (473 F.3d 1080), 1422
Bernard v. County of Suffolk (356 F.3d 495), 1436
Berry v. Valence Tech., Inc. (175 F.3d 699), 1346
Berson v. Applied Signal Tech., Inc. (527 F.3d 982), 1359
Betz v. Trainer Wortham & Co., Inc. (486 F.3d 590), 1346
Betz v. Trainer Wortham & Co., Inc. (519 F.3d 863), 1346
Bielski v. Cabeltron Sys., Inc. (311 F.3d 11), 1359

Billing v. Credit Suisse First Boston (426 F.3d 130), 797
Binder v. Gillespie (184 F.3d 1059), 1332
Birnbaum v. Newport Steel Corp. (193 F.2d 461), 1192
Black v. Finantra Capital, Inc. (418 F.3d 203), 1281
Blatchford v. Native Village of Noatak (501 U.S. 775), 1264
Blau v. Lehman (368 U.S. 403), 719
Blaz v. Belfer (368 F.3d 501), 1192
Blue Chip Stamps v. Manor Drug Stores (421 U.S. 723), 1047, 1192, 1264, 1285, 1332
Board of Governors v. Dimension Fin. Corp. (474 U.S. 361), 894
Bradbury v. SEC (512 F.3d 634), 1232
Bragdon v. Abbott (524 U.S. 624), 1192
Brandaid Mktg. Corp. v. Biss (462 F.3d 216), 1362
Breakaway Solutions, Inc. v. Morgan Stanley & Co., Inc. (2004 Del. Ch. LEXIS 125), 1192
Bristol-Myers Sec. Litig. (2007 Fed. Sec. L. Rep. (CCH) ¶94,447), 1405
Brodsky v. Yahoo! Inc. (592 F. Supp. 2d 1192), 1359
Broudo v. Dura Pharmaceuticals, Inc. (339 F.3d 933), 1285
Brown v. Earthboard Sports USA, Inc. (481 F.3d 901), 29, 1025, 1285, 1310
Brumley v. Touche Ross & Co. (487 N.E.2d 641), 1237
Brunig v. Clark (560 F.3d 292), 1408
Buckeye Check Cashing v. Cardegna (546 U.S. 440), 1376
Burlington Coat Factory Sec. Litig. (114 F.3d 1410), 590
Business Roundtable v. SEC (905 F.2d 406), 573

TABLE OF CASES

CFTC v. Zelener (373 F.3d 861), 267
CSX Corp. v. Children's Inv. Fund Management (UK) (562 F. Supp. 2d 511), 622
Cabletron Systems, Inc. (311 F.3d 11), 1025, 1359
Cada v. Baxter Healthcare Corp. (920 F.2d 446), 1346
Caldwell v. Texas (95 S.W.3d 563), 231
California Pub. Employees Retirement Sys. v. Chubb Corp. (394 F.3d 126), 1359
Cammer v. Bloom (711 F. Supp. 1264), 1281
Cannon v. University of Chicago (441 U.S. 677), 1192, 1264
Capital Gains Research Bureau, Inc., SEC v. (375 U.S. 180), 1232
Caprin v. Simon Transp. Serv., Inc. (2003–2004 Fed. Sec. L. Rep. (CCH) ¶92,692), 1346
Castellano v. Young & Rubicam, Inc. (257 F.3d 171), 841
Cavanagh, SEC v. (445 F.3d 105), 413
Cavanagh, SEC v. (155 F.3d 129), 101
Central Bank of Denver, N.A. v. First Interstate Bank of Denver, N.A. (511 U.S. 164), 1264, 1313, 1332
Central Laborers' Pension Fund v. Integrated Elec. Serv., Inc. (497 F.3d 546), 1025
Ceridian Corp. Sec. Litig. (542 F.3d 240), 1359
Chamber of Commerce v. SEC (412 F.3d 133), 59
Charter Communications, Inc. Sec. Litig. (443 F.3d 987), 1332
Chevron USA Inc. v. Natural Res. Def. Council, Inc. (467 U.S. 837), 894, 957
Chiarella v. United States (445 U.S. 222), 1332

City of Monroe Employees Ret. Sys. v. Bridgestone Corp. (399 F.3d 651), 1025
Cleavinger v. Saxner (474 U.S. 193), 1436
Conley v. Gibson (355 U.S. 41), 1285, 1353
Cornelia I. Crowell GST Trust v. Possis Med., Inc. (519 F.3d 778), 1359
Corporation Relations Group, Inc., SEC v. (Case No. 6:99-cv-1222-Orl.-28KRS), 227
Cort v. Ash (422 U.S. 66), 1264
Credit Suisse Sec. (USA) LLC v. Billing (551 U.S. 264), 797
Credit Suisse First Boston Corp. v. Grunwald (400 F.3d 1119), 1376

DL Capital Group v. NASDAQ Stock Mkt. Inc. (409 F.3d 93), 1430, 1436
Dabit v. Merrill Lynch, Pierce, Fenner & Smith, Inc. (395 F.3d 25), 1192
Dain Rauscher, Inc., SEC v. (254 F.3d 852), 1232
D'Alessio v. N.Y. Stock Exch., Inc. (258 F.3d 93), 1436
D'Alessio v. SEC (380 F.3d 112), 788
Daou Sys., Inc. Sec. Litig. (411 F.3d 1006), 1359
DeBenedictis v. Merrill Lynch & Co., Inc. (492 F.3d 209), 1346
Deephaven Private Placement Trading Ltd. v. Grant Thornton & Co. (454 F.3d 1168), 1240
De la Fuente v. OCI DCI Telecommunications, Inc. (2003–2004 Fed. Sec. L. Rep. (CCH) ¶92,646), 1408
Desiderio v. NASD (191 F.3d 198), 788, 1436

545

Digimarc Corp. Deriv. Litig. (549 F.3d 1223), 727
Digital Island Sec. Litig. (357 F.3d 322), 643
Dodd v. Cigna (12 F.3d 346), 1346
Dolphin & Bradbury, Inc. v. SEC (512 F.3d 634), 1019, 1332
Domestic Sec., Inc. v. SEC (333 F.3d 239), 763
Donoghue v. Centillium Communications, Inc. (2006 Fed. Sec. L. Rep. (CCH) ¶93,824), 692
Dreiling v. American Express Co. (458 F.3d 942), 719
DuBois, Derek L. (Sec. Ex. Act Rel. 48,332), 582
Dura Pharmaceuticals, Inc. Sec. Litig. (452 F. Supp. 2d 1005), 1285
Dura Pharmaceuticals, Inc. v. Broudo (544 U.S. 336), 1285, 1332, 1359

EBC I v. Goldman Sachs & Co. (832 N.E.2d 26), 1232
ECA, Local 134 IBEW Joint Pens. Trust v. JP Morgan Chase (553 F.3d 187), 1359
EP MedSystems, Inc. v. EchoCath, Inc. (235 F.3d 865), 1285
Edelson v. Ch'ien (405 F.3d 620), 1272
Edwards, SEC v. (540 U.S. 389), 248, 251, 256
Emergent Capital Inv. Mgmt., LLC v. Stonepath Group, Inc. (343 F.3d 189), 841, 1285
Enron Corp. Sec., Deriv. & ERISA Litig. (284 F. Supp. 2d 511), 1192
Enron Corp. Sec., Deriv. & ERISA Litig. (310 F. Supp. 2d 819), 438, 1216
Enron Corp. Sec., Deriv. & ERISA Litig. (535 F.3d 325), 1192

Enron Corp. Sec. v. Enron Corp. (439 F. Supp. 2d 692), 1332
Enterprise Mortgage Acceptance Co., LLC Sec. Litig. (391 F.3d 401), 1347
Epstein v. MCA, Inc. (50 F.3d 644), 643
Ernst & Ernst v. Hochfelder (425 U.S. 185), 1285, 1332, 1359
Ernst & Young (Init. Dec. Rel. 249), 194
Evans, United States v. (486 F.3d 315), 1002
Exploration Co. v. United States (247 U.S. 435), 1346
Exxon Mobil Corp. Sec. Litig. (500 F.3d 189), 1347
Ezra Charitable Trust v. Tyco Int'l, Ltd. (466 F.3d 1), 1025

Faye L. Roth Revocable Trust v. UBS Paine, Webber, Inc. (323 F. Supp. 2d 1279), 1216
Feder v. Martin Marietta Corp. (406 F.2d 260), 719
Feins v. Am. Stock Exch., Inc. (81 F.3d 1215), 1436
Finance & Trading LTD v. Rhodia S.A. (2004 Fed. Sec. L. Rep. (CCH) ¶93,046), 1192
Financial Acquisition Partners LP v. Blackwell (440 F.3d 278), 1359
Financial Planning Ass'n v. SEC (482 F.3d 481), 894
Financial Security Assurance, Inc. v. Stephens, Inc. (450 F.3d 1257), 297, 1045, 1047
Financial Sec. Assur., Inc. v. Stephens (500 F.3d 1276), 231, 1047
Finnerty, United States v. (533 F.3d 143), 1332
Firestone Tire & Rubber Co. v. Bruch (489 U.S. 101), 1303

TABLE OF CASES

Fisk v. Superannuities, Inc. (927 F. Supp. 718), 1216
Forrester v. White (484 U.S. 219), 1436
Foss v. Bear, Stearns & Co., Inc. (394 F.3d 540), 1347
Foster v. Wilson (504 F.3d 1046), 1359
Frank v. Dana Corp. (547 F.3d 564), 1025, 1359
Free Enter. Fund v. PCAOB (2007 WL 891,675), 208
Free Enter. Fund v. Pub. Co. Accounting Oversight Bd. (537 F.3d 667), 208
Freeman v. Venner (120 Mass. 424), 1285

Gallus v. Ameriprise Fin., Inc. (561 F.3d 816), 1303
Ganino v. Citizens Utils. Co. (228 F.3d 154), 588
Garfield v. NDC Health Corp. (466 F.3d 1255), 1025
Gartenberg v. Merrill Lynch Asset Mgmt., Inc. (694 F.2d 923), 1303
Gavin v. AT&T Corp. (464 F.3d 634), 1192
Gebhardt v. ConAgra Foods, Inc. (335 F.3d 824), 174, 588, 1285
Geiger v. SEC (363 F.3d 481), 101, 227, 413, 1510
Gemstar-TV Guide Int'l Inc., SEC v. (401 F.3d 1031), 1420
Gerber v. Computer Assoc. Int'l, Inc. (303 F.3d 126), 643
Gerber v. MTC Elec. Tech. (329 F.3d 297), 1398
Gibson v. SEC (561 F.3d 548), 1511
Gilead Sciences Sec. Litig. (536 F.3d 1049), 1285
Ginsburg, SEC v. (362 F.3d 1292), 1051

Glaser v. Enzo Biochem, Inc. (464 F.3d 474), 1285
Glazer Capital Mgmt., LP v. Magistri (549 F.3d 736), 1025
Global Crossing, Ltd. Sec. Litig. (2003–2004 Fed. Sec. L. Rep. (CCH) ¶92,654), 1347
Goldstein v. SEC (451 F.3d 873), 59, 1108
Gordon v. New York Stock Exch., Inc. (422 U.S. 659), 797
Great White Marine & Recreation, Inc., SEC v. (428 F.3d 553), 1054
Green v. Nuveen Advisory Corp. (295 F.3d 738), 1303
Greenhouse v. MCG Capital Corp. (392 F.3d 650), 174
Grippo v. Perazzo (357 F.3d 1218), 1346
Gustafson v. Alloyd Co. Inc. (513 U.S. 561), 1216

Hanly v. SEC (415 F.2d 589), 1232
Happ, SEC v. (392 F.3d 12), 590
Harlow v. Fitzgerald (457 U.S. 800), 1436
Hawk, SEC v. (2007 Fed. Sec. L. Rep. (CCH) ¶94,461), 1310
Hayes Lemmerz Int'l Inc. Equity Sec. Litig. v. Cucuz (271 F. Supp. 2d 1007), 438
Helwig v. Vencor, Inc. (251 F.3d 540), 165, 1025, 1359
Hemispherx Biopharma, Inc. v. Johannesburg Consol. Inv. (553 F.3d 1351), 622
Heritage Bond Litig. (546 F.3d 667), 1398
Herman & MacLean v. Huddleston (459 U.S. 375), 1332
Higginbotham v. Baxter Int'l, Inc. (495 F.3d 753), 1359
Hollinger Int'l, Inc. v. Black (844 A.2d 1022), 200

547

Holmberg v. Armbrecht (327 U.S. 392), 1346

IBP, Inc. v. Alvarez (126 S. Ct. 514), 1192
Imbler v. Pachtman (424 U.S. 409), 1436
Indiana Elec. Workers' Pension Trust Fund IBEW v. Shaw Group (537 F.3d 527), 1025
Instituto de Prevision Militar v. Merrill Lynch & Co. (546 F.3d 1340), 1192
Intelligroup Sec. Litig. (488 F. Supp. 2d 670), 1285
Intelligroup Sec. Litig. (527 F. Supp. 2d 262), 1353
Int'l Bank for Reconstr. & Dev. (2001 SEC LEXIS 1782), 894

J.I. Case Co. v. Borak (377 U.S. 426), 1264
JT Wallenbrock & Assocs., SEC v. (440 F.3d 1109), 1054
J.W. Barclay & Co., Inc., SEC v. (442 F.3d 834), 1310
J&R Marketing, SEP v. General Motors Corp. (549 F.3d 384), 576, 1332
Johnson v. Alijan (490 F.3d 778), 1049, 1310
Johnson, United States v. (510 F.3d 521), 1545
Jones v. Harris Assoc., L.P. (527 F.3d 627), 1303
Jones v. Harris Assoc. (129 S. Ct. 1579), 1303

KMPG Peat Marwick LLP (289 F.3d 109), 231, 643
Kapps v. Torch Offshore, Inc. (379 F.3d 207), 588
Katz v. Gerardi (552 F.3d 558), 1534

Katz v. Image Innovations Holdings, Inc. (542 F. Supp. 2d 269), 1025
Kern, SEC v. (425 F.3d 143), 413
Kern County Land Co. v. Occidental Petroleum Corp. (411 U.S. 582), 687, 692
King v. Pope (91 S.W.3d 314), 231, 643
Kirby, Charles F. (2000 SEC LEXIS 2681), 227
Kircher v. Putnam Funds Trust (547 U.S. 633), 1192
Kircher v. Putnam Funds Trust (373 F.3d 847), 1192
Kircher v. Putnam Funds Trust (403 F.3d 478), 1192
Knollenberg v. Harmonic, Inc. (2005–2006 Fed. Sec. L. Rep. (CCH) ¶93,554), 1359
Koehler v. Brody (483 F.3d 590), 1384
Koenig, SEC v. (557 F.3d 736), 1346
Kramer v. Time Warner Inc. (937 F.2d 767), 643
Krim v. PC Order.Com, Inc. (402 F.3d 489), 1228
Kurz v. Fidelity Mgmt. & Research Co. (556 F.3d 639), 1192
Kutten v. Bank of Am. (530 F.3d 669), 1192

LaGrasta v. First Union Sec., Inc. (358 F.3d 840), 1346
Lampf, Pleva, Lipkind, Prupis & Petigrow v. Gilbertson (501 U.S. 350), 1264
Landgraf v. USI Film Prod. (511 U.S. 244), 1347
Landreth Timber Co. v. Landreth (471 U.S. 681), 259, 267
Lapin v. Goldman Sachs & Co. (2008 Fed. Sec. L. Rep. (CCH) ¶94,842), 1285

TABLE OF CASES

LaSala v. Bordier et Cie (519 F.3d 121), 1192
Lattanzio v. Deloitte & Touche LLP (476 F.3d 147), 958, 1285
Lay, United States v. (566 F. Supp. 2d 652), 1108
Leegin Creative Leather Products v. PSKS (551 U.S. 877), 1332
Lentell v. Merrill Lynch & Co., Inc. (396 F.3d 161), 841, 1137, 1332, 1346
Leonard, United States v. (529 F.3d 83), 251
Lerro v. Quaker Oats Co. (84 F.3d 239), 643
Levi Strauss & Co. Sec. Litig. (527 F. Supp. 2d 965), 438
Lieberman v. Cambridge Partners, LLC (2003–2004 Fed. Sec. L. Rep. (CCH) ¶92,650), 343
Lipkin v. SEC (468 F. Supp. 2d 614), 1430
Litzler v. CC Inv., L.D.C. (362 F.3d 203), 1338
Livent, Inc. Noteholders Sec. Litig. (151 F. Supp. 2d 371), 438
Livid Holdings Ltd. v. Salomon Smith Barney, Inc. (416 F.3d 940), 1346
Lord Abbett Mut. Funds Fee Litig. (553 F.3d 248), 1192
Lowry v. SEC (340 F.3d 501), 1511
Luther v. Countrywide Home Loans Serv., L.P. (533 F.3d 1031), 1534
Lyttle, SEC v. (538 F.3d 601), 1025

MBIA Ins. Corp. v. Royal Indem. Co. (426 F.3d 204), 913
MFS Sec. Corp. v. NYSE, Inc. (142 Fed. Appx. 541), 797
MFS Sec. Corp. v. SEC (380 F.3d 611), 788
Madden v. Cowen & Co. (556 F.3d 786), 1192
Magma Power Co. v. Dow Chem. Co. (136 F.3d 316), 692
Makor Issues & Rights, Ltd. v. Tellabs, Inc. (437 F.3d 588), 576, 1359
Makor Issues & Rights, Ltd. v. Tellabs, Inc. (513 F.3d 702), 1313, 1359
Margolies v. Deason (464 F.3d 547), 1347
Matsushita Elec. Ind. Co. v. Epstein (516 U.S. 367), 643
McCabe v. Ernst & Young, LLP (494 F.3d 418), 1285
McConville v. SEC (465 F.3d 780), 1025, 1430
McMulen v. Fluor Corp. (2003–2004 Fed. Sec. L. Rep. (CCH) ¶92,665), 1359
Media Gen., Inc. v. Tomlin (387 F.3d 865), 590
Media Gen., Inc. v. Tomlin (532 F.3d 854), 1286
Medtronic, Inc. v. Lohr (518 U.S. 470), 1192
Merchant Capital, LLC, SEC v. (483 F.3d 747), 165, 267, 582
Merck & Co. Sec. Litig. (432 F.3d 261), 590, 1384
Merck & Co. Sec., Deriv. & ERISA Litig. (543 F.3d 150), 1346
Merrill Lynch & Co., Inc. (273 F. Supp. 2d 351), 841
Merrill Lynch & Co., Inc. v. Allegheny Energy, Inc. (500 F.3d 171), 1285
Merrill Lynch & Co., Inc. Research Reports (272 F. Supp. 2d 243), 841
Merrill Lynch & Co., Inc. Research Reports (289 F. Supp. 2d 416), 841
Merrill Lynch & Co., Inc. Research Reports (289 F. Supp. 2d 429), 841
Merrill Lynch & Co. Research Reports Sec. Litig. (273 F. Supp. 2d 351), 841

549

Merrill Lynch, Pierce, Fenner & Smith, Inc. v. Curran (456 U.S. 353), 1264
Merrill Lynch, Pierce, Fenner & Smith, Inc. v. Dabit (547 U.S. 71), 1192
Merrill Lynch, Pierce, Fenner & Smith v. Ware (414 U.S. 117), 1376
Metawave Communications Corp. Sec. Litig. (298 F. Supp. 2d 1056), 1359
Metropolitan Sec. Litig. (532 F. Supp. 2d 1260), 1347
Metzler Inv. GMBH v. Corinthian Colleges, Inc. (540 F.3d 1049), 1285
Michel, SEC v. (521 F. Supp. 2d 795), 1002
Miller v. Asensio & Co., Inc. (364 F.3d 223), 1286
Miller v. Champion Enter., Inc. (346 F.3d 660), 1359
Mizzaro v. Home Depot, Inc. (544 F.3d 1230), 1359
Monetta Fin. Serv., Inc. v. SEC (390 F.3d 952), 1430
Mooney, United States v. (401 F.3d 940), 590
Mooney, United States v. (2004 Fed. Sec. L. Rep. (CCH) ¶92,874), 590
Morris v. Wachovia Sec., Inc. (448 F.3d 268), 1408
Morrison v. Madison Dearborn Capital Partners III, L.P. (463 F.3d 312), 692
Morrison v. National Aust. Bank, Ltd. (547 F.3d 167), 1563
Motient Corp. v. Dondero (529 F.3d 532), 1272
Musick, Peeler & Garrett v. Employers Ins. of Wausau (508 U.S. 286), 1264
Mutual Benefits Corp., SEC v. (323 F. Supp. 2d 1337), 272
Mutual Funds Inv. Litig. (384 F. Supp. 2d 845), 1047

NYSE Specialists Sec. Litig. (503 F.3d 89), 1436
Nacchio, United States v. (519 F.3d 1140), 588
National Ass'n of Sec. Dealers, United States v. (422 U.S. 694), 797
New Eng. Health Care Employees Pension Fund v. Ernst & Young, LLP (336 F.3d 495), 1346
New Jersey Carpenters Pension & Annuity Funds v. Biogen Indec, Inc. (537 F.3d 35), 1025, 1359
New York v. Grasso (350 F. Supp. 2d 498), 182
Newman v. Warnaco Group, Inc. (335 F.3d 187), 1346
Newton v. Merrill Lynch, Pierce, Fenner & Smith, Inc. (259 F.3d 154), 1285
Nisselson v. Lernout (469 F.3d 143), 1362
Nolte v. Capital One Fin. Corp. (390 F.3d 311), 577
Northwest Airlines v. Transp. Workers Union of Am. (451 U.S. 77), 1436
Novak v. Kasaks (216 F.3d 300), 1359

O'Hagan, United States v. (521 U.S. 642), 1192, 1285
Oran v. Stafford (226 F.3d 275), 590
Oscar Private Equity Inv. v. Allegiance Telecom, Inc. (487 F.3d 261), 1285
Ottmann v. Hanger Orthopedic Group, Inc. (353 F.3d 338), 1025, 1357
Overton v. Todman & Co., CPAs, P.C. (478 F.3d 479), 958

TABLE OF CASES

Owen v. Independence (445 U.S. 622), 1430

PEC Solutions, Inc. Sec. Litig. (418 F.3d 379), 1359
P. Stolz Family Partnership L.P. v. Daum (355 F.3d 92), 1335
Parmalat Sec. Litig. (376 F. Supp. 2d 472), 1332
Parnes, SEC v. (2001–2002 Fed. Sec. L. Rep. (CCH) ¶91,678), 438
Parnes v. Gateway 2000 (122 F.3d 539), 588
Pasley v. Freeman (100 Eng. Rep. 450), 1285
Perpetual Sec., Inc. v. Tang (290 F.3d 132), 788
Pet Quarters, Inc. v. Depository Trust & Clearing Corp. (559 F.3d 772), 805
Phan, SEC v. (500 F.3d 895), 413
Pinter v. Dahl (486 U.S. 622), 1362
Poyser v. Flora (780 N.E.2d 1191), 231
Press v. Chem. Inv. Servs. Corp. (166 F.3d 529), 1071
Prima Paint Corp. v. Flood & Conklin Mfg. Co. (388 U.S. 395), 1376
Professional Mgmt. Assoc. Inc. Employees' Profit Sharing Plan v. KPMG LLP (345 F.3d 1030), 1408

Qwest Communications Int'l Inc. (2004–2005 Fed. Sec. L. Rep.) (CCH) ¶78,922), 534

Randall v. Loftsgaarden (478 U.S. 647), 1285
Ray v. Citigroup Global Mkt., Inc. (482 F.3d 991), 1285

Refco, Inc. Sec. Litig. (503 F. Supp. 2d 611), 438
Regents of Univ. of Cal. v. Credit Suisse First Boston (USA), Inc. (482 F.3d 372), 1283, 1332
Reves v. Ernst & Young (494 U.S. 56), 256
Ring v. AXA Fin., Inc. (483 F.3d 95), 272, 1192
Robbins v. Koger Prop., Inc. (116 F.3d 1441), 1285
Robinson v. Glynn (349 F.3d 166), 259
Robison v. Via (821 F.2d 913), 1436
Rockies Fund v. SEC (428 F.3d 1088), 1137
Rodriguez-Ortiz v. Margo Caribe, Inc. (490 F.3d 92), 1025
Rombach v. Chang (355 F.3d 164), 1359
Rosenberg v. Gould (554 F.3d 962), 1359
Rosenberg v. MetLife, Inc. (453 F.3d 122), 1430
Rosenberg v. MetLife, Inc. (8 N.Y.3d 359), 1430
Rosenzweig v. Azurix Corp. (332 F.3d 854), 1228
Roth v. Jennings (489 F.3d 499), 622, 704
Rowinski v. Salomon Smith Barney, Inc. (398 F.3d 294), 1192
Royal Dutch Petroleum and the Shell Transport & Trading Co., p.l.c. (Sec. Ex. Act Rel. 50,233), 194
Royer, United States v. (549 F.3d 886), 943, 957, 1332
Rubin v. United States (449 U.S. 424), 1045

Safety-Kleen Bondholders Litig. (2002 U.S. Dist. LEXIS 26,735), 438

551

Salomon Analyst Metromedia Litig. (544 F.3d 474), 1285
Santa Fe Indus., Inc. v. Green (430 U.S. 462), 174, 1332
Sargent, SEC v. (229 F.3d 68), 590
Schaaf v. Residential Funding Corp. (517 F.3d 544), 1353
Schiffer, SEC v. (1998 Fed. Sec. L. Rep. (CCH) ¶90,247), 227
Sears, Wanda P. (Sec. Ex. Act Rel. 58,075), 1484
Semerenko v. Cendant Corp. (223 F.3d 165), 1285
Series 7 Broker Qualification Exam Scoring Litig. (548 F.3d 110), 1436
Shah v. Meeker (435 F.3d 244), 1346
Shapiro v. UJB Fin. Corp. (964 F.2d 272), 1359
Sherman, SEC v. (491 F.3d 948), 449
Shmueli v. City of New York (424 F.3d 231), 1436
Shoreline Dev. Co., SEC v. (2005 Fed. Sec. L. Rep. (CCH) ¶93,356), 243
Siebel Sys., Inc. SEC v. (384 F. Supp. 2d 694), 957
Siepel v. Bank of Am., N.A. (526 F.3d 1122), 1192
Silicon Graphics Inc. Sec. Litig. (183 F.3d 970), 1359
Simpson v. AOL Time Warner Inc. (452 F.3d 1040), 1332
Skilling, United States v. (554 F.3d 529), 1423
Smith v. Pennington (352 F.3d 884), 1047
Smyth, SEC v. (420 F.3d 1225), 1054, 1511
Sofonia v. Principal Life Ins. Co. (465 F.3d 873), 1192
Softpoint, SEC v. (958 F. Supp. 846), 227
Southern Dev. Co. v. Silva (125 U.S. 247), 1285

South Ferry LP, #2 v. Killinger (542 F.3d 776), 1359
Southland Corp. v. Keating (465 U.S. 1), 1376
Southland Sec. Corp. v. INSpire Ins. Solutions, Inc. (365 F.3d 353), 1359
Sparta Surgical Corp. v. NASD (159 F.3d 1209), 1430, 1436
Spielman v. Merrill Lynch, Pierce, Fenner & Smith, Inc. (332 F.3d 116), 1192
Staehr v. Hartford Fin. Serv. Group, Inc. (547 F.3d 406), 1346
Stark Trading v. Falconbridge Ltd. (552 F.3d 568), 1228, 1285
Stavros v. Exelon Corp. (266 F. Supp. 2d 833), 588
Steadman, SEC v. (967 F.2d 636), 1137
Steadman v. SEC (603 F.2d 1126), 1511
Steed Fin. LDC v. Nomura Sec. Int'l, Inc. (2001 Fed. Sec. L. Rep. (CCH) ¶91,552) 1216
Sterlin v. Biomune Sys. (154 F.3d 1191), 1346
Stone & Webster, Inc. Sec. Litig. (414 F.3d 187), 105
Stoneridge Inv. Partners, LLC v. Scientific-Atlanta, Inc. (522 U.S. 148), 1264, 1332
Stringer, SEC v. (2003 U.S. Dist. LEXIS 25,523), 1310
Sudo Properties, Inc. v. Terrebonne Parish (503 F.3d 371), 1346
Suez Equity Investors, L.P. v. Toronto-Dominion Bank (250 F.3d 87), 174, 841
Superintendent of Ins. of N.Y. v. Bankers Life & Casualty Co. (404 U.S. 6), 1192, 1332
Suprema Specialists, Inc. Sec. Litig. (438 F.3d 256), 1240, 1310, 1359

TABLE OF CASES

Syncor Int'l (2007 Fed. Sec. L. Rep. (CCH) ¶94,354), 576
Swierkiewicz v. Sorema N.A. (534 U.S. 506), 1285

Talbot, SEC v. (530 F.3d 1085), 1002
Tambone, SEC v. (550 F.3d 106), 918, 1332
Teachers Retirement Sys. of La. v. Hunter (477 F.3d 162), 1285
Teamsters Local 445 Freight v. Dynex Capital, Inc. (531 F.3d 190), 1025, 1359
Teamsters Local 445 Freight Div. Pension Fund v. Bombardier, Inc. (546 F.3d 196), 1281
Teicher, United States v. (987 F.2d 112), 957
Tellabs, Inc. v. Makor Issues & Rights (551 U.S. 308), 1025, 1353, 1359
Tello v. Dean Witter Reynolds (410 F.3d 1275), 1346
Tello v. Dean Witter Reynolds, Inc. (494 F.3d 956), 1347
Thielbar, SEC v. (2007 Fed. Sec. L. Rep. (CCH) ¶94,436), 1332
Thompson v. Paul (547 F.3d 1055), 913
Thompson v. Thompson (484 U.S. 174), 1264
Touche Ross & Co. v. Redington (442 U.S. 560), 1264
Tracinda Corp. v. DaimlerChrysler (502 F.3d 212), 1408
Tricontinental Indus. v. PricewaterhouseCoopers (475 F.3d 824), 1237, 1285

U.S. Reservation Bank & Trust, SEC v. (2008 Fed. Sec. L. Rep. (CCH) ¶94,804), 241

United Hous. Found., Inc. v. Forman (421 U.S. 837), 256
United Investors Life Ins. Co. v. Waddell & Reed Inc. (360 F.3d 960), 1192
United States of Am. v. SEC (Order No. 05-1240), 59
Universal Express, Inc., SEC v. (475 F. Supp. 2d 412), 101

Vernazza v. SEC (327 F.3d 851), 582, 1511
Virginia Bankshares v. Sandberg (501 U.S. 1083), 577, 1264, 1332

W. J. Howey Co., SEC v. (328 U.S. 293), 231, 248, 256
WHX Corp. (Sec. Ex. Act Rel. 47,980), 643
WHX Corp. v. SEC (362 F.3d 854), 643, 1510
Walt Disney Co. Deriv. Litig. (907 A.2d 693), 165
Weissman v. NASD, Inc. (500 F.3d 1293), 1430, 1436
Whistler Inv. v. Depository Trust & Clearing Corp. (539 F.3d 1159), 805
Wieglos v. Commonwealth Edison Co. (892 F.2d 509), 165
Williamson v. Tucker (645 F.2d 404), 267
Williams Sec. Litig. – WCG Subclass (558 F.3d 1130), 1285
Winer Family Trust v. Queen (503 F.3d 319), 1359
Wolfson, SEC v. (539 F.3d 1249), 1192, 1332
WorldCom Sec. Litig. (496 F.3d 245), 1346

553

WorldCom, Inc. Sec. Litig. (294 F. Supp. 2d 431), 1347
WorldCom, Inc. Sec. Litig. (346 F. Supp. 2d 628), 90, 1232

Xpedior Creditor Trust v. Credit Suisse First Boston (USA) Inc. (341 F. Supp. 2d 258), 1192

Yung v. Lee (432 F.3d 149), 1216

Zandford, SEC v. (535 U.S. 813), 1192, 1332
Zucco Partners, LLC v. Digimarc Corp. (552 F.3d 981), 1359
Zwick, SEC v. (2008 Fed. Sec. L. Rep. (CCH) ¶94,818), 1071